Irene C. Fountas & Gay Su Pinnell

The **Writing Minilessons Book**

Your Every Day Guide for Literacy Teaching

GRADE 2

HEINEMANN
Portsmouth, NH

Heinemann
145 Maplewood Avenue, Suite 300
Portsmouth, NH 03801
www.heinemann.com

Offices and agents throughout the world

The authors and publisher wish to thank those who have generously given permission to reprint borrowed material: Please see the Credits section beginning on page 597.

Photography:
Photo of crocodile on page 387 by © Bill Birtwhistle/Moment/Getty Images

Library of Congress Cataloging in Publication data is on file at the Library of Congress.
Library of Congress Control Number: 2021950802
ISBN: 978-0-325-11881-9

Editors: Kerry L. Crosby and Sue Paro
Production: Cindy Strowman
Production Assistant: Anthony Riso
Cover and Interior Designs: Ellery Harvey and Kelsey Roy
Illustrators: Sarah Snow and Will Sweeney
Typesetter: Sharon Burkhardt
Manufacturing: Erin St. Hilaire and Jaime Spaulding

Printed in the United States of America on acid-free paper

1 2 3 4 5 6 7 8 9 10 LSB 27 26 25 24 23 22
April 2022 Printing / 32608

CONTENTS

2 Genres and Forms

3 Craft

4 Conventions

5 Writing Process

Planning and Rehearsing

Publishing

Introduction

Welcome to *The Writing Minilessons Book, Grade 2*

To second graders, drawing and writing are new and exciting ways to communicate thoughts, ideas, and plans. To you, children's drawing and writing provide opportunities to watch children grow in amazing ways as they explore written language. Through your teaching, children come to understand the power of putting their ideas on paper. As they learn to live like writers, they notice the world around them and see stories in their everyday lives. And now, the journey begins.

Organization of Lessons

In this book, you will find 190 writing minilessons that help children develop as artists and writers. The minilessons are organized across five sections:

- ◗ Section 1: Management (MGT)
- ◗ Section 2: Genres and Forms (GEN)
- ◗ Section 3: Craft (CFT)
- ◗ Section 4: Conventions (CNV)
- ◗ Section 5: Writing Process (WPS)

The sections contain groups of minilessons, or "umbrellas." Within each umbrella, the minilessons are all related to the same big idea so you can work with each concept for several days. The umbrellas are numbered sequentially within each section, and the minilessons are numbered sequentially within each umbrella. Each writing minilesson is identified by section, umbrella, and minilesson. For example, MGT.U1.WML1 indicates the first minilesson in the first umbrella of the Management section.

Content of Lessons: *The Literacy Continuum*

Almost all lessons in this book are based on the behaviors and understandings presented in *The Fountas & Pinnell Literacy Continuum: A Tool for Assessment, Planning, and Teaching*. This volume presents detailed behaviors and understandings to notice, teach for, and support for prekindergarten through middle school, across eight instructional reading, writing, and language contexts. In sum, *The Fountas & Pinnell Literacy Continuum* describes proficiency in reading, writing, and language as it changes over grades and over levels. When you teach the lessons in this book, you are teaching for the behaviors and understandings that second graders need to become proficient readers and writers over time.

Organized for Your Children's Needs

We have provided a suggested sequence of lessons (see pp. 4–5) for you to try out and adjust based on your observations of the children. The sequence provides one path through the lessons. If this is your first time teaching minilessons, you may want to stick to it. However, with 190 lessons to choose from, you will not have time to teach every minilesson in this book. Choose the lessons that make sense for the children in your class and omit any lessons that would be too advanced or too easy. You will be able to locate the lessons easily because they are organized into sections. We organized the lessons into sections for these reasons:

- The children in any given second-grade class will vary greatly in their literacy experiences and development. Lessons organized by topic allow you to dip into the sections to select specific umbrellas or lessons that respond to your students' needs. You can find lessons easily by section and topic through the table of contents.

- Writing is a complex process and involves many levels of learning— from figuring out the idea to communicate, to putting the thinking into language, to thinking about what to draw and write, to the mechanics of getting it on paper. Having the lessons organized by section enables you to focus on the areas that might be most helpful to the children at a specific point in time.

Key Words Used in Minilessons

The following is a list of key terms that we will use as we describe minilessons in the next chapters. Keep them in mind so that together we can develop a common language to talk about the minilessons.

- **Umbrella** A group of minilessons, all of which are directed at different aspects of the same larger category of understanding.

- **Minilesson** A short, interactive lesson to invite children to think about one idea.

- **Principle** A concise statement of the concept children will learn and be invited to apply.

- **Writing** All the kinds of writing, including drawings and approximated spellings, that second-grade children will do, whether they write a list of words, one sentence, or many pages.

- **Mentor Text** A fiction or nonfiction text in which the author or illustrator offers a clear example of the minilesson principle. Children will have heard the text read aloud and talked about it. Mentor texts can be books you have read to them as well as simple texts that you have written or ones that you and the children have written together.

- **Text Set** A group of either fiction or nonfiction books or a combination of both that, taken together, help children explore an idea, a topic, or a type of book (genre). You will have already read the books to them before a lesson. Children will have also made important connections between them.

▶ **Anchor Chart** A visual representation of the lesson concept using a combination of words and images. You create it as you talk with the children. It summarizes the learning and can be used by the children as a reference tool.

The chapters at the beginning of this book help you think about the role of talking, drawing, and writing in second grade, how the lessons are designed and structured, and the materials and resources you will need to teach the lessons.

Suggested Sequence of Lessons

If you are new to second-grade minilessons, you may want to use the Suggested Sequence of Lessons (Figure I-1) for teaching writing minilessons across the year. This sequence weaves in lessons from the different sections so that children receive instruction in all aspects of writing and drawing throughout the school year. Lessons are sequenced in a way we think will support most second-grade children, but you need first to observe what most of your students are doing as talkers, artists, and writers. Then choose the specific lessons that will lead them forward.

Every group of second-graders is different, so it is impossible to prescribe an exact sequence of lessons. However, this sequence will give you a good starting place as you begin to teach the lessons in *The Writing Minilessons Book, Grade 2*.

▶ The number of days assigned to each umbrella suggests how many days you will spend on teaching the minilessons in an umbrella. You may want to give children time in between lessons to apply the lesson during independent writing.

▶ You may not be able to teach a writing minilesson every day, and you may want to spend more time on some concepts than on others by revisiting or repeating lessons according to children's needs and interests.

▶ You want to expose children to a variety of writing and writing techniques early in the year, so you teach quite a few lessons in the first few months. It's also a good idea to revisit and repeat umbrellas. Children will apply the lessons in different ways as they develop their abilities to write and draw across the school year.

If you use *Fountas & Pinnell Classroom™ Shared Reading Collection* (2018), *Interactive Read-Aloud Collection* (2018), or *The Reading Minilessons Book, Grade 2* (2019), note that the Suggested Sequence of Lessons follows the sequences found in these resources to help organize

Months	Texts from *Fountas & Pinnell Classroom™ Shared Reading Collection*	Text Sets from *Fountas & Pinnell Classroom™ Interactive Read-Aloud Collection*	Reading Minilessons (RML) Umbrellas	Writing Minilessons (WML) Umbrellas	Teaching Suggestions for Extending Learning
Months 1 & 2	Animals with Jobs	The Importance of Friendship	MGT.U1: Working Together in the Classroom	**MGT.U1: Working Together in the Classroom (9 days)**	If you are using *The Reading Minilessons Book, Grade 2*, you do not need to teach the lessons that repeat in MGT.U1. Both RML and WML establish basically the same routines. However, be sure to take time to build community in your classroom. The opening page of the writing minilessons umbrella MGT.U1 offers a suggestion for a writing project students might work on throughout the umbrella to get to know each other while practicing these important routines.
		Caring for Each Other: Family	MGT.U2: Using the Classroom Library for Independent Reading	**WPS.U1: Getting Ideas for Writing Through Storytelling, WML1–WML2 (2 days)**	WPS.U1 helps children get to know one another and continue to build community while generating ideas for writing through oral storytelling. Teach the minilessons in WPS.U1 over several days so that children have time to tell stories in between the lessons. Use the time you usually take to teach a minilesson to give children the opportunity to tell their stories. You can also invite them to tell their stories in partnerships and small groups.
	Smokey Bear: A True Story		MGT.U3: Engaging in Classroom Literacy Work		
				MGT.U2: Using Drawing and Writing ...s (3...	MGT.U2 can be taught in conjunction with GEN.U1. You may choose to teach i... or int...t wit...

reading and writing instruction across the year. If you do not have the texts that appear in the lessons as mentor texts, simply pick similar books and examples from your own classroom library or school library. Characteristics of the books used in the lessons are described on the opening page of the umbrellas for the writing minilessons. It is our intention that whenever possible children will have already seen and heard the mentor texts by the time they are used in a lesson. To read more about using the Suggested Sequence of Lessons to plan your teaching, see Chapter 6.

Figure I-1: The complete Suggested Sequence of Lessons is on pages 575–589 in this book and in the online resources.

Chapter 1 | The Role of Writing in Literacy Learning

Writing can contribute to the building of almost every kind of inner control of literacy learning that is needed by the successful reader.

—Marie Clay

LOOK AROUND A SECOND-GRADE CLASSROOM, bustling with the energy of young children. Some children are busy observing, sketching, and writing notes about the latest wonder in the science center. Other children are deep into their research about a topic they love and care about. Still others are off making books. They are writing how-to books, making poetry books, and writing about their favorite memories. Partners read each other their stories and offer suggestions, and the teacher confers with individual writers who are eager to share the latest additions to their writing. The classroom is filled not only with the excitement of exploration but with the tools of literacy.

Children in your second-grade classroom are learning to be part of a community of talkers, scientists, mathematicians, artists, readers, and writers. The writing minilessons in this book play an important role in this process. In the lessons, children will draw and write in many different ways for many different purposes and audiences across the curriculum (Figure 1-1).

Second graders live in a literate world, a world filled with print in all sizes, shapes, and colors for different purposes. They notice print all around them—from road signs and store names to cereal boxes and text messages. These noticings lead them to understand people have a purpose when they write, and they begin to explore how writing can serve their own purposes.

When we talk about a second grader's writing, what do we mean? Of course, you will have a range of writers in your classroom from those who write a few simple sentences to those who can write across several pages. No matter where they are on this continuum, second graders understand that they can communicate a message in pictures and words. You can help them see the power of their messages and stories through your response to their attempts at trying new things in their writing.

The writing minilessons in this book will help children see the stories in their lives and help you provide time and space for them to share their stories orally as well as in written form. The writing minilessons that introduce children to their first writer's notebooks teach them that they can collect ideas for writing anytime and any place. Children begin to live their lives with a writer's eye—seeing ideas for writing in everyday occurrences. If they have daily opportunities to write and draw, they will learn to see themselves as writers and artists.

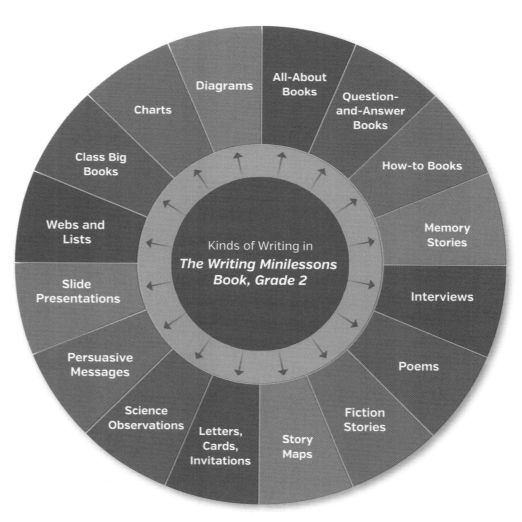

Figure 1-1: Children will have opportunities to write and draw in a variety of ways across the year.

The Writing Minilessons Book, Grade 2

Children Show What They Know

Children learn differently from one another, but all make progress toward the kind of writing they see in books. Observing second graders write and looking at their writing will give you evidence of what they know. Notice whether they

- initiate writing quickly,
- have things to write about,
- choose topics and stories they care about,
- show enthusiasm for their writing,
- draw pictures with details,
- write words with standard and approximated spellings,
- talk about their pictures and messages,
- try out different kinds of writing (different genres and forms),
- write several sentences to communicate a continuous message,
- read what they have written,
- try out new learning in their writing,
- use capitalization and punctuation to clarify their writing, or
- revise, or change, their writing to make it more interesting, more detailed, or clearer.

When you notice what children are doing with writing, you can build on their strengths and help them take the next steps as writers. In Figure 1-2, notice all the things second grader Jemilia is doing in her writing. Also notice areas in which she can grow based on her budding understandings. It is important to note that children take on new behaviors and understandings over time. Your goal in analyzing children's writing is not to "fix" or improve a particular piece of writing (though you might use one piece to teach one or two important new things) but to give children the tools to think in new ways as writers. Analyzing your students' writing gives you direction for what you might teach to lead writers forward. When you meet students where they are and build on their strengths, they are more engaged and interested in learning how to make their writing more like the books they are reading.

Chapter 6 includes information about the tools provided in the online resources to assess your students' writing. *The Fountas & Pinnell Literacy Continuum* and the assessment sections in the writing minilessons will guide your observation of children's writing behaviors and your analysis of their writing pieces. When you take time to talk to writers and read their writing, you learn what they have understood from your teaching, what they have yet to understand, and what you might teach them next.

Children Connect What They Hear, Say, and Write

A child's journey to becoming literate begins at birth. Jemilia has developed the understandings she demonstrates in Figure 1-2 over many years. As caregivers engage the child in language interactions, the child learns to communicate, and this oral language foundation paves the way for learning about written language—reading and writing. All aspects of children's oral and written language—listening, speaking, reading, and writing—develop together and support each other as the young child emerges into literacy.

Figure 1-2: Jemilia's memory book is evidence of what she understands about writing and provides a window into possible next steps.

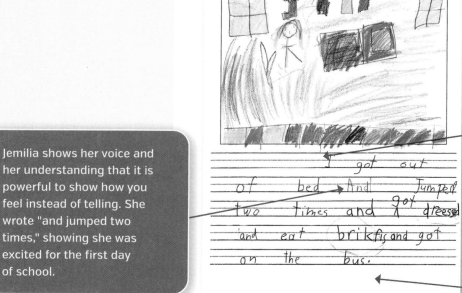

The 1st Day of Second Grade by Jemilia

Yay school

Cover

Jemilia shows her voice and her understanding that it is powerful to show how you feel instead of telling. She wrote "and jumped two times," showing she was excited for the first day of school.

Jemilia understands from her reading that paragraphs are indented. She still needs to learn proper spacing for indents and to return consistently to the margin.

Jemilia understands that writers tell stories from their own lives. A next step for her would be to identify a small moment instead of telling the whole story from start to finish.

I got out of bed and jumped two times and got dressed and ate breakfast and got on the bus.

Jemilia can write several high-frequency words accurately: *when, got, that, but, with, me, and, so.*

Jemilia shows that she understands that writers share their thoughts and feelings about a memory. A next step for Jemilia would be to communicate why this memory is important to her.

Jemilia needs support applying what she knows about words more consistently. Notice she spelled *would* two different ways in consecutive sentences. She also used the suffix *-ed* correctly in *played* but didn't apply the same principle to the word *wanted* above it.

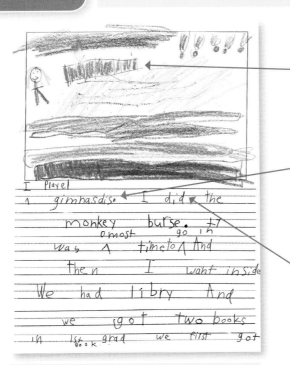

When I got to school, I felt shy and a little scared. I thought that recess would be fun. I thought I would feel better. But no one wanted to play with me. So I played by myself.

Jemilia understands how to draw a background setting (e.g., notice the monkey bars drawn across the top). She would benefit from minilessons focused on drawing people in different positions.

Jemilia demonstrates strength in providing details to support her ideas. She explains that she played gymnastics and monkey bars by herself.

Jemilia seems ready to experiment with choosing more specific verbs in her writing.

I played gymnastics. I did the monkey bars. It was almost time to go in and then I went inside. We had library. And we got two books. In 1st grade, we first got 1 book.

Jemilia shows a beginning understanding of how to use simple transitional words in her writing.

A next step for Jemilia would be learning to make her descriptions more specific. She will benefit from looking at mentor texts and from minilessons that address word choice.

Then we went to lunch. I had home lunch. It was good. When we got back, we did read aloud.

Throughout her piece, Jemilia shows that she understands revision and how to use caret marks to add information. She will benefit from learning other techniques for revision, including how to cut information that does not add to the important ideas.

One of Jemilia's strengths is using using capitalization and punctuation consistently. She is ready to learn how to use different types of punctuation to communicate her voice.

The book was Tacky in Trouble. Then science and then math. Math is my favorite subject. Then we did cleanup. And we went to the bus.

Anytime you and the children write something together—whether labels, descriptions, observations, or stories—thinking and talking come first. Children learn that their thoughts and ideas can be put into language, language can be put into writing, and the writing can be read (Figure 1-3).

Several minilessons in the Writing Process section are dedicated to storytelling and rehearsing writing as part of the planning process. For children to be able to write their stories, they first need to be able to tell their stories. By listening to stories read to them and by telling stories themselves (stories from their own lives or retellings of stories from books), children begin to develop an understanding of story structure. Children develop the ability to use the patterns of language and build strong vocabularies as they listen to and talk about books, ask questions about their classmates' writing, and clarify their own writing for an audience. As they begin to draw and write their oral stories, they have conversations about their writing that deepen their ability to explain their thinking. They learn to put ideas in time order, to elaborate with story details, to develop vocabulary, and to more accurately describe what they want to say. Oral storytelling and rehearsal are not only useful for writing stories. Talking about what to write also helps with nonfiction writing. In WPS.U7: Rehearsing Your Writing, children learn how to say what they have learned about a topic in their own words. Children can more easily move from research to writing when they have opportunities to talk about their learning before writing.

Children Have Opportunities to Write Across the Day

In the second-grade classroom, it is important to carve out a dedicated time for writing as well as to embed writing opportunities into a variety of daily

Figure 1-3: Contributions of writing to literacy learning

The Contributions of Writing to Language, Literacy, and Learning

As children take on literacy in a joyful way, they grow in oral language, reading, and writing. As they write, they

- Move from thoughts to ideas to language to written representation in images or words
- Link spoken language to written language
- Work on communicating meaningful messages
- Say words slowly to hear the individual sounds in words
- Connect sounds with letters
- Learn how print and the structure of written language works
- Read their writing attempts

classroom activities across the curriculum. From the time they enter the literacy-rich classroom, children are engaged in writing. They answer survey questions on charts, create writing pieces with their class members, write explanations for their math solutions, and make sketches of their scientific observations. They talk about what authors do in their books, and they make their own books. Providing second graders with a predictable time to write each day allows them the opportunity to experiment with writing, to make books over several days, and to apply their new learning from writing minilessons. Consider setting aside the following times in your day for writing, and think about how you might build writing across content areas and into other established routines (e.g., independent work time) in your classroom.

Shared/Interactive Writing Time During shared writing, children have an opportunity to collaborate on a piece of writing with you as the scribe. Though shared writing is often a part of writing minilessons, you might also find it helpful to dedicate a time to writing as a whole group a few times a week. The pieces you create as a class can be used as mentor texts during writing minilessons or writing conferences. Some of the children in your class might also benefit from interactive writing, which is the same as shared writing except that children share the pen with you to write letters, word parts, or words. Both shared and interactive writing can be used in a small group or with the whole class.

Independent Writing Time During Writers' Workshop Independent writing time is typically bookended by a writing minilesson and a chance for children to share their writing (Figure 1-4). Children learn about an aspect of writing during a writing minilesson and then have a chance to apply what they learned in that lesson as they write their own text independently for a period of time. The teacher has the opportunity to confer with individual writers or to work with small groups in guided writing (see p. 26 for information about guided writing). Children engage in a variety of writing, especially in making books, which is described in more detail on

Figure 1-4: A writers' workshop structure allows for whole-class learning, individual and small-group instruction from the teacher, independent writing, and whole-class sharing.

Structure of Writers' Workshop

Whole Class	Writing Minilesson	5–10 Minutes
Individuals and Small Groups	Independent Writing Individual Conferences Guided Writing Groups	20–30 minutes (The time will expand to about 45 minutes as children build stamina across the year.)
Whole Class	Group Share	5–10 minutes

pages 56–58. The writers' workshop ends with a whole-group meeting in which children share their writing and, if applicable, the ways they used their new understandings from the writing minilesson. Chapter 2 describes how the writing minilessons in this book follow and support this structure. Using the Management minilessons will help you establish a productive and engaging independent writing time with your second graders.

Independent Work Time During Readers' Workshop After engaging in an inquiry-based reading minilesson, children spend time independently reading and writing about their reading. For example, they might write a weekly letter to their teacher about their reading, record character traits on a web, summarize a story, or make a list of facts they have learned about a topic through reading. During this time, teachers often confer with individual readers as they apply what they learned from the reading minilesson to their independent reading, or they work with small groups in a guided reading lesson. If you find that the children are not yet able to sustain independent reading for the entire reading time, you might find it helpful to use a simple system of four meaningful, productive activities that children complete over the course of the reading time (Figure 1-5).

As children engage in these literacy activities (either at their desks or in an activity center), they have several opportunities to write. They might write about their reading after finishing a book or listening to an audiobook. They might write about their guided reading books as part of a guided reading lesson. During the writing activity, they might make cards, notes, or scientific observations or work on writing related to other instruction in the day. You will want second graders to gradually increase their reading stamina, so be cautious about how much time they spend engaged in activities other than reading. Nevertheless, you can certainly use this time to make important reading and writing connections. A list of materials to support writing in the classroom is shown in Figure 1-6. We provide details for establishing and managing independent work time in both *Guided Reading: Responsive Teaching Across the Grades* (Fountas and Pinnell 2017) and *The Reading Minilessons Book, Grade 2* (Fountas and Pinnell 2019).

Work Time

1. Read a book
2. Listen to a book
3. Work on words
4. Work on writing

Figure 1-5: A simple list can help you manage children's independent work time until they are able to sustain independent reading for the entire reading time.

Children Make Important Literacy Connections

Besides having dedicated times for writing in a writers' workshop, children need to be immersed in a variety of literacy experiences throughout the day so they can make important connections between reading, writing, and word study. In a literacy-building environment, children see print everywhere. They talk and listen to others. They hear books read aloud, read their own books, experience reading and phonics lessons, share poetry, and write and draw about their reading. They learn about and play with language. They make their own books. All of this supports children's writing development.

Figure 1-6: Suggestions for stocking the classroom to encourage writing throughout the day

Stocking the Classroom for Writing

Classroom Spaces	Materials
Classroom Library	• books in labeled tubs organized by topic, author, illustrator, and kind of book (genre) • covers facing out for easy browsing • labels for the tubs written using shared or interactive writing
Writing Center	• pencils, markers, crayons • a variety of paper–different sizes, colors, formats (see online resources) • textured paper for covers • staplers • scissors • glue • premade blank books for bookmaking • sticky notes • white correction tape • name chart, Alphabet Linking Chart, and Consonant Cluster Linking Chart • tub of mentor books to help stimulate ideas • additional writing tools: letter stamps and pads, letter tiles, letter sponges, whiteboards, notebooks, notepads, traceable letters, sandpaper letters, stencils
Art Center (This can be adjacent to the writing center in order to share supplies.)	• paper • paints, markers, colored pencils, crayons (in a variety of colors to provide options for different skin tones and hair colors) • glue • scissors • textured materials (e.g., cloth, ribbed paper, tissue paper) • craft sticks • yarn • tub of books with a variety of interesting art (e.g., collage, found objects, paintings)

Classroom Spaces	Materials
Word Work Center	• blank word cards • very simple wall of words nearby (mostly with children's names and a few high-frequency words) • Alphabet Linking Chart, Consonant Cluster Linking Chart, and name chart • magnetic letters • games • word cards to sort • cookie trays • index cards with textured names; names with dots indicating where to begin tracing
Listening Center	• listening device • clear set of directions with picture clues • multiple copies of books organized in boxes or plastic bags • clipboards and paper to draw responses to books
Science Center	• a range of natural items gathered from outside of school (e.g., rocks, shells, leaves, abandoned bird's nest/beehive, snake's skin) • magnifying glasses • writing tools • paper • rulers • pastels and tracing paper for rubbings • nonfiction books with colorful photographs and drawings of subjects such as animals, foods, families, communities • booklet or notebook labeled *Lab Book* for science observations

Print All Around the Classroom Children live in a world full of print. Just as they see print in their neighborhoods, they walk into a classroom with labels and signs that are meaningful to them. They even participate in making these labels and signs. When you work with children to label parts of the classroom or materials (e.g., writing supplies or tubs of books in the classroom library), you provide a chance for them to produce print that is meaningful and helpful. A word wall (Figure 1-7) that includes children's names (first only or first and last) provides a helpful resource for the writers in your class, especially for those children who are learning English. Keep the word wall active by adding to it regularly (in addition to personal word walls or lists in children's writing folders). As you introduce content-specific vocabulary and high-frequency words (e.g., *after, because, could, their, there*), add them to your word wall. Through minilessons, children learn to use the

EL CONNECTION

> When you teach English learners, you can adjust your teaching—not more teaching, but different teaching—to assure effective learning throughout each lesson. Look for the symbol above to see ways to support English learners.

word wall as a tool to help them generate the spelling of unknown words. During interactive and shared writing, show children how to use the words on the word wall to spell unfamiliar words by using words and parts of words they know (e.g., use the *th* in *then* to start the word *there*).

Interactive Read-Aloud and Shared Reading Reading aloud to children is essential. We call it "interactive" because it is so important for children to talk with each other about the books they hear. They also love shared reading with enlarged print books and charts, reading together from the same book, song, or poem (Figure 1-8). Books they read many times become "theirs." Interactive read-aloud and shared reading expose children to a variety of stories, informational books, songs, and poems. As children listen to and discuss these books and poems, they hear the way written language sounds and start to notice what other writers and illustrators do in their books. When you spend time teaching children to notice how the illustrator designed the cover, the colors used in the illustrations, an interesting choice of words, or the rhythm of a repeating line, they become aware of the author's or illustrator's craft in a simple and authentic way.

Reading Minilessons, Guided Reading, and Independent Reading
Reading minilessons build on the literary understandings developed during interactive read-aloud and shared reading. Children learn more about what illustrators and writers do, how written language sounds, and how stories and information are organized. They learn about the author's message, how print and words work, and about different kinds of writing. They participate in shared writing as they work with you to create anchor charts for reading minilessons and learn how to write and draw about their reading. Children

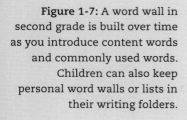

Figure 1-7: A word wall in second grade is built over time as you introduce content words and commonly used words. Children can also keep personal word walls or lists in their writing folders.

grow in all of these understandings as they participate in brief, small-group guided reading lessons in which they read books at their instructional level. Children are also given opportunities throughout the day to read independently. As they engage with a variety of texts independently, children not only apply what they have learned during reading minilessons and guided reading but also make their own discoveries about print, writer's and illustrator's craft, and other literary elements. We have written extensively about reading minilessons and guided reading in *The Reading Minilessons Book, Grade 2* and in *Guided Reading*. Good teaching in reading is essential to the teaching of writing and vice versa. Writing minilessons help children transfer what they have learned in reading to their own writing. In turn, what they learn about writing will make them stronger readers. It is a deeply reciprocal process.

Writing Across the Curriculum Writing plays an important role in the content areas as well (Figure 1-9). Children draw and write as they solve math problems and explain their solutions. They record information during science experiments; they sketch and write their observations in the science center; and they write predictions and wonderings about scientific phenomena. Put a set of magnets with different materials in front of second graders, and they will write predictions for what materials the magnet will attract, they will record what happens, and they will ask questions about how these forces work. Writing, along with talking and reading, is one of the vehicles for learning across the curriculum. Encourage your students to make books in science and social studies—for example, a how-to book for conducting a science experiment, an all-about book about something in history or in your community, or a lab book of science observations. In the Genre and Forms section, you will find several umbrellas that introduce different kinds of writing that can be used across the curriculum. For example, GEN.U6: Making Slide Presentations provides a way for children to display their learning in any of the content areas. In the Writing Process section, as part of the planning process, there is an umbrella that demonstrates how to observe and write like a scientist.

Second graders also have several opportunities throughout the day to write about their reading. You can teach children a variety of ways to respond to their reading through modeled, shared, or interactive writing. Some second-grade teachers use a reader's notebook as a place to collect their children's writing about reading. The writing minilessons in this book focus on having children write their own original pieces, but writing about reading is still an important part of becoming a writer. For minilessons on writing about reading and how to use a reader's notebook with second graders, see *The Reading Minilessons Book, Grade 2*.

Phonics and Phonemic Awareness Through writing minilessons, children have several opportunities to hear individual sounds in words (phonemic awareness) and to connect sounds to letters that represent them (phonics). To explicitly support this learning, second-grade teachers also provide a specific time for daily phonics, spelling, and word study lessons (see *Fountas & Pinnell Phonics, Spelling, and Word Study System, Grade 2*,

Figure 1-9: Examples of children's writing across the curriculum

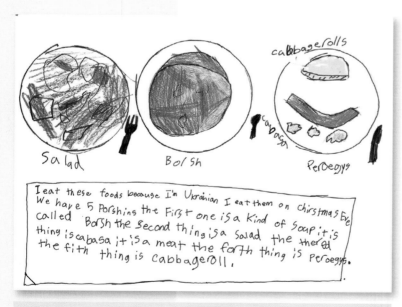

Ivan wrote about his Ukrainian heritage as part of a social studies unit focusing on family traditions and celebrations.

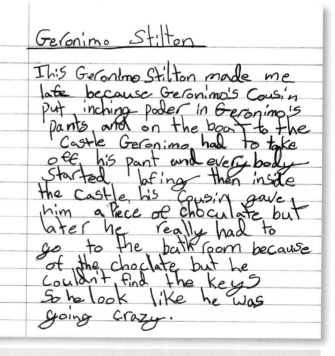

During independent reading, Ryan wrote in his reader's notebook about the humor in a Geronimo Stilton book.

2017). Through inquiry, children learn key principles about the way words work. Additionally, second graders benefit from opportunities to learn the sounds in words through shared reading of songs, poems, and rhymes. The following list has a few simple ways to help children develop in these areas. Many of these activities can be done in the word work center, during morning meeting, or during circle time.

▶ Incorporate songs and poems to help children hear sound patterns in words.

▶ Connect sounds and letters to known words and names.

▶ Demonstrate making words and word parts with magnetic letters.

▶ Make a variety of more sophisticated alphabet books accessible to expand vocabulary and spelling knowledge.

▶ Provide games that focus on a word study principle (e.g., lotto, bingo, concentration) and teach children how to play.

The diagram is of the taproot has thick roots.
Taproots have thick roots with relly long roots with little roots coming off the big roots.
Taproots dont hold alot of soil.

Chul sketched, labeled, and wrote about taproots as part of a science unit on plants and seeds.

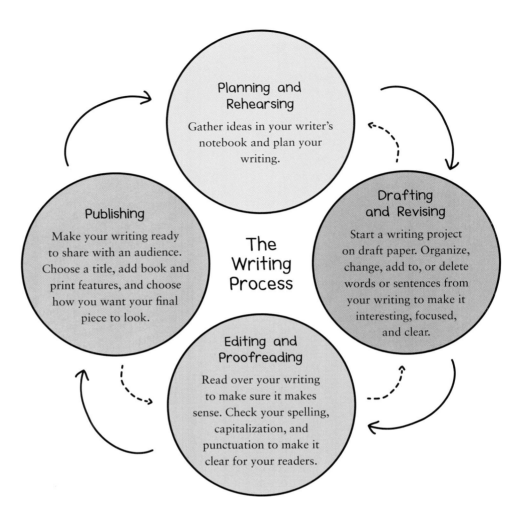

Figure 1-10: The writing process is not linear. Sometimes writers will go forward (the solid arrows) and sometimes they will go back (the dotted arrows) before they move forward again. Individual writers develop their own writing process. Not all writing projects go entirely through to publishing, but all projects provide an opportunity to apply what children are learning in writing minilessons.

Planning and Rehearsing

Gather ideas in your writer's notebook and plan your writing.

The Writing Process

Drafting and Revising

Start a writing project on draft paper. Organize, change, add to, or delete words or sentences from your writing to make it interesting, focused, and clear.

Publishing

Make your writing ready to share with an audience. Choose a title, add book and print features, and choose how you want your final piece to look.

Editing and Proofreading

Read over your writing to make sure it makes sense. Check your spelling, capitalization, and punctuation to make it clear for your readers.

Children Engage in the Writing Process

All writers, regardless of age or experience, engage in the same aspects of the writing process every time they write. Although components of the writing process are usually listed in a sequence, writers can and will use any or all of the components at any point while writing (Figure 1-10). Throughout the process, writers and illustrators often use a writer's notebook to generate ideas, make plans, and try out new craft moves. The lessons in the Writing Process section will help you set up this tool if you want to use it with your students. You can read more about the writing process and the writer's notebook in Chapter 5.

▸ **Planning and Rehearsing** Planning and rehearsing means gathering ideas and talking about them with others. Second graders learn to become intentional planners. They think about their purpose and audience and choose the genre or form of writing that is most effective for their purpose and best communicates their message.

- **Drafting and Revising** This part of the process is focused on getting ideas down on paper and learning how to make changes to improve the writing. Through writing minilessons, children learn the craft moves authors and illustrators make and try them out in their own writing.

- **Editing and Proofreading** For second graders, editing and proofreading means applying what they have learned about the conventions of writing to make their writing clear for their readers.

- **Publishing** This part of the process means sharing a finished piece with an audience. Second grade is a good time to think about broadening these audiences to give students authentic experiences to share their writing. There are a variety of ways to publish both formally and informally using different materials and tools.

Of course, drawing and reading are fundamental parts of this process, as well, and are especially important for second graders. The minilessons in the Writing Process section are designed to support students as they engage in each step of this process.

Children Learn About Writing by Seeing and Doing

Children benefit from seeing examples and demonstrations of drawing and writing before they try drawing and writing on their own. Use modeled, shared, interactive, or guided writing so that children see writing happen.

Modeled Writing

Modeled writing, which includes drawing, has the highest amount of teacher support (Figure 1-11). Children see what it looks like to produce a piece of writing as you demonstrate creating a particular type of writing. As you draw and write, talk through the decisions you are making as an artist or writer. Sometimes, you will have prepared the writing before class, but you will still talk about your thought process for the children. Modeled writing or drawing is often used within a writing minilesson to demonstrate what a particular kind of writing looks like and how it is produced.

Shared Writing

In shared writing, use the children's experiences and language to create writing that they can read. Shared writing is used for most of the charts in the writing minilessons, though you might decide to use modeled or interactive writing. Although you are the scribe who writes the text on

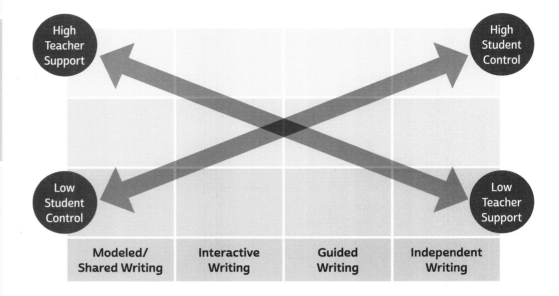

chart paper displayed on an easel or whiteboard, children participate by contributing ideas. First, children talk about their experiences and ideas. Then, you and the children decide together what to say (composing) and how to say it. Moving from thoughts or ideas to saying the words to putting the ideas in print, perhaps with a drawing (constructing), is a process children need to engage in over and over. The process begins with a plan you make together, and then you move to writing the message word by word as the children observe and talk about the process.

Sometimes you will ask the children to say a word slowly to listen for the sounds or a word part and to think about the letters that go with those sounds. It is important for the children to say the word for themselves. Other times, you (with the children's input) will write the word, sentence, or phrase on the chart quickly to keep the lesson moving. Reread what you have written as you go along so that children can rehearse the language structure, anticipate the next word, and check what has been written. The chart then becomes a model, example, or reference for future reading, writing, and discussion (Figure 1-12).

Shared writing is often integrated into writing minilessons but you may want to occasionally carve out a time focused solely on creating a piece of writing with your students. This can be particularly helpful when introducing a new genre. For example, you might spend a day or two writing about a class memory before you embark on GEN.U2: Making Memory Books.

Figure 1-12: In shared writing, the teacher and children come up with the ideas, but the teacher does all the writing.

Interactive Writing

Interactive writing and shared writing are very similar. The only difference is that in interactive writing children "share the pen" by writing letters, word parts, or words (Figure 1-13). Occasionally, while making teaching points that help children attend to various features of letters and words as well as punctuation, invite a child to the easel to contribute a letter, a word, a part of a word, or a type of punctuation. This process is especially helpful to English learners and children who need support with letter/sound relationships and spelling. Consider using interactive writing with small groups of students to support them during independent writing time.

 **EL CONNECTION**

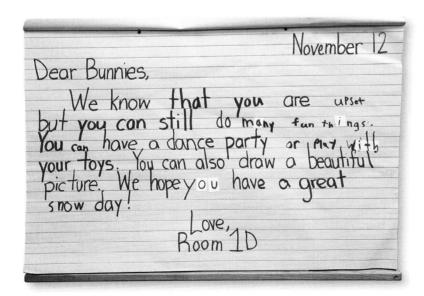

Figure 1-13: In this example of interactive writing, the teacher did most of the writing, but children wrote several high-frequency words that they were learning.

Guided Writing

Guided writing allows for differentiated learning in order to address the common needs of a small, temporary group of students. By conducting conferences with children and examining their writing, you determine which students would benefit from small-group teaching. For example, you may have introduced a new kind of writing to the whole group but notice that there are a few students who need more support to take on the new learning. Or, you have noticed a few students experimenting with writing poetry and you want to support their new interest. In each case, you can pull a guided writing group together to deepen and expand children's understandings. When the new learning is accomplished, the group is disbanded. Whether you are reviewing or teaching something new that the whole class is not quite ready for, the small-group setting of guided writing allows you to closely observe children's writing behaviors and provide specific guidance. Guided writing lessons are brief and focused. Typically a guided writing lesson lasts only ten to fifteen minutes and can take place while the rest of the class is engaged in independent writing (Figure 1-14).

Independent Writing

When children draw and write for themselves, all their understandings about drawing and writing—literacy concepts, word solving, purpose, audience—come together in a way that is visible. Sometimes they will write about their reading. Sometimes they will write in the content areas (e.g., science or social studies). Sometimes they will write from their personal experiences, and other

Figure 1-14: Structure of a guided writing lesson from *The Literacy Quick Guide* (Fountas and Pinnell 2018)

Structure of a Guided Writing Lesson

Teach a Minilesson	Teach a single principle that is useful for a small group of writers at a particular point in time. Keep the lesson brief, and allow student inquiry to drive the learning.
Students Have a Try	Provide a piece of writing, and invite students to apply the new thinking. Support students' learning with additional teaching, as needed. Point out effective applications of the principle by group members.
Students Apply the Principle to Their Own Writing	Invite students to try out the principle using an existing piece of writing or, as appropriate, by beginning a new piece of writing. Students continue to work at the small table as you observe and provide guidance that deepens individual students' understanding of the principle.
Students Share	Invite students to share what they noticed and learned during the lesson. Reinforce the principle, and encourage students to share the next steps they will take in their writing.

times they will write about what they know or have learned about a topic through their observations and research. Through their participation in writing minilessons, children take on new understandings. Through independent writing, they try them out.

Figure 1-15 summarizes the features of modeled writing, shared writing, interactive writing, guided writing, and independent writing. In writing minilessons, you might use any one or more levels of support: modeled, shared, and interactive writing. The ultimate goal of writing minilessons is to support children in developing their own independent drawing and writing.

Figure 1-15: Choose the level of support that helps you reach your goals for the children. These supports apply to both writing and drawing.

Levels of Support for Writing

Type of Writing	Characteristics
Modeled	• Whole class or small group • Teacher composes the text (creates and says the sentences) • Teacher writes the print and/or draws images • Used to demonstrate ideas and refer to • Used as a resource to read
Shared	• Whole class or small group • Teacher and children compose the text (create and say the sentences) • Teacher writes what the children decide together • Used to record ideas to read or refer to • Often included in writing minilessons to show something about writing or drawing
Interactive	• Whole class or small group • Teacher and children plan what to write and/or draw • Teacher and children share the pen to write and illustrate the text • Slows down the writing/drawing and allows focus on specific drawing and writing concepts (e.g., space between words, left-right directionality, features of letters and words, techniques for drawing) • The writing/drawing can be used as a mentor text during writing minilessons and as a reference for independent writing • Often used as a shared reading text later

Type of Writing	Characteristics
Guided	<ul><li>Small group</li><li>Teacher provides a brief lesson on a single writing principle that children apply to their own writing</li><li>Allows for close observation and guidance</li><li>Used to differentiate instruction</li><li>Teaching might involve modeled, shared, or interactive writing</li><li>Similar to a writing minilesson but in a small group setting</li></ul>
Independent	<ul><li>Individuals</li><li>Children decide what to say or draw and then write or illustrate their own texts (mostly through making books)</li><li>Supported by side-by-side talk with the teacher</li><li>Engages children in all aspects of the drawing and writing processes</li></ul>

Levels of Support for Writing (cont.)

Once you get to know the children in your class and understand what they can do on their own and what they can do with your support, you will be able to decide which level of support is most appropriate for a particular purpose. When the processes for each kind of writing are established, you can use them as needed throughout the day.

Chapter 2

What Is a Writing Minilesson?

Every minilesson should end with students envisioning a new possibility for their work, and the key to successful minilessons is helping the group of students sitting in front of us to envision the difference this lesson might make in their work.

—Katie Wood Ray and Lisa Cleaveland

A WRITING MINILESSON IS BRIEF. It focuses on a single writing concept to help children write successfully. A writing minilesson uses inquiry, which leads children to discovering an important understanding that they can try out immediately.

Writing minilessons provide ways to make the classroom a community of learners. They engage children in telling stories and drawing, both of which are foundations of writing. They engage them in making books, writing in a variety of genres, learning about writer's and illustrator's craft, exploring the conventions of writing, and guiding children through the writing process. Writing minilessons help children emerge as readers and writers by thinking about one small understanding at a time and applying it for themselves independently.

> In an **inquiry lesson,** children engage in the thinking and develop the thinking for themselves. They learn from the inside, instead of simply being told what to understand. *Telling* is not the same as teaching.

Five Types of Writing Minilessons

This book has 190 lessons in five color-coded sections (Figure 2-1):

Figure 2-1: The writing minilessons are organized within five sections.

Minilessons in the Management section help children become a strong community of diverse learners who work and learn together peacefully and respectfully. Most of your minilessons at the beginning of the school year will focus on organizing the classroom and building a community in which children feel safe to share ideas and learn about one another. Repeat any of the lessons as needed across the year. A guiding principle: teach a minilesson on anything that prevents the classroom from running smoothly. In these lessons, children will learn

- routines that will help them work well with their classmates,
- ways they can participate,
- the importance of listening, taking turns, and other listening and speaking conventions when in a group, and
- how to gain an ability to work independently as they learn the structures and routines for working and writing together in the classroom (including learning about independent writing time, their writer's notebooks and writing folders, and other tools of writing).

Minilessons in the Genres and Forms section support children by helping them see that they can make their own books like the authors of the books that they read. The first umbrella, Getting Started with Making Books, is designed to get bookmaking up and running in your classroom. As the year progresses, children begin to explore different types of books they can make. They learn how to

- teach others something they know how to do in a how-to book,
- share stories they have told in a memory book, and
- tell what they know about a topic in question-and-answer and all-about books.

Each time children are exposed to a new kind of book, they expand their understanding of ways they can write. They learn more about the way illustrators and authors craft their books. They also learn about other forms of writing, including how to write friendly letters, craft poems, and create slide presentations. The minilessons in this section address behaviors from across the grade 2 Writing continuum in *The Fountas & Pinnell Literacy Continuum*. They address aspects of genre, craft, conventions, and the writing process.

Minilessons in the Craft section help children learn about the decisions writers and illustrators make as they craft their pieces of writing. Through the umbrellas in this section, children explore the way authors use details in their writing to describe the characters and the setting. They look at the ways authors add dialogue to stories and text features to nonfiction writing. They experiment with different ways to start and end their writing and examine the way authors choose words carefully to make their writing interesting and specific. The minilessons in this section address the behaviors and understandings in the Craft section of the grade 2 Writing continuum in *The Fountas & Pinnell Literacy Continuum*.

Minilessons in the Conventions section help children learn "how print works." They learn, for example, that

- letters and sounds are connected,
- you can use what you know about words to write other words,
- every syllable has at least one vowel, and
- words can be broken into syllables.

Other umbrellas in this section touch on properly forming upper- and lowercase letters and learning about punctuation and capitalization. The lessons in this section address the behaviors primarily in the Conventions section of the grade 2 Writing continuum in *The Fountas & Pinnell Literacy Continuum*.

Minilessons in the Writing Process section guide children through the phases of the writing process: planning and rehearsing, drafting and revising, editing and proofreading, and publishing. The minilessons in this section support your students in getting ideas for their writing by teaching them to look for stories in their own lives and in their observations of the world. If you have or wish to have children use writer's notebooks, there are minilessons that offer suggestions for setting up and using a beginning writer's notebook. Other lessons teach second graders to think about why they are writing, whom they are writing for, and what kind of writing will serve their purpose. Finally, minilessons in this section also help children learn how to add to their writing, how to cut and reorganize it, how to proofread it, and, most importantly, how to celebrate it.

Writing Minilessons Are Grouped into Umbrella Concepts

Within each of the five major sections, lessons are grouped in what we call "umbrellas." Each umbrella is made up of several minilessons that are related to the larger idea of the umbrella. Within an umbrella, the lessons build on each other. When you teach several minilessons about the same idea, children deepen their understandings and develop shared vocabulary. These connections are especially helpful to English learners.

In most cases, it makes sense to teach the minilessons in an umbrella one right after another. But for some umbrellas, it makes sense to spread the minilessons over time so that children gain more experience with the first idea before moving on to the next. In this book, lessons are placed together in an umbrella to show you how the lessons build the concept over time.

Figure 2-2: Constructing anchor charts with and in front of your class provides verbal and visual support for all learners.

Anchor Charts Support Writing Minilessons

Anchor charts are an essential part of each writing minilesson (Figure 2-2). They capture children's thinking during the lesson and hold it for reflection at the end of the lesson. The chart is a visual reminder of the big, important ideas and the language used in the minilesson. Each writing minilesson features one sample chart, but use it only as a guideline. Your charts will be unique because they are built from ideas offered by the children in your class.

Each minilesson provides guidance for adding information to the chart. Read through lessons carefully to know whether any parts of the chart should be prepared ahead or whether the chart is constructed during the lesson or left until the end. After the lesson, the charts become a resource for the children to refer to throughout the day and on following days. They are a visual resource for children who need to not only hear but also see the information. Children can revisit these charts as they apply the minilesson principles to their writing or as they try out new routines in the classroom.

Use connecting words to add more information to your writing.

- and
- but
- after

- when
- then
- because

Water Cycle in a Bag

We wanted to see what the water cycle looks like, so we filled a bag with water and sealed it.

The water evaporated because the sun heated it.

After the water evaporated, it "rained" down in the bag.

You can refer to them during guided writing lessons and when you confer with children about their independent writing.

Some of the art you see on the sample charts is available from the online resources to represent concepts that are likely to come up as you construct the charts with children. The downloadable chart art is provided for your convenience. Use it when it applies to the children's responses, but do not let it determine or limit them. Valuing the ideas of the class should be your primary concern.

When you create charts with second graders, consider the following:

Make your charts simple, clear, and organized. Keep the charts simple without a lot of dense text. Provide white space and print neatly in dark, easy-to-read colors.

Make your charts visually appealing and useful. All of the minilesson charts contain visual support, which will be helpful for all children, especially English learners. Children will benefit from the visuals to help them in understanding the concept and in reading some of the words. The drawings are intentionally simple to give you a quick model to draw yourself. You might find it helpful to prepare these drawings on separate pieces of paper or sticky notes ahead of the lesson and tape or glue them on the chart as the children construct their understandings. This time-saving tip can also make the charts look more interesting and colorful, because certain parts will stand out for the children.

 **EL CONNECTION**

Make your charts colorful. The sample minilesson charts are colorful for the purpose of engagement or organization. Color can be useful, but be careful about the amount and type you choose. Color can support English learners by providing a visual link to certain words or ideas. However, color can also be distracting if overused. Be thoughtful about when you choose to use color to highlight an idea or a word on a chart so that children are supported in reading continuous text. Text that is broken up by a lot of different colors can be very distracting for readers. You will notice that the minilesson principle is usually written in black or a dark color across the top of the chart so that it stands out and is easily recognized as the focus of the lesson. In most cases, the minilesson principle is added at the end of the lesson after children have constructed their own understanding of the concept.

Use the charts to support language growth. Anchor charts support language growth in all children, especially English learners. Conversation about the minilesson develops oral language and then connects oral language to print when you write words on the chart, possibly with picture support. By constructing an anchor chart with the children, you provide print that is immediately accessible to them because they helped create it and have ownership of the language. After a chart is finished, revisit it as often as needed to reinforce not only the ideas but also the printed words (Figure 2-3).

Figure 2-3: Characteristics of high-quality anchor charts

Umbrellas and Minilessons Have Predictable Structures

Understanding how the umbrellas are designed and how the minilessons fit together will help you keep your lessons focused and brief. Each umbrella is set up the same way, and each writing minilesson follows the same predictable structure (Figure 2-4). Use mentor texts that you have previously read and enjoyed with the children to streamline the lessons. You will not need to spend a lot of time rereading large sections of the text because the children already know the texts well.

A Closer Look at the Umbrella Overview

All umbrellas are set up the same way. They begin with an overview and end with questions to guide your evaluation of children's understanding of the umbrella concepts plus several extension ideas. In between are the writing minilessons.

At the beginning of each umbrella (Figure 2-5 on page 37), the minilessons are listed and directions are provided to help you prepare to teach them. There are suggestions for books from *Fountas & Pinnell Classroom™ Interactive Read-Aloud Collection* (2018) and *Shared Reading Collection* (2018) to use as mentor texts. There are also suggestions for the kinds of books you might select if you do not have these books.

The Writing Minilessons Book, Grade 2

A Closer Look at the Writing Minilessons

The 190 writing minilessons in this book help you teach specific aspects of writing. An annotated writing minilesson is shown in Figure 2-6 on pages 38–39. Each section is described in the text that follows.

Before the Lesson

Each writing minilesson begins with information to help you make the most of the lesson. There are four types of information:

The Writing Minilesson Principle describes the key idea the children will learn and be invited to apply. The idea for the minilesson principle is based on the behaviors in the grade 2 sections of *The Fountas & Pinnell Literacy Continuum*, but the language has been carefully crafted to be accessible and memorable for children.

The minilesson principle gives you a clear idea of the concept you will help children construct. The lessons are designed to be inquiry-based because the children need to do the thinking to understand the concept for themselves instead of hearing it stated at the beginning.

Structure of a Writing Minilesson	
Minilesson	• Show examples/provide demonstration. • Invite children to talk about their noticings. • Make an anchor chart with clear examples.
Have a Try	• Have children try out what they are learning (usually with a partner).
Summarize and Apply	• Summarize the learning. • Invite children to apply the principle during independent writing time. • Write the minilesson principle on the chart.
Confer	• Move around the room to confer briefly with children.
Share	• Gather children together and invite them to talk about their writing.

Figure 2-4: Once you learn the structure of a writing minilesson, you can create your own minilessons with different examples.

Although we have crafted the language to make it appropriate for the age group, you can shape the language to fit the way your children talk. When you summarize the lesson, be sure to state the principle simply and clearly so that children are certain to understand what it means. State the minilesson principle the same way every time you refer to it.

The Goal of the minilesson is based on a behavior in *The Fountas & Pinnell Literacy Continuum*. Each minilesson is focused on one single goal that leads to a deeeper understanding of the larger umbrella concept.

The Rationale is the reason the minilesson is important. It is a brief explanation of how this new learning leads children forward in their writing journey.

Assess Learning is a list of suggestions of specific behaviors and understandings to look for as evidence that children understand and can apply the minilesson concept. Keep this list in mind as you teach.

Minilesson

The **Minilesson** section provides an example of a lesson for teaching the writing minilesson principle. We suggest some precise language and open-ended questions that will keep children engaged and the lesson brief and focused. Effective minilessons, when possible, involve inquiry. That means children actively think about the idea and notice examples in a familiar piece of writing. They construct their understanding from concrete examples so that the learning is meaningful for them.

Create experiences that help children notice things and make their own discoveries. You might, for example, invite children to look at several nonfiction information books, carefully chosen to illustrate the minilesson principle. Children will know these books because they have heard them read aloud and have talked about them. Often, you can use the same books in several writing minilessons to make your teaching efficient. Invite children to talk about what they notice across all the books.

As second graders explore the mentor text examples using your questions and supportive comments as a guide, make the anchor chart with children's input. From this exploration and the discussion, children come to the minilesson principle. Learning is more powerful and enjoyable for children when they actively search for the meaning, find patterns, talk about their understandings, and share in making the charts. Children need to form networks of understanding around the concepts related to literacy and to be constantly looking for connections for themselves.

A Closer Look at the Umbrella Overview

A list of minilessons is organized under the umbrella title.

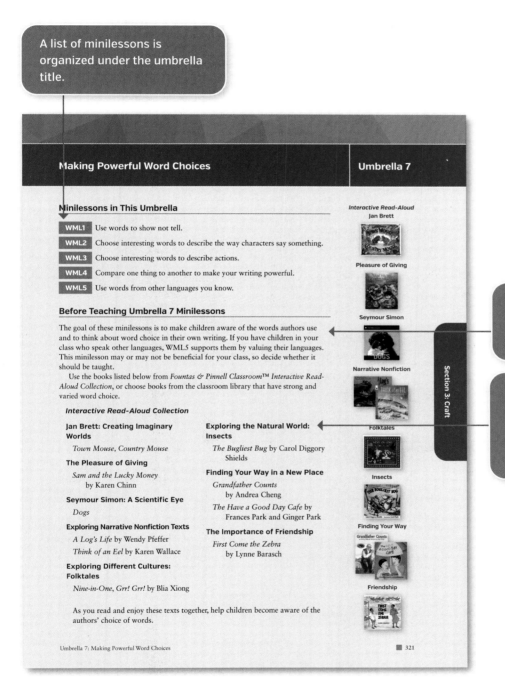

Making Powerful Word Choices

Umbrella 7

Minilessons in This Umbrella

WML1 Use words to show not tell.

WML2 Choose interesting words to describe the way characters say something.

WML3 Choose interesting words to describe actions.

WML4 Compare one thing to another to make your writing powerful.

WML5 Use words from other languages you know.

Before Teaching Umbrella 7 Minilessons

The goal of these minilessons is to make children aware of the words authors use and to think about word choice in their own writing. If you have children in your class who speak other languages, WML5 supports them by valuing their languages. This minilesson may or may not be beneficial for your class, so decide whether it should be taught.

Use the books listed below from *Fountas & Pinnell Classroom™ Interactive Read-Aloud Collection*, or choose books from the classroom library that have strong and varied word choice.

Interactive Read-Aloud Collection

Jan Brett: Creating Imaginary Worlds

Town Mouse, Country Mouse

The Pleasure of Giving

Sam and the Lucky Money by Karen Chinn

Seymour Simon: A Scientific Eye

Dogs

Exploring Narrative Nonfiction Texts

A Log's Life by Wendy Pfeffer

Think of an Eel by Karen Wallace

Exploring Different Cultures: Folktales

Nine-in-One, Grr! Grr! by Blia Xiong

Exploring the Natural World: Insects

The Bugliest Bug by Carol Diggory Shields

Finding Your Way in a New Place

Grandfather Counts by Andrea Cheng

The Have a Good Day Cafe by Frances Park and Ginger Park

The Importance of Friendship

First Come the Zebra by Lynne Barasch

As you read and enjoy these texts together, help children become aware of the authors' choice of words.

Umbrella 7: Making Powerful Word Choices

321

Interactive Read-Aloud
Jan Brett

Pleasure of Giving

Seymour Simon

Narrative Nonfiction

Folktales

Insects

Finding Your Way

Friendship

Section 3: Craft

Prepare for teaching the minilessons in this umbrella with these suggestions.

Use these suggested mentor texts as examples in the minilessons in this umbrella, or use books that have similar characteristics.

Figure 2-5: Each umbrella is introduced by a page that offers an overview of the umbrella.

A Closer Look at a Writing Minilesson

The **Writing Minilesson Principle** is a brief statement that describes what children will be invited to learn and apply.

This code identifies this lesson as the second writing minilesson in the seventh umbrella of the Craft section.

Look for these specific behaviors and understandings as you **assess** children's learning after presenting the lesson.

Important vocabulary used in the minilesson is listed.

Precise language is suggested for teaching the lesson.

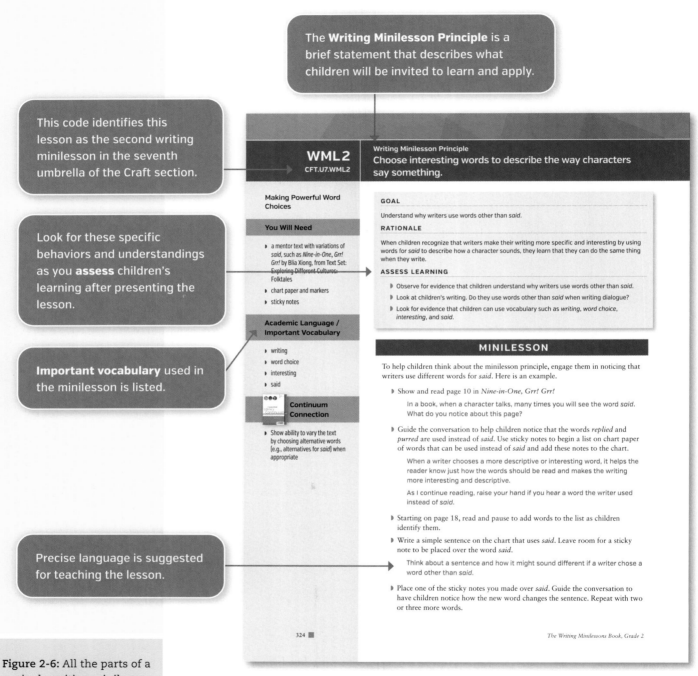

WML2
CFT.U7.WML2

Writing Minilesson Principle
Choose interesting words to describe the way characters say something.

Making Powerful Word Choices

You Will Need

▸ a mentor text with variations of *said*, such as *Nine-in-One, Grr! Grr!* by Blia Xiong, from Text Set: Exploring Different Cultures: Folktales
▸ chart paper and markers
▸ sticky notes

Academic Language / Important Vocabulary

▸ writing
▸ word choice
▸ interesting
▸ said

Continuum Connection

▸ Show ability to vary the text by choosing alternative words (e.g., alternatives for *said*) when appropriate

GOAL
Understand why writers use words other than *said*.

RATIONALE
When children recognize that writers make their writing more specific and interesting by using words for *said* to describe how a character sounds, they learn that they can do the same thing when they write.

ASSESS LEARNING
▸ Observe for evidence that children understand why writers use words other than *said*.
▸ Look at children's writing. Do they use words other than *said* when writing dialogue?
▸ Look for evidence that children can use vocabulary such as *writing, word choice, interesting*, and *said*.

MINILESSON

To help children think about the minilesson principle, engage them in noticing that writers use different words for *said*. Here is an example.

▸ Show and read page 10 in *Nine-in-One, Grr! Grr!*

> In a book, when a character talks, many times you will see the word *said*. What do you notice about this page?

▸ Guide the conversation to help children notice that the words *replied* and *purred* are used instead of *said*. Use sticky notes to begin a list on chart paper of words that can be used instead of *said* and add these notes to the chart.

> When a writer chooses a more descriptive or interesting word, it helps the reader know just how the words should be read and makes the writing more interesting and descriptive.

> As I continue reading, raise your hand if you hear a word the writer used instead of *said*.

▸ Starting on page 18, read and pause to add words to the list as children identify them.
▸ Write a simple sentence on the chart that uses *said*. Leave room for a sticky note to be placed over the word *said*.

> Think about a sentence and how it might sound different if a writer chose a word other than *said*.

▸ Place one of the sticky notes you made over *said*. Guide the conversation to have children notice how the new word changes the sentence. Repeat with two or three more words.

324 ◼

The Writing Minilessons Book, Grade 2

Figure 2-6: All the parts of a single writing minilesson are contained on a two-page spread.

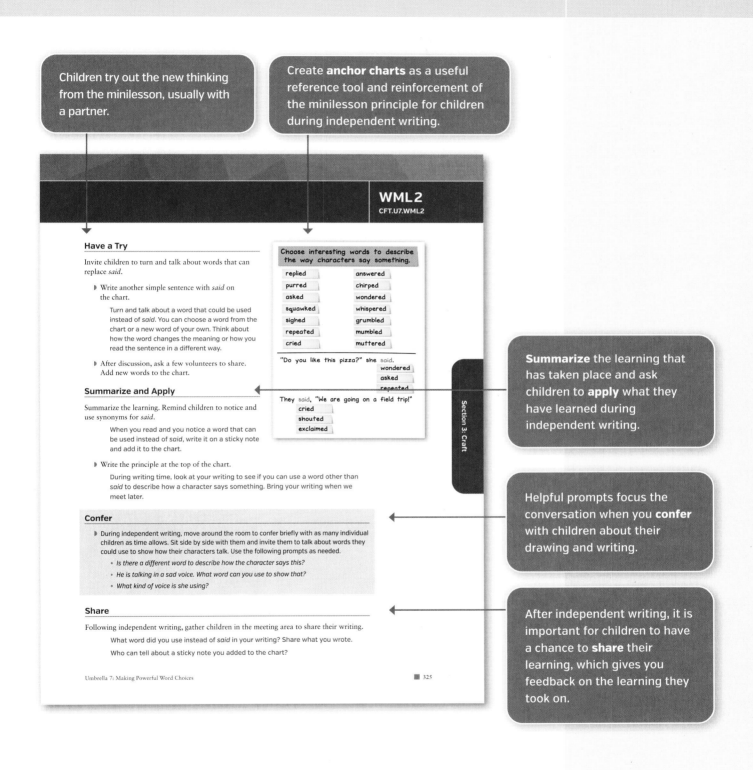

Children try out the new thinking from the minilesson, usually with a partner.

Create **anchor charts** as a useful reference tool and reinforcement of the minilesson principle for children during independent writing.

WML2
CFT.U7.WML2

Section 3: Craft

Have a Try

Invite children to turn and talk about words that can replace *said*.

▶ Write another simple sentence with *said* on the chart.

Turn and talk about a word that could be used instead of *said*. You can choose a word from the chart or a new word of your own. Think about how the word changes the meaning or how you read the sentence in a different way.

▶ After discussion, ask a few volunteers to share. Add new words to the chart.

Summarize and Apply

Summarize the learning. Remind children to notice and use synonyms for *said*.

When you read and you notice a word that can be used instead of *said*, write it on a sticky note and add it to the chart.

▶ Write the principle at the top of the chart.

During writing time, look at your writing to see if you can use a word other than *said* to describe how a character says something. Bring your writing when we meet later.

Choose interesting words to describe the way characters say something.

replied	answered
purred	chirped
asked	wondered
squawked	whispered
sighed	grumbled
repeated	mumbled
cried	muttered

"Do you like this pizza?" she said.
wondered
asked
repeated

They said, "We are going on a field trip!"
cried
shouted
exclaimed

Summarize the learning that has taken place and ask children to **apply** what they have learned during independent writing.

Confer

▶ During independent writing, move around the room to confer briefly with as many individual children as time allows. Sit side by side with them and invite them to talk about words they could use to show how their characters talk. Use the following prompts as needed.

- *Is there a different word to describe how the character says this?*
- *He is talking in a sad voice. What word can you use to show that?*
- *What kind of voice is she using?*

Helpful prompts focus the conversation when you **confer** with children about their drawing and writing.

Share

Following independent writing, gather children in the meeting area to share their writing.

What word did you use instead of *said* in your writing? Share what you wrote.

Who can tell about a sticky note you added to the chart?

Umbrella 7: Making Powerful Word Choices

■ 325

After independent writing, it is important for children to have a chance to **share** their learning, which gives you feedback on the learning they took on.

Children learn more about language when they have opportunities to talk. Writing minilessons provide many opportunities for them to express their thoughts in language, both oral and written, and to communicate with others. The inquiry approach found in these lessons invites more child talk than teacher talk, and that can be both a challenge and an opportunity for you as you work with English learners. However, building talk routines, such as turn and talk, into your writing minilessons can be very helpful in providing opportunities for English learners to talk in a safe and supportive way.

When you ask children to think about the minilesson principle across several stories or informational books that they have previously heard read aloud and discussed, they are more engaged and able to participate because they know the stories and informational books and begin to notice important things about writing through them. Using familiar texts, including some writing that you and the children have created together, is particularly important for English learners. When you select examples for a writing minilesson, choose books and other examples that you know were particularly engaging for the English learners in your classroom. Besides choosing accessible, familiar texts, it is important to provide plenty of wait-and-think time. For example, you might say, "Let's think about that for a minute" before calling for responses.

When working with English learners, look for what the child knows about the concept instead of focusing on faulty grammar or language errors. Model appropriate language use in your responses, but avoid correcting a child who is attempting to use language to learn it. You might also provide an oral sentence frame to get the student response started, for example, *The illustrator chose* _____ *because* _____. Accept variety in pronunciation and intonation, remembering that the more children speak, read, and write, the more they will take on the understanding of grammatical patterns and the complex intonation patterns that reflect meaning in English.

Have a Try

Before children leave the whole group to apply the new thinking during independent writing, give them a chance to try it with a partner or a small group. **Have a Try** is designed to be brief, but it offers you an opportunity to gather information on how well children understand the minilesson goal. In Management lessons, children might quickly practice the new routine that they will be asked to do independently. In the other lessons, children might verbalize how it might be possible to apply the new understanding to their writing. Add further thinking to the chart after the children have had the chance to try out or talk about their new learning. Have a Try is an important step in reinforcing the minilesson principle and moving the children toward independence.

The Have a Try part of the writing minilesson is particularly important for English learners. Besides providing repetition, it gives English learners a safe place to try out the new idea before sharing it with the whole group. These are a few suggestions for how you might support children during this portion of the lesson:

> Pair children with partners that you know will take turns talking.

> Spend time teaching children how to turn and talk. (See MGT.U1: Working Together in the Classroom.) Teach them how to provide wait time for one another, invite the other partner into the conversation, and take turns.

> Provide concrete examples to discuss so that children are clear about what they need to think and talk about. English learners will feel more confident if they are able to talk about a mentor text that they know very well.

> When necessary, provide the oral language structure or language stem for how you want the children to share their ideas. For example, ask them to start with the sentence frame *I noticed the writer* _____ and to rehearse the language structure a few times before turning and talking.

> Imagine aloud how something might sound in a child's writing. Provide children with some examples of how something might sound if they were to try something out in their own writing. For example, you might say something like this: "Marco, you are writing about when you fell off your bike. You could start by drawing yourself on the ground. You could write a speech bubble that says 'OW!!'"

> Observe partnerships involving English learners and provide support as needed.

Summarize and Apply

This part of the lesson includes two parts: summarizing the learning and applying the learning to independent writing.

The **summary** is a brief but essential part of the lesson. It brings together the learning that has taken place through the inquiry and helps children think about its application and relevance to their own learning. Ask children to think about the anchor chart and talk about what they have learned. Involve them in stating the minilesson principle. Then write it on the chart. Use simple, clear language to shape the suggestions. Sometimes, you may decide to summarize the new learning to keep the lesson short and allow enough time for the children to apply it independently. Whether you state the principle or share the construction with the children, summarize the learning in a way that children understand and can remember.

After the summary, the children apply their new understandings to their independent writing. The invitation to try out the new idea must be clear enough for children but "light" enough to allow room for them to have their own ideas for their writing. The application of the minilesson principle should not be thought of as an exercise or task that needs to be forced to fit their writing but instead as an invitation for deeper, more meaningful writing.

We know that when children first take on new learning, they often want to try out the new learning to the exclusion of some of the other things they have learned. When you teach about speech bubbles, for example, expect to see lots of speech bubbles. Encourage children to try out new techniques while reminding them about the other things they have learned.

Before children begin independent writing, let them know that they can apply the new understanding to any writing they do and will have an opportunity to share what they have done with the class after independent writing. Second graders love to share!

Confer

EL CONNECTION

While children are busy independently making books and writing, move around the room to observe and confer briefly with individuals. Sit side by side with them and invite them to talk about what they are doing. In each minilesson, we offer prompts focused on the umbrella concept and worded in clear, direct language. Using direct language can be particularly supportive for English learners because it allows them to focus on the meaning without having to work through the extra talk that we often use in our everyday conversations. Occasionally you will see sentence frames to support English learners in both their talk and their writing.

If a child is working on something that does not fit with the minilesson principle, do not feel limited to the language in this section. Respond to the child in a sincere and enthusiastic way. Remember that the invitation to apply the new learning can be extended another time. This will not be the only opportunity.

General prompts, such as the following, are provided to get children talking so that you can listen carefully to the thinking behind the writing (in using the word *writing* we include *drawing*). Be sure to let children do most of the talking. The one who does the talking does the learning!

▶ *How is your writing going?*

▶ *How can I help you with your writing?*

▶ *What do you think about this piece of writing?*

▶ *What do you want to do next in your writing?*

▶ *What is the best part of your writing (book) so far?*

▶ *Is any part of your writing (book) still confusing for the reader?*

▶ *What would you like to do with this writing (book) when it is finished?*

Observational notes will help you understand how each writer is progressing and provide purposeful, customized instruction every time you talk with children about their writing (Figure 2-7). You can use your notes to plan the content of future minilessons. You can also take pictures of, scan, or make copies of key pieces to discuss with families.

Share

At the end of independent writing, gather children together for the opportunity to **share** their learning with the entire group. During group share, you can revisit, expand, and deepen understanding of the minilesson's goal as well as assess learning. Often, children are invited to bring their drawing and writing to share with the class and to explain how they tried out the minilesson principle. As you observe and talk to children during independent writing, plan how to share by assessing how many children tried the new learning in their writing. If only a few children were able to

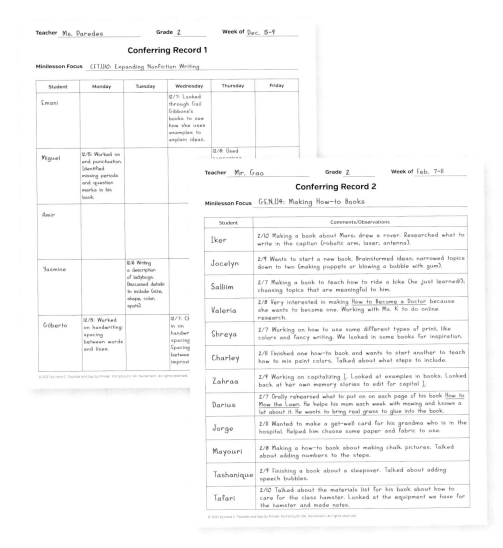

Figure 2-7: Choose one of these downloadable forms to record your observations of children's behaviors and understandings. Visit **fp.pub/resources** to download this and all other online resources.

apply the minilesson principle to their writing, you might ask those children to share with the whole group. However, if you observe most of the class applying the principle, you might have them share in pairs or small groups.

You might also consider inviting children to choose what to share about their writing instead of connecting back to the minilesson principle. For example, one child might share a detail added to make a drawing clearer. Another might share a letter she is writing to her family. Another might read his story to the class.

EL CONNECTION

Share time is a wonderful way to bring the community of learners back together to expand their understandings of writing and of each other as well as to celebrate their new attempts at writing. There are some particular accommodations to support English learners during the time for sharing:

- Ask them to share in pairs before sharing with the group.
- While conferring, help them rehearse the language structure they might use to share their drawing and writing with the class.

Teach the entire class respectful ways to listen to peers and model how to give their peers time to express their thoughts. Many of the minilessons in the Management section will be useful for developing a peaceful, safe, and supportive community of writers.

A Closer Look at the Umbrella Wrap-Up

Following the minilessons in each umbrella, you will see the final umbrella page, which includes a section for assessing what children have learned and a section for extending the learning.

Assessment

The last page of each umbrella, shown in Figure 2-8, provides questions to help you **assess** the learning that has taken place through the entire umbrella. The information you gain from observing what the children can already do, almost do, and not yet do will help inform the selection of the next umbrella you teach. (See Chapter 6 for more information about assessment and the selection of umbrellas.)

Extensions for the Umbrella

Each umbrella ends with several suggestions for **extending** the learning of the umbrella. Sometimes the suggestion is to repeat a minilesson with different examples. Second graders will need to experience some of the concepts more than once before they are able to transfer actions to their independent writing. Other times, children will be able to extend the learning beyond the scope of the umbrella.

A Closer Look at the Umbrella Wrap-Up

Umbrella 7	Making Powerful Word Choices

Assessment

After you have taught the minilessons in this umbrella, observe children in a variety of classroom activities. Use *The Fountas & Pinnell Literacy Continuum* to notice, teach for, and support children's learning as you observe their attempts at writing.

- What evidence do you have of children's new understandings related to word choice?
  - Do children use words that show instead of tell?
  - Are they choosing alternatives to the word *said*?
  - Do they choose interesting verbs?
  - Are they using some figurative language in their writing?
  - Do they sometimes include words from other languages in their writing?
  - Are they using vocabulary such as *writing, word choice, powerful, descriptive, show, tell, interesting, said, action, compare,* and *language*?
- In what ways, beyond the scope of this umbrella, are children's reading and writing behaviors showing an understanding of word choice?
  - Are they varying the ways they begin and end their writing?

Use your observations to determine the next umbrella you will teach. You may also consult Suggested Sequence of Lessons (pp. 575–589) for guidance.

EXTENSIONS FOR MAKING POWERFUL WORD CHOICES

- If you are using *The Reading Minilessons Book, Grade 2* (Fountas and Pinnell 2019), the minilessons in this umbrella would pair well with LA.U9: Analyzing the Writer's Craft.

- Encourage children to use or make up sound words (onomatopoeia) to make their writing more interesting and descriptive.

- Provide opportunities to talk about overused words and have children work together to come up with alternatives.

- Meet with children in small groups to help them make powerful word choices in their writing.

- You may want to repeat WML4 using other types of figurative language, such as metaphor or personification.

332 ■   *The Writing Minilessons Book, Grade 2*

> Gain important information by **assessing** what children have learned as they apply and share their learning of the minilesson principles. Observe and then follow up with individuals in conferences or in small groups in guided writing.

> Optional suggestions are provided for **extending** the learning of the umbrella over time or in other contexts.

Figure 2-8: The final page of each umbrella offers suggestions for assessing the learning and ideas for extending the learning.

- are based on a **writing principle** that is important to teach to second graders
- are based on a **goal** that makes the teaching meaningful
- are **relevant to the specific needs of children** so that your teaching connects with the learners
- are very **brief, concise, and to the point**
- use **clear and specific language** to avoid talk that clutters learning
- stay **focused on a single idea** so children can apply the learning and build on it day after day
- use an **inquiry approach** whenever possible to support active, constructive learning
- often include **shared, high-quality mentor texts** that can be used as examples
- are **well paced** to engage and hold children's interest
- are **grouped into umbrellas** to foster depth in thinking and coherence across lessons
- **build one understanding on another** across several days instead of single isolated lessons
- provide time for children to **"try out" the new concept** before they are invited to try it independently
- engage children in **summarizing the new learning and applying it to their own writing**
- build **important vocabulary** appropriate for children in second grade
- help children **become better artists and writers**
- **foster community** through the development of shared language
- **can be assessed** as you observe children engaged in authentic writing
- **help children understand what they are learning** how to do as artists and writers

Figure 2-9: Characteristics of effective minilessons

Effective Writing Minilessons

The goal of all writing minilessons is to help children think and act like writers and illustrators as they build their capacity for independent writing and drawing across the year. Whether you are teaching lessons about routines, genre, craft, conventions or the writing process, the characteristics of effective minilessons, listed in Figure 2-9, apply.

Writing minilessons can be used to teach anything from telling stories to making books to trying a new craft move and more. Teach a writing minilesson whenever you see an opportunity to nudge the children forward as writers and illustrators.

Chapter 3

Minilessons for Building a Community: Management

*We need a caring classroom community in which multiple perspectives
are developed and used to think critically and expand learning.
We need a community in which children come to appreciate the
value of different perspectives for their own development, in which
they recognize changes in their own and others' thinking and
that that difference is the source for the change.*

—Peter Johnston

INDIVIDUALS LEARN BETTER AND HAVE more fun when they have some
routines for working safely and responsibly. The lessons in Section 1:
Management establish these routines. Children learn how to

- listen,

- take turns,

- show kindness to one another,

- draw and write independently,

- share their writing,

- take care of classroom materials,

> ▶ use their writing folder resources, and

> ▶ use and return materials.

They become independent problem-solvers who can work and play as members of a community.

Building a Community of Writers

Writers need to feel valued and included in a community whose members have learned to trust one another with their stories. The minilessons in the Management section are designed to help children build this trust and learn to include one another in discussions and play. The first lesson in MGT.U1: Working Together in the Classroom (WML1: Get to know your classmates) sets the tone for building this community. As children share who they are, where their families come from, what languages they speak, what foods they eat, and what activities they enjoy, they begin to explore their identities and learn about the identities of others. Self-identity influences the way an individual reads and writes; it impacts the perspective one brings to these literacy experiences. We see this even with our youngest readers and writers. When we celebrate children's unique identities and perspectives, we teach children to value and include one another. This is one of the reasons the share time at the end of independent writing is so important. This time of sharing inspires writing ideas, but it does so much more. It provides a time to celebrate writing and more importantly carves out space to celebrate each writer in the classroom community.

Create a Peaceful Atmosphere

The minilessons in this section will help you establish a classroom environment in which children are confident, self-determined, and kind and in which every child's identity is valued. The lessons are designed to contribute to peaceful activity and shared responsibility. Through the Management minilessons, children learn how to modulate their voices to suit various purposes (from silent to outdoor). They also learn to keep supplies in order, help others, listen to and look at a speaker, and clean up quickly and quietly (Figure 3-1).

All of these minilessons contribute to an overall tone of respect in every classroom activity. They are designed to help you establish the atmosphere you want. Everything in the classroom reflects the children who work there; it is their home for the year.

Teach the minilessons in this section in the order that fits your class needs, or consult the Suggested Sequence of Lessons (pp. 575–589). You may need to reteach some of these lessons because as the year goes on you will be

Tone of
respect

Shared
responsibility

Supplies in
order

Peaceful
Community

Appropriate
voice levels

Help others

Clean up
quickly

Listen to
others

Figure 3-1: Characteristics of a peaceful atmosphere for the community of readers and writers

working in a more complex way. A schedule change or other disruption in classroom operations might prompt a refresher minilesson. Any problem in your classroom should be addressed through minilessons that focus on building a community of learners.

Design the Physical Space

In addition to creating a peaceful atmosphere, prepare the physical space in a way to provide the best support for learning (Figure 3-2). Each umbrella in Section 1: Management will help your second graders become acquainted with the routines of the classroom and help them feel secure and at home. Make sure that the classroom has the following qualities.

▸ **Welcoming and Inviting.** Pleasing colors and a variety of furniture will help. There is no need for commercially published posters or slogans, except for standard references such as the Alphabet Linking Chart (available in online resources) or colorful poetry posters. The room can be filled with the work that the children have produced beginning on day one, some of it in languages other than English. They should see signs of their learning everywhere—shared and interactive writing, charts, drawings of various kinds, and their names. Be sure that children's

Figure 3-2: In an organized classroom, there are places for children to meet and to work. Materials are stored neatly and are easily accessible.

names are at various places in the room—on tables, on cubbies, on a helper's or jobs chart, and on some of the charts that you will make in the minilessons. A wall of framed children's photographs and self-portraits sends the clear message that this classroom belongs to them and celebrates their unique identities. The classroom library should be as inviting as a bookstore or a library. Place books in baskets and tubs on shelves to make the front covers of books visible and accessible for easy browsing. Clearly label the supplies in the writing center so children can see the materials that are available and can access them and return them independently (Figure 3-3). Better yet, have children make labels with you during shared or interactive writing. Children also love to be involved in the naming of the different classroom areas so they truly feel like they have ownership of the classroom. We have seen some classrooms that create space on a low bulletin board with each child's name so that children can choose items to display.

▶ **Organized for Easy Use.** The first thing you might want to do is to take out everything you do not need. Clutter increases stress and noise. Using scattered and hard-to-find materials increases the children's dependence on you. Consider keeping supplies for bookmaking and writing in clearly labeled areas. For example, some teachers organize a writing area where they keep paper, highlighters, staplers, etc. Provide paper and booklets in a variety of different sizes so children can choose the kind of paper they want to use. For example, a simple four-page booklet (two pieces of paper folded in half) or a stapled book folded

horizontally can be made and placed in a tray. You might also provide a selection of templates for writing (available from the online resources). Some teachers choose to have children keep the books or other writing projects they are making in writing folders that are stored in the writing center. Others have them in bins located throughout the room so children can easily access their writing without causing traffic jams.

In the first few days of school, children learn how to get supplies and return supplies. Children who choose to make books can get what they need independently and work at their tables. Some teachers choose to have caddies at tables instead of keeping supplies on a shelf in the writing center so that children can spread out and get started right away.

Work areas are clearly organized with necessary, labeled materials and nothing else. Labels with pictures and words as well as an arrow pointing to where the items belong show children exactly what goes where. Some teachers stick a shape on the shelf that matches the bottom of the container (Figure 3-4). Over the course of the year, introduce different kinds of media into these spaces so children can experiment with collage, 3D materials, and materials that have different textures.

Figure 3-4: A shape on the shelf helps children know where to return materials.

Arrange furniture to create traffic patterns that discourage running, promote safe movement around the room for all children, and allow for easy access to emergency exits. Be sure that all furniture is appropriate for the children's size/height and that children's work is displayed at their eye level so they can appreciate it.

▶ **Designed for Whole-Group, Small-Group, and Individual Instruction.** Writing minilessons are generally provided as whole-class instruction and typically take place at an easel in a meeting space. The space is comfortable and large enough for all children to sit as a group or in a circle. It will be helpful to have a colorful rug. Create some way of helping children find an individual space to sit without crowding one another. (For example, the rug often has squares of different colors.) The meeting space is next to the classroom library so that books are displayed and handy. The teacher usually has a larger chair or seat next to an easel or two so that he can display the mentor texts, make anchor charts, do shared or interactive writing, or place big books for shared reading. This space is available for all whole-group instruction; for example, the children come back to it for group share. In addition to the group meeting space, assign tables and spaces in the classroom for small-group writing instruction. Use low shelving and furniture to define and separate learning areas and to create storage opportunities. Second graders need tables and spaces throughout the classroom where they can work independently and where you can easily set a chair next to a child for a brief writing conference.

Establish Independent Writing

The third umbrella in the Management section helps you establish independent writing time with your second graders. Through the minilessons in this umbrella, children learn the routines needed to be independent and productive. They learn to get started with their writing quickly and quietly. They increase their stamina and become efficient in storing their writing and materials at the end of writing time. Children will learn that writers are never finished. When they finish making a book or working on a piece of writing, they can start another. At the beginning of the year, keep the writing time short (you may even start with just ten minutes of independent time) so they can feel successful right away. Add a few minutes every day until they are able to sustain writing for thirty to forty minutes. Involve the children in setting goals for stretching their writing time and celebrate each time you reach them as a class. You will soon have children begging for more time to do this important work. Second graders also begin to see the value of working on a piece of writing over time. They establish important routines like rereading their writing to think what to do next. Through this umbrella, children also learn that writers receive feedback and guidance from other writers. They learn the routines for conferring with a teacher and how to productively share their writing with an audience at the end of independent writing.

Introduce Writing Tools and Resources

The minilessons in the Management section also introduce children to the tools and resources they will need for independent writing. Choose the minilessons from MGT.U2: Using Drawing and Writing Tools that your students need to use tools properly and independently. It might not seem important, but a short lesson on using markers and glue goes a long way in preserving classroom materials and helping children become increasingly independent. There are also lessons to introduce using scissors and a stapler and lessons about tools that allow writers to revise and add on to their work.

Provide Paper Choices

When you give children the ability to choose from a variety of paper, you teach them to make important decisions as a writer/illustrator. We suggest offering some of the following choices (most available as templates in online resources) throughout the year:

- Paper with picture boxes and lines in varying formats (e.g., picture box on the top/lines on the bottom or picture box on the side with wrapping lines)
- Paper in landscape and portrait layouts
- Paper stapled into booklets (portrait and landscape)
- Paper formatted for text features (e.g., sidebar, table of contents, and materials list)
- Author page
- Dedication page
- Paper in a letter format

Paper choices give children a chance to envision how they want their writing to look. Part of making books is thinking about how you want the print and illustrations to be placed on a page. We have included the lesson MGT.U2.WML3 (Choose your paper) because paper is a tool for writing. However, choosing paper could be introduced or revisited as part of GEN.U1: Getting Started with Making Books.

Introduce the Writing Folder

Children's writing folders serve two purposes. They provide a place for them to keep ongoing writing projects (e.g., a book they are working on or letters they are writing) as well as writing they have finished but might want to return to in the future. We suggest using colored folders with a pocket on each side and fasteners in the middle on which you can place resources for children to use during independent writing (e.g., a personal word list). If you use four different colors for the folders, it is easy to have four students pass out the folders in a short amount of time. Or, place a crate for each of the four colors in different corners of the classroom so that only one fourth of the children go to the crate at a time to retrieve their folders. With four colors, students can quickly recognize their writing folders. The minilessons in MGT.U4: Introducing Writing Folder Resources support children in recording information on finished writing pieces, reflecting on what they have learned about writing, and learning how to use a personal spelling list. These resources give children agency and promote their independence by giving them tools for sustaining their own writing. Templates for these resources are available in the online resources.

The writing folder also helps children view themselves as writers. The record of finished writing pieces gives individual writers a sense of accomplishment and provides a way for you and your students to notice patterns in their writing choices. Use this record to help your writers reflect during writing conferences: Are there different kinds of writing they would like to try? Are they choosing topics they care about? Is there a way to write about the same topic in a different way? Consider expanding writing folder resources over time. For example, you could place a list of high-frequency words and a proofreading checklist (both available in the online resources) after teaching the minilessons in CNV.U2: Learning How to Write Words and WPS.U10: Editing and Proofreading Writing.

When children have writing pieces that they have completed in their writing folders, consider creating hanging file folders in a filing cabinet or crate in which students can store their finished work. This allows them to have their finished writing in one place so they can look back and reflect on their growth periodically. The collection of finished writing is also helpful for you to see children's growth over time and to communicate that growth during conferences with children and with their parents or caregivers.

Chapter 4

Minilessons for Studying Genres and Forms of Writing

*Genre study is where we put all of our reading-like-a-writer
skills together. When we read like writers for genre, we read across a set of
mentor texts and notice many categories of writerly moves including ideas
(what writers generally write about in that genre) and
also craft and structure (how they write about it).*

—Allison Marchetti and Rebekah O'Dell

EXPOSING CHILDREN TO DIFFERENT GENRES, forms, and modes of writing broadens their vision for what writing can be. The minilessons in the Genres and Forms section use inquiry and mentor texts to help students understand the characteristics of different genres and how to use that knowledge when they write. Through the umbrellas in this section, students are also exposed to various forms of writing and composition. Besides learning how to write in the genres of memory story, realistic fiction, informational text, and procedural text, students also learn how to write in various forms and modes. They learn to make picture books, write poems, design slide presentations, write letters, and think about different ways to communicate a persuasive message (e.g., making bumper stickers, designing posters, writing songs, making slogans for a T-shirt or hat).

It is always helpful to support children by reading and studying a genre either before or while writing in a genre. If you have *Fountas & Pinnell Classroom™ Interactive Read-Aloud Collection* (2018) and/or *The Reading Minilessons Book, Grade 2* (2019), use the genre study text sets and the minilesson umbrellas that address genre study to immerse students within a genre and to help them define the genre in their own words. The genre study process, outlined in both the *Interactive Read-Aloud Collection* lessons and *The Reading Minilessons Book, Grade 2*, is designed to help students develop a deep understanding of the characteristics of genres as readers. We have written extensively about this topic and process in our book *Genre Study: Teaching with Fiction and Nonfiction Books* (Fountas and Pinnell 2012).

It is important for children to be exposed to a variety of genres as both readers and writers, and we hope the writing minilesson umbrellas in the Genres and Forms section will further extend their genre understandings. However, we caution you to avoid jumping directly from one genre study to another. Children need time to experiment with different forms of writing. They also need time to choose their own genres based on their purpose and audience. As Ralph Fletcher points out in his book *Joy Write: Cultivating High-Impact, Low-Stakes Writing* (2017), writers need time to play with writing. The lessons in the genre umbrellas are designed to expose children to different characteristics of a genre and offer ways for them to think about writing in them. They are not meant to take students through a rigid sequence of steps for writing in that genre. Writers each have their individual ways of working on writing. You will want to make sure you respect students' own writing processes and topic choices while helping students develop new genre understandings.

Children Love to Make Books

Bookmaking is a powerful way for children to begin exploring different genres and to bring together all their important literacy experiences. Glover (2009) said it well:

> The reason for making books is simple. Books are what children have the greatest vision for, and having a clear vision for what you are making is important in any act of composition. Young children have the clearest vision for making picture books because that is the type of writing that they have seen most. (13)

Invite your students to make their own books, just like the authors of the books they love (Figure 4-1). Children enjoy using blank books (even as simple as a piece of paper folded in half), but you can also offer any of the

Cover

What is a horse
A horse is a big animal. There are wild
horses. They are horses too. Wild
horses gallop more than walking. You
don't see wild horses a lot.

What color are they
Horses can be a lot of different colors
like brown, dark brown, tan, gray,
white. You can tell if it is white or gray
because gray is darker.

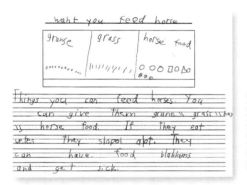

What you feed horses
Things you can feed horses. You can
give them grain, grass, hay, horse
food. If they eat lettuce, they slobber a
lot. They can have food problems and
get sick.

Everything you need for horses
If you want a horse, you need this–a
saddle. A saddle is what you put on a
horse when you are riding. You need
a brush. You need a coat for your
horse.

Actions they do
You have to be careful of the actions
they can do. They can kick you. They
can step on you. They also can make
you fall off if you are not being nice
to them.

variety of optional paper templates for writing from the online resources. The act of making books—we use the term *making* instead of *writing* because some children will protest that they can't write a book—benefits you and the children in lots of ways.

▶ Children see themselves as authors, illustrators, and readers (Figure 4-2).

▶ They develop feelings of independence and accomplishment at having created something that is uniquely theirs.

▶ They begin to try out aspects of craft, such as how to organize their ideas, where to place them on the page, and how to communicate their message effectively.

Figure 4-1: Rose shows her understanding of books with her own nonfiction book about a favorite topic, horses. She included features she has seen in nonfiction books: a cover, pictures with labels, and headings.

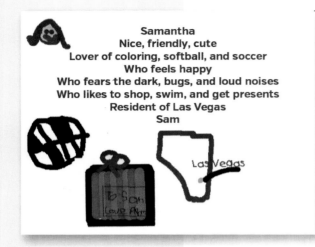

Figure 4-2: Second grader Samantha wrote a poem about herself for the author page of her book.

▶ They build stamina by working on a book over several days.

▶ Writing and reading reinforce one another, so as children make their own books, they become more aware of the decisions that authors and illustrators make in their books.

▶ Children expand their understanding about print, illustrations, and text structure.

▶ The books they write show evidence of what they know about drawing and writing, and you can use that information to decide what they need to learn next.

The minilessons in Genres and Forms umbrella GEN.U1: Getting Started with Making Books introduces the basics of making books. Other umbrellas provide opportunities for children to try making specific kinds of books, including how-to books, question-and-answer books, all-about books (informational books), and memory books.

> Once you treat children as authors and illustrators, and engage them in conversations about how authors and illustrators do things, they notice more and more of those things and wonder how and why authors do them. (Johnston et al. 2020, 14)

Through bookmaking, children also see how their areas of interest can fuel different types of writing. Now that she has written an informational book about horses, Rose might write a memory book about something that happened while horseback riding, or she might make a how-to book to teach how to care for horses. She might even choose to make a collection of poems about horses. When children have opportunities to choose their own topics for bookmaking, they learn about themselves, what they love, and who they are. They are learning how to put themselves on the pages of a book.

Children Learn About Writing Through Poetry

When you teach children to read and write poetry, they learn craft moves that cross over all genres and forms from poetry to prose. They learn how to be precise and efficient in their language, how to create sensory images, how to use figurative language, and how to evoke emotion in a reader. We have written previously that, in a way, everything writers need to know about reading and writing exists within a poem. Second graders benefit from learning to write poetry because it

- helps them appreciate the sound and imagery of language,
- invites them to reflect on themselves and the world in new ways,
- allows them to discover words, sounds, and rhythm in unique, creative ways,
- engages them in "solving" a puzzle as they think about the meaning of a poem, and
- captures the essence of a message or image with a sparse amount of language.

We recommend that you integrate poetry throughout the school year instead of teaching poetry for just a few weeks as part of a unit. Some teachers reserve one day a week during the writers' workshop to hold a poetry workshop (Figure 4-3). During this time, children focus on reading poetry, responding to poetry, and writing their own poetry.

We also recommend you help your students develop a personal poetry book or anthology. In it, they collect poems they love, respond to them through drawing and writing, and write their personal poetry. The first minilesson in GEN.U8: Writing Poetry introduces children to their personal poetry books and provides suggestions for responding to poetry. For example, children might draw a picture, write a reflection about what the poem made them think about, or write their own poem in response.

Figure 4-3: Structure of Poetry Workshop

Structure of Poetry Workshop	
Poet Talk	• Offer advice from a poet or tell about a poet's life.
Poetry Read-Aloud and Writing Minilesson	• Read a poem aloud and teach a minilesson that can be applied to poetry. • Besides the minilessons dedicated to poetry, there are several lessons in the Craft and Writing Process sections that can be taught or retaught with poetry as the focus.
Poetry Projects and Poetry Centers	• Confer with students as they participate in reading, writing, and responding to poems.
Poetry Share	• Allow time for children to share poems they have written or memorized.

Providing students with multiple ways to respond, including with art, makes the poetry experience more meaningful and joyful. Children love making watercolor paintings or collages in response to poems they have read or to ones they have written. Encourage children to perform poems using movement and their voices. When children have opportunities to respond to poetry authentically, they learn more about the characteristics of poetry and how to write it themselves.

Whether students work on poetry during poetry workshop or writers' workshop, they are involved in the same writing process they go through when writing prose (Figure 4-4):

▶ They look at mentor texts (poems).

▶ They apply what they learned in minilessons.

▶ They collect ideas for poetry topics in a writer's notebook.

▶ They draft, revise, and edit their poems.

▶ They create art to accompany their poems.

Some teachers choose to create poetry centers during their poetry workshop.

▶ Consider setting up a center to explore memorable words and phrases from books and poems. Encourage students to write their own poems using the words and phrases as inspiration. Invite children to cut out words from magazines or newspapers and make poems out of them by gluing them in a poetry book or writer's notebook.

▶ Set up a poetry window with clipboards, colored pencils, etc. Outline a portion of the window so students can look through and describe or sketch what they see. Invite them to write poems about the things they see through the poetry window.

▶ Create an illustration or art center where students have access to a variety of art media to illustrate poems they have read or written.

Clouds

Clouds are like cotancandy
fluffy and puffy
trees are like houses
tall and strong
Planets are like Ball
rolling thrght space
oceans are Blanks
wide and long

Figure 4-4: Nico used what he learned in minilessons about comparing one thing to another to write a poem of comparisons.

For more ideas, we highly recommend *Awakening the Heart: Exploring Poetry in Elementary and Middle School* (Heard 1999), *A Place for Wonder: Reading and Writing Nonfiction in the Primary Grades* (Heard and McDonough 2009), and *Poems Are Teachers: How Studying Poetry Strengthens Writing in All Genres* (VanDerwater 2018). Create a culture of poetry in your school: post poems meaningfully on the walls of the school (e.g., poems about food around the cafeteria doors or poems about water around sinks and water fountains); designate a poetry gallery where you invite children to add mentor poems as well as their own poems; create schoolwide poetry readings or share a poem of the day as part of morning announcements. When you immerse children in poetry, you will see the results in their writing across genres.

Experimenting with Writing in New Ways

Children get excited to try out writing that they see in the world. Engagement always increases with authenticity. When you give them multiple ways to compose and offer them new ways to play with their writing, they become more motivated to write, especially when you approach the writing with a spirit of inquiry. Use GEN.U10: Experimenting with Writing in New Ways to spark your own creativity. Approach the learning within this umbrella with your own sense of discovery and wonder. Writing involves composing and there are so many ways to compose whether through images, movement, or words. Allowing yourself and your students to dream up all the ways they might compose something new will reinvigorate the writing happening in your classroom. We recommend that you break up this umbrella across the year, repeat the lessons at different times, and add your own creative ideas.

This umbrella offers children ways to re-envision their writing. In the first minilesson, children learn that they can write about the same topic in different ways. For example, Lilliana loves dogs. She has written a book telling how to take care of dogs, an information book all about dogs, and poems about dogs. Later, Lilliana figures out she can also write fiction about her favorite topic. She decides to write a fairy tale about a dog named Cinderella Puppy. (Figure 4-5). In WML2, students learn how changing perspective in a piece of writing can give it a brand-new twist. They are introduced to the idea of personification and learn how writing from the point of view of an object or animal can be a playful way to inspire new writing. In WML3, children learn that books can inspire new ways to write. Figure 4-6 shows the comic strip Luca was inspired to draw after reading several comic books.

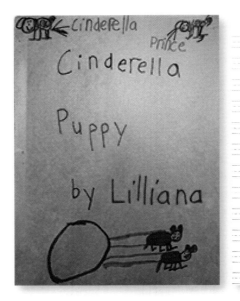

Figure 4-5: Students can write about the same topic in different ways. Lilliana loves dogs. In this book, a dog, Cinderella Puppy, is the main character. In this poem, she wrote lovingly about her own dog.

The last minilesson in this umbrella supports persuasive writing. Most of the persuasive efforts of second graders are best done in the context of reading. There, they give book talks and write book recommendations to share their thoughts about and give reasons to convince their classmates to read books they love (see *The Reading Minilessons Book*). However, in

Figure 4-6: Inspired by the comic books he has read, Luca drew his own comic strip.

this writing minilesson, children think about a message that is important to them and then look at how people market their messages in the world. They brainstorm different ways to compose and share their messages (e.g., developing a logo for merchandise, writing a song, or making a public service announcement poster) for their intended audience.

Children need lots of opportunities to write in different ways so they can envision the importance of writing. Children want to write when they understand that it serves an authentic and meaningful purpose. As you work through the minilessons in the Genres and Forms section, you offer students a range of ways to write and open their eyes to the ways writing can serve a variety of purposes.

Chapter 5

Minilessons for the Study of Craft, Conventions, and Writing Process

One of our primary goals is for children to be self-directed writers who have the ability to follow their own intentions. We want children to be engaged for reasons beyond the fact that they are required to write. We want them to choose projects because they want to entertain their friends or share what they know about a topic or convince someone to do something. Without the ability and opportunity to find authentic writing projects, it will be more difficult for them to become truly self-directed.

— Matt Glover

FOR CHILDREN TO BECOME ENGAGED in the writing process, they have to care about their writing. Teachers of writing know that children are more engaged when they are able to make choices about their writing. Choice comes in many forms. Writers choose the length of their writing, their topic, their purpose, their audience, the kind of writing they will do, and how they will craft it. They make choices about where to put things on the page, how to punctuate a sentence, what to revise and edit, and whether to ultimately publish a piece of writing. If we want to develop authentic writers in our classrooms, we have to provide time, space, and instruction for children to engage in these decisions. The umbrellas and minilessons in the last three sections of this book, Craft, Conventions, and Writing Process, set the stage for you to develop writers who make these decisions, have a sense of agency, and care deeply about their writing work.

Applying Craft, Conventions, and Writing Process Minilessons

The umbrellas in the Craft, Conventions, and Writing Process sections can be used in several ways. They are perfect for selecting when you notice that your children are ready for or in need of a certain lesson. For example, let's say you have noticed that several of your students are starting to organize similar information together in their nonfiction books, and you know they would benefit from learning about headings. So you decide to teach the Craft minilesson on headings or the entire Craft umbrella CFT.U9: Using Text Features in Nonfiction Writing.

Alternatively, you might choose to simply follow the Suggested Sequence of Lessons (pp. 575–589), which weaves the umbrellas from these three sections across the year. Children can apply their new learning about craft to books in a single genre they are all working on (e.g., all-about books) or to books in whatever genres individuals have chosen to work on. Whichever way you decide to use these lessons, be thoughtful about whether your children are writing something that will allow them to try out the minilessons. There are some umbrellas in the Craft section that are quite easy to apply to certain kinds of writing. For example, you might want to introduce CFT.U4: Adding Dialogue to Writing when children are writing memory stories because they can probably imagine what was said at the time of their stories. If they have difficulty applying new learning to their current writing, consider inviting them to revisit finished work in their writing files or folders. They also can apply the new learning to something they have started in their writer's notebooks. Occasionally, you might ask all students to finish or lay aside what they are currently writing in order to try out a principle or genre and return to their unfinished piece later. However, there are several umbrellas in the Craft, Conventions, and Writing Process sections that can be applied across all kinds of writing (e.g., CNV.U4: Using Capital Letters or WPS.U8: Adding Information to Your Writing).

Another thing to consider when you ask children to apply the minilessons from these three sections is the place where most students are in their use of the writing process to create a piece. If most children are just starting a new informational piece, you might teach WPS.U3: Gathering Ideas for Informational Writing. If many children are working on revising their work, you might teach a Craft lesson or a lesson from the drafting and revising part of the Writing Process section. If you want to engage children in editing their work, choose an umbrella from the Conventions section or one of the editing umbrellas in the Writing Process section. Whenever you decide to teach these minilessons, think of it as adding tools to your writers' toolboxes. For many students, you will hand them the right tool at exactly the right time. But others will tuck that tool away and use it when they are ready.

Studying the Craft of Writing

What do we mean when we talk about the craft of writing with second graders? Young children appreciate writer's craft even before they know what it is. They laugh at Helen Lester's humorous characters and word play, they are entertained by Cynthia Rylant's beautiful word choices, or they know how to turn to the exact page they want in a Gail Gibbons book because they have figured out how the book is organized. Through the talk that surrounds interactive read-aloud and shared reading, second graders know a lot about the craft of writing. Craft minilessons take this budding knowledge and pull back the curtain on the decisions authors make to create books that are interesting and exciting to read.

The minilessons in the Craft section are based on the behaviors and understandings in the Craft section of the grade 2 Writing continuum in *The Fountas & Pinnell Literacy Continuum*. It is important to note that minilessons that teach these behaviors and understandings are not limited to the Craft section of this book. There are minilessons that address aspects of craft built into the Genres and Forms section because craft is part of writing in any genre (e.g., telling your memory story in a sequence or organizing your all-about book). Even minilessons in the Conventions section have an aspect of craft to them. For example, capitalization and punctuation have to do with the conventions of writing, but writers also use punctuation and capitalization to communicate their ideas and voice (e.g., using multiple exclamation points to indicate excitement or using all caps to indicate yelling). Whenever writers make decisions about their writing, they are making craft moves. The first umbrella in the Craft section, U1: Reading Like a Writer and Illustrator, sets the stage for noticing writer's and illustrator's craft decisions whenever a book is read. The minilessons in the Craft section allow you to focus specifically on the following aspects of craft, which can be applied across a variety of genres.

Organization

This aspect of craft includes the structure of the whole text—the beginning, the arrangement of ideas, and the ending. In CFT.U5: Exploring Different Ways Authors Start Books and CFT.U6: Exploring Different Ways Authors End Books, you lead the children through an inquiry process using mentor texts to discover how they might try different beginnings and endings in their own writing. In CFT.U9: Using Text Features in Nonfiction Writing, they learn that they can use headings, sidebars, and tables of contents to organize information for their readers. All these minilessons help children learn how to organize and arrange their ideas as writers while also contributing to their understandings as readers.

Idea Development

Idea development is how writers present and support their ideas with examples and details. For second graders, this means thinking about the details they can add to describe where their stories take place and what their characters are like (e.g., CFT.U2: Describing Characters and CFT.U3: Crafting a Setting). It also means they learn how to provide examples to support their ideas and take notes to become an expert on a topic. In CFT.U10: Expanding Nonfiction Writing, children learn how to use personal anecdotes and comparisons to further develop their ideas. Whether they are writing a personal narrative, fiction, or informational text, students learn how to support and develop their ideas from the umbrellas in the Craft section.

Figure 5-1: Lilliana has clearly been inspired to use language she has read in books.

Language Use

This aspect of craft addresses the way writers use sentences, phrases, and expressions to describe events, actions, or information. As your second graders grow in their ability to write words, they can turn more of their attention to using language that sounds like the language in books. Notice how Lilliana used the language she learned from reading fairy tales in her own Cinderella tale (Figure 5-1). Notice how she writes in the middle of her own version of the classic tale "Oh how she wanted to go" to describe how much Cinderella Puppy yearns to go to the ball. She uses the language of traditional tales yet again as she writes the ending. Cinderella Puppy "lived happily ever after" when the glass collar fits. Children also begin to notice how authors use dialogue in speech bubbles and in text. CFT.U4: Adding Dialogue to Writing supports children as they experiment with writing meaningful dialogue in their stories.

Word Choice

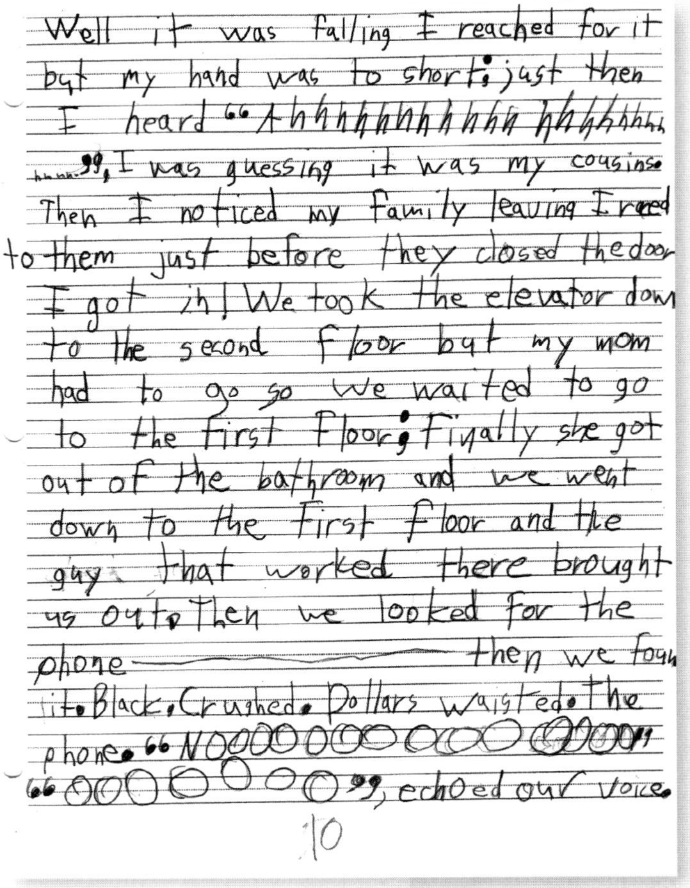

Word choice matters. A writer's choice of a specific word can change the whole meaning of a sentence. Consider the difference between writing *The woman strolled down the road* and *The woman sprinted down the road*. In the first sentence, we understand that the woman must feel pretty relaxed to be strolling along. The latter conveys much more urgency; we wonder what caused her to hurry. Second graders quickly pick up on the importance of word choice once they are taught to pay attention to it. You can begin planting the seeds for this in your interactive read-aloud and shared reading lessons. As you read, linger on a few important words, think aloud about why the author chose them, repeat a word, and simply comment how much you love the author's choice of words. When you heighten children's awareness of how carefully writers choose words, they begin to think about their own word choices (Figure 5-2). One umbrella, CFT.U7: Making Powerful Word Choices, is dedicated to supporting children in taking these early understandings about word choice and applying them to their own writing.

Figure 5-2: In his fiction story about getting lost in the Empire State Building, Keith chose his words carefully. He described the phone they found as not just broken but "crushed." Their voices "echo" as shown by a string of O's.

Voice

It is through the writer's voice that readers get a sense of the author's feelings and passion for a story or topic. Voice is a writer's unique style. The voices of second graders often naturally shine through their writing pieces. They have unique ways of seeing the world, and the way they use their words often conveys this perspective. When children are encouraged to share their feelings in a story or to write the way they talk, they learn important lessons about voice. Voice is also very closely linked to the conventions of writing. When children learn to punctuate their writing with exclamation points, question marks, and even more sophisticated punctuation, their voices become even stronger. In CFT.U8, children learn how to use different styles of print and to talk directly to the reader as other ways to infuse voice into a piece of writing (Figure 5-3).

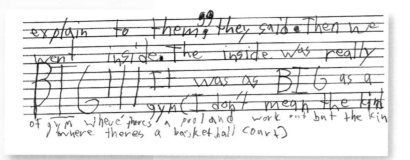

Figure 5-3: Keith's voice comes through at the beginning of his fiction story as the characters step into the Empire State Building. Notice his use of punctuation and the way he made the word BIG larger within the text. His use of parentheses to talk to the reader also demonstrates how much he has learned about voice through minilessons and mentor texts.

Figure 5-4: Santiago teaches how to juggle a soccer ball through a series of pictures.

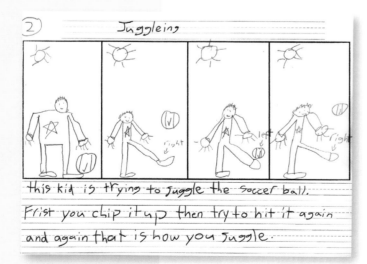

Drawing

Drawing is important and is used at every stage of the writing process. There are several writing minilessons in the Craft section to help you and your children take a close look at illustrator's craft—the decisions illustrators make to communicate their ideas. Through these lessons, children's drawings become increasingly representational and detailed. CFT.U11: Learning to Draw teaches children how to use shapes to draw people in different positions, how to show where a story takes place, and how to draw people consistently on each page. Another minilesson helps them consider how to color things realistically, helping them notice details of skin tone and hair and eye color.

When you teach drawing, you are also nurturing children's development of writing. As children develop their ability to draw representationally, they begin to add details that capture more of a story in both pictures and words. They become more aware of the way illustrators use their drawings to communicate ideas. In Santiago's book about soccer, he used a series of pictures to demonstrate how to complete a soccer move. Through minilessons and mentor texts, he has learned that he can draw people in different positions and that consecutive scenes can be used to demonstrate movement and action (Figure 5-4). Careful examination of mentor texts in the drawing minilessons shows children how to look at the illustrations in books with an illustrator's eye. Santiago has learned to make his words and his drawings work together to convey an idea. In CFT.U12: Adding Information to Illustrations, minilessons focus on many of the craft moves illustrators make, such as using color to show feelings, drawing motion and sound lines, and using layout and perspective to draw attention to important information. The more children learn about drawing, the more they learn about the process of revising their writing. They get excited to add new details to their pictures after talking about their stories and learning new illustration techniques. This in turn impacts the details they add to their writing.

The minilessons in CFT.U13: Using Illustrations and Graphics in Nonfiction Writing help children expand their thinking about illustrations beyond drawing characters and settings. They learn that illustrations can be used to show factual information through detailed drawings, diagrams (Figure 5-5), and photographs. Children love experimenting with different media (e.g., cut paper, found objects, or fabric) to make their illustrations interesting for their readers.

Through CFT.U14: Making Illustrations Interesting, children learn that they can use scenes, borders, and text layout to make their pictures interesting. In Figure 5-6, Alfred made a mobile of volcanos to share facts he learned. When you teach children to draw and use media in interesting ways, they become inspired to use art in their own ways to communicate their messages and ideas.

Teaching the Conventions of Writing

Conventions and craft go hand in hand. They work together to communicate meaning. A writer can have great ideas, understand how to organize them, and even make interesting word choices. But the ideas can get lost if the writer doesn't form letters correctly, spell words in recognizable ways, or use conventional grammar and punctuation. For writing to be valued and understood, writers need to understand the conventions of writing. Sophisticated writers might play with these conventions and sometimes break the rules for their use, but they are aware that they are making an intentional decision to do so.

Teaching conventions to second graders can be tricky. Approach it with a spirit of inquiry and discovery. Children are more motivated to use conventions when they see the rewards of others being able to read and understand their writing. Avoid being so rigid in your teaching of

Figure 5-5: Rachine made a diagram to describe a science experiment involving a hand-built parachute for her how-to book.

Figure 5-6: Alfred included a drawing on one side of the "volcano" and facts on the other to tell what he has learned about this self-chosen topic.

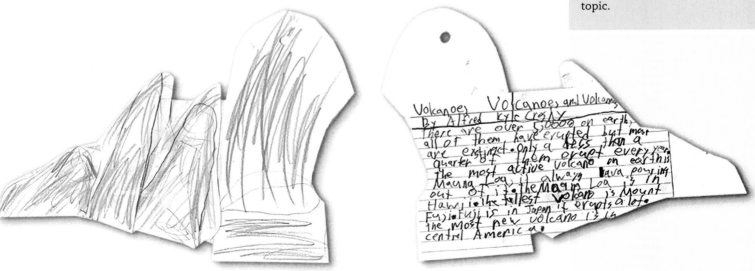

conventions that children are afraid to take risks. Second graders should celebrate their efforts to spell a new word. How limited and boring their writing would be if they used only the words they knew how to spell! The minilessons in the Conventions section are designed to strike a balance between teaching children to write clearly while making them comfortable to take risks with their new learning. The minilessons in this section are based on the behaviors and understandings in the Conventions section of the grade 2 Writing continuum in *The Fountas & Pinnell Literacy Continuum*; however, just like craft, the conventions of writing are not limited to this section. There are aspects of conventions woven into the writing minilessons in every section. The Conventions section, in conjunction with these other sections, addresses the following conventions of writing.

Text Layout

For second graders, text layout might mean making sure that there is proper space between their words and that their letters are proportionate to one another (see CNV.U1: Using Good Handwriting). Children also learn that when they use a computer they can use different font styles and sizes to convey meaning. In addition, learning about text layout involves learning about where to place print and pictures on a page, including placement of headings and titles. When you introduce a variety of paper templates (available in the online resources) that show a variety of ways to lay out a page, you teach them that writers make important choices about where they place print and pictures.

Grammar and Usage

For second graders, grammar and usage are best taught in the context of writing. For example, children experience how to use past, present, and future tenses as they participate in shared and interactive writing. They learn how to use adjectives, adverbs, prepositions, and conjunctions in the act of writing. The more children are engaged in writing and translating their talk into writing, the more experience they will have in using grammar. In later grades, they will more explicitly learn about the rules of grammar. For now, they learn and internalize the conventions of grammar as they read, talk, and write.

Capitalization

Most second graders are at a stage in which they understand the difference between upper- and lowercase letters. They may occasionally use a capital letter in the middle of a word, but for the most part, they understand that capital letters are used for specific reasons. The minilessons in CNV.U4: Using Capital Letters support and expand this understanding. Minilessons reinforce the concepts of using capital letters at the beginning of names, for the first letter of the first word in a sentence, and for most of the words in a title. Children learn to capitalize the first letter in the names of places, days, months, cities, and states.

Punctuation

Second graders learn that punctuation makes their writing readable for others. CNV.U3: Learning About Punctuation helps children further develop their understanding that punctuation also communicates how the reader should read the sentence (e.g., an exclamation point indicates excitement or surprise). This beginning understanding of the role of punctuation provides a foundation for children to see punctuation as a way to craft their messages. Writers communicate voice with punctuation. They communicate emotions—excitement, fear, sadness, confusion. Punctuation is inextricably linked with the craft of writing. When second graders learn the conventions of punctuation, they begin to notice how authors use punctuation in their books. Writing minilessons make children curious about what writers do and eager to imitate what they notice in their own writing.

Spelling

As second graders acquire knowledge of letters, sounds, and words, they use a combination of approximated spelling and conventional spelling in their writing. Encourage children to write the words they know quickly and accurately and to use a range of strategies to make their best attempts at words they do not know. In CNV.U2: Learning How to Write Words, children learn to say words slowly and listen for all the sounds. They learn to break words into syllables to write them, to include a vowel in every syllable, and to use what they know about words to help them spell other words.

These minilessons should accompany a strong phonics, spelling, and word study component in your classroom. The umbrella on spelling in the Conventions section is not meant to be your students' only instruction in spelling. It is meant to *reinforce and supplement* what you are teaching in your phonics, spelling, and word study instruction and help children transfer what they are learning to their writing. Interactive writing can be a powerful tool for students to learn about how words work. Each time you ask children to share the pen, you help them to think about the connections between letters and sounds and bring them directly into the process of constructing words using the strategies explicitly taught in these writing minilessons. The Conventions minilessons and phonics, spelling, and word study lessons you teach all work together to bring children closer to spelling conventionally and making their writing clear to their readers.

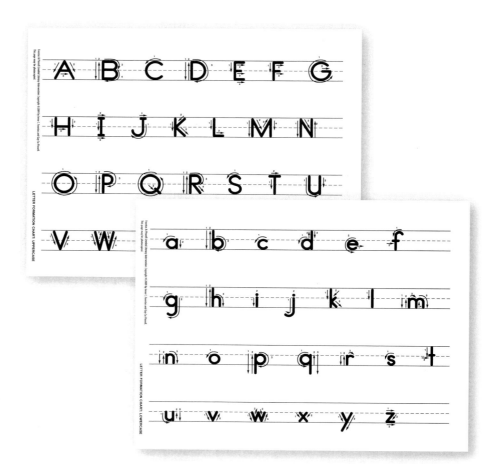

Verbal Path for Letter Formation

Sometimes it helps children to say aloud the directions for "making" a letter. This "verbal path" helps them to understand the directional movement that is essential. In addition, it gives the teacher and child a language to talk through the letter and its features. Here, we suggest language for creating a verbal path to the distinctive features of letters.

Lowercase Letter Formation

a — pull back, around, up, and down
b — pull down, up, around
c — pull back and around
d — pull back, around, up, and down
e — pull across, back, and around
f — pull back, down, and cross
g — pull back, around, up, down, and under
h — pull down, up, over, and down
i — pull down, dot
j — pull down, curve around, dot
k — pull down, pull in, pull out
l — pull down
m — pull down, up, over, down and up, over, and down

n — pull down, up, over, and down
o — pull back and around
p — pull down, up, and around
q — pull back, around, up, and down
r — pull down, up, and over
s — pull back, in, around, and back around
t — pull down and cross
u — pull down, around, up, and down
v — slant down, up
w — slant down, up, down, up
x — slant down, slant down
y — slant in, slant, and down
z — across, slant down, across

Verbal Path for Letter Formation: Lowercase Page 1

Figure 5-7: Use the language of the Verbal Path for Letter Formation consistently to support children in making letters.

Handwriting and Word Processing

Besides being important for legibility, effective handwriting also increases writing fluency so the writer can give more attention to the message and less attention to the mechanics of writing. The minilessons in CNV.U1: Using Good Handwriting support children in developing writing fluency. In this umbrella, particularly in WML1, we use specific language for how to form letters. The language comes from a resource called the Verbal Path for Letter Formation (Figure 5-7), which is available in the online resources. When you consistently use the same direction words, you help children internalize the directions and support their fluency with letter formation.

You can also find an online resource that shows with numbered arrows the strokes for writing each letter. Consider including this resource in your children's writing folders as a reference (Figure 5-8). These minilessons are not intended to replace any handwriting curriculum you already have in place. Feel free to modify these minilessons so they are consistent with the handwriting curriculum you use. Avoid confusing children with conflicting

Figure 5-8: Use the Letter Formation Chart: Uppercase and Letter Formation Chart: Lowercase from online resources to demonstrate how to form letters efficiently.

ways of directing the formation of
letters. The paper choices available
in online resources provide lines with
dashes to support children in their
letter formation, but feel free to use
the paper that is consistent with your
school's handwriting program.

Children will also need to learn
keyboarding skills to increase
their writing fluency. One way to
support children's development of
keyboarding skills is to on occasion
offer the option of "publishing"
a piece of writing on a computer.
Figure 5-9 shows a piece of student's
writing that has been published
on the computer. Unlike most of
the other published pieces in this
second-grade classroom, the teacher

Mercy's Fair-time Adventure

By Jihae

"I hope I win a prize," shouted Mercy. It was Christmas. She hit
one cone. One more turn.

Then a lion appeared out of nowhere. Mercy threw the ball. It hit
Flash the lion in the head. 'I'm going to eat you!" roared Flash. "Sorry,"
whispered Mercy. Flash started to chase the pig Mercy. "Ahh!" cried
Mercy.

She dashed to the merry-go-round. Mercy hopped on. "Hey!"
hollered the man who was waiting for the tickets. "Give me your tickets!"
insisted the man. "Sorry!" squealed Mercy.

Mercy jumped a seat up. Flash was right behind her. Flash's
mouth was watery. Flash jumped a seat, like Mercy did. Flash couldn't
make it. He started to cry. He screamed, 'mommy!" But when Mercy was
at the top, Flash had an idea.

Flash stopped the merry-go-round and started to get Mercy.

Jump. Jump. Jump.

Then Mercy lost her grip. "Ahh!" cried Mercy. She landed on
something. "What is this?" she wondered. She looked under her and it
was just the carousel. "Phew." It was fast, scary, and a little fun. It was
going in circles. Meanwhile, Flash was still trying to look for her.

Then Flash spotted something pink. "Hey! There's the yummy pig."
Flash's heart was pounding so fast that he could hardly breathe. Flash
stomped to the carousel.

Mercy was dizzy when she saw Flash stomping over. But then,
Mercy had an idea! She was going to kick flash.

Flash got to the carousel. Mercy jumped up and kicked Flash in the
head. The security came running and took him away to jail. And Mercy
ran out the door.

and student worked together to polish the piece of writing. In most other
cases, published pieces have been edited but are not perfect. They reflect the
child's current understandings. Mrs. H. offers the chance to publish on the
computer a couple of times a year and places the published books in her
classroom library. In this case, Jihae's piece is part of a class collection of
fiction stories. In the next section on the writing process, we discuss other
ways you might choose to publish a text.

Engaging Children in the Writing Process

After children have experimented with making books, use Writing Process
umbrellas to emphasize that when authors make books, they make
important decisions and sometimes change those decisions to improve their
books. These umbrellas introduce children to the phases of the writing
process (Figure 1-10). They are based on the behaviors and understandings
in the Writing Process section of the grade 2 Writing continuum in *The
Fountas & Pinnell Literacy Continuum*. The umbrellas in the Writing Process
section introduce children to the following phases of the writing process.

Planning and Rehearsing

For children, talk is an important part of planning and rehearsing their writing.
They need to be able to form their ideas into oral language before they can
attempt to put those ideas on paper. Some of the talk is about children's ideas—

what they are writing. Some of the talk is about *why* children are writing and for *whom*—the purpose and the audience. The minilessons in the first umbrella of the Writing Process section, WPS.U1: Getting Ideas for Writing Through Storytelling, support students in getting their ideas out orally before writing. As they tell each other stories, they build community, develop oral language, and generate content for future writing. When children engage in storytelling, they are not only generating ideas for writing but also beginning to see the response of an audience. They think about who will read their writing and begin to ask themselves and each other, "What will the readers need to know? What else should I put in my book to help my readers enjoy and understand it?"

Knowing the purpose for writing often leads to discussions about what type of writing to do and what kind of paper is best for that purpose. For example, if children want to

- say thank you, they might write a note or a letter,

- teach others how to do something, they might write a how-to book,

- create a public service announcement, they might make a poster or a sign, or

- remember an experience or entertain their audience, they might write a story.

In all of these cases, the writer thinks about the purpose, determines what kind of writing will serve that purpose, and then begins to write a message. In Figure 5-10, Jill chose to write a letter to her parents (her audience) to try to convince them to let her stay up late.

In addition to storytelling, children need explicit opportunities to generate and collect ideas for writing during the planning process. From discussions during interactive read-aloud, children understand that writers get their ideas from their own experiences and from what they have learned. Minilessons in the Writing Process section support children in further developing this understanding. Children learn how to gather ideas

Figure 5-10: Jill chose to write a letter to her parents (her audience) to try to convince them to let her stay up late.

Dear Mom + Dad, I would like to stay up later and I would like to read a book at night. I would not come downstairs and I would be good. Stay up 10 more minutes. Please.

I know Kyle is older than me but just 5 or 10 more minutes. I would be so happy! Sincerely, Jill

for both memory writing and informational writing. They discover stories by making webs of their favorite memories, drawing maps of special places, and sketching memories of spending time with people they care about. They learn that they can get ideas from their wonderings, from making lists about topics they know, and from sketching objects in nature. Collecting ideas can be done in a writer's notebook, if you choose to use one with your students. The lessons in WPS.U2: Learning About My First Writer's Notebook will help support you in setting up writer's notebooks for the children and getting them familiar with the ways they can use it. You can read more about writer's notebooks on pages 79–84.

Drafting and Revising

At the beginning of the year, most second-grade writing is focused on just getting something down on the paper. We expect some standard spelling, but we also want children to try using new words, which means that spelling will not be perfect. Drawing is an important way for children to express what they want to say. Talk is especially important for those students whose first language is not English. They need opportunities to rehearse their ideas by telling stories or talking about their ideas before they write. In WPS.U7: Rehearsing Your Writing, you teach children to say their stories aloud before writing them, read and restate information for taking notes, and use oral language to support sequencing when writing procedural text.

As you guide children, they learn that part of the process of getting something down involves rereading and thinking about each word as part of a larger idea. You can show them how to think what they want to say before they draw or write.

Over the course of the year, children learn more about the way words work, talk about the decisions authors make, and make their own informed decisions about how to get their ideas down on paper. Like most writers, you will see your children revise while drafting, changing things as they go. Second graders can be reluctant at first to change something once it is drafted. However, as they learn about revising from the work of authors they love and learn ways that make adding to their writing easier, they get excited about revising to make their writing more interesting to their readers. Revising becomes contagious when children have opportunities to share and celebrate their changes with one another. Minilessons in WPS.U8: Adding Information to Your Writing and WPS.U9: Revising to Focus and Organize Writing offer different ways to revise. They learn to reread their writing to make sure it makes sense and to add new information for more detail or clarification (Figure 5-11).

EL CONNECTION

Figure 5-11: Tim combined two techniques he learned for adding information: he used an asterisk and number to indicate where to place the new information and then cut the new information out as a "spider leg" and taped it in place. Tim was deeply engaged in revising to add feelings to his writing.

Proofreading and Editing

In second grade, your primary goal is guiding children to reread and revisit their work to help them notice what they can do to make their writing and drawings interesting and easy to read. Second graders are learning more and more about print and the way words work every day. You can teach them how to proofread to make sure the words they know are spelled correctly and have them check their writing for punctuation and capitalization. In the last minilesson of WPS.U10: Editing and Proofreading Writing, children are introduced to a proofreading checklist, available in online resources. When you teach your students how to edit their own work, they feel more ownership over the piece and develop a sense of agency.

Publishing

When we say *publish* in second grade, we really mean "share it with others." Children are invited to share their independent drawing and writing daily as they experiment with new ideas taught through the lessons in this book. Publishing might mean having children type or bind their writing with cardboard or other materials to resemble a book. Published books can go into your classroom library for others to check out and read (Figure 5-12). Publishing can also take the form of framing a piece of writing or drawing, displaying it, posting it on a bulletin board, or holding informal writing celebrations. For example, you can have children share their books with another class or with a teacher or administrator, or you can invite families and guests to look at published books.

Second grade is a good time to begin thinking about broadening children's understanding of audience. The minilessons in WPS.U5: Thinking About Purpose and Audience help you and the children think about potential audiences both within the school and in the greater community. Consider asking local government officials, community organizations, or university professors and other experts in a field to listen to your students' writing and provide feedback. For example, one class recently invited a graduate research group from a local university to come to an exhibit of their own bio-inspired inventions. Students stood by their posters

Figure 5-12: You can publish books in a variety of ways. *My Tree Study* is bound with a dowel and a rubber band. *The Time I Cut My Finger* is simply two pieces of construction paper stapled together. Spiral bindings, like for *Soccer*, are also a durable option.

and inventions describing their work to an authentic audience of scientists who provided feedback and asked real questions. The event resembled a poster session at a scientific conference. Sharing their writing and celebrating risks taken and new techniques tried with a range of audiences presents children with the opportunity to see how different audiences react to their writing and how they might approach their writing differently in the future. When we give children the opportunity to share their writing with authentic audiences, their engagement and motivation for writing increase. The widespread use of virtual meetings helps make the world even smaller. Your students can connect with an audience from their local community or from across the world.

Lastly, you can teach your students how to add book and print features like covers, an author page, a dedication, and endpapers as part of the publishing process (WPS.U11: Adding Book and Print Features). In Figure 5-13, Keith wrote a summary and a teaser for the back of his fiction book about the Empire State Building after becoming aware of different book and print features through minilessons and mentor texts.

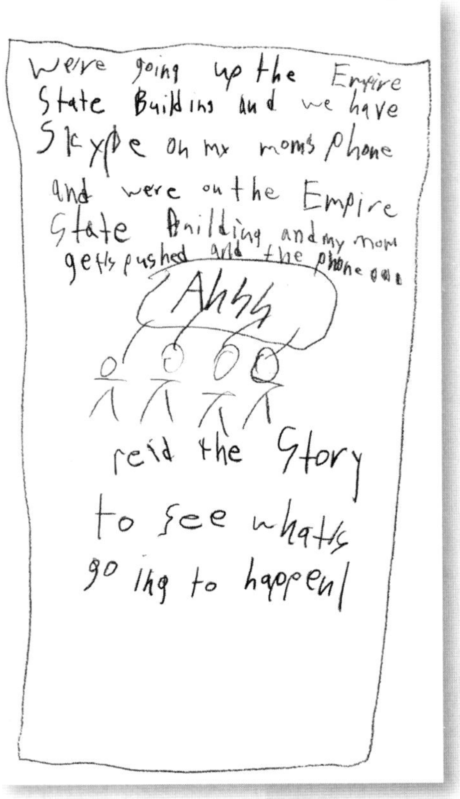

Figure 5-13: As part of the publishing process, Keith wrote a summary and teaser ("read the story to see what's going to happen") for the back of his book.

Using a Writer's Notebook with Second Graders

Author Ralph Fletcher writes, "Keeping a writer's notebook can help you be more alive to the world. It can help you develop the habit of paying attention to the little pictures and images of the world you might otherwise ignore" (Fletcher 1996).

Writers notice, listen, and observe every day, all of the time. They notice everything in their world—what they see, hear, and smell. They use writer's notebooks to collect these observations plus their thinking, their memories, lists, artifacts, and sketches so they can use them as sparks for writing. Writers read and reread their notebooks and add more and more ideas. It is a place for them to experiment with writing and try things out. It is a tool you can offer your students to help them expand and grow as writers.

We recommend introducing a writer's notebook when second graders are writing fluently and are beginning to produce multiple writing projects (e.g., making book after book) relatively quickly. For a typical second grade classroom, we recommend introducing the writer's notebook for the second half of the year, perhaps starting in January. If they are given a writer's notebook too early, it can become yet another thing to manage and can distract from their ongoing bookmaking. A writer's notebook is helpful for jotting down ideas, exploring different techniques, and experimenting with quick writes. Children need to be fluent enough with drawing and writing so that the work in their writer's notebooks does not feel like a writing project in and of itself. Instead, it is a place for experimenting and trying things out and a tool for collecting and selecting ideas for writing projects.

Choosing and Organizing a Writer's Notebook for Second Graders

A simple composition book makes a good choice for a first writer's notebook, but any size notebook will do. You will find many online resources to help you build a notebook in the minilesson umbrellas that refer to a writer's notebook. Consider dividing the writer's notebook into two sections: Getting Ideas and More Writing and Sketching.

In the Getting Ideas section, children can keep an ongoing list of writing ideas (available in online resources) as well as collect ideas through a series of quick writes (see WPS.U3: Gathering Ideas for Informational Writing and WPS.U4: Gathering Ideas for Memory Writing). They can also use this section to glue in poems or passages from books to inspire writing ideas. The More Writing and Sketching section is where children can experiment with new ideas, develop some of the ideas from the first section, make plans, or try out craft moves from minilessons. Most importantly, the writer's notebook can be a place where you have children write every day, even for just five minutes. You can ask them to take out their notebooks at any time of day to get in the habit of daily fluent writing. Once you have taught them some generative ways for getting ideas (e.g., making webs of memories, making maps of special places, making sketches of objects from nature, making lists of favorite topics), you will be able to repeat and extend these lessons to continue gathering ideas. You will find a list of ideas for children to write about in online resources. Be sure to invite them to reread their notebooks frequently, choose an idea, and add more and more.

Using the Writer's Notebook with Other Tools

The writer's notebook is used throughout the writing process. Children use it to collect ideas as they plan for writing, to begin a draft to see if an idea works, and to try out craft moves as they revise their writing (Figure 5-14). The writer's notebook can also be used as a tool to support editing. For example, you might encourage or invite students to try writing a word a few different ways in their notebooks to figure out the spelling. As students publish, they can use their notebooks to develop different book and print features, such as an author page, a dedication, or acknowledgments.

Typically, a writer's notebook is used alongside a writing folder, in which students keep ongoing writing projects. Students often begin a writing project, such as a memory book or a how-to book, by rereading their writer's notebooks for topic ideas. Other times, children will start an idea in their writer's notebooks and discover that they want to expand it into a longer project. They take the idea out of their notebook and choose paper that makes sense for the type of writing they are doing. Children continually use their writer's notebooks as they work on their writing projects to try out different crafting techniques and to continue to collect ideas, especially as peers share their own writing project ideas. Ideas are contagious. Hearing one person's memory story often triggers a related memory for someone else. When children share their writing, encourage them to bring their writer's notebooks so they can capture ideas inspired by their classmates' writing.

Once the writer feels a writing project is complete, we recommend that the finished product (whether published or not) be moved to a storage file somewhere in your classroom. Sometimes teachers ask students to write a reflection about what they learned from the writing project in their writing folder as described earlier. After completing a writing project, children return to their writer's notebooks to continue gathering ideas or to find another idea they want to explore for a writing project.

Figure 5-14: Taj tried out a craft move in her writer's notebook. After a minilesson, she tried a way to *show* how her character was feeling rather than telling how. She then applied the attempt to the fiction book she was writing.

> Character feeling
> Julea felt one wet drop on her face then onther she was crying!

Introducing Your Students to Their First Writer's Notebook

The minilessons in WPS.U2: Learning About My First Writer's Notebook will support you in introducing a writer's notebook to your students. It is important that children understand that the writer's notebook is their own special notebook and should reflect their individuality. To this end, WML1 invites them to decorate the front cover of their writer's notebooks. Encourage them to bring photographs from home (but be wary of sending the notebooks home because it is necessary to have them in the classroom every day), cut out images from magazines, draw their own sketches, or print out online images of things that represent their interests and identities. In WML2, they use a heart map to further explore their own interests and lives and to inspire ideas for writing. Through the minilessons in the rest of the umbrella, you will help children understand how to collect their writing ideas over time on writing lists as well as how to reread their notebooks for ideas. If you choose not to use a writer's notebook with your students, we recommend including the writing list available in the online resources for WPS.U1 in the writing folders so children have somewhere to collect ideas whenever they get them.

Using the Writer's Notebook to Support Bookmaking

The writer's notebook is a wonderful tool for supporting children when they make books. To help them find a topic, teach them to look through their writer's notebooks for ideas. Before you teach children how to write all-about books and memory books, teach some of the lessons in WPS.U3: Gathering Ideas for Informational Writing and WPS.U4: Gathering Ideas for Memory Writing, respectively. One way children might gather ideas for memory stories is to draw maps of special places in their lives (Figure 5-15). In Figure 5-16, notice how Grace used her writer's notebook to make a list of topics in which she feels she has expertise. These lessons will provide a repository of ideas for children to explore so you will never hear, "I don't know what to write." If anything, you will have kids asking you which of their many ideas they should develop. Remind them that they can make

Figure 5-15: Noah made a map of Camp Norwich, which he glued into his writer's notebook. He used this map to think about different memories from the camp and jotted a list of those ideas in his writer's notebook.

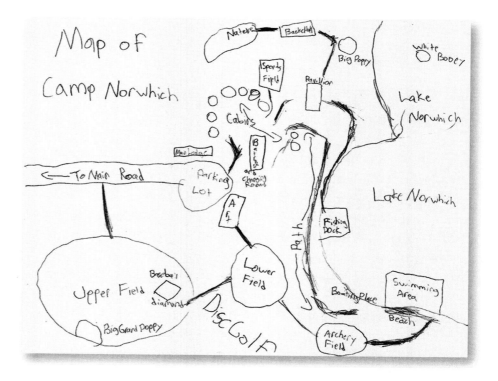

Expert projects

1. hores ❌ yes
2. dogs donot No
3. ~~~~ ballet ❌ ballet
4. I danseing. yes
5. rillr doingt hair do not No
6. plaing school. No
7. swiming No
8. drawing

Figure 5-16: Writer's notebooks can be used to support nonfiction writing.

one book after another. They can also revisit ideas in their notebooks in multiple ways. As we touched on in Chapter 4, the lessons in GEN.U10: Experimenting with Writing in New Ways show students how to revisit ideas they have collected and write about them in different ways.

Children can also use the writer's notebook for trying out certain ideas for their books without committing to them in the book itself. For example, perhaps they want to try drawing a diagram before putting it in a book, or maybe they want to write down three or four different titles for a book before selecting the best one for the front cover. In Figure 5-17, Taj tried out an ending in her notebook before settling on it for her book. The writer's notebook can also be a place in which writers collect notes for their informational books (Figure 5-18). The writer's notebook becomes a playground where they get to exercise their writing muscles in different ways.

Ending
That grabs the reader

Emily start to sit
down on the couch
and started to read a
book.

Figure 5-17: Children can use their writer's notebooks to experiment with part of their writing—for example a character description, a beginning, or an ending—before putting it in a book. Here Taj worked on an ending for the book she was writing.

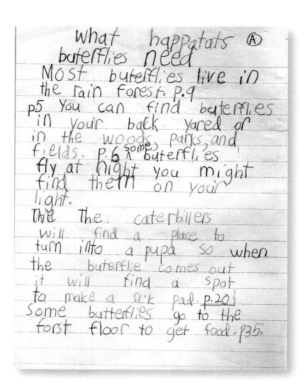

Figure 5-18: Laura used her writer's notebook to collect facts on butterflies for an all-about book. She combined what she learned in both genre and writing process minilessons to take notes in her own words.

So many things contribute to young children's development in writing. When you surround children with literacy activities and print, help them notice what other writers and illustrators do, provide them with time to write, encourage their efforts with enthusiasm, and gently guide them through writing minilessons, you create the right conditions for second graders to grow into confident, engaged writers.

With a choice of so many writing minilessons, how do you decide which lesson to teach when? Most of your decisions will be based on your close observations of the children as they write. What do you see them doing on their own? What might they be able to do with your help? What are they ready to learn? Chapter 6 offers guidance and support for making those decisions.

Chapter 6

6

Putting Minilessons into Action: Assessing and Planning

With assessment, you learn what students know; the literacy continuum will help you think about what they need to know next.

—Irene Fountas and Gay Su Pinnell

WRITING MINILESSONS ARE EXAMPLES OF explicit, systematic teaching that address the specific behaviors and understandings to notice, teach for, and support in *The Fountas & Pinnell Literacy Continuum*. Goals for each lesson are drawn from the sections on Writing; Writing About Reading; Phonics, Spelling, and Word Study; and Oral and Visual Communication. Taken together, the goals provide a comprehensive vision of what children need to become aware of, understand, and apply to their own literacy and learning about writing. Each minilesson lists Continuum Connections, which are the exact behaviors from *The Fountas & Pinnell Literacy Continuum* that are addressed in the lesson.

Figure 6-1 provides an overview of the processes that take place when a proficient writer creates a text and represents what children will work toward across the years. Writers must decide the purpose of a text, their audience, and their message. They think about the kind of writing that will help them communicate the message. They make important craft decisions, such as how to organize the piece, what words to use, and how they want the writing to sound. While keeping the message in their heads, writers must also consider the conventions of writing, such as letter formation, capitalization, punctuation, and grammar. They work through a writing process from planning and rehearsing to publishing. All lessons in this book are directed to helping writers expand their processing systems as they write increasingly complex texts.

Decide Which Writing Minilessons to Teach

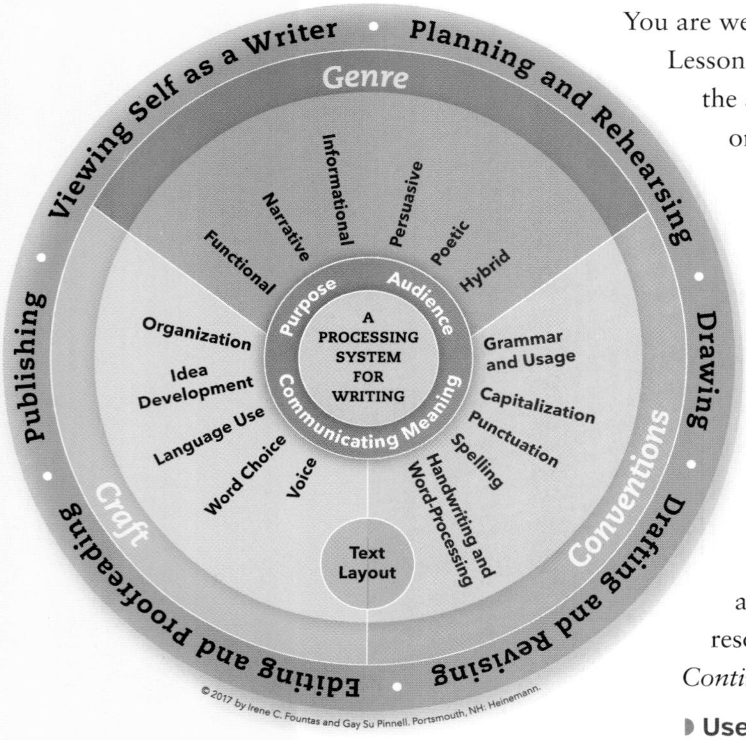

You are welcome to follow the Suggested Sequence of Lessons (discussed later in this chapter; located in the appendix and available as a downloadable online resource). However, first look at the children in front of you. Teach within what Vygotsky (1979) called the "zone of proximal development"—the zone between what the children can do independently and what they can do with the support of a more expert other (Figure 6-2). Teach on the cutting edge of children's present competencies.

Select minilessons based on what you notice the majority of your class needs to learn to develop writing behaviors. Here are some suggestions and tools to help you think about the children in your classroom, the main resource being *The Fountas & Pinnell Literacy Continuum*:

▶ **Use the Writing continuum** to help you observe how children are thinking, talking, and writing/drawing. Think about what they can already do, almost do, and not yet do to select the emphasis for your teaching. Think about the ways you have noticed children experimenting with drawing and bookmaking. Observe children's contributions and participation during writing minilessons, writing conferences, and guided writing. Use the Writing Process section to assess how children are developing their own independent writing process.

- Are they volunteering ideas when you talk about what to write?

- Do they demonstrate confidence in trying to write words they don't yet know how to spell?

- How are children applying some of the things they are learning during writing minilessons to independent writing?

Figure 6-1: The writing wheel diagram, shown full size on the inside back cover, illustrates how the writing process encompasses all aspects of writing.

The Learning Zone

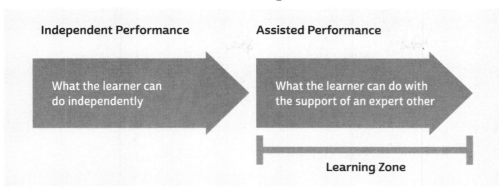

Figure 6-2: Learning zone from *Guided Reading: Responsive Teaching Across the Grades* (Fountas and Pinnell 2017)

▶ **Scan the Writing About Reading continuum** to help you analyze children's drawing and writing in response to the books you have read aloud. This analysis will help you determine next steps for having them respond to the books and poems you read together.

▶ **Review the Phonics, Spelling, and Word Study continuum** to help you evaluate children's phonological awareness, letter knowledge, and understanding of how to write words. These insights will help you make important choices about how to support students using writing minilessons as well as phonics, spelling, and word study lessons.

▶ **Consult the Oral and Visual Communication continuum** to help you think about some of the routines children might need for better communication between peers, especially as they share their writing with one another. You will find essential listening and speaking competencies to observe and teach for.

▶ **Record informal notes** about the interactions you have while conferring or the interactions you see between children as they write and share their writing. Look for patterns in these notes to notice trends in children's drawing and writing. Use *The Fountas & Pinnell Literacy Continuum* to help you analyze your notes and determine strengths and areas for growth across the classroom. Your observations will reveal what children know and what they need to learn next as they build knowledge about writing over time. Each goal becomes a possible topic for a minilesson (see Conferring Record 1 and Conferring Record 2 in Figure 2-7).

▶ **Establish routines for reading your students' writing regularly.** It is helpful to create a system for reading through a few writing folders every day. Some teachers divide the number of writing folders across five days and read through one set each day. As you read your students' writing, make notes about the patterns you see across student writing. What writing principles would the whole group benefit from learning in a writing minilesson? Which principles might be better addressed in a small guided writing group? And, which goals might you want to address in individual conferences?

▶ **Consult district, state, and/or accreditation standards.** Analyze the suggested skills and areas of knowledge specified in your local and state standards. Align these standards with the minilessons suggested in this book to determine which might be applicable within your classroom.

▶ **Use the Assess Learning and Assessment sections** within each lesson and at the end of each umbrella. Take time to assess the children's learning after the completion of each lesson and umbrella. The guiding questions on the last page of each umbrella will help you to determine strengths and next steps for your second graders. Your notes on the online resources shown in the next two sections will also help you make a plan for your teaching.

Use Online Resources for Planning and Teaching

The writing minilessons in this book are examples of how to engage second-grade children in developing the behaviors and understandings of competent writers as described in *The Fountas & Pinnell Literacy Continuum*. Use any of the planning forms in the online resources (**fp.pub/resources**) to help you plan your teaching

The form shown in Figure 6-3 will help you plan each part of a new writing minilesson. You can design a lesson that uses a different set of example texts from the ones suggested in this book, or you can teach a concept in a way that fits the current needs of the children. The form shown in Figure 6-4 will help you plan which lessons to teach over a period of time to address the goals that are important for the children.

The minilessons are here for you to teach according to the instructional needs of your class. You may not be able to use all 190 lessons within the year, but they are there for your selection based on assessment of the needs of your students. Record or check off the lessons you have taught so that you can reflect on the work of the semester and year. You can do this with the Writing Minilessons Record (Figure 6-5).

Figure 6-3: Use the downloadable form to plan your own writing minilessons.

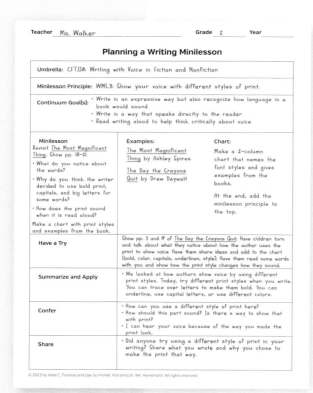

Teacher Ms. Vitella   Grade 2   Year _____

Curriculum Plan: Writing Minilessons

Month January	Writing Minilessons	Comments/Observations	✓ or Date
Week 1	GEN.U7: Writing Friendly Letters WML1: Write a letter to someone for a purpose. WML2: Write the parts of a letter. WML3: Write the important information in your letter. WPS.U4: Gathering Ideas for Memory Writing WML1: Make a web of favorite memories.	1/4: Class is motivated and excited to write friendly letters! Children want to set up a classroom post office. 1/6: Have Eli and Jules work with Mr. Ned on adding information to their letters.	
Week 2	WPS.U4 (continued) WML2: Make a map of an important place and think about the stories that took place there. WML4: Sketch a favorite memory. Revisit GEN.U2: Making Memory Books WML1: Choose a small moment or memory that is important to you.	1/12: Skipped WML3 for now. Will do later. 1/12: Check in with Jax, Sachi, and Summer.	
Week 3	CFT.U12: Adding Meaningful Details to Illustrations WML1: Add details that show how a person feels. WML3: Draw motion or sound lines to show something moving or making noise. WML4: Add details to your drawings to give information. WML5: Draw the picture so the reader knows what is important.	1/21: Have Mr. Ned work in small group with Lenira and Abdullah about adding feelings in pictures and words. 1/25: skipped WML2—covering in art class.	
Week 4	CFT.U7: Making Powerful Word Choices WML1: Use words to show not tell. WML2: Make up words that match a sound. WML3: Choose interesting words to describe the way characters say something. WML4: Choose interesting words to describe actions. WML6: Use words from other languages you know.	1/26: Children really enjoying this umbrella. Making connections to poetry work. 1/27: Skipping WML5—teach when revisit poetry.	

Figure 6-4: Use this downloadable form to make notes about specific writing minilessons for future planning.

Meet Children's Needs and Build on Their Strengths

Figure 6-5: Writing Minilessons Record for Grade 2

If you are new to writing minilessons, you may want to adhere closely to the suggested sequence, but remember to use the lessons flexibly to meet the needs of the children you teach and to build upon their strengths. Base your decisions about when or whether to use certain lessons on what you notice that children can already do, almost do, and not yet do.

▶ Omit lessons that you think are not necessary.

▶ Repeat lessons that you think need more time and instructional attention. Or, repeat lessons using different examples for a particularly rich experience.

▶ Move lessons around to be consistent with the curriculum that is adopted in your school or district.

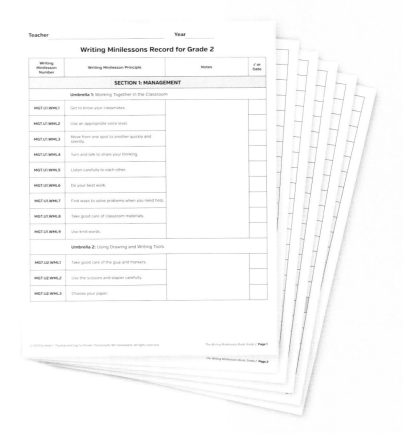

Consider using the analysis tool in Figure 6-6 along with *The Fountas & Pinnell Literacy Continuum* after you have taught the minilessons in a few umbrellas. We suggest using this tool, or one of the other assessment tools offered in the online resources, to focus on one or two pieces of a student's writing. Set aside time to analyze the writing of five students a day. By the end of the week, you will have a snapshot of what the children understand and what they do not yet understand. Use Guide to Observing and Noting Writing Behaviors (Figure 6-7) quarterly as an interim assessment. This observation form comes in two versions, one for individuals and one for the whole class.

Patterns and trends across students' writing will help you plan what to address through whole-group minilessons, small-group guided writing lessons, or individual conferences. Not only will this allow you to be responsive in your teaching, but it will also give you a sense of how to build upon each student's strengths. Consult the Suggested Sequence of Lessons when necessary to decide if you want to wait to teach a particular umbrella, but don't be afraid to be responsive to your learners. You can always repeat or skip lessons if you have decided to teach them before they come up in the sequence.

Figure 6-6: Use this form to analyze student writing to make a plan for future teaching.

Analyzing Student Writing for Planning

Use *The Literacy Continuum* and the Assessment section at the end of each umbrella you have taught to analyze a student's writing for evidence of writing behaviors and understandings.

Name: Jemilia   Grade: 2   Genre: Memory Story   Date: 10/24

Umbrellas Taught: GEN.U2: Making Memory Books, CNV.U2: Learning How to Write Words, CFT.U4: Adding Dialogue to Writing

	Strengths	Next Steps	Plan [IW, WML, GW, IC]
Genre	• Tells a personally meaningful story. • Tells a story in a sequence. • Pictures and writing match. • Includes feelings and emotions.	• Learn how to select a small moment from a longer story.	• GW: Bring together Chao, Marc, and Jemilia to look at small moments in mentor texts.
Craft	• Uses speech bubbles. • Presents ideas clearly—beginning, middle, and end. • Draws background.	• Needs support drawing people in different positions. • Review how to include dialogue in a story. • Needs to learn how to choose more specific and interesting words.	• WML: Teach CFT.U1: Learning to Draw to whole class. • IC: Show how to include dialogue in her writing.
Conventions	• Uses capitals and periods in sentences. • Says words slowly to listen for sounds. • Has several simple high-frequency words in control: when, but, so, with, me, that.	• Needs to increase consistency in spelling high-frequency words (e.g., would). • Needs to learn how to use known words to write unknown words.	• GW: Meet with Jemilia, Kylie, Remi, and Marcel to review using known words to write other words. • IC: Help her proofread her work for inconsistent spelling.
Writing Process	• Gets ideas from life experiences. • Revises by adding information with caret marks.	• Remind her to cross out instead of erase. • Teach other ways of revising, including omitting and changing information.	• IC: Talk about crossing out vs. erasing. • WML: Teach WPS.U4: Revising to Focus and Organize Writing.

IW: Interactive Writing   WML: Writing Minilesson   GW:

Figure 6-7: Use the observation forms about every quarter. One form helps you focus on an individual child. The other form offers a snapshot of the whole class.

Guide to Observing and Noting Writing Behaviors–Individual Student, Grade 2

Guide to Observing and Noting Writing Behaviors–Whole Class, Grade 2

Date: 1/22

Write students' names/initials and the date when each student consistently demonstrates this behavior. Use this form quarterly if possible to assess your entire class.

Behaviors and Understandings	Lucia	Myka	Saeid	Trae	Aiden	Rachel	Manahil	Colin	Hazel	Sasha
Genre										
Make picture books (with pictures and/or words)	11/8	11/8	11/8	11/8	11/8	11/8	11/8	11/8	11/8	11/8
Write a variety of information books (all-about, question-answer books)										
Write books to teach how to do something (how-to books)										
Make memory books	1/22	1/22	1/22	1/22	1/22	1/22	1/22	1/22	1/22	1/22
Write friendly letters										
Experiment with writing poetry	1/22	11/8	1/22	1/22		11/8	1/22	11/10		1/22
Make realistic fiction picture books										
Craft										
Choose a title for writing	11/22	11/22	11/14	11/14	11/14	11/8	11/14	11/14	11/14	11/14
Tell stories in first person about own experience	11/14	11/22	11/14	11/14	11/14	11/8	11/14	11/14	11/14	11/14
Write across several pages, all related to the same story or topic	11/14	1/22	11/14	11/14	11/14	11/8	11/14	11/14	11/14	11/14
Write stories that have a beginning, a series of events, and an ending	11/14	11/22	11/14	11/14	11/14	11/14	11/14	11/14	1/17	11/14
Describe where a story takes place	11/14			11/14			11/14	11/14		11/14
Describe the characters or people in a story	1/17	1/22		1/17	1/22	1/17	1/17	11/14		1/17
Communicate the main points to an audience	11/14	1/17	11/8	11/14	1/17	11/14	1/17	11/14		
Include facts and details in information writing				1/17	1/22	1/17	1/17	1/17	1/17	1/17
Use pictures and words to show feelings.	11/14	1/17	11/14	11/14	11/14	11/14	11/14	11/14	1/17	11/8
Add speech bubbles, thought bubbles, and dialogue	11/14	1/17	11/14	1/17	11/14	1/17	11/14	1/17	11/14	1/22
Write engaging beginnings and endings	1/22			1/22		1/17				
Choose interesting words to express ideas	1/22	1/22		1/22					1/17	1/17

The Writing Minilessons Book, Grade 2 **Page 1**

Understand the Suggested Sequence of Lessons

The Suggested Sequence of Lessons (pp. 575–589 and also in online resources) is intended to establish a strong classroom community early in the year, work toward more sophisticated concepts across the year, and bring together the instructional pieces of your classroom. The learning that takes place during writing minilessons is applied in many situations in the classroom and so is reinforced daily across the curriculum and across the year.

Because many writing minilessons use mentor texts as a starting point, the lessons are sequenced so that they occur after children have had sufficient opportunities to build some clear understandings of aspects of writing through interactive read-aloud and shared reading. From these experiences, you and the children will have a rich set of mentor texts to pull into writing minilessons. If you are using shared and/or interactive writing regularly in your classroom to write together with the class, bring those texts into lessons as other mentor texts. They will be extremely meaningful since you will have developed them collaboratively.

The Suggested Sequence of Lessons follows the suggested sequence of text sets in *Fountas & Pinnell Classroom™ Interactive Read-Aloud Collection* (2018) and books in *Shared Reading Collection* (2018). If you are using either or both of these collections, you are invited to follow this sequence of texts. If you are not using them, the kinds of books children will need to have read are described on the first page of each umbrella in this book.

The text sets in the *Interactive Read-Aloud Collection* are grouped together by theme, topic, author, or genre, not by skill or concept. That's why in many minilessons, we use mentor texts from several different text sets and why the same books are used in more than one umbrella in this book.

We have selected the most concrete and clear examples from the recommended books. In most cases, the minilessons draw on mentor texts that have been introduced within the same month. However, in some cases, minilessons taught later in the year might draw on books you read much earlier in the year. Most of the time, children will have no problem remembering these early books because you have read and talked about them. Sometimes children have responded through art, dramatic play, or writing. Once in a while, you might need to quickly reread a book or a portion of it before teaching the umbrella so it is fresh in the children's minds, but this is not usually necessary. Looking at some of the pictures and talking about the book is enough.

Use the Suggested Sequence to Connect the Pieces

To understand how the Suggested Sequence of Lessons can help you bring these instructional pieces together, let's look at a brief example from the suggested sequence. In month 2, we suggest reading the text sets Memory Stories and Tomie dePaola: Writing from Life from the *Interactive Read-Aloud Collection*. In reading minilessons, children are engaged in understanding aspects of plot. One of the suggestions for extending learning after the Memory Stories text set is to write a memory story. (You do not need any specific books in this text set; use any set of similar books available.) Later, the books from the *Interactive Read-Aloud Collection* and *Shared Reading Collection* become mentor texts in GEN.U2: Making Memory Books. You may choose to write a memory story as a class using shared or interactive writing. A class-made memory story can also serve as one of the mentor texts. These mentor texts help children learn specific understandings about making a memory book, such as choosing a small moment, using pictures and words to show feelings, and telling why the memory is important (Figure 6-8).

Interactive read-aloud and shared/interactive writing experiences give children the background that helps them go deeper when they experience minilessons on specific topics. They are able to draw on their previous experiences with texts to fully understand the concepts in the minilessons.

Figure 6-8: The Suggested Sequence of Lessons helps you connect all the pieces of your classroom instruction and leads to children's own independent writing.

Connecting All the Pieces

Read aloud and enjoy memory stories with the children.

Use shared or interactive writing to write about a class memory.

Teach writing minilessons on specific aspects of memory books.

Have children make their own memory books.

They can then apply this learning to their own independent writing and bookmaking. The Suggested Sequence of Lessons is one way to organize your teaching across the year to make these connections.

Add Writing Minilessons to the Day in Grade 2

After deciding what to teach and in what order to teach it, the next decision is when. In *Fountas & Pinnell Classroom™ System Guide, Grade 2* (2018), you will find frameworks for teaching and learning across a day. Using the schedules and the information in this book as guides, think about when you might incorporate writing minilessons as a regular part of the day in second grade. One suggestion is to provide a dedicated time each day (ideally 50–60 minutes) for independent writing, which begins with a writing minilesson and ends with a share (Figure 1-4).

Second graders thrive on structure, organization, and predictability. When you set routines and a consistent time for writing minilessons and independent writing, you teach children what to expect. They find comfort in the reliability of the structure. Children write joyfully when they know they can count on time to experiment with and explore drawing and writing. They delight in knowing that what they have to say is valued. Writing minilessons build on the joy and enthusiasm children bring to all that they do in the classroom setting.

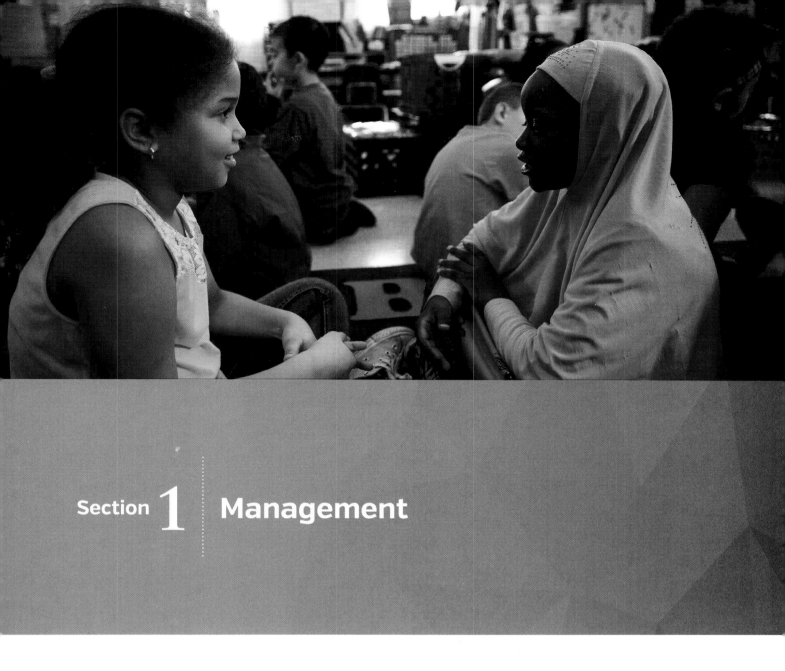

Section 1 | Management

MANAGEMENT MINILESSONS WILL help you set up routines for learning and working together in the classroom. They allow you to teach effectively and efficiently and are directed toward the creation of an orderly, busy classroom in which children know what is expected and how to behave responsibly and respectfully in a community of learners. A class that has a strong feeling of community is a safe place for all children to do their best work and have fun. Most of the minilessons at the beginning of the school year will come from this section.

1 Management

Minilessons in This Umbrella

WML1	Get to know your classmates.
WML2	Use an appropriate voice level.
WML3	Move from one spot to another quickly and silently.
WML4	Turn and talk to share your thinking.
WML5	Listen carefully to each other.
WML6	Do your best work.
WML7	Find ways to solve problems when you need help.
WML8	Take good care of classroom materials.
WML9	Use kind words.

Interactive Read-Aloud
Friendship

Before Teaching Umbrella 1 Minilessons

These minilessons establish an orderly classroom and build a community of writers so that children get to know and learn to trust one another. Note that this umbrella is not focused on rule following; instead, the goal is to create a warm and inviting child-centered classroom. If you are using *The Reading Minilessons Book, Grade 2* (Fountas and Pinnell 2019) and have already taught the first umbrellas in the Management and Literary Analysis sections, you may not need to teach every lesson. Use the books listed below from *Fountas & Pinnell Classroom™ Interactive Read-Aloud Collection* or other books about being part of a caring community.

The inside/outside writing project introduced in WML1 can be continued in Summarize and Apply through the next several lessons. As children finish, they can write about an aspect of their inside or outside selves. Sharing time each day focuses on both classroom management and getting to know each other.

Interactive Read-Aloud Collection
The Importance of Friendship

First Come the Zebra by Lynne Barasch

The Old Woman Who Named Things by Cynthia Rylant

A Weekend with Wendell by Kevin Henkes

This Is Our House by Michael Rosen

As you read and enjoy these texts together, help children

- think about different ways that people work together, and
- talk about different ways to solve problems.

Working Together in the Classroom

You Will Need

- chart paper folded in half from top to bottom and prepared with a sketch or photo of yourself on the front and a few details about yourself on the inside (visible when the paper is unfolded)
- chart paper and markers

Academic Language / Important Vocabulary

- community
- proud
- inside
- outside
- unique
- special

Continuum Connection

- Sustain a conversation with a variety of audiences
- Refrain from speaking over others
- Enter a conversation appropriately

GOAL

Learn to value one another's unique identities as part of a community of learners.

RATIONALE

Children learn to value the special qualities of their classmates when they feel valued for who they are. This appreciation creates a positive classroom community in which children can feel comfortable expressing themselves in writing.

ASSESS LEARNING

- Watch how children interact with one another. How do they get to know their classmates?
- Observe whether children recognize and value special qualities in themselves and others.
- Look for evidence that children can use vocabulary such as *community*, *proud*, *inside*, *outside*, *unique*, and *special*.

MINILESSON

Engage children in a conversation about getting to know and appreciate one another using a sketch or photo of yourself and sharing some things that make you special. Then provide a lesson to help children think about ways they can learn more about each other. Here is an example.

- Show the prepared folded paper.

   What do you notice about this sheet of paper and what's on it?

- Guide children to notice that you are showing what you look like on the *outside*. Point out some special details about the way you look.

- Open the paper so that the inside is showing.

   Here are some things that make me special on the *inside*. These are things that you cannot see when you look at me, but they help you get to know me better.

   During writing time, you are going to work on your own inside/outside project. Fold the paper like I did. Write or draw what you are like on the outside. Open your paper and write or draw what you are like on the inside so that we can get to know each other.

- Ask for children's suggestions about what to draw and write on the outside and then ask about the inside. Write their responses on chart paper.

   How does getting to know each other help our classroom community?

Have a Try

Invite children to turn and talk to get to know each other.

> Turn and tell your partner something about yourself. You may choose one of the things from the list, or you may have a different idea.

▶ After time for discussion, ask one or two volunteers to share what they learned about a classmate. Add any new general categories to the chart.

Summarize and Apply

Summarize the lesson. Write the principle on the chart.

> Today you learned about getting to know each other. During writing time, begin showing who you are on the outside and inside. You will continue working on your inside/outside project for the next few days.

▶ To show their outside selves, children can draw themselves or you could provide photographs of the children. Have them add labels to show the parts that are special to them, such as their hair.

Get to know your classmates.

On the Outside

Draw what you look like on the outside (hair, eyes, clothing).

On the Inside

Write or draw what you are like and what you like to do.
- Things you like to make
- Things you like to do
- Things you do with your family
- Places you like to go
- Languages you speak
- Your favorite thing to do with friends
- One thing that is special about you
- A family tradition

Confer

▶ During independent writing, move around the room to confer briefly with as many individual children as time allows. Sit side by side with them and invite them to talk about what makes them special. Use the following prompts as needed.

- *How does getting to know your classmates help our classroom community?*
- *What is one thing that makes you special?*
- *What are some things you enjoy doing?*

Share

Following independent writing, gather children in the meeting area to share something special about themselves.

> Think about some things you drew and wrote today. Choose one special thing about yourself to share.

Working Together in the Classroom

You Will Need

- chart paper and markers
- To download the following online resource for this lesson, visit **fp.pub/resources**:
  - chart art (optional)

Academic Language / Important Vocabulary

- voice level
- appropriate
- silent
- soft
- normal
- loud

Continuum Connection

- Speak at an appropriate volume
- Refrain from speaking over others
- Adjust speaking volume for different contexts

GOAL

Learn to use an appropriate voice level.

RATIONALE

When you teach children to use appropriate voice levels for different activities, they learn to independently determine which voice level to use and modulate their voices accordingly.

ASSESS LEARNING

- Observe for evidence that children understand why a certain voice level is appropriate for a specific situation.
- Listen as children participate in different activities. Do they adjust their voice levels accordingly?
- Look for evidence that children can use vocabulary such as *voice level*, *appropriate*, *silent*, *soft*, *normal*, and *loud*.

MINILESSON

To help children think about the minilesson principle, engage them in discussing voice levels and in creating an anchor chart. Here is an example.

- Talk about the importance of sometimes using a soft voice and sometimes using a loud voice.

  When you are on the playground, how does your voice sound?

  When you are working on some writing, how does your voice sound?

  Does your voice sound the same when you are on the playground as when you are doing your writing? Why?

  We can talk about the kind of voice to use by using a number. A 0 voice means that you are silent.

- Begin a voice level chart that provides examples to show appropriate voice levels. In the first column, include the numeral *0*, the word *silent*, and a sketch depicting a child who is not speaking.

  What are times at school when you use a 0 voice?

- Add children's examples to the chart.

- Repeat the activity for each voice level. On the chart, indicate that a 1 voice means a soft voice, a 2 voice means a normal voice, and a 3 voice means a loud voice.

Have a Try

Invite children to talk with a partner about using appropriate voice levels.

> With your partner, choose one voice level to talk about. What are some other times when you might use that voice level?

▶ After a brief time for discussion, ask children to share new ideas, and add their ideas to the chart. Have them discuss why using an appropriate voice level is important.

Summarize and Apply

Summarize the lesson.

> Look at the chart. Is there anything that should be moved from one voice level to another? Is there anything that should be added?

> During writing time, use an appropriate voice level while you are working on your inside/outside project and which one to use when you and I talk about your writing.

▶ Keep the voice level chart posted so children can refer to it. The voice level chart will be used in other minilessons in this umbrella.

Our Voice Level Chart

0	1	2	3
Silent	Soft	Normal	Loud
-working alone	-small-group work	-whole-group work	-playground
-independent writing	-partner work	-class meetings	
-hallways	-working with teacher	-shared reading	
		-interactive writing	

Confer

▶ During independent writing, move around the room to confer briefly with as many individual children as time allows. Sit side by side with them and talk with them about the voice levels they are using. Use the following prompts as needed.

- *Look at the chart. What voice level were you using when you were writing?*
- *What voice level should we be using right now?*
- *What voice level will you use when you work with a partner? Why?*

Share

Following independent writing, gather children in the meeting area to talk about the voice levels they used today and to share their inside/outside projects.

> What did you do during writing time today? What voice level did you use?

> Share something that you drew or wrote about yourself today.

Writing Minilesson Principle
Move from one spot to another quickly and silently.

Working Together in the Classroom

You Will Need

- several children prepared to model transitioning
- voice level chart from WML2
- chart paper and markers
- To download the following online resource for this lesson, visit **fp.pub/resources**:
  - chart art (optional)

Academic Language / Important Vocabulary

- quickly
- silently
- voice level

GOAL

Learn to transition from one activity to another in the classroom.

RATIONALE

When you teach children procedures for moving from one spot to another, you encourage independence and promote a positive classroom environment that allows you time to work with children in small groups and individually.

ASSESS LEARNING

- ▶ Observe whether children transition well from one activity to the next.
- ▶ Listen for evidence that children understand why they should move quickly and quietly.
- ▶ Look for evidence that children can use vocabulary such as *quickly*, *silently*, and *voice level*.

MINILESSON

To help children think about the minilesson principle, engage them in a demonstration and discussion of how to transition smoothly between activities. Here is an example.

> Throughout each day, you move around to different places in the classroom. For example, sometimes you work in the meeting area and sometimes you work at your table.

> Today let's watch several classmates as they move around the classroom. Then we can talk about what you notice.

▶ Invite the children you have prepared ahead of time to demonstrate how to move between several places in the classroom, such as from the meeting area to the writing area and then from the writing area to their tables.

> What did you notice about how they moved from one place to another?

▶ As children discuss what they noticed, record their observations of the transition process on chart paper. Prompt them to look back at the voice chart and talk about the voice level used by the volunteers.

> Why is it important that everyone moved quickly and safely and used a 0 voice?

Have a Try

Invite children to talk with a partner about transitioning from one place to another in the classroom.

▶ Decide on a signal to indicate that it is time to transition.

> When I give this signal, please move quickly and with a 0 voice to your table.

▶ Use the transition signal and provide time for the children to move into place.

▶ Repeat one or more times, asking children to move to the meeting area and/or other locations in the classroom.

Summarize and Apply

Summarize the lesson. Write the principle on the chart.

> What did you notice about how everyone moved from one place to another?

> Today, you can continue working on your inside/outside project. When it is time to move to another place, put your materials away carefully and walk quickly and silently.

▶ If children finish their inside/outside project, they can select one idea from it to write more about, or they may choose to write about anything that is special about themselves.

Move from one spot to another quickly and silently.

Walk quickly but do not run.

Use a 0 voice.

Keep your hands and feet in your own space.

Confer

▶ During independent writing, move around the room to confer briefly with as many individual children as time allows. Sit side by side with them and invite them to talk about transitions. Use the following prompts as needed.

- *How will you move back to the meeting area when you finish writing today?*
- *What will you do when it is time to move to a different place in the classroom?*
- *Why is it important to use a 0 voice when you move from one place to another?*

Share

Following independent writing, gather children in the meeting area to talk about how they moved about the classroom and to share what they wrote about themselves.

> Tell about how you moved from one place to another today.

> Share something that you wrote about yourself today.

WML4
MGT.U1.WML4

Writing Minilesson Principle
Turn and talk to share your thinking.

Working Together in the Classroom

You Will Need

- a child prepared to model turn and talk

- two texts that you have read aloud recently, such as *First Come the Zebra* by Lynne Barasch and *The Old Woman Who Named Things* by Cynthia Rylant, from Text Set: The Importance of Friendship

- voice level chart from WML2

- chart paper and markers

- To download the following online resource for this lesson, visit **fp.pub/resources**:
  - chart art (optional)

Academic Language / Important Vocabulary

- turn and talk
- listen
- voice level
- signal
- eye contact
- opinion

Continuum Connection

- Engage actively in conversational routines: e.g., turn and talk

- Take turns when speaking

- Actively participate in the give and take of conversation

- Ask follow-up questions during partner, small-group, and whole-class discussion

- Refrain from speaking over others

GOAL

Develop guidelines for turn and talk.

RATIONALE

Turn and talk routines allow children to express themselves verbally, to engage in conversation with others, and to share opinions. They also have a chance to rehearse their oral language in a safe way before sharing with the class. When children learn and practice procedures for turn and talk, they develop conversational skills that can be applied to speaking within a larger group and in other situations.

ASSESS LEARNING

- Watch and listen to children as they turn and talk. Do they follow the guidelines?

- Observe whether both children in a pair have a chance to talk.

- Look for evidence that children can use vocabulary such as *turn and talk*, *listen*, *voice level*, *signal*, *eye contact*, and *opinion*.

MINILESSON

To help children think about the minilesson principle, choose familiar texts to use in a demonstration of the turn and talk routine. Then engage children in a conversation about what they noticed. Here is an example.

▸ Show the cover of *First Come the Zebra*.

> Sometimes when you write something or read a book, you turn and talk to a partner about your thinking. Today, _____ is my partner, and we are going to turn and talk about interesting parts in *First Come the Zebra*.

> While we turn and talk, watch and listen carefully.

▸ Briefly model the turn and talk procedure. Offer an interesting observation or opinion about the book. Prompt the child to talk about whether she agrees or disagrees with you and why. Use the transition signal when you finish.

> What did you notice about the way we turned and talked? What did we do with our bodies and voices?

> How did we share our opinions?

▸ As children respond, begin a list on chart paper to create turn and talk guidelines. If children mention looking at each other, take into consideration that some children are not comfortable with establishing or able to establish eye contact because of cultural conventions or for other reasons. Adjust the lesson accordingly.

> When you share your thinking with a partner, you can agree or disagree with your partner. Or you can add on to what your partner says. This shows that you are listening carefully to what your partner is saying. Remember to always give reasons for your thinking.

Have a Try

Invite children to apply what they learned about turn and talk with a partner.

▶ Show the cover of *The Old Woman Who Named Things*.

> Turn and talk with your partner to share your thinking about this story. You can look back at the chart to remember the guidelines we made together.

Summarize and Apply

Summarize the lesson. Write the principle on the chart.

> What did you learn about how to turn and talk with a partner? Look at the chart if you need to.

> During writing time today, write about something that makes you special. You can choose one idea from your inside/outside project to write more about, or you can write about a new idea. Later, you will turn and talk with a partner about your writing.

Turn and talk to share your thinking.

- Look at your partner.

- Listen carefully to your partner.

- Wait for your partner to finish before you talk.

- Use a level 1 voice.

- Say whether you agree or disagree with your partner or add on to what your partner said.

- Give reasons for your thinking.

Confer

▶ During independent writing, move around the room to confer briefly with as many individual children as time allows. Sit side by side with them and invite them to talk about how they will share their thinking. Use the following prompts as needed.

- *Look at the chart. What is one thing you will do when you turn and talk?*

- *What voice level will you use during turn and talk?*

- *Why is it important to stop talking and turn back to me when I give the signal?*

Share

Following independent writing, gather children in the meeting area to turn and talk about the writing they did today. Have children bring their writing to the meeting area.

> Turn and talk to your partner about the writing you worked on today. Look at the chart if you need a reminder about the guidelines we made together.

WML5

Writing Minilesson Principle
Listen carefully to each other.

Working Together in the Classroom

You Will Need

- a familiar text about listening and friendship, such as *A Weekend with Wendell* by Kevin Henkes, from Text Set: The Importance of Friendship
- voice level chart from WML2
- chart paper and markers
- To download the following online resource for this lesson, visit **fp.pub/resources**:
  - chart art (optional)

Academic Language / Important Vocabulary

- listen
- speaker
- carefully
- politely
- agree
- disagree

Continuum Connection

- Look at the speaker when being spoken to
- Listen actively to others read or talk about their writing and give feedback
- Listen to and speak to a partner about a given idea, and make a connection to the partner's idea
- Demonstrate respectful listening behaviors
- Listen, respond, and build on the statements of others
- Refrain from speaking over others

GOAL

Learn expectations for listening during small- or whole-group meetings.

RATIONALE

When children learn to listen carefully to each other, they learn to communicate and collaborate effectively. These skills support respectful behavior not just in the classroom but in any social situation.

ASSESS LEARNING

- Observe for evidence that children demonstrate careful listening whether they are in a small group or with the whole group.
- Look for evidence that children can use vocabulary such as *listen*, *speaker*, *carefully*, *politely*, *agree*, and *disagree*.

MINILESSON

To help children think about the minilesson principle, engage them in discussing effective listening behaviors and in creating listening guidelines. Here is an example.

- Briefly revisit a few pages from *A Weekend with Wendell*.

  At first, Sophie and Wendell had trouble with their friendship. How did their friendship change after Wendell listened to what Sophie wanted to do?

- As children share, help them focus on how listening helped the friendship.

  In our classroom, we listen carefully when someone is speaking. What does it look like to be a careful listener?

- Guide the conversation to discuss what a good listener does. Show the voice level chart from WML2 to make the connection between voice level and listening. These suggested prompts may be helpful:
  - *What does your body look like when you are listening?*
  - *When you are listening, what voice level do you use?*
  - *When you listen, what are you thinking about?*
  - *How can you agree or disagree politely?*
  - *What do you do when you have a question?*
  - *How can you show that you listened to what someone said?*

- As children provide ideas, write them on chart paper. If children mention looking at the speaker, take into consideration that some children may not be comfortable with establishing or able to establish eye contact because of cultural conventions or for other reasons. Adjust the lesson accordingly.

- Keep the chart posted.

The Writing Minilessons Book, Grade 2

Have a Try

Invite children to turn and talk about careful listening.

> What is something you can say to your partner to show that you are listening? Turn and talk to your partner about that. Remember to listen carefully!

▶ After time for discussion, ask a few volunteers to share.

Summarize and Apply

Summarize the lesson. Write the principle at the top of the chart.

> What are some ways to show you are listening carefully?

> Today, you can continue drawing and writing about something that makes you special, or you can begin something new. As you work today, remember to be a careful listener when someone else is speaking. You can look at the chart to help you remember how.

Listen carefully to each other.

Look at the person who is speaking.

Listen silently when someone else is speaking.

Think about what the speaker says.

Say something to the speaker.

I agree with you because _____

Confer

▶ During independent writing, move around the room to confer briefly with as many individual children as time allows. Sit side by side with them and invite them to talk about careful listening. Use the following prompts as needed.

- *How can you show that you are listening carefully when someone is speaking?*
- *What are some ways you can agree or disagree politely with what someone says?*
- *What voice level do you use when someone is speaking? Why?*

Share

Following independent writing, gather children in the meeting area to talk about careful listening and to share their writing.

> Talk about a time today when you were a good listener.

> Share something you wrote about that makes you special.

Section 1: Management

Writing Minilesson Principle
Do your best work.

Working Together in the Classroom

You Will Need

- four children prepared in advance to model the principle
- chart paper and markers
- To download the following online resource for this lesson, visit **fp.pub/resources**:
  - chart art (optional)

Academic Language / Important Vocabulary

- best
- focus
- independent
- routine

Continuum Connection

- Produce a reasonable quantity of writing within the time available
- Write with independent initiative and investment
- Listen with attention during instruction, and respond with statements and questions

GOAL

Learn to start working promptly, stay focused, and produce high-quality work.

RATIONALE

When you help children learn ways to do their best work, you promote their independence and support their being proud of and motivated by what they do.

ASSESS LEARNING

- Observe for evidence that children understand classroom routines for working independently.
- Notice whether children can articulate why it is helpful to follow routines in order to do their best work.
- Look for evidence that children can use vocabulary such as *best*, *focus*, *independent*, and *routine*.

MINILESSON

To help children think about the minilesson principle, engage them in a short demonstration of how to do their best work. Here is an example.

- In advance, prepare four children to demonstrate going to their table, taking out writing materials, starting right away, and staying focused.

  When you are working independently, there are things you can do to do your best work. Watch and listen carefully as a few volunteers do their best work.

- Ask the four volunteers to go to the writing area and begin working on their writing. After a brief time, have the volunteers return to the meeting area as the other children observe how they put away materials and then move quickly and silently as they return.

  What did you notice about how your classmates worked?

- As children respond, make a list on chart paper using general categories. Guide the conversation to help children notice how the volunteers did their best work.

  When you look at writing that a classmate has done, what are some ways you can tell that he did his best work?

- Prompt the conversation to help children think of examples (e.g., crossing out a misspelled word and rewriting it neatly instead of making a hole in the paper with vigorous erasing).

Have a Try

Invite children to turn and talk about the importance of doing their best work.

> What does your best work look like? Turn and talk to your partner about that. You can look at the chart for ideas.

▶ After time for discussion, ask a few volunteers to share.

Summarize and Apply

Summarize the lesson. Write the principle on the chart.

> Today you talked about different ways to do your best work. During writing time today, you can continue something you are working on, or you can begin writing about something that makes you special. As you work, think about different ways to do your best work.

 Get to work right away.

 Follow directions.

 Stay focused.

Work quietly.

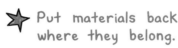 Put materials back where they belong.

Confer

▶ During independent writing, move around the room to confer briefly with as many individual children as time allows. Sit side by side with them and invite them to talk about doing their best work. Use the following prompts as needed.

- *What can you do to make sure you get started right away on your writing?*
- *Talk about how your best work looks.*
- *What will you do when writing time is over?*

Share

Following independent writing, gather children in the meeting area to talk about doing their best work and to share their writing.

> What is one thing you did today to do your best work?

> Share what you drew or wrote about yourself today.

Writing Minilesson Principle

Find ways to solve problems when you need help.

Working Together in the Classroom

You Will Need

- a familiar book that shows independent problem solving, such as *The Old Woman Who Named Things* by Cynthia Rylant, from Text Set: The Importance of Friendship
- chart paper and markers
- To download the following online resource for this lesson, visit **fp.pub/resources**:
  - chart art (optional)

Academic Language / Important Vocabulary

- problem solve
- reread
- directions
- help
- questions
- emergency

GOAL

Find ways to solve problems independently when help is needed.

RATIONALE

Helping children learn to independently choose and implement problem-solving strategies encourages independence and allows time for you to work with other children.

ASSESS LEARNING

- ▶ Notice whether children can come up with different ways to solve problems on their own.
- ▶ Observe whether children can articulate reasons why it is important to try to solve problems independently.
- ▶ Look for evidence that children can use vocabulary such as *problem solve*, *reread*, *directions*, *help*, *questions*, and *emergency*.

MINILESSON

To help children think about the minilesson principle, engage them in a discussion of how to problem solve independently. Here is an example.

- ▶ Show the cover and briefly revisit pages 20–29 of *The Old Woman Who Named Things*.

  What problem did the woman have, and how did she solve it?

- ▶ Briefly support a conversation to help children identify that the woman lost the dog and she had to come up with a name and find and identify the dog.

  Just like the woman in the story, it is important to learn to solve some problems on your own. This is especially true when I am working with other children. What are some ways you can try to solve a problem on your own?

- ▶ Engage children in a discussion of different problems they might have and solutions they could try. Prompt the conversation as needed. Some suggestions are below.

  - *What if you do not know what supplies or materials you need?*
  - *What if you are not sure what to do next?*
  - *What if you finish early?*

- ▶ As children provide solutions, record their ideas on chart paper using generalized language. The chart can remain posted so you can add to it as you observe children engaged in problem solving or as they suggest new ideas.

- ▶ Briefly discuss what an emergency is and that it is okay to interrupt the teacher if there is an emergency.

Have a Try

Invite children to turn and talk about solving problems.

> Why is it important to try to solve problems on your own? Turn and talk about that.

▶ After time for discussion, ask a few volunteers to share.

Summarize and Apply

Summarize the lesson. Write the principle at the top of the chart.

> Today during writing time, you can continue working on something you already started, or you can begin something new. If you have a question when you are writing today, look at the chart for ways to solve your problem. Later, we will share how you solved problems on your own.

Confer

▶ During independent writing, move around the room to confer briefly with as many individual children as time allows. Sit side by side with them and invite them to talk about solving problems on their own. Use the following prompts as needed.

- *If you can't remember the directions, how can you solve that problem?*
- *What can you do if you do not know how to spell a word?*
- *Look back at the chart. What is one way you can solve a problem on your own?*

Share

Following independent writing, gather children in the meeting area to talk about problem solving and to share their writing.

> Did anyone solve a problem on your own today? Tell about that.

> Share something you drew or wrote about yourself today.

Find ways to solve problems when you need help.

Reread the directions.

Use a level 1 voice to ask someone in this class.

Review what you have done so far.

Keep working until the teacher can help you.

Section 1: Management

Writing Minilesson Principle
Take good care of classroom materials.

Working Together in the Classroom

You Will Need

- a familiar book that shows a child taking care of (or not taking care of) materials, such as *A Weekend with Wendell* by Kevin Henkes, from Text Set: The Importance of Friendship
- two children prepared ahead of time to model taking care of materials
- voice chart from WML2
- chart paper and markers
- To download the following online resource for this lesson, visit **fp.pub/resources**:
  - chart art (optional)

Academic Language / Important Vocabulary

- materials
- supplies
- properly
- return

Continuum Connection

- Listen to, remember, and follow directions with multiple steps

GOAL

Learn to take good care of classroom materials and supplies and return them independently.

RATIONALE

Helping children understand the importance of taking good care of shared materials, including returning them to where they belong, promotes a positive classroom community by guaranteeing that everyone will have materials to use that are in good condition.

ASSESS LEARNING

- Observe children as they handle materials and supplies. Do they treat the materials and supplies carefully and with respect?
- Listen to what children say about why caring for materials is important in the classroom community.
- Look for evidence that children can use vocabulary such as *materials*, *supplies*, *properly*, and *return*.

MINILESSON

To help children think about the minilesson principle, engage them in a demonstration and conversation about taking good care of classroom materials. Here is an example.

- Show pages 4–5 in *A Weekend with Wendell*.

  What do you notice about the way that Wendell is using Sophie's toys?

- Have a brief discussion about how Wendell is being careless and making a mess. Have children talk about how Sophie is probably feeling about that.

  In our classroom community, we share many materials and supplies. Watch closely as _____ and _____ get the materials they need to do their work. When they finish working, we will talk about what they did.

- Provide a few minutes for the prepared children to demonstrate getting and returning writing materials. Point out that the materials are labeled to show where they belong.

  What did you notice?

  What are some ways you can take good care of the materials and supplies when you use them?

- Record responses on chart paper.

  When you are cleaning up, what voice should you use?

Have a Try

Invite children to turn and talk about the importance of taking care of classroom materials and supplies.

> Choose one item on the chart. Turn and talk about why it is important.

▶ After time for discussion, ask a few volunteers to share.

Summarize and Apply

Summarize the lesson. Write the principle at the top of the chart.

> During writing time today, you can continue working on something you already started, or you can begin a new piece of writing about something that makes you special. If you use any classroom materials or supplies when you work, remember to take good care of them. At the end of writing time, return materials quickly to where they belong and use a 0 voice. Later, we will talk about how you took good care of the materials.

> ### Take good care of classroom materials.
>
> • Get your materials.
>
> • Use them carefully.
>
> • Return them to where they belong.
>
> • Keep them clean and neat.

Confer

▶ During independent writing, move around the room to confer briefly with as many individual children as time allows. Sit side by side with them and invite them to talk about taking care of classroom materials. Use the following prompts as needed.

• *How will you take good care of materials and supplies today?*

• *I notice you are using some classroom supplies for writing today. What will you do with them when you are finished?*

• *What can you do to keep materials and supplies clean and neat?*

Share

Following independent writing, gather children in the meeting area to talk about taking good care of classroom materials. Give them an opportunity to share their writing.

> How did you show that you are taking good care of materials today?

> Share something you drew or wrote about yourself today.

Writing Minilesson Principle
Use kind words.

Working Together in the Classroom

You Will Need

- a familiar book that relates to respectful conversation, such as *This Is Our House* by Michael Rosen, from Text Set: The Importance of Friendship
- chart paper and markers

Academic Language / Important Vocabulary

- words
- respect
- kind
- conversation

Continuum Connection

- Use conventions of respectful conversation
- Enter a conversation appropriately
- Listen and respond to a partner by agreeing, disagreeing, or adding on, and explaining reasons
- Express and reflect on their own feelings and recognize the feelings of others
- Refrain from speaking over others

GOAL

Learn to use language to facilitate discussion, express opinions, and show respect.

RATIONALE

When children learn to listen and respond respectfully to communicate their opinions and feelings, they contribute to a positive learning community and learn to show empathy and concern for others.

ASSESS LEARNING

- Observe whether children can agree and disagree respectfully.
- Listen to children talking to one another. Do they use kind words?
- Look for evidence that children can use vocabulary such as *words*, *respect*, *kind*, and *conversation*.

MINILESSON

To help children think about the minilesson principle, engage them in a conversation about how to use words in a positive way in the classroom. Here is an example.

- Briefly revisit pages 1–2 and 21 of *This Is Our House*.

  What do you notice about how George talked to the other children?

- Revisit pages 22–24.

  What type of words were better?

- Have a brief discussion about how using words in a positive way helped George and the other children get along better.

  In our classroom, we can choose kind words when we talk and work together to show respect for each other. What are some kind words we can say to each other in the classroom?

- Guide the conversation to help children think of words and phrases that are kind and respectful. As they provide suggestions, make a list on chart paper of examples of positive communication.

Have a Try

Invite children to turn and talk about using words in a positive way.

> Look at the chart and think about one way you might use kind words today. Turn and talk to your partner about some times when you might use the words on the chart.

▶ After time for discussion, ask a few volunteers to share.

Summarize and Apply

Summarize the lesson. Write the principle on the chart.

> Today, continue working on drawing or writing about yourself or begin something new. As you work, use kind words whenever you can. Using kind words will help make our classroom a place where you can all work together. Look at the chart to remember ideas.

Use kind words.
Please.
Thank you.
Excuse me.
Hi, my name is _____. What's your name?
You're welcome.
Do you want to work with us?
We can share.
I agree because _____.
I disagree because _____.

Confer

▶ During independent writing, move around the room to confer briefly with as many individual children as time allows. Sit side by side with them and invite them to talk about using kind words. Use the following prompts as needed.

- *How can you use kind words to share what you are thinking?*
- *What could you say to someone new in our class?*
- *When might you say "thank you" to someone?*
- *How can you agree or disagree in a kind way?*

Share

Following independent writing, gather children in the meeting area to talk about their experiences using or hearing kind words and to share their writing.

> Tell about a time you used kind words today or someone said a kind word to you.

> Share a time that a classmate used kind words today.

> Share something you drew or wrote about yourself today.

Assessment

After you have taught the minilessons in this umbrella, observe children in a variety of classroom activities. Use *The Fountas & Pinnell Literacy Continuum* to notice, teach for, and support children's learning as you observe their attempts at building a classroom community.

▶ What evidence do you have of new understandings children have developed related to working together in the classroom?

- How are children getting to know each other?
- Are they using appropriate voice levels?
- Do they move in an efficient manner to the meeting area?
- Do they follow turn and talk procedures?
- Are they actively listening when others are speaking?
- Can they begin working right away and stay focused?
- Do they use a variety of problem-solving strategies?
- Do they take care of classroom materials and keep the room organized?
- Do they choose kind words?
- Are they using vocabulary such as *community*, *proud*, *unique*, *special*, *voice level*, *appropriate*, *listen*, *turn and talk*, *signal*, *eye contact*, *opinion*, *carefully*, *politely*, *agree*, *disagree*, *classmates*, *goals*, *focus*, *problem solve*, *conversation*, and *respect*?

▶ In what ways, beyond the scope of this umbrella, are children building a classroom community whose members work well together?

- Are they learning to respect and value one another by listening to each other's stories?
- Do they understand what to do during independent writing time?

Use your observations to determine the next umbrella you will teach. You may also consult Suggested Sequence of Lessons (pp. 575–589) for guidance.

EXTENSIONS FOR WORKING TOGETHER IN THE CLASSROOM

▶ Revisit different classroom activities with the whole class, asking volunteers to role-play how responsible classroom community members act.

▶ Ask children to review voice levels before and after an activity, especially as new activities are introduced.

▶ Embed problem-solving strategies within classroom activities.

Minilessons in This Umbrella

WML1 Take good care of the glue and markers.

WML2 Use the scissors and stapler carefully.

WML3 Choose your paper.

Before Teaching Umbrella 2 Minilessons

Organize the writing center at the start of the school year. Begin with just a few materials so that children can easily learn where they are located and know where to return them. As children gain experience, you can increase the mix of items. Select containers for supplies and label them with words and pictures and label the areas where the containers will be stored. Provide space for glue, markers, scissors, staplers, staple removers, pencils, pens, colored pencils, blank paper of different sizes, and blank paper stapled into books.

Note that there are different formats of books. *Booklet* refers to paper that is either folded or bound to look like a book for reading. Books can also be written across pages and stapled in one corner. Refer to the online resources for a variety of paper templates that might be useful as children learn to make different kinds of books. Repeat WML3 as needed to introduce new paper options.

Section 1: Management

WML1

MGT.U2.WML1

Writing Minilesson Principle
Take good care of the glue and markers.

Using Drawing and Writing Tools

You Will Need

- glue stick and/or glue bottle
- markers (multiple sets in multiple colors)
- designated, labeled containers in the writing center for storing glue sticks and markers
- paper for gluing/drawing
- chart paper and markers
- To download the following online resource for this lesson, visit **fp.pub/resources**:
  - chart art (optional)

Academic Language / Important Vocabulary

- location
- return
- materials
- glue
- markers
- click

Continuum Connection

- Listen to, remember, and follow directions with multiple steps
- Ask questions when directions are not clearly understood
- Compare personal knowledge and experiences with what is heard

GOAL

Learn the routines for using glue and markers.

RATIONALE

When children learn how to properly care for glue and markers, they take ownership, resulting in everyone in the classroom having the materials they need. It is important to teach explicit steps for taking care of the classroom supplies.

ASSESS LEARNING

- ▶ Look for evidence that children know where to find markers and glue and where to return them.
- ▶ Observe whether children know how to use glue and markers appropriately.
- ▶ Look for evidence that children can use vocabulary such as *location*, *return*, *materials*, *glue*, *markers*, and *click*.

MINILESSON

Prior to teaching this lesson, make sure children have had multiple experiences using markers and glue and know where they are located in the classroom. To help children learn to use them properly, engage them in a short demonstration. Here is an example.

> If I would like to glue something onto a piece of paper, tell me how I would do that.

▶ As children provide each step, gather paper and glue and model the process.

> If I want to draw on this picture using markers, talk about how I would do that.

▶ Using children's suggestions, model the process of using markers carefully.

▶ As you go through the procedures for using glue and markers, prompt the children to discuss each step. Some suggestions are below.

- *Why do you press down with the marker carefully and not too hard or too softly?*
- *Why do you twist the top of the glue bottle and dab on a tiny amount?*
- *Why do you turn up the glue stick just a little?*
- *What do you do when you are finished using glue (markers)?*
- *Show how you can make the* click! *sound when you put on the cap.*

Have a Try

Invite children to turn and talk about using glue and markers in the classroom.

> Turn and talk to your partner about why you might use glue or markers. How will you use them carefully?

Summarize and Apply

Summarize the lesson.

> What are some important things to remember about using glue and markers?

▸ As children offer suggestions, guide the conversation and write each step on chart paper. When finished, write the principle at the top.

> Today during writing time, if you make a book or a picture, you might decide to use glue or markers. If you do, think about what we talked about and look at the chart to remember how to take good care of the glue and markers.

Take good care of the glue and markers.

Glue Stick
- Remove cap.
- Turn it up a little.
- Place a little glue on paper.
- Turn it down a little.
- Put the cap on.

Glue Bottle
- Twist cap a little.
- Turn bottle upside down.
- Squeeze a little glue onto paper.
- Twist cap closed.
- Return the glue.

Markers
- Remove cap.
- Put the cap on the end.
- Press down carefully onto paper.
  ~Click!~
- Put the cap on.
- Return the markers.

Markers

Confer

▸ During independent writing, move around the room to confer briefly with as many individual children as time allows. Sit side by side with them and invite them to talk about using glue and markers. Use the following prompts as needed.

- *Show how to twist or turn the glue cap.*
- *Why is it important not to press on the marker too little (too much)?*
- *How do you know the glue stick (marker) cap is on?*
- *How do you know the glue bottle cap is closed?*
- *Where will you put the glue (marker) when you finish?*

Share

Following independent writing, gather children in the meeting area to share experiences using glue and markers.

> If you used glue (a marker) today, tell one way you took good care of it.

Section 1: Management

Writing Minilesson Principle

Use the scissors and stapler carefully.

Using Drawing and Writing Tools

You Will Need

- scissors, stapler, and paper for modeling
- scissors and staplers (one set per student pair)
- several pieces of paper for each pair
- designated, labeled container for storing scissors and staplers
- chart paper and markers
- To download the following online resource for this lesson, visit **fp.pub/resources**:
  - chart art (optional)

Academic Language / Important Vocabulary

- scissors
- stapler
- firmly
- carefully
- safe

Continuum Connection

- Listen to, remember, and follow directions with multiple steps
- Ask questions when directions are not clearly understood
- Compare personal knowledge and experiences with what is heard

GOAL

Learn to use scissors and staplers safely.

RATIONALE

When children learn how to properly handle and use scissors and staplers, they keep themselves and others safe and they gain independence. They also learn that they can take risks in their writing because they can use scissors and staplers to revise their writing by cutting out sentences that don't fit or adding more information on a new page.

ASSESS LEARNING

- ▶ Look for evidence that children use scissors and staplers carefully and safely.
- ▶ Look for evidence that children can use vocabulary such as *scissors*, *stapler*, *firmly*, *carefully*, and *safe*.

MINILESSON

Prior to teaching this lesson, make sure children have had a variety of experiences using scissors and staplers and know where they are located in the classroom. Decide whether children will staple their books once in the left corner or three times along the left side. To help them learn to use scissors and staplers appropriately, engage them in a short demonstration. Here is an example.

▶ Hold up a pair of scissors and several pieces of paper for cutting.

   Watch what I do with this pair of scissors.

▶ Model the correct way to sit and hold the scissors and then use them to cut a piece of paper. Demonstrate walking with and properly passing the scissors to someone. Include a demonstration of how to cut paper into strips (spider legs) for adding information to a page.

   Turn and talk about what you noticed.

▶ After time for discussion, ask children to share. Guide a conversation about safety rules. Use children's ideas to make a list about using scissors safely.

▶ Hold up a stapler and paper for stapling.

   Watch what I do with this stapler.

▶ Repeat the modeling process with the stapler. Include how to line up the pages so they are even, keep fingers out of the way, use two hands (one atop the other), push down firmly, and check to see that the staple went through the paper.

   What did you notice?

▶ Make a list on chart paper of what children noticed.

Have a Try

Invite children to practice using scissors and staplers in pairs.

▶ Pass out scissors, staplers, and paper to each pair and have them practice.

> Take turns with your partner using the scissors and stapler carefully. Remember to use two hands and listen for the click when you use the stapler. Look at the list we made to help you remember how to use scissors and staplers safely and properly.

▶ Provide enough time for each child to briefly use the scissors and stapler.

Summarize and Apply

Summarize the lesson.

> Today you learned how to use scissors and staplers carefully.

▶ Add a principle to each chart.

> What are some things you did when you used them with your partner?

> During writing time, you may want to use scissors or a stapler. You can look at the chart to help you remember how to use them carefully.

Confer

▶ During independent writing, move around the room to confer briefly with as many individual children as time allows. Sit side by side with them and invite them to demonstrate using scissors and staplers. Use the following prompts as needed.

- *Please pass the scissors to me.*
- *Show me how you hold scissors when you walk.*
- *Show how you will use the stapler to make a book.*
- *How can you use the stapler to add more pages?*

Share

Following independent writing, gather children in the meeting area to talk about using scissors and staplers.

> Who used the scissors or a stapler today? Tell about that.

Use the scissors carefully.

Sit in a chair.

Cut away from you.

Turn the handle out to pass the scissors.

Hold the scissors in a safe way when you walk.

Use the stapler carefully.

Line up the paper.

Put the paper in the stapler.

click!

Use two hands and press down firmly. Click once.

Check the staples.

Writing Minilesson Principle
Choose your paper.

Using Drawing and Writing Tools

You Will Need

- children's writing samples that use different types of paper (e.g., a book, a map, a brochure, a glossary)
- examples of paper (taped onto chart paper on the left)
- chart paper and markers
- To download the following online resource for this lesson, visit **fp.pub/resources**:
  - paper templates (optional)

Academic Language / Important Vocabulary

- kinds
- example
- paper

Continuum Connection

- Understand that layout of print and illustrations is important in conveying the meaning of a text
- Understand that illustrations play different roles in a text: e.g., increase reader's enjoyment, add information, show sequence or step-by-step process
- Listen to, remember, and follow directions with multiple steps

GOAL

Learn that writers choose the kind of paper to suit the writing they will do.

RATIONALE

When children begin to think about what kind of paper to use, they understand that writers choose the paper that suits their writing purposes. This lesson can be taught whenever introducing new paper might be helpful, such as when children are making books.

ASSESS LEARNING

- Look for evidence that children recognize that writers select a particular kind of paper depending on what they are writing.
- Observe whether they choose paper that is appropriate for what they are writing.
- Look for evidence that children can use vocabulary such as *kinds*, *example*, and *paper*.

MINILESSON

Prior to teaching, ensure that children are familiar with different kinds of paper (with respect to size, color, thickness, layout, etc.), including appropriate paper templates from the online resources, and know where the paper is located in the classroom. To help children select paper that is appropriate for what they are writing, engage them in a short demonstration and inquiry-based lesson. Here is an example.

- Show examples of the children's writing on different kinds of paper.

  Here are examples of different kinds of paper that you can use for writing. What do you notice about them?

- Use the paper samples on the chart along with the following prompts as needed to help children think about choosing paper to achieve their purpose for writing. Include a discussion about what different kinds of paper can be used for.

  - *What kind of writing could you do with this folded piece of paper?*
  - *How can you use big paper like this for your writing?*
  - *What could you write using these stapled pages?*
  - *If you want to make a book, what paper would you choose?*
  - *What type of paper could you use to make a poster (thank you card, letter)?*
  - *Why do you think this writer chose paper that has boxes and lines?*

- As children talk about ways to use each kind of paper, record their answers on the chart paper.

  Writers get to choose how they want their books or pieces of writing to look. When you write, choose the paper that is best for what you want to write.

Have a Try

Invite children to turn and talk about choosing paper for different purposes.

> Turn and talk about which kind of paper you think you might use today. How will you use it?

Summarize and Apply

Summarize the lesson. Remind children to choose the kind of paper that best fits their writing.

▶ Write the principle at the top of the chart.

> During writing time, choose the kind of paper that is best for your writing. Bring your writing to share when we meet later.

Confer

▶ During independent writing, move around the room to confer briefly with as many individual children as time allows. Sit side by side with them and invite them to talk about choosing different kinds of paper. Use the following prompts as needed.

- *[Hold up a paper example.] For what purpose could you use this type of paper?*
- *What kind of paper might work well for a travel brochure?*
- *What paper will you choose to make that book?*

Share

Following independent writing, gather children in the meeting area to share experiences using different kinds of paper.

> What kind of paper did you choose today? Show what you made and talk about your paper choice.

Assessment

After you have taught the minilessons in this umbrella, observe children in a variety of classroom activities. Use *The Fountas & Pinnell Literacy Continuum* to notice, teach for, and support children's learning as you observe their writing and drawing.

▶ What evidence do you have of new understandings children have developed related to using drawing and writing tools?

- Do children use glue properly?
- Are they taking care of the markers?
- Do they use scissors and staplers carefully and safely?
- Is their choice of paper appropriate for the kind of writing they are doing?
- Are they using vocabulary such as *location*, *return*, *materials*, *glue*, *markers*, *scissors*, *stapler*, *click*, *tool*, and *paper*?

▶ In what ways, beyond the scope of this umbrella, are children showing an understanding of best practices for writing and learning together in the classroom community?

- Are children engaging in bookmaking?
- Are they using a variety of drawing and writing tools to write and illustrate books?
- Do they make illustrations in a thoughtful way?

Use your observations to determine the next umbrella you will teach. You may also consult Suggested Sequence of Lessons (pp. 575–589) for guidance.

EXTENSIONS FOR USING DRAWING AND WRITING TOOLS

▶ Revisit WML3 using different kinds of paper as the need arises throughout the year (e.g., when learning about a dedication page, an author page, a table of contents).

▶ Provide different kinds of creative paper choices for children to use (e.g., gift tags, invitations, grocery lists, greeting cards).

▶ If children encounter problems with the materials, provide a brief demonstration with possible solutions (e.g., stapler is jammed or runs out of staples; glue bottle is dry).

Minilessons in This Umbrella

WML1 Get started on your writing quickly and quietly.

WML2 Write until the end of writing time.

WML3 Put your writing in your writing folder.

WML4 Talk with your teacher or other writers about your writing.

WML5 Share your writing with an audience.

WML6 Return your writing materials to the places they belong.

Before Teaching Umbrella 3 Minilessons

We recommend that children have the opportunity for independent writing time every day. Learning the routines for independent writing will help children build self-confidence by achieving a sense of agency and responsibility for their own work while also allowing time for you to work with individual children or small guided-writing groups. Opportunities and invitations for writing are discussed on pages 13–15. Minilessons in the Craft and Conventions sections provide instruction about how to teach specific writing skills.

Before teaching the minilessons in this umbrella, organize the classroom writing center to facilitate easy access to materials. Materials may include but are not limited to paper, pens, pencils, crayons, markers, and staplers. As children become familiar with these materials, introduce other materials and tools, such as different kinds of paper, a hole punch, tape, glue sticks, and scissors. The minilessons in MGT.U2: Using Drawing and Writing Tools provide helpful background for the minilessons in this umbrella. Additional organizational tips are to have children keep their writing folders and other literacy materials in a personal box (e.g., magazine storage box) or have children use folders in four or five different colors stored in crates. Assign children a color and keep each color in a separate corner of the classroom to alleviate traffic jams when children retrieve their folders. When writing folders become too full, move each child's finished writing to a hanging file folder, which will become a resource for viewing the child's progress through the year (see p. 54).

Writing Minilesson Principle
Get started on your writing quickly and quietly.

Establishing Independent Writing

You Will Need

▸ a child prepared to demonstrate getting writing materials and starting quickly and quietly

▸ chart paper and markers

▸ To download the following online resource for this lesson, visit **fp.pub/resources**:

■ chart art (optional)

Academic Language / Important Vocabulary

▸ writing time

▸ writing folder

▸ quickly

▸ quietly

▸ reread

Continuum Connection

▸ Listen to, remember, and follow directions with multiple steps

GOAL

Learn a routine for beginning independent writing quickly and quietly.

RATIONALE

Teaching children to begin independent writing quickly and quietly promotes independence and a sense of responsibility, allows the class to function efficiently, and gives you time to confer with individual children or small groups.

ASSESS LEARNING

▸ Notice whether children get ready for independent writing quickly, quietly, and independently.

▸ Look for evidence that children can use vocabulary such as *writing time*, *writing folder*, *quickly*, *quietly*, and *reread.*

MINILESSON

Consider having children store their folders and other literacy materials in a personal box (e.g., a magazine storage box). Another idea is to use folders in four or five different colors stored in hanging folders in crates. Assign children a color and keep each color in a separate corner of the classroom to alleviate traffic jams when children retrieve their folders. To help children learn the routine for independent writing, engage them in a short demonstration and discussion. Here is an example.

> During writing time, you will learn about writing, spend some time writing on your own, and then come together to share what you wrote. _____ is going to show how to get started when you write on your own.

▸ Invite the child prepared to demonstrate the routine for independent writing to come forward and get started.

> What did you notice about how she got started? What did she do first?

> What could you hear when she went to get her writing folder and materials?

> How quickly did she get started?

> What did she do before she started writing?

> Why do you think she reread what she had already written first?

▸ Make a list of guidelines based on children's responses on chart paper.

Have a Try

Invite children to talk to a partner about the routine for independent writing.

> Turn and talk to your partner about how you will get started during writing time.

▶ After children turn and talk, invite a few children to share their responses. Clarify the routine if necessary.

Summarize and Apply

Write the principle at the top of the chart. Summarize the learning and remind children to follow the routine for getting started with independent writing.

> Today when you work on making books, practice what you just learned about getting started during writing time. Look at the chart if you need help remembering what to do.

Confer

▶ During independent writing, move around the room to confer briefly with as many individual children as time allows. Sit side by side with them and invite them to talk about getting started with their drawing and writing. Use prompts such as the following as needed.

- *What materials do you need for your writing and drawing today?*
- *Did you reread what you wrote yesterday? How did it help you with your writing today?*
- *What are you going to write about today?*
- *You got started with your writing quickly and quietly today.*

Share

Following independent writing, gather children in the meeting area to talk about getting started with independent writing.

> How did you get started during writing time today?

> How did getting started quickly and quietly help you do your best work during writing time?

Get started on your writing quickly and quietly.

Start quickly and quietly.

Get your writing folder.

Get your writing and drawing materials.

Reread your writing so you know what to write next.

Begin to draw and write.

WML2
MGT.U3.WML2

Writing Minilesson Principle
Write until the end of writing time.

Establishing Independent Writing

You Will Need

- chart paper and markers
- To download the following online resource for this lesson, visit **fp.pub/resources**:
  - chart art (optional)

Academic Language / Important Vocabulary

- writing time
- add
- reread
- detail

Continuum Connection

- Produce a reasonable quantity of writing within the time available
- Write with independent initiative and investment

GOAL

Learn how to work independently and build stamina during independent writing.

RATIONALE

Teaching children to write independently and to use all of the time at their disposal allows them to develop as writers and build their stamina for and interest in writing.

ASSESS LEARNING

- Observe children during independent writing. Are they able to work independently?
- Notice whether children work on their writing for the whole independent writing time.
- Look for evidence that children can use vocabulary such as *writing time*, *add*, *reread*, and *detail*.

MINILESSON

To help children learn to work independently and build stamina during independent writing, engage them in a discussion about using the entire amount of time allotted for drawing and writing. Here is an example.

> During writing time, some of you stop drawing and writing before writing time is over. What are some things you might do if you think you have finished the book you're working on?

- Record responses on chart paper.
- As needed, prompt children to think about actions such as checking the pictures, rereading the words, adding more words or pictures, adding more details to the pictures, thinking about what to write about next, and starting a new book.
- Remind children to refer to the My Ideas for Writing list (see WPS.U1: Getting Ideas Through Storytelling) to help them decide what to write about next.
- Explain how children will know how much time they have left during independent writing. You might use a timer or tell them what time writing time will end. Gradually increase the length of the time for writing as children become comfortable with the routine and build stamina.

Have a Try

Invite children to talk to a partner about what they will do during independent writing.

> Turn and talk to your partner about what you will do if you think you've finished writing before writing time is over.

Summarize and Apply

Write the principle at the top of the chart. Summarize the learning and remind children to write until the end of independent writing.

> Whenever you think you have finished writing, there is always something more you can do. Check to see whether you need to add more words or pictures to make your writing or drawing clearer to your readers. Or, you can start writing a new book. Remember to keep writing until writing time is over.

> **Write until the end of writing time.**
>
> Check your pictures.
>
> Reread your writing.
>
> Add words or pictures.
>
> Add more details to your pictures.
>
> Decide what to write about next.
>
> Start a new book.

Confer

▸ During independent writing, move around the room to confer briefly with as many individual children as time allows. Sit side by side with them and invite them to talk about their writing. Use the following prompts as needed.

- *Do you think you have finished your book? What might you do next? Look at the chart we made.*

- *Did you reread your writing? Is there anything else you could add to your book to make it clearer for your readers?*

- *What did you draw on this page? What details could you add to your drawing?*

- *Do you want to look at your My Ideas for Writing list to help you decide what to write about next?*

Share

Following independent writing, gather children in the meeting area and invite them to share how they stayed busy.

> Give a thumbs-up if you wrote until the end of writing time.

> If you thought you were finished with your book before the end of writing time, what did you do next?

WML3
MGT.U3.WML3

Put your writing in your writing folder.

Establishing Independent Writing

You Will Need

- a child prepared to demonstrate putting writing in a writing folder
- a writing folder for each child (folders with a pocket on each side are preferable)
- chart paper and markers
- To download the following online resource for this lesson, visit **fp.pub/resources**:
  - chart art (optional)

Academic Language / Important Vocabulary

- organized
- writing folder
- finished
- unfinished

Continuum Connection

- Listen to, remember, and follow directions with multiple steps

---

GOAL

Learn to keep writing organized within a writing folder.

RATIONALE

Teaching children to put their writing in a writing folder encourages them to be organized and builds a routine for independent writing that makes it easier to write more, confer with other writers, and share writing. When writing folders become too full, have children move finished pieces to a hanging file folder.

ASSESS LEARNING

- Notice whether children demonstrate keeping their writing organized in their writing folders.
- Look for evidence that children can use vocabulary such as *organized*, *writing folder*, *finished*, and *unfinished*.

MINILESSON

The writing folders should have a pocket on each side and clasps in the center to hold useful resources. Organize the way the folders are stored, either in children's personal boxes or in crates fitted with hanging folders (see Before Teaching). To help children learn the routine for putting away their writing in their writing folders, engage them in a short demonstration and discussion. Here is an example.

> At the end of writing time, put your writing away in your writing folder so that your writing will be organized. Why do you think it's important to keep your writing organized?

> Keeping your writing organized will make it easier to find it later. _____ will show how to use a writing folder.

- Invite the participating child to demonstrate how to store papers in a writing folder.

  > What did you notice about how _____ put his writing into his writing folder?

  > The folder has two sides with pockets. Where did _____ put his writing?

  > _____, why did you put your writing on that side?

- Help children understand that one side of the folder is for unfinished writing and the other side is for finished writing. You may want to put a full smiley face on the finished work side and half of a smiley face on the unfinished side.

Have a Try

Invite children to talk to a partner about what they will do at the end of writing time.

> What will you do with your writing at the end of writing time? Turn and talk to your partner about this.

▶ After time for discussion, invite a few children to share their thinking. Use their responses to make a list of guidelines on chart paper.

Summarize and Apply

Summarize the learning and remind children to put their writing in their writing folders.

> What should you do with your writing when writing time is over?

▶ Write the principle at the top of the chart.

> Today you learned what to do with your writing at the end of writing time. At the end of writing time today, remember to put your writing in your writing folder. Then bring your folder to share when we meet later.

Put your writing in your writing folder.

Unfinished   Finished

Put unfinished writing in the left pocket.

Put finished writing in the right pocket.

Make sure you can see the front.

Confer

▶ During independent writing, move around the room to confer briefly with as many individual children as time allows. Sit side by side with them and invite them to talk about their writing folders. Use prompts such as the following if needed.

- *Talk about what you have in your writing folder.*
- *Are you finished with this book, or will you work on it again another day? Where should you put it?*
- *Why is it important to keep your writing organized?*

Share

Following independent writing, gather children in the meeting area to share how they used their writing folders.

> What did you do with your writing at the end of writing time?

> How did you decide which side of your folder to put it in?

Writing Minilesson Principle
Talk with your teacher or other writers about your writing.

Establishing Independent Writing

You Will Need

- a child prepared to demonstrate a writing conference
- chart paper and markers
- To download the following online resource for this lesson, visit **fp.pub/resources**:
  - chart art (optional)

Academic Language / Important Vocabulary

- writing time
- writer

Continuum Connection

- Understand that other writers can be helpful in the process
- Change writing in response to peer or teacher feedback
- Understand the role of the writer, teacher, or peer writer in conference

GOAL

Understand that writers find it helpful to talk about their writing with another person.

RATIONALE

When children read their writing aloud, they can listen for what they are communicating to others. Talking to you or their classmates about their writing can give children an audience that provides feedback for how they can improve their writing.

ASSESS LEARNING

- Notice how children discuss their writing with you.
- Look for evidence that children can use vocabulary such as *writing time* and *writer*.

MINILESSON

To help children understand why and how to talk to another person about their writing, engage them in a short demonstration of a writing conference. Select in advance a child who is willing and able to talk with you in front of the class. Here is an example.

- Sit on a low chair with the prepared child in front of the class.

  Please read your writing aloud, _____.

- As you talk with the child, model some of the language you might use to support the writers in your classroom, such as the following:

  - *You wrote about celebrating the holiday at your uncle's house. I like the interesting words you used to describe the food you ate, like* juicy *and* delicious.

  - *I'm wondering how you were feeling during this time.*

  - *Was there one part that was more interesting than the rest? Could you say more about that?*

  - *Will your readers need to know more about* _____? *You might want to explain it a little more clearly.*

  - *What details could you add to your pictures?*

  - *Do you have any questions for me? Is there anything you need help with?*

  - *What might you work on next?*

Have a Try

Invite children to talk to a partner about what they observed.

> What did you notice when _____ and I talked? Turn and talk about what you noticed.

▶ After time for discussion, invite several children to share what they noticed. Record responses on chart paper.

Summarize and Apply

Write the principle at the top of the chart. Summarize the learning and remind children that talking about their writing helps them grow as writers.

> Why do you think it's important to talk about your writing? How can it help you grow as a writer?

> Today during writing time, I will sit with some of you just like I sat with _____. You will read your writing to me, and then we will talk about what you might work on next to grow as a writer. Some of you might want to talk with a classmate about your writing. Your classmate might have some questions for you to help you make your writing better.

Talk with your teacher or other writers about your writing.

Writer	Teacher/Other Writers
• Read your writing aloud. Show the pictures.	• Listen to the writer read.
• Tell what you want help with.	• Help the writer.
• Tell what you will add to your book and why.	• Tell what you are wondering about the writing.
• Answer questions.	• Ask questions.

Confer

▶ During independent writing, move around the room to confer briefly with as many individual children as time allows. Sit side by side with them and invite them to talk about their writing. Use prompts such as the following.

> • I am wondering _____. Would you like to write something about that?

> • What could you add to help readers understand _____?

> • Why did you decide to draw _____ on this page? Are there any details you could add?

> • What do you want help with today?

Share

Following independent writing, gather children in the meeting area to talk about their writing conferences.

> Raise your hand if you talked with someone about your writing today.

> How was it helpful?

Section 1: Management

Writing Minilesson Principle
Share your writing with an audience.

Establishing Independent Writing

You Will Need

- an example book you have written
- chart paper and markers
- To download the following online resource for this lesson, visit **fp.pub/resources**:
  - chart art (optional)

Academic Language / Important Vocabulary

- audience
- ideas

Continuum Connection

- Understand that other writers can be helpful in the process
- Change writing in response to peer or teacher feedback
- Show confidence when presenting
- Look at the audience (or other person) while talking
- Listen actively to others read or talk about their writing and give feedback
- Demonstrate respectful listening behaviors

GOAL

Learn that an audience can provide feedback and new ideas.

RATIONALE

Helping children understand why and how to share their writing with each other helps them generate and expand their ideas for improving their writing, build on each other's comments, and strengthen their listening and writing skills.

ASSESS LEARNING

- Notice whether children listen respectfully to their peers and give constructive feedback.
- Observe whether children use peer feedback to develop their writing.
- Look for evidence that children can use vocabulary such as *audience* and *ideas*.

MINILESSON

Before teaching this minilesson, make sure children are familiar with the concepts taught in MGT.U1: Working Together in the Classroom, particularly WML2, WML4, and WML5. To help children understand how to share their writing, engage them in an inquiry-based lesson. Here is an example.

> Writers often share their writing with an audience, or a group of people who watch and listen to the writing being read aloud. Today, you will be my audience as I read aloud a book that I wrote. After I share my writing with you, we will talk about what I did as a writer and what you did as my audience.

- Read aloud the example book that you prepared. Model strong presentation skills, such as using a strong voice and making eye contact with the audience.

  > What did you notice about how I shared my writing with you? What did I do?

  > What did you do as my audience?

- As needed, use questions such as the following to prompt discussion. If children mention looking at the audience, take into consideration that some children may not be comfortable with establishing or able to establish eye contact because of cultural conventions or for other reasons. Adjust the lesson accordingly.

  - *What did you notice about my voice?*
  - *Where did I (you) look?*
  - *How did you show that you were listening to me?*
  - *What did we do after I finished reading?*
  - *What did you ask me? What did I ask you?*

- Record children's responses about the roles of the writer and the audience on chart paper.

Have a Try

Invite children to talk to a partner about why it is helpful to share writing with an audience.

> How can sharing your writing with an audience help you become a better writer? Turn and talk to your partner about this.

▶ After time for discussion, invite several children to share their thinking.

Summarize and Apply

Write the principle at the top of the chart. Summarize the learning and remind children why it is important to share writing with an audience.

> Sharing your writing with an audience can help you get ideas and grow as a writer. As you write today, think about how you will share your writing with an audience. After writing time, some of you will have a chance to share your writing with an audience.

Share your writing with an audience.	
Writer	**Audience**
• Read your book aloud and show the pictures.	• Listen carefully to the writer.
• Use a strong, clear voice.	• Look at the writer.
• Look at the audience.	• Give your opinion.
• Ask for help if you need it.	• Help the writer.
• Answer the audience's questions.	• Ask questions.

Confer

▶ During independent writing, move around the room to confer briefly with as many individual children as time allows. Sit side by side with them and invite them to talk about their writing. Use prompts such as the following if needed.

- *Can you read your writing aloud?*
- *Is there anything you need help with?*
- *I like how you _____. What could you add to tell more about _____?*
- *How will you share your book with an audience? Look at the chart we made if you need help remembering what to do.*

Share

Following independent writing, gather children in the meeting area. Invite several children to practice what they learned about sharing their writing with an audience.

> Raise your hand if you would like to share your writing with an audience.

> Is there anything you want help with, _____?

> Does anyone have any questions or comments for _____?

Section 1: Management

WML6

MGT.U3.WML6

Writing Minilesson Principle
Return your writing materials to the places they belong.

Establishing Independent Writing

You Will Need

- two or three children prepared to demonstrate putting away writing materials
- chart paper and markers
- To download the following online resource for this lesson, visit **fp.pub/resources**:
  - chart art (optional)

Academic Language / Important Vocabulary

- writing time
- materials
- writing folder
- personal box

Continuum Connection

- Listen to, remember, and follow directions with multiple steps

GOAL

Learn the routine of putting materials away at the end of writing time.

RATIONALE

Teaching children to put away their writing materials helps them create an organized learning environment. This builds the children's independence and allows them to quickly find their materials.

ASSESS LEARNING

- Notice whether children carefully put away their materials at the end of independent writing.
- Look for evidence that children can use vocabulary such as *writing time*, *materials*, *writing folder*, and *personal box*.

MINILESSON

Before this minilesson, children should already be familiar with the materials in the writing center and how they are organized. To help children learn how to put away their writing materials, engage them in a short demonstration. Right before teaching the lesson, ask two or three children to place their writing materials at their writing spots.

> What materials do we have in the writing center?

> What do you notice about how our writing materials are organized? How do you know where each type of material belongs?

> Why do you think it's important for writers to keep their materials organized?

> It's important to keep your writing materials organized so you can find them easily and start writing quickly and quietly. A few of your classmates are now going to show you what to do with your writing materials at the end of writing time.

▶ Invite the children prepared to demonstrate to pick up the writing materials that they placed at their writing spots and put them away.

> What did you notice your classmates do?

Use the following suggested questions to prompt further discussion:

- *Where did they put their materials? Why did they put them there?*
- *Where did they put their writing?*
- *How did they place the writing in their folders? Then what did they do?*
- *How did it sound when they were putting their materials away?*

▶ Record children's responses on chart paper.

Have a Try

Invite children to talk to a partner about what to do at the end of independent writing.

> What will you do at the end of writing time? Turn and talk to your partner about this.

▶ After time for discussion, invite a few children to share their responses.

Summarize and Apply

Help children summarize the learning. Remind them to put away their writing materials at the end of independent writing.

> Why is it important to return your materials to the places they belong when writing time is over?

▶ Write the principle at the top of the chart.

> Remember to put your materials away at the end of writing time today and every day. However, if you would like to share your writing when we meet later, bring the writing you are working on. You can put it away later.

Return your writing materials to the places they belong.

- Put your materials away where they belong.

- Put your writing in your writing folder.

- Put your folder where it belongs.

- Put everything away quickly and quietly.

Confer

▶ During independent writing, move around the room to confer briefly with as many individual children as time allows. Sit side by side with them and invite them to talk about what they will do at the end of writing time. Use prompts such as the following if needed.

- *What will you do at the end of writing time?*
- *Where will you put your finished writing?*
- *Where will you put your writing folder? Look at the chart we made.*
- *Where do the pencils go?*

Share

Following independent writing, gather children in the meeting area. Invite several children to share their writing and talk about what they did at the end of writing time.

> Raise your hand if you would like to share your writing today.

> What did you do with your writing materials at the end of writing time?

Assessment

After you have taught the minilessons in this umbrella, observe children as they prepare for, progress through, and conclude independent writing time each day. Use *The Fountas & Pinnell Literacy Continuum* to notice, teach for, and support children's learning as you observe their attempts at reading and writing.

▶ What evidence do you have of new understandings children have developed related to the routines for independent writing time?

- Do children get started on their writing quickly and quietly?
- Are they able to sustain working for the whole independent writing time?
- Is the writing inside children's writing folders organized?
- How are they talking with you about their writing?
- How are they sharing their writing with an audience to get ideas?
- Are the writing materials returned to the places they belong?
- Do they understand and use vocabulary such as *reread*, *organized*, *ideas*, *audience*, and *materials*?

▶ In what other ways, beyond the scope of this umbrella, are children getting started with independent writing?

- Are they using drawing and writing tools appropriately?
- Are they using the resources in their writing folder?

Use your observations to determine the next umbrella you will teach. You may also consult Suggested Sequence of Lessons (pp. 575–589) for guidance.

EXTENSIONS FOR ESTABLISHING INDEPENDENT WRITING

▶ Teach children to use the resources in their writing folder, such as a list of finished writing, a list of ideas for writing, a personal word list, guidelines for writing time, and a proofreading checklist. See online resources for minilessons in MGT.U4: Introducing Writing Folder Resources.

▶ Show children what to do with their finished pieces when their writing folder gets too full.

▶ When children share, help them progress from statements like "I like your writing" to statements like "The words you used helped me make a picture in my mind of _____."

Minilessons in This Umbrella

WML1 List your finished writing.

WML2 Write what you learned from your writing.

WML3 Add to your personal word list.

Before Teaching Umbrella 4 Minilessons

Before teaching the minilessons in this umbrella, prepare a writing folder for each child. Folders should have two pockets with fasteners, which you will use to attach the resources used in this umbrella. The information that children record on the resources pages (My Finished Writing and My Words—both found in the online resources) can be used during writing conferences. When you meet with guided writing groups, have children fill in something they have learned from doing their writing.

As you think about how children will organize their writing, consider labeling the pockets *Finished* (possibly with a smiley face) and *Unfinished* (possibly with half of a smiley face). Children can store their writing folders in a personal box (e.g., a magazine storage box) with other literacy items. Another idea is to use folders in four or five different colors stored in crates. Assign children a color and keep each color in a separate corner of the classroom to alleviate traffic jams when children retrieve their folders. These ideas are introduced in MGT.U3: Establishing Independent Writing, which you may want to complete before this umbrella.

Use the book from the following text set in *Fountas & Pinnell Classroom™ Interactive Read-Aloud Collection*, or use books from your classroom library, including at least one that lists the author's previously published books.

Interactive Read-Aloud Collection
Caring for Each Other: Family

Super-Completely and Totally the Messiest! by Judith Viorst

As you read and enjoy books together, help children

- think about ideas for their own writing,

- notice that some authors write more than one book, and

- notice how the accuracy of the spelling and the clear spacing between words makes it easier for the reader to read.

Introducing Writing Folder Resources

You Will Need

- a familiar book that contains a list of other books written by the author, such as *Super-Completely and Totally the Messiest!* by Judith Viorst, from Text Set: Caring for Each Other: Family

- a writing folder for each child with a My Finished Writing chart fastened inside

- chart paper with an example My Finished Writing chart drawn on or attached and filled in

- markers

- To download the following online resource for this lesson, visit **fp.pub/resources**:
  - My Finished Writing

Academic Language / Important Vocabulary

- finished
- completed

Continuum Connection

- Select an appropriate title for a poem, story, or informational book

- Listen to, remember, and follow directions with multiple steps

---

GOAL

Learn how to keep track of finished writing to reflect on progress across the year.

RATIONALE

A finished writing list allows children to communicate to you when they believe a piece of writing is complete so you can plan further instruction for them. It allows them and you to reflect on their writing across the year, and it also provides information for you when you discuss children's progress in writing.

ASSESS LEARNING

- Observe children's ability to create and maintain a list of finished writing.
- Notice if children are appropriately evaluating the completeness of their writing.
- Look for evidence that children can use vocabulary such as *finished* and *completed*.

MINILESSON

Before the lesson, prepare for each child a writing folder with My Finished Writing fastened inside. To help children think about the minilesson principle, display a page in a familiar book that lists other books written by the same author. Then show and discuss your own completed My Finished Writing chart. Here is an example.

- Show the cover of *Super-Completely and Totally the Messiest!* and then turn to the "Also by Judith Viorst" page in the front matter.

  What do you see on this page?

  This is a list of other books written by the author, Judith Viorst.

  You can make a list of your finished writing, too!

- Display the example My Finished Writing prepared before class.

  What do you see on the list?

  I wrote a number, the title of each piece of writing, and the date I completed it. Whenever I finish a new piece of writing, I will add it to my list. There is another row in the chart, but we will look at that later.

Have a Try

Invite children to talk to a partner about finished writing they could add to their lists.

> Think about books you have written this year. What finished writing could you list on a chart like this? Turn and talk to your partner.

▸ After time for discussion, invite a few children to share titles. Explain that they will learn how to fill in the rest of the chart later.

▸ Save the chart for WML2.

Summarize and Apply

Invite them to list the titles of their finished writing on the online resource My Finished Writing.

▸ Display a child's writing folder open to My Finished Writing.

> Whenever you finish a piece of writing, write the title and date on My Finished Writing, which is in your writing folder. Before you start writing today, take a moment to write on the chart the title of the last thing you finished writing.

My Finished Writing

#	Title	Date Completed
1	All About Dinosaurs	9/15
	What I learned how to do as a writer:	
2	My Poor Ankle!	9/29
	What I learned how to do as a writer:	
3	Then Came Wesley	10/8
	What I learned how to do as a writer:	
4	Grandma and I	10/18
	What I learned how to do as a writer:	

Confer

▸ During independent writing, move around the room to confer briefly with as many individual children as time allows. Sit side by side with them and invite them to talk about using the resources in their writing folders.

- *Take out the last book you finished writing. What is it called?*
- *Did you add that book to your list?*
- *What is your new book about? What is a title that matches that?*

Share

Following independent writing, ask children to bring their writing folders to the meeting area and share their lists of finished writing with a partner.

> Share your list of finished writing with your partner.

Introducing Writing Folder Resources

You Will Need

- a writing folder for each child with My Finished Writing inside
- chart from WML1 with more lines filled in
- markers
- To download the following online resource for this lesson, visit **fp.pub/resources**:
  - My Finished Writing

Academic Language / Important Vocabulary

- title
- learned
- writer

Continuum Connection

- Discuss what is being worked on as a writer
- Talk about oneself as a writer
- State what was learned from each piece of writing

GOAL

Reflect on what was learned from a piece of writing.

RATIONALE

When children keep a record of what they have learned from their writing, they learn to reflect on their writing. This helps them see their progress in writing more easily, giving them more confidence in their writing ability. It also helps them view themselves as writers and think about what to work on next. It gives you important information about children's progress that you can use to inform your teaching.

ASSESS LEARNING

- Observe for evidence that children can thoughtfully reflect on what they have learned from their writing.
- Look for evidence that children can use vocabulary such as *title*, *learned*, and *writer*.

MINILESSON

WML1 was about how to fill in part of My Finished Writing. This minilesson is about how to fill in the rest of it. Show and discuss an example chart that you have filled in to model for children how to reflect on what they have learned from working on their writing. Here is an example.

- Display the example My Finished Writing, prepared before class.

  You learned how to make a list of your finished writing on your My Finished Writing chart. Today we are going to talk about how to fill in the part that says *What I learned how to do as a writer*.

  What do you notice about what I learned from my writing?

  I wrote down new things I did in my writing, like adding dialogue or using a sidebar.

  How can writing down what you learned from your writing help you?

  Writing what you learned from your writing helps you think about the progress you have made as a writer and what you want to work on next.

Have a Try

Invite children to talk to a partner about what they learned from their last piece of writing.

> Think about the last piece of writing you finished. What did you learn how to do as a writer? Turn and talk to your partner about this.

▶ After time for discussion, invite a few children to share what they learned.

Summarize and Apply

Invite children to reflect on writing they have already completed before moving on to a new piece of writing.

▶ Display a child's writing folder open to My Finished Writing.

> Keep track of all the pieces of writing that you do. Sometimes I will ask you to write what you learned how to do when you did your writing. Before you start writing today, take a moment to write something you learned how to do from your last piece of writing.

	My Finished Writing	
#	Title	Date Completed
1	All About Dinosaurs	9/15
	What I learned how to do as a writer: I tried using a sidebar to give more information.	
2	My Poor Ankle!	9/29
	What I learned how to do as a writer: I learned how to write a good story about something small.	
3	Then Came Wesley	10/8
	What I learned how to do as a writer: I used words that showed the order of events.	
4	Grandma and I	10/18
	What I learned how to do as a writer: I added talking to my writing to make it more interesting.	

Confer

▶ During independent writing, move around the room to confer briefly with as many individual children as time allows. Sit side by side with them and invite them to talk about using the resources in their writing folders.

- *What is the title of the last book you wrote?*
- *What did you learn how to do from writing that book?*
- *Did you try anything new when you wrote it?*

Share

Following independent writing, ask children to bring their writing folders to the meeting area.

> Who would like to share what you learned from your last piece of writing?

> It is so interesting to think about what you can learn when you write.

Writing Minilesson Principle

Add to your personal word list.

Introducing Writing Folder Resources

You Will Need

▸ a sample piece of your writing with standard spelling

▸ a writing folder for each child, with My Words printed as two-page spreads and fastened inside

▸ chart paper prepared with a portion of the My Words resource drawn on or attached

▸ markers

▸ To download the following online resource for this lesson, visit **fp.pub/resources**:

  ▪ My Words

Academic Language / Important Vocabulary

▸ spell

▸ personal

▸ frequently

Continuum Connection

▸ Use simple resources to help in spelling words or check on spelling (word walls, personal word lists)

▸ Use beginning reference tools: e.g., word walls, personal word lists, or word cards to assist in word choice or checking spelling

▸ Understand that the more accurate the spelling and the clearer the space between words, the easier it is for the reader to read it

GOAL

Learn how to add a new word to a personal word list to use for future reference.

RATIONALE

When you help children develop a list of words they use often, they can use the list as a reference to support writing accurately, fluently, and independently.

ASSESS LEARNING

▸ Notice if children refer to their personal word list when writing.

▸ Look for evidence that children can use vocabulary such as *spell*, *personal*, and *frequently*.

MINILESSON

Before the lesson, prepare for each child a writing folder with My Words fastened inside so that it opens in two-page spreads. Consider writing a couple of words on children's lists ahead of time to get them started. Demonstrate adding words to the chart. Here is an example.

▸ Display the sample piece of writing that you prepared before class.

> What do you notice about how I spelled the words?

> The words are spelled the same way they are spelled in books. How does it help the reader if you spell words the same way they are spelled in books?

▸ Display the prepared chart and a copy of My Words fastened inside a child's writing folder.

> The big chart shows just part of what you will have in your writing folder. What do you see on the chart?

> Each box has an uppercase (capital) and lowercase (small) letter of the alphabet. What do you think you will write in each box?

> If you talk to me about your writing and we notice you use the word *friend* a lot, I could write *friend* on your personal word list so that you can learn to spell it yourself.

▸ Demonstrate writing the word *friend* on the chart.

> Where else can you look if you're not sure how to spell a word or if you think you have not spelled it right?

▸ Direct children's attention to resources in the room, such as dictionaries and a word wall. Explain that children can also ask you for help with spelling.

Have a Try

Invite children to talk to a partner about other words they could add to their personal word lists.

> Turn and talk to your partner. What are some other words you use a lot in your writing that you might want on your personal word list?

▶ After time for discussion, ask a few children to share words. Add them to the chart if they begin with the letters shown. Remind children that their charts have the full alphabet.

Summarize and Apply

Write the principle at the top of the chart. Remind children to add words to their personal word lists.

▶ Display a child's writing folder open to My Words.

> When you and I talk about your writing together, notice if we talk about how to spell some words that you like to use in your writing. Those are the words I can help you write on your personal word list.

> You can use resources like a word wall, a dictionary, or your personal word list to write a word or check your spelling.

Add to your personal word list.

My Words		My Words	
Aa	Bb	Cc	Dd
Ee	Ff friend	Gg	Hh
Ii	Jj	Kk	Ll
Mm	Nn	Oo	Pp

Confer

▶ During independent writing, move around the room to confer briefly with as many individual children as time allows. Sit side by side with them and invite them to talk about the resources in their writing folders. Use the following prompts as needed.

- *Have you spelled all the words in your writing the same way they are spelled in books? Are there any words you're not sure about?*

- *Where can you look to find out how to spell that word?*

- *I notice you write the word _____ a lot. Let's add _____ to your personal word list. That will help you learn to write that word quickly. [Teacher writes word to ensure legibility and correct spelling.]*

Share

Following independent writing, gather children in the meeting area. Ask several volunteers to share a word from their personal word lists.

> How will it help you to have a personal word list?

Section 1: Management

Assessment

After you have taught the minilessons in this umbrella, observe children as they prepare for, progress through, and conclude independent writing time each day. Use *The Fountas & Pinnell Literacy Continuum* to notice, teach for, and support children's learning as you observe their reading and writing.

▶ What evidence do you have of new understandings children have developed related to the writing folder resources?

- Do children add the title of each finished work to a chart in their writing folder?

- Are they able to think and write about what they have learned how to do from doing their writing?

- When they are writing, do they add to and refer to a personal word list?

- Do they understand and use vocabulary such as *ideas*, *finished*, *completed*, *spell*, *personal*, and *frequently*?

▶ In what other ways, beyond the scope of this umbrella, are children using and thinking about writing?

- Do they refer to the resources in their writing folders when they make books?

- Do they look in their folders to choose a piece of writing to celebrate?

Use your observations to determine the next umbrella you will teach. You may also consult Suggested Sequence of Lessons (pp. 575–589) for guidance.

EXTENSIONS FOR INTRODUCING WRITING FOLDER RESOURCES

▶ If you are planning to have children use a writer's notebook, you might want children to glue My Ideas for Writing in their notebooks (see WPS.U2: Learning About My First Writer's Notebook).

▶ Place a high-frequency word list (use your own or download a list from the online resources) in each writing folder. While children should not stop writing every time they think a word might be on the list, they can be taught to refer to it (sparingly) while writing. Or, they can learn to check spelling afterward. Likewise, you can introduce a proofreading list to the writing folder (see WPS.U10.WML5).

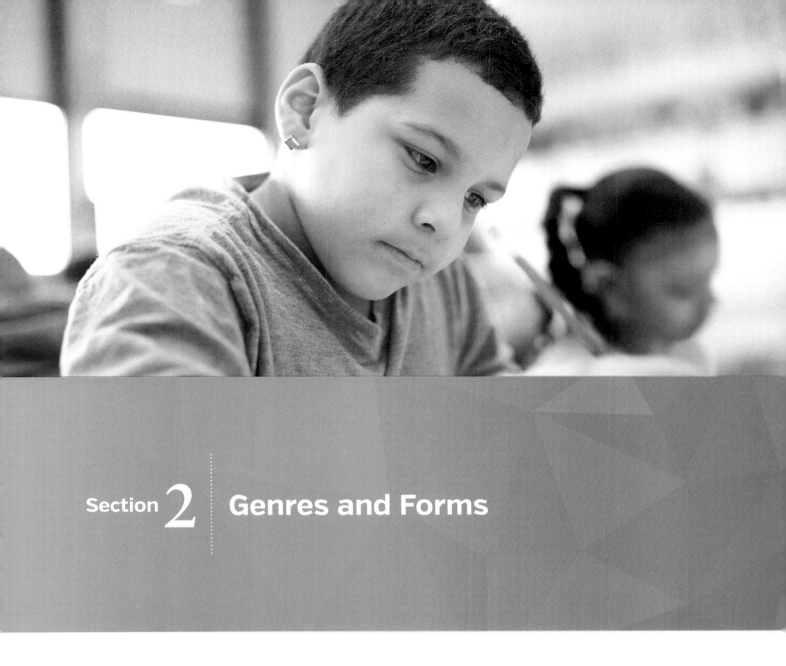

Section 2 | Genres and Forms

Exposure to various genres and forms of writing broadens children's vision for what their writing can be. The minilessons in this section support children by helping them see that they can express themselves in writing in a variety of ways. They learn to make books, such as memory books and all-about books, and to write in other forms, such as friendly letters and poems.

2 Genres and Forms

Minilessons in This Umbrella

WML1 Make a book with pictures and words.

WML2 Write your name and the date on your book.

WML3 Plan what to tell on each page.

WML4 Decide when your book is finished.

Before Teaching Umbrella 1 Minilessons

Before teaching, children will benefit from having experienced at least some of the minilessons in WPS.U1: Getting Ideas for Writing Through Storytelling and from having heard and enjoyed various types of books, including fiction, wordless, pattern, and nonfiction. When children make their books, they can use plain paper or any of the paper templates from online resources that are appropriate.

   It is a good idea to make a picture book of your own to use as a model for the lessons. Prepare a simple booklet of stapled-together paper. Choose any topic and write a short book that has words and corresponding pictures on each page. Include a blank cover. For published mentor texts, consider the following books from *Fountas & Pinnell Classroom™ Shared Reading Collection*, or choose books from the classroom library.

Shared Reading Collection

   Smokey Bear: A True Story by Hannah Cales

   Animals with Jobs by Charlotte Rose

   Side by Side: A True Story by Linda Ruggieri

As you read and enjoy these texts together, help children notice that

- writers and illustrators make books,

- there are words and/or pictures on every page, and

- writers tell about different things in their books.

Shared Reading

Section 2: Genres and Forms

Writing Minilesson Principle
Make a book with pictures and words.

Getting Started with Making Books

You Will Need

- a variety of familiar picture, wordless, alphabet, and informational books
- a prepared book of your own (see Before Teaching)
- chart paper and markers
- To download the following online resource for this lesson, visit **fp.pub/resources**:
  - paper templates (optional)

Academic Language / Important Vocabulary

- author
- pictures
- words

Continuum Connection

- Create a picture book as one kind of writing
- Write a continuous message on a simple topic
- Understand that when both writing and drawing are on a page, they are mutually supportive, with each extending the other
- Take on both approximated and conventional writing independently
- Write with independent initiative and investment

GOAL

Make books using drawing and a combination of approximated and conventional writing.

RATIONALE

As you introduce children to making books, they begin to view themselves as writers and illustrators, which builds their excitement and endurance for writing. They learn the power of their own ideas, and they learn that drawing and writing can communicate ideas to others.

ASSESS LEARNING

- Notice whether children understand that the words and pictures in a book are related.
- Look for evidence that children recognize that they can make their own books.
- Look for evidence that children can use vocabulary such as *author*, *pictures*, and *words*.

MINILESSON

Use familiar books that have both pictures and words and a book you made for this umbrella to generate a discussion about the features of books in preparation for children to make their own books. Below is an example. Provide plain paper or any paper templates in the online resources that are appropriate for children's books.

- Display the books you have gathered.

  What is the same about these books?

- Guide the conversation to help children notice that the pages in the books have pictures and/or words and that the pictures and words go together to tell a story or give information.

  What are some things that make a book good for you to read?

- As children share ideas, begin a list on chart paper that shows qualities of good books.

- Show the pages of the book you made.

  What do you notice about this book that I wrote?

- Help children notice that it shares features of the other books they looked at: on each page, you drew a picture and wrote the words that go with the picture.

  Because I wrote this book, I am the author. Authors write all types of books and you can, too.

Have a Try

Invite children to turn and talk about a story they might like to draw and write.

> Turn and talk about a book you could write. What could you write about? What pictures could you draw?

▶ After time for discussion, ask a few children to share. Guide the conversation as needed to help them explore what type of book they might like to make.

Summarize and Apply

Summarize the lesson. Remind children that they can make many types of books. Write the principle at the top of the chart and read the list.

> You will make lots of books this year. Your books will have some of the good things we talked about. Today during writing time, plan the pictures and words for your book. When you are ready, start making your book.

▶ This minilesson is intended as an introduction to making books. Some of the children in your class may be excited to get started, while others may want to just write down ideas.

Make a book with pictures and words.

Good books . . .

- have words

- have pictures that go with the words

- tell interesting facts

- are about interesting characters

- are funny or sad or spooky

- help you learn about something

Confer

▶ During independent writing, move around the room to confer briefly with as many individual children as time allows. Sit side by side with them and invite them to talk about making books. Use the following prompts as needed.

- *What will your book be about?*
- *Tell more about your book.*
- *What happened first . . . next . . . after that?*
- *What will you draw to go with the words on this page?*

Share

Following independent writing, gather children in the meeting area to share their writing.

▶ Have each child share an idea for a picture book. Then ask if anyone started writing a book.

> Who started a book today? Share what you made.

WML2

GEN.U1.WML2

Writing Minilesson Principle
Write your name and the date on your book.

Getting Started with Making Books

You Will Need

- several mentor texts, such as the following from *Shared Reading Collection*:
  - *Smokey Bear: A True Story* by Hannah Cales
  - *Animals with Jobs* by Charlotte Rose
- a prepared book of your own
- a blank booklet (paper stapled together)
- books children have made or are working on
- markers

Academic Language / Important Vocabulary

- author
- illustrator
- name
- date
- front cover

Continuum Connection

- Talk about oneself as a writer

GOAL

Understand that it is important to include the author's name and the date the book was made.

RATIONALE

Build children's ownership of their writing and their identity as writers by reminding them that the author's name goes on the cover. Writing the date helps you and the children observe progress in writing across the year.

ASSESS LEARNING

- Notice whether children know that the author's name is on the cover of a book.
- Look at children's books. Are they writing their names and the date on them?
- Look for evidence that children can use vocabulary such as *author, illustrator, name, date,* and *front cover.*

MINILESSON

To help children think about the minilesson principle, show the covers of a number of published books. Consider using enlarged texts so the author's name is large enough for the children to see. Refer to the book you made for this umbrella. Here is an example.

- Display familiar books, such as *Smokey Bear: A True Story* and *Animals with Jobs*. Read the name of the author while pointing to it on each cover.

  Here is the title of the book. What is right below it?

  The author's name is here after the word *by*. The cover of *Smokey Bear* has another name, the illustrator's name.

- Show the copyright year on the copyright page of each book.

  Each book has a date in it that tells when the book was published.

- Attach your booklet with a blank cover to the easel. Model the process of adding your name and date to the cover. Write the month, day, and year, and encourage children to do the same.

  Because you are the author, you will write your name and date on the cover of the books you make. Write the word *by*, your name, and the date first. Authors often wait until after a book is finished to think of a title. After you write your book, add a title and a picture to the cover.

Have a Try

Distribute the books children have written or are working on. Ask them to think about where on the cover they will write their names and the date.

> Show your partner where you will write your name and the date. Or if your book already has the name and date, show your partner where you wrote those on your cover.

Summarize and Apply

Summarize the lesson. Remind children to write their names and the date on the books they make.

> What can you do to be sure your readers know who wrote the book and when it was written?

▶ Write the principle at the top of the chart.

> Today you will work on a book you have already started or you will start making a new book. When you make the cover of your book, be sure to write the word *by*, your name, and the date with the month, day, and year. Bring your book to share when we meet later.

Confer

▶ During independent writing, move around the room to confer briefly with as many individual children as time allows. Sit side by side with them and invite them to talk about making books. Use the following prompts as needed.

- *Write your name [date] here.*
- *Where can you look to check the date?*
- *Where will you write your name? Where will you leave space to add the title later?*

Share

Following independent writing, gather children in the meeting area to share their writing.

▶ Ask each child who made a cover to hold it up for everyone to see.

> Who would like to share what you have written so far in your book?

WML3
GEN.U1.WML3

Writing Minilesson Principle
Plan what to tell on each page.

Getting Started with Making Books

You Will Need

- a mentor text, such as *Side by Side: A True Story* by Linda Ruggieri, from *Shared Reading Collection*
- a prepared book of your own
- chart paper and markers

Academic Language / Important Vocabulary

- page
- plan
- order

Continuum Connection

- Tell one part, idea, or group of ideas on each page of a book
- Write and/or draw about one idea on a page or across several pages of a book

---

GOAL

Plan what to put on each page so the pictures and words match.

RATIONALE

When children learn that part of making a book is planning what goes on each page, they realize that a book has many parts and they must make the decision about which part to draw and write on each page. This minilesson is a beginning form of rehearsal.

ASSESS LEARNING

- Notice whether children know how to plan what goes on each page of their books.
- Observe whether children add pictures to support the corresponding text on each page.
- Look for evidence that children can use vocabulary such as *page*, *plan*, and *order*.

MINILESSON

To help children think about the minilesson principle, use mentor texts with pictures to show how authors make logical decisions about what to put on each page. Here is an example.

- Briefly paraphrase what happens in *Side by Side: A True Story*. As you turn through a few pages, talk about each part of the story across your fingers (thumb for the first part, pointer finger for the next, etc.) to model how children will tell their stories across their fingers.

  First the author introduces Tarra the elephant. Then she introduces Tarra's best friend, a dog named Bella. Each part is on one page.

- Show the pages again, this time asking children how the pictures and words go together.

- Show the prepared story you wrote.

  To write my story, first I thought about the story I wanted to tell.

- Begin a list on chart paper of the planning steps. Add this first step, using general language. Continue modeling your writing thought process as you show your book, adding each step to the chart.

  Then I told my story across my fingers. That helped me decide the order of my book and plan what to put on the first page, what to put on the next page, and so forth. When I drew the pictures, I made sure that they matched what the words said.

  When you make books, you will want to do each of the things on this list, too.

- Help children understand that if they have a lot to tell about something, they might need to use or add another page.

Have a Try

Invite children to talk about a book idea with their partners. Have them think about the steps they would use to plan the pages of their books.

> Practice telling your partner a short story, perhaps about something you did before school, across your fingers. After you tell the story, talk about what you could put on the first page.

▶ After time for discussion, ask a few volunteers to share.

Summarize and Apply

Summarize the lesson. Remind children to plan what goes on each page of their books. Write the principle at the top of the chart.

> Today you will work on a book you have already started or you will start making a new book. If you are ready to write a new book, tell the story across your fingers to help plan what will go on each page before you start writing.

Plan what to tell on each page.

Decide what to write about.

Think about the order.

Tell about one part of the story on each page.

Make sure your pictures match your words.

Confer

▶ During independent writing, move around the room to confer briefly with as many individual children as time allows. Sit side by side with them and invite them to talk about making books. Use the following prompts as needed.

- *What story do you want to tell? Tell it across your fingers.*
- *What will you tell on the first page? on the next page?*
- *What will you draw for this part of the story?*
- *What words could go with that drawing?*

Share

Following independent writing, gather children in the meeting area to share their writing.

> With a partner, share the book you are working on. Tell how you planned what to write and draw on each page.

Writing Minilesson Principle
Decide when your book is finished.

Getting Started with Making Books

You Will Need

- a prepared book of your own
- a child's book
- chart paper and markers

Academic Language / Important Vocabulary

- decide
- finished

Continuum Connection

- Produce a reasonable quantity of writing within the time available
- Write with independent initiative and investment

GOAL

Understand when a book is finished and when to start another one.

RATIONALE

Some children will decide that their books are finished before checking to be sure the work is complete. Teach children how to decide when a book is finished to build a foundation for revising and proofreading and editing. Teach them options for what to do next to support them as independent writers.

ASSESS LEARNING

- Observe for evidence that children can evaluate when they have finished making a book.
- Notice evidence that children know what to do when they have finished making a book.
- Look for evidence that children can use vocabulary such as *decide* and *finished*.

MINILESSON

To help children think about the minilesson principle, use the book you created and a child's book to demonstrate thinking about whether a book is finished. Here is an example.

- Show and read the book you wrote.

  I think my book is finished, but I should check to be sure. Listen as I think aloud.

- Model the thinking process. As you do, begin a list on chart paper of the steps to think about: reread the book, check the words, and check the pictures.

- Show the child's book.

  Here is _____'s book. It might be finished, or it might not be. What can she do to find out?

  She can reread the book, check the words, and check the pictures.

  When you reread your book, think about whether you told everything that the reader needs to know. If you didn't, you might need to add some words to your book. Check the pictures to be sure that all the important information is there.

- You may want to weave the following ideas into the conversation.

  - *Even if you are able to add more to the end, it isn't always necessary.*

  - *Ask yourself if you have told everything that is important and made sure pictures are complete.*

  - *Sometimes, you might be working on a book that you haven't finished, but you want to stop and start writing a new one. Most times, you will want to finish so you have the good feeling of finishing a book.*

Have a Try

Invite children to turn and talk about what to do when they decide they have finished a book.

> If you have already reread your book and checked the words and pictures, what could you do next? Turn and talk to your partner about that.

▶ After time for discussion, ask volunteers to share. Make sure children are clear on what they need to know when they finish a book (e.g., where to put finished books, where to get a new booklet, how to think of a new idea).

Summarize and Apply

Summarize the lesson. Remind children to make sure their books are finished before starting new books. Write the principle at the top of the chart.

> How do you know when your book is finished?

> If you think your book is finished, look at the chart to make sure. When you are sure, put the book away, get another booklet, and start planning a new book.

Confer

▶ During independent writing, move around the room to confer briefly with as many individual children as time allows. Sit side by side with them and listen as they talk about making books. Use the following prompts as needed.

- *Look at the chart. What should you do next?*
- *I notice you are starting a new book. Let's look at your last book and think about what to do to make sure it is finished.*
- *What can you add to the pictures to help the reader understand more?*

Share

Following independent writing, gather children in the meeting area to share their writing.

> How did you know when you were finished with your book? Let's look at the chart.

Decide when your book is finished.

 Reread the book.

 Check the words.
Have you told what the reader needs to know?

 Check the pictures.
Are they complete?

Section 2: Genres and Forms

Assessment

After you have taught the minilessons in this umbrella, observe children as they make books. Use *The Fountas & Pinnell Literacy Continuum* to notice, teach for, and support children's learning as you observe their attempts at writing.

▶ What evidence do you have of children's new understandings related to making books?

  • Are children aware that they can make their own books?

  • Do they write their names and the date on the front cover?

  • Are there pictures and/or words on each page?

  • Can you tell that they are planning what to put on each page?

  • Do they understand the routine of what to do when they think their book is finished?

  • Are they using vocabulary such as *author, front cover, pictures, words, illustrator,* and *finished*?

▶ In what ways, beyond the scope of this umbrella, are children showing an interest in making books?

  • Are they thinking about different types of books they would like to make?

  • Are they showing an interest in adding details to illustrations to give more information?

Use your observations to determine the next umbrella you will teach. You may also consult Suggested Sequence of Lessons (pp. 575–589) for guidance.

EXTENSIONS FOR GETTING STARTED WITH MAKING BOOKS

▶ As you read aloud, take time to share an author's website or to read notes about the author to emphasize that books are written by real people.

▶ Gather several books by the same author. Help children understand that a writer can write more than one book.

▶ Gather together a guided writing group of several children who need support with the same aspect of making books.

▶ This umbrella can be extended by teaching about rehearsal (see WPS.U7: Rehearsing Your Writing).

Minilessons in This Umbrella

WML1 Choose a small moment or memory that is important to you.

WML2 Tell the story you remember.

WML3 Draw and write your story in the order it happened.

WML4 Use pictures and words to show your feelings.

WML5 Tell why the story is important.

Before Teaching Umbrella 2 Minilessons

The goal of this umbrella is to help children understand that they can make a memory book about anything they have experienced. Guide them to focus on a small moment in time so that they can write about it in detail in their memory books. You can have children work on one memory book throughout the umbrella and apply these lessons to that one piece, or you might prefer to have them work on several memory books across the umbrella.

Prior to teaching these minilessons, it would be helpful to have taught at least some of the minilessons in WPS.U1: Getting Ideas for Writing Through Storytelling. Children can use their lists to help them define small moments. If you have *The Reading Minilessons Book, Grade 2* (Fountas and Pinnell 2019), LA.U3: Studying Authors and Illustrators and LA.U23: Understanding Characters' Feelings, Motivations, and Intentions pair well with the minilessons in this umbrella. For mentor texts, use memory stories from the classroom library or ones that you have created with the class. Also consider the following books from *Fountas & Pinnell Classroom™ Interactive Read-Aloud Collection.*

Interactive Read-Aloud Collection

Memory Stories

I Love Saturdays y domingos by Alma Flor Ada

When I Was Young in the Mountains by Cynthia Rylant

The Rainbow Tulip by Pat Mora

Bigmama's by Donald Crews

Caring for Each Other: Family

Big Red Lollipop by Rukhsana Khan

Finding Your Way in a New Place

Mango, Abuela, and Me by Meg Medina

Tomie dePaola: Writing from Life

The Art Lesson

As you read and enjoy these texts together, help children

• connect the stories to memories in their own lives,

• notice the sequence of story events, and

• talk about what the words and pictures reveal about feelings.

Interactive Read-Aloud
Memory Stories

Family

Finding Your Way

Tomie dePaola

Section 2: Genres and Forms

Writing Minilesson Principle
Choose a small moment or memory that is important to you.

Making Memory Books

You Will Need

- several familiar memory stories, such as *Big Red Lollipop* by Rukhsana Khan, from Text Set: Caring for Each Other: Family
- chart from WPS.U1.WML4
- children's copies of My Ideas for Writing from WPS.U1
- chart paper drawn to look like Ideas for Memory Stories
- markers
- To download the following resource for this lesson, visit **fp.pub/resources**:
  - Ideas for Memory Stories

Academic Language / Important Vocabulary

- memory
- writer's notebook
- small moment

Continuum Connection

- Select a meaningful topic
- Select "small moments" or experiences and share thinking and feelings about them
- Reread a writer's notebook to select and develop a topic

GOAL

Understand that writers write stories based on small moments or memories that are important to them.

RATIONALE

To make their writing interesting, authors choose to write about small moments. Writing about a small moment instead of a longer time allows them to write in more detail, making their small moments come alive for their readers.

ASSESS LEARNING

- Look for evidence that children understand what a small moment is.
- Notice where children get their ideas for writing.
- Notice evidence that children can use vocabulary such as *memory*, *writer's notebook*, and *small moment*.

MINILESSON

Use familiar stories to demonstrate that authors write stories to tell about their own memories. Help children focus their memories on one small moment instead of a long event. Here is an example.

- Show the cover of *Big Red Lollipop* and revisit pages 10–15.

  What do you notice about what the author, Rukhsana Khan, chose to write about?

  Rubina and Sana don't always get along. The author used one birthday party as an example to show that.

  The author did not write about years of their lives. What do you notice about how much time passed in the writer's story?

- Guide children to understand that the author chose to write about small moments.

  Instead of telling what happened over a long stretch of time, the writer tells about something important that happened in a short space of time.

Have a Try

Invite children to help you choose a small moment from your list of ideas for writing.

▷ Use the chart from WPS.U1 (My Ideas for Writing) to model the process of choosing a small moment from a list of larger ideas. Emphasize that limiting a memory story to a small moment allows the writer to include lots of detail to help the reader imagine being there.

> Here's my list of writing ideas. Writing about my little brother, for example, would be a really long book! I need to choose something small or a little piece to tell about. The day we brought him home from the hospital is something I still remember.

▷ Record the idea on prepared chart paper.

▷ Tell a little bit about the other ideas so that children can help you choose small moments or a small piece to write about. Do as many as needed to help them understand the idea of choosing a small moment.

Summarize and Apply

Summarize the lesson. Have children list ideas for small moments on their own Ideas for Memory Stories lists.

> Today during writing time, look at your list of writing ideas. Think about the small moments or a small piece you could write about. Write those ideas on Ideas for Memory Stories.

Confer

▷ During independent writing, move around the room to confer briefly with as many individual children as time allows. Sit side by side with them and invite them to talk about ideas for memory stories. Use the following prompts as needed.

• *Tell more about this memory. What is a small piece you could write about?*

• *You talked about _____. Is there one small moment or small piece that you could write about?*

Share

Following independent writing, gather children in the meeting area to share their ideas for memory stories.

> Share a memory that you thought about today. Tell a few details about that memory and why you think it would be a good idea for a book.

My Ideas for Writing

1. My little brother
2. When I fell down and hurt myself
3. Getting a piano
4. Things I did with Grammy
5. Rebuilding houses
6. Mrs. Connolly the librarian
___
___

Ideas for Memory Stories

1. Bringing my brother home from the hospital
2. How I got my scar — Emergency Room
3. The day we got a piano
4. Riding the subway for the first time
5. Working on a house for the Chavez family
6. When Mrs. Connolly retired — My favorite Librarian

Writing Minilesson Principle
Tell the story you remember.

Making Memory Books

You Will Need

- a familiar memory story that has an example of oral storytelling, such as *I Love Saturdays y domingos* by Alma Flor Ada, from Text Set: Memory Stories

- chart paper featuring a picture of an open hand

- children's copies of Ideas for Memory Stories (WML1)

- To download the following online resource for this lesson, visit **fp.pub/resources**:
  - chart art (optional)

Academic Language / Important Vocabulary

- memory
- aloud
- remember

Continuum Connection

- Tell details about the most important moments in a story or experience while eliminating unimportant details

- Understand that a story from your life is usually written in first person (using *I* or *we*)

- Usually write in first person to achieve a strong voice

- Present ideas and information in a logical sequence

GOAL

Tell the important events in a story orally to an audience.

RATIONALE

Telling a story orally is a way of rehearsing one's writing (see WPS.U7.WML1), which helps children work out how best to tell the story before committing the words to paper. Telling a story across their fingers helps children plan what to draw and write on each page.

ASSESS LEARNING

- Notice whether children are able to orally tell about a memory.
- Notice the questions children ask. Do they help the writer clarify the story?
- Look for evidence that children can use vocabulary such as *memory*, *aloud*, and *remember*.

MINILESSON

Model how to tell a memory story (using words like *first*, *next*, *then*, *after that*, and *at the end*), and engage children in a conversation about oral storytelling. Here is an example.

▶ Show and read page 16 in *I Love Saturdays y domingos*.

  What is Grandpa doing here?

▶ Guide them to notice that Grandpa is telling stories aloud about his memories.

  I can tell a story aloud about my memories, too. Telling my story aloud will help me think about how to draw and write my story better. I am going to tell it across my fingers. For each finger, I'll tell an important part of my story. Later, I can write what I told on the first finger on the first page and so on.

▶ Choose a personal memory from the chart in WML1 and tell a story about it, modeling how you can tell it across your fingers. Use the prepared chart paper to show how each part of your story connects to a finger. Include the most important events, where you were, and the people you were with.

▶ After you tell your story, engage children in a conversation about what they noticed. The following prompts may be helpful.

  - *Why did I use the word* I *(we)?*
  - *What questions can you ask that might help me come up with more ideas?*
  - *What did you notice about the people in the story?*
  - *What did you notice about where the story took place?*
  - *Did I tell only the most important things that happened in the story? Are there parts of the story that I could leave out next time? Talk about that.*

Have a Try

Invite children to turn and talk about a memory story.

▶ Make sure children have their copies of Ideas for Memory Stories.

> Choose one memory from your Ideas for Memory Stories list that you might like to make a memory book about. Turn and tell your partner a few details of your story.

▶ After each partner has had a chance to tell a story, ask a few volunteers to share their stories.

Summarize and Apply

Summarize the lesson. Remind children to tell a memory story.

▶ Write the principle at the top of the chart. Pair children up so that each has a partner different from the one in Have a Try.

> During writing time, tell your partner a story across your fingers to help you think about how you will draw and write the story in a book. Then let your partner tell a story. After your partner finishes, tell what you understood about the story and what you are wondering about it. If you are ready, start writing your memory book.

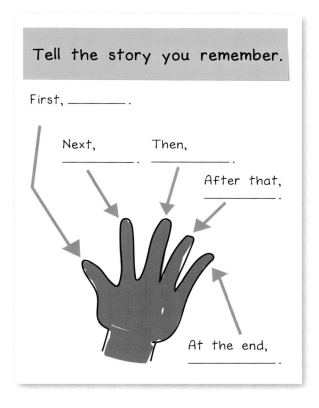

Confer

▶ During independent writing, move around the room to confer briefly with as many individual children as time allows. Sit side by side with them and invite them to tell memory stories across their fingers. Use the following prompts as needed.

- *Tell the story across your fingers. Write what you tell on your thumb on the first page.*
- *What ideas do you have for a story?*
- *As you tell your story, listen for ways to make it better when you write it.*
- *Why would you use the words* I *and* we *in your memory story?*
- *What details could you add to make the story come alive?*

Share

Following independent writing, gather children in the meeting area to share their stories.

> Who would like to share a memory story? Tell it across your fingers.

WML3
GEN.U2.WML3

Writing Minilesson Principle
Draw and write your story in the order it happened.

You Will Need

- several familiar memory stories told sequentially, such as the following:
  - *Mango, Abuela, and Me* by Meg Medina, from Text Set: Finding Your Way in a New Place
  - *The Art Lesson* by Tomie dePaola, from Text Set: Tomie dePaola: Writing from Life
- several pages of a memory story you have written, attached to chart paper
- chart paper and markers

Academic Language / Important Vocabulary

- order
- beginning
- middle
- end
- details

Continuum Connection

- Use words that show the passage of time
- Tell details about the most important moments in a story or experience while eliminating unimportant details
- Present ideas and information in a logical sequence

GOAL

Understand that the pictures and writing in a story occur in chronological order.

RATIONALE

When children learn that authors tell stories in sequential order, they realize that the order of events in a story is important.

ASSESS LEARNING

- Look for evidence that children understand that stories are told in chronological order.
- Observe whether they recognize words that show the passage of time.
- Notice whether they are including important details and eliminating those that are unnecessary.
- Notice evidence that children can use vocabulary such as *order*, *beginning*, *middle*, *end*, and *details*.

MINILESSON

Use familiar stories and your own original story to engage children in thinking and talking about chronological order in memory stories. Here is an example.

- Ahead of time, write and sketch a simple story about a small moment in your own life in sequential order. The story used in this minilesson is just an example.
- Show and revisit the first few pages of *Mango, Abuela, and Me*, guiding children to notice that the author is telling a memory story about her grandmother, whom she is meeting for the first time. Then revisit several pages in the middle and the last page.
- Engage children in a conversation about the sequence of events in the book, using a few prompts about the beginning, middle, and end of the story. Here are some examples:
  - *Why did the author decide to begin the story this way?*
  - *What happened next? What happened after that?*
  - *Why do you think the author ended the story this way?*
  - *What do you notice about the order of the story events?*
- Repeat with another memory story that is written in chronological order, such as *The Art Lesson*.

Have a Try

Invite children to turn and talk about whether a memory story is written sequentially.

> Listen as I read my memory story. Then talk to your partner about the order of the events.

▎ Read the story across your fingers. Have children turn and talk.

> What did you notice about the order of events?

> Are there any words that show the order?

▎ Ask volunteers to add numbers to the chart to show the story sequence.

▎ Save this memory story to use in WML4.

Summarize and Apply

Summarize the lesson. Write the principle at the top of the chart. Remind children to draw and write their stories in the order they happened.

> What did you learn about writing memory stories?

> During writing time today, you can tell a story to a partner or to me. Tell the story across your fingers if that will help. When you are ready to write, go ahead and start your memory book.

Confer

▎ During independent writing, move around the room to confer briefly with as many individual children as time allows. Sit side by side with them and invite them to talk about their memory stories. Use the following prompts as needed.

- *Tell the story across your fingers to help plan your writing.*
- *Read your story. Is it written in the right order?*
- *Is there a word you could use to show the order?*

Share

Following independent writing, gather children in the meeting area to share their writing. Choose volunteers whose memory books are written in sequential order.

> As you listen to a few memory stories, think about how you know the memory story is in the right order.

Draw and write your story in the order it happened.

1. The day my baby brother came home, he cried. Wesley cried a lot!

2. I tried rocking him, but he kept crying. I rocked some more. I rocked too hard, and he fell out. I felt terrible!

3. Then Mom came running. She started to yell at me, but she saw that Wesley was bleeding. I started to cry.

4. After that, Mom gathered us up and we rushed to the hospital.

5. When we got home, I was so happy knowing Wesley was OK. I will love him and take care of him forever!

Writing Minilesson Principle
Use pictures and words to show your feelings.

Making Memory Books

You Will Need

- several familiar memory stories that show feelings, such as *I Love Saturdays y domingos* by Alma Flor Ada and *When I Was Young in the Mountains* by Cynthia Rylant, from Text Set: Memory Stories

- a page of the memory story from WML3, attached to chart paper

- two cut-out arrows

- tape or glue stick

- chart paper and markers

Academic Language / Important Vocabulary

- memory
- feelings
- tell
- show

Continuum Connection

- Understand that the writer can look back or think about the memory or experience and share thoughts and feelings about it

- Select "small moments" or experiences and share thinking and feelings about them

- Understand that a story from your life is usually written in first person (using *I* or *we*)

GOAL

Understand that pictures and words can show feelings.

RATIONALE

Teaching children to add pictures and words to show feelings when making a book helps them learn that authors reveal information in a variety of ways.

ASSESS LEARNING

- Look for evidence that children recognize that authors show feelings through words and pictures.

- Observe whether they add pictures and words to show emotion in their own writing.

- Notice evidence that children can use vocabulary such as *memory*, *feelings*, *tell*, and *show*.

MINILESSON

Use familiar stories that show emotion through words and illustrations to engage children in thinking and talking about making memory books. Here is an example.

- Revisit pages 8–11 from *I Love Saturdays y domingos*.

  Turn and talk about how the girl and her grandmothers are feeling and how you know.

- After time for a brief discussion, ask children to share. Guide the conversation to describe the characters' feelings, including being joyful, loving, proud, amazed, and interested. Help them move beyond merely using simple words, such as *happy* and *sad*, as they discuss feelings throughout this lesson.

  Now think about the words and illustrations and the feelings in *When I Was Young in the Mountains*.

- Read and show the last four pages.

  What do you notice?

- Guide the conversation to help children identify the facial expressions and body language that show feelings such as contentment, relaxation, and a sense of belonging. Highlight text such as, "I never wanted to go anywhere else in the world," and talk about how the author shows that the girl is content without specifically saying it.

  A writer can show feelings through words and pictures.

Have a Try

Invite children to turn and talk about how to show their feelings through pictures and words.

▶ Show the prepared chart paper. The chart in this lesson is only an example.

> Here is the end of my story. How do you think I was feeling? How can you tell? Turn and talk to your partner about that.

▶ After time for a brief discussion, have volunteers attach arrows pointing to the parts of the chart that show emotion, such as the facial expressions (picture) and the words.

> What other words could describe how I was feeling?

Summarize and Apply

Summarize the lesson. Remind children to show their feelings through words and pictures when they make books.

> What can you do to show your feelings?

▶ Write the principle at the top of the chart.

> Today during writing time when you work on your memory book, add words and pictures to show your feelings. Bring your book to share when we meet later.

Use pictures and words to show your feelings.

When we got home, I was so happy knowing Wesley was OK. I will love him and take care of him forever!

Confer

▶ During independent writing, move around the room to confer briefly with as many individual children as time allows. Sit side by side with them and invite them to talk about using words and pictures to convey emotion. Use the following prompts as needed.

- *Point to a place in your memory book that shows your feelings.*
- *What word tells about your feelings? Is there another word you could use?*
- *How were you feeling in this part of the story? How can you show that?*

Share

Following independent writing, gather children in the meeting area to share their writing.

> Who would like to share your memory book?

> Share a place in your memory book that shows your feelings.

Writing Minilesson Principle

Tell why the story is important.

Making Memory Books

You Will Need

- several familiar memory stories that reveal something important about the author, such as *Bigmama's* by Donald Crews, *The Rainbow Tulip* by Pat Mora, and *I Love Saturdays y domingos* by Alma Flor Ada, from Text Set: Memory Stories

- two memory books written by children

- chart paper and markers

Academic Language / Important Vocabulary

- memory
- important
- show

Continuum Connection

- Write in a way that shows the significance of the story

- Reveal something important about self or about life

GOAL

Write in a way that shows the importance of the story.

RATIONALE

When children understand that writers choose to tell a story because it is important, they realize that they can select their own important memory stories to write about. They can also think about ways to show why the story is important through words and illustrations.

ASSESS LEARNING

- Look for evidence that children understand that writers choose important stories to tell.
- Observe whether children show through words and illustrations the importance of the memories they write about.
- Notice evidence that children can use vocabulary such as *memory*, *important*, and *show*.

MINILESSON

Use mentor texts to show how authors reveal why their stories are important. Then help children think and talk about how to show that their own memory stories are important. Here is an example.

- Ahead of time, choose two memory books that children are working on that have covers and titles, or choose two completed memory books that show something about the writer.

- Revisit a few pages from *Bigmama's*, including the last page.

  How did the writer show this story is important? Turn and talk in threes about that.

- After time for a brief discussion, ask volunteers to share. Help them identify words and illustrations that reveal something about the author. On chart paper, make a note about what the author reveals.

- Revisit a few pages from *The Rainbow Tulip*. Emphasize the sentences on page 27 when the mother and daughter talk about being different.

  How did the writer show this memory story is important?

- Add to the chart.

- Repeat with *I Love Saturdays y domingos*, revisiting a few pages including pages 2–3. Add to the chart.

  When writers tell something about themselves in a memory story, they show why the story was important for them to write.

Have a Try

Invite children to turn and talk about how writers can show that a memory story is important to tell.

▶ Read the two memory stories that children have written.

> Turn and talk to your partner about these memory stories. How do the writers show why the story is important to them?

▶ After time for discussion, have the writers share why the story is important to them. Add to the chart.

Summarize and Apply

Summarize the lesson. Write the principle at the top of the chart. Remind children to show through words and pictures why the story is important.

> Today during writing time when you work on your memory book, think about why the story is important to you. Include words and pictures that show something about yourself and why the story is important. Bring your book to share when we meet later.

Tell why the story is important.	
Memory Story	Why the Story Is Important
BIGMAMA'S Donald Crews	The writer is an adult and lives in the city, but he remembers how he loved spending time with his big family in the country.
The Rainbow	The writer learns that being different is OK.
I Love Saturday y domingos	The writer's grandparents are different from each other, but she loves spending time with all of them.
Kick and Score	Soccer is important to the writer. She is excited when she scores her first goal.
Taking Care of Buster	The writer wants a dog but first has to learn how to take care of one. Now he feeds and walks him. That makes him proud.

Confer

▶ During independent writing, move around the room to confer briefly with as many individual children as time allows. Sit side by side with them and invite them to talk about their memory stories. Use the following prompts as needed.

• *Why did you choose to write about this memory?*

• *What words or pictures will you include to show why this story is important to you?*

• *What will your memory book show about you?*

Share

Following independent writing, gather children in the meeting area to share their memory books.

> What words or pictures in _____'s memory book show something important about her?

> How do you know that this story is important to _____?

Assessment

After you have taught the minilessons in this umbrella, observe children as they draw, write, and talk about their writing. Use *The Fountas & Pinnell Literacy Continuum* to notice, teach for, and support children's learning as you observe their attempts at making books.

▶ What evidence do you have of new understandings children have developed related to making memory books?

- Are children selecting small moments for their memory books?
- Can they tell the story orally before writing?
- Do they draw and write story events in chronological order?
- Do they use pictures and words to show feelings when they make books?
- Are they showing why the story is important by telling something about themselves?
- Are they using vocabulary such as *memory, writer's notebook, remember, moment, aloud, order, beginning, middle, end, details, feelings, tell, show,* and *important*?

▶ In what ways, beyond the scope of this umbrella, are children showing an understanding of best practices for making books?

- Are children ready to add dialogue to their stories?
- Are they able to select a piece of writing to share with an audience?

Use your observations to determine the next umbrella you will teach. You may also consult Suggested Sequence of Lessons (pp. 575–589) for guidance.

EXTENSIONS FOR MAKING MEMORY BOOKS

▶ Point out the words (pronouns) that authors use to show that they are telling the story, such as *I, me, my, we, us,* and *our.*

▶ As you read stories that authors have written about their own lives, engage children in conversations about how the authors told the stories, showed emotion, and revealed important information about themselves.

▶ Teach CFT.U4: Adding Dialogue to Writing so that children can add conversations to their memory stories.

Minilessons in This Umbrella

WML1   Make an all-about book.

WML2   Plan your all-about book.

WML3   Become an expert on your topic.

WML4   Use your plan to write your book.

WML5   Think about how to get your reader interested in your topic.

Before Teaching Umbrella 3 Minilessons

Prepare blank booklets (four to eight stapled pages with a cover) for children to use to make all-about books. Use plain paper or any of the appropriate paper templates in the online resources. Store the booklets in the writing center.

Before teaching this umbrella, you may want to teach WPS.U3: Gathering Ideas for Informational Writing. If you wish to expand on this umbrella, you might also consider teaching CFT.U9: Using Text Features in Nonfiction Writing and CFT.U13: Using Illustrations and Graphics in Nonfiction Writing, but these can also be taught when you revisit Making All-About Books as suggested in the Suggested Sequence of Lessons (pp. 575–589).

Read aloud a variety of engaging nonfiction books. You may use the following books from *Fountas & Pinnell Classroom™ Interactive Read-Aloud Collection* and *Shared Reading Collection* or informational books from your classroom library.

Interactive Read-Aloud Collection
Exploring the Natural World: Insects

Bugs A to Z by Caroline Lawton

Bugs for Lunch by Margery Facklam

Seymour Simon: A Scientific Eye

Frogs

Shared Reading Collection

Busy Beavers by Mary Ebeltoft Reid

As you read and enjoy these texts together, help children

- understand that the books provide information about a single topic,

- notice how the authors organize information, and

- think about how the authors engage and interest their readers.

Interactive Read-Aloud
Insects

Seymour Simon

Shared Reading

Section 2: Genres and Forms

Writing Minilesson Principle
Make an all-about book.

You Will Need

- familiar nonfiction books that provide information about a single topic, such as the following:
  - *Busy Beavers* by Mary Ebeltoft Reid, from *Shared Reading Collection*
  - *Frogs*, from Text Set: Seymour Simon: A Scientific Eye
  - *Bugs A to Z* by Caroline Lawton, from Text Set: Exploring the Natural World: Insects
- chart paper and markers
- To download the following online resource for this lesson, visit **fp.pub/resources**:
  - chart art (optional)

Academic Language / Important Vocabulary

- all-about book
- author
- topic
- fact
- information

Continuum Connection

- Understand how to write a factual text from mentor texts
- Write about a topic keeping the audience and their interests involved
- Select own topics for informational writing and state what is important about the topic
- Choose topics that one knows about, cares about, or wants to learn about

GOAL

Identify the characteristics of an all-about book (informational text) and select a topic for an all-about book.

RATIONALE

Noticing and naming the characteristics of all-about books will help children construct their own all-about books. From writing all-about books, children will learn that they can share their knowledge with an audience.

ASSESS LEARNING

- Observe children as they write all-about books and talk about their writing.
- Notice whether children can explain why they chose a particular topic to write about.
- Look for evidence that they can use vocabulary such as *all-about book*, *author*, *topic*, *fact*, and *information*.

MINILESSON

To help children think about the principle, have them notice and name the characteristics of all-about books. Here is an example.

- Show the cover of *Busy Beavers* and read the title.

  What is this book about?

  This book is called an all-about book because the author tells all about beavers. The topic of this book is beavers.

- Show the covers of *Frogs* and *Bugs A to Z*.

  What topics are these books about?

  These all-about books tell all about frogs and bugs.

  What have you noticed about all-about books? How do the authors of these books help you learn about the topic?

- Record children's responses on chart paper. As needed, show some pages from each book and direct children's attention to specific elements (e.g., the illustrations).

Have a Try

Invite children to talk to a partner about their ideas for all-about books.

> You can write an all-about book like the books you just looked at. What are some topics you know and care about that you might like to write a book about? Turn and talk to your partner about your topics.

▶ After children turn and talk, invite a few children to share their ideas.

Summarize and Apply

Summarize the learning and remind children to think about a topic for an all-about book.

▶ Write the principle at the top of the chart.

> What did you learn about all-about books today?

> Today during writing time, look through your writer's notebook for topics you could use to write an all-about book. Write a list of three or four topics you know and care a lot about. You might also write down a few things you already know about each topic. Bring your list to share when we come back together.

> ### Make an all-about book.
>
> - The author writes about one topic.
> - The author knows and cares a lot about the topic.
> - The book has facts and information about the topic.
> - The book has photos or illustrations to help you learn more about the topic.
> - Each part of the book is about something different but is still about the main topic.

Confer

▶ During independent writing, move around the room to confer briefly with as many individual children as time allows. Sit side by side with them and invite them to talk about their plans for making all-about books. Use the following prompts as needed.

- *What topics do you know a lot about?*
- *What would you like to learn more about?*
- *What could you write in a book about that?*

Share

Following independent writing, gather children in the meeting area.

▶ Ask children to each share one topic they wrote on their lists. Then ask several children about their topics.

> Why did you choose that topic?

Making All-About Books

You Will Need

▶ a familiar informational book, such as *Busy Beavers* by Mary Ebeltoft Reid, from *Shared Reading Collection*

▶ chart paper prepared with a blank web

▶ markers

▶ To download the following online resource for this lesson, visit **fp.pub/resources**:

- Web

Academic Language / Important Vocabulary

▶ all-about book

▶ plan

▶ web

Continuum Connection

▶ Introduce information in categories

▶ Tell one part, idea, or group of ideas on each page of a book

▶ Organize information according to purpose

GOAL

Learn how to use a web to organize and plan an all-about book.

RATIONALE

When you teach children how to use a web to organize and plan an all-about book, they begin to understand how to organize information in a logical way, and they are better prepared to start writing their all-about books.

ASSESS LEARNING

▶ Observe children as they plan their all-about books.

▶ Notice whether children can use a web to organize information.

▶ Look for evidence that they can use vocabulary such as *all-about book*, *plan*, and *web*.

MINILESSON

To help children think about the principle, model how to use a web to organize and plan an all-about book. Here is an example.

▶ Show the cover of *Busy Beavers*.

> I really enjoyed learning about beavers from this book! I've decided to write my own all-about book about beavers so I can share what I learned with other people. Before I begin to write my book, I will plan what I want to write about.

▶ Show the web you prepared.

> I can use a web to plan my all-about book. Since my book will be about beavers, I will write *Beavers* in the center. Now I need to think about what I want to write on the topic. I found it interesting to learn about the lodges beavers live in, so I could write one part of my book about their lodges.

▶ Write *Beaver lodges* in one circle of the web.

> What else could I write about in an all-about book about beavers? What do you find interesting about beavers?

▶ Help children generate subtopics about beavers. Add them to the web.

Have a Try

Invite children to talk to a partner about additional subtopics.

> What else could we write about beavers? Turn and talk to your partner about what else we could add to the web.

▸ After time for discussion, invite a few pairs to share their ideas. Add to the web as appropriate.

▸ Save the chart for WML3.

Summarize and Apply

Help children summarize the learning and remind them to use a web to organize and plan their all-about books. Children can make their own webs, or you can make copies of the web template in the online resources. If children are using a writer's notebook, they can use it for their webs.

> Before you start writing an all-about book, what should you do?

▸ Write the principle at the top of the chart.

> Today during writing time, think about what you'd like to write about in your all-about book and use a web to plan your book. Bring your web to share when we come back together.

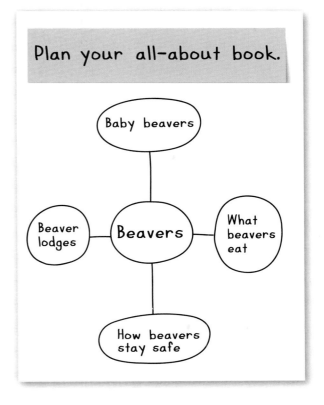

Plan your all-about book.

Baby beavers

Beaver lodges — Beavers — What beavers eat

How beavers stay safe

Confer

▸ During independent writing, move around the room to confer briefly with as many individual children as time allows. Sit side by side with them and invite them to talk about planning their all-about books. Use prompts such as the following as needed.

- *What would you like to write about _____?*
- *What do you find interesting about _____?*
- *What are some things you know about _____?*

Share

Following independent writing, gather children in the meeting area to share their writing.

> What are you going to write about in your book?

> Talk about how you made a plan for your writing.

Making All-About Books

You Will Need

- a familiar informational book, such as *Busy Beavers* by Mary Ebeltoft Reid, from *Shared Reading Collection*
- the chart from WML2
- markers

Academic Language / Important Vocabulary

- all-about book
- topic
- expert
- research
- note

Continuum Connection

- Understand that to write a factual text, the writer needs to become very knowledgeable about a topic
- Provide interesting details that develop a topic
- Provide information that teaches readers about a topic
- Gather and internalize information and then write in one's own words
- Select information that will support the topic
- Take notes or make sketches to help in remembering or generating information

GOAL

Gather information about the topic and take brief, concise notes.

RATIONALE

When you teach children to conduct research for their all-about books, they begin to understand that nonfiction authors must first learn about a topic before they can write about it. They learn that anyone can become an expert on a topic with the right tools. Before teaching this lesson, consider teaching WPS.U7.WML2 so that children learn to say what they learn in their own words.

ASSESS LEARNING

- Observe for evidence of what children understand about taking notes.
- Look for evidence that they can use vocabulary such as *all-about book*, *topic*, *expert*, *research*, and *note*.

MINILESSON

To help children think about the principle, model gathering information about a topic and taking brief, concise notes. Here is an example.

- Show the cover of *Busy Beavers* and the web from WML2.

  Here's the web we made for an all-about book about beavers. Today, we will continue to plan the book by becoming experts on beavers. Does anyone know what an expert is?

  An expert is someone who knows a lot about a certain topic. How could we become experts on beavers?

  One way is to do research about beavers. I found some information online about beavers. I also have this book, *Busy Beavers*. We decided to write about beaver lodges in one part of the book. I'm going to look for the part about lodges in *Busy Beavers*.

- Turn to pages 2–3 of *Busy Beavers*.

  Here it says that beaver parents build their lodges in ponds. I'm going to write a note that says *ponds* on the web to help me remember this fact. It also says that beavers make their lodges out of sticks, which they glue together with mud. I can write *sticks and mud* to help me remember this.

  What did you notice about how I gathered information about beavers?

- Record children's responses below the web.

Have a Try

Invite children to talk to a partner about how to take notes.

▶ Read aloud page 6 of *Busy Beavers*.

> What could we write on the web so we remember what beavers eat? Turn and talk to your partner about this.

▶ After children turn and talk, invite a few pairs to share their thinking. Add the notes to the web.

▶ Save the chart for WML4.

Summarize and Apply

Summarize the learning. Remind children to ask for your help to find books and online resources.

> How will you know what to write in your all-about book?

▶ Write the principle at the top of the chart.

> During writing time today, become an expert on your topic. Look for information about your topic in books or online. Then write short notes on your web to help you remember the information.

Become an expert on your topic.

- Baby beavers
- Beaver lodges
  - ponds
  - sticks and mud
- Beavers
- What beavers eat
  - leaves
  - bark
  - sticks
- How beavers stay safe

- Do research about your topic.
- Look for information about the ideas on your web.
- Write short notes on your web to help you remember the information.

Confer

▶ During independent writing, move around the room to confer briefly with as many individual children as time allows. Sit side by side with them and invite them to talk about their all-about books. Use the following prompts as needed.

- *Where might you find information about _____?*
- *What does that book (website) say about _____?*
- *What could you write on your web to help you remember that?*
- *Remember that a note should just be a few words, not a whole sentence.*

Share

Following independent writing, gather children in the meeting area to talk about their research.

> What did you learn about your topic today?

> How will you remember what you learned?

WML4

GEN.U3.WML4

Writing Minilesson Principle
Use your plan to write your book.

Making All-About Books

You Will Need

- the chart from WML3
- chart paper and markers
- To download the following online resource for this lesson, visit **fp.pub/resources**:
  - chart art (optional)

Academic Language / Important Vocabulary

- all-about book
- plan

Continuum Connection

- Introduce information in categories
- Use some vocabulary specific to the topic
- Tell one part, idea, or group of ideas on each page of a book
- Gather and internalize information and then write in one's own words

GOAL

Learn how to move from planning to writing.

RATIONALE

When you teach children to use their plans to write their all-about books, they will know exactly what they are going to write about and be able to transition quickly and smoothly to writing. They will also better understand the purpose and benefits of planning writing.

ASSESS LEARNING

- Observe how (whether) children use their plans to write their books.
- Look for evidence that they can use vocabulary such as *all-about book* and *plan*.

MINILESSON

To help children think about the principle, model using a plan to begin writing an all-about book. Here is an example.

- Show the chart from WML3.

  Here's the plan for an all-about book on the topic of beavers. Now, we're ready to begin writing the book. Let's start by writing a page about beaver lodges. I wrote *ponds* to help remember that beavers build their lodges in ponds. I can start by writing something about that.

- Begin writing about beaver lodges on chart paper, reading aloud as you write.

  What else could we write on this page?

- Use shared writing to write a few more sentences. Remind children to refer to the plan if necessary.

Have a Try

Invite children to talk to a partner about how to use a plan to start writing.

> What did you notice about how I started writing about beaver lodges? How did I use the plan? Turn and talk to your partner about this.

▶ After children turn and talk, invite several pairs to share their responses. Record them on a separate sheet of chart paper.

Summarize and Apply

Summarize the learning and remind children to use their plans to write their all-about books.

▶ Write the principle at the top of the chart.

> Today during writing time, start writing your all-about book. Remember to use your plan. Bring your writing to share when we meet later.

Confer

▶ During independent writing, move around the room to confer briefly with as many individual children as time allows. Sit side by side with them and invite them to talk about writing their all-about books. Use prompts such as the following as needed.

- *Look at your plan. What is the first thing you want to write about?*
- *What notes did you take about that?*
- *How could you write that?*
- *What other information could you give about that?*

Share

Following independent writing, gather children in the meeting area to share their writing.

> Who would like to share what you wrote today?

> How did you use your plan to help you write your book?

Beaver Lodges

A beaver home is called a lodge. Beaver parents build lodges in ponds. The lodges are made of sticks. Beavers use mud to glue the sticks together.

Use your plan to write your book.

- Look at your plan.

- Decide what part to write first.

- Use your notes to remember what you learned.

- Start writing!

Think about how to get your reader interested in your topic.

Making All-About Books

You Will Need

▶ familiar nonfiction books with a variety of engaging features, such as the following:

- *Bugs for Lunch* by Margery Facklam, from Text Set: Exploring the Natural World: Insects

- *Busy Beavers* by Mary Ebeltoft Reid, from *Shared Reading Collection*

- *Bugs A to Z* by Caroline Lawton, from Text Set: Exploring the Natural World: Insects

▶ chart paper and markers

Academic Language / Important Vocabulary

▶ all-about book
▶ reader
▶ interested
▶ topic

Continuum Connection

▶ Understand that the writer may work to get readers interested in a topic

▶ Write a piece that is interesting and enjoyable to read

▶ Write about a topic keeping the audience and their interests involved

▶ Show enthusiasm and energy for the topic

▶ Tell about a topic in an interesting way

GOAL

Use mentor texts to learn ways to get readers interested in a topic.

RATIONALE

When children notice different ways that nonfiction authors engage their readers, they are likely to try the same techniques in their own all-about books.

ASSESS LEARNING

▶ Observe children as they talk about nonfiction books. Can they identify different ways that authors get readers interested in a topic?

▶ Notice whether children experiment with these techniques in their own writing.

▶ Look for evidence that they can use vocabulary such as *all-about book*, *reader*, *interested*, and *topic*.

MINILESSON

To help children think about the principle, lead them in an inquiry-based lesson around different ways that nonfiction authors engage readers. Here is an example.

▶ Show the cover of *Bugs for Lunch* and read the title. Read the first page.

> Does the first page of this book make you want to read the rest of the book and find out more? Why or why not?

> How does the author get you interested in the topic?

▶ Record children's responses on chart paper.

▶ Show the cover of *Busy Beavers* and read the title. Turn to page 7 and read the text in the speech bubble.

> How does the author of this book make the book interesting and fun to read?

▶ Add responses to the chart.

▶ Show pages 12–13 of *Busy Beavers*. Point to and read the sound words "Crack!" and "Splash!"

> What does the author do on this page to get you interested in the topic?

▶ Add responses to the chart.

Have a Try

Invite children to talk to a partner about how another author gets readers interested in a topic.

▸ Show a few pages of of *Bugs A to Z*.

How does the author of this book get readers interested in the topic of bugs? Turn and talk to your partner about how the author makes it interesting.

▸ After children turn and talk, invite a few pairs to share their responses. Add to the chart.

Summarize and Apply

Summarize the learning and remind children to think about how to get their readers interested in their topic.

Besides writing what you know about a topic, what else do you need to think about when you write your all-about book?

▸ Write the principle at the top of the chart.

Work on your all-about book during writing time today. Think about how to get your readers interested in your topic. You can try some of the ways we talked about. Bring your all-about book to share when we come back together.

Think about how to get your reader interested in your topic.

- Ask questions to make the reader think.
- Use speech bubbles.
- Tell fun facts.
- Choose interesting words.
- Write words in different colors and SIZES.
- Write an alphabet book about your topic.

Section 2: Genres and Forms

Confer

▸ During independent writing, move around the room to confer briefly with as many individual children as time allows. Sit side by side with them and invite them to talk about their all-about books. Use prompts such as the following as needed.

- *How might you get readers interested in _____?*
- *Is there anything on the chart that you would like to try?*
- *What questions could you ask your readers?*
- *What interesting words could you use to tell about _____?*

Share

Following independent writing, gather children in the meeting area to share their books.

Who would like to share your all-about book?

What did you do to get your readers interested in the topic?

Assessment

After you have taught the minilessons in this umbrella, observe children as they explore making books. Use *The Fountas & Pinnell Literacy Continuum* to notice, teach for, and support children's learning as you observe their attempts at writing.

▶ What evidence do you have of children's new understandings related to making all-about books?

- Are children making all-about books on their own?

- Do they conduct research and take notes?

- Do they plan their all-about books and use their plans to write their books?

- In what ways are they experimenting with different ways of getting readers interested in a topic?

- Do they understand and use vocabulary such as *all-about book*, *topic*, and *information*?

▶ In what other ways, beyond the scope of this umbrella, are children ready to explore nonfiction writing?

- Are children ready to make other kinds of nonfiction books (e.g., how-to books, question-and-answer books)?

- Are they using illustrations and graphics in their nonfiction writing?

Use your observations to determine the next umbrella you will teach. You may also consult Suggested Sequence of Lessons (pp. 575–589) for guidance.

EXTENSIONS FOR MAKING ALL-ABOUT BOOKS

▶ Some children might want to present the information in a slide presentation (see GEN.U6: Making Slide Presentations) or video format.

▶ Teach children how to add text and organizational features, such as a table of contents, captions, or sidebars, to their nonfiction texts.

▶ When children show an interest in a topic, help them learn more by providing resources and encouraging them to make an all-about book with their newly acquired knowledge.

▶ Teach children to think about not only the front cover but also the back cover. Have them notice the kind of information and illustration that is often found on a back cover and add it to their books.

Minilessons in This Umbrella

WML1 Make a book to teach something.

WML2 Write words and draw pictures to show the order of what to do.

WML3 Make a list of materials.

Before Teaching Umbrella 4 Minilessons

Prior to teaching these minilessons, make sure children have engaged in making or doing something that they could teach to others (e.g., preparing a snack or riding a bike) and have talked about those activities. Prepare blank booklets (six to eight stapled pages including a cover), or provide paper templates for how-to books from the online resources for children to use. Store the booklets or paper templates in the writing center.

Read aloud a variety of how-to texts and use them as mentor texts for the minilessons in this umbrella. You may use the following book from *Fountas & Pinnell Classroom™ Shared Reading Collection*, or you might use other how-to texts from your classroom library. Recipes from cookbooks and directions on the backs of boxes or on websites are other good sources of examples for these lessons.

Shared Reading Collection

A Piñata Fiesta by Adrián Garcia Montoya

As you read and enjoy how-to texts together, help children

- identify what the reader can learn from the text,
- discuss how the illustrations support the written directions,
- notice whether the steps are numbered, and
- notice if the writer included a list of materials.

Making How-to Books

You Will Need

- a familiar how-to book, such as *A Piñata Fiesta* by Adrián Garcia Montoya, from *Shared Reading Collection*
- chart paper and markers
- To download the following online resource for this lesson, visit **fp.pub/resources**:
  - paper templates (optional)

Academic Language / Important Vocabulary

- how-to book
- steps
- materials

Continuum Connection

- Understand that a procedural text helps people know how to do something
- Understand how to craft procedural writing from mentor texts
- Write a procedural how-to book

GOAL

Notice the characteristics of how-to books and think of ideas for making a how-to book.

RATIONALE

This minilesson is a general inquiry into how-to books and gets students started with making their own how-to books.

ASSESS LEARNING

- Look for evidence of what children know about how-to books.
- Observe whether children choose to write how-to books about activities that are interesting and familiar to them.
- Look for evidence that they can use vocabulary such as *how-to book*, *steps*, and *materials*.

MINILESSON

To prepare children to make how-to books independently, engage them in an inquiry-based lesson around the characteristics of how-to books. Below is an example. You might want children to use any of the appropriate paper templates from the online resources when they start making their how-to books.

- Display the cover of *A Piñata Fiesta* and read the title.

  Let's talk about this book. What is the topic?

  What does it teach you how to do?

- Display pages 8–9.

  What information do you learn from this part of the book?

- Display pages 10–11.

  What do you learn from these pages?

  How did the author make it easy for you to understand how to make a piñata?

  How did the author show you the order of the steps you need to follow?

- Record children's noticings on chart paper.

  A Piñata Fiesta is a how-to book. What is a how-to book?

  Let's make a list of the parts.

Have a Try

Invite children to talk to a partner about their ideas for how-to books.

> Think of something you know how to do and would like to teach to other people. Turn and talk to your partner about that.

▶ After time for discussion, invite several children to share their ideas. Record them on the chart.

Summarize and Apply

Help children summarize what they learned about how-to books. Have them choose an idea and begin planning a how-to book during independent writing time.

> What did you learn today about how-to books?

▶ Write the principle at the top of the chart.

> During writing time today, choose a topic for your how-to book. You can look at the chart for ideas. You might also look in your writer's notebook for ideas. Think about how you will teach readers to do something. If you have time, start writing your book.

Make a book to teach something.

What We Notice About How-to Books	Ideas for How-to Books
• A list of <u>materials</u>	• Make tacos
• <u>Steps</u> to follow	• Ride a bicycle
• <u>Numbers</u> to show the order	• Draw a cat
• <u>Clear words and pictures</u> for each step	• Make a paper airplane
	• Have a lemonade stand

Confer

▶ During independent writing, move around the room to confer briefly with as many individual children as time allows. Sit side by side with them and invite them to talk about plans for their how-to books. Use the following prompts as needed to get children started.

- *Think about something you could teach other people to do.*
- *What ideas in your writer's notebook could you use to make a how-to book?*
- *What materials will people need?*
- *What steps will they need to follow?*
- *What will your pictures be?*

Share

Following independent writing, gather children in the meeting area to talk about their plans for making how-to books.

> What will you teach in your how-to book?

> Why did you decide to write a how-to book about that?

Writing Minilesson Principle
Write words and draw pictures to show the order of what to do.

Making How-to Books

You Will Need

- a familiar how-to book, such as *A Piñata Fiesta* by Adrián Garcia Montoya, from *Shared Reading Collection*
- a topic for a how-to book that is familiar to all the children (e.g., how to wash your hands)
- chart paper and markers
- To download the following online resources for this lesson, visit **fp.pub/resources**:
  - chart art (optional)
  - paper templates (optional)

Academic Language / Important Vocabulary

- how-to book
- order
- steps

Continuum Connection

- Understand how drawings can help the reader understand information
- Include a picture to illustrate a step in a procedure
- Write a procedural how-to book

GOAL

Use pictures and words in a logical order to teach how to do something.

RATIONALE

When children notice that how-to books include sequentially organized steps with clear written and visual information, they are better prepared to include the same when they write their own how-to books. They develop the ability to clearly present information in a logical order. Consider teaching WPS.U7.WML3 before you teach this lesson so that children learn to rehearse directions before they write them.

ASSESS LEARNING

- Look for evidence that children understand why it is important to present the steps in a how-to book in a logical order.
- Observe whether children's how-to books include sequentially organized (and numbered) steps with clear written and visual information.
- Look for evidence that they can use vocabulary such as *how-to book*, *order*, and *steps*.

MINILESSON

To help children think about the minilesson principle, use a mentor text to engage children in an inquiry-based lesson around how to write the steps in a how-to book. Then use shared writing to model writing the steps in a how-to book. Here is an example.

- Display pages 10–11 of *A Piñata Fiesta*.

  The author of this how-to book explains how to make a piñata. What do you notice?

  The author wrote the steps you need to follow. The steps are numbered to show the order. Each step has clear words and pictures to help you know what to do. You will do the same thing when you write your own how-to book. First, let's write a how-to book together about how to wash your hands. What is the first thing you have to do when you wash your hands?

  What number should we write before the first step?

  What could we draw to help readers understand what to do?

- Using children's responses, write and draw a picture for the first step on chart paper. Then continue in a similar manner with the rest of the steps. Point out that when children make their own how-to books they can put one step on each page.

Have a Try

Invite children to talk to a partner about the steps they will write in their own how-to books.

> Think about the how-to book you are working on. What steps will you write? What order will you put them in? What pictures could you draw to help readers understand the steps? Turn and talk to your partner about your ideas.

▶ Save the chart for WML3.

Summarize and Apply

Help children summarize the learning. Then have them work on their own how-to books during independent writing time. You might want to select appropriate paper templates from the online resources for children to use to make their how-to books.

> What did you learn today about making a how-to book?

▶ Write the principle at the top of the chart.

> During writing time today, work on the how-to book you started thinking about. Write words and draw pictures to show the order of what to do. Bring your how-to book to share when we come back together.

Write words and draw pictures to show the order of what to do.

How to Wash Your Hands

Step 1: Wet your hands.

Step 2: Put soap on your hands.

Step 3: Scrub your hands for 20 seconds.

Step 4: Rinse your hands.

Step 5: Dry your hands.

Confer

▶ During independent writing, move around the room to confer briefly with as many individual children as time allows. Sit side by side with them and invite them to talk about the steps in their how-to books. Use the following prompts as needed.

- *What is the first step readers have to follow?*
- *How can you write that in a way that will be easy to understand?*
- *What could you draw to show readers what to do?*
- *What is the next step?*

Share

Following independent writing, gather children in the meeting area to share their how-to books.

> Who would like to share the steps in your how-to book?

> How did you decide what order to put the steps in?

Writing Minilesson Principle
Make a list of materials.

Making How-to Books

You Will Need

- a familiar how-to book, such as *A Piñata Fiesta* by Adrián Garcia Montoya, from *Shared Reading Collection*
- the chart created during WML2
- chart paper and markers
- To download the following online resources for this lesson, visit **fp.pub/resources**:
  - chart art (optional)
  - Paper Template: Materials List (optional)

Academic Language / Important Vocabulary

- how-to book
- list
- materials

Continuum Connection

- Understand that lists are a functional way to organize information
- Understand that a procedural text often includes a list of what is needed to do the procedure
- Make a list in the appropriate form with one item under another

GOAL

Understand that sometimes writers include a list of materials needed to complete the instructions in a how-to book.

RATIONALE

Thinking about the materials needed for their how-to books will prompt children to think about the book from the reader's perspective. What will the reader need to complete the steps? Thinking like a reader will help children develop the ability to clearly and effectively communicate their ideas in writing.

ASSESS LEARNING

- Notice whether children understand the importance of a materials list.
- Observe whether children include a clear list of materials in their how-to books.
- Look for evidence that they can use vocabulary such as *how-to book*, *list*, and *materials*.

MINILESSON

To help children think about the minilesson principle, use a mentor text to engage them in an inquiry-based lesson around creating a list of materials for a how-to book. Then use shared writing to model creating a list of materials. Here is an example.

- Display pages 8–9 of *A Piñata Fiesta*.

  What do you notice about these pages?

  How did the author make it easy to understand what you need to make a piñata?

  Why is it important for a how-to book to include a list of the materials you need?

- Display the chart created during WML2.

  Yesterday we started to write a how-to book about how to wash your hands. Let's write a list of the materials you need to wash your hands. What should we put on our list of materials?

- Use children's responses to create a list of materials (including both words and pictures) on chart paper. If needed, read aloud each step to help children think about what materials are needed.

Have a Try

Invite children to talk to a partner about the materials they will list in their own how-to books.

> Some how-to books do not have a list of materials, but if the book is about making something, it probably will have one. Think about the how-to book you're working on. Will the reader need any materials? Which ones? Turn and talk to your partner about this.

Summarize and Apply

Help children summarize the learning. Then have them work on their own how-to books during independent writing time. You might want children to use the paper template from the online resources to make their materials lists.

> What did you learn today about making a how-to book?

▶ Write the principle at the top of the chart.

> During writing time today, work on your how-to book. If the reader will need any materials, add a list of materials to your book. Bring your how-to book to share when we come back together.

Confer

▶ During independent writing, move around the room to confer briefly with as many individual children as time allows. Sit side by side with them and invite them to talk about making a materials list for their how-to books. Use prompts such as the following as needed.

- *Let's reread the steps you wrote. What materials will the reader need to do this step? Add that to your list of materials.*
- *What else will the reader need to follow your directions?*
- *Reread your list of materials. Are you sure it has everything the reader will need?*
- *How will the list of materials help the reader?*

Share

Following independent writing, gather children in the meeting area to share their materials lists.

> Who added a list of materials to your how-to book today?

> What did you put on the list?

Assessment

After you have taught the minilessons in this umbrella, observe children as they explore making books. Use *The Fountas & Pinnell Literacy Continuum* to notice, teach for, and support children's learning as you observe their attempts at reading and writing.

▶ What evidence do you have of new understandings children have developed related to making how-to books?

- Can children explain the purpose of a how-to book?
- Do they create how-to books independently?
- Do their how-to books contain numbered steps, illustrations, and a list of materials?
- Do they understand and use vocabulary related to making a how-to book, such as *how-to book*, *order*, *steps*, *list*, and *materials*?

▶ In what other ways, beyond the scope of this umbrella, are children exploring making books?

- Are children revising their writing?
- Do they add features, such as sidebars or headings, to their books?

Use your observations to determine the next umbrella you will teach. You may also consult Suggested Sequence of Lessons (pp. 575–589) for guidance.

EXTENSIONS FOR MAKING HOW-TO BOOKS

▶ Have children follow a recipe for a healthy snack that has several steps and then talk about the steps with a partner. Following this, they can make a how-to book to share the recipe with their families.

▶ Talk to children about things they do at school or at home and encourage them to make a how-to book to teach someone something they have done (e.g., play four square, play a drum, make a paper boat, make hummus).

▶ If you read aloud how-to books, directions, or recipes that do not have numbered steps, have children use sticky notes to add numbers to show the order. Explain that how-to books might or might not have numbered steps.

▶ As children engage in social studies projects and science activities, use shared writing to make a list of materials. Afterward, you might encourage children to make their own how-to book about the activity.

▶ Have children trade how-to books with a partner and follow the directions in each other's books.

▶ Teach children how to give an oral presentation about how to do something.

Minilessons in This Umbrella

WML1 Notice the kinds of questions in question-and-answer books.

WML2 Write a repeating question for your topic.

WML3 Write different questions for your topic.

WML4 Find answers to your questions.

WML5 Write a question-and-answer book.

Before Teaching Umbrella 5 Minilessons

Children will benefit from doing these lessons later in the year so they will have learned about a wide variety of topics that they can use for writing question-and-answer books. In the first two minilessons, they will learn that there are two types of question-and-answer books: those with a repeating question and those with different questions. The first four minilessons lead children to the culminating minilesson in which they will apply what they have been learning to make a question-and-answer book. Prepare blank booklets (six to eight stapled pages with a cover) or use any paper templates available in the online resources that are appropriate. Store the materials for children in the writing center.

Prior to teaching these lessons, gather a variety of question-and-answer books and nonfiction books, both published mentor texts and children's writing. You might also choose the following books from *Fountas & Pinnell Classroom™ Shared Reading Collection.*

Shared Reading Collection

Bigger or Smaller? by Brenda Iasevoli

Animals with Jobs by Charlotte Rose

Rain Forest Surprises by Kelly Martinson

Surprises on a Coral Reef by Kelly Martinson

Surprises on the Savanna by Kelly Martinson

As you read and enjoy these texts together, help children

- notice that the books have questions and answers,

- recognize that all of the pages are related to the same topic, and

- observe how the author provides information to the reader in an interesting way.

Section 2: Genres and Forms

Writing Minilesson Principle
Notice the kinds of questions in question-and-answer books.

Making Question-and-Answer Books

You Will Need

- several question-and-answer books, such as the following from *Shared Reading Collection*:
  - *Bigger or Smaller?* by Brenda Iasevoli
  - *Animals with Jobs* by Charlotte Rose
- chart paper and markers

Academic Language / Important Vocabulary

- question
- answer
- question-and-answer book
- topic
- repeating question
- different questions

Continuum Connection

- Understand that the writer may work to get readers interested in a topic
- Understand how to write a factual text from mentor texts
- Understand that an informational text is ordered by logic (sequences, ideas related to each other)
- Understand how the purpose of the writing influences the selection of genre
- Generate and expand topic through talk with peers and teacher
- Form questions to answer about a topic

GOAL

Understand that question-and-answer books have two kinds of questions.

RATIONALE

This minilesson is a general inquiry that helps children become aware that informational books have different organizations. They learn that authors make decisions about how to present information to their readers in engaging and interesting ways and that they can make similar decisions when they make their own books. The following minilessons explore children's noticings further.

ASSESS LEARNING

- Look for evidence of what children understand about question-and-answer books.
- Notice evidence that children can use vocabulary such as *question*, *answer*, *question-and-answer book*, *topic*, *repeating question*, and *different questions*.

MINILESSON

Before this lesson, children should have heard and read a variety of informational books, including question-and-answer books. Use text examples to help them notice types of question-and-answer books. Here is an example.

- Show the covers of *Bigger or Smaller?* and *Animals with Jobs*.

  What are the topics of these books?

- Briefly revisit the topics. Reread the question on pages 7, 9, and 11 in *Bigger or Smaller?*

  What question did the author ask?

  The author asked the same question throughout the book. This book has a *repeating question*.

- If needed, point out to children that even though one word changed each time (i.e., the name of the animal or plant), the author always asked the same question (i.e., which animal or plant is bigger and which is smaller).

- Write on the chart paper *Repeating Question* with a definition and the question.

- Reread the question on pages 7, 9, and 11 in *Animals with Jobs*.

  What do you notice about the questions on these pages?

  The author changed the question each time. She asked different questions about the animals, such as "Why do water buffaloes like muddy water?" and "Are these horses special?" This book has different questions.

- Record similar information about different questions on the chart.

Have a Try

Invite children to turn and talk about question-and-answer books.

▶ Choose a topic to get children thinking about types of questions. Here is an example.

> If you were going to make a question-and-answer book about animal homes, you could have a repeating question like *Where does this _____ live?* Or, you could have different questions like *Why do birds build their homes in trees?* What other questions can you think of?

▶ Write examples on the chart.

Summarize and Apply

Summarize the lesson. Remind children to think about what they would like to write about in a question-and-answer book. Children can make their lists in their writer's notebooks or on paper and stored in their writing folders.

▶ Help children understand that the question-and-answer format helps readers get interested in a topic. Write the principle at the top of the chart.

> Today during writing time, make a list of topics you could make a question-and-answer book about. Bring your list to share when we meet later.

Notice the kinds of questions in question-and-answer books.	
Repeating Question	**Different Questions**
the same question every time	a different question every time
• Is this _____ bigger or smaller than you are? • Where does this _____ live? ? ?	• Why do water buffaloes like muddy water? • Are these horses special? • Why do birds build their homes in trees? • Where does a mouse live? ? ? ? ?

Confer

▶ During independent writing, move around the room to confer briefly with as many individual children as time allows. Sit side by side with them and invite them to share their ideas for a question-and-answer book. Use the following prompts as needed.

- *What topic are you interested in writing about?*
- *What are some questions you might ask?*
- *Will you ask a repeating question or different questions?*

Share

Following independent writing, gather children in the meeting area to share an idea with a partner before sharing with the whole class.

> What topic are you interested in writing about? How did you think of that idea?

Section 2: Genres and Forms

WML2

GEN.U5.WML2

Writing Minilesson Principle
Write a repeating question for your topic.

Making Question-and-Answer Books

You Will Need

▸ a familiar question-and-answer book with a repeating question, such as *Bigger or Smaller?* by Brenda Iasevoli, from *Shared Reading Collection*

▸ chart paper and markers

Academic Language / Important Vocabulary

▸ question

▸ answer

▸ question-and-answer book

▸ topic

▸ repeating question

Continuum Connection

▸ Understand how to write a factual text from mentor texts

▸ Understand that the writer may work to get the reader interested in a topic

▸ Learn ways of using language and constructing texts from other writers (reading books and hearing them read aloud) and apply understandings to one's own writing

▸ Explore relevant questions in talking about a topic

GOAL

Write a repeating question to explore one kind of question-and-answer book.

RATIONALE

When children understand that using a repeating question is one way to make a question-and-answer book, they realize that as writers, they have choices about the kinds of books they will make.

ASSESS LEARNING

▸ Notice whether children can identify a repeating question in a mentor text.

▸ Look at children's writing to check their understanding of how to use a repeating question.

▸ Look for evidence that children can use vocabulary such as *question*, *answer*, *question-and-answer book*, *topic*, and *repeating question*.

MINILESSON

Use text examples to help children make a list of some sample repeating questions that they might use in their question-and-answer books. Here is an example.

▸ Revisit the questions on several pages of *Bigger or Smaller?* ("Is this _____ bigger or smaller than you are?")

> In this question-and-answer book, what question is asked again and again?

> Talk with a partner about that kind of question.

▸ Begin a list on chart paper with examples of repeating questions that can be used in a question-and-answer book. Start the list with *Is this _____ bigger or smaller than _____?*

> What are some other repeating questions the writer might have decided to use in a question-and-answer book that compares different animals?

▸ As children suggest repeating questions, add generic forms of the questions to the chart.

▸ Model how you might use a repeating question for a topic. This is one example.

> I would like to make a question-and-answer book that shows different kinds of homes. If I use a repeating question, I might ask something like *What kind of home is this?* I could write the question on one page and then make a flap to hide the answer. What are some different types of homes I could show under the flap for the answer?

▸ Add to the chart, using a generic form of the question.

Have a Try

Invite children to talk to a partner about repeating questions in question-and-answer books.

> What is another repeating question you might use in a question-and-answer book? Turn and talk about that.

▶ Ask a few children to share ideas. Guide the conversation and add to the chart.

Summarize and Apply

Summarize the learning. Then have children experiment with repeating questions. Children can write their questions in their writer's notebooks or on paper, which can be stored in their writing folders.

▶ Write the principle at the top of the chart.

> During writing time, make a list of repeating questions you might use in your question-and-answer book. You will use your list to help decide whether a repeating question will work well in your book. You might want to write some answers if you know them. Bring your list to share when we meet later.

Write a repeating question for your topic.

Is this _____ bigger or smaller than _____?

Is this _____ heavier or lighter than _____?

Is this _____ faster or slower than _____?

What kind of _____ is this?

What am I?

Whose _____ is this?

What will you see when _____?

What says _____?

What is a _____?

What color is a _____?

Confer

▶ During independent writing, move around the room to confer briefly with as many individual children as time allows. Sit side by side with them and invite them to talk about their plans for writing a question-and-answer book. Use the following prompts as needed.

- *What topic will you write about in your question-and-answer book?*
- *Share your idea for a repeating question.*
- *Let's talk about some answers you might use for your repeating question.*

Share

Following independent writing, gather children in the meeting area. Ask a few volunteers to share a few questions they might ask.

> Share the topic you will choose for your question-and-answer book and a repeating question you might ask.

Writing Minilesson Principle
Write different questions for your topic.

Making Question-and-Answer Books

You Will Need

- several familiar question-and-answer books with different questions, such as the following from *Shared Reading Collection*:
  - *Rain Forest Surprises* by Kelly Martinson
  - *Surprises on a Coral Reef* by Kelly Martinson
- chart paper and markers

Academic Language / Important Vocabulary

- question
- answer
- question-and-answer book
- topic
- different questions

Continuum Connection

- Understand how to write a factual text from mentor texts
- Understand that the writer may work to get the reader interested in a topic
- Learn ways of using text and constructing language from other writers (reading books and hearing them read aloud) and apply understandings to one's own writing
- Explore relevant questions in talking about a topic

GOAL

Write different questions to explore one kind of question-and-answer book.

RATIONALE

When children learn that using different questions is one way to construct a question-and-answer book, they realize that as writers they can make decisions about what kind of books they make.

ASSESS LEARNING

- ▶ Notice whether children can identify different questions in a mentor text.
- ▶ Look at children's writing to check their understanding of how to use different questions.
- ▶ Look for evidence that children can use vocabulary such as *question*, *answer*, *question-and-answer book*, *topic*, and *different questions*.

MINILESSON

Use text examples to help children make a list of some sample different questions to get them thinking about questions they might use in their question-and-answer books. Here is an example.

- ▶ Revisit the questions on several pages of *Rain Forest Surprises*.

  What do you notice about the questions in this book?

- ▶ Guide children to notice that each question is different. The questions do not repeat.

- ▶ Repeat the process with *Surprises on a Coral Reef*.

- ▶ To help children think about what readers might want to know about a topic, model a writer's thinking process. Think aloud as you come up with a new question for a mentor text. This is one example.

  I'm thinking about other things a reader might want to know about rain forests. Many rain forest plants are unique, so a reader might find facts about the plants interesting. I am going to add the question *What is the tallest plant in the Amazon rain forest?* to the chart.

- ▶ Write the new question on chart paper.

Have a Try

Invite children to turn and talk about different questions (and their answers) in question-and-answer books.

> Think about some other things people might like to know about rain forests or coral reefs. You could think of more questions and answers about rain forest plants, or you might have other ideas. In class, we talked about how coral reefs are in danger of being destroyed, so you might ask questions about that. Turn and talk about some questions and answers.

▶ Ask a few children to share ideas. Record questions on the chart.

Summarize and Apply

Summarize the learning. Then have children experiment with different questions in a writer's notebook or on paper, which can be stored in their writing folders.

▶ Write the principle at the top of the chart.

> Today during writing time, make a list of different questions you might use in a question-and-answer book. You will use your list to help you decide whether different questions will work well in your book. If you know any answers, you can write those down, too. Bring your list to share when we meet later.

Topic	Questions
Rain forest plants	What is the tallest plant in the Amazon rain forest?
	What plant covers the ground in the Amazon rain forest?
	How much water do rain forest plants need?
Coral reefs	Are coral reefs alive?
	Why are coral reefs in danger?
	How can we protect coral reefs?

Write different questions for your topic.

Confer

▶ During independent writing, move around the room to confer briefly with as many individual children as time allows. Sit side by side with them and invite them to talk about their plans for writing a question-and-answer book. Use the following prompts as needed.

- *What topic will you use for your question-and-answer book?*
- *Share ideas for different questions you might ask in your book.*
- *Let's talk about some answers you might use for your different questions.*

Share

Following independent writing, gather children in the meeting area to share their writing.

> Share the topic you will use for your question-and-answer book and a few different questions you might ask.

Making Question-and-Answer Books

You Will Need

- familiar question-and-answer books, such as the following from *Shared Reading Collection*:
  - *Surprises on the Savanna* by Kelly Martinson
  - *Animals with Jobs* by Charlotte Rose
- chart paper and markers
- To download the following online resource for this lesson, visit **fp.pub/resources**:
  - chart art (optional)

Academic Language / Important Vocabulary

- question-and-answer book
- topic
- research
- internet
- interview
- expert

Continuum Connection

- Understand that to write a factual text, the writer needs to become very knowledgeable about a topic
- Understand how to write a factual text from mentor texts
- Form questions to answer about a topic
- Gather information (with teacher assistance) about a topic from books or other print and media resources while preparing to write about it

GOAL

Use resources to find answers to questions.

RATIONALE

Teaching children that they can find answers in a variety of places will build a foundation of using different sources of information to explore a topic in depth. They also become more independent once they know how to find answers for themselves.

ASSESS LEARNING

- Look for evidence that children can identify resources to use for finding answers.
- Observe whether children are attempting to independently find answers to their questions.
- Notice evidence that children can use vocabulary such as *question-and-answer book*, *topic*, *research*, *internet*, *interview*, and *expert*.

MINILESSON

Use text examples to help children think about how writers find answers to questions they have, and guide children in identifying ways they can find answers. Here is an example.

- Gather several examples of question-and-answer books on a variety of topics.
- Show the cover and a few pages of *Surprises on the Savanna*.

  > What topic does the author of *Surprises on the Savanna* want you to learn about?

  > The writer gives information about animals that live on the African savanna. Before writing *Surprises on the Savanna*, the writer needed to find answers to the questions she had. Can you think of one place the writer might have looked to find answers to her questions?

- Guide children to understand that authors can look in books to learn facts before writing their own books. Begin a list on chart paper of ways children can find answers to questions.
- Repeat the process using a question-and-answer book on another topic, such as *Animals with Jobs*, to prompt the conversation. Help children identify other ways to find information (e.g., use the internet, interview someone, ask an expert). Add to the list.

  > It's a good idea to look in more than one place for answers. Sometimes you may not find the answers you are looking for in one place, but other places may have different information, and you can learn more about your topic.

Have a Try

Invite children to talk to a partner about how they might find answers to questions for their question-and-answer books.

> What is your question-and-answer book about? Turn and tell your partner. Then talk about where you might look to find answers to the questions in your book.

▶ Ask a few children to share ideas. During this conversation, guide them to identify the question(s) they will be using and at least one place to look for answers.

Summarize and Apply

Summarize the learning. Then have children begin looking for answers to their questions.

▶ Write the principle at the top of the chart.

> Writers look in different places to find information to write about. During writing time, look at the question(s) you have about your topic. Think about at least one way you might find answers to your question(s). Write down your ideas about where to look. If you know a place in the classroom you can look for answers, you can begin looking.

Find answers to your questions.

- Look in books.

- Use the internet.

- Interview someone.

- Ask an expert.

Confer

▶ During independent writing, move around the room to confer briefly with as many individual children as time allows. Sit side by side with them and invite them to talk about their question-and-answer books. Use the following prompts as needed.

- *What topic are you writing about?*
- *Would you like me to help you use the computer to find an answer?*
- *Let's look in the classroom library for some books about your topic.*

Share

Following independent writing, gather children in the meeting area. Ask a few volunteers to share the way they found or will find answers to their questions.

> What is one question you have about your topic?

> Where will (did) you look to find an answer?

Section 2: Genres and Forms

Writing Minilesson Principle
Write a question-and-answer book.

Making Question-and-Answer Books

You Will Need

- two pages of a question-and-answer book that you have prepared
- chart paper and markers
- To download the following online resource for this lesson, visit **fp.pub/resources**:
  - chart art (optional)

Academic Language / Important Vocabulary

- question-and-answer book
- decide
- informational
- page
- topic

Continuum Connection

- Understand that the writer may work to get readers interested in a topic
- Write about a topic keeping the audience and their interests involved
- Provide interesting details that develop a topic
- Understand that layout of print and illustrations is important in conveying the meaning of a text
- Choose topics that are interesting to the writer
- Select own topics for informational writing and state what is important about the topic

GOAL

Make decisions about content and format to write a question-and-answer book.

RATIONALE

Children have been learning about two ways to organize the information in a question-and-answer book. Now they will apply all their learning to make their decisions about the topic, the kinds of questions to ask, and how to arrange the information on the pages. When children learn that writers have many choices when they make books, they begin to take ownership over their own writing and gain confidence in making decisions about what and how to write.

ASSESS LEARNING

- Examine children's question-and-answer books for evidence of what they understand about this text structure.
- Look for evidence that children can use vocabulary such as *question-and-answer book*, *decide*, *informational*, *page*, and *topic*.

MINILESSON

To prepare children to write their question-and-answer books, engage them in a conversation about the decisions they must make. Refer to the work that children have done previously to get ready to write their books. Below is an example. Children will begin writing their books today, but it will take several days to finish the books.

> You have been thinking about repeating questions, different questions, and places to find answers to your questions. Today you will make some decisions about the question-and-answer book you will start writing.
>
> What is the first thing I need to decide for my question-and-answer book?

▸ Write your topic on chart paper.

> What is the next thing I need to decide?
>
> I need to decide what kind of questions to use. I have decided to use different questions in my book.

▸ Write the kind of question you will use on the chart.

> Now that I've decided on my topic and the kind of questions, I need to think about where I might look for some answers. Where do you think I could look?

▸ Record ideas on the chart.

> Finally, I need to think about how my book will look. Should I put the question at the top of the page and the answer at the bottom? Or, should I put the question on one page and the answer on the next? Maybe I could put the answer under a flap. Here's what I decided.

▸ Write your decision on the chart and show the pages of your prepared book.

Have a Try

Invite children to talk to a partner about question-and-answer books.

> Look at the chart to start thinking about what you will decide about your question-and-answer book. Turn and talk to your partner about your ideas.

▶ Ask a few children to share their decisions for their question-and-answer books.

Summarize and Apply

Summarize the learning. Then have children write their question-and-answer books.

▶ Write the principle at the top of the chart.

> Today, you will start writing your question-and-answer book. Use your lists of questions and answers to help you. Think about how you want to show the questions, answers, and illustrations on the pages. It may take you a few days to finish your book, and that's OK. Bring the pages you finish today to share when we meet later.

Confer

▶ During independent writing, move around the room to confer briefly with as many individual children as time allows. Sit side by side with them and invite them to talk about their question-and-answer books. Use the following prompts as needed.

- *Talk about your question-and-answer book.*
- *What type of questions will you ask in your question-and-answer book?*
- *Point to where you will place the information on the page. How did you decide that?*

Share

Following independent writing, gather children in the meeting area. Select several volunteers to share the question-and-answer books they are working on.

> How did you choose the topic for your book?

> Tell about how you decided to ask repeating (different) questions.

Assessment

After you have taught the minilessons in this umbrella, observe children as they make books. Use *The Fountas & Pinnell Literacy Continuum* to notice, teach for, and support children's learning as you observe their writing and drawing.

▶ What evidence do you have of children's new understandings related to making question-and-answer books?

- Can they distinguish between the two kinds of question-and-answer books?

- How well are they able to identify sources of information for the answers to their questions?

- Do their question-and-answer books show evidence of a good understanding of the question-and-answer structure?

- Are they using vocabulary such as *question, answer, question-and-answer book, topic, repeating question, different questions, topic, research, internet, interview, expert, page,* and *informational*?

▶ In what ways, beyond the scope of this umbrella, are children showing an interest in making books?

- Do children reread their books to see whether anything should be added?

- Are they thinking about purpose and audience as they plan their books?

Use your observations to determine the next umbrella you will teach. You may also consult Suggested Sequence of Lessons (pp. 575–589) for guidance.

EXTENSIONS FOR MAKING QUESTION-AND-ANSWER BOOKS

▶ Support children in their research tasks by assisting with internet use or library searches. Engage the help of the school librarian for children's research.

▶ Organize an opportunity for children to share their question-and-answer books with another class.

▶ When you observe children showing an interest in a topic, guide them to explore that interest further by writing an all-about book.

▶ Help children notice other text features in nonfiction books and encourage them to try the features in their own writing (e.g., table of contents, captions, author's note). Teach minilessons from CFT.U9: Using Text Features in Nonfiction Writing. If you are using *The Reading Minilessons Book, Grade 2* (Fountas and Pinnell 2019), see LA.U17: Using Text Features to Gain Information.

Minilessons in This Umbrella

WML1 Choose and research a topic.

WML2 Plan your presentation.

WML3 Write the words for your slides.

WML4 Add pictures, sound, and video to make your presentation interesting.

WML5 Practice and present your presentation.

Before Teaching Umbrella 6 Minilessons

Children will benefit from multiple ways to compose and share their ideas. A slide presentation is a format that allows for multimodal composition, as it can include a combination of words, images, video, and audio. The lessons in this umbrella take children through the process of creating a slide presentation, from planning all the way through to presenting. In each lesson, you will use shared writing to work collaboratively with children to create a class presentation. (Alternatively, you can display a model slide presentation that you have created and guide children to notice the choices you made.) During independent writing time, children will have the opportunity to create their own slide presentations.

Depending on the technology available in your classroom, you may choose to have children make their presentations directly in slideshow software or on paper or poster board (using one page or poster per slide). You might also have children create rough drafts of their presentations on paper and later convert them to digital presentations.

Before teaching this umbrella, it would be helpful to have taught GEN.U3: Making All-About Books to give children a sense of organization and structure. In addition, teach any or all minilessons in WPS.U3: Gathering Ideas for Informational Writing and read aloud a variety of nonfiction books (e.g., simple biographies, informational texts) to provide ideas for presentation topics. You might refer to the following texts from *Fountas & Pinnell Classroom™ Interactive Read-Aloud Collection* or to nonfiction books from the library.

Interactive Read-Aloud Collection
Simple Biography

Manfish: A Story of Jacques Cousteau by Jennifer Berne

Gail Gibbons: Exploring the World Through Nonfiction

Penguins!

As you read and enjoy these texts together, help children

- talk about what topics they find most interesting and why, and
- notice how the authors structure and present information.

Interactive Read-Aloud
Simple Biography

Gail Gibbons

Section 2: Genres and Forms

Writing Minilesson Principle
Choose and research a topic.

Making Slide Presentations

You Will Need

- an example writer's notebook with ideas for writing
- a writer's notebook for each child
- chart paper and markers
- To download the following online resource for this lesson, visit **fp.pub/resources**:
  - chart art (optional)

Academic Language / Important Vocabulary

- slide presentation
- research
- topic

Continuum Connection

- Reread a writer's notebook to select and develop a topic
- Choose topics that one knows about, cares about, or wants to learn about
- Make brief oral reports that demonstrate understanding of a topic

GOAL

Choose a topic one knows about, cares about, or wants to learn about for a slide presentation.

RATIONALE

When you help children understand the range of topics they could choose for a slide presentation, they are more likely to choose a topic they are enthusiastic about and do their best work. It will be helpful to have taught WPS.U3: Gathering Ideas for Informational Writing before this lesson.

ASSESS LEARNING

- Observe whether children carefully consider potential topics for a slide presentation and choose one that interests them.
- Notice whether children research their topics using books and/or approved websites.
- Look for evidence that children can use vocabulary such as *slide presentation*, *research*, and *topic*.

MINILESSON

To help children think about the minilesson principle, model using a writer's notebook to brainstorm ideas for a slide presentation. Here is an example.

> Today, we're going to start to make a slide presentation together. A slide presentation is a special kind of presentation that you can make on a computer or on poster board. Each slide has information about the topic. You can use words, pictures, sounds, and videos to tell about the topic. First, we will choose a topic for our presentation. I'm going to look through my writer's notebook to get some ideas.

- Model looking through a writer's notebook to gather ideas for a presentation, as in the example below.

> After I read the book *Penguins!* by Gail Gibbons, I wrote that I wonder what sounds penguins make. It would be interesting to do a presentation about penguins. I also made a list of topics I know a lot about. I wrote that I know a lot about how to decorate cakes—I could do a presentation about how to decorate a cake. I also wrote that I'd like to write about Jacques Cousteau after I read his biography, *Manfish*.

- Record each idea on chart paper. Invite children to contribute their own ideas to the list. Then have children vote on the topic that will be used for the class presentation.

Have a Try

Invite children to browse their writer's notebooks and brainstorm ideas for a presentation with a partner.

▶ Make sure children have their writer's notebooks.

> We will make a slide presentation together, and you will also make a slide presentation of your own. Look through your writer's notebook to find ideas for a topic. Then turn and talk to a partner about your ideas.

Summarize and Apply

Write the principle at the top of the chart. Read it to children. Summarize the learning and remind them to choose a topic they care about.

> Today during writing time, choose a topic for your slide presentation. Make sure to choose a topic that you really care about and are excited to tell others about. Once you've chosen a topic, you can start to research your topic. You can use books or websites to find information about your topic. I will help you if you need help.

Choose and research a topic.

Topic Ideas for a Slide Presentation

A Topic That Interests You:

- penguins
- honeybees
- the moon

How to Do Something:

- decorate a cake
- use a paddleboard
- take care of a puppy

A Person That Interests You:

- Jacques Cousteau
- Celia Cruz
- Zora Hurston

Confer

▶ During independent writing, move around the room to confer briefly with as many individual children as time allows. Sit side by side with them and invite them to talk about their ideas for a slide presentation. Use prompts such as the following if needed.

- *What would you like to make a slide presentation about? Can you think of a topic that you're really interested in?*
- *Let's look through your writer's notebook (writing folder) for ideas.*
- *Why did you choose that topic?*
- *Do you think you will find enough information about that topic? Or do you need to think about a different topic?*

Share

Following independent writing, gather children in the meeting area to talk with a partner about their topics before sharing with the whole class.

> Who would like to share the topic you chose for your slide presentation?

> Did you start to research your topic? What did you learn?

Making Slide Presentations

You Will Need

- a chosen topic for a class presentation (see WML1)
- a book about the chosen topic, for example, *Penguins!* from Text Set: Gail Gibbons: Exploring the World Through Nonfiction
- a computer with slideshow software or several sheets of paper
- chart paper and markers
- To download the following online resource for this lesson, visit **fp.pub/resources**:
  - chart art (optional)

Academic Language / Important Vocabulary

- slide presentation
- organize
- plan
- information

Continuum Connection

- Maintain a clear focus on the important or main ideas
- Present ideas and information in a logical sequence
- Speak to one topic at a time, and stay on topic
- Have a clear beginning and conclusion
- Make brief oral reports that demonstrate understanding of a topic
- Demonstrate understanding of a topic by providing relevant facts and details

GOAL

Organize information for a presentation across slides.

RATIONALE

When you teach children how to plan a slide presentation, they begin to think about how to organize information in a logical sequence. When they begin to write, they will have an easier time deciding what to write on each slide. Before this lesson, your class should have already decided on a topic for a class presentation (see WML1).

ASSESS LEARNING

- Observe whether children plan their slide presentations before beginning to write.
- Notice whether they organize information in a logical sequence.
- Look for evidence that children can use vocabulary such as *slide presentation*, *organize*, *plan*, and *information*.

MINILESSON

To help children think about the minilesson principle, use shared writing to guide them through the process of planning a slide presentation. Here is an example that focuses on penguins, but your class may use a different topic. You can use slideshow software for this lesson or plan the presentation on sheets of paper attached to chart paper.

> Yesterday, we decided to make a slide presentation about penguins because we learned a lot about penguins from the book *Penguins!* by Gail Gibbons. Today, we will plan our presentation. To plan a slide presentation, decide what kind of information to put on each slide and what order to put it in. Think about what you learned about penguins. What could the first slide of our presentation be about?

- Help children understand that the purpose of the first slide is to introduce the topic.

> The first slide could answer the question *What are penguins?* I'll write that on the first slide.

- Use shared writing to plan a few more slides. Save the plan for WML3.

> What did you notice about how we planned our presentation?

> What should you remember to do when you plan your own presentation?

- Prompt children's thinking as necessary. Record responses on a clean sheet of chart paper.

The Writing Minilessons Book, Grade 2

Have a Try

Invite children to talk to a partner about how they might organize their own presentations.

> Think about the topic that you chose for your own presentation. How might you organize information about that topic? Turn and talk to your partner.

Summarize and Apply

Write the principle at the top of the chart. Summarize the learning and remind children to plan slide presentations before they start to write.

> Why is it important to plan your presentation before you start to write?

> Today during writing time, plan your presentation on sheets of paper [or on a computer]. Decide what you will write about on each slide. Remember to put the information in an order that makes sense.

Confer

▶ During independent writing, move around the room to confer briefly with as many individual children as time allows. Sit side by side with them and invite them to talk about planning their slide presentations. Use prompts such as the following if needed.

- *What will you write about on the first slide?*
- *How are you going to organize the information in your presentation?*
- *Is _____ related to _____? Remember that every slide should be about your main topic.*
- *Why did you decide to put the slide about _____ before the slide about _____?*

Share

Following independent writing, gather children in the meeting area to talk about their plans.

> Who would like to share your plan for a presentation?

> Why did you decide to organize the information like that?

Plan your presentation.

- Stay on topic. Make each slide about the same topic.
- Make each slide about an important or main idea.
- Put information that goes together on the same slide.
- Put the information in an order that makes sense.

What Are Penguins?

What Are Penguins?   Kinds of Penguins

Sounds Penguins Make   Where Penguins Live

WML3

GEN.U6.WML3

Writing Minilesson Principle
Write the words for your slides.

You Will Need

- the planning slides from WML2
- a book about the chosen topic, for example, *Penguins!* from Text Set: Gail Gibbons: Exploring the World Through Nonfiction
- a computer with slideshow software or several sheets of paper
- chart paper and markers
- To download the following online resource for this lesson, visit **fp.pub/resources**:
  - chart art (optional)

Academic Language / Important Vocabulary

- slide presentation

Continuum Connection

- Maintain a clear focus on the important or main ideas
- Present ideas and information in a logical sequence
- Speak to one topic at a time, and stay on topic
- Vary language according to purpose
- Have a clear beginning and conclusion

GOAL

Write ideas clearly with vocabulary appropriate to the topic.

RATIONALE

When you teach children how to write the words for a slide presentation, they learn that different writing conventions are followed for different forms of writing. Using fewer words on slides is easier for the audience to comprehend, so there might be incomplete sentences and bulleted lists.

ASSESS LEARNING

- Notice whether they focus on the topic, use content vocabulary appropriately, and follow the conventions for using print on slides.
- Look for evidence that children can use vocabulary such as *slide presentation*.

MINILESSON

To help children think about the minilesson principle, use shared writing to guide children through the process of writing a slide presentation. The example below focuses on penguins, but your class may use a different topic. You can write directly in slideshow software or on sheets of paper taped to chart paper.

> Let's talk about our class slide presentation about penguins. We know the main kinds of information we want to present. Today, we will write our slides.

- Show the plan made during WML2.

> What did we decide to write about on our first slide?

> We decided to introduce the topic of penguins by explaining what they are and giving a few basic facts about them. What do you think we should write first?

- Use children's responses to help you write the first slide.
- Continue in a similar manner with at least one more slide. Read aloud the text on each slide.

> What did you notice about how we wrote the words for our slides?

- Prompt children's thinking with questions such as the following:
  - *How did we know what to write about on each slide?*
  - *Did we write only in complete sentences?*
  - *Did we fill the whole slide with words? Why not?*
  - *What special words did we use to tell about penguins?*
  - *Did we write a lot of details?*
- Record children's responses on chart paper to create guidelines for using print on slides.

Have a Try

Invite children to talk to a partner about what to write on the next slide.

> What do you think we should write on our next slide? Turn and talk to your partner.

▶ After time for discussion, invite several pairs to share. Use shared writing to write another slide. Save the slides for WML4.

Summarize and Apply

Write the principle at the top of the chart. Summarize the learning. Then have children work on adding words for their slides.

> Today during writing time, start to write the words for your own slide presentation. What will you remember to do when you write the words?

> If you need help remembering, look at the presentation and the chart we made together. You can also ask me for help.

Confer

▶ During independent writing, move around the room to confer briefly with as many individual children as time allows. Sit side by side with them and invite them to talk about their slide presentations. Use prompts such as the following if needed.

- *Let's look at your plan. What did you decide to write about on the first slide?*
- *What do you want to write about that?*
- *What is the best way to write that? Could you write a list?*
- *You can give more details when you talk about your slides.*

Share

Following independent writing, gather children in the meeting area to talk about their writing.

> What did you write about on your slides today?

> How is writing a slide presentation different from writing a book?

What Are Penguins?
- Penguins are a type of bird.
- They live in the Southern Hemisphere.
- They can swim but not fly.
- They have feathers and flippers.

Kinds of Penguins
- Adélie penguin
- King penguin
- Emperor penguin

Sounds Penguins Make
- Penguins call out to find their mates.

Where Penguins Live

Write the words for your slides.

- Follow your plan.
- Focus on the main ideas.
- Leave space around the print.
- Use words that are specific to the topic.
- You don't have to use complete sentences.
- Write lists.

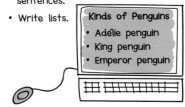

Kinds of Penguins
- Adélie penguin
- King penguin
- Emperor penguin

Add pictures, sound, and video to make your presentation interesting.

You Will Need

- the slides from WML3 with different kinds of media added (images, audio, and video)
- chart paper and markers
- To download the following online resource for this lesson, visit **fp.pub/resources**:
  - chart art (optional)

Academic Language / Important Vocabulary

- slide presentation
- sound
- video

Continuum Connection

- Use props, illustrations, images, or other digital media to enhance a presentation

GOAL

Enhance presentations with a variety of media (illustrations, images, or digital media).

RATIONALE

When children add media to a slide presentation, they begin to understand how writers make choices about how best to enhance and clarify information with different types of media.

ASSESS LEARNING

- Observe whether children know how to find images, audio, and video and add them to slide presentations.
- Notice whether they choose appropriate media that enhance and/or clarify their written content.
- Look for evidence that children can use vocabulary such as *slide presentation*, *sound*, and *video*.

MINILESSON

Before this lesson, add a variety of media to the presentation used in this umbrella. Also, make sure you are familiar with how children can search for multimedia safely and decide how you will facilitate the process of letting children add multimedia to their presentations. To help children think about the minilesson principle, display the prepared presentation and engage children in a discussion about the media you chose and why. Here is an example.

> You can add pictures, sound, and video to your slide presentation to make it more interesting and help people learn more about the topic. I started to add pictures, sound, and video to our class presentation about penguins.

- Display a slide to which you added images.

  What did I add to this slide?

  Why do you think I added pictures to this slide?

  What will the pictures help people understand?

  What do you notice about where I put each picture on the slide?

- Display a slide to which you added audio or video. Play the audio or video.

  What did I add to this slide?

  Why do you think I added sound/video instead of pictures to this slide?

  What will the sound/video help people understand?

  What are some things you should think about when you are adding pictures, sound, and video to your own presentation?

- Record children's responses on chart paper.

Have a Try

Invite children to talk to a partner about what media to include on the next slide.

▶ Display another prepared slide that does not yet have media.

> Look at this slide we wrote together. What pictures, sound, or video could we add to make it more clear or interesting? Turn and talk to your partner about that.

▶ After time for discussion, invite several pairs to share their thinking. Then demonstrate searching for media and choosing what to add to the slide.

Summarize and Apply

Write the principle at the top of the chart. Summarize the learning and remind children to think about how to use pictures, sound, and video to make their presentations more interesting.

> Today during writing time, think about how you could add pictures, sound, and video to your presentation to make it more clear and interesting.

▶ The amount of time necessary for children to add media to their presentations will depend on the technology available.

Confer

▶ During independent writing, move around the room to confer briefly with as many individual children as time allows. Sit side by side with them and invite them to talk about their slide presentations. Use prompts such as the following if needed.

- *What could you add to this slide to help your audience better understand _____?*
- *Would a picture, a sound, or a video work best on this slide? Why?*
- *What could you search for to find pictures (sound, video) like that?*
- *Where on the slide are you going to put that picture? Why?*

Share

Following independent writing, gather children in the meeting area to talk about the progress of their slide presentations.

> Raise your hand if you added pictures, sound, or video to your presentation today.

> What did you add and why?

What Are Penguins?
- Penguins are a type of bird.
- They live in the Southern Hemisphere.
- They can swim but not fly.
- They have feathers and flippers.

Kinds of Penguins
- Adélie penguin
- King penguin
- Emperor penguin

Sounds Penguins Make
- Penguins call out to find their mates.

Where Penguins Live

Add pictures, sound, and video to make your presentation interesting.

Think about . . .
- If a picture, sound, or video would make the information more clear or interesting
- What kind of picture, sound, or video you need
- Where you could find the picture, sound, or video
- Where to place it on the slide

Writing Minilesson Principle

Practice and present your presentation.

You Will Need

- a completed digital slide presentation (see WML4)
- index cards with prepared notes for the presentation
- chart paper and markers
- blank index cards
- To download the following online resource for this lesson, visit **fp.pub/resources**:
  - chart art (optional)

Academic Language / Important Vocabulary

- slide presentation
- notes
- practice
- present

Continuum Connection

- Have a plan or notes to support the presentation
- Speak about a topic with enthusiasm
- Tell stories and present information in an interesting way
- Show confidence when presenting
- Vary speaking voice for emphasis

GOAL

Prepare notes and present the topic with enthusiasm, confidence, and a strong voice.

RATIONALE

When children prepare notes for and practice their slide presentations, they are better able to communicate their ideas effectively.

ASSESS LEARNING

- ▶ Notice if children refer to notes, speak with enthusiasm and confidence, and vary their speaking voices for emphasis.
- ▶ Look for evidence that they can use vocabulary such as *slide presentation*, *notes*, *practice*, and *present*.

MINILESSON

To help children think about the minilesson principle, model presenting a slide presentation and engage children in a discussion about what they noticed. Here is an example.

- ▶ Display the completed slide presentation.

  We worked together to create this slide presentation about penguins. Before class, I practiced the presentation and now I'm going to present it to you. You will be my audience. Watch what I do.

- ▶ Present the presentation, modeling speaking with confidence and enthusiasm, referring to notes, and varying your speaking voice for emphasis.

  What did you notice about how I presented the presentation?

- ▶ Use questions such as the following, as needed, to prompt children's thinking:
  - *What did you notice about my voice?*
  - *How fast or slowly did I speak?*
  - *How quietly or loudly did I speak?*
  - *Did I sound interested in what I was talking about?*
  - *Did I read from the slides?*
  - *How did I remember what to say?*
  - *Did I change my voice when I said certain words? How?*
  - *Where did I look?*

- ▶ If children mention looking at the audience, take into consideration that some children may not be comfortable with establishing or able to establish eye contact because of cultural reasons or for other reasons.

Have a Try

Invite children to talk to a partner about how to present a slide presentation.

> How will you get ready to present your slide presentation? What will you remember to do when you are presenting? Turn and talk to your partner about this.

▶ After children turn and talk, invite several pairs to share their thinking. Record responses on chart paper.

Summarize and Apply

Write the principle at the top of the chart. Read it to children. Summarize the learning and remind them to practice their slide presentations.

> During writing time today, think about what you want to say when you present your slide presentation. Make notes to help you remember what you want to say. Then practice your presentation with a partner or with me.
> When we come back together, some of you will have the chance to present to the whole class.

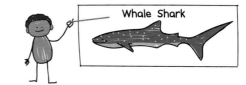

Practice and present your presentation.

- Practice what you're going to say before presenting.
- Look at your notes to help you remember what to say.
- Speak loudly enough for your audience to hear you, but not too loudly.
- Speak at the right speed—not too fast or too slow.
- Say every word clearly.
- Change your voice to show that an idea is important.
- Look at your audience.
- Sound excited and interested!

Whale Shark

Confer

▶ During independent writing, move around the room to confer briefly with as many individual children as time allows. Sit side by side with them and listen as they prepare for and practice their slide presentations. Use prompts such as the following if needed.

- *What do you want to say about this slide? Write down what you want to say on an index card so you don't forget.*
- *Can you speak a little louder? I don't want to miss anything!*
- *You changed your voice for the word _____ to show that it is important.*

Share

Following independent writing, gather children in the meeting area to start presenting their slide presentations. You may want to set aside a block of time for children to make their presentations, or you might have a few children present each day for several days.

> Who would like to present your slide presentation to the class?

> Does anyone have any questions or comments for _____?

Section 2: Genres and Forms

Assessment

After you have taught the minilessons in this umbrella, observe children as they create and present their slide presentations. Use *The Fountas & Pinnell Literacy Continuum* to notice, teach for, and support children's learning as you observe their written and oral communication skills.

▶ What evidence do you have of children's new understandings related to making a slide presentation?

- Do children choose and research topics they are interested in?
- Do they plan their presentations before they begin writing?
- Are they able to arrange their slides in a logical sequence?
- Are the ideas written in clear language with appropriate vocabulary?
- How effective is their use of images, video, and sound?
- Do they practice their presentations and prepare notes?
- Do they present with enthusiasm, confidence, and a strong voice?
- Do they understand and use vocabulary such as *slide presentation*, *topic*, *research*, and *present*?

▶ In what other ways, beyond the scope of this umbrella, are children experimenting with different modes of composition?

- Do they show an interest in creating different types of books?
- Are they writing poetry?
- Are they recording scientific observations?

Use your observations to determine the next umbrella you will teach. You may also consult Suggested Sequence of Lessons (pp. 575–589) for guidance.

EXTENSIONS FOR MAKING SLIDE PRESENTATIONS

▶ Invite guest speakers to present to the class using a slide presentation. Afterward, ask children what they noticed about the presentations.

▶ Regularly include slide presentations as part of your lessons in various subjects (e.g., math, science, social studies). Help children notice the different ways you can present information in a slide presentation (e.g., graphs, maps, tables).

▶ Teach children how to cite the sources of information and media included in slide presentations.

▶ Give children regular opportunities to create and present slide presentations on a variety of topics, both informational and personal (e.g., all about my family, what it was like to go to a new school).

Minilessons in This Umbrella

WML1	Write a letter to someone for a reason.
WML2	Write the parts of a letter.
WML3	Write the important information in your letter.

Before Teaching Umbrella 7 Minilessons

Functional writing includes letters, lists, directions, and labels. When children have experiences with functional writing, they understand that people write for authentic purposes. Friendly letters are used to give information, to invite, and to give thanks. They may take forms other than traditional letters, such as emails, invitations, cards, or notes. Consider using Paper Template: Letter from the online resources if you think it will help children learn to write a friendly letter.

If you are using *The Reading Minilessons Book, Grade 2* (Fountas and Pinnell 2019) you may choose to teach WAR.U3: Writing Letters About Reading. Use the books listed below from *Fountas & Pinnell Classroom™ Interactive Read-Aloud Collection*, or choose books from the classroom library.

Interactive Read-Aloud Collection

Finding Beauty in the World Around You

Wanda's Roses by Pat Brisson

The Importance of Friendship

A Weekend with Wendell by Kevin Henkes

Finding Your Way in a New Place

Home at Last by Susan Middleton Elya

Jan Brett: Creating Imaginary Worlds

Comet's Nine Lives

As you read and enjoy these texts together, help children

- notice details in the letters, and
- observe different reasons for why people write letters.

Interactive Read-Aloud
Finding Beauty

Friendship

Finding Your Way

Jan Brett

Section 2: Genres and Forms

Writing Minilesson Principle
Write a letter to someone for a reason.

GOAL

Understand that different types of letters have different purposes, audiences, and tones.

RATIONALE

When children understand why people write letters, they begin to think about what they could write in a letter and understand that they can write with purpose and authenticity.

ASSESS LEARNING

- Observe for evidence of what children understand about friendly letters.

- Look for evidence that children can use vocabulary such as *friendly letter*, *invite*, *thanks*, *opinion*, *reason*, and *purpose*.

MINILESSON

To help children plan and begin writing letters independently, provide examples of different forms of friendly letters (e.g., letters, notes, invitations, cards, emails) and help them think about why people write friendly letters. Here is an example.

- Ahead of time, prepare a sample traditional friendly letter on chart paper (e.g., a letter from a child to a grandparent).

- Show and read aloud the prepared sample friendly letter.

  What do you notice about this letter? Turn and talk about that.

- After time for discussion, guide children in a conversation about the writer's reason for writing the letter. Generalize the purpose of the letter and characterize a friendly letter.

  Sydney wrote to her grandfather to say hello and share information about her life. It is an example of a friendly letter because it is written in a way that sounds like she is talking to her grandfather.

- Begin two lists on chart paper: one with different types of friendly letters, and one with different purposes of friendly letters.

- Show text examples of a variety of types of friendly letters. Use the examples below from books and/or samples from the online resources. Discuss each kind with children and then add to the list on the chart. Here are some examples:

  - Invitation: *Wanda's Roses* (page 19)

  - Note: *A Weekend with Wendell* (page 18)

  - Letter: *Home at Last* (pages 15–16)

  - Message: *Comet's Nine Lives* (pages 9, 25)

Have a Try

Invite children to turn and talk about an idea they have for writing a letter.

> Think about why you might write a letter. Turn and tell your partner.

▸ After time for discussion, ask a few children to share their ideas. Add new ideas to the chart.

Summarize and Apply

Summarize the learning. Have children begin writing a letter during independent writing.

> You can write a friendly letter for many different reasons.

▸ Write the principle on the top of the chart.

> During writing time, choose a reason for writing a friendly letter. Begin writing when you are ready. Look at the chart if you need ideas. Bring your writing to share when we meet later.

Confer

▸ During independent writing, move around the room to confer briefly with as many individual children as time allows. Sit side by side with them and invite them to talk about writing a friendly letter. Use the following prompts as needed.

- *What type of friendly letter are you writing?*
- *What is the reason for your letter?*
- *Let's look back at the chart for some ideas.*

Share

Following independent writing, gather children in pairs in the meeting area to share their friendly letters.

> Turn to your partner and read what you wrote today.

April 14

Dear Grandpa,
    I am so excited for you to come visit this summer! I am taking swimming lessons. By the time you come, I will be a great swimmer. I can't wait to show you how I can hold my breath and turn my head. I also will be a rock in the school play. It sounds funny, but the rock talks!

Love,
Sydney

Write a letter to someone for a reason.

Types of Friendly Letters	Reasons
Letter	• Say hello and share some news.
Invitation	• Give information.
	• Say thank you.
Card	• Invite to an event.
Note	• Ask how someone is feeling.
	• Tell an opinion.
Email	• Plan an activity.
	• Share thoughts about a book or movie.
	• Ask for help with a problem.

WML2

GEN.U7.WML2

Writing Minilesson Principle
Write the parts of a letter.

You Will Need

- a mentor text, such as *Wanda's Roses* by Pat Brisson, from Text Set: Finding Beauty in the World Around You
- chart paper prepared with a sample friendly letter that shares your thinking about the book
- sticky notes
- marker
- highlighter tape (optional)

Academic Language / Important Vocabulary

- friendly letter
- signature
- greeting
- P.S.
- closing
- comma

Continuum Connection

- Understand that the sender and the receiver must be clearly shown
- Understand that a friendly letter has parts (date, salutation, closing signature, and sometimes *P.S.*)
- Understand how to learn about writing notes, cards, invitations, emails, and friendly letters by noticing the characteristics of examples
- Write to a known audience or a specific reader
- Write a friendly letter with all parts

GOAL

Understand and write the parts of a letter including the date, greeting (salutation), closing, signature, and sometimes a P.S.

RATIONALE

When children learn how to write friendly letters by looking at examples, they understand that friendly letters have parts and it is important to include each part when writing one.

ASSESS LEARNING

- Notice evidence that children understand the parts of a friendly letter.
- Observe whether children include each part of a friendly letter in their letters.
- Look for evidence that children can use vocabulary such as *friendly letter*, *greeting*, *closing*, *signature*, *P.S.*, and *comma*.

MINILESSON

To help children understand the parts of a friendly letter, provide a brief interactive lesson that uses a model letter. Here is an example.

- Ahead of time, prepare a sample friendly letter on chart paper to share your thinking about a familiar book. Include the date, greeting, closing, signature, and a P.S.

- Show the prepared friendly letter along with the cover of the book that the letter is about.

  Listen as I read the friendly letter that I wrote to you about *Wanda's Roses*.

- Read all parts of the letter, pointing to each as you do.

  What do you notice about this letter?

- Guide the conversation to help children notice that the letter is like a conversation and is written by you (the sender) to the children (the receivers).

  Look at the different parts of this letter. Turn and talk about what you notice.

- After time for conversation, ask volunteers to point to the different parts of the letter. As they do, place a sticky note beside the date, greeting, closing, signature, and P.S. Write the name of each part of the letter on the corresponding sticky note. Point out that a P.S. is sometimes included in a letter when you have a little extra something to say.

  Who can point to the sender's name and the receiver's name?

  Who can show the commas after the greeting and the closing?

- You may choose to use highlighter tape to point out the commas after the greeting and the closing as well as to assist children in noticing the parts of the letter.

Have a Try

Invite children to turn and talk about the parts of a friendly letter.

> Turn and talk about what you will write for the different parts of your friendly letter.

▶ After time for a brief discussion, ask a few children to share. Ask them to identify where they will write each part on the page.

Summarize and Apply

Summarize the lesson. Remind children to include each part in a friendly letter. Write the principle at the top of the chart.

> During writing time, write a friendly letter or continue working on one you have already started. Remember, you can share your thoughts about a book if you wish, or you can write to a friend or someone in your family who lives in a different place. Bring your writing to share when we meet later.

Write the parts of a letter.

Dear Class, **greeting**   January 15 **date**

    The book <u>Wanda's Roses</u> was special to me because it was about following your dreams. Wanda had an idea to make something beautiful out of a place that was not so pretty. She learned a lot about gardening on her own, but she also asked for help from others. Along the way, she made many friends.

    I enjoyed reading this book. It helped me think about how wonderful things can start from just a small idea.

             From, **closing**

             Mr. Flores **signature**

P.S. Would you like to plant some flower seeds in our classroom? **P.S.**

Confer

▶ During independent writing, move around the room to confer briefly with as many individual children as time allows. Sit side by side with them and invite them to talk about their friendly letters. Use the following prompts as needed.

- *Show where you will write the greeting and closing on your letter.*
- *Whose name will go in the greeting and whose name will go in the signature?*
- *What words will you use for the closing?*
- *Point to where you will add commas in your letter.*

Share

Following independent writing, gather children in the meeting area. Ask a few volunteers to share their friendly letters.

> Who would like to share the friendly letter you worked on today?

> Show where you placed each part of the friendly letter on the page.

Write the important information in your letter.

Writing Friendly Letters

You Will Need

- several mentor texts that show examples of friendly letters, such as the following:
  - *Wanda's Roses* by Pat Brisson, from Text Set: Finding Beauty in the World Around You
  - *Comet's Nine Lives* by Jan Brett, from Text Set: Jan Brett: Creating Imaginary Worlds
- chart paper prepared with a sample friendly letter that shares your thinking about a book
- highlighter or highlighter tape

Academic Language / Important Vocabulary

- friendly letter
- important
- information

Continuum Connection

- Write notes, cards, invitations, and emails for a variety of purposes
- Understand that a note or card should include short greetings and relevant information
- Include important information in the communication

GOAL

Understand and write the important information in a letter.

RATIONALE

When children learn to include important information in a friendly letter, they will think about the letter's purpose and include important details as they write their own friendly letters.

ASSESS LEARNING

- ▶ Observe for evidence of what children understand about friendly letters.
- ▶ Look at children's letters. Do children include relevant details in their friendly letters?
- ▶ Look for evidence that children can use vocabulary such as *friendly letter*, *important*, and *information*.

MINILESSON

To help children think about the minilesson principle, demonstrate how to include important information in a friendly letter. Here is an example.

- ▶ Ahead of time, prepare a sample friendly letter on chart paper to share your thinking about a familiar book. Include important information. An alternative would be to do this lesson over a couple of days and write a letter together with shared writing.

- ▶ Show and read a sample friendly letter in a mentor text, such as the invitation in *Wanda's Roses* on page 19.

  What do you notice about the information Wanda included?

- ▶ Guide the conversation to help children notice that this is an invitation and that it includes important information.

  An invitation is a type of friendly letter. Wanda included the important information, such as the place, date, and time.

- ▶ Show the chart paper with the prepared friendly letter, along with the cover of the book that the letter is about.

  What important information do you notice in this friendly letter that I have written to you?

- ▶ As children discuss, highlight the words that help children identify and recognize the important information that is included in the letter, including the evidence of your thinking about the book. Also note the date, greeting, closing, signature, and commas.

Have a Try

Invite children to turn and talk about including important information in a friendly letter.

> What important information will you include in the friendly letter you are writing? Turn and talk to your partner about that.

▶ After time for discussion, ask a few volunteers to share ideas.

Summarize and Apply

Summarize the lesson. Remind children to include important information in the friendly letters they are working on. Write the principle at the top of the chart.

> During writing time, work on a friendly letter about a book. Think about the important information you want to write in your letter.

Confer

▶ During independent writing, move around the room to confer briefly with as many individual children as time allows. Sit side by side with them and invite them to talk about their letters. Use the following prompts as needed.

- *What are you writing about in your letter?*
- *What important information will you include in your friendly letter?*
- *Reread your letter to check the important information.*

Share

Following independent writing, gather children in the meeting area. Ask a few volunteers to share their friendly letters.

> Who would like to share your friendly letter?

> What important information did you include in your friendly letter?

Write the important information in your letter.

March 17

Dear Class,

I read the book <u>Comet's Nine Lives</u> by Jan Brett. I thought a lot about Comet's journey trying to find a nice home. It was sad when Comet was made to feel like he didn't belong. For example, at the ice cream shop, only dogs were allowed to enjoy the ice cream. Another example was when Comet was not wanted in the theater, even though he was just trying to be close to the actor.

I felt relieved when the book had a happy ending. Comet ended up exactly where he started, which was by the lighthouse on Nantucket Island. I guess home is really wherever you feel like you belong.

Your teacher,
Mr. Flores

Assessment

After you have taught the minilessons in this umbrella, observe children in a variety of classroom activities. Use *The Fountas & Pinnell Literacy Continuum* to notice, teach for, and support children's learning as you observe their attempts at writing letters.

▶ What evidence do you have of new understandings children have developed related to writing friendly letters?
- Do children understand the reasons for writing friendly letters?
- Do their letters include the date, greeting, closing, and signature?
- Are children including important information in their letters?
- Are they using vocabulary such as *friendly letter, invite, thanks, opinion, purpose, greeting, closing, signature, P.S., comma, important,* and *information*?

▶ In what ways, beyond the scope of this umbrella, are children engaged in writing?
- Do they show an interest in more functional writing, such as writing directions in a how-to book?
- Are they interested in writing memory stories?

Use your observations to determine the next umbrella you will teach. You may also consult Suggested Sequence of Lessons (pp. 575–589) for guidance.

EXTENSIONS FOR WRITING FRIENDLY LETTERS

▶ Discuss with children different words to use when closing a letter (e.g., *love, sincerely, from*) and when each is appropriate.

▶ Have children work with a partner to write letters to people in their community (e.g., a request letter or thank you note to the librarian, a get well card to a classmate).

▶ Sit side by side at the computer with children as they write an email to a fam14y member.

Minilessons in This Umbrella

WML1   Collect poems in your own poetry book.

WML2   Poems look and sound different from other types of writing.

WML3   Some poems rhyme, but many do not.

WML4   Observe the world to get ideas for poems.

WML5   Place words on a page to make them look like a poem.

WML6   Use your senses to describe something.

WML7   Use a word or phrase from other writing to make a poem.

Before Teaching Umbrella 8 Minilessons

These minilessons help children notice characteristics of poems that they can try out when they write poems on their own. The focus of this umbrella is to help children respond to poems, understand that poets make decisions when they write, and notice different characteristics of poems. Prior to teaching these minilessons, provide opportunities for children to read and talk about many types of poetry, including those with rhyme, repetition, rhythm, and sensory language and those without. For some lessons, you might need to use books with which the class is not yet familiar. Read selected poems now, and study them more in depth later.

Use the books listed below from the *Fountas & Pinnell Classroom™ Interactive Read-Aloud Collection*, or choose poetry books from the classroom library.

Interactive Read-Aloud Collection

Exploring the Natural World: Insects

The Bugliest Bug by Carol Diggory Shields

Bugs for Lunch by Margery Facklam

Simple Biography

The Pot That Juan Built by Nancy Andrews-Goebel

Exploring the Natural World: The Earth

Our Big Home: An Earth Poem by Linda Glaser

River Story by Meredith Hooper

On Earth by G. Brian Karas

The Importance of Determination

Earrings! by Judith Viorst

As you read and enjoy these texts together, help children

- notice the way the words sound,
- observe the way the words look on the page, and
- notice sensory language.

Interactive Read-Aloud
Insects

Simple Biography

The Earth

Determination

Writing Minilesson Principle
Collect poems in your own poetry book.

Writing Poetry

You Will Need

- chart paper prepared with a poem you have selected
- chart paper prepared with an original poem written in response to the first poem and attached to the first of two columns (covered)
- markers
- a selection of poems, poetry books, and/or poetry charts
- notebooks (one per child) that will be used for gathering and responding to poetry
- To download the following online resource for this lesson, visit **fp.pub/resources**:
  - chart art (optional)

Academic Language / Important Vocabulary

- poem
- poet
- poetry book
- gather
- respond

Continuum Connection

- Understand poetry as a unique way to communicate about and describe feelings, sensory images, ideas, or stories
- Sometimes borrow specific words or phrases from writing and make them into a poem
- Notice what makes writing effective and name the craft or technique

GOAL

Create a personal poetry anthology to learn about writing poetry.

RATIONALE

When children collect poems and respond to them, they learn to read and appreciate poetry as well as become aware of which poems appeal to them. They also learn that their opinions about poetry have value.

ASSESS LEARNING

- Observe children's writing behaviors to look for evidence that they are responding to poetry in a variety of ways.
- Look for evidence that children can use vocabulary such as *poem*, *poet*, *poetry book*, *gather*, and *respond*.

MINILESSON

Before teaching, provide children with multiple experiences listening to and reading poetry. Model the process of gathering and responding to poetry to get them started on making their own poetry books. Here is an example.

- Read and briefly discuss the prepared poem.

  This is a poem that I really like. I could write it or glue a copy in my poetry book, but I've put it here so you can see it. After I find a poem I like, there are different ways I can respond to it.

- Uncover the new poem, which relates to the original, on the second chart.

  How did I respond to the poem?

- Guide the conversation to help children recognize that you responded to a poem you liked by writing a new, related poem. In the second column, add *Write a new poem*.

  Sometimes, I might respond to a poem in a different way, such as writing about what I was thinking as I read the poem. What are some things you thought about when I read the poem to you?

- Use shared writing to jot down children's ideas in the first column, guiding the discussion as needed. Add *Write what you thought about when you read the poem* to the second column.

  Another way to respond is to make a sketch about what you pictured in your mind when you read or heard the poem. Who would like to do that?

- Have a volunteer make a sketch about the poem. Add *Draw a picture* to the chart.

Have a Try

Invite children to turn and talk about poetry books.

▶ Show the blank notebooks that children will be using for gathering and responding to poems. Provide poems, poetry books, and/or poetry charts with which children are familiar.

> In a little while, you will each get your own poetry book. Turn and talk about a poem you might put in your book and respond to the poem. Tell your partner whether you would like to write a new poem, write what you were thinking, or draw a picture. If you can't think of a poem, look through these poems.

▶ After time for discussion, ask a few volunteers to share.

Summarize and Apply

Summarize the learning. Remind children to use their poetry books for gathering and responding to poems.

> Your poetry book is a place to collect poems and respond to them.

▶ Write the principle on the top of the chart. Distribute the poetry books and keep the familiar poems accessible.

> During writing time, start working on your poetry book. Look at the chart for ideas.

Confer

▶ During independent writing, move around the room to confer briefly with as many individual children as time allows. Sit side by side with them and invite them to talk about poems. Use the following prompts as needed.

- *Let's look through these poems to choose one you like for your poetry book.*
- *How will you respond to this poem?*
- *Tell about your sketch. How did you decide what to draw?*

Share

Following independent writing, gather children in pairs in the meeting area.

> Turn to your partner. Show how you responded to a poem.

"To a Butterfly"
by William Wordsworth

I've watched you now a full half-hour
Self-poised upon that yellow flower;
And, little Butterfly! indeed
I know not if you sleep or feed.
How motionless!—not frozen seas
More motionless! and then
What joy awaits you, when the breeze
Hath found you out among the trees,
And calls you forth again!

Collect poems in your own poetry book.

Responses	Ways to Respond
Butterfly, oh my! How still and lovely you sit. Flap your wings for me!	Write a new poem.
I think of butterflies as always moving, but this poem is about a butterfly that is not moving. I can picture the butterfly and the flower in my mind. I like how the wind makes the butterfly move.	Write what you thought about when you read the poem.
	Draw a picture

Writing Minilesson Principle
Poems look and sound different from other types of writing.

You Will Need

- several mentor texts with poems or poetic language, such as the following:
  - *The Bugliest Bug* by Carol Diggory Shields, from Text Set: Exploring the Natural World: Insects
  - *Our Big Home: An Earth Poem* by Linda Glaser and *River Story* by Meredith Hooper, from Text Set: Exploring the Natural World: The Earth
  - *The Pot That Juan Built* by Nancy Andrews-Goebel, from Text Set: Simple Biography
- chart paper and markers
- sticky notes
- chart paper prepared with a poem you will be using for this lesson
- To download the following online resource for this lesson, visit **fp.pub/resources**:
  - chart art (optional)

Academic Language / Important Vocabulary

- poem
- poet
- poetic language
- look
- sound

Continuum Connection

- Understand poetry as a way to communicate about and describe feelings, sensory images, ideas, or stories
- Understand the way print and space work in poems

GOAL

Notice the characteristics of poems and try writing one.

RATIONALE

Helping children recognize some characteristics of poetry will widen their understanding of the decisions they can make when writing a poem (e.g., word choice, rhymes, layout).

ASSESS LEARNING

- Observe children's writing behaviors for evidence of trying out new ideas in their own poems.
- Observe for evidence that children notice features of different poems.
- Look for evidence that children can use vocabulary such as *poem*, *poet*, *poetic language*, *look*, and *sound*.

MINILESSON

Before teaching, read and enjoy poetry with the children in your class. If children are not familiar with the mentor texts in this lesson, read them aloud several times before teaching the lesson. If possible, show poems in an enlarged format so children can easily see layouts and word placements. Here is an example.

> As I share a few poems from books you know, think about some of the things you notice.

- Show and read pages 13 and 15 from *The Bugliest Bug*.

  > What do you notice about how this poetic language looks (sounds)?

- Guide the conversation to help children notice some characteristics of poetry. Encourage them to include characteristics learned through their prior experiences with poetry. Write each characteristic named on a sticky note and place it on chart paper.

- Repeat with other poetic examples, such as the following:
  - *The Pot That Juan Built*, page 5
  - *Our Big Home: An Earth Poem*, page 6
  - *River Story*, pages 8–9

  > Poets write many different types of poems. When you are writing your own poems, you can make lots of choices about the topic you write about, how the words will sound, and where you will place them on the page.

- Keep the chart posted as children continue writing poems throughout this umbrella.

Have a Try

Invite children to turn and talk about characteristics of poetry.

▸ Display the prepared poem and read it aloud.

> Think about the things you noticed about the poems you looked at. Look at the chart if you need a reminder. Turn and talk about which of those things you notice in this poem.

▸ After time for discussion, ask a volunteer to choose a sticky note from the chart of characteristics and place it beneath the poem. Repeat until all of the sticky notes with relevant characteristics have been placed.

▸ Save the sticky note chart for WML3 and the poem for WML7.

Summarize and Apply

Summarize the learning. Have children write a poem with some of the characteristics they talked about. Write the principle on the top of the chart.

> During writing time, you will start writing a poem. It can be about anything. Think about how you want your poem to look and sound. Bring your poem to share when we meet later.

Confer

▸ During independent writing, move around the room to confer briefly with as many individual children as time allows. Sit side by side with them and invite them to talk about their poems. Use the following prompts as needed.

- • *What will your poem be about?*
- • *Where on the page will you start writing your poem?*
- • *Will your poem rhyme or not rhyme?*
- • *Let's look at the chart and talk about what things you would like to include in your poem.*

Share

Following independent writing, gather children in the meeting area. Ask a few volunteers to share their poems.

> Who would like to share the poem you are working on?

> Let's look at the chart and think about what things _____'s poem includes.

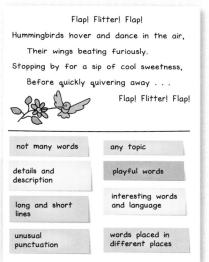

Section 2: Genres and Forms

Writing Minilesson Principle
Some poems rhyme, but many do not.

Writing Poetry

You Will Need

- chart paper prepared with a rhyming poem and a non-rhyming poem
- highlighters or highlighter tape in several colors
- two sticky notes, one labeled *Rhyme* and one labeled *No Rhyme*
- several examples of rhyming and non-rhyming poems from any source
- the sticky note chart from WML2
- chart paper and markers
- To download the following online resource for this lesson, visit **fp.pub/resources**:
  - chart art (optional)

Academic Language / Important Vocabulary

- writing
- poem
- rhyme

Continuum Connection

- Understand that a writer can create different types of poems: e.g., rhyming poems, unrhyming poems
- Understand that poems may look and sound different from one another
- Understand that poems do not have to rhyme

GOAL

Understand that some poems rhyme and some do not.

RATIONALE

Often, *poem* and *rhyme* are considered one and the same, but that is not always the case. When children learn that poems do not have to rhyme, they are free to write and be creative about different ways to craft poems.

ASSESS LEARNING

- Observe children's writing for evidence of understanding that poems sometimes rhyme and sometimes do not.
- Look for evidence that children can use vocabulary such as *writing*, *poem*, and *rhyme*.

MINILESSON

Use examples of both rhyming and non-rhyming poetry to help children understand that some poems rhyme and some do not. Here is an example.

- Show the prepared chart and read the rhyming poem aloud.

  What do you notice about the words in this poem?

- If needed, reread the poem and guide children to recognize the rhyming words. Add (or have a child add) the sticky note for *Rhyme* near the rhyming poem.

  What words do you hear that rhyme?

- As children identify the rhyming pairs, ask a volunteer to indicate the pairs. Use different highlighters or highlighter tape for each pair.

- Read the non-rhyming poem aloud.

  What do you notice about the words in this poem?

- Guide the children to recognize that there are no rhyming words. Add the sticky note for *No Rhyme* near the non-rhyming poem.

- As needed, repeat with several more examples of rhyming and non-rhyming poems.

Have a Try

Invite children to turn and talk about different rhyming and non-rhyming poems.

> Listen as I read these two poems.

▶ Read an example of a rhyming poem and a non-rhyming poem that you have selected.

> What did you notice about the words in these poems?

Summarize and Apply

Summarize the learning. During independent writing, remind children that they can write a poem either with or without rhyme. Write the principle at the top of the chart.

> During writing time, work on a poem you have started or begin a new one. Think about whether you want your poem to rhyme or not. Look at the chart we made before (WML2) and think about how you want your poem to look and sound. Bring your poem to share when we meet later.

Confer

▶ During independent writing, move around the room to confer briefly with as many individual children as time allows. Sit side by side with them and invite them to talk about their poems. Use the following prompts as needed.

- *Will the poem you are working on have rhyming words?*
- *What is your poem about?*
- *Look at the chart (WML2). What will you include in the poem you are working on?*

Share

Following independent writing, gather children in the meeting area. Ask a few volunteers to share their poetry.

> Who would like to share the poem you are working on?

> What do you notice about _____'s poem?

Some poems rhyme, but many do not.

Rhyme

A tiny seed planted just right,
Not a breath of air, not a ray of light.
Rain falls softly to and fro,
And now the seed begins to grow.

No Rhyme

Down low, beneath the light.
A little seed lies buried and still.
Raindrops fall
     drip
       drip
         drip.
And green life peeks out of the darkness.

Section 2: Genres and Forms

Writing Minilesson Principle
Observe the world to get ideas for poems.

Writing Poetry

You Will Need

- several mentor texts with poetic language and topics that children can observe in their world, such as the following:

  - *Our Big Home: An Earth Poem* by Linda Glaser and *River Story* by Meredith Hooper, from Text Set: Exploring the Natural World: The Earth

  - *The Pot That Juan Built* by Nancy Andrews-Goebel, from Text Set: Simple Biography

  - *Earrings!* by Judith Viorst, from Text Set: The Importance of Determination

- chart paper and markers

- To download the following online resource for this lesson, visit **fp.pub/resources**:

  - chart art (optional)

Academic Language / Important Vocabulary

- writing
- observe
- poem
- idea

Continuum Connection

- Closely observe the world (animals, objects, people) to get ideas for poems

- Write poems that convey feelings or images

- Look for ideas and topics in personal experiences, shared through talk

- Observe carefully events, people, settings, and other aspects of the world to gather information on a topic

GOAL

Observe the world to find topics for writing poetry.

RATIONALE

When children understand that writers get ideas for poetry by noticing the world around them, they begin to observe their own environment and think about ideas they could use for writing poems.

ASSESS LEARNING

- Notice whether children are able to think of ideas for their poems by observing the world around them.

- Look for evidence that children can use vocabulary such as *writing*, *poem*, *observe*, and *idea*.

MINILESSON

To help children think about the minilesson principle, use poetry about topics children might notice in their world. Here is an example.

- Show the cover of *Our Big Home: An Earth Poem* and read page 4.

  Where do you think the writer got her idea for this poem?

  What might you notice in nature that you could write about in a poem?

- As children provide ideas, start a list on chart paper. You might want to create general categories for the observations, such as *Nature*, *Places*, *People*, and *Things People Do*.

- Show and read pages 17–18 of *The Pot That Juan Built*.

  Where might the writer have been to get the idea for this story?

- Add to the chart.

  As I read a few more examples, think about what things the writers might have observed in the world around them to write this poetic language.

- Repeat with several more poetic examples, such as the following:

  - *River Story,* pages 11, 18, 19

  - *Earrings!* pages 3–6

Have a Try

Invite children to turn and talk about using their observations to find ideas for their poems.

> Turn and talk to your partner about what else you could observe and then write about in a poem.

▶ After time for discussion, ask a few volunteers to share. Add to the chart.

Summarize and Apply

Summarize the learning. During independent writing, remind children to observe the world to think of ideas for their poems. Write the principle at the top of the chart.

> We talked about getting ideas for poems from observing the world around us. During writing time, work on a poem you have started or begin a new one. If you need an idea for your poem, think of something you have observed and write about what you noticed. Bring your poem to share when we meet later.

Observe the world to get ideas for poems.

Nature	People
rain	child
river	dentist
insects	grandmother
moon	aunt
flowers	

Things People Do

Places

Places	Things People Do
desert	row boats
park	take the dog on a walk
backyard	go to the market
jewelry store	play jump rope
	swim in a lake

Confer

▶ During independent writing, move around the room to confer briefly with as many individual children as time allows. Sit side by side with them and invite them to talk about their poems. Use the following prompts as needed.

- *What is something you observe when you are outside? You can write a poem about that.*
- *Let's talk about some things you have observed that you might write a poem about.*
- *Look at the chart. Is there something on the chart that gives you an idea for a poem?*

Share

Following independent writing, gather children in the meeting area. Ask a few volunteers to share the poem they are working on.

> Who would like to share the poem you are working on?

> What do you notice about _____'s poem?

Section 2: Genres and Forms

Writing Minilesson Principle
Place words on a page to make them look like a poem.

You Will Need

- several mentor texts with words placed on the pages in a poetic way, such as the following:

  - *The Bugliest Bug* by Carol Diggory Shields and *Bugs for Lunch* by Margery Facklam, from Text Set: Exploring the Natural World: Insects

  - *Earrings!* by Judith Vorst, from Text Set: The Importance of Determination

  - *Our Big Home: An Earth Poem* by Linda Glaser and *On Earth* by G. Brian Karas, from Text Set: Exploring the Natural World: The Earth

- pocket chart

- two sets of word cards with words from the poem you will be using for this lesson

- tape

- chart paper and markers

- document camera (optional)

Academic Language / Important Vocabulary

- pause
- line
- shape
- page

Continuum Connection

- Understand the way print and space work in poems

- Place words on a page to look like a poem

- Use line breaks and white space when writing poems

GOAL

Think about where to place words on the page when writing a poem.

RATIONALE

When children recognize that writers think about where to place words on a page, they understand that they can show the reader how they want their poem to look or to be read by making choices about where they place the words on a page.

ASSESS LEARNING

- Look at children's poems to evaluate their understanding of word placement in a poem.

- Look for evidence that children can use vocabulary such as *pause*, *line*, *shape*, and *page*.

MINILESSON

To help children think about the minilesson principle, use examples of poetry that show different ways that the words of a poem can be placed on a page. Here is an example.

- Show and read page 3 of *The Bugliest Bug*. Emphasize how you pause at the end of lines. If possible, project the page so children can easily see how the words are placed.

  What do you notice about how the words are placed on this page?

- Guide the conversation so children notice that you paused at the end of lines. Help them recognize that the writer has placed the words on the page to look like a poem and in a way that helps the reader know how to read the poem.

- Repeat with other poem examples, such as the following:

  - *Bugs for Lunch*, page 12
  - *Earrings!* pages 16–17
  - *Our Big Home: An Earth Poem*, page 4
  - *On Earth*, page 23

- Place one set of the poetry word cards in a pocket chart as one long sentence and read it to the children as a continuous sentence.

  What do you notice about how the words are placed and how they sound?

- Reposition the word cards in the pocket chart to look like a poem. Read the poem.

  What do you notice about how the words are placed now?

- Attach the second set of cards to chart paper in a different placement and repeat the activity (e.g., if you previously made a shape poem with the cards, this time you might place them in lines).

Have a Try

Invite children to turn and talk about the way the words in poems are placed on a page.

> There are many choices poets make about how they place the words in their poems. What ideas do you have about a way the words to this poem could be placed? Turn and talk about that.

▶ After time for discussion, ask a volunteer to share. Change the position of the cards.

Summarize and Apply

Summarize the learning. Have children think about where they will place the words of a poem they are working on. Write the principle on the top of the chart.

> Poets think about how they want a poem to be read before they place the words on the page. During writing time, think about how you will place the words on the page so your writing looks like a poem. Bring your poem to share when we meet later.

Confer

▶ During independent writing, move around the room to confer briefly with as many individual children as time allows. Sit side by side with them and invite them to talk about their poems. Use the following prompts as needed.

- *Show where you will begin (end) your poem on this page.*
- *How do you want your poem to sound when it is read aloud?*
- *What ideas do you have for where the words should go on the page?*
- *Show me the parts of the page that will be empty (without words).*

Share

Following independent writing, gather children in the meeting area. Ask a few volunteers to share their poetry.

> Who would like to share the poem you are working on?

> What do you notice about _____'s poem?

Section 2: Genres and Forms

Writing Minilesson Principle
Use your senses to describe something.

Writing Poetry

You Will Need

- several mentor texts with sensory poetic language, such as the following:
  - *The Pot That Juan Built* by Nancy Andrews-Goebel, from Text Set: Simple Biography
  - *Our Big Home: An Earth Poem* by Linda Glaser, from Text Set: Exploring the Natural World: The Earth
- several pictures of objects that can be described using one or more senses
- chart paper prepared with five columns, each one with a heading: *Object, Looks, Sounds, Smells, Feels*
- markers
- To download the following online resources for this lesson, visit **fp.pub/resources**:
  - Senses Chart
  - chart art (optional)

Academic Language / Important Vocabulary

- writing
- poem
- poet
- senses
- describe

Continuum Connection

- Understand the importance of specific word choice in poetry
- Use language to describe how something looks, smells, tastes, feels, or sounds

---

GOAL

Use senses to describe something in a poem.

RATIONALE

Encouraging children to use their senses to describe something in a poem expands the possibilities of what they can write about and how to write about it.

ASSESS LEARNING

- Observe whether children recognize that writers use sensory language in poetry.
- Look at children's poems. Notice whether or how children use their senses to describe things.
- Look for evidence that children understand and use vocabulary such as *writing*, *poem*, *poet*, *senses*, and *describe*.

MINILESSON

Use examples of poetic language and several objects to help children recognize that poets use their senses to describe things in their poems. Here is an example.

- Show the cover and read page 9 of *The Pot That Juan Built*.

  What are some of the words the author used to describe the rocks and the fire?

- Guide the conversation to help them notice the sensory words (e.g., *red*, *black*, *crackling*, *sizzling*, *flickered*, *flared*).

- Show the cover of *Our Big Home: An Earth Poem*.

  Listen as I read from *Our Big Home: An Earth Poem*.

- Show and read pages 12–13.

  What do you notice about the way the poet described the wind?

- Guide the conversation so children identify the sensory language. Begin filling in the prepared chart with the item being described (wind) and the sensory words used.

  Linda Glaser used her senses (sight, sound, smell, touch) to think of words that would help you imagine what she was describing. When you write poems, think about what you want your readers to imagine they can see, hear, smell, and touch.

Have a Try

Invite children to turn and talk about using their senses to describe something.

▶ Show a few pictures of familiar objects that lend themselves to being described by multiple senses (e.g., ice cream, garbage truck)

> What words can you use to describe how this looks? Sounds? Smells? Feels?

▶ After time for discussion, ask a few volunteers to share. Add to the chart.

▶ As needed, talk about how some things can be described using only some of your senses (e.g., you cannot touch the sky).

Summarize and Apply

Write the principle at the top of the chart. Some children might find it helpful to use a Senses Chart as they work on their poems during independent writing.

> During writing time, work on a poem you have already started or begin a new poem. Think about your topic. How can you describe it for your readers? Use your senses to think about words you could use. Bring your poem to share when we meet later.

Use your senses to describe something.				
Object	Looks	Sounds	Smells	Feels
Wind	Stirs the grass Shakes the trees	Whooshes	Rain Fresh air	Sweeps Swirls Blows kids' hair
Ice cream	White or brown or green or pink	Slurp	Vanilla Chocolate Mint	Cold Wet
Garbage truck	Big and heavy looking Red letters on the side	Roar of the engine Crunching of trash	Exhaust Garbage	

Confer

▶ During independent writing, move around the room to confer briefly with as many individual children as time allows. Sit side by side with them and invite them to talk about their poems. Use the following prompts as needed.

- *What are you writing about? What does it look (sound, smell, feel) like?*
- *What words can you use to describe that?*
- *Is there a different word you could use to help your reader imagine your topic?*
- *Let's fill in a Senses Chart together.*

Share

Following independent writing, gather children in the meeting area to share their poems.

> Turn to your partner and read your poem. After you share, talk about how you used your senses to write your poem.

Writing Minilesson Principle
Use a word or phrase from other writing to make a poem.

Writing Poetry

You Will Need

- a mentor text, such as *River Story* by Meredith Hooper, from Text Set: Exploring the Natural World: The Earth
- document camera (optional)
- the poem you prepared from WML2
- chart paper and markers

Academic Language / Important Vocabulary

- writing
- poem
- poet
- borrow
- word
- phrase

Continuum Connection

- Understand that a poem can be created from other kinds of texts
- Write poems from other kinds of texts (story, informational text)
- Sometimes borrow specific words or phrases from writing and make them into a poem
- Borrow a word, phrase, or a sentence from another writer
- Use memorable words or phrases

GOAL

Use a specific word or phrase from other writing to make a poem.

RATIONALE

When children learn that poets sometimes use specific words or phrases from other writing, they begin to think about ways they can use language in their poems.

ASSESS LEARNING

- Observe for evidence that children understand that writers sometimes borrow language or ideas from other writing.
- Look at children's poems. Are they using words or phrases from other writing?
- Look for evidence that children can use vocabulary such as *writing*, *poem*, *poet*, *borrow*, *word*, and *phrase*.

MINILESSON

To help children understand that they can use a word or phrase from another piece of writing as a basis for poetry, use mentor and class examples and engage children in shared writing. Here is an example.

- Ahead of time, gather the poem written on chart paper for WML2, or use another poem that you or the children have previously written.

  Sometimes, you can borrow a word or a phrase (a few words) from another piece of writing to use for a poem. Let's think about the words on this page and decide how we could make a new poem.

- Show and read aloud page 27 of *River Story*. If possible, project the page.

  What phrase might be good to borrow to make a new poem?

- Guide the children to select a phrase from the mentor text to use for making a new poem. Then, use shared writing to write a poem using the phrase. The chart shows one example.

- Show and read the poem written on chart paper from WML2.

  Sometimes, you might want to use a word that you have written before in a story or another poem. Let's look at a poem we read and think whether there is a word or phrase that we could borrow and use for a new poem.

- Guide the children as they select a word or phrase. Then, engage them in shared writing, making a new poem that uses the term. The chart shows one example.

Have a Try

Invite children to turn and talk about ideas for using borrowed words and phrases for poetry writing.

> Think about where you might look to borrow a word or phrase to use for a poem. Turn and talk about your ideas.

▶ Prompt the conversations as needed. After time for discussion, ask a few volunteers to share.

Summarize and Apply

Summarize the learning. Remind children to think about using a borrowed word or phrase to make a poem. Write the principle at the top of the chart.

> During writing time, think about a word or phrase you might borrow from other writing. Then make a poem using the borrowed word or phrase. You might choose a word from another writer, or you might choose a word or phrase from something you have written. Bring your poem to share when we meet again.

Use a word or phrase from other writing to make a poem.

Borrowed phrase: "sea winds"
(from River Story, page 27)

Blow sea winds, blow
  Across the wide, blue water
    I wish I could catch a ride with you
      To a faraway island adventure.

Borrowed word: hummingbirds
(from "Flap! Flitter! Flap!")

Hummingbirds are quick quick quick!
Ducks like to quack quack quack!
Chickens like to scratch scratch scratch!
But I just like to kick kick kick!

Confer

▶ During independent writing, move around the room to confer briefly with as many individual children as time allows. Sit side by side with them and invite them to talk about their poems. Use the following prompts as needed.

- *Tell me about the poem you are working on.*
- *Let's look at something you have written and talk about a word you might use to make a new poem.*
- *What word or phrase are you borrowing for your poem?*

Share

Following independent writing, gather children in the meeting area. Ask a few volunteers to share their poetry.

> Who would like to share the poem you are working on?

> What do you notice about _____'s poem?

Assessment

After you have taught the minilessons in this umbrella, observe children in a variety of classroom activities. Use *The Fountas & Pinnell Literacy Continuum* to notice, teach for, and support children's learning as you observe their attempts at writing poetry.

▶ What evidence do you have of new understandings children have developed related to writing poetry?

- Are children using a poetry book to gather and respond to poems?
- Do children recognize that poems look and sound different from other types of writing?
- Do they recognize that some poems rhyme and some do not?
- Are they observing the world around them to get ideas for poems?
- Can they use their senses to describe something?
- Are they able to borrow a word or phrase from another piece of writing to make a poem?
- Are they using vocabulary such as *writing*, *poem*, *poet*, *poetry book*, *gather*, *respond*, *poetic language*, *look*, *sound*, *rhyme*, *observe*, *idea*, *page*, *senses*, *describe*, *borrow*, *word*, and *phrase*?

▶ In what ways, beyond the scope of this umbrella, are children showing readiness for writing poetry?

- Do they show an interest in independently writing different types of poetry?
- Are they thinking about how to add to and delete from what they have written?

Use your observations to determine the next umbrella you will teach. You may also consult Suggested Sequence of Lessons (pp. 575–589) for guidance.

EXTENSIONS FOR WRITING POETRY

▶ Provide opportunities to share poetry with children from other classrooms.

▶ Place a variety of picture and word (noun) cards in a basket to help children think of new topics for making poetry.

▶ If you are using *The Reading Minilessons Book, Grade 2* (Fountas and Pinnell 2019) you may choose to teach LA.U9: Analyzing the Writer's Craft.

Minilessons in This Umbrella

WML1 Think about your own experiences for ideas.

WML2 Sketch and quickly write about the main character.

WML3 Plan the problem, what happens, and how it gets solved.

WML4 Think of a real place to describe the setting.

WML5 Write a realistic fiction story.

Interactive Read-Aloud
Realistic Fiction

Before Teaching Umbrella 9 Minilessons

Children stretch their ability to imagine when they have opportunities to experiment with writing both realistic fiction and fantasy. Children love to write fantastical stories, and we should make space to listen to and honor those stories. However, we recommend spending instructional time in minilessons on teaching realistic fiction because children will be able to build on their experience of writing memory stories. Writing fantasy involves many sophisticated understandings that we think are better left for explicit teaching in the upper grades. Provide children with time to write any type of fiction they want, as it will help build engagement, writing identity, and stamina. However, for the purposes of this umbrella, the focus is on realistic fiction.

Before teaching the minilessons in this umbrella, we recommend teaching children how to use a writer's notebook. We suggest having children do their thinking in WML1–WML4 in a writer's notebook (see WPS.U2: Learning About My First Writer's Notebook). These minilessons will come together in WML5 when children start to write their own realistic fiction stories. Before children write their stories independently, you might want to use shared writing to compose a realistic fiction story together.

Also, make sure to read and discuss a variety of realistic fiction stories that the children will enjoy. Use the following texts from *Fountas & Pinnell Classroom™ Interactive Read-Aloud Collection* or any other realistic fiction stories.

Interactive Read-Aloud Collection

Exploring Realistic Fiction

Happy Like Soccer by Maribeth Boelts

Amelia's Road by Linda Jacobs Altman

As you read and enjoy realistic fiction together, help children

- notice how the author describes the characters and setting,

- retell the main events in a story, and

- explain how a realistic fiction story is similar to real life.

Writing Minilesson Principle

Think about your own experiences for ideas.

Writing Fiction

You Will Need

- a familiar realistic fiction story, such as *Happy Like Soccer* by Maribeth Boelts, from Text Set: Realistic Fiction
- a writer's notebook with a list of ideas for stories based on personal experiences
- a writer's notebook for each child
- chart paper and markers

Academic Language / Important Vocabulary

- experience
- idea
- realistic fiction

Continuum Connection

- Look for ideas and topics in personal experiences, shared through talk
- Use a writer's notebook or booklet as a tool for collecting ideas, experimenting, planning, sketching, or drafting
- Reread a writer's notebook to select and develop a topic

GOAL

Use personal experiences to get ideas for realistic fiction.

RATIONALE

When children understand that they can get ideas for writing stories from personal experiences, they find it easier to come up with ideas for their writing. They are also more likely to construct realistic plots.

ASSESS LEARNING

- ▶ Observe whether children use personal experiences (or those of friends or family) as the basis for realistic fiction stories.
- ▶ Notice whether children understand that their story does not need to be completely faithful to the real-life experience that inspired it.
- ▶ Look for evidence that they can use vocabulary such as *experience*, *idea*, and *realistic fiction*.

MINILESSON

To help children think about the minilesson principle, model looking through a writer's notebook and thinking aloud about story ideas from personal experiences. Here is an example.

▶ Show the cover of *Happy Like Soccer*. Read the title.

> Remember this book? It is a realistic fiction story about a girl who plays soccer. A realistic fiction story is a made-up story that could actually happen in real life. How do you think the author got this idea for the story?

▶ Accept children's responses. Then share the dedication.

> I think the author got the idea from her own life. What do you think?

> I want to write my own realistic fiction story. I've been writing a list of ideas for stories in my writer's notebook so I don't forget them. One of my ideas is about a character whose dog gets lost. I thought of this idea because my dog got lost last year. Another idea I have is about a character who sings in a talent show. I thought of this idea when I went to a talent show at my son's school.

▶ Record each idea discussed on chart paper.

> What do you notice about my ideas for realistic fiction stories? Where did I get my ideas?

> You can get ideas for stories from things that have happened to you or to your friends or family. Your story doesn't have to be exactly the same as what happened in real life. It's your story, and you decide what happens!

> I'm going to think some more about these ideas to decide which one I could write a story about.

Have a Try

Invite children to talk to a partner about their own ideas for realistic fiction.

> Think about things that have happened to you or to people you know. Maybe you had a problem or a challenge and figured out what to do. Maybe you did something that was new to you or hard to do. A character in a story could have a similar experience. Turn and talk to your partner about your ideas.

▶ After children turn and talk, invite several children to share their ideas. Add them to the chart.

Summarize and Apply

Write the principle at the top of the chart. Summarize the learning and remind children to think about their own experiences to get ideas for realistic fiction.

> During writing time today, spend some more time thinking about your own experiences for ideas for writing realistic fiction. Make a list of your ideas in your writer's notebook. If you have time, you can start writing a story about one of your ideas.

> **Think about your own experiences for ideas.**
>
> I could write a story about...
> - a character whose dog gets lost
> - a character who sings in a talent show
> - a character who was late for school
> - a character whose house was damaged by a bad storm
> - a character who finds something that someone else lost
> - a character's first day of school

Confer

▶ During independent writing, move around the room to confer briefly with as many individual children as time allows. Sit side by side with them and invite them to talk about their ideas for their stories. Use prompts such as the following as needed.

> • *What's the funniest (strangest, happiest, most exciting) thing that's ever happened to you? Does that give you any ideas for a story?*

> • *Remember that you're using your experiences only for ideas. Your story doesn't have to be exactly the same as what happened to you.*

> • *Tell me about what happened when _____. What part of that story could you change when you write a realistic fiction story?*

Share

Following independent writing, gather children in the meeting area. Have each child share one idea for realistic fiction.

> Who would like to share an idea you have for a realistic fiction story?

WML2

GEN.U9.WML2

Writing Minilesson Principle
Sketch and quickly write about the main character.

Writing Fiction

You Will Need

- a familiar realistic fiction book with strong character development, such as *Happy Like Soccer* by Maribeth Boelts from Text Set: Exploring Realistic Fiction

- chart paper and markers

Academic Language / Important Vocabulary

- realistic fiction
- main character

Continuum Connection

- Describe characters by how they look and what they do

GOAL

Describe the main characters by how they look and what they do.

RATIONALE

When children notice how authors develop and describe characters, they begin to understand how they can create believable characters in their own stories. When they plan their characters before beginning to write, they are more likely to write stories with consistent, well-developed characters.

ASSESS LEARNING

- Observe whether children plan their main characters before beginning to write realistic fiction.

- Notice whether they can describe both external and internal characteristics of their characters.

- Look for evidence that they can use vocabulary such as *realistic fiction* and *main character*.

MINILESSON

To help children think about the minilesson principle, use shared writing to model sketching and describing the main character of a familiar realistic fiction story. Here is an example.

- Show the cover of *Happy Like Soccer* and read the title.

  Who is the main character in this story?

  What is Sierra like?

- Guide children's thinking with questions such as the following, as needed:

  - *What does she look like?*
  - *What is she like on the inside?*
  - *What does she like to do?*
  - *How does she feel when she plays soccer?*
  - *What makes Sierra sad?*
  - *What does she want?*

- Use children's responses to sketch Sierra and write a brief description of her on chart paper.

  The author probably thought about what Sierra was going to be like before she wrote the story. When you write a realistic fiction story, think about what your main character will be like.

Have a Try

Invite children to talk to a partner about the character.

> Is there anything else you think we should write about Sierra or add to our sketch? Turn and talk to your partner about your ideas.

▶ After children turn and talk, invite a few children to share their thinking. Add new suggestions to the chart.

Summarize and Apply

Summarize the learning and remind children to sketch and quickly write about the main character before writing a realistic fiction story.

> Before they write a story, authors think about what the main character will be like. Taking a few minutes to sketch and quickly write about the main character will help you get ready to write your story.

▶ Write the principle at the top of the chart.

> During writing time today, think about a story you'd like to write. Decide who the main character will be. In your writer's notebook, sketch the main character and quickly write some notes about what the character is like on the outside and on the inside. When you write notes, you don't have to write whole sentences.

Sketch and quickly write about the main character.

Book: Happy Like Soccer
Main character: Sierra
What is she like on the outside?
- Soccer uniform
- Dark, curly hair in a ponytail

What is she like on the inside?
- Loves playing soccer
- Loves her aunt
- Feels like she does not fit in with her teammates
- Sad because her aunt can't come to her games
- Wishes she had someone to cheer for her

Confer

▶ During independent writing, move around the room to confer briefly with as many individual children as time allows. Sit side by side with them and invite them to talk about their ideas for characters. Use prompts such as the following as needed.

- *What are you going to write a story about?*
- *Who is the main character in your story?*
- *What is the character's name?*
- *What is the character like on the inside (outside)?*

Share

Following independent writing, gather children in the meeting area to talk about their characters.

> Who would like to share something about the main character in your story?

Section 2: Genres and Forms

Writing Minilesson Principle
Plan the problem, what happens, and how it gets solved.

Writing Fiction

You Will Need

▸ a familiar realistic fiction book with a clear and simple problem-solution plot, such as *Happy Like Soccer* by Maribeth Boelts from Text Set: Exploring Realistic Fiction

▸ chart paper and markers

Academic Language / Important Vocabulary

▸ problem
▸ solved
▸ event

Continuum Connection

▸ Understand that a fiction text may involve one or more events in the life of a main character

▸ Understand that a writer uses various elements of fiction (e.g., setting, plot with problem and solution, characters) in a fiction text

▸ Understand the difference between developing a narrative (or plot) and giving information about a topic in categories

▸ Structure a narrative and sustain writing to develop it logically

GOAL

Plan the plot of the story, including the problem, events, and resolution.

RATIONALE

When children notice that plots in realistic fiction stories are generally structured with a clear problem, logically sequenced events, and a resolution, they begin to understand how to develop plots in their own stories. When they plan their plots before beginning to write, they are more likely to write stories with coherent, well-organized plots.

ASSESS LEARNING

▸ Observe for evidence of what children understand about planning the plot of a story.

▸ Look for evidence that children can use vocabulary such as *problem*, *solved*, and *event*.

MINILESSON

To help children think about the minilesson principle, engage them in an inquiry-based lesson around the plot in a familiar realistic fiction story. Here is an example.

▸ Show the cover of *Happy Like Soccer*. Read the title.

> What problem does the main character, Sierra, have in this story?

▸ Record the problem on chart paper.

> What happens in the story?

▸ Review parts of the book as necessary to help children retell the main events of the story in chronological order. Add each major event to the chart.

> At the end of the story, how is Sierra's problem solved? What does she do?

▸ Add the solution to the chart.

> In most realistic fiction stories, the main character faces a problem. The author tells about the problem at the beginning of the story. In the middle of the story, the character tries to solve the problem. The events in the story are what the character does and what happens to the character. At the end of the story, the problem is usually solved. Before you write a realistic fiction story, plan the problem, what happens, and how the problem gets solved.

Have a Try

Invite children to talk to a partner about the plot of their story.

> Yesterday, you wrote about the main character in your story. Now, think about the problem that your main character might face. Turn and talk to your partner about your ideas.

▸ After time for discussion, invite a few volunteers to share their ideas.

Summarize and Apply

Summarize the learning and remind children to plan the plot of their story before they begin to write.

> What did you learn today about writing realistic fiction stories?

▸ Write the principle at the top of the chart. Read it to children.

> During writing time today, think more about the story you are working on. In your writer's notebook, plan the problem, what happens, and how it gets solved.

Plan the problem, what happens, and how it gets solved.	
BEGINNING	**Problem** Sierra is sad that her aunt can't come to her games because she has to work on Saturdays.
MIDDLE	**Events** • Sierra plays in a soccer game while her aunt is at work. • Sierra's aunt gets a Saturday off work. • It starts to rain, so the game is canceled.
END	**How the Problem Is Solved** Sierra asks her coach to schedule the game on a Monday at the lot by her apartment.

Confer

▸ During independent writing, move around the room to confer briefly with as many individual children as time allows. Sit side by side with them and invite them to talk about their ideas for their stories. Use prompts such as the following as needed.

- *Tell me about the main character in your story.*
- *What problem will the character have?*
- *What will the character do to try to solve the problem?*
- *How will the problem be solved in the end?*

Share

Following independent writing, gather children in the meeting area to talk about their stories.

> Who would like to tell us about the problem in your story?

> What will happen in your story? How will the problem be solved?

Writing Fiction

You Will Need

- two or three familiar realistic fiction books with different settings, such as the following from Text Set: Exploring Realistic Fiction:

  - *Happy Like Soccer* by Maribeth Boelts

  - *Amelia's Road* by Linda Jacobs Altman

- chart paper and markers

- To download the following online resource for this lesson, visit **fp.pub/resources**:

  - chart art (optional)

Academic Language / Important Vocabulary

- realistic fiction
- setting

Continuum Connection

- Describe the setting with appropriate detail

GOAL

Use a real place to choose and describe the setting.

RATIONALE

When children think about a real place when they are choosing a setting for a realistic fiction story, they are more likely to write stories with realistic settings and describe them with appropriate detail.

ASSESS LEARNING

- Observe for evidence that children understand how thinking of a real place can help them create a setting for a realistic fiction story.

- Notice whether they use appropriate details to describe their settings.

- Look for evidence that they can use vocabulary such as *realistic fiction* and *setting*.

MINILESSON

To help children think about the minilesson principle, engage them in an inquiry-based lesson around the settings of two or three familiar realistic fiction stories. Here is an example.

- Show the cover of *Happy Like Soccer*, and then show pages 13–14.

  Where does the main character in this book live?

  What is her city like?

- Record children's responses on chart paper.

  Does the city where she lives seem like a real place?

  Have you ever been to a place that looks like this? Where?

- Show the cover of *Amelia's Road*, and then show pages 3–4.

  Where does this story take place?

  What is this place like?

- Add children's responses to the chart.

  The place where a story happens is called the setting. What have you noticed about the settings in realistic fiction books?

  Realistic fiction books happen in real places, or places that seem like they could be real. When you are choosing a setting for your realistic fiction story, think about a real place that you've been to or know a lot about. That will help you think of the kind of details you should include to describe and draw the place for your readers.

Have a Try

Invite children to talk to a partner about the setting of their stories.

> Where will your story take place? Think about a real place where your story could happen. Turn and talk to your partner about it.

▶ After children turn and talk, invite a few volunteers to share their thinking.

Summarize and Apply

Summarize the learning and remind children to choose a real place for the setting when they write realistic fiction.

> What did you learn today about writing realistic fiction stories?

▶ Write the principle at the top of the chart. Read it to children.

> During writing time, continue to think about your realistic fiction story. Choose a real place for the setting. Write about what the setting is like in your writer's notebook. You can also draw a picture of it.

Think of a real place to describe the setting.

In a City
- Lots of buildings close together
- Sidewalks
- An empty lot
- Bus stop

In the Country
- Long roads
- Big farms
- Little houses
- Lots of trees

Confer

▶ During independent writing, move around the room to confer briefly with as many individual children as time allows. Sit side by side with them and invite them to talk about their ideas for settings. Use prompts such as the following as needed.

- *What is your story about?*
- *Where does your story take place?*
- *Is that a real place? Have you been there (or to a place like that) before?*
- *What is that place like?*

Share

Following independent writing, gather children in the meeting area to talk about their settings.

> Who would like to tell about the setting in your story?

Writing Minilesson Principle
Write a realistic fiction story.

Writing Fiction

You Will Need

- several familiar realistic fiction books
- chart paper and markers

Academic Language / Important Vocabulary

- realistic fiction
- setting
- character
- problem

Continuum Connection

- Write a simple fiction story, either realistic or fantasy
- Understand that writers can learn to craft fiction by using mentor texts as models
- Structure a narrative and sustain writing to develop it logically
- Begin to develop a sense of the language of different genres

GOAL

Write a simple realistic fiction story.

RATIONALE

When children use realistic fiction mentor texts as models, they develop an understanding of the conventions and characteristics of realistic fiction. They can then apply these understandings to writing their own realistic fiction stories.

ASSESS LEARNING

- Look at children's stories for evidence that they understand the characteristics of realistic fiction.
- Look for evidence that children can use vocabulary such as *realistic fiction*, *setting*, *character*, and *problem*.

MINILESSON

To help children think about the minilesson principle, use mentor texts to engage them in an inquiry-based lesson around the characteristics of realistic fiction. Here is an example.

- Show the covers of several familiar realistic fiction books.

  We have been reading and talking about realistic fiction stories. What have you noticed about realistic fiction? What makes a good realistic fiction story?

- Record children's responses on chart paper. As needed, prompt their thinking with questions such as the following:
  - *What have you noticed about the characters in realistic fiction stories?*
  - *How do authors help you get to know the characters?*
  - *What kinds of settings have you seen in realistic fiction stories?*
  - *How do authors describe the settings?*
  - *What kinds of things happen in realistic fiction stories?*
  - *What keeps you interested in reading a realistic fiction story?*
  - *What can you learn from reading realistic fiction?*

Have a Try

Invite children to talk to a partner about writing realistic fiction.

> Think about what you have noticed about realistic fiction stories. What will you remember to do when you write your own realistic fiction story?

▷ After time for discussion, invite several children to share their responses.

Summarize and Apply

Summarize the learning and remind children to think about the characteristics of realistic fiction when they write.

> During writing time today, start writing your realistic fiction story. Use the notes you made in your writer's notebook to help remember your plan. Look at the chart we made today to help remember how to write a good realistic fiction story. Bring your writing to share when we meet later.

What makes a good realistic fiction story?

- The characters seem like real people.
- The author describes what the main character is thinking and feeling.
- The settings are real places, or seem like they could be real.
- The author uses words that help you make a picture of the setting in your mind.
- The main character has a problem that is solved at the end.
- You want to read the story to see how the problem will be solved.
- The story can teach you important lessons about life.

Confer

▷ During independent writing, move around the room to confer briefly with as many individual children as time allows. Sit side by side with them and invite them to talk about their realistic fiction stories. Use prompts such as the following as needed.

- *How will you start your story?*
- *What happens first in your story? What happens next?*
- *How can you describe the setting? Look at what you wrote about the setting in your writer's notebook.*
- *What is the main character like? How will you describe the character?*

Share

Following independent writing, gather children in the meeting area to share their writing.

> Who would like to share what you have written so far?

> Does anyone have any questions for _____ about the story?

Assessment

After you have taught the minilessons in this umbrella, observe children as they explore writing fiction. Use *The Fountas & Pinnell Literacy Continuum* to notice, teach for, and support children's learning as you observe their writing development.

▶ What evidence do you have of children's new understandings related to writing realistic fiction?

- Do children get inspiration from personal experiences for their fiction writing?
- How well do they plan their stories before beginning to write?
- Are their characters believable?
- Are their plots realistic and logically sequenced?
- Do they choose and describe realistic settings?
- Do children understand and use vocabulary such as *realistic fiction*, *character*, *problem*, *setting*, and *event*?

▶ In what other ways, beyond the scope of this umbrella, are children exploring writing fiction?

- Would they benefit from learning more about describing characters or settings?
- Are they exploring different ways to write beginnings?
- Are they experimenting with interesting word choices?

Use your observations to determine the next umbrella you will teach. You may also consult Suggested Sequence of Lessons (pp. 575–589) for guidance.

EXTENSIONS FOR WRITING FICTION

▶ Use umbrellas in the Craft section such as CFT.U2: Describing Characters and CFT.U3: Crafting a Setting to help children explore different aspects of writing fiction in greater depth.

▶ Use shared writing to help children explore various aspects of writing fiction collaboratively before doing so independently.

▶ Show children a photo or illustration of an interesting person or setting, and encourage them to describe the character/setting and include it in a story.

▶ Suggest that children write alternative versions of their favorite stories (for example, by changing the ending of a familiar story, writing a sequel, or placing the main character in a different situation).

Minilessons in This Umbrella

WML1   Revisit an old topic in a new way.

WML2   Write with a different set of eyes.

WML3   Use a book to inspire a new way to write.

WML4   Find a new way to share a message.

Before Teaching Umbrella 10 Minilessons

The minilessons in this umbrella are designed to help children apply what they have learned about writing to forms of writing that are typically outside of the usual. This umbrella is intended to infuse new energy into writing and can be broken up and used at different times of the year to inspire new forms of writing.

To help children experiment with the concepts taught in these minilessons, you will need to collect mentor texts for the type of writing children choose and provide them with those mentor texts. It will be helpful to have taught CFT.U1: Reading Like a Writer and Illustrator before teaching this umbrella. This will help children be able to look at mentor texts for ideas. For WML2 and WML3, use the following texts from *Fountas & Pinnell Classroom™ Interactive Read-Aloud Collection*, or choose suitable books from your classroom library.

Interactive Read-Aloud Collection
Exploring the Natural World: Insects

Bugs for Lunch by Margery Facklam

Facing Challenges

Courage by Bernard Waber

As you read and enjoy these and other texts together, help children

- notice interesting choices the author or illustrator made,
- identify the author's message, and
- talk about their own ideas for writing that were inspired by the book.

Interactive Read-Aloud
Insects

Facing Challenges

Section 2: Genres and Forms

WML1

GEN.U10.WML1

Writing Minilesson Principle
Revisit an old topic in a new way.

Experimenting with Writing in New Ways

You Will Need

- a few examples of teacher- and/ or student-written texts that explore a previous topic in a new genre or form
- chart paper and markers

Academic Language / Important Vocabulary

- revisit
- topic

Continuum Connection

- Select the genre for the writing based on the purpose: e.g., friendly letter, procedural text, fiction, memoir, expository text, poetry
- Select from a variety of forms: e.g., notes, cards, letters, invitations, email; books with illustrations and words, alphabet books, label books, question and answer books, illustration-only books; poems
- Choose topics that are interesting to the writer
- Tell about a topic in an interesting way
- Reread a writer's notebook to select and develop a topic
- Write in a variety of genres across the year

GOAL

Write about a previous topic in a different genre or form.

RATIONALE

Some children may choose to write about their same favorite topic repeatedly. When you show them that they can write about the same topic in different ways, they grow as writers by experimenting with different forms and genres while still indulging their passion and enthusiasm for a particular topic.

ASSESS LEARNING

- Observe children as they write and talk about their writing.
- Notice whether children write about the same topic using different genres or forms.
- Look for evidence that they can use vocabulary such as *revisit* and *topic*.

MINILESSON

To help children think about the principle, show and discuss examples of writing that revisit a previous topic in a new way. Help children create a list of different forms and genres of writing. Here is an example.

- Show and discuss two (or more) examples of texts you have written about the same topic in different genres.

  > I wrote a memory story about making naan with my grandmother. I loved writing about this topic, so I thought about different ways I could write about it again. I decided to write a how-to book about how to make naan. I also wrote a letter to my grandmother about this memory.

- Record on chart paper each form of writing discussed.
- If possible, show and discuss an example of a student-written piece of writing that revisits an old topic in a new way.

  > _____ loves writing about dinosaurs and wrote an all-about book about dinosaurs and a comic strip about dinosaurs. What are some other ways to write about dinosaurs?

- Add each new form of writing discussed to the chart, generalizing them as necessary.
- Repeat with other examples, if available.

  > If there's a topic that you love writing about, try writing about it again in a new way.

Have a Try

Invite children to talk to a partner about their own ideas for writing about a topic in a new way.

> Think about a topic that you've enjoyed writing about. How could you write about the same topic in a new way? Turn and talk to your partner about your ideas.

▶ After children turn and talk, invite several children to share their ideas. Add any new forms of writing to the chart.

Summarize and Apply

Summarize the learning and suggest that children revisit an old topic in a new way.

> Today we talked about how you can get new ideas for writing by revisiting an old topic.

▶ Write the principle at the top of the chart.

> Today during writing time, look through the writing you have finished to find a topic you enjoy writing about. Then think about how you can write about that topic in a new way. Look at our chart to remind yourself of different ways you can write about your topic.

Revisit an old topic in a new way.

- Memory story
- Song
- How-to book
- Fiction story
- Recipe
- Poem
- Letter
- Slide presentation
- All-about book
- Question-and-answer book
- Comic strip
- Blog post

Confer

▶ During independent writing, move around the room to confer briefly with as many individual children as time allows. Sit side by side with them and invite them to talk about their ideas for writing about a topic in a new way. Use prompts such as the following as needed.

- *What is a topic that you really like to write about?*
- *How did you write about that topic before?*
- *What is another way you could write about that topic?*
- *Would you like to write a poem about that topic?*

Share

Following independent writing, gather children in the meeting area to share their writing.

> Did anyone write about an old topic in a new way today?

> How did you write about that topic before? How did you write about it today?

Section 2: Genres and Forms

WML2
GEN.U10.WML2

Writing Minilesson Principle
Write with a different set of eyes.

Experimenting with Writing in New Ways

You Will Need

- *Bugs for Lunch* by Margery Facklam from Text Set: Exploring the Natural World: Insects
- chart paper and markers
- To download the following online resource for this lesson, visit **fp.pub/resources**:
  - chart art (optional)

Academic Language / Important Vocabulary

- point of view
- different set of eyes

Continuum Connection

- Tell about a topic in an interesting way
- Take risks as a writer

GOAL

Use personification to write from a different perspective.

RATIONALE

When you teach children how to use personification to write from a different perspective, they begin to think about perspective and point of view in their fiction writing. This can also give children plenty of new ideas for their writing and breathe new life into their writing.

ASSESS LEARNING

- Observe for evidence that children understand writing from a different perspective.
- Notice whether children experiment with using personification to write from a different perspective.
- Look for evidence that they can use vocabulary such as *point of view* and *different set of eyes*.

MINILESSON

To help children think about the principle, use shared writing to model using personification to write from a different perspective. Make sure children understand the figurative meaning of seeing through a "different set of eyes." Here is an example.

- Show the cover of *Bugs for Lunch* and read the title. Then read pages 1–5.

  This book asks you to imagine who you could be if you ate bugs for lunch. It says that you could be a bird, a spider, or a bat! This gave me an idea for writing. We could imagine that we are a bird that eats bugs for lunch, and write from the point of view of the bird.

  When you write from the point of view of something or someone else, you imagine that you are that person, animal, or thing, and you write as if that other person, animal, or thing is doing the writing.

  If you were a bird writing about eating bugs for lunch, what would you write?

- Use shared writing to write, on chart paper, at least a few sentences from the perspective of a bird. Point out the use of the pronoun *I* because the writing is from the point of view of the bird.

- If necessary, guide children's thinking with questions such as the following:
  - *What might a bird think about eating bugs for lunch?*
  - *What might a bird say about how they taste?*
  - *How would a bird find food?*

Have a Try

Invite children to talk to a partner about their ideas for using personification.

> When you write, you don't always have to write as yourself. You can write with a different set of eyes by pretending to be an animal or an object. What animal or object would you like to pretend to be in your writing? Turn and talk to your partner about your ideas.

▶ After children turn and talk, invite several children to share their ideas. Record them on the chart.

Summarize and Apply

Write the principle at the top of the chart. Read it to children. Summarize the learning and remind children to try writing with a different set of eyes.

> During writing time today, try writing with a different set of eyes. In other words, you will write as if you are an animal or an object. Write about what that animal or object would think about and experience. Bring your writing to share when we come back together.

Write with a different set of eyes.

For lunch today, I went hunting for worms. I ate so many earthworms. I even caught a giant grasshopper! It was so crunchy and delicious. I am so full now . . . time for a nap!

I can write with the eyes of . . .

* A bug that is being hunted by a bird
* My pet cat
* A tree
* My house
* A car

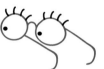

Confer

▶ During independent writing, move around the room to confer briefly with as many individual children as time allows. Sit side by side with them and invite them to talk about writing with a different set of eyes. Use prompts such as the following as needed.

* *What animal or object would you like to pretend to be?*
* *What might a _____ think about?*
* *How might a _____ feel when _____?*
* *How would a _____'s experience be different from yours?*

Share

Following independent writing, gather children in the meeting area to share their writing.

> Did you write with a different set of eyes today? Who or what did you pretend to be?

> Would you like to read aloud your writing?

Writing Minilesson Principle

Use a book to inspire a new way to write.

Experimenting with Writing in New Ways

You Will Need

- a book with an interesting form or style that could inspire children's writing, such as *Courage* by Bernard Waber, from Text Set: Facing Challenges

- chart paper and markers

- To download the following online resource for this lesson, visit **fp.pub/resources**:
  - chart art (optional)

Academic Language / Important Vocabulary

- inspire
- example
- author

Continuum Connection

- Show evidence of using language from storybooks and informational books that have been read aloud

- Learn ways of using language and constructing texts from other writers (reading books and hearing them read aloud) and apply understandings to one's own writing

- Borrow a word, phrase, or a sentence from another writer

- Get ideas from other books and writers about how to approach a topic

GOAL

Try a new form of writing inspired by a book.

RATIONALE

When you encourage children to be inspired by other authors, they can experiment with different forms and styles of writing. They also learn that writers and other creators do not work in a vacuum—they are all inspired and influenced by others, and that is part of the beauty of creativity. This lesson focuses on a form of writing inspired by one particular book, but it can be repeated with many different books and styles of writing.

ASSESS LEARNING

- Observe children as they write and talk about their writing.

- Notice whether children try new forms of writing as inspired by books they have read.

- Look for evidence that they can use vocabulary such as *inspire*, *example*, and *author*.

MINILESSON

To help children think about the principle, use shared writing to model trying a new form of writing inspired by a book. Here is an example.

- Show the cover of *Courage* and read the title. Read the first several pages.

  How does the author of this book tell about courage?

  The author tells about courage by beginning each sentence with "Courage is . . ." and giving an example of things that take courage to do. This book inspired me to try writing in the same way, and I think we could write a book like this. Ours could be called *Friendship.* How would we start each sentence?

- Write *Friendship is* on a chart paper.

  What could we write about friendship? What are some examples of things that friends might do?

- Use children's responses to write several sentences following this format.

Have a Try

Invite children to talk to a partner about their ideas for writing.

> We were inspired by Bernard Waber to write about friendship in the way he wrote about courage. What other feelings or ideas could you write about in this way? Turn and talk to your partner about your ideas.

▶ After time for discussion, invite several children to share their ideas. Record them on the chart.

Summarize and Apply

Summarize the learning and remind children to try new forms of writing as inspired by books.

> What new way of writing did we talk about today?

▶ Write the principle at the top of the chart.

> During writing time today, try writing a book that is inspired by *Courage* or another book that you've read. Bring your writing to share when we meet later.

Use a book to inspire a new way to write.

Friendship
by Mr. A's Class

Friendship is sharing.

Friendship is always being there for your friends.

Friendship is playing games together.

Friendship is standing up for your friends when someone is mean to them.

Friendship is letting your friend have the last chocolate milk.

- Love
- Happiness
- Family
- Hope
- Fear

Confer

▶ During independent writing, move around the room to confer briefly with as many individual children as time allows. Sit side by side with them and invite them to talk about trying a new form of writing. Use prompts such as the following as needed.

- *Would you like to write a book inspired by* Courage?
- *What feeling or idea would you like to write about? Look at our chart for ideas.*
- *What are some examples of things that make you feel _____?*
- *What are some things people do that show _____?*

Share

Following independent writing, gather children in the meeting area to share their writing.

> Turn and share your writing with a partner. Be sure to tell which book inspired your writing.

WML4

GEN.U10.WML4

Writing Minilesson Principle
Find a new way to share a message.

Experimenting with Writing in New Ways

You Will Need

- several examples of multimodal texts (e.g., T-shirts, magnets, posters, songs, bumper stickers) that communicate a message (e.g., "Save the Whales")
- chart paper and markers

Academic Language / Important Vocabulary

- message
- share

Continuum Connection

- Choose topics that are interesting to the writer
- Tell about a topic in an interesting way
- Communicate the significance of the topic to an audience
- Understand writing as a vehicle to communicate something the writer thinks

GOAL

Choose a message and share it through a multimodal form of writing.

RATIONALE

Encourage children to think creatively not just about the content of their writing but also the form. For example, you might expose children to forms of multimodal writing. Multimodal writing has a component, such as visual or oral, in addition to or instead of writing. Learning to match the form of writing to the purpose and audience results in more effective writing. Understanding that there are many ways to convey a message gives children the opportunity to share their opinions about issues or topics they feel passionate about. It also sets the stage for opinion and persuasive writing in the future.

ASSESS LEARNING

- Observe children as they write and talk about their writing.
- Notice whether children try using different forms of multimodal writing to communicate a message.
- Look for evidence that they can use vocabulary such as *message* and *share.*

MINILESSON

To help children think about the principle, use several mentor texts to engage children in an inquiry-based lesson around multimodal forms of writing that communicate a message. Here is an example.

- Show one mentor text that communicates a message (e.g., a "Save the Whales" bumper sticker or an anti-littering poster).

    What do you think this is?

    Why do you think someone made this bumper sticker?

    The author of this bumper sticker wants readers to take actions to help save whales. The message is that saving the whales is important. An author's message is the important idea the author wants to share.

- Write the message and form of writing discussed on chart paper.

    What are some other important messages that you might want to share with an audience?

- List children's suggestions on the chart.

    If you have a message that you want people to really notice, what are some ways that you can get that message across? For example, what have you seen or heard that was meant to send a message?

Have a Try

Invite children to talk to a partner about the messages they would like to share.

> Authors can share messages in lots of different ways. What is a message that you would like to share about something that is important to you? How might you share that message? Turn and talk to your partner about your ideas.

▶ After children turn and talk, invite several children to share their ideas. Add any new ideas to the chart.

Summarize and Apply

Write the principle at the top of the chart. Read it to children. Summarize the learning and remind children to try different ways of sharing a message.

> What did you learn today about how authors can share messages?

> During writing time today, think about a message you would like to share and the best way to share it. Bring your writing to share when we come back together.

Find a new way to share a message.

Message

- Saving the whales is important.
- Littering is bad for the planet.
- War is bad.
- It's important to recycle.
- Adopt a dog.
- Be kind to people.

Getting the Message Out

- Bumper sticker
- Poster
- T-shirt
- Song
- Magnet
- Sign
- Script for a play or video

Your Message Here!

Confer

▶ During independent writing, move around the room to confer briefly with as many individual children as time allows. Sit side by side with them and invite them to talk about the best way to share a message. Use prompts such as the following as needed.

- *What message would you like to share?*
- *Are there any issues or topics that you care a lot about?*
- *How would you like to share that message? Would you like to make a T-shirt/bumper sticker/magnet?*
- *What is the best way to get your message across to your audience?*

Share

Following independent writing, gather children in the meeting area to share their writing.

> Who would like to share your writing?

> What message did you share? Why did you choose that message?

Assessment

After you have taught the minilessons in this umbrella, observe children as they explore different ways of writing. Use *The Fountas & Pinnell Literacy Continuum* to notice, teach for, and support children's learning as you observe their attempts at writing.

▶ What evidence do you have of children's new understandings related to experimenting with writing in new ways?

- Have children tried writing about a previous topic in a different genre or form?

- Have they experimented with using personification to write from a different perspective?

- Have they tried a new form of writing as inspired by a book?

- Are they able to choose an effective and appropriate way of conveying a message?

- Do children understand and use vocabulary such as *topic*, *inspire*, and *message*?

▶ In what other ways, beyond the scope of this umbrella, are children exploring the writing process?

- Are they publishing their writing in different ways?

- Are they sharing their writing with an audience?

Use your observations to determine the next umbrella you will teach. You may also consult Suggested Sequence of Lessons (pp. 575–589) for guidance.

EXTENSIONS FOR EXPERIMENTING WITH WRITING IN NEW WAYS

▶ Regularly give children opportunities to write in the same style or genre as a book you have read aloud.

▶ Invite children to write their own version of a familiar trickster tale.

▶ Help children experiment with digital forms of content creation as appropriate—for example, blog post, slideshow, podcast, or video.

▶ Read aloud *This Plus That: Life's Little Equations* by Amy Krouse Rosenthal and then challenge children to create their own "word equations."

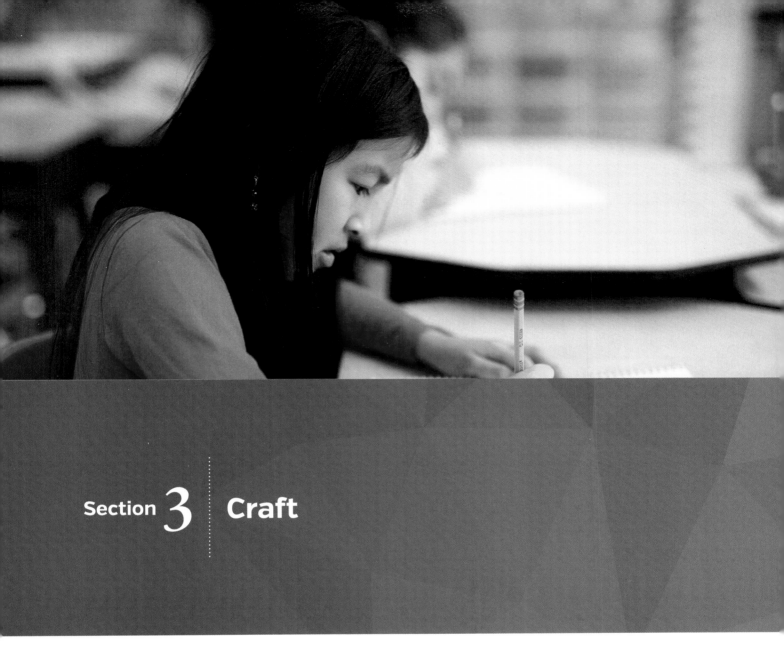

Section 3 | Craft

THROUGH THE TALK that surrounds interactive read-aloud and shared reading, second graders learn a lot about the craft of writing. The minilessons in this section take this budding knowledge and pull back the curtain on the decisions authors and illustrators make (e.g., choosing powerful words, using dialogue, drawing borders, using close-ups) to create books that are interesting and exciting to read.

Minilessons in This Umbrella

WML1 Notice the decisions writers make.

WML2 Notice the decisions illustrators make.

WML3 Try something you notice writers and illustrators do.

Before Teaching Umbrella 1 Minilessons

The minilessons in this umbrella are designed to help children notice elements of author's craft and illustrator's craft that they can try in their own bookmaking. Teach the first two lessons over several days, as children will need time to explore and participate in each inquiry over time. When you notice children are gaining confidence in reading like a writer and an illustrator, they may be ready to try some of the same crafting decisions in their own writing (WML3). Repeat lessons throughout the year as children get to know different authors and illustrators, tailoring the lessons to the author or illustrator you are studying.

Read and discuss engaging books with a variety of writing and illustration styles. Give children plenty of opportunities to study multiple books by the same author or illustrator. If you are using *The Reading Minilessons Book, Grade 2* (Fountas and Pinnell 2019), LA.U3: Studying Authors and Illustrators provides a foundation for this umbrella. Consider using the following books from *Fountas & Pinnell Classroom™ Interactive Read-Aloud Collection*, or choose books from your classroom library.

Interactive Read-Aloud Collection

Caring for Each Other: Family

Pecan Pie Baby by
 Jacqueline Woodson

The Wednesday Surprise by
 Eve Bunting

Big Red Lollipop by Rukhsana Khan

Finding Your Way in a New Place

The Have A Good Day Cafe by
 Frances Park and Ginger Park

Mango, Abuela, and Me by
 Meg Medina

Memory Stories

When I Was Young in the Mountains
 by Cynthia Rylant

The Importance of Friendship

*Horace and Morris but Mostly
 Dolores* by James Howe

First Come the Zebra by
 Lynne Barasch

As you read and enjoy these texts together, help children

- notice and discuss interesting examples of author's and illustrator's craft, and

- discuss how the decisions writers make can help with their own writing.

Interactive Read-Aloud
Family

Finding Your Way

Memory Stories

Friendship

Section 3: Craft

Writing Minilesson Principle
Notice the decisions writers make.

You Will Need

- several familiar books that exemplify author's craft, such as the following:
  - *Pecan Pie Baby* by Jacqueline Woodson and *The Wednesday Surprise* by Eve Bunting, from Text Set: Caring for Each Other: Family
  - *The Have A Good Day Cafe* by Frances Park and Ginger Park, from Text Set: Finding Your Way in a New Place
  - *When I Was Young in the Mountains* by Cynthia Rylant, from Text Set: Memory Stories
  - *Horace and Morris but Mostly Dolores* by James Howe, from Text Set: The Importance of Friendship
- several books for each pair of children that have recognizable craft moves they could try in their own writing
- chart paper and markers
- sticky notes

Academic Language/ Important Vocabulary

- decision
- notice

Continuum Connection

- Attend to the language and craft of other writers (mentor texts) in order to learn more as a writer
- Notice what makes writing effective and name the craft or technique

---

GOAL

Read familiar books and notice crafting decisions writers make.

RATIONALE

Once children become aware of and can name the ways that authors craft their books, they can begin to apply some of the same crafting decisions and techniques to their own writing.

ASSESS LEARNING

- Listen to children as they talk about books. Can they identify examples of author's craft?
- Look for evidence that children can use vocabulary such as *decision* and *notice*.

MINILESSON

To help children think about the minilesson principle, use mentor texts or samples of your own writing, children's writing, or class shared writing to guide them to notice the authors' craft decisions. Here is an example.

- Show *Pecan Pie Baby* and read pages with text separated out from the rest, such as pages 1 and 4.

  > What do you notice about Jacqueline Woodson's writing?

  > Why do you think she made that decision?

- Record children's responses on chart paper.
- Think aloud about how you might use this in your own writing.

  > I might try this in my own writing. If I were writing about seeing all the guests waiting for me at a surprise party, I could separate out the words "I was stunned!" to let the reader know how I was feeling.

- Discuss other decisions in a similar manner with a few more familiar books, such as *The Have a Good Day Cafe* (words in another language), *When I Was Young in the Mountains* (repetition of "When I was young in the mountains"), or *Horace and Morris but Mostly Dolores* (ellipses).

Have a Try

Use a book that has a good example of author's craft, such as *The Wednesday Surprise*.

▶ Review a few pages of *The Wednesday Surprise*.

Turn and talk about something Eve Bunting did that makes her book interesting or something that helps you understand the story.

▶ After children turn and talk, invite a few children to share their thinking. Add to the chart. Save the chart for WML3.

Summarize and Apply

Summarize the learning. Provide books for each pair of children to look in to notice the authors' decisions.

▶ Write the principle at the top of the chart.

Writers make decisions when they write their books. During writing time, look in books with a partner to find examples. Ask each other these questions: What did the writer do to make the writing interesting? What did the writer do to help the reader understand more? Mark the places where you notice decisions the writer made with a sticky note so we can talk about them when we meet later.

Notice the decisions writers make.		
Author	**Writers' Decision**	**Why?**
Jacqueline Woodson	Placed some of the words separate from other words	Helps the reader stop and think about how the character might feel
Frances Park and Ginger Park	Included words from their home language	Makes the writing more authentic Shares details from the authors' culture
Cynthia Rylant	Repeated important words or phrases	Shows that an idea is important
James Howe	Added an ellipsis (. . .)	Creates suspense or interest
Eve Bunting	Used dialogue or talking Waited to tell what the surprise would be	Shares information through conversation Makes the reader read to find out

Confer

▶ During independent writing, move around the room to confer briefly with as many pairs of children as time allows. Sit side by side with them and invite them to talk about writers' decisions that they can try in their own writing. Use prompts such as those below if needed, following each with "Why might the writer have done that?" and/or "How might you try that in your own writing?"

- *What decision do you notice the writer made in this part of the book?*
- *How did the writer decide to place the words on the page?*
- *How did the writer decide to begin [end] this book?*

Share

Following independent writing, gather children in the meeting area. Ask each set of partners to share the writers' decisions they noticed.

Talk about the writers' decisions you noticed.

Writing Minilesson Principle
Notice the decisions illustrators make.

You Will Need

- several familiar books that exemplify illustrator's craft, such as the following:

  - *Pecan Pie Baby* by Jacqueline Woodson and *Big Red Lollipop* by Rukhsana Khan, from Text Set: Caring for Each Other: Family

  - *Mango, Abuela, and Me* by Meg Medina, from Text Set: Finding Your Way in a New Place

  - *First Come the Zebra* by Lynne Barasch, from Text Set: The Importance of Friendship

- several books for each pair of children that have recognizable craft moves they could try in their own illustrations

- chart paper and markers

- sticky notes

Academic Language/ Important Vocabulary

- decisions
- illustrators
- illustrations
- notice

Continuum Connection

- Attend to the nuances of illustrations and how they enhance a text in order to try them out for oneself

---

GOAL

Study illustrations from familiar books and notice the craft decisions that illustrators make.

RATIONALE

Once children become aware of and can name ways that illustrators craft their illustrations, they can begin to apply some of the same crafting decisions to their own drawings.

ASSESS LEARNING

- Listen to children as they talk about books. Can they identify examples of illustrator's craft?

- Look for evidence that children can use vocabulary such as *decisions*, *illustrators*, *illustrations*, and *notice*.

MINILESSON

To help children think about the minilesson principle, use mentor texts to guide them to notice illustrators' craft decisions in books they know. Here is an example.

- Show the cover of *Pecan Pie Baby* and read the title. Show the illustration of Gia's bedroom.

  > Sophie Blackall illustrated this book. Why do you think she decided to illustrate the bedroom this way?

- Record children's responses on chart paper.

- Show the cover of *Big Red Lollipop* and read the title. Show a page with thought bubbles.

  > Sophie Blackall also illustrated this book! Look closely at this illustration. What do you notice?

  > Why do you think the illustrator decided to use thought bubbles in her drawings?

- Add responses to the chart.

- Think aloud about the decisions.

  > I might try this in my own books. If I were writing about imagining all the fun things I would do at the beach, I could draw a picture of myself with a thought bubble that shows me building a sandcastle, like Sophie Blackall did.

- Continue in a similar manner with the illustrations in *Mango, Abuela, and Me* (whole-page drawings).

Have a Try

Use a book that has a good example of illustrator's craft, such as *First Come the Zebra*, to help children think more about reading like an illustrator.

> Look at the illustration at the beginning of *First Come the Zebra*. What do you notice about the illustrator's decision to show the sky? Turn and talk to your partner.

▶ After children turn and talk, invite a few children to share their thinking about the illustrator's decisions. Add to the chart. Save the chart for WML3.

Summarize and Apply

Summarize the learning. Provide books for each pair of children to look in for decisions the illustrators made.

▶ Write the principle at the top of the chart.

> Illustrators make decisions when they illustrate books. During writing time, look in books with a partner to find more examples. Ask each other these questions: What did the illustrator do to make the illustrations more interesting? How did the illustrator use the picture to tell more of the story? Mark the illustrator's decisions you notice with a sticky note so we can talk about them when we come back together.

Notice the decisions illustrators make.

Illustrator	What decision did the illustrator make?	Why?
Sophie Blackall	Drew lots of details, like the book on Gia's bed and the toys in her room	Shows what the character likes and where the story takes place
	Used thought bubbles	Shows what a character is thinking
		Gives more information
	Drew small lines	Shows something is moving
Angela Dominguez	Filled the pages	Shows whole scenes
		Shows where the story takes place
Lynne Barasch	Drew a morning sky	Shows the time of day
	Used watercolors	Gives a feeling of peace

Confer

▶ During independent writing, move around the room to confer briefly with as many pairs of children as time allows. Sit side by side with them and invite them to talk about illustrators' crafting decisions. Use prompts such as the following if needed, following each with "Why might the illustrator have done that?" and/or "How might you try that in your own books?"

- *What decisions did the illustrator make about what to illustrate?*
- *What do you notice about how the illustrations are placed on the page?*

Share

Following independent writing, gather children in the meeting area. Ask each set of partners to share the illustrators' decisions they noticed.

> What did you notice about the illustrator's decisions?

WML3

CFT.U1.WML3

Writing Minilesson Principle
Try something you notice writers and illustrators do.

Reading Like a Writer and Illustrator

You Will Need

- charts from WML1 and WML2
- your own or a student's sample writing, with a number of craft moves
- chart paper and markers

Academic Language/ Important Vocabulary

- writers
- illustrators
- illustrations
- text
- decisions

Continuum Connection

- Learn ways of using language and constructing texts from other writers (reading books and hearing them read aloud) and apply understandings to one's own writing
- Attend to the nuances of illustrations and how they enhance a text in order to try them out for oneself
- Be willing to work at the craft of writing, incorporating new learning from instruction

GOAL

Choose crafting decisions of writers and illustrators to try out when making books.

RATIONALE

As children notice the crafting decisions that authors and illustrators make, they can begin to try them out in their own books. This experimentation sets the foundation that writers become stronger as they learn from and try out the decisions of others.

ASSESS LEARNING

- ▶ Listen to children as they talk about books. Are they reading like a writer (an illustrator)?
- ▶ Notice whether children try out crafting decisions that they have noticed other authors and illustrators using.
- ▶ Look for evidence that children can use vocabulary such as *writers*, *illustrators*, *illustrations*, *text*, and *decisions*.

MINILESSON

To help children notice the decisions writers and illustrators make so they can try them out in their own writing, engage them in a discussion of a sample of writing. Here is an example.

▶ Display the charts from WML1 and WML2.

> Authors and illustrators make decisions about what they write or draw. What decisions do you remember seeing in books?

▶ As children respond, point to their noticings on the chart, or add new ones.

> How could you try that in your own writing? your own illustrations?

▶ Think aloud about how you might use a decision in your own writing and/or illustrations or in a child's writing. Add noticings to the new chart.

> Listen as I read Antoine's writing.

> *THUMP! "What was that noise?" I wondered. It was snow that had fallen from the rooftop. My family was already out of bed. Then my mother said "We're going to shovel the snow today!" I quickly got ready. "Wow, that's a lot of snow!" said my older brother. We got the shovels from the garage and started shoveling the snow.*

> What do you notice Antoine tried? After noticing writers sometimes use dialogue, or conversations, in their writing, Antoine chose to try this in his own writing to make it even more meaningful to the reader. He also added a word to help the reader hear what was happening in that part of his story.

Have a Try

Invite children to talk to a partner about the crafting decisions they will try in their own writing.

> What do you want to try in your own writing or illustrations? Turn and talk about that.

▶ After children turn and talk, invite several to share their thinking. Add to the chart. Prioritize those children who are not sure for a side-by-side talk in a writing conference.

Summarize and Apply

Remind children to try the crafting decisions authors and illustrators use in their own writing. Write the principle at the top of the chart.

> Think about what you have noticed authors and illustrators do in books. What could you try in your own writing? You can also look at the chart for ideas. Be prepared to share when we come back together.

Try something you notice writers and illustrators do.

	What will you try today when you write or illustrate?
Antoine	Dialogue, sound word
Aleena	Repeating important words or phrases
Katey	Speech bubbles
Benjamin	Lines to show movement
Jaliyah	Sound words
Chun	Dialogue
Ian	Background details in illustration
Devin	Some words in Spanish

Confer

▶ During independent writing, move around the room to confer briefly with as many individual children as time allows. Sit side by side with them and invite them to talk about trying a craft move in their own writing. Use prompts such as the following if needed.

- *What will you try that you have learned from looking at another author's writing? Show where you plan to do that in your book.*

- *What have you already tried that you learned from another illustrator?*

- *What will you try next that you have learned from looking at another illustrator's drawing? Where do you plan to include that in your writing?*

Share

Gather children in the meeting area to share with a partner what they did as writers and illustrators. Invite a few children to share with the class what their partners tried. Add new ideas to the chart along with children's names.

> What did you hear from your classmates that you might try in your writing?

Assessment

After you have taught the minilessons in this umbrella, observe children as they write and talk about their writing. Use the behaviors and understandings in *The Fountas & Pinnell Literacy Continuum* to notice, teach for, and support children's learning as you observe their attempts at writing and drawing.

▪ What evidence do you have of children's new understandings related to reading like a writer and illustrator?

  • Can children notice and talk about the decisions that writers and illustrators make?

  • What craft decisions are they trying in their own writing and illustrations?

  • Do they understand and use vocabulary such as *decision*, *notice*, *writers*, and *illustrators*?

▪ In what other ways, beyond the scope of this umbrella, are children ready to expand their writing?

  • Are they beginning to share their writing with others?

  • Are they using a writing folder or writer's notebook?

Use your observations to determine the next umbrella you will teach. You may also consult Suggested Sequence of Lessons (pp. 575–589) for guidance.

EXTENSIONS FOR READING LIKE A WRITER AND ILLUSTRATOR

▪ Continue adding to the charts created during these minilessons as children notice more examples of crafting decisions that authors and illustrators make. Refer to these charts across the year as you explore similar ideas in different umbrellas.

▪ Apply this umbrella to nonfiction writing and illustrations, such as in informational texts.

▪ When you notice a child trying out an interesting crafting decision, share the work with other children to look at with an eye toward reading like a writer and illustrator.

Minilessons in This Umbrella

WML1 Tell how characters look.

WML2 Tell what characters do.

WML3 Tell what characters think.

WML4 Tell what characters say.

Before Teaching Umbrella 2 Minilessons

Before teaching, provide plenty of opportunities for children to make independent writing and drawing choices and to make their own books. Read and discuss books with detailed character descriptions shown through words and illustrations. While including character descriptions in writing most often involves writing fiction, you may want to point out to children that this also applies to real-life characters in a memory story.

If you have *The Reading Minilessons Book, Grade 2* (Fountas and Pinnell 2019), umbrellas that are related to these minilessons are LA.U23: Understanding Characters' Feelings, Motivations, and Intentions and LA.U24: Understanding Character Traits. For mentor texts, use fiction books that have well-developed characters. Consider the following books from *Fountas & Pinnell Classroom™ Interactive Read-Aloud Collection*, or choose fiction books from the classroom library.

Interactive Read-Aloud Collection

Living and Working Together: Community

For You Are a Kenyan Child by Kelly Cunnane

The Library by Sarah Stewart

Armando and the Blue Tarp School by Edith Hope Fine

Exploring Realistic Fiction

Amelia's Road by Linda Jacobs Altman

As you read and enjoy these texts together, help children

- notice how characters are described, and
- talk about what actions, thoughts, and dialogue reveal about characters.

Interactive Read-Aloud
Community

Realistic Fiction

Section 3: Craft

Writing Minilesson Principle
Tell how characters look.

Describing Characters

You Will Need

- a mentor text with words that describe how a character looks, such as *For You Are a Kenyan Child* by Kelly Cunnane, from Text Set: Living and Working Together: Community
- chart paper and colored markers

Academic Language / Important Vocabulary

- character
- look

Continuum Connection

- Describe characters by how they look and what they do
- Use examples to make meaning clear to readers
- Be willing to work at the craft of writing, incorporating new learning from instruction

GOAL

Notice how an author describes a character to help the reader picture the character.

RATIONALE

Being able to imagine what a character looks like adds to the enjoyment and understanding of a story. By noticing how writers use language to describe how a character looks, children learn ways that they can describe a character's physical characteristics in their own writing.

ASSESS LEARNING

- ▷ Notice evidence that children understand the importance of describing characters in a story.
- ▷ Look for evidence that children are describing how characters look in their own writing.
- ▷ Look for evidence that children can use vocabulary such as *character* and *look*.

MINILESSON

To help children think about the minilesson principle, use a mentor text to show how writers use language to describe how a character looks. Here is an example.

- ▷ Show the cover of *For You Are a Kenyan Child*.

  What are some words you might use to tell how the boy looks?

- ▷ Help children describe the boy's physical characteristics and clothing in the illustration.

  Looking at the illustrations is one way to know how a character looks. Another way is to make a picture in your mind. Listen as I read about a few characters. Think about the words the writer used.

- ▷ Without showing the illustrations, read the first sentence on page 7. Write the words that describe the character on chart paper.

  Who would like to quickly sketch the picture you made in your mind of what Bashir looks like?

- ▷ Support a volunteer to quickly sketch the character next to the words. If having a child draw will take too long, you can share the pen or make the sketch yourself following children's suggestions.

- ▷ Repeat with Grandmother on page 16.

  Let's look at the way the illustrator drew the characters and compare the illustrations to our sketches.

- ▷ Briefly show the illustrations and talk about the similarities and differences.

  The way that you tell about your characters is important for your readers.

Have a Try

Invite children to turn and talk about describing the characters in their own stories.

> Think about a character in the story you are writing or thinking about writing. Turn to your partner and tell how the character looks.

▶ After time for discussion, ask a few volunteers to share their character descriptions. Encourage children to ask questions if they would like to know more details about how a character looks.

Summarize and Apply

Summarize the lesson. Remind children to describe their characters when they write.

> What can you do to help your readers picture the characters in your story?

▶ Write the principle at the top of the chart.

> Today if you are working on a story, use words to show how a character looks. If you are getting ready to write a story, you can write some notes in your writer's notebook about how a character looks. Bring your writing to share when we meet later.

Tell how characters look.

| Bashir | "red and yellow beanie on his long loopy hair" | |
| Grandmother | "plump as a hen" | |

Confer

▶ During independent writing, move around the room to confer briefly with as many individual children as time allows. Sit side by side with them and invite them to talk about describing characters. Use the following prompts as needed.

- *How does this character look?*
- *What are some words you might add to tell how the characters look?*
- *What else can you say about how this character looks?*

Share

Following independent writing, gather children in the meeting area to share their writing.

> Who would like to share how you used words to tell about a character?

> Do you have any questions about the way _____'s character looks?

Describing Characters

You Will Need

- a mentor text that describes a character's actions, such as *The Library* by Sarah Stewart, from Text Set: Living and Working Together: Community

- chart paper and markers

Academic Language / Important Vocabulary

- character
- describe
- do
- actions

Continuum Connection

- Describe characters by what they do, say, and think and what others say about them

- Show through language instead of telling

- Be willing to work at the craft of writing, incorporating new learning from instruction

---

GOAL

Learn to describe characters through their actions.

RATIONALE

When children recognize that a writer can use behavior to help readers infer something about a character, they recognize that they have different ways they can share information about a character in their own writing.

ASSESS LEARNING

- Notice whether children understand that writing about a character's actions is one way a writer can show something about a character.

- Look for evidence that children sometimes write about a character's actions.

- Look for evidence that children can use vocabulary such as *character*, *describe*, *do*, and *actions*.

MINILESSON

To help children think about the minilesson principle, use a mentor text to show that a character's actions reveal information about the character and to help children think about how to use a character's actions in their own writing. Here is an example.

- Show and revisit the last few pages of *The Library*.

  Elizabeth Brown gave all of her books away to the town for a library. What does this tell you about what Elizabeth is like as a person?

- Guide the conversation to help children recognize that the action shows that she is kind and giving. Begin a chart that states the action and what it reveals about the character.

- Choose another character trait that is familiar to the children in your class. Then model the thinking a writer might do when deciding what actions to write about to show that trait. This is just an example.

  If I am going to write a story about a little sister who feels jealous of her big sister, I would think about how the little sister might act and some things she might do. For example, I could write that the little sister uses her big sister's backpack without asking. This could show that she is jealous that she doesn't have a backpack of her own.

- Add the example to the chart.

  What are some other things the girl might do that show she is jealous of her sister?

- Support the conversation to help children talk about actions a writer could write about to show that the girl is jealous. Add to the chart.

Have a Try

Invite children to turn and talk about describing characters through their actions.

> What action could show that a character is honest? Turn and talk about that.

▶ Allow a short time for discussion.

> Now turn and talk about an action that could show that a character is feeling hungry.

▶ Ask volunteers to share their ideas and add them to the chart.

Summarize and Apply

Summarize the lesson. Remind children to write about a character's actions.

> When you use actions to show something about a character, you are showing the reader what the character is like instead of just telling.

▶ Write the principle at the top of the chart.

> Today during writing time, if you are working on a story, include your character's actions. If you are getting ready to write a story, write some notes in your writer's notebook about what a character might do. Bring your writing to share when we meet later.

Tell what characters do.

Character's Actions	What the Character Is Like
• Donates her books so others can read them	• Kind and giving (Elizabeth Brown)
• Uses her sister's backpack • Follows her sister and her sister's friends around • Says things that are not nice	• Jealous of big sister
• Returns lost money • Tells the truth even when the person might get punished	• Honest
• Asks when dinner will be ready • Asks for a snack	• Hungry

Confer

▶ During independent writing, move around the room to confer briefly with as many individual children as time allows. Sit side by side with them and invite them to talk about characters. Use the following prompts as needed.

- *What are some ways you can show how this character feels?*
- *How will your readers know what kind of person this character is?*
- *Can you add details about what the character is doing?*

Share

Following independent writing, gather children in the meeting area to share their writing.

> Who wrote about a character's actions today? Share what you wrote.

Writing Minilesson Principle
Tell what characters think.

You Will Need

- a mentor text that reveals a character's thoughts, such as *Amelia's Road* by Linda Jacobs Altman, from Text Set: Exploring Realistic Fiction
- chart paper and markers

Academic Language / Important Vocabulary

- character
- think
- thoughts
- feelings

Continuum Connection

- Describe characters by what they do, say, and think and what others say about them
- Show through language instead of telling
- Use examples to make meaning clear to readers
- Be willing to work at the craft of writing, incorporating new learning from instruction

GOAL

Learn to describe characters by writing their thoughts.

RATIONALE

When children recognize that writers reveal something about a character by sharing the character's inner thoughts, they realize that they have another way to describe the characters in their stories.

ASSESS LEARNING

- Notice evidence that children understand that a character's thoughts reveal something about the character.
- Look for evidence that children sometimes write about a character's thoughts.
- Look for evidence that children can use vocabulary such as *character*, *think*, *thoughts*, and *feelings*.

MINILESSON

To help children think about the minilesson principle, use a mentor text to show that a character's thoughts reveal information about the character. Here is an example.

- Revisit the first four pages of *Amelia's Road*.

  What is Amelia thinking about?

  Amelia is thinking that she does not like long roads because they lead to places she doesn't want to live. As I read, give a thumbs-up every time you notice what Amelia is thinking.

- Begin a three-column chart with the character's name and what she is thinking in the first two columns. Read through the pages to find several more examples, stopping to have volunteers share Amelia's thoughts. Add to the chart.

  The writer, Linda Jacobs Altman, wrote about Amelia's thoughts and feelings to help you know more about her. What do you learn about Amelia from knowing her thoughts?

- Guide the conversation. Add what the thoughts reveal to the third column.

- Choose a fiction story topic to use as a model. This is an example.

  If I want to write about a boy who loves soccer and wants to win the soccer game, I might write that he is thinking about how excited he is about playing. Or he might be thinking how it would feel to score a goal. What else might he be thinking?

- Add your ideas to the chart and then add a few of the children's ideas.

Have a Try

Invite children to turn and talk about writing about what characters think.

> Turn and talk about what a girl might be thinking on the first day at a new school.

▸ Guide the discussions as needed. Ask volunteers to share and add to the chart.

Summarize and Apply

Summarize the lesson. Remind children that they can write about characters' thoughts.

> What can writers do to show what their characters are like?

▸ Write the principle at the top of the chart.

> Today during writing time, if you are writing a story, decide if you want to write what your characters are thinking. If you are getting ready to write a story, write some notes in your writer's notebook about what a character's thoughts might be. Bring your writing to share when we meet later.

Tell what characters think.

Character	What the Character Is Thinking	What This Shows
Amelia	• Doesn't like long roads • Wants to stay at this new school • That her parents don't know exactly when or where she was born	• Amelia wants to belong.
Boy playing soccer	• How excited he is for the game • How it would feel to score a goal • Hopes his friend passes him the ball	• The boy likes soccer and wants to win.
Girl on the first day at a new school	• Hopes there's someone to sit with at lunch • Wonders what the teacher will be like	• The girl is nervous.

Confer

▸ During independent writing, move around the room to confer briefly with as many individual children as time allows. Sit side by side with them and invite them to talk about describing characters. Use the following prompts as needed.

- *What is this character thinking about?*
- *How could this character's thoughts help your reader learn more?*
- *Tell about the thoughts this character has. You could add that to your story.*

Share

Following independent writing, gather children in the meeting area to share their writing.

> Who wrote about a character's thoughts today? Share what you wrote.

> How do the character's thoughts help you learn more about the character in _____'s story?

Describing Characters

You Will Need

- a mentor text that has dialogue, such as *Armando and the Blue Tarp School* by Edith Hope Fine, from Text Set: Living and Working Together: Community
- two short pieces of writing on chart paper with dialogue to show two different feelings, the second piece covered
- markers

Academic Language / Important Vocabulary

- character
- talk
- say

Continuum Connection

- Describe characters by what they do, say, and think and what others say about them
- Show through language instead of telling
- Use examples to make meaning clear to readers
- Be willing to work at the craft of writing, incorporating new learning from instruction

GOAL

Learn to describe characters through their dialogue.

RATIONALE

When children become aware that dialogue reveals information about a character, they learn they can include dialogue in their own writing as a way to show more about the character.

ASSESS LEARNING

- Notice evidence that children understand that writers can use dialogue to reveal information about a character.
- Look for evidence that children are trying out the use of dialogue to show how a character feels.
- Look for evidence that children can use vocabulary such as *character*, *talk*, and *say*.

MINILESSON

To help children think about the minilesson principle, use a mentor text to show that a character's dialogue reveals information about the character. Here is an example.

> Listen and think about the words Armando says as I read a few pages from *Armando and the Blue Tarp School*.

- Revisit and read the dialogue from pages 2, 12, and 25, pausing after each page to ask children what they noticed.

> What do Armando's words help you understand about him?

- Help children understand what Armando's words reveal about him (e.g., he is excited to see Señor David, he longs to attend school, he is joyous that a new school has been built).

> Writers can write what a character says to help readers understand more about the character.

- Show and read the first prepared piece.

> What do you notice about what the character says?

- Guide the conversation to help children focus on the dialogue. On the chart, write children's suggestions about what it shows about the character.

Have a Try

Invite children to turn and talk about what dialogue can reveal about a character.

▶ Uncover and read the second prepared piece of writing.

> How does this writing show you something different about Sindra? Turn and talk that.

▶ After time for discussion, ask volunteers to share. Add to the chart.

Summarize and Apply

Summarize the lesson. Remind children to think about including dialogue in their writing.

> What can you do to show something about your characters?

▶ Write the principle at the top of the chart.

> Today during writing time, think about including what a character says. Bring your writing to share when we meet later.

Tell what characters say.	
What the Character Says	What the Words Show
Sindra brushed her hair slowly. When her grandma opened the door, Sindra cried, "Oh, Grandma, I can't do my hair bow, so I want to stay home and skip the party. Maybe I will stay home all week. Or forever."	Sindra doesn't want to go to the party. She might be nervous.
As fast as she could, Sindra brushed her hair and put in her bow. When her grandma opened the door, Sindra exclaimed, "Grandma, I'm ready! Can we please leave now so I can be the first one at the party?"	Sindra is excited and happy about going to the party.

Confer

▶ During independent writing, move around the room to confer briefly with as many individual children as time allows. Sit side by side with them and invite them to talk about describing characters. Use the following prompts as needed.

- *What could this character say to show how he is feeling?*
- *What do you want your readers to know about this character? How can you show that?*
- *What will this character's words show about her?*

Share

Following independent writing, gather children in the meeting area to share their writing.

> Who included talking in your writing today? Share what you wrote.

> What did you learn about the character from what the character says in _____'s writing?

Assessment

After you have taught the minilessons in this umbrella, observe children in a variety of classroom activities. Use *The Fountas & Pinnell Literacy Continuum* to notice, teach for, and support children's learning as you observe their attempts at writing.

▶ What evidence do you have of children's new understandings related to describing characters?

  • How are children describing the characters in their stories? Do they include descriptions, actions, thoughts, or dialogue?

  • Are they using vocabulary such as *character*, *describe*, *look*, *do*, *actions*, *think*, *thoughts*, *feelings*, *talk*, and *say*?

▶ In what ways, beyond the scope of this umbrella, are children showing an interest in writing fiction?

  • Do children's illustrations support what they write and vice versa?

  • Are children using quotation marks when they write dialogue?

  • Are they able to write with voice?

Use your observations to determine the next umbrella you will teach. You may also consult Suggested Sequence of Lessons (pp. 575–589) for guidance.

EXTENSIONS FOR DESCRIBING CHARACTERS

▶ Once children have learned to describe the characters in their stories, encourage them to look at their drawings to make sure they support the text. Children might also find more details to write about by studying their drawings.

▶ Gather together a guided writing group of several children who need support in adding character descriptions.

▶ Repeat WML4 with examples of what other characters say and what that reveals about the main character. Use the online resource Planning a Minilesson to capture your planning notes.

Minilessons in This Umbrella

WML1 Use words and illustrations to show where and when the story happens.

WML2 Use your senses of smell and hearing to show where the story happens.

WML3 Draw and write about clothing, food, and language to show where and when the story happens.

Before Teaching Umbrella 3 Minilessons

When writing, children often focus on the characters and what they do but neglect to think about or show where and when the story takes place. The goals of this umbrella are to help them recognize that writers use language and illustrations to show details about the setting and that they can do the same in their own writing. While setting can apply to fiction or nonfiction (e.g., memoir, narrative nonfiction), there will be some aspects of setting that will not be appropriate for some nonfiction writing. As this naturally arises, have a conversation with children to discuss whether setting is relevant. Introduce the word *setting* if the children in your class are ready.

Before teaching the minilessons in this umbrella, read and discuss a variety of picture books that have detailed and informative illustrations and descriptive language. If you have *The Reading Minilessons Book, Grade 2* (Fountas and Pinnell 2019), you might teach the minilessons in LA.21: Thinking About Where Stories Take Place. For mentor texts, use the following books from *Fountas & Pinnell Classroom™ Interactive Read-Aloud Collection*. Also consider using books with settings from the classroom library or that you have created with the class.

Interactive Read-Aloud Collection

The Pleasure of Giving

> *Those Shoes* by Maribeth Boelts
>
> *Sam and the Lucky Money* by Karen Chinn
>
> *My Rows and Piles of Coins* by Tololwa M. Mollel
>
> *The Birthday Swap* by Loretta Lopez

Jan Brett: Creating Imaginary Worlds

> *Town Mouse, Country Mouse*

> *Honey . . . Honey . . . Lion! A Story from Africa*

Exploring Different Cultures: Folktales

> *Why the Sky Is Far Away: A Nigerian Folktale* by Mary-Joan Gerson

Finding Beauty in the World Around You

> *Last Stop on Market Street* by Matt de la Peña
>
> *The Gardener* by Sarah Stewart

As you read and enjoy these texts together, help children

- notice details in the words and drawings that relate to time and place, and

- connect the setting to children's experiences (when an opportunity presents itself naturally in a text).

Interactive Read-Aloud
Pleasure of Giving

Jan Brett

Folktales

Finding Beauty

Section 3: Craft

WML1

CFT.U3.WML1

Writing Minilesson Principle
Use words and illustrations to show where and when the story happens.

Crafting a Setting

You Will Need

- several familiar texts that show a setting, such as the following:

  - *Those Shoes* by Maribeth Boelts, from Text Set: The Pleasure of Giving

  - *Town Mouse, Country Mouse* and *Honey . . . Honey . . . Lion! A Story from Africa* by Jan Brett, from Text Set: Jan Brett: Creating Imaginary Worlds

  - *Why the Sky Is Far Away: A Nigerian Folktale* by Mary-Joan Gerson, from Text Set: Exploring Different Cultures: Folktales

- chart paper and markers

- document camera (optional)

- To download the following online resource for this lesson, visit **fp.pub/resources**:

  - chart art (optional)

Academic Language / Important Vocabulary

- place
- time
- draw
- describe
- details
- setting (optional)

Continuum Connection

- Understand that a writer uses various elements of fiction (e.g., setting, plot with problem and solution, characters) in a fiction text

- Use drawings and sketches to represent people, places, things, and ideas in the composing, revising, and publishing process

---

GOAL

Include details in words and pictures to show the setting.

RATIONALE

Helping children become aware of the setting of a story will help them learn how they can inform their readers about the setting in their own books. Some children put more detail into their drawings than into their writing. Having them draw and then write will help those children write a more robust description of the setting. Decide whether it is appropriate to introduce the word *setting* to the children in your class.

ASSESS LEARNING

- Look for evidence that children recognize that writers include details about the setting in both words and illustrations and that they can do the same in their own writing.

- Look for evidence that children can use vocabulary such as *place*, *time*, *draw*, *describe*, *details*, and *setting* (optional).

MINILESSON

To help children think about the minilesson principle, use mentor texts in which the setting is revealed through words and illustrations. Be sure to show the illustrations; project the pages if you can so children can see the details in the illustrations. Here is an example.

- Show and read pages 13–14 in *Those Shoes*.

  How do the writer and illustrator help you understand where the story takes place and when it is happening?

- Engage children in a discussion about the details in the writing and drawings (e.g., "ride the bus," apartment building, items in thrift shop window). On chart paper, begin a list of details the children notice that reveal the setting. Use generative language instead of language that is specific to a particular story.

- Show and read pages 5–8 in *Town Mouse, Country Mouse*.

  What do you notice about where this story takes place?

- Guide the conversation to help children notice that the writer uses words and illustrations to show that the location changes from the city to the country.

- Show and read pages 26–29 in *Why the Sky Is Far Away: A Nigerian Folktale*.

  What words help you picture where and when the story is happening?

- As needed, point out the details in the writing and illustrations that reveal time of day, weather, and rural African setting.

Have a Try

Invite children to turn and talk about using words and illustrations to describe the setting.

▶ Show and read pages 18–19 in *Honey . . . Honey . . . Lion!*

Turn and talk about the information that Jan Brett gives about how the grass looks.

▶ After time for discussion, ask volunteers to share. Add to the chart.

Summarize and Apply

Summarize the lesson. Remind children to include details that reveal the setting in their writing and drawings.

How can you let your readers know where and when your story is taking place?

▶ Write the principle at the top of the chart.

Today during writing time, use words and drawings to show your readers where and when your story happens. If you have started to draw, you can add details to your illustration and then write a description based on the picture. If you have not started drawing, remember to put details about the place in your pictures. Bring your writing to share when we meet later.

> **Use words and illustrations to show where and when the story happens.**
>
> • Draw and write about details that show where the story takes place.
>
> • Draw and write about buildings to show what the place is like.
>
> • Draw and write about plants that show the place or time of year.
>
> • Tell information to show the way something looks (not just "grass" but a "field of golden bristle grass").

Section 3: Craft

Confer

▶ During independent writing, move around the room to confer briefly with as many individual children as time allows. Sit side by side with them and invite them to talk about their settings. Use the following prompts as needed.

• *What can you do to help your readers understand where the story takes place?*

• *What details could you add to this drawing to show the time of day (year)?*

• *Let's talk about some words you might include to show the time and place.*

Share

Following independent writing, gather children in the meeting area to share their writing.

Turn to your partner. Share words or pictures you included that show where or when your story takes place.

WML2
CFT.U3.WML2

Writing Minilesson Principle
Use your senses of smell and hearing to show where the story happens.

Crafting a Setting

You Will Need

- several familiar texts that use sensory words to describe the setting, such as the following:
  - *Last Stop on Market Street* by Matt de la Peña, from Text Set: Finding Beauty in the World Around You
  - *Sam and the Lucky Money* by Karen Chinn, from Text Set: The Pleasure of Giving
- chart paper and markers
- children's writing (one per child or pair of children)
- To use the following resource for this lesson, visit **fp.pub/resources**:
  - chart art (optional)

Academic Language / Important Vocabulary

- place
- time
- senses
- smell
- sound
- setting (optional)

Continuum Connection

- Understand that a writer uses various elements of fiction (e.g., setting, plot with problem and solution, characters) in a fiction text
- Describe a setting and how it is related to the writer's experiences
- Show through language instead of telling

GOAL

Use sensory details, including onomatopoeia, to describe the setting.

RATIONALE

Teaching children to use their senses to describe the setting gives them a way to access details to write a richer description. Whereas WML1 focuses on sight, this minilesson focuses on smell and sound.

ASSESS LEARNING

- Observe for evidence that children recognize that they can use their senses when they describe the setting.
- Look at children's writing. Are they are trying to use some sensory words to describe the setting?
- Look for evidence that children can use vocabulary such as *place*, *time*, *senses*, *smell*, *sound*, and *setting* (optional).

MINILESSON

To help children include sensory details to craft their settings, look at and discuss examples in mentor texts. Here is an example.

> Listen as I read some pages in *Last Stop on Market Street*. Listen for words that the writer, Matt de la Peña, used to help you picture the setting. Put your thumb up when you notice details that describe sounds or smells in the story.

- Show and read pages 5–10 in *Last Stop on Market Street*. Pause when children put their thumbs up and ask volunteers to share their noticings. They might notice the smell and sound of the rain, the sound of the bus, and the sounds of laughter and a guitar playing.

> Now think about the sounds and smells that Karen Chinn described in *Sam and the Lucky Money*. Put your thumb up when you notice something.

- Show and read pages 3–4 and pages 7–10. Pause as children put their thumbs up and ask them to share the sensory details they noticed, such as the sound of drums and cymbals and the smell of smoke, sweet egg tarts, and coconut pastries.

- You may also want to have children notice details in the illustrations that help them imagine the setting.

Have a Try

Invite children to turn and talk about using smell and sound to reveal the setting.

▶ Give children a sample of their writing (or one sample per pair of children).

> What smells and sounds might the characters in your story notice? Turn and talk about that.

▶ Prompt the conversations as needed to help children think of specific sounds and smells. After time for discussion, ask volunteers to share details of sounds or smells that they could add to their writing. Write their ideas on chart paper.

Summarize and Apply

Summarize the lesson. Remind children to include sensory details in their writing to reveal the setting. Write the principle at the top of the chart.

> During writing time, think about the words or illustrations you can use to show what the characters hear or smell. You might include sound words or other words to describe the sounds and smells so that the reader can better understand where or when the story happens. Bring your writing to share when we meet later.

Use your senses of smell and hearing to show where the story happens	
Sounds	**Smells**
chug-chug—train	burning smell of smoke
crackle—flames	cheesy nachos
buzz-buzz—fly	car exhaust
vroom—car engine	dirty socks
sizzle—hot dogs in a pan	french fries

Confer

▶ During independent writing, move around the room to confer briefly with as many individual children as time allows. Sit side by side with them and invite them to talk about describing the setting. Use the following prompts as needed.

- *What are some sound words you might use to show where your story takes place?*
- *What does it smell like in this place?*
- *What sounds and smells does this character notice?*
- *Picture yourself in the place. What do you hear [smell]?*

Share

Following independent writing, gather children in the meeting area to share their writing.

> Who would like to share your story?

> What words do you notice in _____'s writing that show sounds and smells?

Writing Minilesson Principle
Draw and write about clothing, food, and language to show where and when the story happens.

Crafting a Setting

You Will Need

- several mentor texts that have word and illustration details that show setting, such as the following:
  - *The Gardener* by Sarah Stewart, from Text Set: Finding Beauty in the World Around You
  - *My Rows and Piles of Coins* by Tololwa M. Mollel and *The Birthday Swap* by Loretta Lopez, from Text Set: The Pleasure of Giving
- chart paper and markers
- children's writing (one per child or pair of children)

Academic Language / Important Vocabulary

- place
- time
- details
- setting (optional)

Continuum Connection

- Understand that a writer uses various elements of fiction (e.g., setting, plot with problem and solution, characters) in a fiction text
- Describe a setting and how it is related to the writer's experiences
- Show through language instead of telling

GOAL

Draw and write about clothing, food, and language to reveal the setting.

RATIONALE

Authors and illustrators can convey a sense of place and time by writing or drawing about clothing and food and by using words from the language of the setting. When children become aware of examples in the books they read and hear, they realize that they can try these techniques in their own writing.

ASSESS LEARNING

- Look at children's writing. Do they sometimes show the setting by drawing and writing about clothing and food or by using words from the language of the setting?
- Notice evidence that children can use vocabulary such as *place*, *time*, *details*, and *setting* (optional).

MINILESSON

To help children think about the minilesson principle, use mentor texts and an interactive discussion about how they can reveal setting through words and illustrations. Here is an example.

- Show a few pages from *The Gardener.*

  How do you know where and when this story takes place?

- Engage children in a conversation about the clothing and how it shows that the story takes place long ago. Begin a list on chart paper that shows the details in the illustrations that help reveal the setting.

- Show and read pages 3–4 in *My Rows and Piles of Coins.*

  What information does the writer include in the words and pictures to show the place and time?

- Help children notice details in the clothing and food that show the setting. Point out that because Tanzania is modern today, the writer was showing that this story takes place some years ago. Also point out that the writer used words from another language to help you think about the words the characters might hear. Add to the chart.

  Listen as I read some pages from *The Birthday Swap*, and think about the details in the clothing, food, and language that give you information about the setting.

- As you show and read pages 1–12, pause throughout to engage children in conversation. As children mention details that relate to setting, add them to the chart.

Have a Try

Invite children to turn and talk about details that show the setting.

▶ Give children a sample of their writing (or one sample per pair of children).

> What clothing, food, or language details could you add to show the time and place? Turn and talk about that.

▶ After time for discussion, ask a few volunteers to share.

Summarize and Apply

Summarize the lesson. Remind children to draw or write details to reveal setting.

> How can you show the reader where and when a story happens?

▶ Write the principle at the top of the chart.

> Today during writing time, look to see if drawing or writing about clothing, food, or language would help the reader understand where and when your story is happening. If those details are not important for your story, do not include them. Bring your writing to share when we meet later.

▶ If children speak a language other than English at home, suggest that they use some words from it in their writing if it helps the reader understand the setting.

Draw and write about clothing, food, and language to show where and when the story happens.		
Clothing	Food	Language
hats, shoes, dresses, purses, uniform (long ago)	roasted peanuts, chapati, rice cakes, sambusa (Tanzania)	written letters (long ago)
head wrap, warm weather clothing (Tanzania)	burritos, tacos, flautas, fruit stand (Mexico)	chapati, sambusa (Tanzania)
shorts, lightweight shirts (warm climate in Mexico)		maracas, sombreros, piñata (Mexico)

Confer

▶ During independent writing, move around the room to confer briefly with as many individual children as time allows. Sit side by side with them and invite them to talk about crafting a setting. Use the following prompts as needed.

- *What kinds of clothes would these characters wear?*
- *What types of foods would they eat?*
- *Are there any words the characters might say that would show the place or time?*

Share

Following independent writing, gather children in the meeting area to share their writing.

> Who would like to share your story?

Assessment

After you have taught the minilessons in this umbrella, observe children in a variety of classroom activities. Use *The Fountas & Pinnell Literacy Continuum* to notice, teach for, and support children's learning as you observe their attempts at writing and drawing.

▶ What evidence do you have of children's new understandings related to setting?

- Are children showing the setting through words and illustrations?
- Do they include sensory language relating to smell and sound to show the setting?
- Do they include setting details, such as clothing, food, and words from the language of the setting?
- Are they using vocabulary such as *place*, *time*, *draw*, *describe*, *details*, *senses*, *smell*, and *sound*?

▶ In what ways, beyond the scope of this umbrella, are children showing an interest in writing and drawing?

- Do children show an interest in adding picture details that connect to the text?
- Are they willing to revise their writing to improve it?

Use your observations to determine the next umbrella you will teach. You may also consult Suggested Sequence of Lessons (pp. 575–589) for guidance.

EXTENSIONS FOR CRAFTING A SETTING

▶ Once children have learned to write with details, encourage them to look at their drawings to make sure they support the way the setting is described in words.

▶ Have children study their drawings to notice other things they may write about the setting.

▶ Talk with children about the details they could add to their illustrations to show more about where the story is taking place.

▶ Encourage them to study the background illustrations in books to get ideas from the illustrators.

▶ Refer to CFT.U7: Making Powerful Word Choices to help children think about the language they use to describe a setting.

Minilessons in This Umbrella

WML1 Show talking with speech bubbles. Show thinking with thought bubbles.

WML2 Add talking to make your writing more interesting.

WML3 Include action with talking in your writing.

Before Teaching Umbrella 4 Minilessons

Prior to teaching these minilessons, make sure children have experienced a variety of fiction books with dialogue. Choose as mentor texts the following books from *Fountas & Pinnell Classroom™ Interactive Read-Aloud Collection*, or use other text examples of dialogue from the classroom library or from class shared writing.

Interactive Read-Aloud Collection

Caring for Each Other: Family

Pecan Pie Baby by Jacqueline Woodson

Big Red Lollipop by Rukhsana Khan

Super-Completely and Totally the Messiest! by Judith Viorst

The Importance of Friendship

Horace and Morris but Mostly Dolores by James Howe

Finding Your Way in a New Place

Mango, Abuela, and Me by Meg Medina

As you read and enjoy these texts together, help children notice

- the way the writers show what the characters say and think,
- when writers include dialogue to increase drama, move the plot along, or show how characters feel, and
- that writers include action directly before and/or after characters speak.

Interactive Read-Aloud
Family

Friendship

Finding Your Way

Section 3: Craft

Writing Minilesson Principle

Show talking with speech bubbles.
Show thinking with thought bubbles.

Adding Dialogue to Writing

You Will Need

- several mentor texts that have speech and thought bubbles, such as the following:
  - *Pecan Pie Baby* by Jacqueline Woodson and *Big Red Lollipop* by Rukhsana Khan, from Text Set: Caring for Each Other: Family
  - *Horace and Morris but Mostly Dolores* by James Howe, from Text Set: The Importance of Friendship
- chart paper prepared with a large speech bubble and a large thought bubble
- markers

Academic Language / Important Vocabulary

- speech bubble
- thought bubble
- talking
- thinking

Continuum Connection

- Use dialogue as appropriate to add to the meaning of the story
- Add ideas in thought bubbles or dialogue in quotation marks or speech bubbles to provide information, provide narration, or show thoughts and feelings

GOAL

Use speech bubbles to show talking and thought bubbles to show thinking.

RATIONALE

Speech and thought bubbles make the readers' experience of reading a story more interesting. Teaching children to add speech and thought bubbles to their own writing is a visual way to introduce the idea of dialogue.

ASSESS LEARNING

- Notice evidence of what children understand about speech bubbles and thought bubbles.
- Look at children's writing. Are they using speech bubbles and thought bubbles?
- Look for evidence that children can use vocabulary such as *speech bubble*, *thought bubble*, *talking*, and *thinking*.

MINILESSON

To help children think about including speech or thought bubbles in their own writing, provide an inquiry-based lesson with examples and then model the process. Here is an example.

- Show the cover of *Pecan Pie Baby*. Show the pages with speech bubbles.

  How did the illustrator show what the characters are saying?

  Why do you think the illustrator chose to use speech bubbles?

- Engage children in a brief conversation about speech bubbles.
- Show pages with speech bubbles in *Horace and Morris but Mostly Dolores*.

  What do you notice about how the author placed speech bubbles in the illustrations?

- Help children recognize the way the speech bubbles point to the speaker's mouth. Guide them to understand that this helps them to know what each character says.
- Show and read the pages with thought bubbles in *Big Red Lollipop*.

  Now think about what the illustrator did in *Big Red Lollipop*.

  What do you notice about the bubbles?

  Rubina has a thought bubble with pictures inside to show what she is thinking in her head. If the author decided to put words in the thought bubble instead of pictures, what words might Rubina be thinking?

- Mention that thought bubbles can be drawn in different ways. Often they look like clouds with little circles leading to the character.

The Writing Minilessons Book, Grade 2

Have a Try

Invite children to turn and talk about using speech and thought bubbles.

▶ Show and read pages 15–16 of *Pecan Pie Baby* where Gia is listening to a story in school. Turn to the prepared chart paper.

> If the author added a speech bubble here, what might Gia say? Turn and talk to your partner.

▶ After time for discussion, ask a few children to share. Using their ideas, fill in the speech bubble. Repeat this process for a thought bubble, using pages 13–14 where Gia is sitting on her bed while her uncles put the crib together.

Summarize and Apply

Summarize the learning. Remind children to add speech bubbles and thought bubbles to their own writing.

> How can you show what characters are saying and thinking in your stories?

▶ Write the principle at the top of the chart.

> During writing time, take a look at the writing you are working on, think about how you might include a speech bubble or a thought bubble, and add that to your writing. Bring your writing to share when we meet later.

Show talking with speech bubbles.
Show thinking with thought bubbles.

Speech bubbles	Thought bubbles

I don't want to talk about being a big sister.

I don't want to share my room with the baby.

Confer

▶ During independent writing, move around the room to confer briefly with as many individual children as time allows. Sit side by side with them and invite them to talk about using dialogue in their books. Use the following prompts as needed.

- *What is this person saying [thinking]?*
- *Is there a place in this drawing where you could add a speech [thought] bubble?*
- *How can you show what the people are saying or thinking?*

Share

Following independent writing, gather children in the meeting area to share their writing.

> Turn to your partner to share what you wrote today. Point out a speech bubble or thought bubble if you added one to your writing.

Writing Minilesson Principle
Add talking to make your writing more interesting.

Adding Dialogue to Writing

You Will Need

- several mentor texts with dialogue, such as the following from Text Set: Caring for Each Other: Family:
  - *Super-Completely and Totally the Messiest!* by Judith Viorst
  - *Pecan Pie Baby* by Jacqueline Woodson
- chart paper prepared with book titles and dialogue
- labeled sticky notes: *Adds drama, Moves story forward, Shows feelings*
- highlighter

Academic Language / Important Vocabulary

- story
- talking
- thoughts
- feelings
- drama
- quotation marks

Continuum Connection

- Use dialogue as appropriate to add to the meaning of the story
- Show through language instead of telling
- Use quotation marks to show simple dialogue or to show what someone said
- Add ideas in thought bubbles or dialogue in quotation marks or speech bubbles to provide information, provide narration, or show thoughts and feelings

GOAL

Understand that dialogue adds meaning and interest to a story.

RATIONALE

When children notice how writers include dialogue to enhance drama, move the plot forward, or show how characters feel, they begin to think about ways to add dialogue to their own writing to make it more interesting.

ASSESS LEARNING

- Look at children's writing. Are they including dialogue?
- Look for evidence that children can use vocabulary such as *story, talking, thoughts, feelings, drama,* and *quotation marks.*

MINILESSON

To help children think about how writers include dialogue in their stories, provide an inquiry-based lesson. Here is an example.

- Show *Super-Completely and Totally the Messiest!* and read page 4.

  Why did Judith Viorst include talking here?

  It's exciting when everything is falling out of the closet! There is a lot of drama. The talking makes the writing interesting.

- Place the sticky note labeled *Adds drama* on the chart.
- Show *Pecan Pie Baby* and read page 3.

  Why did the author use dialogue here?

- Place the sticky note labeled *Moves story forward* on the chart.

  An author can have the characters talk to let readers know what is happening in the story or to move the story forward. The author could have written something like this: "Gia wanted to get rid of her old stuff, but her mother said they needed it for the baby." How would that be different from what the author wrote?

- Talk with children about the purpose of the talking on pages 22–23. Place the sticky note labeled *Shows feelings* on the chart.

Have a Try

Invite children to turn and talk about including dialogue in a story.

> When you are reading, how can you tell that a person is talking? Turn and talk to your partner about that.

▶ Ask volunteers to highlight the quotations marks in the dialogue on the chart.

Summarize and Apply

Summarize the lesson. Remind children that they can add dialogue to their writing.

> A writer adds talking to a story for a reason. The writer might want to add drama or move the story forward. The writer might want to show how the characters are feeling.

▶ Write the principle at the top of the chart. Read it aloud.

> During writing time, think about what the people in your story might say to each other and how that could make your writing more interesting. Remember to put quotation marks around what people say to let the reader know who is talking. Bring your writing to share when we meet later.

Add talking to make your writing more interesting.

Book	Talking	Why did the author include talking here?
messfest!	"Don't do it!" I hollered. "Stop! Watch out! Oh no!"	Adds drama
PECAN PIE Baby	"I don't know why we have to keep my old stuff," I said. "You do too know why," my mama said back. "Because there's going to be another baby coming soon."	Moves story forward
	"I'm so sick of that DING-DANG BABY!"	Shows feelings

Confer

▶ During independent writing, move around the room to confer briefly with as many individual children as time allows. Sit side by side with them and invite them to talk about using dialogue in their books. Use the following prompts as needed.

- *What could the people say to each other?*
- *Talk about this part of your story. How might you add talking to show how that character is feeling? to add drama? to move the story forward?*
- *How can you show which person is speaking?*

Share

Following independent writing, gather children in the meeting area to share their experiences writing dialogue.

> How did you decide what your characters should say? Share what you wrote.

> What ideas did you hear from your classmates that you might try in your writing?

WML3
CFT.U4.WML3

Writing Minilesson Principle
Include action with talking in your writing.

Adding Dialogue to Writing

You Will Need

- several mentor texts with dialogue, such as the following:
  - *Mango, Abuela, and Me* by Meg Medina, from Text Set: Finding Your Way in a New Place
  - *Big Red Lollipop* by Rukhsana Khan, from Text Set: Caring for Each Other: Family
- chart paper prepared with excerpts
- two colors of highlighters
- markers

Academic Language / Important Vocabulary

- talking
- action

Continuum Connection

- Use dialogue as appropriate to add to the meaning of the story
- Add ideas in thought bubbles or dialogue in quotation marks or speech bubbles to provide information, provide narration, or show thoughts and feelings

---

GOAL

Understand that dialogue is often broken up with narration or action.

RATIONALE

When children notice how writers break up dialogue with narration or action, they begin to see how dialogue can move a story along, and they can begin to try this in their own writing.

ASSESS LEARNING

- Notice evidence that children understand that dialogue is often broken up with narration or action.
- Look at children's writing. Are they adding actions to the dialogue?
- Look for evidence that children can use vocabulary such as *talking* and *action*.

MINILESSON

To help children understand that sometimes authors use action or narration to break up dialogue, use mentor texts and provide an inquiry-based lesson. Here is an example.

- Show *Mango, Abuela, and Me.* Show and read pages 21–22.

  I am going to read this again and highlight some parts of it.

- Read the same passage prewritten on the chart. Think aloud as you highlight what the characters say in blue and what they do in orange.

  The author wrote what the character was saying and what the character was doing—an action—at the same time. That makes the writing interesting and moves the story along.

- Repeat this process with pages 16–17 of *Big Red Lollipop.*

  What was the writer showing here with the dialogue? Why do you think the writer did this?

- Briefly discuss why authors include action with dialogue in their stories.

  A writer breaks up dialogue with action or narration for a reason. The writer might want to make the talking seem more natural. Think about when you talk. Sometimes you are doing something while you are talking. Telling what the characters are doing when they speak makes the story more interesting and helps the reader picture what is happening in the story.

Have a Try

Invite children to turn and talk about adding dialogue and narration in a purposeful way.

▶ Talk to children about an experience at school.

> Yesterday at recess Sammy and Yazid were playing catch with the football. If we were to write a book about that, what might Sammy and Yazid say? What action would you write between the dialogue? Turn and talk about what these friends might be saying and doing.

▶ After listening to pairs, ask a few volunteers to share. Use their ideas to add dialogue and action to the chart. Highlight the dialogue and action, as before.

Summarize and Apply

Summarize the lesson. Remind children to add dialogue and action in a purposeful way.

> How can you make the dialogue in your writing more interesting?

▶ Write the principle at the top of the chart.

> During writing time, try breaking up the dialogue with what is happening in the story or what the characters are doing. This helps the reader picture what is happening. Bring your writing to share when we meet later.

> **Include action with talking in your writing.**
>
> "Buenas tardes, Mango," Abuela says, opening his cage door when I get home from school.
>
> "Good afternoon," I say, and give him a seed. Soon Mango calls to me even before we open his cage.
>
> from <u>Mango, Abuela, and Me</u> by Meg Medina
>
> ---
>
> I shove aside the coats and boots. "I'm going to get you!" Quick as a rat, she scoots through my legs and runs around and around the living room, the dining room, the kitchen, yelling, "Am!! Am!! Help! Help!"
>
> from <u>Big Red Lollipop</u> by Rukhsana Khan
>
> ---
>
> At recess Sammy got ready to throw the football. "Go long!" she yelled to Yazid.
>
> Yazid ran across the field. "I got it!"

Confer

▶ During independent writing, move around the room to confer briefly with as many individual children as time allows. Sit side by side with them and invite them to talk about adding dialogue and action to their books. Use the following prompts as needed.

- *Talk about what is happening in this part of your story. What are the characters doing? What are they saying? How might you add that to your writing?*

- *You have people talking in your story. What might you add to show what is happening while the characters are talking?*

Share

Following independent writing, gather children in the meeting area to share their writing.

> Who added talking and action to your story today? Share what you wrote.

> How does this help the reader picture what is happening?

Assessment

After you have taught the minilessons in this umbrella, observe children as they write. Use *The Fountas & Pinnell Literacy Continuum* to notice, teach for, and support children's learning as you observe their attempts at reading and writing.

▶ What evidence do you have of children's new understandings related to dialogue?

- Do children understand that they can use speech and thought bubbles in their writing?

- Do they understand how to write dialogue in their stories?

- How do they use dialogue to make their writing more interesting?

- Do they include action before and/or after dialogue?

- Do they understand and use vocabulary related to writing dialogue, such as *speech bubble*, *thought bubble*, *talking*, *thinking*, *quotation marks*, *action*, *story*, *thoughts*, *feelings*, and *drama*?

▶ In what ways, beyond the scope of this umbrella, are children thinking about writing stories?

- When children incorporate dialogue, are they using punctuation and speaker tags? Do they use words other than *said*?

- Are they beginning to revise their writing to add what the characters think and say?

Use your observations to determine the next umbrella you will teach. You may also consult Suggested Sequence of Lessons (pp. 575–589) for guidance.

EXTENSIONS FOR ADDING DIALOGUE TO WRITING

▶ Notice dialogue in interactive read-aloud texts and children's writing, and continue to add to the chart in WML2. Add new examples of reasons authors use dialogue.

▶ Have children act out what is happening in their stories, including what the characters are saying. Ask them to think about what they were doing as they spoke and to add that to their dialogue.

▶ Have children engage in readers' theater and then write about the conversations as a way to incorporate dialogue in their stories.

▶ Talk about using speaker tags (e.g., *shouted*, *whispered*, *cried*, *laughed*) to show how a character says something.

Minilessons in This Umbrella

WML1 Start your writing with talking.

WML2 Start your writing with a feeling.

WML3 Start your writing by describing the setting.

WML4 Start your writing with a question.

WML5 Start your writing with an interesting fact.

WML6 Start your writing with a sound word.

Before Teaching Umbrella 5 Minilessons

Before teaching this umbrella, make sure children have had many opportunities to read, discuss, and write their own books in a variety of fiction and nonfiction genres. These lessons will help children talk about the decisions writers make about how to start their books and support children in deciding how to start their own books. The way an author begins a book is often called the lead.

Guide children to understand that some beginnings may be more suited for fiction and some for nonfiction. Use the books listed below from *Fountas & Pinnell Classroom™ Interactive Read-Aloud Collection* and *Shared Reading Collection*, or choose books from the classroom library.

Interactive Read-Aloud Collection

Caring for Each Other: Family

Pecan Pie Baby by Jacqueline Woodson

Big Red Lollipop by Rukhsana Khan

Tomie dePaola: Writing from Life

Bill and Pete Go Down the Nile

Strega Nona

Exploring the Natural World: Insects

When Lightning Comes in a Jar by Patricia Polacco

The Bugliest Bug by Carol Diggory Shields

Bugs for Lunch by Margery Facklam

Bugs A to Z by Caroline Lawton

Exploring Narrative Nonfiction Texts

Cactus Hotel by Brenda Z. Guiberson

Salmon Stream by Carol Reed-Jones

Think of an Eel by Karen Wallace

Shared Reading Collection

Night of the Ghost Crabs by Reese Brooks

Inside a Cow by Catherine Friend

As you read and enjoy these texts together, help children

• notice the ways authors try to get the reader's attention, and

• observe the way the stories begin.

Tomie dePaola

Insects

Bugs A to Z by Caroline Lawton

Narrative Nonfiction

Shared Reading

Section 3: Craft

WML1

CFT.U5.WML1

Start your writing with talking.

Exploring Different Ways Authors Start Books

You Will Need

- several books that begin with talking, such as the following:
  - *Pecan Pie Baby* by Jacqueline Woodson, from Text Set: Caring for Each Other: Family
  - *Bill and Pete Go Down the Nile* by Tomie dePaola, from Text Set: Tomie dePaola: Writing from Life
- chart paper prepared with a short piece of writing (see first chart on next page)
- chart paper and markers
- To download the following online resource for this lesson, visit **fp.pub/resources**:
  - chart art (optional)

Academic Language / Important Vocabulary

- book
- beginning
- talking

Continuum Connection

- Use a variety of beginnings to engage the reader

GOAL

Understand that writers can begin a book with someone talking.

RATIONALE

When children understand that writers make decisions about how to begin a book, they realize that they, too, can make writing choices by varying how they begin their own books. You might want to point out that, often, beginning a book with talking may be better suited to fiction books, though it might be used in some informational books.

ASSESS LEARNING

- Observe for evidence that children recognize that writers make decisions about how they begin a book.
- Look at children's writing. Do they sometimes start their books with dialogue?
- Look for evidence that children understand and use vocabulary such as *book*, *beginning*, and *talking*.

MINILESSON

To help children think about the minilesson principle, use familiar books and modeling to engage them in noticing that a writer may choose to begin a book with someone talking. Below is an example. To support this lesson, see CNV.U3.WML2 for a lesson on punctuating dialogue.

- Ahead of time, prepare a simple, short piece of writing (about four sentences) on chart paper. This text will be used throughout this umbrella as a starting point to support children's exploration of the different beginnings they might use as they write books.

- Show the cover and read the first page of *Pecan Pie Baby*.

  What do you notice about the way the writer, Jacqueline Woodson, decided to start this book?

- Guide the conversation to help children recognize that Gia and her mom are talking.

  Gia and her mom are talking about some of Gia's clothes that are too small for her.

- Repeat the activity using *Bill and Pete Go Down the Nile*.

  You can try starting your own writing with talking. You can begin an informational piece with talking, but mostly you will start stories with talking.

Have a Try

Invite children to turn and talk about starting a piece of writing with talking.

▶ Show the prepared short text and read it to the children.

> How could you begin this story with talking? Turn and talk to your partner about that.

▶ As needed, support the conversation to get it started. After time for discussion, ask a few volunteers to share. Record their suggestions on chart paper.

Summarize and Apply

Summarize the lesson. Encourage children to begin their writing with someone talking. Write the principle at the top of the chart.

> Today, you can begin a new piece of writing or continue one you are working on. Think about how to start your book. Could you start your writing with someone talking? Bring your writing to share when we meet later.

Confer

▶ During independent writing, move around the room to confer briefly with as many individual children as time allows. Sit side by side with them and invite them to talk about how to start their writing. Use the following prompts as needed.

- *How would you like to start your book?*
- *What is one way you could use talking to begin your story?*
- *What else could the characters say?*

Share

Following independent writing, gather children in the meeting area in groups of three to share the beginning of their writing.

> Share the beginning of your book. Talk about how you made your decision to start your book that way.

My sister and I went to the park to watch the ducks. We sat by the edge of a pond so we could see them swim. The ducklings were dunking and paddling behind their mother. We laughed as we watched their silly duck moves.

Start your writing with talking.

When we got to the park, my sister said, "Let's head over to the pond to see the ducks."

"I hope the ducks are at the park today," I said.
"Me too. The babies are always so funny," my sister said.

"I see the ducks over in the pond. Let's go!"

Exploring Different Ways Authors Start Books

You Will Need

- several books that begin with a feeling, such as the following:
  - *Big Red Lollipop* by Rukhsana Khan, from Text Set: Caring for Each Other: Family
  - *When Lightning Comes in a Jar* by Patricia Polacco, from Text Set: Exploring the Natural World: Insects
- the prepared short text used in WML1
- chart paper and markers

Academic Language / Important Vocabulary

- book
- beginning
- feeling

Continuum Connection

- Use a variety of beginnings to engage the reader

GOAL

Understand that writers can begin a book with a feeling.

RATIONALE

When children learn different ways to begin writing a book, they expand their thinking about the independent decisions they can make about their writing. You might want to point out that, often, beginning a book with a feeling may be better suited to fiction books.

ASSESS LEARNING

- Observe for evidence that children recognize that writers make choices about how they begin a book.
- Look at children's writing. Do they sometimes start their books with a feeling?
- Look for evidence that children can use vocabulary such as *book*, *beginning*, and *feeling*.

MINILESSON

To help children think about the minilesson principle, use familiar books and modeling to engage children in noticing that a writer may choose to begin a book with a feeling. Here is an example.

- Show the cover and read the first page of *Big Red Lollipop*.

  What do you notice about the way that the writer, Rukhsana Khan, decided to start this book?

- Guide the conversation to help children recognize that the book begins with the reader learning that a girl is excited about something as she runs home from school. Help them understand that being excited is a feeling.

  The story begins with the reader learning that the girl is so excited about something that she runs all the way home from school. Why might this be a good way to begin a story?

- Help them understand that the reader wants to keep reading to learn why this girl is so excited.

- Repeat the activity using *When Lightning Comes in Jar*.

  What do you notice about how the author, Patricia Polacco, decided to begin this book?

Have a Try

Invite children to turn and talk about using a feeling to begin a piece of writing.

▶ Show the prepared short text used in WML1 and read it to the children.

> How could you begin this story with a feeling? Turn and talk to your partner about that.

▶ As needed, support the conversation to get it started. After time for discussion, ask a few volunteers to share. Record their suggestions on chart paper.

▶ Support children in describing feelings as precisely as they can (i.e., choosing words beyond *happy*, *sad*, and *mad*).

Summarize and Apply

Summarize the lesson. Encourage children to start their writing with a feeling.

> Remember that there are different ways to start your writing.

▶ Write the principle at the top of the chart.

> Today, you can begin a new piece of writing or continue one you are working on. Think about whether you want to start your writing with a feeling. If you do, add it to your writing. Bring your writing to share when we meet later.

Confer

▶ During independent writing, move around the room to confer briefly with as many individual children as time allows. Sit side by side with them and invite them to talk about how they want to start their writing. Use the following prompts as needed.

- *How would you like your book to start?*
- *How are the characters feeling at the beginning of your book?*
- *What is a word that describes how they are feeling?*
- *What could the characters do to show how they are feeling?*

Share

Following independent writing, gather children in the meeting area. Ask a few volunteers to share the beginning of their writing.

> Who started a writing piece with a feeling? Share the beginning of your book.

My sister and I went to the park to watch the ducks. We sat by the edge of a pond so we could see them swim. The ducklings were dunking and paddling behind their mother. We laughed as we watched their silly duck moves.

Start your writing with a feeling.

I love the baby ducks! They are so much fun to watch.

My favorite time is when my sister and I go to the park to see the baby ducks.

I have been waiting so long to see the baby ducks at the park. Finally, the day has arrived.

Section 3: Craft

WML3

CFT.U5.WML3

Writing Minilesson Principle
Start your writing by describing the setting.

Exploring Different Ways Authors Start Books

You Will Need

▸ several books that begin with a description of the setting, such as the following:

- *Strega Nona* by Tomie dePaola, from Text Set: Tomie dePaola: Writing from Life

- *Cactus Hotel* by Brenda Z. Guiberson and *Salmon Stream* by Carol Reed-Jones, from Text Set: Exploring Narrative Nonfiction Texts

▸ the prepared short text used in the first two WMLs

▸ chart paper and markers

Academic Language / Important Vocabulary

▸ setting

▸ describe

▸ place

▸ weather

▸ time

Continuum Connection

▸ Use a variety of beginnings to engage the reader

GOAL

Understand that writers can begin a book with a description of the setting.

RATIONALE

When children learn that they can begin a book with a description of when and where something happened, they understand that they have many choices to make in their writing.

ASSESS LEARNING

▸ Observe for evidence that children recognize that writers make choices about how they begin a book.

▸ Look at children's writing. Do they sometimes choose to start a book by describing the setting?

▸ Look for evidence that children can use vocabulary such as *setting*, *describe*, *place*, *weather*, and *time*.

MINILESSON

To help children think about the minilesson principle, use familiar books and modeling to engage children in noticing that a writer may choose to begin a book with a description of place, weather, or time. Here is an example.

▸ Show the cover and read the first page of *Strega Nona*.

> What do you notice about the way that the writer, Tomie dePaola, decided to start this book?

▸ Guide the conversation to help children recognize that the book begins with a description of the time and place in which Strega Nona lived.

> The story begins with a description of the place from long ago and far away where Strega Nona lived. Is it a good beginning for this type of story? Why?

▸ Help children understand that this is a fictional fairy tale, so describing the time and place helps the reader identify the type of story they will be reading.

▸ Show the cover and read the first page of *Cactus Hotel*.

> What do you notice about how the writer, Carol Reed-Jones, decided to begin this book?

▸ Help children understand that in an informational book, the weather and place might be a good choice for beginning the book. Also point out that the author lets readers know that it is daytime, and talk about why this is useful.

▸ Show the cover and read the first two pages of *Salmon Stream*.

> How did the writer choose to begin this nonfiction book?

> Why do you think she described the stream in the forest?

Have a Try

Invite children to turn and talk about starting a book by describing where and when something happened.

▶ Show the prepared short text from the first two minilessons and read it to the children.

> How could you begin this story by describing where and when it happened? Turn and talk to your partner about that.

▶ As needed, support the conversation to get it started. After time for discussion, ask a few volunteers to share. Record their suggestions on chart paper.

▶ Support children to include ideas for beginnings that include place, weather, and time.

Summarize and Apply

Summarize the lesson. Encourage children to begin their writing piece by describing when or where something happened. Write the principle at the top of the chart.

> Today, you can begin a new piece of writing or continue one you are working on. Think about if you want to start your writing with a description of the place, weather, or time. Bring your writing to share when we meet later.

Confer

▶ During independent writing, move around the room to confer briefly with as many individual children as time allows. Sit side by side with them and invite them to talk about how to start their writing. Use the following prompts as needed.

- *How would you like to start your book?*
- *Where (when) does your story take place? How can you let your readers know that?*
- *How could you use the weather to begin your writing?*

Share

Following independent writing, gather children in the meeting area. Ask a few volunteers to share the beginning of their writing.

> Who started a book by describing the setting? Share the beginning of your book.

My sister and I went to the park to watch the ducks. We sat by the edge of a pond so we could see them swim. The ducklings were dunking and paddling behind their mother. We laughed as we watched their silly duck moves.

Start your writing by describing the setting.

We sat down on the green grass by the sandy edge of the pond.

Hooray! It was finally warm enough to wear shorts again. I looked around and saw that the trees were full of new leaves as the fuzzy, yellow baby ducks swam in the warm pond water.

When I was little, my sister used to take me to the park on Saturday mornings in the spring to watch the ducks.

Section 3: Craft

Writing Minilesson Principle
Start your writing with a question.

Exploring Different Ways Authors Start Books

You Will Need

- several books that begin with a question, such as the following from Text Set: Exploring the Natural World: Insects:
  - *The Bugliest Bug* by Carol Diggory Shields
  - *Bugs for Lunch* by Margery Facklam
- the prepared short text used in the previous minilessons
- chart paper and markers

Academic Language / Important Vocabulary

- book
- beginning
- question

Continuum Connection

- Use a variety of beginnings to engage the reader

GOAL

Understand that writers can begin a book with a question.

RATIONALE

When children learn that they can begin a book with a question, they think about what questions a reader might have and what a reader might like to read about. They learn that a question can catch the reader's attention.

ASSESS LEARNING

- ▸ Observe for evidence that children understand that writers make decisions about how they begin a book.
- ▸ Look at children's writing. Do they sometimes choose to begin a book with a question?
- ▸ Look for evidence that children can use vocabulary such as *book*, *beginning*, and *question*.

MINILESSON

To help children think about the minilesson principle, use familiar books and modeling to engage children in noticing that a writer may choose to begin a book with a question. Here is an example.

- ▸ Show the cover and read the first page of *The Bugliest Bug*.

  What do you notice about the way this writer decided to begin this book?

  Why do you think she made that choice?

- ▸ Guide the conversation to help children recognize that the author wrote questions. Help them notice that the questions make a rhyme and that they show that the reader might be learning about different bugs.

- ▸ Show the cover and read the first page of *Bugs for Lunch*.

  What do you notice about the way the author, Carol Diggory Shields, decided to begin this book?

  Why do you think she made that choice?

- ▸ Help them recognize that the question shows that the reader might learn about different animals that eat bugs. Guide children to realize that writers begin books with questions to get readers interested in reading more.

Have a Try

Invite children to turn and talk about starting a book with a question.

▶ Show the prepared short text used in the previous minilessons and read it to the children.

> How could you begin this story with a question? Turn and talk to your partner about that.

▶ As needed, support the conversation to get it started. After time for discussion, ask a few volunteers to share. Record their suggestions on chart paper.

▶ Encourage children to include questions that might be good for both fiction and nonfiction writing.

Summarize and Apply

Summarize the lesson. Encourage children to begin their writing piece by asking a question. Write the principle at the top of the chart.

> Today, you can begin a new piece of writing or continue one you are working on. Think about whether you want to start your book with a question. If so, add the question. Bring your writing to share when we meet later.

Confer

▶ During independent writing, move around the room to confer briefly with as many individual children as time allows. Sit side by side with them and invite them to talk about how to start their books. Use the following prompts as needed.

- *How would you like to start your book?*
- *What question might get the reader interested in reading your book?*
- *What question could this character ask?*
- *What question might the reader have?*

Share

Following independent writing, gather children in the meeting area. Ask a few volunteers to share the beginning of their writing.

> Who started a book with a question? Share the beginning of your book.

My sister and I went to the park to watch the ducks. We sat by the edge of a pond so we could see them swim. The ducklings were dunking and paddling behind their mother. We laughed as we watched their silly duck moves.

Start your writing with a question.

Have you ever noticed how ducks dunk their heads into the water when they swim?

What is your favorite thing to see at the park?

Why do baby ducklings swim so close to their mother?

WML5

CFT.U5.WML5

Writing Minilesson Principle
Start your writing with an interesting fact.

Exploring Different Ways Authors Start Books

You Will Need

- several books that begin with an interesting fact, such as the following:
  - *Think of an Eel* by Karen Wallace, from Text Set: Exploring Narrative Nonfiction Texts
  - *Bugs A to Z* by Caroline Lawton, from Text Set: Exploring the Natural World: Insects
  - *Night of the Ghost Crabs* by Reese Brooks, from *Shared Reading Collection*
- the prepared short text used in previous minilessons
- chart paper and markers

Academic Language / Important Vocabulary

- book
- beginning
- interesting
- fact

Continuum Connection

- Use a variety of beginnings to engage the reader

GOAL

Understand that writers can begin a book with an interesting fact.

RATIONALE

When children learn that they can begin a book with an interesting fact, they have another tool for starting their stories. Choosing the interesting fact prompts children to think about how best to engage their readers. It focuses attention on the audience.

ASSESS LEARNING

- ▶ Observe for evidence that children understand that writers make choices about how they begin a book.
- ▶ Look at children's writing. Do they sometimes decide to begin a book with an interesting fact?
- ▶ Look for evidence that children can use vocabulary such as *book*, *beginning*, *interesting*, and *fact*.

MINILESSON

To help children think about the minilesson principle, use familiar books and modeling to engage children in noticing that a writer may choose to begin a book with an interesting fact. Here is an example.

- ▶ Read the first pages of several books that begin with an interesting fact, such as page 1 of *Think of an Eel*, page 4 of *Bugs A to Z*, and page 2 of *Night of the Ghost Crabs*.

  Turn and talk about what you notice about the way these authors decided to begin these books.

- ▶ After time for discussion, ask volunteers to share their noticings. Support the conversation by helping children identify that each book begins with an interesting fact.

  These writers wrote an interesting fact to get the reader interested in learning more about eels, bugs, and ghost crabs.

  What kinds of books might begin with an interesting fact?

- ▶ Guide the conversation to talk about how interesting facts may be more helpful when beginning an informational book than a fiction book.

Have a Try

Invite children to turn and talk about starting a book with an interesting fact.

▶ Show the prepared short text used in the previous minilessons and read it to the children.

> How could you begin this writing with an interesting fact? Turn and talk to your partner about that.

▶ As needed, support the conversation to get it started. After time for discussion, ask a few volunteers to share. Record their suggestions on chart paper.

Summarize and Apply

Summarize the lesson. Encourage children to begin their writing piece with an interesting fact. Write the principle at the top of the chart.

> Today, you can begin a new piece of writing or continue one you are working on. Think about the ways you know to start your writing. You might want to start your book with an interesting fact. Bring your writing to share when we meet later.

Confer

▶ During independent writing, move around the room to confer briefly with as many individual children as time allows. Sit side by side with them and invite them to talk about how to begin their writing. Use the following prompts as needed.

- *How would you like to start your book?*
- *What is the most interesting fact you learned about your topic?*
- *What fact do you think will get your readers interested in reading about _____?*

Share

Following independent writing, gather children in the meeting area. Have them share in pairs before asking several children to share with the class.

> Turn to your partner and read the beginning of your book.

> What did you hear from your partner that you might try in your own writing?

My sister and I went to the park to watch the ducks. We sat by the edge of a pond so we could see them swim. The ducklings were dunking and paddling behind their mother. We laughed as we watched their silly duck moves.

Start your writing with an interesting fact.

Ducklings are born without feathers. Instead, they have a fuzzy covering all over their bodies.

Ducklings stay with their mother until they are about two months old.

Ducks dunk their head into the water to scoop up plants and insects.

Writing Minilesson Principle
Start your writing with a sound word.

Exploring Different Ways Authors Start Books

You Will Need

- a book that begins with a sound word, such as *Inside a Cow* by Catherine Friend, from *Shared Reading Collection*
- the prepared short text used in previous minilessons
- chart paper and markers

Academic Language / Important Vocabulary

- book
- beginning
- sound word

Continuum Connection

- Use a variety of beginnings to engage the reader

GOAL

Understand that writers can begin a book with a sound word.

RATIONALE

When children understand that they can begin a book with a sound word, they learn that a variety of beginnings can capture a reader's attention right from the start.

ASSESS LEARNING

- Observe for evidence that children understand that writers make choices about how they begin a book.
- Look at children's writing. Do they sometimes decide to begin a book with a sound word?
- Look for evidence that children can use vocabulary such as *book*, *beginning*, and *sound word*.

MINILESSON

To help children think about the minilesson principle, use a familiar book and modeling to engage children in noticing that a writer may choose to begin a book with a sound word. Here is an example.

- Show the cover and read the first page of *Inside a Cow*, emphasizing the sound words: "Crunch. Crunch. Crunch."

  What do you notice about the way this writer, Catherine Friend, decided to begin this book?

- Talk about how using sound words might get a reader's attention and make the reader want to turn the page.

  What are some examples of when sound words might be a good choice for beginning a book?

- Guide the conversation to help children talk about different examples for using sound words to begin a book. Help them realize that sound words might be good in nonfiction books (e.g., sounds animals make in a book about animals) and also in fiction books (e.g., sounds of horns honking to describe a setting as a busy city).

- Also point out that sound words can be a clever way to begin a book, but they should not be overused.

Have a Try

Invite children to turn and talk about starting a book with a sound word.

▶ Show the prepared short text used in the previous minilessons and read it to the children.

> How could you begin this writing with a sound word? Turn and talk to your partner about that.

▶ As needed, support the conversation to get it started. After time for discussion, ask a few volunteers to share. Record their suggestions on chart paper.

Summarize and Apply

Summarize the lesson. Encourage children to begin their writing piece with a sound word. Write the principle at the top of the chart.

> Today, you can begin a new piece of writing or continue one you are working on. Think about the ways you know to start a book. You might want to start your book with a sound word. Bring your writing to share when we meet later.

Confer

▶ During independent writing, move around the room to confer briefly with as many individual children as time allows. Sit side by side with them and invite them to talk about how to begin their writing. Use the following prompts as needed.

- *How would you like to start your book?*
- *Is there a sound word that might be good to use at the beginning?*
- *What sounds could your character be hearing?*
- *What sounds might go with the facts you will be writing about?*

Share

Following independent writing, gather children in pairs in the meeting area. Then ask a few volunteers to share the beginning of their writing.

> How did you start your book? Read the beginning aloud.

My sister and I went to the park to watch the ducks. We sat by the edge of a pond so we could see them swim. The ducklings were dunking and paddling behind their mother. We laughed as we watched their silly duck moves.

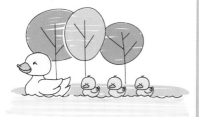

Start your writing with a sound word.

Quack, quack!

"Wheeeee!" My sister and I both screamed as we ran to the pond.

Splash! I could hear the baby ducks dunking and swimming before I even saw them.

Section 3: Craft

Assessment

After you have taught the minilessons in this umbrella, observe children in a variety of classroom activities. Use *The Fountas & Pinnell Literacy Continuum* to notice, teach for, and support children's learning as you observe their attempts at writing.

▶ What evidence do you have of new understandings children have developed related to writing the beginning of their books?

- Do they understand that writers make decisions about how to begin a book?

- Are they using a variety of ways to start their books?

- Are they using vocabulary such as *book*, *beginning*, *talking*, *feeling*, *describe*, *time*, *place*, *weather*, *question*, *interesting*, *fact*, and *sound word*?

▶ In what ways, beyond the scope of this umbrella, are children showing an interest in making books?

- Do they need help punctuating dialogue?

- Are they thinking about the ways writers choose to end books?

Use your observations to determine the next umbrella you will teach. You may also consult Suggested Sequence of Lessons (pp. 575–589) for guidance.

EXTENSIONS FOR EXPLORING DIFFERENT WAYS AUTHORS START BOOKS

▶ As you read aloud, help children notice the ways writers choose to begin books. Ask children to share their opinions about which ways they think work well and why.

▶ Have children revise the beginning of a piece of shared writing that the class created together.

▶ Pull together a small group of children who would benefit from guided instruction on starting their books in different ways.

▶ If you are using *The Reading Minilessons Book, Grade 2* [Fountas and Pinnell 2019] you may choose to teach RML3 on sound words in LA.U9: Analyzing the Writer's Craft.

Minilessons in This Umbrella

WML1 End your book with a feeling.

WML2 End your book with talking.

WML3 End your book with a call to action.

WML4 End your book by telling what you learned or how you changed.

Before Teaching Umbrella 6 Minilessons

Often, children give their attention to the middle of a book without a thought to how it might begin or end. By guiding them to give attention not only to the middle of a story but also to the beginning and ending, you show that all parts of their own books can benefit from strong writing.

Guide children to understand that not every type of ending introduced in this umbrella will fit what they are working on. For the minilessons, examples are provided using children's writing and shared writing samples, although you can also use an example you write yourself. Use the books listed below from *Fountas & Pinnell Classroom™ Interactive Read-Aloud Collection*, or choose books that have strong beginnings and endings from the classroom library.

Interactive Read-Aloud Collection

The Pleasure of Giving

Sam and the Lucky Money by Karen Chinn

The Birthday Swap by Loretta Lopez

Caring for Each Other: Family

The Wednesday Surprise by Eve Bunting

Two Mrs. Gibsons by Toyomi Igus

Pecan Pie Baby by Jacqueline Woodson

Finding Beauty in the World Around You

Something Beautiful by Sharon Dennis Wyeth

Last Stop on Market Street by Matt de la Peña

Exploring the Natural World: Insects

The Bugliest Bug by Carol Diggory Shields

The Importance of Friendship

First Come the Zebra by Lynne Barasch

This Is Our House by Michael Rosen

Exploring Narrative Nonfiction Texts

Salmon Stream by Carol Reed-Jones

Seymour Simon: A Scientific Eye

Dolphins

As you read and enjoy these texts together, help children

- notice different ways authors begin and end their books, and
- observe which types of endings go best with which types of books.

Interactive Read-Aloud
The Pleasure of Giving

Family

Finding Beauty

Insects

Friendship

Narrative Nonfiction

Seymour Simon

Section 3: Craft

Exploring Different Ways Authors End Books

You Will Need

- several books that end with a feeling, such as the following:

  - *Sam and the Lucky Money* by Karen Chinn and *The Birthday Swap* by Loretta Lopez, from Text Set: The Pleasure of Giving

  - *The Wednesday Surprise* by Eve Bunting, from Text Set: Caring for Each Other: Family

- a prepared short piece of writing (projected or written on chart paper)

- document camera (optional)

- chart paper and markers

Academic Language / Important Vocabulary

- book
- ending
- choice
- feeling

Continuum Connection

- Use a variety of endings to engage and satisfy the reader

GOAL

Understand that writers can end their books with a feeling.

RATIONALE

When children understand that writers make decisions about how to end a book, they realize that they, too, can make writing choices by varying how they end their own books.

ASSESS LEARNING

- Look for evidence that children recognize that writers make decisions about how they end their books.
- Observe whether they sometimes choose to end a book with a feeling.
- Look for evidence that children can use vocabulary such as *book, ending, choice,* and *feeling.*

MINILESSON

To help children think about the minilesson principle, use familiar books and modeling to engage them in noticing that a writer may choose to end a book with a feeling. Here is an example.

- Ahead of time, select a writing sample that can be projected or written on chart paper. The example shown uses a child's piece of writing, but you might use shared or teacher writing. This writing sample will also be used for WML2.

- Show the cover and read the last page of text in *Sam and the Lucky Money*.

  What do you notice about the way the writer, Karen Chinn, ended this book?

- Guide the conversation to help children recognize and name the type of ending chosen by the author.

  At the end of the story, Sam feels he is lucky and feels really good about what he decided to do with his money. What name could you give to this type of an ending?

  The writer decided to end this story with a feeling.

- Repeat the activity using *The Birthday Swap* and *The Wednesday Surprise*.

  What do you notice about how the authors decided to end these books?

  What type of stories might be good to end with a feeling?

- As needed, guide the conversation to help children discuss the types of stories that might be good choices to sometimes end with a feeling (e.g., realistic fiction, memory stories).

Have a Try

Invite children to turn and talk about using a feeling to end a piece of writing.

▶ Show the prepared writing sample and read it to the children.

> What is another way you could end this story with a feeling? Turn and talk to your partner about that.

▶ As needed, support the conversation to get it started. You might have children discuss and name the way the sample piece of writing ends (e.g., feeling happy).

▶ After time for discussion, ask volunteers to share. Record suggestions on chart paper.

Summarize and Apply

Summarize the lesson. Encourage children to end their book with a feeling. Write the principle at the top of the chart.

> Today, you can begin a new piece of writing or continue one you are working on. Think about whether you want to end your writing with a feeling. If you are making a book that would not be good for ending with a feeling, it is okay to choose a different type of ending. Remember, you are the writer, so you can decide what type of ending is best.

Confer

▶ During independent writing, move around the room to confer briefly with as many individual children as time allows. Sit side by side with them and invite them to talk about how they might end their books. Use the following prompts as needed.

- *How would you like to end your book?*
- *What is one way you could use a feeling to end your writing piece?*
- *How are the characters feeling at the end of your book?*
- *What is a word that describes how they are feeling?*

Share

Following independent writing, gather children in the meeting area. Ask a few volunteers to share their books.

> Did anyone end your book with a feeling? Share the ending of your book.

> Is anyone thinking of writing an ending that shows a feeling? Tell about that.

I love birthday parties!
Here's a story about mine. First we went into a makup and cloths store I was turning 8. First I went into a dressing room to change into something they had. Then we had sanwitces and a cake for dinner. After that I opend my presents. My favorite was from my baby-sitter. It was clay that you could desighn and put beuds on it and it would harden. Finally the party was over and I went home. That was such a great party. I hop I can come back

---

End your book with a feeling.

I was so happy just thinking about my best birthday party ever.

I loved it so much that I can hardly wait to begin planning next year's birthday party!

After that busy day, I fell asleep as soon as I got into bed with a huge smile on my face.

WML2

CFT.U6.WML2

Writing Minilesson Principle
End your book with talking.

Exploring Different Ways Authors End Books

You Will Need

- several books that end with talking, such as the following:
  - *Something Beautiful* by Sharon Dennis Wyeth and *Last Stop on Market Street* by Matt de la Peña, from Text Set: Finding Beauty in the World Around You
  - *The Bugliest Bug* by Carol Diggory Shields, from Text Set: Exploring the Natural World: Insects
- the writing sample used in WML1
- document camera (optional)
- chart paper and markers

Academic Language / Important Vocabulary

- book
- ending
- choice
- talking

Continuum Connection

- Use a variety of endings to engage and satisfy the reader

GOAL

Understand that writers can end their books with talking.

RATIONALE

When children understand that writers make decisions about how to end a book, they realize that they, too, can make writing choices by varying how they end their own books.

ASSESS LEARNING

- Look for evidence that children recognize that writers make decisions about how they end their books.
- Observe whether children sometimes choose to end a book with talking.
- Look for evidence that children can use vocabulary such as *book*, *ending*, *choice*, and *talking*.

MINILESSON

To help children think about the minilesson principle, use familiar books and modeling to engage them in noticing that a writer may choose to end a book with talking. Here is an example.

- Show the cover and read the ending of *Something Beautiful*.

  What do you notice about the way the writer ended this book?

- Guide the conversation to help children recognize and name the type of ending chosen by the author.

  At the end of the story, the girl and her mom are having a conversation. One way to end a story is with the characters talking, like Sharon Dennis Wyeth did in *Something Beautiful*.

- Repeat the activity using *Last Stop on Market Street* and *The Bugliest Bug*.

  What do you notice about how the authors decided to end these books?

  What type of stories might be good to end with talking?

- As needed, guide the conversation to help children discuss the types of stories that might be good choices to sometimes end with talking (e.g., realistic fiction, memory stories, fantasy).

Have a Try

Invite children to turn and talk about using talking to end a piece of writing.

▶ Show the prepared writing sample from WML1 and read it to the children.

> How could you end this story with talking? Turn and talk to your partner about that.

▶ As needed, support the conversation to get it started. After time for discussion, ask a few volunteers to share. Record their suggestions on chart paper.

Summarize and Apply

Summarize the lesson. Encourage children to end their writing piece with someone talking.

> What is one way to end your book?

▶ Write the principle at the top of the chart.

> Today, you can begin a new piece of writing or continue one you are working on. Think about whether you want to end your writing with someone talking. Bring your writing to share when we meet later.

Confer

▶ During independent writing, move around the room to confer briefly with as many individual children as time allows. Sit side by side with them and invite them to talk about how they might end their books. Use the following prompts as needed.

- *How would you like to end your book?*
- *What is one way you could use talking to end your writing?*
- *What else could the characters say?*

Share

Following independent writing, gather children in the meeting area. Ask a few volunteers to share the ending of their writing.

> Who ended a writing piece with someone talking? Share the ending of your book.

> Is anyone thinking of ending a book with talking? Tell about that.

I love birthday parties!
Here's a story about mine. First we went into a makup and cloths store I was turning 8. First I went into a dressing room to change into something they had. Then we had sanwitces and a cake for dinner. After that I opend my presents. My favorite was from my baby-sitter. It was clay that you could desighn and put beuds on it and it would harden. Finally the party was over and I went home. That was such a great party. I hop I can come back.

End your book with talking.

I told my cat, Nala, all about the party. "It was the best party ever, but I just wish you could've been there to see it."

The last thing I said before bed was, "Mom, when can we start planning next year's birthday?"

"Thank you, Dad, for giving me my best birthday party," I said. Dad said, "You're welcome. I'm glad you had fun."

WML3
CFT.U6.WML3

Writing Minilesson Principle
End your book with a call to action.

Exploring Different Ways Authors End Books

You Will Need

- several fiction and nonfiction books that end with a call to action, such as the following:
  - *First Come the Zebra* by Lynne Barasch, from Text Set: The Importance of Friendship
  - *Dolphins* by Seymour Simon, from Text Set: Seymour Simon: A Scientific Eye
  - *Salmon Stream* by Carol Reed-Jones, from Text Set: Exploring Narrative Nonfiction Texts
- a prepared short piece of writing (projected or written on chart paper) by you or by a child
- document camera (optional)
- chart paper and markers

Academic Language / Important Vocabulary

- book
- ending
- choice
- call to action
- hope
- wish

Continuum Connection

- Use a variety of endings to engage and satisfy the reader

GOAL

Understand that writers can end their books with a call to action.

RATIONALE

When children understand that writers make decisions about how to end a book, they realize that they, too, can make writing choices by varying how they end their own books.

ASSESS LEARNING

- Observe whether children sometimes choose to end a book with a call to action.
- Look for evidence that children can use vocabulary such as *book*, *ending*, *choice*, *call to action*, *hope*, and *wish*.

MINILESSON

To help children think about the minilesson principle, use familiar books and modeling to engage them in noticing that a writer may choose to end a book with a call to action. Here is an example.

- Show the cover and read the last few pages of *First Come the Zebra*.

  What do you notice about the way the writer, Lynne Barasch, ended this book?

  Abaani and Haki know that sharing with each other brings peace, and they hope the others will begin to share like they did. Notice the words the writer used on the last page.

- Reread the last sentence, emphasizing "the boys hope," and then define *call to action*.

  The words *hope* and *peaceful* show that the boys want something good for the future. It is a call to action to do something that will make the world a better place.

- Show and read the last page in *Dolphins*.

  What do you notice about how Seymour Simon ended this book?

- Guide the conversation to help children recognize that the ending is a call to action and that the writer listed specific things people can do to help dolphins.

- Repeat with "How You Can Help" at the end of *Salmon Stream*.

- Discuss which types of books might end with a call to action (e.g., informational or all-about books, realistic fiction).

Have a Try

Invite children to turn and talk about using a call to action to end a piece of writing.

▶ Show the prepared writing sample and read it to the children.

How could you end this story with a call to action? Turn and talk to your partner about that.

▶ As needed, support the conversation to get it started.

▶ After time for discussion, ask volunteers to share. Record suggestions on chart paper. Save the writing sample for WML4.

Summarize and Apply

Summarize the lesson. Encourage children to end their writing with a call to action. Write the principle at the top of the chart.

Today, you can begin a new piece of writing or continue one you are working on. Think about whether you want to use a call to action for an ending. Bring your writing to share when we meet later.

Confer

▶ During independent writing, move around the room to confer briefly with as many individual children as time allows. Sit side by side with them and invite them to talk about how they might end their writing. Use the following prompts as needed.

• *How would you like to end your book?*

• *What is one way you could use a call to action to end your writing piece?*

• *Let's talk about whether ending with a call to action would work well with the type of writing you are doing.*

Share

Following independent writing, gather children in groups of three in the meeting area. Then ask a few volunteers to share the ending of their writing.

Share the end of your book with your group.

Did you hear an idea that you could use in your own writing? What is it?

WHOOOO! WHOOO!

We heard the sounds coming from over the hill as we approached the spot for our visit with an expert. Suddenly, we saw a huge owl sitting on the arm of our guide, Tandy Yeow. Tandy is a real-life bird of prey rehabilitator. She rescues and cares for injured birds and then releases them back into the wild. We saw a great horned owl, a bald eagle, and a merlin. At the end, we met Bobo, a peregrine falcon that Tandy found when it was sick and hungry. Tandy nursed it back to health. Soon Bobo will return to the wild!

End your book with a call to action.

It is important to help protect endangered and threatened species any chance you get.

You can help birds of prey by learning more about them. Go to a wildlife park or any open area and watch and learn.

See if there is a rehabilitation center near you. If so, you can visit and volunteer with your family.

Section 3: Craft

Writing Minilesson Principle

End your book by telling what you learned or how you changed.

You Will Need

- several books that end with a lesson learned or with a character changing, such as the following:

  - *Two Mrs. Gibsons* by Toyomi Igus and *Pecan Pie Baby* by Jacqueline Woodson, from Text Set: Caring for Each Other: Family

  - *This Is Our House* by Michael Rosen, from Text Set: The Importance of Friendship

- the writing sample used in WML3

- chart paper and markers

Academic Language / Important Vocabulary

- book
- ending
- choice
- lesson
- change

Continuum Connection

- Use a variety of endings to engage and satisfy the reader

GOAL

Understand that writers can end their books by telling what they learned or how they changed.

RATIONALE

When children understand that writers make decisions about how to end a book, they realize that they, too, can make writing choices by varying how they end their own books.

ASSESS LEARNING

- Observe for evidence that children recognize how writers choose to end their books.

- Look for evidence that children choose to end a book with something they learned or how they changed.

- Look for evidence that children can use vocabulary such as *book*, *ending*, *choice*, *lesson*, and *change*.

MINILESSON

To help children think about the minilesson principle, use familiar books and modeling to engage them in noticing that a writer may choose to end a book by showing a lesson learned or a change. Here is an example.

- Show the cover and read the ending of *Two Mrs. Gibsons*.

  What do you notice about the way the writer, Toyomi Igus, ended this book?

- Guide the conversation to help children recognize that the ending shows how the girl, who is the author, learned a lesson about families when she was young. Help them name this type of ending.

  The writer learned that all families are unique and that even though people are different from each other, they can still have things in common. Sometimes, a story ends with something the writer learned or a way that the writer changed.

- Repeat the activity using *Pecan Pie Baby* and *This Is Our House*.

  What do you notice about how the authors decided to end these books?

- Prompt the conversation as needed, continuing to name the type of ending. Help children recognize that this type of ending could be used in both fiction and nonfiction books (e.g., biographies).

- As needed, talk about how writers show lessons they learned or ways they changed. Point out that in fiction stories it might be a character that learns something or changes.

Have a Try

Invite children to turn and talk about ending a book with something they learned or with a way they changed.

▶ Show the prepared writing sample from WML3 and read it to the children.

> Think of another way you could end this writing piece. You could tell something you learned. Turn and talk about that.

▶ As needed, support the conversation to get it started. Then provide discussion time. Ask several volunteers to make suggestions. Record on chart paper.

Summarize and Apply

Summarize the learning. Invite children to end their books with something they learned. Write the principle at the top of the chart.

> Today, you can begin a new book or continue one you have already started. Think about whether you would like to end your book by telling what you learned or how you changed. If you are writing a story, you might want to tell what a character learned or how a character changed. If so, add that to your book. Bring your writing to share when we meet later.

Confer

▶ During independent writing, move around the room to confer briefly with as many individual children as time allows. Sit side by side with them and invite them to talk about how they might end their writing. Use the following prompts as needed.

- *How would you like to end your book?*
- *What did you learn from the experience you wrote about?*
- *What do you want your reader to learn?*
- *What lesson do the people in your book learn (or how do they change)?*

Share

Following independent writing, gather children in the meeting area. Ask several children to share the books they are working on.

> Who ended a book with something you learned? Share how you ended your book.

WHOOOO! WHOOO!

We heard the sounds coming from over the hill as we approached the spot for our visit with an expert. Suddenly, we saw a huge owl sitting on the arm of our guide, Tandy Yeow. Tandy is a real-life bird of prey rehabilitator. She rescues and cares for injured birds and then releases them back into the wild. We saw a great horned owl, a bald eagle, and a merlin. At the end, we met Bobo, a peregrine falcon that Tandy found when it was sick and hungry. Tandy nursed it back to health. Soon Bobo will return to the wild!

End your book by telling what you learned or how you changed.

We learned that all birds of prey have hooked beaks, a strong, powerful grip, sharp eyesight, and wide, powerful wings.

We were amazed to learn that birds of prey live in all parts of the world.

Our favorite bird of prey was the peregrine falcon because it is the fastest!

Instead of thinking of birds of prey as scary, we now know that they are special and it is important to take care of them and their environment.

It was surprising to learn that many birds of prey are endangered or threatened.

We learned that meat-eating birds of prey are called raptors.

Assessment

After you have taught the minilessons in this umbrella, observe children in a variety of classroom activities. Use *The Fountas & Pinnell Literacy Continuum* to notice, teach for, and support children's learning as you observe their attempts at writing.

▶ What evidence do you have of children's new understandings related to writing the ending of a book?

- Do children understand that writers make decisions about how to end a book?

- Are they choosing to end books in a variety of ways (e.g., with a feeling, with talking, with a wish or call to action, with a lesson learned)?

- Are they using vocabulary such as *book*, *ending*, *choice*, *feeling*, *talking*, *call to action*, *hope*, *wish*, *lesson*, and *change*?

▶ In what ways, beyond the scope of this umbrella, are children showing an interest in making books?

- Do they show an interest in making both fiction and nonfiction books?

- Are they thinking about the ways writers choose to begin books?

Use your observations to determine the next umbrella you will teach. You may also consult Suggested Sequence of Lessons (pp. 575–589) for guidance.

EXTENSIONS FOR EXPLORING DIFFERENT WAYS AUTHORS END BOOKS

▶ You may want to repeat a lesson by introducing other ways to end a book (e.g., with a question; with additional facts; with a surprise ending; with a circular ending). Consider using the online resource Planning a Writing Minilesson to guide your planning.

▶ As you read aloud, help children notice the ways writers choose to end books and why they may have made those decisions. Talk about which endings are most satisfying and why.

▶ As children begin to include dialogue in their writing, teach them appropriate punctuation (see CNV.U3: Learning About Punctuation).

▶ Gather baskets of books and have children work in pairs to think about and name the way the authors ended the books. Encourage them to talk about what they liked or what they found to be effective.

Minilessons in This Umbrella

WML1 Use words to show not tell.

WML2 Choose interesting words to describe the way characters say something.

WML3 Choose interesting words to describe actions.

WML4 Compare one thing to another to make your writing powerful.

WML5 Use words from other languages you know.

Before Teaching Umbrella 7 Minilessons

The goal of these minilessons is to make children aware of the words authors use and to think about word choice in their own writing. If you have children in your class who speak other languages, WML5 supports them by valuing their languages. This minilesson may or may not be beneficial for your class, so decide whether it should be taught.

Use the books listed below from *Fountas & Pinnell Classroom™ Interactive Read-Aloud Collection*, or choose books from the classroom library that have strong and varied word choice.

Interactive Read-Aloud Collection

Jan Brett: Creating Imaginary Worlds

Town Mouse, Country Mouse

The Pleasure of Giving

Sam and the Lucky Money by Karen Chinn

Seymour Simon: A Scientific Eye

Dogs

Exploring Narrative Nonfiction Texts

A Log's Life by Wendy Pfeffer

Think of an Eel by Karen Wallace

Exploring Different Cultures: Folktales

Nine-in-One, Grr! Grr! by Blia Xiong

Exploring the Natural World: Insects

The Bugliest Bug by Carol Diggory Shields

Finding Your Way in a New Place

Grandfather Counts by Andrea Cheng

The Have a Good Day Cafe by Frances Park and Ginger Park

The Importance of Friendship

First Come the Zebra by Lynne Barasch

As you read and enjoy these texts together, help children become aware of the authors' choice of words.

Interactive Read-Aloud

Jan Brett

Pleasure of Giving

Seymour Simon

Narrative Nonfiction

Folktales

Insects

Finding Your Way

Friendship

Making Powerful Word Choices

You Will Need

- fiction and nonfiction mentor texts with examples of language that shows instead of tells, such as the following:
  - *Town Mouse, Country Mouse* by Jan Brett, from Text Set: Jan Brett: Creating Imaginary Worlds
  - *Sam and the Lucky Money* by Karen Chinn, from Text Set: The Pleasure of Giving
  - *Dogs* by Seymour Simon, from Text Set: Seymour Simon: A Scientific Eye
- chart paper and markers
- document camera (optional)
- To download the following online resource for this lesson, visit **fp.pub/resources**:
  - chart art (optional)

Academic Language / Important Vocabulary

- writing
- word choice
- powerful
- descriptive
- show
- tell

Continuum Connection

- Show through language instead of telling
- Learn ways of using language and constructing texts from other writers (reading books and hearing them read aloud) and apply understandings to one's own writing

GOAL

Show through language instead of telling.

RATIONALE

When children understand that writers use language to show instead of tell what or how something is, they begin to think about finding alternative ways to say things to help readers make pictures in their minds.

ASSESS LEARNING

- Observe for evidence that children understand the concept of using language to show instead of tell.
- Observe children's writing behaviors for evidence that children are trying out varied and interesting words in order to show not tell.
- Look for evidence that children can use vocabulary such as *writing*, *word choice*, *powerful*, *descriptive*, *show*, and *tell*.

MINILESSON

To help children think about the minilesson principle, use mentor text examples to demonstrate what it means to use language to show instead of tell. Here is an example.

> Make a picture in your mind of what is happening in the story as I read aloud to you.

▶ Read page 6 in *Town Mouse, Country Mouse*.

> Who are you picturing saying "Sauces and ham"?
>
> How do you know it's a cat? The words do not say, "A cat said, 'Sauces and ham.'"

▶ Support the conversation to help children notice that the writer used an interesting way to let the reader know a cat was threatening the mice.

> Jan Brett used the words "purring loudly" to let you know that a cat was nearby. She used words showing you what the cat was doing instead of telling you that a cat was there.

▶ Repeat with several more examples, stopping to help children notice and talk about the specific words the writers used to show rather than tell. Some examples are below.

- Sam and the Lucky Money, *page 4 (e.g., "Sam had to look out for elbows and shopping bags" shows that Sam was small in a crowded place).*
- Dogs, *page 19 (e.g., "Some terriers even won medals for their service in the British army" shows that terriers are loyal).*

Have a Try

Invite children to turn and talk about how writers can choose powerful words.

▶ Write and read a simple first-person statement with language that declares a feeling.

> This statement tells how I was feeling. Turn and talk about some ways you could use words to show instead of tell how I was feeling.

▶ As needed, prompt the conversations by asking children how things might look, sound, and feel and by providing a few scenarios in which you might be having that feeling.

▶ After time for discussion, ask volunteers for ideas. Using their suggestions, write examples on the chart of language that shows instead of tells.

Summarize and Apply

Summarize the learning. Remind children to use language to show instead of tell, especially when they write stories. Write the principle at the top of the chart.

> Today we talked about how sometimes writers don't tell you exactly what they mean or how a character feels. Instead, they show you by writing about actions or feelings. During writing time, try writing to show instead of tell.

Use words to show not tell.

I felt scared.

I could feel the hairs on my neck stand up. I dared not open my eyes.

The sound started as a low roar, but it got louder and louder as it came closer and closer.

Around every corner, it seemed like a new terror jumped out and grabbed me.

"Boo!"
It was the last thing I heard as I dropped my candy and ran.

Confer

▶ During independent writing, move around the room to confer briefly with as many individual children as time allows. Sit side by side with them and invite them to talk about word choice. Use the following prompts as needed.

- *What is another way you could say this that shows instead of tells?*
- *What do you want your readers to picture when they read this part?*
- *Let's talk about some words that describe what you want your readers to see.*

Share

Following independent writing, gather children in the meeting area. Ask a few volunteers to share their writing.

> Did anyone try writing to show instead of tell? How did it go?

Writing Minilesson Principle
Choose interesting words to describe the way characters say something.

Making Powerful Word Choices

You Will Need

- a mentor text with variations of *said*, such as *Nine-in-One, Grr! Grr!* by Blia Xiong, from Text Set: Exploring Different Cultures: Folktales
- chart paper and markers
- sticky notes

Academic Language / Important Vocabulary

- writing
- word choice
- interesting
- said

Continuum Connection

- Show ability to vary the text by choosing alternative words (e.g., alternatives for *said*) when appropriate

GOAL

Understand why writers use words other than *said*.

RATIONALE

When children recognize that writers make their writing more specific and interesting by using words for *said* to describe how a character sounds, they learn that they can do the same thing when they write.

ASSESS LEARNING

- Observe for evidence that children understand why writers use words other than *said*.
- Look at children's writing. Do they use words other than *said* when writing dialogue?
- Look for evidence that children can use vocabulary such as *writing*, *word choice*, *interesting*, and *said*.

MINILESSON

To help children think about the minilesson principle, engage them in noticing that writers use different words for *said*. Here is an example.

- Show and read page 10 in *Nine-in-One, Grr! Grr!*

  In a book, when a character talks, many times you will see the word *said*. What do you notice about this page?

- Guide the conversation to help children notice that the words *replied* and *purred* are used instead of *said*. Use sticky notes to begin a list on chart paper of words that can be used instead of *said* and add these notes to the chart.

  When a writer chooses a more descriptive or interesting word, it helps the reader know just how the words should be read and makes the writing more interesting and descriptive.

  As I continue reading, raise your hand if you hear a word the writer used instead of *said*.

- Starting on page 18, read and pause to add words to the list as children identify them.

- Write a simple sentence on the chart that uses *said*. Leave room for a sticky note to be placed over the word *said*.

  Think about a sentence and how it might sound different if a writer chose a word other than *said*.

- Place one of the sticky notes you made over *said*. Guide the conversation to have children notice how the new word changes the sentence. Repeat with two or three more words.

Have a Try

Invite children to turn and talk about words that can replace *said*.

▶ Write another simple sentence with *said* on the chart.

Turn and talk about a word that could be used instead of *said*. You can choose a word from the chart or a new word of your own. Think about how the word changes the meaning or how you read the sentence in a different way.

▶ After discussion, ask a few volunteers to share. Add new words to the chart.

Summarize and Apply

Summarize the learning. Remind children to notice and use synonyms for *said*.

When you read and you notice a word that can be used instead of *said*, write it on a sticky note and add it to the chart.

▶ Write the principle at the top of the chart.

During writing time, look at your writing to see if you can use a word other than *said* to describe how a character says something. Bring your writing when we meet later.

Choose interesting words to describe the way characters say something.

replied	answered
purred	chirped
asked	wondered
squawked	whispered
sighed	grumbled
repeated	mumbled
cried	muttered

"Do you like this pizza?" she said.
wondered
asked
repeated

They said, "We are going on a field trip!"
cried
shouted
exclaimed

Confer

▶ During independent writing, move around the room to confer briefly with as many individual children as time allows. Sit side by side with them and invite them to talk about words they could use to show how their characters talk. Use the following prompts as needed.

- *Is there a different word to describe how the character says this?*
- *He is talking in a sad voice. What word can you use to show that?*
- *What kind of voice is she using?*

Share

Following independent writing, gather children in the meeting area to share their writing.

What word did you use instead of *said* in your writing? Share what you wrote.

Who can tell about a sticky note you added to the chart?

Writing Minilesson Principle
Choose interesting words to describe actions.

Making Powerful Word Choices

You Will Need

- mentor texts with examples of interesting verbs, such as the following:
  - *The Bugliest Bug* by Carol Diggory Shields, from Text Set: Exploring the Natural World: Insects
  - *A Log's Life* by Wendy Pfeffer, from Text Set: Exploring Narrative Nonfiction Texts
- chart paper and markers
- sticky notes

Academic Language / Important Vocabulary

- writing
- word choice
- action
- interesting
- descriptive

Continuum Connection

- Vary word choice to create interesting description and dialogue

---

GOAL

Understand that writers use specific verbs to make their writing more descriptive and interesting.

RATIONALE

When children recognize that writers make their writing more interesting and descriptive by using specific verbs to describe how someone is acting or what they are doing, they learn that they can do the same when they write.

ASSESS LEARNING

- Observe for evidence that children understand why writers use specific verbs.
- Look at children's writing. Do they use specific verbs to describe the action?
- Look for evidence that children can use vocabulary such as *writing*, *word choice*, *action*, *interesting*, and *descriptive*.

MINILESSON

To help children think about the minilesson principle, engage them in noticing that writers use different words to show actions. Here is an example.

> Think about the words the writer chose as I read aloud to you.

▶ Show and read the first paragraph on page 3 in *The Bugliest Bug*.

> What do you notice about the words the writer chose to show an action?

▶ Define and discuss the term *action*, as well as the meanings of the various action words that children identify. As children share ideas, use sticky notes to begin a list on chart paper of interesting action words.

▶ Continue using sticky notes to add words that children notice as you show and read pages 5 and 11. Engage them in a conversation about the specific definitions of some words to help them understand the importance of word choice. An example is below.

> Think about the difference between *billowed* and *swayed*. *Billowed* means to fill with air, get larger, and move outward. *Swayed* means to move back and forth. Why do you think the writer decided to write that "The curtain billowed and swayed" instead of just "The curtain moved"? How does it change the meaning?

▶ Support children's thinking by helping them understand that using descriptive action words helps the reader picture exactly what type of movement is going on and makes the writing more interesting.

▶ Repeat with pages 14 and 17 in *A Log's Life*.

Have a Try

Invite children to turn and talk about using interesting action words.

▸ Write two simple sentences on chart paper that use common action words, such as *went* and *get*. Read the sentences.

> Turn and talk about how you could choose an action word to replace the words *went* and *get* to make a more interesting and descriptive sentence.

▸ After time for discussion, have volunteers come up and replace *went* or *get* with a different word by covering up the word with a sticky note. If children suggest words not on the chart, add them.

Summarize and Apply

Summarize the learning. Remind children to notice and use interesting verbs.

> When you notice an interesting action word, write it on a sticky note and add it to the chart.

▸ Write the principle at the top of the chart.

> During writing time, look at your writing to see if you can use an interesting word to describe a character's action.

Choose interesting words to describe actions.

buzzed	slithered	swarmed
billowed	swayed	clacked
whirled	sang	twirled
curtsied	flipped	applauded
licked	rush	crawls
settle	snap	click

I ~~went~~ down the sidewalk.
 flipped
 twirled
 tiptoed

I ~~get~~ out of bed in the morning.
 fall
 flip
 crawl

Confer

▸ During independent writing, move around the room to confer briefly with as many individual children as time allows. Sit side by side with them and invite them to talk about action words. Use the following prompts as needed.

- *Is there a more interesting way you could describe what this character is doing?*
- *What other word could you use to show how the person is moving?*
- *Let's talk about some words you could use to show this action.*

Share

Following independent writing, gather children in the meeting area to share their writing.

> Who would like to share an interesting word you used to show an action?

> Who added a sticky note to the chart today? Share the word you added.

Writing Minilesson Principle
Compare one thing to another to make your writing powerful.

Making Powerful Word Choices

You Will Need

- fiction and nonfiction mentor texts with examples of similes, such as the following:

  - *Sam and the Lucky Money* by Karen Chinn, from Text Set: The Pleasure of Giving

  - *A Log's Life* by Wendy Pfeffer and *Think of an Eel* by Karen Wallace, from Text Set: Exploring Narrative Nonfiction Texts

- chart paper and markers

- chart paper prepared with a short story that has no figurative language

Academic Language / Important Vocabulary

- writing

- word choice

- powerful

- compare

Continuum Connection

- Notice and understand how an author uses literary language, including some figurative language

- Use memorable words or phrases

- Show through language instead of telling

- Use examples to make meaning clear to reader

GOAL

Use similes to compare one thing to another to make writing clear and interesting.

RATIONALE

When children understand that writers sometimes use words that compare to provide clarity or enjoyment for the reader, they begin to think about using comparative language in their own writing.

ASSESS LEARNING

- Observe for evidence that children understand why writers use similes (comparisons).

- Look at children's writing. Are they making an effort to use similes?

- Notice whether children can use vocabulary such as *writing*, *word choice*, *powerful*, and *compare*.

MINILESSON

To help children understand the minilesson principle, use mentor texts and provide an interactive lesson. Here is an example.

- Ahead of time, write a short story with no figurative language. Leave space between the lines so you can edit the writing.

  > Think about the writer's words as I read from a page of *Sam and the Lucky Money*.

- Show and read the second paragraph on page 12.

  > How does the writer help you paint a picture in your mind of how the lion float moved?

  > The writer compared the lion float to a giant centipede. Writers use the words *like* or *as* to compare two things.

- Begin a list of examples by writing the simile on chart paper and highlight *like*.

  > Listen and think about how a few other writers compare two things to help you understand something better and to make the writing more interesting.

- Use other text examples of similes and guide the conversation to help children understand the two things being compared and to identify the words *like* or *as*. Add each to chart paper. Some suggestions are below.

  - *A Log's Life*, page 24

  - *Think of an Eel*, pages 1, 3, 4

Have a Try

Invite children to turn and talk about making writing more powerful by adding words that compare.

▶ Show and read the prepared story.

> I can make my story more interesting and descriptive by comparing one thing to another. Turn and talk about how I might do that. Use your imagination!

▶ As needed, prompt the conversations. After time for discussion, ask a few volunteers for suggestions and add in the similes.

Summarize and Apply

Summarize the learning. Remind children to use language that compares one thing to another when they write. Write the principle at the top of the first chart.

> We talked about how to make writing more interesting and descriptive by comparing one thing to another. Today, think about if there is a way you can do this in your own writing, and try it out. Bring your writing when we meet later.

Confer

▶ During independent writing, move around the room to confer briefly with as many individual children as time allows. Sit side by side with them and invite them to talk about comparing one thing to another in their writing. Use the following prompts as needed.

- *What can you compare this to?*
- *Let's talk about some words you can use to compare one thing to another.*
- *Use the words* like *or* as *to compare this to something else.*

Share

Following independent writing, gather children in the meeting area. Ask a few volunteers to share their writing.

> Who used language to compare one thing to another? Share what you wrote.

Compare one thing to another to make your writing powerful.

	lion wove **like** a giant centipede
	earthworms turn the soil just **as** a shovel does
	swims **like** a fish slides **like** a snake looks **like** a willow leaf looks clear **as** a crystal teeth **like** a saw blade eats **like** a horse

One day, I went to the lake. As soon as

I got off my bike,

as quickly as a race car.
I saw a bird dive toward the water. It

flew away with a fish hanging out of its

mouth. What a way to start my day!

I spread out my blanket and took off my

My toes in the sand felt like sausages wrapped in a pancake with sugar sprinkles all over.
shoes. ~~I loved feeling the warm sand on~~

~~my toes.~~ I knew that this was going to

be a great day.

WML5
CFT.U7.WML5

Writing Minilesson Principle
Use words from other languages you know.

Making Powerful Word Choices

You Will Need

- mentor texts with words in other languages, such as the following:
  - *Grandfather Counts* by Andrea Cheng and *The Have a Good Day Cafe* by Frances Park and Ginger Park, from Text Set: Finding Your Way in a New Place
  - *First Come the Zebra* by Lynne Barasch, from Text Set: The Importance of Friendship
- chart paper and markers

Academic Language / Important Vocabulary

- writing
- word choice
- language

Continuum Connection

- Add words, phrases, or sentences to make the writing more interesting or exciting for readers
- Add words, phrases, or sentences to provide more information to readers
- Attend to the language and craft of other writers (mentor texts) in order to learn more as a writer

GOAL

Use words from languages other than English to make writing interesting and authentic.

RATIONALE

When children understand that writers sometimes use words from other languages, they begin to think about including words from other languages they speak. Using words from other languages contributes to the sense of the setting and adds authenticity to the characters. It also shows children that their languages are valued.

Translanguaging is used by multilingual speakers as a way to draw meaning from all of the languages they know. By encouraging multilingual children to include other languages in their writing, they are provided the opportunity to write more fluently.

ASSESS LEARNING

- Notice whether children talk about reasons writers sometimes use words from other languages.
- Observe children's writing for evidence of words or phrases from other languages.
- Look for evidence that children can use vocabulary such as *writing*, *word choice*, and *language*.

MINILESSON

To help children understand the minilesson principle, use mentor texts and provide an interactive lesson. Here is an example.

> Think about the writer's words as I read a few pages from these books.

- Show and read page 2 from *Grandfather Counts* and page 2 from *The Have a Good Day Cafe*.

  > What do you notice about these two books?

  > Both of these families have a grandparent who speaks another language, so the families speak more than one language when they are together.

- Show and read pages 13–16 from *First Come the Zebra*.

  > What do you notice about the words in this story?

- Guide the conversation to help children recognize that there are words from Swahili, which is a language spoken in Kenya, where the story takes place.

  > Why do you think the writer included Swahili words in this story?

- As children share ideas, begin a list on chart paper of some reasons why a writer might include words from other languages in their writing.

- Let children know that they can include one word or a phrase or two. Also communicate that not all children in the class speak another language, and that is okay because everyone has different things to add to their stories.

Have a Try

Invite children to turn and talk about using words from other languages in stories.

> Turn and talk about some other reasons that writers might sometimes include words from other languages in their stories.

▷ After time for discussion, ask volunteers to share. Add to the chart.

Summarize and Apply

Summarize the learning. Remind children to try including words from other languages in their writing. Write the principle on the top of the chart.

> We talked about how writers sometimes use words from other languages. Today, think about whether a word from another language you know would be good to use in your writing and try it out.

> ### Use words from other languages you know.
>
> Use words from other languages to. . .
>
> - capture an idea when you can't think of a word in English.
> - tell something about a character or setting.
> - make a story more interesting to the reader.
> - make your own unique voice shine through.
> - help more people read and understand the writing.

Confer

▷ During independent writing, move around the room to confer briefly with as many individual children as time allows. Sit side by side with them and invite them to talk about including words from other languages in their writing. Use the following prompts as needed.

- *Is there a word you know that might explain this in a different way?*
- *What word in another language might fit here to show more about the character?*
- *Let's talk about some ways you might say this by using a sentence from another language you speak.*

Share

Following independent writing, gather children in the meeting area. Ask a few volunteers to share their writing.

> Who included a word from another language in your writing? Share what you wrote.

Assessment

After you have taught the minilessons in this umbrella, observe children in a variety of classroom activities. Use *The Fountas & Pinnell Literacy Continuum* to notice, teach for, and support children's learning as you observe their attempts at writing.

▶ What evidence do you have of children's new understandings related to word choice?

- Do children use words that show instead of tell?
- Are they choosing alternatives to the word *said*?
- Do they choose interesting verbs?
- Are they using some figurative language in their writing?
- Do they sometimes include words from other languages in their writing?
- Are they using vocabulary such as *writing, word choice, powerful, descriptive, show, tell, interesting, said, action, compare,* and *language*?

▶ In what ways, beyond the scope of this umbrella, are children's reading and writing behaviors showing an understanding of word choice?

- Are they varying the ways they begin and end their writing?

Use your observations to determine the next umbrella you will teach. You may also consult Suggested Sequence of Lessons (pp. 575–589) for guidance.

EXTENSIONS FOR MAKING POWERFUL WORD CHOICES

▶ If you are using *The Reading Minilessons Book, Grade 2* (Fountas and Pinnell 2019), the minilessons in this umbrella would pair well with LA.U9: Analyzing the Writer's Craft.

▶ Encourage children to use or make up sound words (onomatopoeia) to make their writing more interesting and descriptive.

▶ Provide opportunities to talk about overused words and have children work together to come up with alternatives.

▶ Meet with children in small groups to help them make powerful word choices in their writing.

▶ You may want to repeat WML4 using other types of figurative language, such as metaphor or personification.

Minilessons in This Umbrella

WML1 Speak directly to the reader.

WML2 Show your voice with punctuation.

WML3 Show your voice with different styles of print.

Before Teaching Umbrella 8 Minilessons

Voice is the authentic connection between talking and writing, so throughout this umbrella it is important to encourage children to read their writing aloud and listen to how it sounds. Children can recognize that their personalities can shine through their writing by thinking about how authors do this in mentor texts. Support the link by helping them recognize that they can write in a way that is similar to talking but also understand that writing differs from talking. Before teaching, it is recommended that you teach CNV.U3: Learning About Punctuation so that children have an opportunity to explore when to use punctuation before trying it out as a way to show voice.

Use the books listed below from *Fountas & Pinnell Classroom™ Interactive Read-Aloud Collection* and *Shared Reading Collection*, or choose books from the classroom library. Big books are helpful, but you can project the page of text or write a sentence from the text on chart paper.

Interactive Read-Aloud Collection

Helen Lester: Learning a Lesson

Author: A True Story

All for Me and None for All

Princess Penelope's Parrot

Facing Challenges

Courage by Bernard Waber

Roller Coaster by Marla Frazee

Shared Reading Collection

A Piñata Fiesta by Adrián Garcia Montoya

Bigger or Smaller? by Brenda Iasevoli

Busy Beavers by Mary Ebeltoft Reid

As you read and enjoy these texts together, help children

- notice what is unique about the way the author writes,
- observe the way punctuation and styles of print are used, and
- talk about whether it feels like the writer is speaking directly to the reader.

Interactive Read-Aloud
Helen Lester

Facing Challenges

Shared Reading

Section 3: Craft

Writing with Voice in Fiction and Nonfiction

You Will Need

▸ fiction and nonfiction mentor texts with examples of using voice to speak directly to the reader, such as the following:

- *A Piñata Fiesta* by Adrián Garcia Montoya, from *Shared Reading Collection*

- *Author: A True Story* by Helen Lester, from Text Set: Helen Lester: Learning a Lesson

- *Courage* by Bernard Waber, from Text Set: Facing Challenges

▸ chart paper and markers

▸ prepared chart paper with something you have written in a way that speaks directly to readers

▸ highlighter or highlighter tape

▸ To download the following online resource for this lesson, visit **fp.pub/resources**:

- chart art (optional)

Academic Language / Important Vocabulary

▸ voice   writing

▸ speak   directly

Continuum Connection

▸ Write in a way that speaks directly to the reader

▸ Read writing aloud to help think critically about voice

GOAL

Write in a way that speaks directly to the reader.

RATIONALE

When children learn that writers can write in a way that speaks directly to readers, they begin to think about how their writing sounds and try to incorporate their own voices into their writing.

ASSESS LEARNING

▸ Notice whether children recognize that a writer can show voice by speaking directly to a reader.

▸ Look at children's writing for evidence that they are trying to speak directly to readers.

▸ Look for evidence that children can use vocabulary such as *voice*, *speak*, *writing*, and *directly*.

MINILESSON

To help children think about the minilesson principle, use mentor texts that have writing that speaks directly to the reader. Here is an example.

▸ Ahead of time, begin a story on chart paper that uses your authentic voice.

▸ Show and read page 2 in *A Piñata Fiesta*.

> Turn and talk about what you notice about how this writing sounds.

▸ After time for discussion, ask volunteers to share their thinking. Guide the conversation to help children notice that it sounds like the writer is speaking directly to the reader.

> The writer uses words like *lots of* and *you* to make it sound like he is talking to the readers the way he would talk to people he knows.

▸ Repeat with page 6. Point out that the writing sounds like the way the author might sound if he was talking directly to you about smashing a piñata.

> Listen as I read a few pages from *Author: A True Story*. Notice the way Helen Lester's writing sounds.

▸ Read pages 5–7 in *Author: A True Story* using a conversational reading style.

> What do you notice about the writer's voice?

▸ Point out the way the writer sounds like she is having a conversation with the reader.

▸ Repeat with pages 3–9 in *Courage*.

> Voice is what makes your writing strong. Your voice is something that belongs only to you. It shows your personality. One way you can show voice is by writing in a way that speaks directly to the reader.

Have a Try

Invite children to turn and talk about using voice in their writing by speaking directly to a reader.

▶ Read the prepared chart.

> Does my writing sound like it speaks directly to my readers–to you? How do you know? Turn and talk to your partner about that.

▶ After time for discussion, ask volunteers to highlight parts that speak directly to the reader (e.g., questions, the word *you*).

> What is a sentence I could write to end my writing?

▶ Add children's suggestions to the chart.

Summarize and Apply

Summarize the learning. Have children try speaking directly to the reader as they write. Write the principle at the top of the chart.

> We have been talking about how writers show voice by writing like they are talking directly to the reader. When you write today, you might want to try using your voice in this way. Bring your writing to share when we meet later.

Speak directly to the reader.

What is orange with black stripes? You guessed it, a tiger! What do you know about tigers? For example, did you know that a tiger can live for over twenty years in the wild? Most cats don't like to swim, but tigers do. They like being in the water and are very good swimmers.

Don't you think tigers are great?
I love tigers!
What is your favorite animal?
Now you know about tigers!

Confer

▶ During independent writing, move around the room to confer briefly with as many individual children as time allows. Sit side by side with them and invite them to talk about voice. Use the following prompts as needed.

- *What are you writing about today?*
- *Read this sentence the way you want a reader to read it.*
- *Let's talk about some ways you might say that so it sounds like you are talking to the reader.*

Share

Following independent writing, gather children in the meeting area to share their writing.

> Did anyone write in a way that sounds as if you are talking to the reader? Share what you wrote.

Writing Minilesson Principle
Show your voice with punctuation.

You Will Need

- several mentor texts that show examples of using punctuation to show voice, such as the following:

  - *Roller Coaster* by Marla Frazee and *Courage* by Bernard Waber, from Text Set: Facing Challenges

  - *All for Me and None for All* by Helen Lester, from Text Set: Helen Lester: Learning a Lesson

  - *Bigger or Smaller?* by Brenda Iasevoli, from *Shared Reading Collection*

- chart paper and markers

- document camera (optional)

- basket of books that have examples of different ways authors use punctuation to show voice

- sticky notes

Academic Language / Important Vocabulary

- voice

- punctuation

Continuum Connection

- Use punctuation to make the text clear, effective, and interesting, and to support voice

- Read writing aloud to help think critically about voice

GOAL

Use a variety of punctuation to show voice.

RATIONALE

Punctuation marks are used in conventional ways, but used creatively they can be considered author's craft. By studying how authors use punctuation to show expression as well as meaning, children learn that they can do the same.

ASSESS LEARNING

- Examine children's writing for evidence that they are trying to use punctuation to convey meaning and show voice.

- Look for evidence that children can use vocabulary such as *voice* and *punctuation* as well as names of punctuation as needed (e.g., *parentheses*, *quotation marks*, *ellipsis*).

MINILESSON

To help children think about using punctuation to convey voice, provide mentor text examples and an interactive discussion. Below is an example. Make sure children can see the punctuation by writing sentences on chart paper or projecting the pages.

- Show page 10 of *Roller Coaster*. Read the sentences, emphasizing the way that the words in parentheses are meant to be read with humor.

  > What do you notice that the writer, Marla Frazee, did on this page?

- Guide the conversation to help children recognize that the writer used parentheses to create meaning and to show voice.

- Show page 12. Read with emphasis, highlighting the way punctuation shows how the page should be read with meaning.

  > What are your thoughts about what the writer did on this page?

- Guide the conversation. On chart paper, begin a list of text examples that demonstrate a writer's use of punctuation to show voice and add these two examples. After writing each, have children join in as you read the examples with emphasis.

- Repeat the activity using pages 25 and 27 in *All for Me and None for All* and page 5 in *Bigger or Smaller?*

- Add to the chart and read aloud the examples together.

Have a Try

Invite children to turn and talk about using punctuation to show voice.

▶ Show the first sentence on page 11 in *Courage*.

Turn and talk about what the author did here.

▶ After time for discussion, ask children to share their thoughts about how the writer uses punctuation to convey meaning and show voice. Add to the chart.

Summarize and Apply

Summarize the learning. Have children look for interesting ways writers have used punctuation to show voice. Write the principle at the top of the chart.

During writing time, work with a partner to look for different ways writers have used punctuation to show voice. You can look in a book you are reading or choose a book from the basket. Be sure to read the words aloud in the way you think the writer wanted you to. Add a sticky note to the pages with examples and bring the book when we meet.

▶ You may want to spend several days studying mentor texts to help children understand the minilesson principle before they begin to apply it to their own writing.

Show your voice with punctuation.	
ROLLER COASTER	(Now it is too late for anyone to change their mind.) S-l-o-w-l-y the train is pulled up the hill. Clickity, clackity. Clickity, clackity. Up. Up. Up. And then . . .
ALL FOR ME AND NONE FOR ALL	He was about to dig in . . . But wait. Or taken it. Or snatched it. Or grabbed it. "All . . ."
Bigger or Smaller?	Is this lemur bigger or smaller than you are? Smaller!
COURAGE	Courage is mealtime and desperately hoping it's not "Chunky Chunks" in "real" gravy again.

Confer

▶ During independent writing, move around the room to confer briefly with as many individual children as time allows. Sit side by side with them and invite them to talk about the ways writers use punctuation to show voice. Use the following prompts as needed.

- *What punctuation choices did this writer make?*
- *Talk about how the writer's voice sounds in this book.*
- *Read this page in the way you think the writer wanted you to.*

Share

Following independent writing, gather children in the meeting area to share their writing.

Who found an example of when a writer used punctuation to show voice? Share the page and read it the way the writer wanted it to be read.

Section 3: Craft

WML3
CFT.U8.WML3

Writing Minilesson Principle
Show your voice with different styles of print.

Writing with Voice in Fiction and Nonfiction

You Will Need

- several mentor texts with examples of using different styles of print, such as the following:
    - *Princess Penelope's Parrot, Author: A True Story*, and *All for Me and None for All* by Helen Lester, from Text Set: Helen Lester: Learning a Lesson
    - *Busy Beavers* by Mary Ebeltoft Reid, from *Shared Reading Collection*
- chart paper and markers
- document camera (optional)

Academic Language / Important Vocabulary

- voice
- style
- capitalization
- italics
- bold

Continuum Connection

- Read writing aloud to help think critically about voice
- Write in an expressive way but also recognize how language in a book would sound
- Use underlining and bold print to convey meaning

GOAL

Use different styles of print to convey meaning and support voice.

RATIONALE

When children learn they can use different styles and sizes of print to convey meaning and support voice, they understand that writers have a variety of tools they can use to express themselves, and they might be inspired to use different styles of print in their own writing. If appropriate for your class, you might mention that different fonts (e.g., Helvetica, Times New Roman) can be used when using a computer.

ASSESS LEARNING

- Examine children's writing to see whether they are experimenting with styles of print.
- Look for evidence that children can use vocabulary such as *voice*, *style*, *capitalization*, *italics*, and *bold*.

MINILESSON

To help children think about how writers use different styles of print to show voice, use mentor text examples and provide an interactive lesson. Below is an example. Make sure children can see the print by writing sentences on chart paper or projecting the pages.

- Show page 6 of *Princess Penelope's Parrot*.

    What do you notice about the words on the page?

- Support a conversation about how capitalization of those words conveys the idea that Penelope is selfish. Helen Lester's funny writing style comes through, and the reader knows to read "Gimme" with emphasis. As children talk, begin a two-column chart that shows the styles and text examples.

- Repeat with page 29 in *Author: A True Story*. Add to the chart.

- Show and read pages 1 and 26 in *All for Me and None for All*.

    What do you notice?

    Why do you think the writer decided to use italics (slanted print)?

- Support a discussion about how the writer used italics to show voice. Add to the chart.

- Show pages 2–3 and 4–5 in *Busy Beavers*.

    What do you notice about the print on pages 2 and 4 and the print in the speech bubbles?

    How might the orange print sound different from the black print when it is read aloud?

Have a Try

Invite children to turn and talk about how a writer uses styles of print to show voice.

▶ Show page 4 in *All for Me and None for All*.

What do you notice about the print on this page? How did Helen Lester use it to show voice? Turn and talk about that.

▶ After time for discussion, ask children to share. Write the sentence on the chart. Have children read it aloud with you emphasizing "HOG."

Summarize and Apply

Summarize the learning. Have children try using different styles of print to show voice.

What can print show in your writing?

▶ As children share, list their ideas on chart paper. Guide children to come up with a principle, and add it to the chart.

Today during writing time, you might decide to try different styles of print in your writing. If there are words you want the reader to read a certain way, you can trace over your letters to make them bold, slant (or underline) your letters, write all capital letters, or use different colors. Bring your writing when we meet later.

Capitalization	GIMME, GIMME, GIMME. anyTIME anyWHERE anyTHING
Italics	*his* theirs *Should* he? *Would* he? *Could* he?
Color and Style	And the lodge has secret doors under the water. The doors are secret so predators can't find a way inside.
Bold	What a **HOG!**

Show your voice with different styles of print.

What Print Can Show

• Humor

• The writer's personality

• What a character is like

• What a character is thinking

• How to read the words to sound like the character

• Important words

Confer

▶ During independent writing, move around the room to confer briefly with as many individual children as time allows. Sit side by side with them and invite them to talk about voice. Use the following prompts as needed.

• *How can you use a different style of print here?*

• *How should this part sound? Is there a way to show that with print?*

• *Can you read this part aloud?*

Share

Following independent writing, gather children in the meeting area. Ask a few volunteers to share their writing.

Did anyone try using a different style of print in your writing? Share what you wrote.

Section 3: Craft

Assessment

After you have taught the minilessons in this umbrella, observe children in a variety of classroom activities. Use *The Fountas & Pinnell Literacy Continuum* to notice, teach for, and support children's learning as you observe their attempts at writing.

▶ What evidence do you have of children's new understandings related to voice?

- Do children understand what it means to speak directly to the reader when they write?

- Do they recognize that writers express voice with creative use of punctuation and print styles?

- Are they using vocabulary such as *voice*, *speak*, *writing*, *directly*, *punctuation*, *style*, *capitalization*, *italics*, and *bold*?

▶ In what ways, beyond the scope of this umbrella, are children's reading and writing behaviors showing an understanding of voice?

- Are children looking for ways to make their illustrations interesting?

- Do they need to learn more about using punctuation?

Use your observations to determine the next umbrella you will teach. You may also consult Suggested Sequence of Lessons (pp. 575–589) for guidance.

EXTENSIONS FOR WRITING WITH VOICE IN FICTION AND NONFICTION

▶ Show children how to select different fonts and font sizes on the computer. Encourage creative use of fonts and print styles but also caution against the use of too many of either.

▶ Use shared writing to create a class story. Experiment with using different punctuation or print styles on one or more sentences from the story. Talk about how changing the punctuation or print style changes how the words would be read.

▶ As you read aloud both fiction and nonfiction texts, pause to have a conversation about the author's voice and what choices the author made to show it.

Minilessons in This Umbrella

WML1 Use headings to tell what a part is about.

WML2 Make a table of contents for your book.

WML3 Use sidebars to give extra information.

WML4 Write captions under pictures.

Before Teaching Umbrella 9 Minilessons

In addition to using published mentor texts in these minilessons, consider providing a mentor text that children in your class can relate to by writing your own informational book or using shared writing to write one with the children. You might want to teach or revisit GEN.U3: Making All-About Books alongside this umbrella so children can apply the text features taught in this umbrella to their own all-about books.

Read and discuss engaging nonfiction books with a variety of text features, including headings, sidebars, tables of contents, and captions. Use the following texts from *Fountas & Pinnell Classroom™ Interactive Read-Aloud Collection* and *Shared Reading Collection*, or choose nonfiction books from the classroom or school library.

Interactive Read-Aloud Collection
Gail Gibbons: Exploring the World Through Nonfiction

The Moon Book

Simple Biography

Snowflake Bentley by Jacqueline Briggs Martin

Shared Reading Collection

Busy Beavers by Mary Ebeltoft Reid

Amazing Nests by Mary Ebeltoft Reid

As you read and enjoy these texts together, help children

- notice headings and talk about what each page or section is about,
- discuss information provided in sidebars and captions, and
- use the table of contents to find information.

Interactive Read-Aloud
Gail Gibbons

Simple Biography

Shared Reading

Section 3: Craft

Writing Minilesson Principle
Use headings to tell what a part is about.

You Will Need

- a familiar nonfiction book that has headings, such as *The Moon Book* by Gail Gibbons, from Text Set: Gail Gibbons: Exploring the World Through Nonfiction

- a familiar nonfiction book that does NOT have headings, such as *Busy Beavers* by Mary Ebeltoft Reid, from *Shared Reading Collection*

- sticky notes

- chart paper and markers

Academic Language / Important Vocabulary

- nonfiction
- heading
- page
- author

Continuum Connection

- Use headings, a table of contents, and other features to help the reader find information and understand how facts are related

- Understand how to use layout, spacing, and size of print to create titles, headings, and subheadings

---

GOAL

Write headings that tell the reader what to expect from sections of text.

RATIONALE

When you help children notice headings in books, they begin to understand that nonfiction authors group together related details on a page or in a section. They learn to structure their own nonfiction texts in a similar way and to use headings to help the reader know what to expect. Before or after this lesson, it would be helpful to also teach WPS.U9: Revising to Focus and Organize Writing, particularly WML5: Group similar ideas together.

ASSESS LEARNING

- Listen to children as they talk about nonfiction books. What do they understand about headings?

- Notice whether children use headings in their own nonfiction texts.

- Look for evidence that children can use vocabulary such as *nonfiction*, *heading*, *page*, and *author*.

MINILESSON

To help children think about the minilesson principle, engage them in an inquiry-based lesson around headings in a familiar nonfiction book. Then demonstrate how to add headings to a book that does not already have them. Here is an example.

- Show the cover of *The Moon Book* and read the title. Read page 13, and then point to the heading.

  What do you notice about these words at the top of the page?

  How do they look different from the other words on the page?

  This is a heading. A heading is usually bigger or darker than the other words on the page, and it is sometimes in a different color or a different font. What does the heading tell you?

  The heading tells you what the page or part of the book is about. This heading tells us that this part is about the phases of the moon.

- Turn to page 16, and invite a volunteer to point to and read aloud the heading.

  What do you think this part of the book will be about?

  How do headings help you when you read or write nonfiction?

- Record children's responses on chart paper.

Have a Try

Invite children to talk to a partner about adding a heading.

▶ Show the cover of *Busy Beavers* and read the title. Show page 6. Read the page aloud.

> This book doesn't have headings. What heading could we add to this page to help readers know what it is about?

▶ After children turn and talk, invite several pairs to share their ideas. Agree on a heading, and use a sticky note to add it to the page. Add headings to a few other pages if time allows.

Summarize and Apply

Summarize the learning. Remind children to think about using headings when they write nonfiction.

> Why do nonfiction authors use headings?

▶ Write the principle at the top of the chart.

> You can use headings when you write your own nonfiction books. If you work on a nonfiction book during writing time today, see if there is a place you could add a heading. Bring your writing to share when we meet later.

Confer

▶ During independent writing, move around the room to confer briefly with as many individual children as time allows. Sit side by side with them and invite them to talk about adding headings to their books. Use prompts such as the following as needed.

- *What is this page (part) of your book about?*
- *What heading could you add to this page?*
- *How will you make the heading look different from the other words on the page?*
- *What are you going to write about on this page? You can add a heading now to help you organize your ideas before you write.*

Share

Following independent writing, gather children in the meeting area to share their headings. Have children hold up a page with a heading so that everyone can see. Then select several children to read their headings aloud.

> What do you think this part of _____'s book is about?

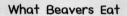

Use headings to tell what a part is about.

How Do Headings Help?

- tell what the page or part is about

- help readers find information

- organize the author's ideas

What Beavers Eat

Beavers make sure their family has good food to eat. They gather lots of leaves, bark, and sticks and carry them home. The family eats some of the food. But they save some for winter too.

Section 3: Craft

Writing Minilesson Principle
Make a table of contents for your book.

You Will Need

- a familiar nonfiction book that has a table of contents and page numbers, such as *Amazing Nests* by Mary Ebeltoft Reid, from *Shared Reading Collection*

- a sample nonfiction book written by you, the whole class, or an individual child

- chart paper and markers

Academic Language / Important Vocabulary

- page numbers

- table of contents

Continuum Connection

- Use headings, a table of contents, and other features to help the reader find information and understand how facts are related

- Incorporate nonfiction text features (captions, labels, insets, sidebars, table of contents) into writing

GOAL

Understand that writers include a table of contents as an organizational tool for the reader.

RATIONALE

When you help children notice and think about tables of contents in nonfiction books, they begin to understand that a table of contents helps readers find information. They learn that they can include a table of contents in their own nonfiction books.

ASSESS LEARNING

- Listen to children as they talk about nonfiction books. What do they understand about a table of contents?

- Notice whether children know how to make a table of contents.

- Look for evidence that children can use vocabulary such as *page numbers* and *table of contents*.

MINILESSON

To help children think about the minilesson principle, engage them in noticing the characteristics and purpose of a table of contents in a familiar nonfiction book. Then demonstrate how to make one. Here is an example.

- Show the cover of *Amazing Nests* and display the table of contents.

  What is this part of the book called?

  This is the table of contents. Let's read it together.

- Point to each element as you read it.

  What information does the table of contents tell you?

  It tells you the name of each part of the book and the page number it starts on. The table of contents is always at the beginning of a book.

  Why do you think authors sometimes put a table of contents in their books? How does the table of contents help you as a reader?

- Display a class-written nonfiction text or one written by you or an individual child.

  We can make a table of contents for this book.

- If the pages are not numbered, add page numbers. Explain that it's important to be sure the pages are in the correct order and numbered before making a table of contents.

- Write *Table of Contents* at the top of a sheet of chart paper. With children's input, create a table of contents.

Have a Try

Invite children to talk to a partner about how to make a table of contents.

> You can make a table of contents for your own books, too. What will you have to remember to do when you make one? Turn and talk to your partner about this.

▶ After time for discussion, invite several pairs to share their thinking. Record responses on chart paper.

Summarize and Apply

Summarize the learning. Remind children that they can include a table of contents in their own books.

> What did you learn today about making a table of contents?

▶ Write the principle at the top of the chart.

> If you are working on a nonfiction book today, try making a table of contents for it. Make sure you number your pages first. If you're not finished with your book, you can add the table of contents when you finish. Bring your writing to share when we meet later.

Confer

▶ During independent writing, move around the room to confer briefly with as many individual children as time allows. Sit side by side with them and invite them to talk about adding a table of contents to their books. Use prompts such as the following to help them make a table of contents as appropriate.

- *Where should you put the table of contents?*
- *What do you need to write on the table of contents?*
- *What is the first part of your book called? What page is it on?*
- *How will your table of contents help the reader?*

Share

Following independent writing, gather children in the meeting area to share their writing.

> Who would like to share your table of contents with the class?

> How did you make it?

Table of Contents

Where Penguins Live 1

Different Kinds of Penguins . . . 2

The Parts of a Penguin 4

What Penguins Eat 6

Penguin Babies 7

Make a table of contents for your book.

- Reread your writing.

- Make sure the pages are in the correct order.

- Number the pages.

- Write the name of each part of the book and the page number it starts on.

Using Text Features in Nonfiction Writing

You Will Need

- a familiar nonfiction book that has sidebars, such as *Snowflake Bentley* by Jacqueline Briggs Martin, from Text Set: Simple Biography
- a sample nonfiction book written by you or the whole class (a shared writing piece)
- chart paper and markers

Academic Language / Important Vocabulary

- sidebar
- nonfiction
- information
- author

Continuum Connection

- Incorporate nonfiction text features (captions, labels, insets, sidebars, table of contents) into writing

GOAL

Write sidebars to provide extra information to the reader about the topic.

RATIONALE

When you help children notice and think about sidebars in nonfiction books, they learn that they, too, can use sidebars to give extra information in their own books. They begin to think about what other information readers might need or want to know about the topic.

ASSESS LEARNING

- Listen to children as they talk about nonfiction books. What do they understand about sidebars?
- Notice whether children include sidebars in their own nonfiction books.
- Look for evidence that children can use vocabulary such as *sidebar*, *nonfiction*, *information*, and *author*.

MINILESSON

To help children think about the minilesson principle, engage them in an inquiry-based lesson around sidebars in a familiar nonfiction book. Then demonstrate how to add a sidebar by creating one for an existing text. Here is an example.

- Show the cover of *Snowflake Bentley* and read the title. Read pages 2–3. Then point to and read the sidebar on page 2.

    What do you notice about these words? How do they look different from the other words on these pages?

    These words are on the side of the page in a box called a sidebar. What does the sidebar tell you about?

    What does the sidebar have to do with the other information on these pages?

    These pages tell about how Willie Bentley enjoyed snowstorms when he was a young boy in Vermont, and the sidebar gives extra facts about where he grew up and how much it snows there.

    Why do you think the author decided to include sidebars in her book?

    The author of this book used sidebars to give extra facts about the information in the main part of the biography.

- Guide children to think about using sidebars in their own writing.

    You can use sidebars when you write your own nonfiction books. What should you think about when you want to make a sidebar?

- Record responses on chart paper.

Have a Try

Invite children to talk to a partner about what to write in a sidebar.

▸ Display a class-written nonfiction text or a sample text written by you. Read one page aloud.

> What extra facts might be interesting to include in a sidebar about different kinds of penguins? Turn and talk to your partner about what we might write.

▸ After time for discussion, invite several pairs to share their ideas. You might demonstrate writing the sidebar on a separate piece of paper and gluing it in the book.

Summarize and Apply

Summarize the learning. Remind children to think about including sidebars when they write nonfiction.

> What did you learn today about using sidebars?

▸ Write the principle at the top of the first chart.

> If you are working on a nonfiction book today, try adding a sidebar to give extra information. Think about what the reader might like to know in addition to the information in the main text. Bring your book to share when we come back together.

Confer

▸ During independent writing, move around the room to confer briefly with as many individual children as time allows. Sit side by side with them and invite them to talk about adding sidebars to their books. Use prompts such as the following as needed.

- *What is this page about?*
- *What else might readers want to know about that?*
- *Where on the page would you like to put the sidebar?*
- *Remember to make sure the information in the sidebar relates to the rest of the information on the page.*

Share

Following independent writing, gather children in the meeting area to share their writing.

> If you wrote a sidebar, hold up the page so we can see it.

> Why did you decide to put that information in a sidebar?

Use sidebars to give extra information.

- Decide what else readers might want or need to know about the topic.

- Use a sidebar to give extra facts or information.

> **Did You Know?**
>
> A sidebar looks like this!

- Make sure the sidebar is about the same topic or idea as the main part of the book.

Different Kinds of Penguins

There are seventeen different kinds of penguins. The emperor penguin is the biggest penguin. The smallest is the little blue penguin.

> **Fun Fact**
> The little blue penguin is sometimes called the fairy penguin because of its small size. It is only one foot tall!

Section 3: Craft

Writing Minilesson Principle
Write captions under pictures.

Using Text Features in Nonfiction Writing

You Will Need

- a familiar nonfiction book that contains image captions, such as *Amazing Nests* by Mary Ebeltoft Reid, from *Shared Reading Collection*
- a sample nonfiction book written by you or the whole class (through shared writing) or chart paper prepared with a sample nonfiction text and illustration
- chart paper and markers

Academic Language / Important Vocabulary

- nonfiction
- information
- caption

Continuum Connection

- Write captions under pictures
- Incorporate nonfiction text features (captions, labels, insets, sidebars, table of contents) into writing

GOAL

Write captions under pictures to provide more information for the reader.

RATIONALE

When children notice and think about captions in nonfiction books, they learn that they can add captions to images to give additional information. They develop the ability to communicate information through different means.

ASSESS LEARNING

- Observe for evidence that children understand the purpose of captions and can distinguish them from other types of text.
- Look to see whether children include clear captions in their own nonfiction books.
- Look for evidence that children can use vocabulary such as *nonfiction*, *information*, and *caption*.

MINILESSON

To help children think about the minilesson principle, use a mentor text to engage children in an inquiry-based lesson around captions. Then use shared writing to model adding a caption to an image. Here is an example.

- Display page 6 of *Amazing Nests*. Point to the photo's caption and read it aloud.

    This is a caption. A caption is words near a picture that tell more about the picture. What does this caption tell you about?

- Continue in a similar manner with the captions on pages 9 and 10. Help children understand that captions add additional information beyond what is included in the main text.

- Display a class-written nonfiction text or a sample text written by you. Read one page aloud. Help children compose a caption for the illustration. For example:

    Let's add a caption to our illustration of a mother penguin and baby penguin. What could we write to help readers understand what is happening in the picture?

- Use children's responses to write a caption.

Have a Try

Invite children to talk to a partner about captions they might add to their own nonfiction books.

▶ Direct children to retrieve a nonfiction book they have been working on or have already written.

Look at your nonfiction book. What captions could you add to your pictures to give extra information? Turn and talk to your partner about your ideas.

▶ After time for discussion, invite a few children to share their thinking.

Summarize and Apply

Summarize the learning. Remind children to think about including captions when they write nonfiction.

What did you learn today about captions? How are they helpful for the reader?

▶ Write the principle at the top of the chart.

During writing time today, try adding a caption to at least one of the pictures in your nonfiction book. Bring your book to share when we come back together.

Write captions under pictures.

Caption → The chick stays warm under its mother's brood pouch.

Penguin babies are called chicks. Chicks are very small. They are covered in soft, gray down.

Confer

▶ During independent writing, move around the room to confer briefly with as many individual children as time allows. Sit side by side with them and invite them to talk about adding captions to their books. Use prompts such as the following as needed.

• *What does that picture show?*

• *Do you want to write a caption under it?*

• *What could the caption say?*

• *Remember that the caption should be different from the other words on the page. What extra information could you give in the caption?*

Share

Following independent writing, gather children in the meeting area to share their writing.

Who would like to share a caption you wrote?

Assessment

After you have taught the minilessons in this umbrella, observe children as they write and talk about their writing. Use *The Fountas & Pinnell Literacy Continuum* to notice, teach for, and support children's learning as you observe their attempts at writing.

▶ What evidence do you have of children's new understandings related to using text features in nonfiction writing?

- Do children use headings to tell what each part of a book is about?
- Do they use sidebars and captions to give extra information?
- Do they understand how to make a table of contents?
- Is there evidence children can use vocabulary such as *heading*, *sidebar*, *table of contents*, and *caption*?

▶ In what other ways, beyond the scope of this umbrella, are children ready to develop their nonfiction writing?

- Are they ready to learn about making different types of nonfiction books?
- Are they ready to learn how to add more details and examples to their nonfiction writing?
- Are they experimenting with using different types of graphics in nonfiction?

Use your observations to determine the next umbrella you will teach. You may also consult Suggested Sequence of Lessons (pp. 575–589) for guidance.

EXTENSIONS FOR USING TEXT FEATURES IN NONFICTION WRITING

▶ Teach children how to revise a table of contents if they make substantial changes to a book after making the table of contents.

▶ Guide children to notice subheadings in books and invite them to use them in their own books.

▶ Teach children how to make headings, sidebars, a table of contents, and other text features on a computer.

▶ Guide children to notice glossaries in nonfiction books, and help them make their own.

▶ If you use *The Reading Minilessons Book, Grade 2* (Fountas and Pinnell 2019), note that LA.U17: Using Text Features to Gain Information looks at text features through the lens of a reader.

Minilessons in This Umbrella

WML1   Give examples for your ideas.

WML2   Use words to give the reader a picture.

WML3   Tell how two things are the same or different.

WML4   Tell about an experience from your life to teach more about a topic.

Before Teaching Umbrella 10 Minilessons

Before teaching the minilessons in this umbrella, it would be helpful to teach WPS. U3: Gathering Ideas for Informational Writing. It would also be helpful to teach WPS.U8: Adding Information to Your Writing so children understand the mechanics of adding the techniques taught in this umbrella to their in-process writing.

Continue to display charts created during other umbrellas related to nonfiction writing for children to refer to. Point out that they will use what they have already learned about nonfiction writing alongside these new techniques. Also, you may consider writing your own nonfiction book or writing one with the children through shared writing to use as an example in these minilessons.

Read and discuss engaging nonfiction books. Use the following texts from *Fountas & Pinnell Classroom™ Interactive Read-Aloud Collection* and *Shared Reading Collection*, or choose books from your classroom library.

Interactive Read-Aloud Collection
Seymour Simon: A Scientific Eye

Frogs

Dogs

Cats

Exploring Narrative Nonfiction Texts

Cactus Hotel by Brenda Z. Guiberson

Shared Reading Collection

A Raindrop's Journey by Paloma Jae

The Perfect Beak by Stephanie Petron Cahill

The Amazing Seahorse by Andrea Young

As you read and enjoy these texts together, help children

- notice ways in which authors describe information to the reader,

- notice descriptive language authors use to help the reader picture more about a topic, and

- consider the breadth of ideas that authors share about one topic as a way to understand how much one can write on a topic.

Interactive Read-Aloud
Seymour Simon

Narrative Nonfiction

Shared Reading

Section 3: Craft

Writing Minilesson Principle
Give examples for your ideas.

Expanding Nonfiction Writing

You Will Need

- familiar nonfiction books, such as *Frogs* and *Dogs* by Seymour Simon, from Text Set: Seymour Simon: A Scientific Eye

- excerpts from books written on pieces of paper and attached to chart paper (or projected)

- a sample nonfiction book written by you, the whole class, or an individual child

- document camera (optional)

- chart paper and markers

Academic Language / Important Vocabulary

- examples

- ideas

- sentence

Continuum Connection

- Introduce ideas followed by supportive details and examples

- Use examples to make the meaning clear to readers

- Select information that will support the topic

- Select details that will support a topic or story

- Add words, phrases, or sentences to provide more information to readers

GOAL

Use specific details to tell more about a topic.

RATIONALE

When you help children notice that writers (of all genres) use examples in their writing to support a reader's comprehension, they begin to try this in their own writing.

ASSESS LEARNING

- Observe children as they talk about nonfiction books. Do they show that they understand the purpose of using examples to help explain an idea?

- Notice whether children use specific examples in their own nonfiction texts.

- Look for evidence that children can use vocabulary such as *examples, ideas,* and *sentence.*

MINILESSON

To help children think about the minilesson principle, engage them in an inquiry-based lesson around using examples to explain an idea or a word. Here is an example.

- Show the cover of *Frogs* and read the title. Attach the prepared excerpt to the chart paper or project it. Read the excerpt.

    Can you figure out what wetlands are from this sentence? How?

    You might not know the word *wetlands*, but you probably know at least one of these words: *lakes, ponds, marshes.* These examples help you understand *wetlands.*

- Read aloud the excerpt from *Dogs.*

    How does Seymour Simon explain what specially trained breeds of dogs are and how they help people?

- After time for discussion ask a few children to share. Underline the examples and write their noticings on the chart.

Have a Try

Invite children to talk to a partner about adding examples to a piece of nonfiction writing by you, a child, or the whole class.

▶ Write the first sentence from your book (for example, about roller skating) on the chart.

> I want to give the reader examples for my idea. What examples could I add to my writing? Turn and talk about that.

▶ After children turn and talk, invite several pairs to share their ideas. Agree on a few sentences and add them to the chart.

Summarize and Apply

Help children summarize the learning. Remind them to think about using specific examples in their writing.

> What can you do to help your readers understand what you are writing about?

▶ Write the principle at the top of the chart and read it aloud.

> If you work on a nonfiction book during writing time today, see if there is a place you could add examples. Be prepared to share your writing with your partner.

Give examples for your ideas.

They usually live near slow-moving bodies of water, or **wetlands**, <u>such as lakes, ponds, and marshes.</u>
—from <u>Frogs</u> by Seymour Simon

• Examples listed within one sentence

Specially trained breeds of working and herding <u>dogs help people</u> all over the world. <u>German shepherds and sheepdogs</u> herd sheep and cattle. <u>Malamutes and huskies</u> pull sleds across the snow in Alaska. <u>Doberman pinschers and rottweilers</u> act as watchdogs. <u>Saint Bernards</u> can locate people lost in the snow.
—from <u>Dogs</u> by Seymour Simon

• One sentence followed by several sentences with examples

For roller skating you need some safety equipment. One thing you need is a helmet to protect your head. You also need kneepads. They will help protect your knees if you fall. Elbow pads will protect your arms.

Confer

▶ During independent writing, move around the room to confer briefly with as many individual children as time allows. Sit side by side with them and invite them to talk about adding examples to their books. Use prompts such as the following if needed.

• *Talk about what you want to teach your reader. What are examples that go with that idea?*

• *How might you tell the reader more about that by giving examples?*

• *I wonder, what are examples of _____? How could you add that?*

Share

Following independent writing, gather children in the meeting area to share their writing with a partner. Listen in on conversations. Then bring the class back together.

> What ideas did you hear from your classmates that you might try in your writing?

Writing Minilesson Principle
Use words to give the reader a picture.

Expanding Nonfiction Writing

You Will Need

- several familiar nonfiction books, such as the following:

  - *A Raindrop's Journey* by Paloma Jae and *The Perfect Beak* by Stephanie Petron Cahill, from *Shared Reading Collection*

  - *Cactus Hotel* by Brenda Z. Guiberson, from Text Set: Exploring Narrative Nonfiction Texts

- excerpts from books written on strips of paper and attached to chart paper (or projected)

- highlighter

- chart paper and markers

- To download the following online resource for this lesson, visit **fp.pub/resources**:

  - chart art (optional)

Academic Language / Important Vocabulary

- describe
- details

Continuum Connection

- Introduce ideas followed by supportive details and examples

- Tell about a topic in an interesting way

- Select information that will support the topic

- Select details that will support a topic or story

- Add words, phrases, or sentences to provide more information to readers

GOAL

Use descriptive details to create a picture for the reader.

RATIONALE

When you help children notice that writers (of all genres) use descriptive details in their writing to paint a picture that brings a topic to life for the reader, they begin to try this in their own writing.

ASSESS LEARNING

- Observe children as they talk about nonfiction books. Do they understand why a writer uses descriptive details?

- Notice whether children add descriptive details to their own writing.

- Look for evidence that children can use vocabulary such as *describe* and *details*.

MINILESSON

To help children think about the minilesson principle, engage them in noticing descriptive details that create a picture in a familiar nonfiction book. Here is an example.

- Show the cover of *A Raindrop's Journey*. Read the title and a short excerpt. Attach the excerpt to chart paper or project it.

  Can you picture in your mind what is happening to the raindrop?

  How does the writer help you do that?

- Highlight (or have a child highlight) the words that help the reader picture what is happening to the raindrop.

  What do these words describe?

- Record children's responses on the chart.

- Repeat this process with several more excerpts from books, such as *Cactus Hotel* and *The Perfect Beak*.

- Guide children to think about using descriptive details that create a picture in their own writing.

  What are some things you can do as a writer to think about what words to use to give the reader a picture of an idea?

- Add ideas to a new sheet of chart paper.

The Writing Minilessons Book, Grade 2

Have a Try

Invite children to talk to a partner about using words to give the reader a picture.

> I want to help my readers picture how roller skating looks. I will demonstrate roller skating for you.

> What words would help the reader picture what it looks like to roller skate? Turn and talk about that.

▸ After children turn and talk, invite several pairs to share their ideas. Agree on a few sentences and add them to the chart.

Summarize and Apply

Help children summarize the learning. Remind them that they can use description in their own books to give the readers a picture in their minds.

> What can you do to help your readers understand more about your topic?

▸ Write the principle at the top of the chart and read it aloud.

> Today as you write, think about what words you can use to give the readers a picture in their minds. Be prepared to share your writing with a partner.

Confer

▸ During independent writing, move around the room to confer briefly with as many individual children as time allows. Sit side by side with them and invite them to talk about using description to give the reader a picture. Use prompts such as the following as needed.

- *What do you want your reader to understand about your topic? How might you describe it to help the reader picture it?*
- *Draw a quick sketch of that idea. What words will help your reader picture it?*
- *Act out that idea. What words will help your reader picture it?*
- *Let's find a book with drawings or photos to help you picture that idea.*

Share

Following independent writing, gather children in the meeting area to share their writing with a partner. Listen in on conversations. Then bring the class back together.

> What ideas did you hear from your classmates that you might try in your writing?

Use words to give the reader a picture.

One spring day, a big raindrop was up in a storm cloud. Suddenly, it fell down from the cloud. It blew left and right, as it fell through the air with many other raindrops.
—from _A Raindrop's Journey_ by Paloma Jae

· Movement

[The cactus] weighs eight tons—about as much as five automobiles.
—from _Cactus Hotel_ by Brenda Z. Guiberson

· Size

A hummingbird's beak is like a long, thin straw.
—from _The Perfect Beak_ by Stephanie Petron Cahill

· Shape

Ways to Help You Write a Description

· Act out the ideas.

· Make a quick sketch.

· Look at a picture in a book.

When you roller skate, bend your knees. Push hard on one foot at a time. Swing your arms. Be sure to look where you are going!

Writing Minilesson Principle
Tell how two things are the same or different.

Expanding Nonfiction Writing

You Will Need

- several familiar nonfiction books, such as the following:
  - *The Perfect Beak* by Stephanie Petron Cahill and *The Amazing Seahorse* by Andrea Young, from *Shared Reading Collection*
  - *Frogs*, *Cats*, and *Dogs* by Seymour Simon, from Text Set: Seymour Simon: A Scientific Eye
- excerpt from books written on strips of paper
- highlighter
- chart paper and markers

Academic Language / Important Vocabulary

- same
- different
- topic

Continuum Connection

- Introduce ideas followed by supportive details and examples
- Select information that will support the topic
- Select details that will support a topic or story
- Add words, phrases, or sentences to provide more information to readers

GOAL

Compare and contrast one thing with another to provide more information to the reader.

RATIONALE

Comparing and contrasting two things is a very useful way to help readers understand a new concept. When you help children notice how writers (of all genres) use comparison and contrast in their writing as a way to help the reader understand a topic more deeply, they begin to try this in their own writing.

ASSESS LEARNING

- Observe children as they talk about nonfiction books. Do they understand how a writer uses comparison and contrast to tell more about a topic?
- Notice whether children use comparison and contrast in their own nonfiction books.
- Look for evidence that children can use vocabulary such as *same*, *different*, and *topic*.

MINILESSON

To help children think about the minilesson principle, engage them in noticing comparison and contrast in familiar nonfiction books. Here is an example.

- Show the cover of *The Perfect Beak*. Read the title and a short excerpt. Attach the excerpt to the chart.

  > What did the author do to teach you more about the topic?

- Add children's responses to the chart.

  > The author compared birds' beaks to objects that you might know so that you will understand what the beaks are like.

- Highlight (or have a child highlight) the words in the excerpt that show comparison.

- Repeat this process with more texts, such as *The Amazing Seahorse* and *Frogs*. Point out that in *Frogs*, the author shows how things are different.

Have a Try

Invite children to talk to a partner about comparison and contrast. Provide half the pairs with an excerpt from *Cats* (use the sentences on page 13 that contrast "smelling" nerve endings in cats and humans) and half with an excerpt from *Dogs* (use the sentence on page 7 that compares senses in dogs and humans).

> Turn and talk about what Seymour Simon did to teach you more about the topic.

▶ After children turn and talk, invite several pairs to share their ideas.

Summarize and Apply

Help children summarize the learning. Remind them to think about using comparison and contrast as they write nonfiction.

> How can you help your readers understand what something is like?

▶ Write the principle at the top of the chart.

> Today as you write, think about what is the same or different about your topic and something else. Write about that as a way to help your reader learn more about your topic. Be prepared to share your writing with your partner.

Tell how two things are the same or different.	
A beak is like a tool. A blue jay's beak is like a nutcracker. A heron's beak is like a fishing spear. — from <u>The Perfect Beak</u> by Stephanie Petron Cahill	• Beaks are like tools.
A seahorse's tail is like a monkey's tail. — from <u>The Amazing Seahorse</u> by Andrea Young	• A seahorse's tail is similar to a monkey's tail.
Most frogs have bulging eyes, smooth skin, long hind legs, and webbed feet, and live in or near water. Most toads live on land, have dry skin with warts and stubby bodies with short hind legs, and are less active. — from <u>Frogs</u> by Seymour Simon	• Frogs and toads are different.

Confer

▶ During independent writing, move around the room to confer briefly with as many individual children as time allows. Sit side by side with them and invite them to talk about helping their readers understand the topic. Use prompts such as the following if needed.

- *What is something that is the same as your topic? How are they the same? What could you write to explain that to the reader?*

- *What is something that is different from your topic? How are they different? What could you write to explain that to the reader?*

Share

Following independent writing, gather children in the meeting area to share their writing with a partner. Listen in on the conversations. Then bring the class back together.

> What ideas did you hear from your classmates that you might try in your writing?

WML4

CFT.U10.WML4

Writing Minilesson Principle
Tell about an experience from your life to teach more about a topic.

Expanding Nonfiction Writing

You Will Need

- children's samples of writing that contain life experiences that taught more about their topic
- sample of a nonfiction book written by you
- highlighter
- chart paper and markers

Academic Language / Important Vocabulary

- experience
- explain
- topic

Continuum Connection

- Introduce ideas followed by supportive details and examples
- Select information that will support the topic
- Select details that will support a topic or story
- Add words, phrases, or sentences to provide more information to readers

GOAL

Use details from personal experience to explain more about a topic.

RATIONALE

When children notice and think about how authors (of all genres) use details from personal experience to explain more about a topic, they learn another way to engage the reader. They learn to use these details in their own writing.

ASSESS LEARNING

- Notice whether children understand the purpose of using details from their personal experience in nonfiction texts.
- Observe whether children include personal experience to explain more about a topic in their own nonfiction books.
- Look for evidence that children can use vocabulary such as *experience*, *explain*, and *topic*.

MINILESSON

To help children notice how a writer uses information from personal experience to explain more about a topic, use a child's writing, or your own writing. Here is an example.

- Display the first writing sample on chart paper.

  Ava is writing a book about soccer. This part is about places to play soccer. Listen as I read it aloud. Notice what she does to provide information about the topic.

- Read the sample. Highlight children's noticings.

  Ava's experience helped us learn more about where you can play soccer.

- Repeat with a second writing sample.

  Lucas wrote about bicycle safety. How did he use an experience from his life to give more information?

- Demonstrate adding information to your own nonfiction writing by telling about an experience from your life that explains your idea. Show the book you have written about roller skating.

  In my book about roller skating, I can tell about my own roller skating experiences as a way to teach you more. When I went roller skating on the bike trail, I had to be very careful. There were people running and riding their bikes all along the trail. When I went roller skating at an indoor rink, it was easier because everyone was roller skating. I can add that to my writing as a way to teach you more about my topic.

Have a Try

Invite children to talk to a partner about an experience from their lives that explains an idea they are writing about in a nonfiction book.

▶ Direct children to retrieve a nonfiction book they have been working on or have already written.

Think about the nonfiction topic you have chosen for your book. Turn and talk to your partner about an experience you have had that would help your reader understand your topic.

▶ After time for discussion, invite a few children to share their thinking. Assure children that not everyone has had an experience related to their topic.

Summarize and Apply

Summarize the learning. Remind children to think about including experiences from their lives that explain their ideas.

What can you do to teach your readers more about a topic?

▶ Write the principle at the top of the chart.

During writing time today, reread what you have written. Is there a place where you can add a personal experience? Will you need a new piece of paper? Bring your book to share when we come back together.

> ### Tell about an experience from your life to teach more about a topic.
>
> #### Places to Play Soccer
>
> Where can you play soccer? You can play on a field. You can also play soccer at the park. All you need is a goal and a soccer ball. My brother and I play soccer in our backyard. We don't have a goalie net so we use two buckets to mark where the goal should be.
>
> #### Bicycle Safety
>
> Bicycle safety gear is important. The gear you need is kneepads, elbow pads, and a bicycle helmet. The most important thing is a helmet. It really helps protect a rider's head during a crash. When I go to ride my bike my dad always asks if I have my helmet. He wants to be sure I am safe.

Section 3: Craft

Confer

▶ During independent writing, move around the room to confer briefly with as many individual children as time allows. Sit side by side with them and invite them to talk about expanding their nonfiction writing. Use prompts such as the following if needed.

- *What section of your book are you working on? Do you have a personal experience that would explain more to your reader? Talk about that experience. Add that to your writing.*

- *What personal experience do you have with your topic? How might that help your reader learn more? Where will you write that in your book?*

Share

Following independent writing, gather children in the meeting area to share their writing.

Who would like to share your writing?

Assessment

After you have taught the minilessons in this umbrella, observe children as they write and talk about their writing. Use *The Fountas & Pinnell Literacy Continuum* to notice, teach for, and support children's learning as you observe their attempts at writing.

▶ What evidence do you have of children's new understandings related to nonfiction writing?

- Do children give examples for their ideas? Are the examples appropriate?
- How clear are their descriptions?
- How successfully do they use comparison and contrast to expand their nonfiction writing?
- Do they tell about an experience from their lives to teach more about a topic?
- Is there evidence children can use vocabulary such as *examples*, *ideas*, *details*, *same*, *different*, *experience*, and *explain*?

▶ In what other ways, beyond the scope of this umbrella, are children ready to expand their nonfiction writing?

- Are they using description to give the reader a picture in narrative writing?
- Have they thought about the illustrations and graphics in their nonfiction books?

Use your observations to determine the next umbrella you will teach. You may also consult Suggested Sequence of Lessons (pp. 575–589) for guidance.

EXTENSIONS FOR EXPANDING NONFICTION WRITING

▶ Study introductions of informational books. Support children in writing a beginning that encourages the reader to continue reading.

▶ Study conclusions of informational books. Support children in writing a satisfying conclusion for their informational books.

▶ Study fun facts or sidebars. Encourage children to include fun facts or sidebars in their writing.

▶ Remind children to think about what their reader might be wondering about a topic as a way to expand or elaborate on their writing.

▶ Encourage children to think about different text structures they might incorporate as ways to elaborate or expand on their writing (e.g., a question-and-answer section rather than a whole question-and-answer book; a how-to section rather than a how-to book).

Minilessons in This Umbrella

WML1   Use shapes to draw people.

WML2   Draw people in different positions.

WML3   Draw people in a place.

WML4   Add color to your picture.

WML5   Make people look the same on every page.

Before Teaching Umbrella 11 Minilessons

Before teaching the minilessons in this umbrella, read and discuss a variety of picture books with different styles of illustrations and provide plenty of opportunities for children to independently draw and color without restrictions. Share a diverse collection of realistic fiction so children have exposure to the different ways illustrators use color and show movement in drawings. It would be helpful to share books with illustrations and with photographs of people. Because this umbrella focuses on drawing people, you will want to teach these minilessons as children are working on books that have people in them, perhaps picture books, memory books, or fiction books.

For mentor texts, use fiction books that have detailed illustrations of people, such as the following books from *Fountas & Pinnell Classroom™ Interactive Read-Aloud Collection* or books from the classroom library.

Interactive Read-Aloud Collection
Caring for Each Other: Family

Big Red Lollipop by Rukhsana Khan

Super-Completely and Totally the Messiest! by Judith Viorst

Pecan Pie Baby by Jacqueline Woodson

The Wednesday Surprise by Eve Bunting

The Importance of Friendship

First Come the Zebra by Lynne Barasch

Finding Your Way in a New Place

Home at Last by Susan Middleton Elya

Mango, Abuela, and Me by Meg Medina

The Have a Good Day Cafe by Frances Park and Ginger Park

As you read and enjoy these texts together, help children

- notice and talk about the illustrations,
- notice details in the background,
- notice the illusion of sound and motion, and
- talk about the colors in the illustrations.

Interactive Read-Aloud
Family

Friendship

Finding Your Way

Section 3: Craft

Writing Minilesson Principle
Use shapes to draw people.

Learning to Draw

You Will Need

- several familiar books with illustrations of people that can be easily broken down into shapes, such as the following:
  - *Big Red Lollipop* by Rukhsana Khan, from Text Set: Caring for Each Other: Family
  - *First Come the Zebra* by Lynne Barasch, from Text Set: The Importance of Friendship
- tracing paper, pencils, and a document camera or overhead transparencies and markers

Academic Language / Important Vocabulary

- draw
- shape
- oval

Continuum Connection

- Use drawings and sketches to represent people, places, things, and ideas in the composing, revising, and publishing process

GOAL

Understand that shapes can be used to draw people.

RATIONALE

Drawing people can be difficult. Teaching children to start with basic shapes will help them draw more easily and more representationally, which will assist them in getting their ideas onto paper. More accurate and detailed drawings may prompt children to include details from their illustrations in their writing.

ASSESS LEARNING

- Notice whether children try to make their drawings of people look realistic.
- Watch children draw. Are they using shapes to draw people?
- Look for evidence that children can use vocabulary such as *draw*, *shape*, *oval*, and any other vocabulary related to the names of specific shapes.

MINILESSON

To help children think about the minilesson principle, use several mentor texts to talk about drawings of people. Then model how to use shapes to draw people. Here is an example.

- Show pages 12 and 14 of *Big Red Lollipop*.

  What shapes do you see that make up Rubina's and Sana's body parts?

- Use your finger to trace over the body parts, showing how the body can be broken down into circles, ovals, rectangles, and angles.

  The illustrator used shapes to draw these people. Notice what I do as I use shapes to draw Haki in *First Come the Zebra*.

- Show page 26. Use your finger to trace the body parts of Haki. As you do, help children see beyond his white shirt and shorts to notice the ovals for his head and upper and lower body and the rectangles and angles for his neck, arms, and legs. Quickly sketch the shapes.

  What do you notice about what I have drawn?

  Characters need clothes to look real. Watch as I add clothes over the shapes.

- Attach a piece of tracing paper (or an overhead transparency) on top of the body-part shapes so they show through. Ask the children for guidance as to what shapes to draw for the clothing. Finish the drawing by adding facial features, hair, hands, and feet so that the shapes mostly do not show anymore. You will show the children how to add color to this drawing in WML4.

- As an alternative, you could invite the children to come up and draw the shapes or the clothing on chart paper.

Have a Try

Invite children to turn and talk about drawing people.

> Think about the way we drew Haki. You can draw anyone using shapes. Think about a person or some people you might like to draw. Turn and talk about how you might do that.

Summarize and Apply

Summarize the lesson. Remind children to use shapes when they draw people.

> How can you learn to draw people?

▶ Write the principle at the top of the chart.

> During writing time, draw a person. Remember to use ovals, rectangles, and angles in your drawings.

▶ If the children in your class are ready, you can show them how they can draw the shapes lightly with a pencil, draw the clothes over the shapes, and then erase the shapes. Otherwise, they can make a finished drawing by attaching a piece of tracing paper over the shapes and drawing the clothes on the tracing paper.

▶ Save the chart for WML4.

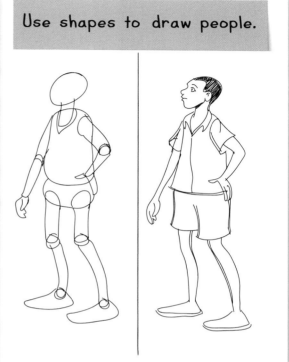

Use shapes to draw people.

Confer

▶ During independent writing, move around the room to confer briefly with as many individual children as time allows. Sit side by side with them and invite them to talk about drawing people. Use the following prompts as needed.

- *Let's look closely at some illustrations (photographs) of people in books from our classroom library. What body shapes do you see?*
- *What shapes do you see in the clothing?*
- *Show how you can use those shapes in your drawing.*

Share

Following independent writing, gather children in the meeting area to share their drawings.

▶ Ask all children to hold up their pictures for everyone to see.

▶ Select several volunteers to talk about their pictures.

WML 2

CFT.U11.WML2

Writing Minilesson Principle

Draw people in different positions.

Learning to Draw

You Will Need

- several familiar books with illustrations of people in various positions, such as the following:
  - *Home at Last* by Susan Middleton Elya, from Text Set: Finding Your Way in a New Place
  - *Super-Completely and Totally the Messiest!* by Judith Viorst, from Text Set: Caring for Each Other: Family
- tracing paper, pencils, and a document camera or overhead transparencies and markers

Academic Language / Important Vocabulary

- draw
- shape
- position
- seated
- behind
- in front

Continuum Connection

- Use drawings and sketches to represent people, places, things, and ideas in the composing, revising, and publishing process

GOAL

Understand that shapes can help show people in different positions.

RATIONALE

After children understand how to draw people using shapes, they can be taught to place the shapes to depict people in different positions. This allows them to illustrate their stories with characters engaged in any activity or situation.

ASSESS LEARNING

- Watch children draw. Are they using shapes to draw people in different positions?
- Look for evidence that children can use vocabulary such as *draw*, *shape*, *position*, *seated*, *behind*, and *in front*.

MINILESSON

To help children think about the minilesson principle, use mentor texts to talk about how illustrators draw people in different positions, and model how to do that. Here is an example.

- Show page 2 of *Home at Last*.

  What do you notice about how the illustrator drew the positions of the people?

- Guide the conversation to help children recognize that Ana is in front of her parents and that the parents are holding the babies.

  Let's look at some other pages and notice how the illustrator drew the people.

- Show and talk about pages 3–4 and 7–8. Point out how the illustrator drew some people seated and some standing, and some in front of and behind each other.

  Let's look at another book to see how the illustrator drew different positions. I will draw like the illustrator.

- Show pages 1, 5, and 12 in *Super-Completely and Totally the Messiest!* Ask volunteers to come up and point to the parts of the illustrations that show kneeling, sitting, and falling. Point out the angles that show movement.
- Turn to page 19 and begin drawing Sophie in the middle of the page taking a step. Start with the head and use ovals for body parts. Talk aloud about positioning as you draw.
- After you draw the shapes, use children's suggestions to finish the drawing on a piece of tracing paper or overhead transparency attached over the shape drawing.

Have a Try

Invite children to turn and talk about how to draw another position.

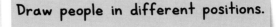

▶ Show page 15 in *Super-Completely and Totally the Messiest!* Ask a volunteer to stand the way Sophie is standing with an arm outstretched.

> Turn and talk about what shapes you see in the drawing of Sophie and in your classmate.

▶ Guide the conversation to help children recognize how the illustrator used shapes and drew Sophie in a position that is similar to how a person might look in real life.

Summarize and Apply

Summarize the lesson. Remind children to draw people in positions that match what they are doing in the story.

> How can you make the illustrations of the characters in your stories more realistic?

▶ Write the principle at the top of the chart.

> Today during writing time, try drawing the same person in two different positions. Bring your drawings to share when we meet later.

Confer

▶ During independent writing, move around the room to confer briefly with as many individual children as time allows. Sit side by side with them and invite them to talk about drawing people. Use the following prompts as needed.

- *Let's look in some books to see how the people are standing (sitting). How do the legs look?*
- *Where should you put the ovals for the person's legs (arms)?*
- *Which way should this angle point? Try to make the leg (arm) point in the same direction as the leg (arm) in the picture.*

Share

Following independent writing, gather children in the meeting area to share their drawings.

> Who would like to show a drawing of a person that you made today?

> Tell about what you were thinking as you drew the picture.

Section 3: Craft

Learning to Draw

You Will Need

- several familiar books that show detailed settings and perspective, such as the following:

  - *Mango, Abuela, and Me* by Meg Medina, from Text Set: Finding Your Way in a New Place

  - *First Come the Zebra* by Lynne Barasch, from Text Set: The Importance of Friendship

  - *Big Red Lollipop* by Rukhsana Khan, from Text Set: Caring for Each Other: Family

- chart paper and colored markers

- document camera (optional)

- To download the following online resource for this lesson, visit **fp.pub/resources**:

  - chart art (optional)

Academic Language / Important Vocabulary

- draw
- background
- close
- place
- detail

Continuum Connection

- Use drawings and sketches to represent people, places, things, and ideas in the composing, revising, and publishing process

---

GOAL

Learn to draw people in a setting.

RATIONALE

When children learn to give attention to drawing the background, they provide the reader with information about the setting. When they place people against a background, they have to think about the size and position of the people relative to the background (perspective).

ASSESS LEARNING

- Notice whether children understand that the background has important details.

- Observe for evidence of what children understand about perspective.

- Look for evidence that children can use vocabulary such as *draw*, *background*, *close*, *place*, and *detail*.

MINILESSON

Use mentor texts with backgrounds to engage children in a discussion about what can be learned from an illustration's background, and model drawing a background. If possible, project the pages. Here is an example.

- Show page 1 of *Mango, Abuela, and Me*.

  What do the details in this illustration tell you?

  You know who is in the illustration and where they are. Turn and talk to your partner about how you know if the people are inside or outside of the house.

- After time for a brief discussion, ask several children to share their thinking.

  The illustrator made the characters big. They look close to us. The illustrator wants to introduce us to the family.

- Show pages 9–10.

  What do you notice about this illustration?

  Here, the illustrator made the characters look small and far away to show that they are feeling sad that they can't speak to one another.

- Show pages 9–10 in *First Come the Zebra*.

  What do you notice about where the people are in this illustration?

- Guide the conversation to help them notice how the illustrator drew Abaani larger and at the front of the illustration and in front of the fencing. Point out that the other people are smaller. They look farther away and less important.

  How would you draw people to look close or far away?

- Record children's responses on chart paper.

Have a Try

Invite children to turn and talk about drawing people in a setting.

▶ Show the first page of *Big Red Lollipop*.

Turn and talk about what the illustrator is showing you in this illustration. How do you know?

▶ After discussion, ask volunteers to share. Children should note that Rubina has already run through the neighborhood, leaving it behind.

Summarize and Apply

Summarize the lesson. Remind children to think about the background when they draw. Write the principle at the top of the chart.

When illustrators draw people in a place, they think about what they want to show. Where is the person? Is the person close or far away?

These are questions you will think about when you draw today during writing time. Bring the illustrations you are working on to share when we meet.

▶ Some children may be ready to draw the illustrations for a story they are already writing, while others will want to experiment with drawing people in a setting first.

Draw people in a place.

To Make People Look . . .	Draw Them . . .
• Close	• Larger
• Far away	• Smaller

Confer

▶ During independent writing, move around the room to confer briefly with as many individual children as time allows. Sit side by side with them and invite them to talk about drawing. Use the following prompts as needed.

- *Tell me about this drawing.*
- *How will you show who is close and who is far away?*
- *What can you draw in the background to show where the story takes place?*

Share

Following independent writing, gather children in the meeting area to share their drawings.

Who would like to share the picture you drew today? Tell us about it.

What do you notice about the people in _____'s drawing?

Learning to Draw

You Will Need

- several familiar books with colorful illustrations of people and backgrounds, such as the following:
  - *The Have a Good Day Cafe* by Frances Park and Ginger Park, from Text Set: Finding Your Way in a New Place
  - *Pecan Pie Baby* by Jacqueline Woodson, from Text Set: Caring for Each Other: Family
  - *First Come the Zebra* by Lynne Barasch, from Text Set: The Importance of Friendship
- the black-line sketch from WML1
- markers, crayons, or paints of different colors, including representations of different skin tones and hair colors

Academic Language / Important Vocabulary

- drawing
- color
- diversity
- real
- illustration
- illustrator

Continuum Connection

- Create drawings that employ careful attention to color or detail

GOAL

Understand that color in pictures helps the reader understand more about the story.

RATIONALE

As children study the way illustrators intentionally use color (e.g., to make people and objects look realistic or fanciful, to highlight an important object), they realize that they can use color in similar ways in their own drawings.

ASSESS LEARNING

- Notice how children use color in their drawings.
- Observe whether children are choosing color to depict their characters in accurate ways.
- Look for evidence that children can use vocabulary such as *drawing*, *color*, *diversity*, *real*, *illustration*, and *illustrator*.

MINILESSON

To help children think about the minilesson principle, use mentor texts and engage them in an inquiry-based lesson around color. Then demonstrate adding color to a drawing. Here is an example.

- Show pages 13–14 of *The Have a Good Day Cafe*.

  What do you notice about the colors in this illustration?

  Why do you think the illustrator used so many different colors?

- Support a conversation about color choice in skin tone, hair, clothing, and background, helping children notice diversity of tones.

- Repeat the conversation using pages 15–16 and pages 23–24 in *Pecan Pie Baby*.

  What do you notice about the colors on these pages?

  When you choose colors to match the way people and things actually look, your drawings look real. Real people have diversity in skin tones and hair colors, and you can show that in your drawings.

  Watch as I add color to a drawing.

- Show the black-line sketch you made in WML1 and page 26 in *First Come the Zebra*, which has the original illustration. Say your thought process aloud as you choose colors and add them to the figure's face, hair, clothing, and other parts.

- As an alternative, you may decide to let children choose the colors without looking back at the original illustration.

  What did you notice I thought about when I added color to this drawing of Haki?

Have a Try

Invite children to turn and talk about what colors they will use for an illustration.

> What colors will you add to a drawing you are working on? Turn and talk to your partner about what your colors will show.

▶ After time for discussion, invite a few children to share their ideas.

Summarize and Apply

Summarize the lesson. Remind children to think about color in their illustrations. Write the principle at the top of the chart.

> Today during writing, you can work on your book. As you draw pictures for your book, remember to think carefully about what colors to use.

▶ As an alternative, children might choose to add color to a black-line drawing they have already made.

Add color to your picture.

Confer

▶ During independent writing, move around the room to confer briefly with as many individual children as time allows. Sit side by side with them and invite them to talk about drawing. Use the following prompts as needed.

- *What thinking did you do when you made these color choices?*
- *What color[s] could you choose to make this look real?*
- *Do these characters have the same color hair and skin? How will you show the diversity of skin and hair color?*

Share

Following independent writing, gather children in the meeting area to share their drawings.

> Turn to your partner to share your picture. Tell about the colors and how you made the color choices.

Section 3: Craft

Writing Minilesson Principle
Make people look the same on every page.

Learning to Draw

You Will Need

- several familiar texts with illustrations of human characters, such as the following:
  - *The Wednesday Surprise* by Eve Bunting, from Text Set: Caring for Each Other: Family
  - *Home at Last* by Susan Middleton Elya and *Mango, Abuela, and Me* by Meg Medina, from Text Set: Finding Your Way in a New Place

- on chart paper, a prepared simple sketch of a person, with room to add another

- markers, crayons, or paints of different colors

Academic Language / Important Vocabulary

- people
- character
- same
- recognize
- height
- illustrator

Continuum Connection

- Use drawings and sketches to represent people, places, things, and ideas in the composing, revising, and publishing process

- Create drawings that are related to the written text and increase readers' understanding and enjoyment

GOAL

Understand that it is important to draw people consistently on every page.

RATIONALE

When children learn that characters are drawn consistently throughout a book so that readers don't get confused, they learn to draw characters consistently in their own books.

ASSESS LEARNING

- Notice whether children try to draw characters consistently throughout their books.
- Look at children's drawings. Is there evidence that they think about a character's size when drawing the character on different pages?
- Look for evidence that children can use vocabulary such as *people*, *character*, *same*, *recognize*, *height*, and *illustrator*.

MINILESSON

To help children think about the minilesson principle, use mentor texts and demonstrate drawing a character consistently. Here is an example.

- Show the cover of *The Wednesday Surprise* and then show page 27.

  How do you know that the characters on the cover are the same characters on this page?

- Turn to pages 30–31.

  What clues did the illustrator give you to help you recognize Anna and Grandma?

- Help children see the consistency in the features.

- Show page 19 in *Home at Last*.

  Notice how tall Mia is next to her mother. She comes almost to her shoulder. How tall should Mia be standing next to her mother in other pictures?

- Have children point on their own bodies to indicate about how tall Mia would be when standing next to her mom. Show page 29.

  How consistent was the illustrator in showing Mia's size? Tell what you notice.

- Show pages 3–4 in *Mango, Abuela, and Me*.

  The illustrator drew Mia and Abuela in Mia's bedroom. What would the illustrator have included on other pages so you recognize Mia, Abuela, and the bedroom?

- Turn to pages 27–28 and support children in noticing consistencies in the characters and the background.

Have a Try

Invite children to turn and talk about consistency in drawings.

▶ Show the prepared sketch.

> I have drawn a person and now I'm going to draw the person again, but I'm going to change it a little. Let's say she is going to a soccer game, so she puts on a uniform. What should stay the same and what might be different? Turn and talk about that.

▶ After time for discussion, ask volunteers to share. Using children's suggestions, draw the character in the new outfit, showing how the person can still be recognized.

Summarize and Apply

Summarize the lesson. Remind children to make people look the same on every page.

> How can you help your readers recognize the characters throughout your book?

▶ Write the principle at the top of the chart.

> Today you learned that a reader has to be able to recognize characters throughout a book. When you work on the drawings in your book today, remember to draw characters so readers can recognize them on each page.

Make people look the same on every page.

Confer

▶ During independent writing, move around the room to confer briefly with as many individual children as time allows. Sit side by side with them and invite them to talk about drawing. Use the following prompts as needed.

- *Who is this character? Show where you have drawn this person before.*
- *What will you add to show that this is the same person as on the page before?*
- *How will you make this person the same on each page?*

Share

Following independent writing, gather children in the meeting area to share their drawings.

> Share two pages of your book to show a character that looks the same on both pages.

Assessment

After you have taught the minilessons in this umbrella, observe children when they illustrate their books. Use *The Fountas & Pinnell Literacy Continuum* to notice, teach for, and support children's learning as you observe their attempts at drawing and writing.

▶ What evidence do you have of children's new understandings related to drawing?

- Are children noticing and using shapes to draw people?
- Do they attempt to draw people in different positions?
- Do they try to be consistent with the way they draw their characters throughout the story?
- Can you tell from children's drawings of people in a place that children understand perspective?
- Are they purposeful about choosing which colors to use?
- Are they using vocabulary such as *draw*, *shape*, *position*, *seated*, *behind*, *in front*, *color*, *face*, *diversity*, *illustration*, *illustrator*, and *background*?

▶ In what ways, beyond the scope of this umbrella, are children showing an interest in drawing?

- Are they trying out different drawing and writing tools?
- Are they noticing drawings in the books they read and thinking about the choices that the illustrators made?

Use your observations to determine the next umbrella you will teach. You may also consult Suggested Sequence of Lessons (pp. 575–589) for guidance.

EXTENSIONS FOR LEARNING TO DRAW

▶ Support children as they try drawing people from the back and side. Ask a child to model moving in different ways and have children talk about what they notice before trying to draw the person on paper.

▶ During interactive read-aloud, invite children to notice how the illustrators used color and showed people against backgrounds.

▶ Teach children how to draw motion or sound lines and how to use colors to show a feeling (see CFT.U12: Adding Information to Illustrations).

Minilessons in This Umbrella

WML1   Add information to show how a person feels.

WML2   Use colors to show a feeling.

WML3   Draw motion or sound lines to show something moving or making noise.

WML4   Add information to your drawings to show more about people and places.

WML5   Show what is important in your picture.

Before Teaching Umbrella 12 Minilessons

Teach the minilessons in this umbrella when they are relevant to what children are doing. They can be taught in any order. In addition to these minilessons, there are other lessons that support children when they draw illustrations. CFT.U1.WML2 is a general inquiry-based lesson discussing the decisions that illustrators make.

Give children plenty of opportunities to make their own books. Read and discuss enjoyable books with detailed and informative illustrations. Use the following texts from *Fountas & Pinnell Classroom™ Interactive Read-Aloud Collection* and *Shared Reading Collection*, or choose illustrated books from the classroom library.

Interactive Read-Aloud Collection

The Pleasure of Giving

Those Shoes by Maribeth Boelts

My Rows and Piles of Coins
by Tololwa M. Mollel

Exploring Different Cultures: Folktales

How Chipmunk Got His Stripes
by Joseph Bruchac and
James Bruchac

The Empty Pot by Demi

Finding Beauty in the World Around You

Something Beautiful
by Sharon Dennis Wyeth

Last Stop on Market Street
by Matt de la Peña

Caring for Each Other: Family

Pecan Pie Baby
by Jacqueline Woodson

Big Red Lollipop by Rukhsana Khan

Finding Your Way in a New Place

Mango, Abuela, and Me
by Meg Medina

Shared Reading Collection

The Boy Who Cried Wolf: An Aesop Fable retold by David Edwin

As you read and enjoy these texts together, help children notice

- the specific details illustrators put into illustrations to support the story, and

- how illustrators draw their illustrations so the reader knows what is important.

Interactive Read-Aloud
Pleasure of Giving

Folktales

Finding Beauty

Family

Finding Your Way

Shared Reading

Writing Minilesson Principle
Add information to show how a person feels.

Adding Information to Illustrations

You Will Need

- several texts with illustrations that reflect feelings, such as the following:
  - *Those Shoes* by Maribeth Boelts and *My Rows and Piles of Coins* by Tololwa M. Mollel, from Text Set: The Pleasure of Giving
  - *The Empty Pot* by Demi, from Text Set: Exploring Different Cultures: Folktales
- chart prepared in advance with book titles
- markers

Academic Language / Important Vocabulary

- information
- feelings
- characters
- illustration

Continuum Connection

- Create drawings that employ careful attention to color or detail
- Create drawings that are related to the written text and increase readers' understanding and enjoyment
- Add details to drawings to add information or increase interest

GOAL

Draw characters' faces and bodies to reflect how the characters are feeling.

RATIONALE

When children notice illustrators often reflect how a character is feeling in how they draw the character's face and/or body, they begin to understand how these details help them to enjoy stories more and gain a deeper understanding of the story. They can then begin to try this in their own illustrations.

ASSESS LEARNING

- Observe for evidence that children recognize that characters' faces and bodies can reflect how the characters are feeling.
- Notice how children communicate emotion in the characters they draw.
- Look for evidence that children can use vocabulary such as *information*, *feelings*, *characters*, and *illustration*.

MINILESSON

To help children think about the minilesson principle, use familiar texts to engage them in noticing how details in characters' faces and bodies convey feelings. Here is an example.

- Show the cover of *Those Shoes* and read the title.

    What do you notice the illustrator did on the cover to show you how Jeremy feels?

    What information do you notice the illustrator put in Jeremy's facial expression?

    What do you notice about his body?

    What kind of feeling do you get when you look at this picture?

- Add responses to the chart paper.
- Repeat this process with the illustration of Jeremy and his grandmother on pages 11–12.

    What information do you notice in this illustration that helps you know how Jeremy feels? his grandmother?

- Repeat this process with *The Empty Pot*, using page 20.

Have a Try

Invite children to talk to a partner about the feelings shown in another illustration.

▶ Show pages 28–29 of *My Rows and Piles of Coins*.

Turn and talk to your partner about how you think the people in this illustration are feeling and what makes you think so.

▶ After children turn and talk, ask a few to share. Write their responses on the chart.

Summarize and Apply

Summarize the learning and remind children that they can add information to show how a person feels to their own illustrations.

What can you do to show how the people in your writing are feeling?

▶ Write the principle at the top of the chart and read it aloud.

Today as you begin to write, reread your story and look at the illustrations. Think about how the people in your story feel. Add information or change the characters' faces or bodies to show those feelings and help your readers understand more. Think about this as you begin new books, too. Bring your writing to share when we meet later.

Add information to show how a person feels.

Book Title	What does the face or body look like?	What feeling does that show?
Those Shoes	Sad face Walking away Hands in pockets Slumped shoulders	Sad
	Smiling face Boy pulling his grandmother's arm toward something Boy running	Excited
	Grandmother's eyes wide open	Surprised
The Empty Pot	Holding his head in his hands Sitting with elbows on knees Straight-line mouth	Disappointed
My Rows and Piles of Coins	Smiling faces Adults looking at the boy	Happy Proud

Confer

▶ During independent writing, move around the room to confer briefly with as many individual children as time allows. Sit side by side with them and invite them to talk about adding information to their illustrations. Use prompts such as the following as needed.

• *Read your story aloud. What were you feeling in that part? How can you draw your facial expression to help your reader to know that? How can you show that in the way you draw your arms and legs?*

• *The facial expression of this character looks _____. Your character must feel _____.*

Share

Following independent writing, gather children in the meeting area with their writing. Invite several children to share their illustrations.

Talk about how you drew a character's face or body.

Writing Minilesson Principle
Use colors to show a feeling.

Adding Information to Illustrations

You Will Need

- several texts with illustrations that convey feelings, such as the following from Text Set: Finding Beauty in the World Around You:
  - *Something Beautiful* by Sharon Dennis Wyeth
  - *Last Stop on Market Street* by Matt de la Peña
- chart prepared in advance with column headings *Colors* and *How the Colors Make You Feel*
- markers and tape
- multicolored crayons or pencils

Academic Language / Important Vocabulary

- feelings
- color
- illustration

Continuum Connection

- Create drawings that employ careful attention to color or detail
- Create drawings that are related to the written text and increase readers' understanding and enjoyment
- Add details to drawings to add information or increase interest

GOAL

Add colors to drawings to convey a certain tone or feeling to the pictures.

RATIONALE

When children notice that colors can be used in illustrations to show feelings and help the reader gain deeper understanding of the story, they can begin to try this in their own illustrations.

ASSESS LEARNING

- Observe whether children recognize that color can be used to show a feeling.
- Notice children's use of color to represent a feeling in their own illustrations.
- Look for evidence that children can use vocabulary such as *feelings*, *color*, and *illustration*.

MINILESSON

To help children think about the minilesson principle, use familiar texts to engage them in noticing how color can be used in an illustration to show feelings. Here is an example.

- Show the cover of *Something Beautiful*. Read and show pages 1–4.

  What do you notice about the colors the illustrator used here?

  Why do you think she used those colors? What kind of feeling do you get from the use of those colors?

- Add noticings to the chart.
- Repeat this process with the last two pages of *Something Beautiful*.

  When you read, notice the colors in the illustrations. Sometimes they are used to tell you more about how characters are feeling. You can use colors to show a feeling when you make books, too.

- Repeat this process with *Last Stop on Market Street*, using pages 17–18.

Have a Try

Invite children to talk to a partner about how they might use color to show feelings.

> Talk about how you would feel if someone special were moving away. What colors would help readers understand that feeling? Then talk about how you would you feel if that person came back to visit. What colors would help readers understand that feeling?

▶ After children turn and talk, ask a few to share.

Summarize and Apply

Summarize the learning and remind children that they can add color to illustrations to show a feeling in their own books.

> What did you notice about how color can be used in illustrations?

▶ Write the principle at the top of the chart.

> Today as you begin to write, reread your story.
> Think about how you or the other people in your story feel. Add some color to the illustrations to show that feeling. Think about this as you begin new books, too. Bring your writing to share when we meet later.

Use colors to show a feeling.	
Colors	**How the Colors Make You Feel**
Brown Gray	• sad • fearful
Bright colors **White** Light Blue	• hopeful • happy
Bright Blue Bright Orange	• calm • happy

Confer

▶ During independent writing, move around the room to confer briefly with as many individual children as time allows. Sit side by side with them and invite them to talk about the colors in their illustrations. Use prompts such as the following to support children as needed.

- *Read your story aloud. What were you feeling in that part? What color might you add to help your reader know what you were feeling?*
- *What color are you thinking of adding to your illustration? What feeling will that show?*

Share

Following independent writing, gather children in the meeting area to share their illustrations with a partner. Then choose several children to share with the group.

> What color did you use to show that feeling?

> What ideas did you hear from your classmates that you might try in your writing?

Writing Minilesson Principle
Draw motion or sound lines to show something moving or making noise.

Adding Information to Illustrations

You Will Need

- several texts with illustrations that use motion and/or sound lines, such as the following:
  - *Pecan Pie Baby* by Jacqueline Woodson and *Big Red Lollipop* by Rukhsana Khan, from Text Set: Caring for Each Other: Family
  - *The Boy Who Cried Wolf* retold by David Edwin, from *Shared Reading Collection*
- chart paper prepared with two columns
- labeled sticky notes: *Motion Lines* and *Sound Lines*
- markers
- To download the following online resource for this lesson, visit **fp.pub/resources**:
  - chart art (optional)

Academic Language / Important Vocabulary

- motion lines
- sound lines

Continuum Connection

- Create drawings that employ careful attention to color or detail
- Create drawings that are related to the written text and increase readers' understanding and enjoyment
- Add details to drawings to add information or increase interest

GOAL

Add motion or sound lines to show something moving or making noise in a picture.

RATIONALE

When children notice how lines are used in illustrations to indicate motion and sound, they will understand how this technique helps them to enjoy stories more and gain a deeper understanding of the stories. They can then begin to try this technique in their own illustrations.

ASSESS LEARNING

- ▶ Observe whether children recognize that lines can be used to show movement or sound.
- ▶ Notice children's use of lines to represent something in their own illustrations moving or making a sound.
- ▶ Look for evidence that children can use vocabulary such as *motion lines* and *sound lines*.

MINILESSON

To help children think about the minilesson principle, use familiar texts to engage them in noticing how lines can be used in an illustration to indicate motion or sound. Here is an example.

- ▶ Show *Pecan Pie Baby* and then show and read pages 7–8.

  What do you notice about this illustration?

  Why do you think the illustrator placed those small lines in the illustrations? What do those lines show you?

- ▶ Invite children to place the sticky note labeled *Motion Lines* at the top of the first column on the prepared chart paper. Add a sketch or two in the column to illustrate motion.

- ▶ Repeat this process with page 10 of *The Boy Who Cried Wolf* to point out how the illustrator showed sound.

  How did the illustrator show you that the boy is shouting?

Have a Try

Invite children to turn and talk to a partner about what the lines mean.

▶ Show pages 8–9 in *Big Red Lollipop*. After a moment, draw children's attention to the child in the upper right corner.

> Turn and talk to your partner about what the lines mean.

▶ After children turn and talk about what the lines show.

Summarize and Apply

Summarize the learning and remind children that they can use sound and motion lines in their own books.

> How do illustrators show movement and sound?

▶ Write the principle at the top of the chart.

> Today as you begin to write, reread your story. Look for a place to try using motion lines or sound lines. Think about this as you begin new books, too. Bring your writing to share when we meet later.

Draw motion or sound lines to show something moving or making noise.

| Motion Lines | Sound Lines |

Confer

▶ During independent writing, move around the room to confer briefly with as many individual children as time allows. Sit side by side with them and invite them to talk about adding information to their illustrations. Use prompts such as the following as needed.

- *Read your story aloud. Who or what was moving in this part of the story? How can you add motion lines to help the reader understand that?*

- *Read your story aloud. What sounds did you hear in this part of the story? How can you add sound lines to help the reader understand that?*

Share

Following independent writing, gather children in the meeting area with their writing. Invite several children to share their illustrations.

> How did you use motion or sound lines in your drawings?

WML4
CFT.U12.WML4

Writing Minilesson Principle
Add information to your drawings to show more about people and places.

Adding Information to Illustrations

You Will Need

- several texts with detailed illustrations, such as the following:
  - *Those Shoes* by Maribeth Boelts and *My Rows and Piles of Coins* by Tololwa M. Mollel, from Text Set: The Pleasure of Giving
  - *Something Beautiful* by Sharon Dennis Wyeth, from Text Set: Finding Beauty in the World Around You
- chart prepared in advance with book titles
- markers
- five sticky notes, three labeled *Place* and one each labeled *Person* and *Weather*

Academic Language / Important Vocabulary

- information

Continuum Connection

- Create drawings that employ careful attention to color or detail
- Create drawings that are related to the written text and increase readers' understanding and enjoyment
- Add details to drawings to add information or increase interest

GOAL

Add specific details to drawings to give information about the people or the places in the story.

RATIONALE

When children notice details in illustrations, they begin to understand how these details help them enjoy stories more and understand the story better. They can then begin to try this in their own illustrations.

ASSESS LEARNING

- ▶ Observe for evidence that children recognize that specific details in drawings give information about the people or places in the story.
- ▶ Notice children's use of specific details in their own illustrations.
- ▶ Observe for evidence that children can use vocabulary such as *information*.

MINILESSON

To help children think about the minilesson principle, use familiar texts to engage them in noticing how specific details can be used in an illustration to show more about people, places, or weather. Here is an example.

- ▶ Show the cover of *Those Shoes* and pages 19–20.

  What information do you notice in the illustration?

  What did the illustrator draw to help you know more about this person?

  What does the information in the illustration tell you about where this part of the story takes place?

- ▶ Add responses to the chart paper.

  The illustrator added information in the drawing to show what Jeremy's room looks like and that Jeremy loves dinosaurs.

- ▶ Repeat this process with the illustration on pages 3–4 in *My Rows and Piles of Coins*. Then discuss how the illustration tells the reader about the place and the weather.

  What information did the illustrator add to show where Saruni is?

  What information did the illustrator add to show the weather?

- ▶ Repeat this process with pages 1–2 in *Something Beautiful*.

Have a Try

Use sticky notes to label the *Place*, *Person*, or *Weather* examples on the chart.

> The illustrations in *Those Shoes* tell you more about a place and a person in the story. I will label those with these sticky notes. Turn and talk to your partner. What does the information in the other illustrations tell you more about?

▶ After children turn and talk, ask a few to share. Place sticky notes in the appropriate places on the chart.

Summarize and Apply

Summarize the learning and remind children to include information in their own illustrations.

> How can your drawings show more about people and places?

▶ Write the principle at the top of the chart.

> Today as you get started with your writing, reread your story and look at the illustrations. Think of information you could add. Think about this as you begin new books, too. Bring your writing to share when we meet later.

Add information to your drawings to show more about people and places.

Book Title	Information	What the Information Tells You	What the Information Describes
Those Shoes	Furniture Dinosaurs Clothes hanging in closet	The boy is in his bedroom. The boy loves dinosaurs.	Place Person
My Rows and Piles of Coins	Outside Bags of goods Short-sleeved dresses/shirts Shorts	They are in an outdoor market. It is warm there.	Place Weather
Something Beautiful	Brick walls Windows Broken glass Garbage cans	The area outside the building needs cleaning up.	Place

Section 3: Craft

Confer

▶ During independent writing, move around the room to confer briefly with as many individual children as time allows. Sit side by side with them and invite them to talk about adding information to their drawing and writing. Use prompts such as the following as needed.

- *Read your story aloud. Talk about the people in your story. How can you add information to help the reader understand more about this person?*
- *Read your story aloud. Talk about the places in your story. How can you add information to help the reader understand more about this place?*

Share

Following independent writing, gather children in the meeting area to share their writing.

> What information did you add to your drawings?

> What ideas did you hear from your classmates that you might try in your writing?

Writing Minilesson Principle

Show what is important in your picture.

Adding Information to Illustrations

You Will Need

- several texts with illustrations that draw the reader's attention to what is important, such as the following:

  - *How Chipmunk Got His Stripes* by Joseph Bruchac and James Bruchac and *The Empty Pot* by Demi, from Text Set: Exploring Different Cultures: Folktales

  - *Mango, Abuela, and Me* by Meg Medina, from Text Set: Finding Your Way in a New Place

- chart paper and markers

- To download the following online resource for this lesson, visit **fp.pub/resources**:

  - chart art (optional)

Academic Language / Important Vocabulary

- illustration
- illustrator

Continuum Connection

- Create drawings that employ careful attention to color or detail

- Create drawings that are related to the written text and increase readers' understanding and enjoyment

GOAL

Use different techniques to draw the reader's attention to what is important.

RATIONALE

When illustrators decide how to illustrate part of a story, they think about whether a character or object needs to be shown as more important than other characters or objects. When children become aware of this kind of thinking and the techniques that illustrators use to show importance, they learn more ways to make their illustrations meaningful.

ASSESS LEARNING

- Observe whether children recognize that making decisions about what details to include in one's illustrations helps draw the reader's attention to what is important.

- Notice children's use of this technique in their own illustrations.

- Look for evidence that children can use vocabulary such as *illustration* and *illustrator*.

MINILESSON

To help children understand the minilesson principle, use familiar texts to engage children in noticing how an illustrator draws the reader's attention to what is important. Discuss how they can apply these techniques to their own writing and illustrations. Here is an example.

- Show *How Chipmunk Got His Stripes*. Then show and read pages 1–2 and pages 5–6.

  Look closely. What do you notice about how the illustrator drew the bear? What does that help you understand about the bear?

  What could you do in your own illustrations to show that something is important?

- Record on the chart as children share their thinking.

- Repeat this process with page 29 in *Mango, Abuela, and Me*.

  What information does the illustrator include here? What does that help you to understand at this part of the story?

  What could you try in your own illustrations to show how two people care about each other?

Have a Try

Invite the children to talk with a partner about how an illustrator shows what is important.

▶ Show pages 26–27 in *The Empty Pot*.

This illustration shows when Ping brings his empty pot to the Emperor. What do you notice? What is the illustrator showing you? Turn and talk about that.

▶ After children turn and talk, ask a few to share. Add noticings to the chart.

Summarize and Apply

Help children summarize the learning. Remind children to think about how they can use these techniques in their own books.

What did you learn about how you can draw the pictures in your books?

▶ Write the principle at the top of the chart.

Today as you begin to write, reread your story so far. Think about what is important at that point in the story. How will you draw your picture to help the reader know that? Think about this as you begin new books, too. Bring your writing to share when we meet later.

Show what is important in your picture.		
What does the illustration show?	What do the illustrations help you understand?	What can you do to try this?
	The strength, size, and importance of the bear	Draw an object or character big/large.
	They care very much about each other.	Draw close-ups of characters.
	The Emperor and Ping are the most important in this part of the story.	Leave out the background.

Confer

▶ During independent writing, move around the room to confer briefly with as many individual children as time allows. Sit side by side with them and invite them to talk about adding details to illustrations. Use prompts such as the following as needed.

- *Talk about the story you are writing. What is important in this part? What illustrations will you draw so the reader understands that?*

- *You focus on _____ in your picture. That helps the reader understand that _____ is important.*

Share

Following independent writing, gather children in the meeting area with their writing. Invite them to share with a partner. Then select several children to share their illustrations with the class.

What ideas did you hear from your classmates that you might try in your writing?

Assessment

After you have taught the minilessons in this umbrella, observe children as they draw, write, and talk about their writing. Use the behaviors and understandings in *The Fountas & Pinnell Literacy Continuum* to notice, teach for, and support children's learning as you observe their attempts at drawing and writing.

▶ What evidence do you have of children's new understandings related to adding information to illustrations?

- Do children add information to show how a person feels?
- Do they use colors to convey a certain feeling or tone?
- Do they use motion or sound lines to show something moving or making noise?
- What kinds of information do children show about the people or the places in the story?
- Do they draw pictures so the reader focuses on what is important?
- Do they notice and use vocabulary such as *feelings*, *character*, *illustration*, *color*, *motion lines*, *sound lines*, *information*, *illustrator*, and *illustration*?

▶ In what other ways, beyond the scope of this umbrella, are the children showing an interest in adding meaningful information to illustrations?

- Do they use details when they illustrate nonfiction?
- Are they using speech and thought bubbles?

Use your observations to determine what you will teach next. You may also consult Suggested Sequence of Lessons (pp. 575–589) for guidance.

EXTENSIONS FOR ADDING INFORMATION TO ILLUSTRATIONS

▶ Use mentor texts to explore how colors change from one page to the next to indicate a change in feeling or tone.

▶ To build ownership, make a display of children's illustrations that use motion or sound lines or that use perspective.

▶ Gather together a guided writing group of several children who need support in a specific area of writing, such as adding information to their illustrations.

▶ If you are using *The Reading Minilessons Book*, Grade 2 (Fountas and Pinnell 2019), consider teaching or reviewing LA.U26: Studying Illustrations in Fiction Books, which develops the concepts of this umbrella through the lens of a reader.

Minilessons in This Umbrella

WML1 Use photographs in your nonfiction book.

WML2 Look at pictures in books and try to include some of the same details.

WML3 Draw diagrams to give information.

WML4 Use close-ups to show details from a bigger picture.

WML5 Use maps and legends to give readers information.

Before Teaching Umbrella 13 Minilessons

Read aloud a variety of engaging, illustrated nonfiction books about different topics and give children plenty of opportunities to experiment with creating their own nonfiction books. For mentor texts, choose nonfiction books that include photographs, diagrams, maps with legends, and different styles of illustration. Use the following books from *Fountas & Pinnell Classroom™ Shared Reading Collection*, or choose other suitable nonfiction books.

Shared Reading Collection

Big Bites by Nicole Walker

The Amazing Seahorse by Andrea Young

Eaglets in the Nest by Annette Bay Pimentel

Busy Beavers by Mary Ebeltoft Reid

A Raindrop's Journey by Paloma Jae

As you read and enjoy these texts together, help children

- notice whether each book has photographs or illustrations,

- look closely at the pictures and share details that they notice,

- notice and understand maps and diagrams, and

- discuss how the images help them better understand the book's topic.

Shared Reading

Section 3: Craft

Using Illustrations and Graphics in Nonfiction Writing

You Will Need

- a familiar nonfiction book with photographs, such as *Big Bites* by Nicole Walker, from *Shared Reading Collection*

- a page from a nonfiction book or chart paper prepared with a photograph and text; cover the photograph

- a collection of other photographs (e.g., taken yourself, printed from the internet, or cut out from magazines)

- markers

Academic Language / Important Vocabulary

- nonfiction
- photograph
- author

Continuum Connection

- Use illustrations and book and print features (e.g., labeled pictures, diagrams, table of contents, headings, sidebars, page numbers) to guide the reader

- Use illustrations (e.g., drawings, photographs, diagrams) to provide information

GOAL

Understand that photographs make books interesting and help readers understand more about a topic.

RATIONALE

When children understand why and how authors use photographs in nonfiction books, they learn to study them for details and begin to use them in their own books.

ASSESS LEARNING

- Look for evidence that children understand that the photographs provide information about the topic.

- Notice whether children experiment with using photographs in their own nonfiction books.

- Look for evidence that children can use vocabulary such as *nonfiction*, *photograph*, and *author*.

MINILESSON

To help children think about the minilesson principle, use mentor texts to demonstrate the use of photographs in nonfiction books. Here is an example.

- Display the cover of *Big Bites* and read the title. Show several pages.

  This nonfiction book has a lot of pictures! What do you notice about the pictures in this book? What kind of pictures are they?

  This book has photographs. Some nonfiction books have drawings, some have photographs, and some have both. How are a drawing and a photograph different?

  Why might photographs sometimes be more helpful than drawings?

  Photographs let the reader know *exactly* how something looks in real life, which is very helpful in a book about a science topic. What do the photographs in this book help you learn more about?

  Authors use photographs in nonfiction books to help you learn more about the topic of the book. You can use photographs in your books, too.

Have a Try

Invite children to talk to a partner about a photograph in a nonfiction book.

▶ Show a page from a nonfiction book (or one that you have prepared on chart paper). Make sure the photograph is covered. Read the text aloud.

> There is a photograph hidden under this piece of paper. What do you think the photograph shows? Turn and talk to your partner about this.

▶ After children turn and talk, invite a few children to share their predictions. Reveal the photograph and talk about how the photograph adds meaning to the text.

Summarize and Apply

Summarize the learning. Remind children that they can include photographs in their own nonfiction books.

> Why do authors sometimes decide to use photographs in their nonfiction books?

▶ Write the principle at the top of the chart. Read it aloud.

> Today during writing time, work on a nonfiction book. Look for a page that could use a photograph. Bring your book to share when we meet later.

Use photographs in your nonfiction book.

Crocodiles have about 60 to 100 teeth. When crocodiles lose a tooth, they can grow a new one to replace it. They can replace each of their teeth up to 50 times!

Confer

▶ During independent writing, move around the room to confer briefly with as many individual children as time allows. Sit side by side with them and invite them to talk about illustrating nonfiction. Use prompts such as the following if needed.

- *What is this page about? Would a photograph help readers learn more about that? What should the photograph show? Let's think about where to find a photograph.*

- *Why did you choose that photograph?*

- *How will that photograph help readers learn about _____?*

Share

Following independent writing, gather children in the meeting area to share their writing.

> Who would like to share a photograph in your nonfiction book?

> Why did you choose that photograph?

Writing Minilesson Principle
Look at pictures in books and try to include some of the same details.

You Will Need

- a familiar nonfiction book with detailed photographs or illustrations, such as *The Amazing Seahorse* by Andrea Young, from *Shared Reading Collection*
- chart paper and markers or crayons

Academic Language / Important Vocabulary

- nonfiction
- illustration
- drawing
- detail

Continuum Connection

- Use illustrations and book and print features (e.g., labeled pictures, diagrams, table of contents, headings, sidebars, page numbers) to guide the reader
- Use illustrations (e.g., drawings, photographs, diagrams) to provide information
- Create drawings that employ careful attention to color or detail
- Create drawings that are related to the written text and increase readers' understanding and enjoyment

GOAL

Use other illustrators' pictures to get ideas for adding details to drawings.

RATIONALE

When children look closely at illustrations in books and copy some of the details they see, they develop their observational skills and create richer, more informational illustrations for their nonfiction books.

ASSESS LEARNING

- Notice how children choose the details to include in their illustrations.
- Look for evidence that children can use vocabulary such as *nonfiction*, *illustration*, *drawing*, and *detail*.

MINILESSON

Demonstrate looking closely at an illustration in a nonfiction book and drawing some of the same details in your own drawing. Here is an example.

- Show the cover of *The Amazing Seahorse* and read the title. Show page 15.

  I'm writing a book about sea creatures, and I want to include a section about seahorses. I will start by drawing an illustration of a seahorse. I want to make sure my seahorse looks real, so I'm going to look closely at the photograph in this book and draw what I see.

- On chart paper, draw a seahorse similar to the one on page 15. Think aloud as you try to replicate each of the details shown in the photograph.

  I see that the seahorse has a long, rectangular snout. I'm going to give my seahorse a snout like that. I'm also going to give it a small black eye like the one in the photograph. And I will put a small fin on its back. I will also give it a curled-up tail, just like the tail in the book.

- Stop before adding certain details (e.g., the plates).

  What did you notice about how I drew my seahorse?

Have a Try

Invite children to talk to a partner about what else to add to the drawing.

> Look closely at the seahorse in the book. Are any details missing from my drawing? What should I add? Turn and talk to your partner about this.

▶ After children turn and talk, invite a few pairs to share their thinking. Complete the drawing using the children's suggestions.

Summarize and Apply

Help children summarize the learning. Remind them to look at pictures to get ideas for their own illustrations.

> What can help you draw illustrations for nonfiction books?

▶ Write the principle at the top of the chart. Read it aloud.

> During writing time today, work on a nonfiction book. Look at illustrations in other books to help you with your own illustrations. Bring your book to share when we come back together.

Look at pictures in books and try to include some of the same details.

Confer

▶ During independent writing, move around the room to confer briefly with as many individual children as time allows. Sit side by side with them and invite them to talk about illustrating nonfiction. Use prompts such as the following if needed.

- *What are you going to draw on this page?*
- *Where could you look for a picture of a _____ to get ideas for your drawing?*
- *What details do you notice in that picture?*
- *Can you draw those details in your own illustration?*

Share

Following independent writing, gather children in the meeting area to share their nonfiction books.

> Raise your hand if you looked at a picture in a nonfiction book to get ideas for your illustrations. What details from the book did you include in your illustration?

Using Illustrations and Graphics in Nonfiction Writing

You Will Need

- familiar nonfiction books with diagrams, such as the following from *Shared Reading Collection*:
  - *Busy Beavers* by Mary Ebeltoft Reid
  - *Eaglets in the Nest* by Annette Bay Pimentel
  - *A Raindrop's Journey* by Paloma Jae
- a simple drawing of an animal, such as the drawing of a seahorse from WML2
- markers

Academic Language / Important Vocabulary

- nonfiction
- diagram

Continuum Connection

- Use illustrations and book and print features (e.g., labeled pictures, diagrams, table of contents, headings, sidebars, page numbers) to guide the reader
- Use illustrations (e.g., drawings, photographs, diagrams) to provide information

GOAL

Learn how to draw diagrams to give information.

RATIONALE

When children study diagrams in nonfiction books and think about why the diagrams were included, they learn that they, too, can create diagrams to give more information about a topic.

ASSESS LEARNING

- ▶ Observe for evidence of what children know about diagrams.
- ▶ Notice whether children try creating diagrams for their own nonfiction books.
- ▶ Look for evidence that children can use vocabulary such as *nonfiction* and *diagram*.

MINILESSON

To help children think about the minilesson principle, use mentor texts to demonstrate how diagrams can be used to give information. Here is an example.

▶ Display the cover of *Busy Beavers* and read the title. Show page 5.

  What do you notice about this illustration?

  What does the illustration help you understand?

  This is a special kind of illustration called a diagram. It shows you what a beaver's lodge looks like, and the labels and arrows help you understand what each thing is in the picture.

▶ Display the cover of *Eaglets in the Nest* and read the title. Show page 8.

  This is also a diagram. What do you notice about it? What does it help you understand?

▶ Display the cover of *A Raindrop's Journey* and read the title. Show page 15.

  What does this diagram help you understand?

  What are you noticing about diagrams? What would you say a diagram is?

  A diagram is a kind of illustration that shows the parts of something or how something works. A diagram usually has both pictures and words. Why do you think nonfiction authors use diagrams?

  A diagram makes it easier to understand a complicated idea. Sometimes words or drawings aren't enough—you need both.

Have a Try

Invite children to talk to a partner about how to make a diagram.

▶ Show a simple drawing of an animal, such as the seahorse drawing from WML2.

> We can turn this picture into a diagram to help readers learn more about seahorses. What could we add to our drawing to turn it into a diagram? Turn and talk to your partner about this.

▶ After children turn and talk, invite a few pairs to share their ideas. Label the body parts.

Summarize and Apply

Help children summarize the learning. Remind them that they can include diagrams in their own nonfiction books.

> Why might you draw a diagram in your nonfiction book?

▶ Write the principle at the top of the chart.

> During writing time today, work on a nonfiction book. Think about whether you could include a diagram to show the parts of something or how something works. Bring your writing to share when we meet later.

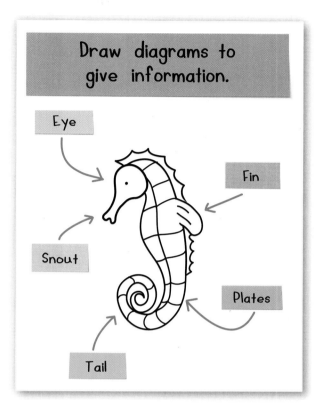

Draw diagrams to give information.

Eye

Fin

Snout

Plates

Tail

Confer

▶ During independent writing, move around the room to confer briefly with as many individual children as time allows. Sit side by side with them and invite them to talk about illustrating nonfiction. Use prompts such as the following if needed.

• *Could you add a diagram to help readers understand more about _____?*

• *What could the diagram show?*

• *What words could you write on the diagram?*

• *Where on the page might you put the diagram? Or do you want to put it on a page of its own?*

Share

Following independent writing, gather children in the meeting area to share their writing.

> Who would like to share a diagram you made today?

> What does your diagram show? What will it help readers learn?

Writing Minilesson Principle
Use close-ups to show details from a bigger picture.

Using Illustrations and Graphics in Nonfiction Writing

You Will Need

- a familiar nonfiction book with close-up illustrations or photographs, such as *The Amazing Seahorse* by Andrea Young, from *Shared Reading Collection*

- a simple sketch on chart paper of an animal, such as a cat

- markers

- To download the following online resources for this lesson, visit **fp.pub/resources**:

  - chart art (optional)

  - paper templates (optional)

Academic Language / Important Vocabulary

- nonfiction
- close-up
- detail
- illustration

Continuum Connection

- Use illustrations and book and print features (e.g., labeled pictures, diagrams, table of contents, headings, sidebars, page numbers) to guide the reader

- Use illustrations (e.g., drawings, photographs, diagrams) to provide information

GOAL

Use close-ups to magnify one part of a bigger picture.

RATIONALE

When children notice close-up illustrations in nonfiction books and think about why they are included, they learn that they, too, can use close-ups to show one part of an illustration in greater detail.

ASSESS LEARNING

- Observe for evidence that children understand the purpose of a close-up.

- Notice whether children try creating close-up illustrations for their own nonfiction books.

- Look for evidence that children can use vocabulary such as *nonfiction*, *close-up*, *detail*, and *illustration*.

MINILESSON

To help children think about the minilesson principle, use a mentor text to demonstrate how and why close-ups are used in nonfiction. Below is an example. You might want to have children use the close-up paper template when they write their nonfiction books.

- Show the cover of *The Amazing Seahorse* and read the title. Show page 14. Point to the close-up of the armadillo's plates.

  What do you notice about this box?

  What does the box help you understand?

  The photograph in the little box is called a close-up. Why do you think it's called that?

  A close-up shows one small part of the bigger picture as if you've moved closer to it. Why might this be helpful to the reader?

  A close-up helps you see one part of the picture in more detail. When might it be helpful to include a close-up in a nonfiction book?

Have a Try

Invite children to talk to a partner about how to create a close-up.

▶ Show a simple sketch of an animal, such as a cat.

> I drew this picture of a cat for my book, and I would like to add a close-up to it. What could I show in the close-up? What part of the cat might readers want to see in more detail? Turn and talk to your partner about this.

▶ After children turn and talk, invite a few pairs to share their thinking. Demonstrate drawing a close-up. Ask children what details to include.

Summarize and Apply

Help children summarize the learning. Remind them that they can use close-ups in their own nonfiction books.

> Why do illustrators sometimes decide to use close-ups in nonfiction books?

▶ Write the principle at the top of the chart.

> Today during writing time, work on a nonfiction book. Think about whether you could use a close-up to show details from a bigger picture. Bring your book to share when we come back together.

Use close-ups to show details from a bigger picture.

Confer

▶ During independent writing, move around the room to confer briefly with as many individual children as time allows. Sit side by side with them and invite them to talk about illustrating nonfiction. Use prompts such as the following if needed.

- *Would it be helpful to readers to show one part of the illustration in more detail? Which part?*
- *Would you like to add a close-up to show that part?*
- *What details will you show in the close-up?*

Share

Following independent writing, gather children in the meeting area to share their illustrations.

> Did anyone add a close-up to an illustration today? What does your close-up show?

Writing Minilesson Principle
Use maps and legends to give readers information.

Using Illustrations and Graphics in Nonfiction Writing

You Will Need

▸ a familiar nonfiction book with a map and legend, such as *Eaglets in the Nest* by Annette Bay Pimentel, from *Shared Reading Collection*

▸ a simple hand-drawn map (with a legend) of your local area prepared on chart paper

▸ markers

▸ tracing paper

Academic Language / Important Vocabulary

▸ nonfiction

▸ map

▸ legend

▸ information

Continuum Connection

▸ Use illustrations and book and print features (e.g., labeled pictures, diagrams, table of contents, headings, sidebars, page numbers) to guide the reader

▸ Use illustrations (e.g., drawings, photographs, diagrams) to provide information

GOAL

Use maps and legends to provide more information for the reader.

RATIONALE

When children study maps in nonfiction books, they learn how to read maps and understand why they are helpful. They also learn that they, too, can use maps and legends to provide more information for the reader.

ASSESS LEARNING

▸ Observe for evidence of what children know about maps and legends.

▸ Notice whether children try creating maps and legends for their own nonfiction books.

▸ Look for evidence that children can use vocabulary such as *nonfiction*, *map*, *legend*, and *information*.

MINILESSON

To help children think about the minilesson principle, use mentor texts to demonstrate how maps and legends can be used to give information. Here is an example.

▸ Show the cover of *Eaglets in the Nest* and read the title. Turn to page 2. Point to the map.

> What kind of picture is this?

> This is a special kind of picture called a map. What is a map?

> This map shows part of the world: North America, Central America, and a little bit of South America. The author used this map to give information about bald eagles. What information does the map show about bald eagles?

> It shows where in the world bald eagles live. Who can point to the part of the map where bald eagles live?

▸ Help children understand that the legend gives information about what is shown in the map.

> A legend helps you understand what the map shows. In this legend, there is a red circle next to "places bald eagles live." The same red color is used on the map to show where bald eagles live.

▸ Show the map you prepared of your local area.

> I am writing a nonfiction book about our area, so I made this map of it. What do you notice about my map? What does it show?

Have a Try

Invite children to talk to a partner about the map of your local area.

> Is anything missing from my map? What could we add? Turn and talk to your partner about your ideas.

▶ After time for discussion, invite several pairs to share their ideas. Using children's responses, demonstrate adding at least one more place (e.g., a bank, doctor's office, movie theater) to the map and legend.

Summarize and Apply

Help children summarize the learning. Remind them that they can include maps and legends in their own nonfiction books.

> Why do authors sometimes use maps and legends in nonfiction books?

▶ Write the principle at the top of the chart.

> Today during writing time, work on a nonfiction book. Think about whether you could include a map and legend to give your readers more information about the topic. If so, draw a map of the place you want to show, or ask me for help in finding one. Bring your book to share when we come back together.

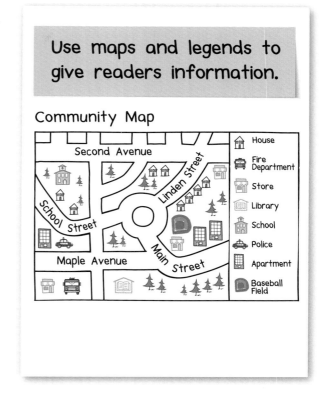

Use maps and legends to give readers information.

Community Map

Confer

▶ During independent writing, move around the room to confer briefly with as many individual children as time allows. Sit side by side with them and invite them to talk about illustrating nonfiction. Use prompts such as the following if needed.

- *What is your book about? Could you add a map to help readers understand more about that?*
- *What place do you want your map to show? Let's see if we can find a map of that place.*
- *Where on the page do you want to put the map?*
- *Do you want to add a legend to your map? What information will the legend give?*

Share

Following independent writing, gather children in the meeting area to share their writing.

> Did anyone draw a map today? What does your map show?

Assessment

After you have taught the minilessons in this umbrella, observe children as they write, draw, and talk about their writing and drawing. Use *The Fountas & Pinnell Literacy Continuum* to notice, teach for, and support children's learning as you observe their writing and drawing.

▶ What evidence do you have of children's new understandings related to illustrating nonfiction?

- Do children include photographs in their nonfiction books?
- Do they look at pictures in nonfiction books to get ideas for the details in their own drawings?
- Do they include diagrams and maps in their nonfiction books?
- Do they use close-ups to show details from a bigger picture?
- Do they understand and use vocabulary such as *nonfiction*, *photograph*, *detail*, *diagram*, *map*, and *legend*?

▶ In what other ways, beyond the scope of this umbrella, are children working on nonfiction books?

- Are they attempting to write different kinds of nonfiction books?
- Are they trying to add text and organizational features to their nonfiction books?

Use your observations to determine the next umbrella you will teach. You may also consult Suggested Sequence of Lessons (pp. 575–589) for guidance.

EXTENSIONS FOR USING ILLUSTRATIONS AND GRAPHICS IN NONFICTION WRITING

▶ Invite children to bring in photographs from home to use in their nonfiction books. You might also consider helping children look online for photographs or take their own photographs.

▶ Help children write captions for the photographs in their nonfiction books.

▶ Discuss other types of graphics in nonfiction books (e.g., graphs, charts, and infographics). Invite children to include these types of graphics in their own books.

▶ Gather together a guided writing group of several children who need support in a specific area of writing, such as adding various kinds of illustrations to their nonfiction books.

Minilessons in This Umbrella

WML1   Use borders to make your pages interesting.

WML2   Use scenes to show action and details.

WML3   Place illustrations in interesting ways on the page.

WML4   Place words in interesting ways on the page.

Before Teaching Umbrella 14 Minilessons

Teach the minilessons in this umbrella when they are relevant to the needs of the class rather than sequentially. Provide time for children to experiment with each technique before introducing another. Provide blank paper to children so they learn to make decisions about orientation (portrait or landscape) and to visualize how and where they will place illustrations and words.

Read and discuss picture books that illustrate a variety of art techniques. Use the following books from *Fountas & Pinnell Classroom™ Interactive Read-Aloud Collection* (along with the entire text set Steve Jenkins: Exploring the Animal World), or choose books from your classroom library that have interesting features.

Interactive Read-Aloud Collection

Steve Jenkins: Exploring the Animal World

I See a Kookaburra! Discovering Animal Habitats Around the World by Steve Jenkins & Robin Page

Facing Challenges

Abuela's Weave by Omar S. Castañeda

Courage by Bernard Waber

Jan Brett: Creating Imaginary Worlds

Comet's Nine Lives

Honey . . . Honey . . . Lion! A Story from Africa

Exploring the Natural World: Insects

The Bugliest Bug by Carol Diggory Shields

Caring for Each Other: Family

Big Red Lollipop by Rukhsana Khan

Pecan Pie Baby by Jacqueline Woodson

Living and Working Together: Community

The Library by Sarah Stewart

The Importance of Determination

Earrings! by Judith Viorst

As you read and enjoy these texts together, help children talk about how illustrators make their illustrations interesting.

Interactive Read-Aloud
Steve Jenkins

Facing Challenges

Jan Brett

Insects

Family

Community

Determination

Section 3: Craft

Writing Minilesson Principle
Use borders to make your pages interesting.

Making Illustrations Interesting

You Will Need

- books with pages that have borders, such as the following:
  - *Abuela's Weave* by Omar S. Castañeda, from Text Set: Facing Challenges
  - *Comet's Nine Lives* by Jan Brett, from Text Set: Jan Brett: Creating Imaginary Worlds
  - *Honey...Honey...Lion!* by Jan Brett, from Text Set: Jan Brett: Creating Imaginary Worlds
- a prepared story of your own
- chart paper and markers

Academic Language/ Important Vocabulary

- borders
- page
- author
- illustrator

Continuum Connection

- Provide important information in illustrations
- Add details to drawings to add information or increase interest
- Create drawings that employ careful attention to color or detail
- Create drawings that are related to the written text and increase readers' understanding and enjoyment

GOAL

Understand that writers and illustrators can use borders to help tell the story or provide information.

RATIONALE

When you help children notice how illustrators use borders around the edge of a page to add interest to the page and meaning to the text, they can experiment with the same technique in their own writing.

ASSESS LEARNING

- Notice whether children try using borders in their writing.
- Look for evidence that children can use vocabulary such as *borders*, *page*, *author*, and *illustrator*.

MINILESSON

To help children think about the minilesson principle, use mentor texts to show how illustrators use borders to create interest and meaning. Here is an example.

- Show the cover of *Abuela's Weave* and read the title. Show a few of the pages with decorative borders at the bottom.

  Think about the setting of this story. How do the borders help you understand the setting?

  In *Abuela's Weave*, the setting is the country Guatemala, and the borders show some of the patterns weavers make there.

- Repeat this process with page 1 of *Comet's Nine Lives*.

  On this page, Jan Brett writes about a cat who lives on an island, and the border matches the setting.

- Share a a page of your prepared story.

  My story is about when my uncle took us all to the beach. What could I draw as the border on my page to show the setting?

- Agree on a border and then draw it on the page.

Have a Try

Show the cover of *Honey . . . Honey . . . Lion!* Read the title and a few pages, being sure children look carefully at the borders and the larger illustrations.

> Turn and talk to your partner. Why do you think Jan Brett chose to use these borders in this book?

▶ Invite a few children to share their ideas.

> The borders show which animal will arrive next.

> Let's look at another page from my story. What border could help the reader know the next page will be about the beach?

▶ Sketch a border, talking about how the border makes the page interesting. Save your story for WML2.

Summarize and Apply

Help children summarize the learning. Remind them that they can use borders in their own books.

> How can you make your pages interesting?

▶ Write the principle at the top of the chart. Read it aloud.

> Today as you work, think about how you might use a border to make your pages more interesting. Your border can match the setting of your story, or it might show what will happen next in the story. You might begin with a blank page, or you can add a border to a finished page. Bring your book to share when we meet later.

Use borders to make your pages interesting.

Borders can match the setting or the action.

My cousins and I enjoyed a day at the beach.

Borders can tell you what might happen next in the story.

We headed out in my uncle's car. The car was so packed it looked like we were moving away!

Confer

▶ During independent writing, move around the room to confer briefly with as many individual children as time allows. Sit side by side with them and invite them to talk about their writing. Use prompts such as the following if needed.

- *What type of story are you working on today? What kind of border might you add?*
- *Which would support your story best: a border that matches the setting of the story or a border that shows what might happen next?*

Share

Following independent writing, gather children in the meeting area to share their writing.

> Who would like to share an illustration you made using a border?

WML2
CFT.U14.WML2

Writing Minilesson Principle
Use scenes to show action and details.

Making Illustrations Interesting

You Will Need

- books with illustrations that use scenes, such as the following:
  - *Earrings!* by Judith Viorst, from Text Set: The Importance of Determination
  - *Pecan Pie Baby* by Jacqueline Woodson, from Text Set: Caring for Each Other: Family
- your story from WML1
- a chart prepared in advance with excerpts from the books
- markers

Academic Language/ Important Vocabulary

- scenes
- author
- details
- illustrator
- action

Continuum Connection

- Understand that when both writing and drawing are on a page, they are mutually supportive, with each extending the other
- Provide important information in illustrations
- Add details to drawings to add information or increase interest
- Create drawings that employ careful attention to color or detail

GOAL

Understand that writers and illustrators can use scenes to show action and detail.

RATIONALE

Help children notice how illustrators draw scenes to add small details that are not mentioned in the writing. They can use this technique in their own writing, which leaves more room for important parts of the message in the text.

ASSESS LEARNING

- ▶ Notice whether children try using scenes in their illustrations.
- ▶ Look for evidence that children can use vocabulary such as *scenes*, *details*, *action*, *author*, and *illustrator*.

MINILESSON

To help children think about the minilesson principle, use mentor texts and your own writing (from WML1) to show how authors/illustrators use scenes to show action and details that are not described in the text. Here is an example.

- ▶ Show the cover of *Earrings!* and read the title. Read and show page 21.

  What do you notice the illustrator did here?

  How are the illustrations the same as the words? How are they different?

- ▶ Help children understand that the words say that the girl can be nice, but the illustrations show how. Write responses on the chart.

- ▶ Repeat this process with *Pecan Pie Baby*, showing and reading pages 13–14.

  What do the scenes tell you about the story?

- ▶ Help children understand that the illustrations show the uncles figuring out how to put things together for the baby, showing how busy and excited most everyone is about the baby. Point out how small and alone the girl looks in the corner. Write children's thoughts on the chart.

- ▶ Demonstrate how you might show action in your own writing. Read your story aloud.

  How can I use scenes to illustrate this part of my story?

- ▶ Sketch children's ideas on the chart.

Have a Try

Invite partners to talk about how they could use scenes in their books to show details or action.

> Where in the book you are working on could you use scenes to show details or action? Turn and talk to your partner about what you might draw.

▶ After children turn and talk, invite a few children to share their ideas.

Summarize and Apply

Help children summarize the learning. Remind them that they can use scenes in their own books.

> What did you discover about authors and illustrators today?

▶ Write the principle at the top of the chart.

> Today as you work, think about how you might draw scenes in your book to show action or details, such as how characters are feeling. Bring your book to share when we meet later.

Use scenes to show action and details.	
What the Words Say	**What the Illustrations Show**
<u>Earrings</u> Like, be nice to my little brother	Some ways that the girl could be nice to her brother
<u>Pecan Pie Baby</u> One Saturday, a huge box came and all afternoon my uncles were in my room, scratching their heads.	How the uncles feel (puzzled but excited) and how the girl feels (unhappy and alone)
The drive to the beach took a long time.	

Confer

▶ During independent reading, move around the room to confer briefly with as many individual children as time allows. Sit side by side with them and invite them to talk about their writing. Use the following prompts as needed.

- *What part of your story are you working on? How might you draw scenes to show the reader those details?*
- *Reread parts of your story and think, "Would using scenes help my reader understand more about the action or more about the details?"*
- *What are you hoping to show in your scenes? How will that help the reader understand the action or details of your story?*

Share

Following independent writing, gather children in the meeting area to share how they used scenes in their books.

> Who would like to share a page where you drew scenes? How did you decide to use scenes for this part of your story?

Umbrella 14: Making Illustrations Interesting

WML3

CFT.U14.WML3

Writing Minilesson Principle
Place illustrations in interesting ways on the page.

Making Illustrations Interesting

You Will Need

- books with interesting placement of illustrations on the page, such as the following:
  - *Big Red Lollipop* by Rukhsana Khan, from Text Set: Caring for Each Other: Family
  - *The Library* by Sarah Stewart, from Text Set: Living and Working Together: Community
- chart paper and markers
- To download the following online resource for this lesson, visit **fp.pub/resources**:
  - chart art (optional)

Academic Language/ Important Vocabulary

- place
- placement
- illustrator
- illustration
- author

Continuum Connection

- Understand that layout of print and illustrations is important in conveying the meaning of a text
- Understand that when both writing and drawing are on a page, they are mutually supportive, with each extending the other

GOAL

Understand that the layout of the illustrations and the print is important.

RATIONALE

Illustrators can enhance the meaning of a text by placing or sizing their illustrations in a certain way. When you help children notice this, they will not only understand more about what they are reading, but they can also use this craft technique when they make their own books.

ASSESS LEARNING

- Listen to how children explain why they placed an illustration on a page a certain way.
- Look for evidence that children can use vocabulary such as *place*, *placement*, *illustrator*, *illustration*, and *author*.

MINILESSON

To help children think about the minilesson principle, use mentor texts to show examples of illustration placement that brings more meaning to a text. Make sure children understand the meaning of *place* as used in this lesson. Here is an example.

- Show the cover of *Big Red Lollipop* and pages 14–15.

  What do you notice about the illustration on these pages?

  Why do you think the illustrator decided to draw the picture like that?

  It's an interesting view. The illustrator drew only Sana's legs and feet on the page, so we know she is running quickly away from her sister.

- Write responses on the chart paper. Then show pages 18–19.

  Look at these two pages. Why do you think the illustrator decided to draw Ami on one page and Rubina on the other page?

- Help children understand Ami looks big and angry and is staring right at Rubina, who looks smaller. The illustrator drew only part of Rubina, but enough to show how she feels. Write responses on the chart.

- Show and read page 3 of *The Library*, pointing out the small drawing of the flashlight next to the text.

  Why did the illustrator place the illustration here?

- Repeat this process with page 6 and the pencil. Add to the chart.

Have a Try

Invite the children to talk to a partner about how they might place illustrations in their books.

> Turn and talk to your partner about how you could place illustrations in your book to look interesting and also help your readers understand more about your writing.

> ▶ After children turn and talk, invite a few children to share.

Summarize and Apply

Help children summarize the learning. Remind them to think about how to place illustrations.

> What did you learn about the decisions illustrators make?

> ▶ Write the principle at the top of the chart.

> Today as you write, think about how to place illustrations in ways that look interesting and also help the reader understand more about your writing. You might begin with a blank page, or you can add to a page you have already begun. Bring your book to share when we meet later.

Place illustrations in interesting ways on the page.	
How the Illustrations Are Placed	**What the Placement Shows**
Trailing off the page	Someone is running quickly
	Someone is running away
Across two pages	One character looks bigger
	How the characters feel
Right next to the words	Adds meaning
	Makes the page look interesting

Confer

> ▶ During independent writing, move around the room to confer briefly with as many individual children as time allows. Sit side by side with them and invite them to talk about their writing. Use the following prompts as needed.

> • *What are you hoping the reader will think about on this page? How can you place the illustrations to help the reader think?*

> • *Could an illustration on the edge of your paper help the reader understand this part of your story?*

> • *How might creating small, simple illustrations next to the words help the reader?*

Share

Following independent writing, gather children in the meeting area to share how they placed illustrations in their books. If possible, share different examples of placement.

> Talk about how you decided to place illustrations in your book.

Writing Minilesson Principle
Place words in interesting ways on the page.

Making Illustrations Interesting

You Will Need

▸ books with interesting placement of words on the page, such as the following:

- *Courage* by Bernard Waber, from Text Set: Facing Challenges

- *The Bugliest Bug* by Carol Diggory Shields, from Text Set: Exploring the Natural World: Insects

- *I See a Kookaburra!* by Steve Jenkins & Robin Page, from Text Set: Steve Jenkins: Exploring the Animal World

▸ chart paper and markers

▸ To download the following online resource for this lesson, visit **fp.pub/resources**:

- chart art (optional)

Academic Language/ Important Vocabulary

▸ place

▸ placement

▸ word

▸ illustrator

▸ author

Continuum Connection

▸ Understand that layout of print and illustrations is important in conveying the meaning of a text

▸ Understand that when both writing and drawing are on a page, they are mutually supportive, with each extending the other

GOAL

Understand that the layout of the print and illustrations is important.

RATIONALE

Authors can enhance the meaning of a text by placing the print in certain ways. When you help children notice this, they will not only understand more about what they are reading, but they can also use this craft technique when they make their own books.

ASSESS LEARNING

▸ Look for evidence of what children understand about word placement.

▸ Observe for evidence that children can use vocabulary such as *place, placement, word, illustrator,* and *author.*

MINILESSON

To help children think about the minilesson principle, use mentor texts to show examples of word placement that add meaning to a text. Here is an example.

▸ Show the cover of *Courage* and read the title. Show some pages so that children can observe the print and illustrations.

> What do you notice about the placement of the words?

> There are just a few words at the bottom or top of each page. The illustration takes up most of the page. Why do you think the author made this decision?

▸ Next, show the cover of *The Bugliest Bug* and read the title. Show and read page 11.

> What do you notice about the words and the illustrations on this page?

> How does the placement of the words help you read them?

▸ Write the idea on chart paper.

▸ Show a few pages of *The Bugliest Bug* that have lots of text on them and then show the last page.

> The author made decisions about the number of words and the size of the words on the last page. What did you notice about the author's decisions?

> These words are important. How do you think the author wants you to read them?

▸ Add to the chart.

Have a Try

Invite children to turn and talk about word placement.

▶ Show the cover of *I See a Kookabura!* and read the title. Show the peacock worm on page 8 and the sea urchin on page 9. Invite children to talk to a partner about the interesting shape of the words.

> Turn and talk to your partner. What do you notice about the way the words are placed on these pages?

▶ After children turn and talk, invite a few children to share. Talk about what the placement of the words shows. Add to the chart.

Summarize and Apply

Help children summarize the learning. Remind them to think about where they place the words in their books.

> What can you do with the words in your book to make your writing interesting?

▶ Write the principle at the top of the chart. Read it aloud.

> Before you begin to write today, think about how you can place the words on the page to make your writing interesting and to help the reader understand more about your writing. You might begin with a blank page, or you can add to a page you have already begun. Bring your book to share when we meet later.

Place words in interesting ways on the page.	
How the Words Are Placed	**What the Placement Shows**
At the bottom or top	Makes the illustration look important
Spaced apart	Slows down how you read the rhyme
One sentence, bigger print *(Use bigger print.)*	Shows how important the sentence is and how to read the sentence
Shaped like animals *snake*	Makes the page fun to read

Confer

▶ During independent writing, move around the room to confer briefly with as many individual children as time allows. Sit side by side with them and invite them to talk about their writing. Use the following prompts as needed.

- *How are you thinking about placing the words on the page? Why?*
- *How are you thinking about placing the words on the page with your illustrations?*

Share

Following independent writing, gather children in the meeting area to share their writing. If possible, have children who tried different ways of placing their words share.

> How did you think about placing words on the page in your book?

Assessment

After you have taught the minilessons in this umbrella, observe children as they draw, write, and talk about their drawing and writing. Use *The Fountas & Pinnell Literacy Continuum* to notice, teach for, and support children's learning as you observe their attempts at writing and illustrating.

▶ What evidence do you have of children's new understandings related to making illustrations interesting?

- Do children use borders to make their pages interesting?
- Are they using scenes to show action and details?
- Are they thoughtful about the placement of the illustrations and words?
- Do they understand and use vocabulary such as *illustration, illustrator, placement, borders,* and *author?*

▶ In what other ways, beyond the scope of this umbrella, are children ready to expand their bookmaking techniques?

- Are they creating text features (e.g., table of contents, caption) for their books?
- Are they revising their writing to make it more focused?

Use your observations to determine the next umbrella you will teach. You may also consult Suggested Sequence of Lessons (pp. 575–589) for guidance.

EXTENSIONS FOR MAKING ILLUSTRATIONS INTERESTING

▶ Discuss how author/illustrators use lift-the-flap techniques to make their writing interesting. Look at books such as *Manfish: A Story of Jacques Cousteau* by Jennifer Berne, *Honey . . . Honey . . . Lion!* by Jan Brett (both from *Interactive Read-Aloud Collection*), and *Bigger or Smaller?* by Brenda Iasevoli (from *Shared Reading Collection*) and discuss why an author/illustrator might use the technique. Provide materials for children to try this in their own writing.

▶ Share other books from your collections that use interesting techniques, such as pop-up illustrations. Provide materials for children to try this in their own writing.

▶ Explore illustrations in nonfiction books when writing nonfiction texts. Use books such as *The Honey Makers* by Gail Gibbons and *Bugs for Lunch* by Margery Facklam to explore borders, and examples from Text Set: Steve Jenkins: Exploring the Animal World to discuss collage, interesting placement of illustrations, and scenes. (The books mentioned here are from *Interactive Read-Aloud Collection*.)

▶ Collaborate with the school art teacher as you explore creating illustrations with your children.

Section 4 | Conventions

A WRITER CAN have great ideas, understand how to organize them, and even make interesting word choices. But the ideas can get lost if the writer doesn't form letters correctly, spell words in recognizable ways, or use conventional grammar and punctuation. For writing to be valued and understood, writers need to understand the conventions of writing. The minilessons in this section are designed to strike a balance between teaching children to write clearly and making them comfortable about taking risks with their writing. Teach these lessons whenever you see that children are ready for them.

4   Conventions

Minilessons in This Umbrella

WML1   Write letters clearly.

WML2   Make letters the right size in a word.

WML3   Use good spacing.

Before Teaching Umbrella 1 Minilessons

The lessons in this umbrella help children focus on legibility and fluency by exposing them to the specific motor movements and techniques that will help them become efficient writers. The goal is to have children write with smooth movements and proportionality so that they can focus on message, craft, conventions, and process. Children shift from having to think about the mechanics of forming the letters, which slows them down, and move toward writing with more automaticity and fluency.

Lined paper is recommended for handwriting practice. Paper with a top and bottom solid line along with a dotted middle line is a good choice. Other paper choices can be provided, including blank unlined paper and paper with solid lines. The paper templates in the online resources provide some possibilities. You can also fold unlined paper, which gives the writer an idea of how to use space for lines of print without visible lines on the page.

As children develop fluency in their handwriting, it is important to be consistent in the language you use to describe the verbal path, which helps them internalize the most efficient way to write letters. Online resources, such as Alphabet Linking Chart and Verbal Path for Letter Formation, provide the information needed to teach or review how to form each letter.

It is not necessary to teach these lessons consecutively, so feel free to teach them when your observations indicate a readiness or need for a particular concept. For WML3, model spacing using an enlarged text, such as the following from *Fountas & Pinnell Classroom™ Shared Reading Collection*.

Shared Reading Collection

Side by Side: A True Story by Linda Ruggieri

As you read and enjoy these texts together, help children

- notice the size of tall and short letters,
- notice that the writing begins on the left side of the page, and
- notice the space between letters, words, and lines.

Writing Minilesson Principle
Write letters clearly.

Using Good Handwriting

You Will Need

- handwriting sentence strips
- tape
- sticky notes
- chart paper and markers
- To download the following online resources for this lesson, visit **fp.pub/resources**:
  - Verbal Path for Letter Formation
  - Alphabet Linking Chart
  - Letters Made in Similar Ways

Academic Language / Important Vocabulary

- smoothly
- direction words
- left
- right
- clearly

Continuum Connection

- Form upper- and lowercase letters efficiently and proportionately in manuscript print

---

GOAL

Follow the verbal path to form letters efficiently.

RATIONALE

When children learn to be consistent in how they form letters, they are able to write clearly, legibly, and with fluency. Fluent writing allows them to spend more time thinking about what they are writing rather than how.

ASSESS LEARNING

- Look for evidence that children follow the verbal path to form letters clearly.
- Notice evidence that children can use vocabulary such as *smoothly*, *direction words*, *left*, *right*, and *clearly*.

MINILESSON

Help children understand the importance of writing with efficiency and fluency. Support the lesson as needed with one or more of the online resources listed in You Will Need. Here is an example.

- Attach handwriting sentence strips to chart paper. Write a short sentence or two that include a combination of tall and short letters. Write the letters clearly and smoothly, saying the verbal path as you write a few letters.

  Take a look at the way I have written the letters and words in these sentences. What are some things you notice?

- Engage children in a discussion about how you said the direction words as you made the letters and placed the letters carefully on the lines. Have them note tall and short letters and the start and stop positions.

  I am going to add another sentence. Notice what I do.

- Compose a sentence that contains a few letters that are difficult for some of the children in your class to write, such as *d* or *y*. As you write, help children connect the difficult letters to letters they know. Use the verbal path to model your thinking. This is an example.

  An *o* is a letter you can write smoothly. Knowing how to make the letter *o* can help you write the letter *d*. To make the letter *o*, pull back and around. To make the letter *d*, pull back and around to make *o*, and then go up and down to make the letter *d*.

- Repeat the process with several letters, such as showing how a *v* can help write *y* and an *l* can help write *b*.

- As needed, continue in this way, discussing the verbal path, tall/short letters, and letters with straight lines/curves/circles.

Have a Try

Invite children to practice making letters with a partner and talk about how knowing some letters can help them write other letters.

> Turn and talk to your partner about the way you make letters. Practice with your finger in the air (or on the carpet) and say the words that help you make the letters.

▶ As needed, assist with the verbal path language.

▶ After time for discussion, ask volunteers if any letters helped them write other letters. Write a few of their examples on separate sticky notes.

Summarize and Apply

Summarize the lesson. Remind children to think about the verbal path when they write and to use letters they know to write other letters.

▶ Write the principle on a blank piece of chart paper and read it aloud.

> What are some tips we talked about today that will help you write quickly and clearly?

▶ As children provide ideas, write them on the chart. Add the sticky notes to the chart.

> Today during writing time, practice writing smoothly and clearly. Look at the chart for tips that will help. Bring your writing when we meet together later.

Confer

▶ During independent writing, move around the room to confer briefly with as many individual children as time allows. Sit side by side with them and observe if they are writing clearly. Use the following prompts as needed.

- *Is there a letter you know that might help to write this letter?*
- *Let's say the words that help write the letter _____ (use the verbal path).*
- *Is this a short letter or a tall letter? Does this letter have straight lines, curves, or circles?*

Share

Following independent writing, gather children in the meeting area to share their writing.

> Show a partner a letter that helped you write another letter.

I took my dog for a walk. Then we went home.

I drank some water because I was very thirsty.

Write letters clearly.

* Say the words that help you write the letter.
* Write the letters on the lines.
* Use letters you know to help you write other letters.

o helps with d	v helps with y
c helps with g	l helps with b

Section 4: Conventions

Writing Minilesson Principle
Make letters the right size in a word.

You Will Need

- chart paper prepared with a few sentences that use words common in your classroom and include a combination of tall, short, and sinking letters
- handwriting sentence strips for the chart and for each pair of children
- markers
- highlighter or highlighter tape

Academic Language / Important Vocabulary

- letters
- words
- size
- height
- sink

Continuum Connection

- Form upper- and lowercase letters efficiently and proportionately in manuscript print

GOAL

Use what is known about writing letters to fluently write letters of proportional size in words.

RATIONALE

When children learn to pay attention to letter size within words and write in an efficient and proportional manner, they are better able to get their message across to a reader.

ASSESS LEARNING

- Look for evidence that children understand that the size of letters in words matters.
- Observe whether children write letters of proportional size.
- Notice evidence that children can use vocabulary such as *letters*, *words*, *size*, *height*, and *sink*.

MINILESSON

Use high-frequency and commonly used words in sentences to demonstrate and discuss proper proportionality and placement of letters. Make sure children understand the term *sink* is used in relationship to letters that hang below the line. Here is an example.

- Read the sentences on the prepared chart paper aloud, pointing to each word.

  Take a look at these sentences. What do you notice about the letters?

- Support the conversation to help children notice tall letters, short letters, and letters that sink.

- Point out a few tall letters (e.g., *f*, *k*, *d*).

  What do you notice about the *f* in *family* (*k* and *d* in *weekend*)?

- Have a few volunteers use highlighter tape to mark the letters.

  Why is it important that the tall letters are all the same height?

- Ask children what they notice about the size of the short letters (e.g., *c*, *a*, *o*), having them point to the tops and bottoms.

- Repeat with letters that sink below the line (e.g., *y*, *p*, *g*), having children use highlighter tape to mark the sinking letters.

- Depending on your class, you may want to include uppercase (capital) letters in the discussion, or you may decide to save that for another time.

Have a Try

Invite children to engage with a partner in making letters proportional in size.

▶ Pass out a sentence strip and a pencil to each pair of children.

> With a partner, take turns writing a sentence. You can use one of the sentences we talked about today, or you can write a new sentence together.

▶ After time for a brief discussion, have volunteers share what they notice about the letters they wrote.

Summarize and Apply

Summarize the lesson. Remind children to make letters the right size in a word.

> Why is it important to make your letters the right size in a word?

▶ Write the principle at the top of the chart.

> Today during writing time, make your letters the right size. Look to see that each type of letter (tall, short, sinking) is the same size.

Make letters the right size in a word.

My family went to the movies this weekend. My favorite part of going to the movies is eating popcorn. I sat next to my cousin.

Confer

▶ During independent writing, move around the room to confer briefly with as many individual children as time allows. Sit side by side with them and observe whether they are making their letters proportional in size. Use the following prompts as needed.

- *Find tall (short, sinking) letters. Are they the same size?*
- *Why do you make sure your letters are the right size?*
- *How can you use these lines to help you make your letters?*

Share

Following independent writing, gather children in the meeting area to share their writing.

> Who would like to share your writing?

> Show a place where you made the letters the right size.

WML3

CNV.U1.WML3

Writing Minilesson Principle
Use good spacing.

Using Good Handwriting

You Will Need

- a familiar enlarged text, such as *Side by Side: A True Story* by Linda Ruggieri, from *Shared Reading Collection*
- highlighter tape
- chart paper and markers

Academic Language / Important Vocabulary

- appropriate
- words
- lines
- spacing
- within
- between

Continuum Connection

- Form upper- and lowercase letters efficiently and proportionately in manuscript print

GOAL

Leave proper spacing between letters, words, and lines.

RATIONALE

Spacing impacts readability. When you teach children to write with appropriate spacing, you teach them that the appearance of their writing is important in helping the reader understand the message.

ASSESS LEARNING

- Observe for evidence that children understand why appropriate spacing of letters, words, and lines is important.
- Look for evidence that children leave an appropriate space between letters, words, and lines.
- Notice evidence that children can use vocabulary such as *appropriate, words, lines, spacing, within,* and *between.*

MINILESSON

Prior to teaching this lesson, make sure children are able to differentiate between a letter, a word, a line, and a sentence. To help them think about the minilesson principle, use an enlarged text to help them notice the spacing between letters, words, and lines. Here is an example.

- Show and read page 8 of *Side by Side: A True Story*. Point under each word as you read.

  Notice the first sentence. How many words are in the sentence?

  There are seven words. How do you know?

- Guide children to talk about the small space between each letter and the large space between each word.

  What do you notice about the lines?

- Guide children to notice the number of lines on the page and the horizontal space between each line.

  Tarra and Bella are two friends who like to do things together. Let's write a sentence about something that friends do together. As I write, notice what I do.

- Write a sentence on chart paper, using two fingers to hold the space between words.

- Ask children for another sentence. As you write, emphasize how you are leaving good spaces between letters, words, and lines. The chart shows an example.

Have a Try

Invite children to talk to a partner about ideas for another sentence.

> Turn and talk to your partner about writing a sentence that tells something else friends like to do together.

▶ Ask volunteers for suggestions. Choose one or two more sentences to write. Invite two or three children to show you where to leave good space between letters, words, or lines.

Summarize and Apply

Summarize the lesson. Remind children to use good spacing when they write. Add the principle to the chart.

> What did you learn about good spacing?

▶ Invite a couple of volunteers to use highlighter tape to show examples of good spacing between words and between lines.

> When you write today, make sure you leave a good space between letters, words, and lines.

Use good spacing.

Friends like to make things together.

You can make a fort with towels

and sheets at a friend's house.

Friends can make popcorn for

a snack.

Section 4: Conventions

Confer

▶ During independent writing, move around the room to confer briefly with as many individual children as time allows. Sit side by side with them and observe whether they are using good spacing. Use the following prompts as needed.

- *Where will you start the next word (letter, line)?*
- *Leave a space to help your reader understand what you have written.*
- *Put the next word (letter, line) here.*

Share

Following independent writing, gather children in the meeting area to share their writing.

> Who would like to share the writing you did today?

> Show a place where you used good spacing on your paper.

Umbrella 1: Using Good Handwriting

Assessment

After you have taught the minilessons in this umbrella, observe children in a variety of classroom activities. Use *The Fountas & Pinnell Literacy Continuum* to notice, teach for, and support children's learning as you observe their attempts at writing.

▶ What evidence do you have of children's new understandings related to using good handwriting?

- Are children learning to write their letters quickly and clearly?
- Do they make letters the right size within a word?
- Do they use appropriate spacing between letters, words, and lines?
- Are they using vocabulary such as *smoothly*, *direction words*, *left*, *right*, *clearly*, *size*, *height*, *sink*, *words*, *lines*, *spacing*, *within*, and *between*?

▶ In what ways, beyond the scope of this umbrella, are children showing an understanding of best practices for the conventions of writing?

- Do children have ways that they can figure out how to write unfamiliar words?
- Are they willing to share their writing with others?

Use your observations to determine the next umbrella you will teach. You may also consult Suggested Sequence of Lessons (pp. 575–589) for guidance.

EXTENSIONS FOR USING GOOD HANDWRITING

▶ Gather together a small guided writing group of children who are struggling with a similar aspect of handwriting.

▶ Provide materials to help children with letter formation (e.g., stencils or plastic forms for tracing, sand, salt, modeling clay, wax sculpting sticks).

▶ Have children sort magnetic letters by different visual features. See Ways to Sort Magnetic Letters (in online resources) for suggestions.

▶ Spend a few minutes during the day having children make a letter in the air or on the rug to provide gross motor practice before the small motor practice of writing on a page.

Minilessons in This Umbrella

WML1 Say words slowly to listen for all the sounds.

WML2 Break words into syllables to write them.

WML3 Every syllable has at least one vowel.

WML4 Use what you know about words to write new words.

WML5 Write words that you know quickly.

Before Teaching Umbrella 2 Minilessons

This umbrella is designed to support children in learning how to write words so they grow more independent in their writing. Use shared writing to provide a scaffold for children to go from sounds to symbols. Children will also benefit from familiarity with letter-sound relationships and some work with phonograms.

As you teach these lessons, refer to classroom resources such as a word wall, ABC chart, and/or name chart, as well as items from each child's writing folder such as a smaller ABC chart, a smaller name chart, and/or a personal word list.

As you read and enjoy texts together, especially shared reading texts, help children follow along with the text as you read it by using a pointer to point under the words. Occasionally, have them

- clap the syllables in a multisyllable word,

- point to vowels in words, and

- point out words that they know.

Section 4: Conventions

WML1

CNV.U2.WML1

Writing Minilesson Principle
Say words slowly to listen for all the sounds.

Learning How to Write Words

You Will Need

- picture cards of words that have consonant clusters
- consonant cluster chart
- pocket chart
- blank word cards
- sentence strip
- markers
- To download the following online resources for this lesson, visit **fp.pub/resources**:
  - Consonant Cluster Linking Chart
  - Verbal Path for Letter Formation
  - chart art (optional)

Academic Language / Important Vocabulary

- word
- sounds
- letter
- slowly
- listen

Continuum Connection

- Say a word slowly to hear the sounds in sequence

GOAL

Say a word slowly to listen for all the sounds in sequence.

RATIONALE

When you teach children to say words slowly, they learn to isolate and identify the sounds they hear. Making the connection between a letter or a group of letters and the sounds they represent is key for both writing and reading.

ASSESS LEARNING

- Observe for evidence that children can say a word slowly and hear the first, middle, and ending sounds.
- Notice whether children can identify the letter or letters that go with a sound.
- Look for evidence that children can use vocabulary such as *word*, *sounds*, *letter*, *slowly*, and *listen*.

MINILESSON

To help children think about the minilesson principle, use picture cards of words that have easily identifiable sounds and include digraphs and consonant clusters. Here is an example.

- Display a picture card in a pocket chart (e.g., *trash*).

  Look at this picture. What word can we write to explain this picture?

  Say the word *trash* slowly to listen for all the sounds.

- Say the word aloud slowly, emphasizing the first two sounds.

  What two sounds do you hear first in *trash*?

  What are the letters that go with those two sounds?

- Have children find the letters on the consonant cluster chart. Record the letters on a word card.

- Repeat this process for the rest of the word, having children say the word slowly with you so that they can hear all the sounds in order. Remind them that two consonants together in a word can stand for one sound (*sh*).

- Run your finger underneath the finished word as you say it slowly and emphasize all the letter sounds. Place the card in the pocket chart.

- Repeat the process for a few more picture cards.

Have a Try

Invite children to work with a partner to listen for and identify the sounds in another word, such as *skunk*.

> What word could we write for this picture?
>
> Turn and talk to your partner about the first two sounds you hear in the word *skunk* and the letters that stand for those sounds. What sound do you hear next?

 Ask volunteers to share the sounds they heard in the correct order. Write the word on a card.

 Check the word by running your finger underneath it and saying all of the sounds slowly. Place the card in the pocket chart.

Summarize and Apply

Summarize the learning. Remind children to listen carefully for all the sounds in words as they write.

 Write the principle on a sentence strip and add it to the top of the pocket chart.

> When you write a word, make sure to say it slowly to listen for all the sounds before you write it. Be sure to write the letters in the order that you hear them.

Confer

 During independent writing, move around the room to confer briefly with as many individual children as time allows. Sit side by side with them and invite them to talk about their writing. Use the following prompts and the Verbal Path for Letter Formation as needed.

- *Say the word slowly so you can hear the sounds [model].*
- *What do you hear first? next? after that?*
- *You can think about the sound(s) and write the letter(s).*

Share

Following independent writing, gather children in the meeting area to share their writing.

> Who would like to share your writing?
>
> Point to a word you wrote. How did you know which letters to write?

Writing Minilesson Principle
Break words into syllables to write them.

Learning How to Write Words

You Will Need

- pocket chart
- picture cards of three- or four-syllable words that have easy-to-hear sounds and syllable breaks
- blank word cards
- a word card or whiteboard for each pair of children
- sentence strip
- markers
- To download the following online resource for this lesson, visit **fp.pub/resources**:
  - chart art (optional)

Academic Language / Important Vocabulary

- parts
- word
- syllable
- clap

Continuum Connection

- Take apart multisyllable words to spell the parts accurately or close to accurately
- Understand and talk about the concept of a syllable
- Hear, say, clap, and identify syllables in words with three or more syllables: e.g., *an/oth/er*, *bi/cy/cle*
- Say a word slowly to hear the sounds in sequence
- Use syllables to help spell a word

GOAL

Clap syllables and listen for the sounds to assist in writing unfamiliar words.

RATIONALE

When you teach children to say words slowly, they hear the syllables and understand that some words are short (one syllable) and other words are longer (two or more syllables). Clapping syllables emphasizes the breaks in words and offers a tool to assist in writing longer, unfamiliar words.

ASSESS LEARNING

- Observe for evidence that children can say and clap syllables in multisyllable words.
- Notice if children use syllables to break apart words when writing.
- Look for evidence that children can use vocabulary such as *parts*, *word*, *syllable*, and *clap*.

MINILESSON

To help children think about the minilesson principle, use picture cards representing multisyllable words with easily identifiable syllable breaks. Here is an example.

- Display a picture card of a three-syllable word and place it in a pocket chart (e.g., *strawberry*).

    Look at this picture. What is this?

    It is a strawberry. When you say the word *strawberry*, you can clap the parts you hear. Each part is called a syllable.

- Demonstrate saying and clapping *strawberry*.

    How many parts, or syllables, do you hear in the word *strawberry*?

    Strawberry has three syllables, so I clapped three times.

    To write the word *strawberry*, say the first syllable slowly and write the letters for the sounds you hear. Say *straw* with me slowly. What sound do you hear first? next? last?

- Record the letters for the first syllable on a word card. Then have children clap the syllables in *strawberry*, this time stressing the second syllable and listening for the sounds in *ber*. Record the second syllable.

    When you need to write a word you don't know how to write, try clapping the parts and then working on one syllable at a time.

- Repeat this process for the third syllable, *ry*. Record the third syllable and place the card in the pocket chart. Run your finger underneath the word as you emphasize all of the letter sounds.

- Repeat this process for additional picture cards for words that have easy-to-hear syllables, such as *violin*, *reporter*, and *hamburger*.

Have a Try

Invite children to work with a partner to clap the syllables in multisyllable words.

▶ Give each pair a blank word card or whiteboard. Show the picture of an umbrella.

> Say the word *umbrella* slowly with your partner and clap the syllables you hear. Turn and talk to your partner about the number of parts you hear. Say the parts slowly and talk about the sounds you hear and the letters that stand for those sounds. Write the word.

▶ Invite volunteers to share what they have written. Place a correctly spelled word card in the pocket chart. If children are ready, have them try a four-syllable word, such as *caterpillar*.

Summarize and Apply

Summarize the learning. Remind children to break words into syllables to help spell them.

> What can you do to make writing new words easier?

▶ Write the principle on a sentence strip and place it at the top of the pocket chart.

> When you write a new word that has more than one syllable, clap the syllables. Then say each syllable slowly so that you can write the letters for the sounds you hear.

Confer

▶ During independent writing, move around the room to confer briefly with as many individual children as time allows. Sit side by side with them and invite them to talk about their writing. Use the following prompts as needed.

- *Listen for the parts. Clap the parts you hear.*
- *Listen for the sounds you hear in the first (next, last) part.*

Share

Following independent writing, gather children in the meeting area to share their writing.

> Did you write a word with more than two syllables? What did you do?

Writing Minilesson Principle
Every syllable has at least one vowel.

Learning How to Write Words

You Will Need

- chart paper and markers
- a word card or whiteboard for each pair of children
- tape
- highlighter or highlighter tape
- sticky note labeled *Vowels*

Academic Language / Important Vocabulary

- sound
- consonant
- syllable
- letter
- vowel

Continuum Connection

- Understand and talk about the concept of a syllable
- Understand and talk about the fact that each syllable contains one vowel sound

GOAL

Understand that every syllable has at least one vowel.

RATIONALE

Understanding the terms *consonant* and *vowel* allows children to talk about letters and how words are made up of them. To help them write unfamiliar multisyllabic words, teach children which letters are vowels and that every syllable in a word contains at least one vowel.

ASSESS LEARNING

- Look at children's writing to see whether at least one vowel is included in every syllable.
- Look for evidence that children can use vocabulary such as *sound*, *consonant*, *syllable*, *letter*, and *vowel*.

MINILESSON

To help children think about the minilesson principle, begin by ensuring they are familiar with the terms *vowel* and *consonant*. Then discuss identifying and writing vowels in each syllable of a word. Here is an example.

- Write the vowels *a, e, i, o, u,* and *y* on chart paper.

  Say these letters with me as I point under each one.

  Does anyone know what these letters are called?

  These are vowels. All of the other letters in the alphabet are called consonants.

- Add the sticky note labeled *Vowels* next to the list of vowels on the chart.
- Write three multisyllable words on the chart.

  Read each word with me as I point to it.

- Place a line between the syllables to indicate the breaks.

  What are you noticing about the letters in each syllable?

- Highlight the vowel in each syllable.

  Every syllable has at least one vowel. When you write a word that is new to you, you have to write at least one vowel in each syllable.

- Write another multisyllable word on the chart, this time with the children.

  Let's write the word *alligator* together. Say it slowly with me and clap the syllables. Say the first part slowly, *al.* What letter comes first? What letter comes next?

- Repeat this process with the word *Saturday.*

Have a Try

Invite children to work with a partner to clap the syllables and listen for and identify the letters for the sounds they hear. Remind them to include at least one vowel in each syllable.

> Say the word *detective* slowly with your partner. Clap the syllables and turn and talk to your partner about the sounds you hear in each syllable and the letters that stand for those sounds. Write the word together on a word card (whiteboard).

▶ Tape a correctly spelled card from a pair of children to the chart, or write the word on the chart. Ask a volunteer to come up to the chart and point to the vowels. Highlight them.

Summarize and Apply

Summarize the learning. Remind children to use what they know about vowels to write new words.

> What did you learn about syllables?

▶ Write the principle at the top of the chart.

> When you write a word, it has to have at least one vowel in each syllable. Write consonants and vowels for the sounds you hear in the order you hear them.

Every syllable has at least one vowel.

Vowels   a   e   i   o   u   y

sun / rise

an / i / mal

wat / er / mel / on

al / li / ga/ tor

Sat / ur / day

de/tec/tive

Confer

▶ During independent writing, move around the room to confer briefly with as many individual children as time allows. Sit side by side with them and invite them to talk about their writing. Use the following prompts as needed.

- *Clap the syllables in the word (model).*
- *Say each syllable slowly.*
- *You need a vowel in each syllable.*
- *Write the letters for the sounds you hear.*

Share

Following independent writing, gather children in the meeting area to share their writing.

> Who can point to a new word you wrote? Does each syllable have at least one vowel?

Section 4: Conventions

Writing Minilesson Principle
Use what you know about words to write new words.

Learning How to Write Words

You Will Need

▸ chart paper and markers

Academic Language / Important Vocabulary

▸ letter
▸ word
▸ ending
▸ beginning
▸ sound

Continuum Connection

▸ Change an onset or rime to read or write other words: e.g., *br-ing*, *th-ing* (change *br* to *th*), *br-ing*, *br-own* (change *ing* to *own*)

▸ Use known word parts (some are words) to solve unknown larger words: e.g., *in/into*; *can/canvas*

GOAL

Use knowledge of known words to write unknown words.

RATIONALE

Teaching children to read and write every individual word in a language would be a huge, time-consuming, and impossible task. A more efficient approach is to teach children to use what they know (known words or parts of words, such as a letter, a cluster of letters, or a phonogram pattern) to understand something new. This equips them with tools to solve new words when they read and write.

ASSESS LEARNING

▸ Observe for evidence that children can use what they know to write unknown words.

▸ Look for evidence that children can use vocabulary such as *letter*, *word*, *ending*, *beginning*, and *sound*.

MINILESSON

To help children think about the minilesson principle, choose words that children know well (from the word wall if you have one) and demonstrate using them to write new words. Here is an example.

▸ Write the word *night* on chart paper.

> This is a word that you know well. Say it with me slowly: *night*.

▸ Write the word *might* on the chart directly below *night*.

> What do you notice about these two words?

> How do you think I knew how to write *might*?

> I used the word *night* and put an *m* at the beginning instead of an *n* to make the word *might*.

▸ Point under the letters as you guide children to understand that you used what you knew about the sound of the letter *m* and the word *night*.

▸ Repeat this process with other *-ight* phonograms such as the words *light*, *right*, *sight*, *bright*, and *flight*. If time permits, repeat this process with the word *kind*.

▸ Model how to use a known word, such as *be*, to write unfamiliar words.

> Let's think how you can use the word *be* to write the word *behind*.

▸ Write *be*. Help children say the rest of the word slowly to hear the sounds. Finish writing *behind*.

▸ Repeat with the word *between*.

Have a Try

Invite children to talk to a partner about using the word *an* to write other words.

> This is the word *an*. Turn and talk to your partner. What letter can you add to the beginning of *an* to write a new word?

▶ Write children's words on the chart. Ask if anyone knows the letter that could be added to the end of *an* to make *ant*.

Summarize and Apply

Summarize the learning. During independent writing, remind children to use what they know about words to write words that are unfamiliar to them.

> What is something you can do to help you write new words?

▶ Write the principle at the top of the chart. Read it aloud.

> When you want to write a new word, think about words you already know to help you write the new word. Bring your writing to share when we meet later.

Use what you know about words to write new words.			
night	**kind**	**be**	**an**
might	bind	behind	man
light	wind	between	pan
right	blind		ant
sight	grind		
bright			
flight			

Confer

▶ During independent writing, move around the room to confer briefly with as many individual children as time allows. Sit side by side with them and invite them to talk about their writing. Use the following prompts as needed.

- *What can you do if you don't know how to write a word?*
- *Do you know another word that starts (ends) like that?*
- *What word do you know that could help you write the word?*

Share

Following independent writing, gather children in the meeting area.

> Turn and talk to a partner about a new word you wrote. How did you know what letters to write?

Writing Minilesson Principle
Write words that you know quickly.

Learning How to Write Words

You Will Need

- chart paper and markers
- highlighter or highlighter tape
- To download the following online resource for this lesson, visit **fp.pub/resources**:
  - High-Frequency Word List

Academic Language / Important Vocabulary

- word
- quickly
- write
- spell

Continuum Connection

- Correctly spell approximately two hundred familiar high-frequency words, words with regular letter-sound relationships (including consonant blends and digraphs and some vowel patterns), and commonly used endings and reflect spelling in final drafts

- Recognize and use longer high-frequency words, some with more than one syllable: e.g., *after*, *around*, *before*, *their*, *there*, *these*, *very*, *which*

GOAL

Write known high-frequency words quickly and accurately.

RATIONALE

When you teach children to write high-frequency words quickly and accurately, they can share their thoughts in writing more fluently and begin to use these words as anchors to monitor and check their writing and reading. They will also be able to devote more time to writing words they do not know and to getting their messages across.

ASSESS LEARNING

- Observe for evidence that children can write high-frequency words quickly and accurately.
- Look for evidence that children can use vocabulary such as *word*, *quickly*, *write*, and *spell*.

MINILESSON

To help children think about the minilesson principle, engage in shared writing about a class memory, such as a field trip. If you have a class word wall, refer to it in the lesson.

- Help children to choose a class memory to write about together.

  Remember when we visited the public library together? Let's write about what we learned at the library. Turn and talk to your partner. What is something you learned from our visit to the public library?

- Invite volunteers to share. Work with the children to decide what to write.

  What should our first sentence be?

- While recording the sentence, stop before writing a high-frequency word and ask a volunteer to locate the word on the word wall.

  You know some of the words that we wrote because they are on our word wall and you see them in the books that we read. You know them very well.

- Continue soliciting and writing several sentences.

- Help volunteers highlight the words they know well (e.g., *our*, *went*, *to*, *the*, *so*, *that*, *it*, *has*).

  Who would like to highlight two words in these sentences that you know well?

  Who can point to these highlighted words on the word wall?

- Invite children to write a few high-frequency words in the air or on the carpet.

  You can write these words quickly because you know them very well. You don't need to spend a lot of time thinking about how to write them.

Have a Try

Invite children to practice writing words they know quickly by adding another sentence to the story on the chart.

> What is another sentence we can add?

▶ With children, decide on one more sentence. Write the sentence, perhaps inviting a child to write a well-known high-frequency word. The other children can practice writing the word in the air or on the carpet.

Summarize and Apply

Summarize the learning. During independent writing time, remind children to write the words they know quickly as they write. Add the principle to the chart.

> When you do your own writing and you write a word that you have seen and used a lot, remember to write it quickly the way you know how. Look at the word wall if you need to remember how to write a word. Be sure you write words so that you and others can read them.

Write words that you know quickly.

Public Library Information

Our class went to the public library so that we could learn about everything that it has to offer.

We need to fill out an application to get a library card.

After we get a card, we can borrow books to take home.

We can take out other things, too.

We can borrow DVDs, CDs, audiobooks, and book/CD packages.

They even have e-books!

Confer

▶ During independent writing, move around the room to confer briefly with as many individual children as time allows. Sit side by side with them and invite them to talk about their writing. Use the following prompts as needed.

- *What are you going to write about today?*
- *Read this page aloud. Is there a word that you were able to write quickly?*
- *Find the word _____ on the word wall.*
- *Write the word _____ quickly.*

Share

Following independent writing, gather children in the meeting area. Invite individual children to share their writing.

> Who would like to share your writing?

> Is there a word that you were able to write quickly?

Assessment

After you have taught the minilessons in this umbrella, observe children as they draw, write, and talk about their writing. Use the behaviors and understandings in *The Fountas & Pinnell Literacy Continuum* to notice, teach for, and support children's learning as you observe their attempts at writing words.

▶ What evidence do you have that children have learned ways to write unfamiliar words?

- Are children saying words slowly to listen for all the sounds?
- Do they break apart words into syllables and listen for sounds?
- Do they understand that every syllable has at least one vowel?
- Is there evidence that children use what they know about words to write new words?
- Can they write known words quickly?
- Do they understand and use vocabulary such as *letter*, *word*, *parts*, *syllable*, *consonant*, *vowel*, *ending*, *beginning*, and *sounds*?

▶ In what other ways, beyond the scope of this umbrella, are the children developing as writers?

- Would children benefit from keeping a personal word list and other resources in their writing folders?
- Are they ready to select a piece of writing to share with an audience?

Use your observations to determine the next umbrella to teach. You may also consult Suggested Sequence of Lessons (pp. 575–589) for guidance.

EXTENSIONS FOR LEARNING HOW TO WRITE WORDS

▶ To help children listen for sounds, use an audio device and have them record and then listen to several words that contain easy-to-hear sounds, including consonant clusters and digraphs.

▶ Continue to use shared writing to demonstrate slowly articulating unknown words and writing predominant sounds in sequence.

▶ Place games in the word work center to practice recognizing and writing high-frequency words, understanding syllables, or building words from a phonogram.

▶ Gather together a guided writing group of several children who need support in a specific area of writing.

▶ Gather together a small group of children to engage in interactive writing sessions to support their specific writing needs.

Minilessons in This Umbrella

WML1   Use punctuation to end a sentence.

WML2   Use quotation marks to show what someone said.

WML3   Use commas to separate words in a list.

WML4   Use an apostrophe to show something belongs to someone.

WML5   Use an ellipsis to show a pause or to build excitement.

Before Teaching Umbrella 3 Minilessons

Punctuation marks are used in conventional ways, but used creatively they can be considered author's craft. Writers carefully choose the punctuation that best helps them express the messages they are communicating. Teach each minilesson when you observe that children would benefit from it. Prior to teaching these minilessons, make sure children have had experiences reading and discussing books with a variety of punctuation marks. Before WML2, it is recommended that you teach CFT.U4: Adding Dialogue to Writing to acquaint children with the idea of dialogue before learning to punctuate it.

Use the books listed below from *Fountas & Pinnell Classroom™ Interactive Read-Aloud Collection* and *Shared Reading Collection*, or choose books with good examples of punctuation use from the classroom library. Enlarged texts are helpful so that children can clearly see the punctuation; however, you can also achieve this goal by projecting a page or by writing a sentence from a text on chart paper.

Interactive Read-Aloud Collection

Exploring the Natural World: Insects

When Lightning Comes in a Jar by Patricia Polacco

Shared Reading Collection

Busy Beavers by Mary Ebeltoft Reid

Paws and Claws by Arlene Block

A Raindrop's Journey by Paloma Jae

Inside a Cow by Catherine Friend

As you read and enjoy these texts together, help children

- observe the way your voice changes in response to different punctuation marks, and

- talk about the writer's intention in choosing a particular punctuation mark.

Interactive Read-Aloud
Insects

Shared Reading

Section 4: Conventions

Writing Minilesson Principle
Use punctuation to end a sentence.

Learning About Punctuation

Learning About Punctuation

You Will Need

- mentor text, such as Paws and Claws by Arlene Block, from *Shared Reading Collection*
- chart paper
- colored markers
- highlighter tape (optional)

Academic Language / Important Vocabulary

- punctuation
- sentence
- end mark
- period
- question mark
- exclamation point

Continuum Connection

- Use periods, exclamation marks, and question marks as end marks
- Read one's writing aloud and think where punctuation would go

GOAL

Use periods, exclamation marks, and question marks to end sentences.

RATIONALE

To convey their messages clearly, children need to know that a sentence ends with a period, a question mark, or an exclamation point. When they recognize that end marks convey meaning, they learn to use punctuation in meaningful and effective ways.

ASSESS LEARNING

- Observe children's writing for appropriate use of end marks.
- Look for evidence that children can use vocabulary such as *punctuation*, *sentence*, *end mark*, *period*, *question mark*, and *exclamation point*.

MINILESSON

To help children understand the minilesson principle, engage them in a discussion about why writers use end marks and how they can use them in their own writing. Here is an example.

- Show page 4 of *Paws and Claws*.

    What do you notice about the end of these sentences?

- As children identify each period, point underneath it.

    Why do you think the writer decided to add a period at the end of each sentence?

- Guide the conversation, helping them recognize that the period shows the end of a sentence, or one complete idea.

- Repeat the activity with question marks (page 16) and exclamation points (page 3).

- Guide children to recognize that a question mark shows that a question is being asked and an exclamation point shows excitement or surprise.

    Why do you think the writer chose to use different end marks for different sentences?

- Engage children in a conversation about end marks. Here are some helpful prompts:

    - *When do writers use this mark?*

    - *What does this mark tell the reader?*

    - *When will you write a period (question mark, exclamation point)?*

- You may choose to have volunteers come up and identify the end marks using highlighter tape.

Have a Try

Invite children to turn and talk about end marks by having them make sentences about something that interests them (e.g., something they do on weekends).

> What sentences could tell what you do on weekends? What questions could you ask? Turn and talk to a partner about that. Also talk about what end mark you would use.

▶ After time for discussion, ask several volunteers to share their sentences. As they do, write the sentences in the left-hand column on chart paper, using a different color for sentences with each type of end mark. Ask volunteers to share what the end marks show, and add responses to chart in the right-hand column.

Summarize and Apply

Summarize the learning. Remind children to add punctuation to the end of each sentence they write. Write the principle at the top of the chart.

> During writing time, think about whether you want to end a sentence with a period, a question mark, or an exclamation point. Bring your writing to share when we meet later.

Use punctuation to end a sentence.		
I play soccer. I help at my family's store.	●	complete thoughts
What do you like to do on weekends? Do you like to go on walks?	?	asking questions
I love biking! I can't wait to go to my aunt's house!	!	strong emotion excitement

Confer

▶ During independent writing, move around the room to confer briefly with as many individual children as time allows. Sit side by side with them and invite them to talk about using punctuation. Use the following prompts as needed.

- *Choose a sentence to read and talk about how you decided which end mark to use.*
- *How will this end mark help the reader?*
- *Where will you put the period [question mark, exclamation point]?*
- *How do you know when a sentence is finished?*

Share

Following independent writing, gather children in the meeting area to share their writing.

> Turn and talk to a partner about some of the punctuation you used in your writing.

Writing Minilesson Principle
Use quotation marks to show what someone said.

Learning About Punctuation

You Will Need

- a mentor text that has quotation marks, such as *When Lightning Comes in a Jar* by Patricia Polacco, from Text Set: Exploring the Natural World: Insects
- chart paper and markers
- document camera (optional)
- highlighter or highlighter tape
- To download the following online resource for this lesson, visit **fp.pub/resources**:
  - chart art (optional)

Academic Language / Important Vocabulary

- punctuation
- talking
- quotation marks
- opening
- closing
- comma

Continuum Connection

- Use quotation marks to show simple dialogue or to show what someone said

---

GOAL

Use quotation marks to show dialogue.

RATIONALE

Children learn about adding dialogue to their stories in CFT.U4: Adding Dialogue to Writing. Learning about how to punctuate dialogue will help them make their writing clear to their readers.

ASSESS LEARNING

- Observe children's writing for evidence that they know how and why to use quotation marks.
- Look for evidence that children can use vocabulary such as *punctuation*, *talking*, *quotation marks*, *opening*, *closing*, and *comma*.

MINILESSON

To help children understand the minilesson principle, engage them in a discussion about why writers use quotation marks and how they can use them in their own writing. Here is an example.

- Prior to this lesson, children should have explored using dialogue in their writing. They are now ready to think about how punctuation marks are used to show dialogue.

- Project page 1 of *When Lightning Comes in a Jar* or write the dialogue section on chart paper in advance.

  Take a look and listen as I read this page from *When Lightning Comes in a Jar*.

- Show page 1. Read portions of dialogue as necessary to point out the quotation marks.

  What do you notice about the punctuation on this page?

- Engage children in noticing that the characters are talking to each other and that Patricia Polacco used quotation marks, along with commas, questions marks, and periods, to show their dialogue. Guide the conversation to help children understand where to place the punctuation marks. Some suggested prompts are below.

  - *Which part of the sentence shows what someone said?*
  - *Where are the opening (closing) quotation marks placed?*
  - *What do you notice about where other punctuation marks are placed?*

Have a Try

Invite children to turn and talk about quotation marks.

> What do you like to eat? Turn and talk to your partner about your favorite foods.

▶ After time for discussion, ask a few volunteers to share their statements.

> First, I will write what I asked you. Where should I put the quotation marks?

▶ Then write the children's sentences on the chart, pausing to talk about the punctuation.

▶ Read each sentence aloud and ask a volunteer to highlight the quotation marks.

Summarize and Apply

Summarize the learning. Remind children to use quotation marks to show that someone is talking.

> In your writing, how can you show that someone is talking?

▶ Write the principle at the top of the chart.

> If your writing includes people talking, remember to use quotation marks around the words that the people say. Bring your writing to share when we meet later.

> Use quotation marks to show what someone said.

"What do you like to eat?" asked Mrs. G.

"My favorite food is pizza," said Tonia.

"I like to eat posole," said Jailyn.

"I eat lots and lots of carrots!" said Joseph.

"I like spicy noodles!"

Confer

▶ During independent writing, move around the room to confer briefly with as many individual children as time allows. Sit side by side with them and invite them to talk about using punctuation. Use the following prompts as needed.

- *Did you include talking in your writing? Read that part and show what punctuation you used.*
- *How will these quotation marks help the reader?*
- *Where will you put the quotation marks to show that someone is talking?*

Share

Following independent writing, gather children in the meeting area to share their writing.

> Who used quotation marks to show someone talking? Read and show the part of your writing that includes quotation marks to your partner.

WML3

CNV.U3.WML3

Writing Minilesson Principle
Use commas to separate words in a list.

Learning About Punctuation

You Will Need

- mentor texts that have several examples of series commas, such as the following:
  - *Busy Beavers* by Mary Ebeltoft Reid, from *Shared Reading Collection*
  - *When Lightning Comes in a Jar* by Patricia Polacco, from Text Set: Exploring the Natural World: Insects
- chart paper and markers
- highlighter or highlighter tape
- document camera [optional]
- To download the following online resource for this lesson, visit **fp.pub/resources**:
  - chart art [optional]

Academic Language / Important Vocabulary

- punctuation
- comma
- list

Continuum Connection

- Use commas to separate items in a series

GOAL

Use commas to separate items in a series.

RATIONALE

When children learn that commas are used to separate items in a series, they acquire another way of using punctuation to make their writing clear.

ASSESS LEARNING

- Observe children's writing to see whether they use commas to separate items in a series.
- Look for evidence that children can use vocabulary such as *punctuation*, *comma*, and *list*.

MINILESSON

To help children understand the minilesson principle, use examples from a mentor text to illustrate the use of commas in a series. Show or project the pages or write the sentences on chart paper. Here is an example.

- Show page 4 from *Busy Beavers*.

  Listen as I read a sentence from *Busy Beavers*: "Kits eat, sleep, and play inside the lodge." What three things do the kits do?

  What do you notice about the punctuation in this sentence?

- Point out the commas. Ask a volunteer to highlight the commas on the chart or in the book (with highlighter tape). Then continue with the next sentence.

  What is it like inside the lodge?

  How is this sentence similar to the first sentence we discussed?

- Read and show or write this sentence from page 30 of *When Lightning Comes in a Jar*: "We'll eat scrumptious Jell-O and meatloaf, play baseball and croquet, spit watermelon seeds, and scrawl new measurements."

  What do you notice about how this sentence is punctuated?

- Engage children in noticing that this time the commas separate groups of words. Ask a child to highlight the commas.

  How do commas help you read the words in a list?

- Guide the conversation to help children understand that writers use commas to separate the items in a list.

Have a Try

Invite children to interactively write sentences that need commas to separate items in a list.

> Share with me three or more things that you saw or did on the playground today.

▶ As a volunteer shares, write the sentence on chart paper, omitting the commas in the list.

> Now we need commas to separate the words in the list. Who can come up and add the commas as I read the sentence?

▶ Have a volunteer use a marker to write in the commas as you read the sentence. Pause each time a comma should be added. Then, read the entire sentence, still pausing slightly at each comma.

▶ Repeat with several examples.

Summarize and Apply

Summarize the learning. Remind children to use commas for words in a list. Write the principle at the top of the chart.

> Today you talked about placing commas between words in a list. During writing time, if you write words in a list, remember to add a comma between each item. Bring your writing when we meet later.

Use commas to separate words in a list.

Kits eat, sleep, and play inside the lodge.

It is warm, dry, and safe inside.

We'll eat scrumptious Jell-O and meatloaf, play baseball and croquet, spit watermelon seeds, and scrawl new measurements.

I saw the principal, swings, and two basketball hoops.

I saw ants, bees, leaves, and flowers.

I kicked a ball, walked around the playground, and went down the slide.

I played with Juan, Kieran, Skyler, and Sydney.

Confer

▶ During independent writing, move around the room to confer briefly with as many individual children as time allows. Sit side by side with them and invite them to talk about using punctuation. Use the following prompts as needed.

• *Will you include a list of items in your writing today? How will you use commas?*

• *How will these commas help the reader?*

• *Read the sentence that has items in a list with commas in between.*

Share

Following independent writing, gather children in the meeting area. Ask a few volunteers to share their writing.

> Who used commas to separate items in a list? Share the part of your writing that includes the commas and the list of items.

Section 4: Conventions

Writing Minilesson Principle
Use an apostrophe to show something belongs to someone.

You Will Need

- several mentor texts that have examples of apostrophes that show possession, such as the following from *Shared Reading Collection*:
  - *Paws and Claws* by Arlene Block
  - *A Raindrop's Journey* by Paloma Jae
- chart paper and markers

Academic Language / Important Vocabulary

- punctuation
- apostrophe
- belongs

Continuum Connection

- Use apostrophes in contractions and many possessives

GOAL

Use apostrophes to show possession.

RATIONALE

This lesson focuses on apostrophes used to show possession; however, you may want to help children make the distinction between apostrophes that show possession and those that are used to make contractions.

ASSESS LEARNING

▶ Observe children's writing to see if they are using apostrophes to show possession.

▶ Look for evidence that children can use vocabulary such as *punctuation*, *apostrophe*, and *belongs*.

MINILESSON

To help children understand the minilesson principle, use examples from mentor texts to illustrate how apostrophes are used to show possession. Here is an example.

▶ Show and read page 7 in *Paws and Claws*.

> Whose paws are these?
>
> How do you know?

▶ Guide the children to notice the apostrophe that shows possession.

> When you want to show that something belongs to someone or something, use an apostrophe and an s, just like the writer did when she wrote "polar bear's paws."

▶ On chart paper, make a two-column chart. In the left-hand column, write *polar bear's paws*, pausing before the apostrophe.

> Who would like to come to the chart and finish this word so that it shows that the paws belong to the polar bear?

▶ Add the word *paws*. Then write *the paws belong to the polar bear* in the right-hand column,

▶ Repeat with the possessives on pages 13 and 15. Add to the chart.

▶ On a different day, you may want to repeat this lesson with examples of words that end with *s'*.

Have a Try

Invite children to turn and talk about apostrophes.

▶ Show the cover of *A Raindrop's Journey*.

> Turn and talk about what you notice about the title of this book.

▶ After time for discussion, ask volunteers to share their thinking. Guide the conversation to have them notice the apostrophe and why the writer might have used it in the title. Add to the chart.

Summarize and Apply

Summarize the learning. Remind children to use apostrophes to show possession.

> What does an apostrophe show?

▶ Write the principle at the top of the chart.

> When you write today, remember to use an apostrophe to show that something belongs to someone. Bring your writing to share when we meet later.

Use an apostrophe to show something belongs to someone.	
polar bear's paws	the paws belong to the polar bear
woodchuck's home	the home belongs to the woodchuck
bat's claws	the claws belong to the bat
raindrop's journey	the journey belongs to the raindrop

Confer

▶ During independent writing, move around the room to confer briefly with as many individual children as time allows. Sit side by side with them and invite them to talk about using punctuation. Use the following prompts as needed.

- *Show a place in your writing where something belongs to someone or something.*
- *How will this apostrophe help the reader?*
- *Point to where you will put the apostrophe and the* s.

Share

Following independent writing, gather children in the meeting area. Ask a few volunteers to share their writing.

> Who used an apostrophe in your writing today? Share the part of your writing with an apostrophe.

Learning About Punctuation

You Will Need

- several mentor texts that have examples of ellipses, such as the following from *Shared Reading Collection*:
  - *A Raindrop's Journey* by Paloma Jae
  - *Inside a Cow* by Catherine Friend
- chart paper and markers
- To download the following online resource for this lesson, visit **fp.pub/resources**:
  - chart art (optional)

Academic Language / Important Vocabulary

- punctuation
- ellipsis
- pause
- build suspense
- surprise
- excitement

Continuum Connection

- Understand and use ellipses to show pause or anticipation, often before something surprising

GOAL

Use an ellipsis to show a pause or build excitement in a writing piece.

RATIONALE

Learning how to use an ellipsis allows children to add an element of excitement or suspense to their writing. Using an ellipsis in this way not only adds interest to their writing but also contributes to voice.

ASSESS LEARNING

- Observe children's writing to see if they sometimes use an ellipsis to indicate a pause or to build excitement.
- Look for evidence that children can use vocabulary such as *punctuation, ellipsis, pause, build suspense, surprise,* and *excitement*.

MINILESSON

To help children understand the minilesson principle, use mentor texts to help them notice and talk about ellipses. Here is an example.

- Show page 10 of *A Raindrop's Journey*.

  What do you notice about the punctuation marks?

  Listen as I read this part of *A Raindrop's Journey*.

- Read the sentence with the ellipsis.

  What did I do with my voice when I got to the part with three dots?

- Guide the conversation to help the children notice the ellipsis and how you paused before you read the words after it.

  An ellipsis looks like three periods with space between them. The writer used an ellipsis here to show that we should pause before reading the rest of the sentence.

- Show and read the sentence with the ellipsis on page 16 of *Inside a Cow*. Emphasize the pause at the ellipsis.

  Why do you think the writer placed an ellipsis here?

- Guide the conversation to help children recognize that the writer used the ellipsis to build suspense for what would come next.

Have a Try

Invite children to turn and talk about ellipses.

> If I want to write about getting a surprise new puppy, what are some things I might write? Turn and talk about that.

▶ After time for discussion, ask volunteers to share ideas, providing support as needed. Then arrange the words in a way that uses an ellipsis to build suspense or excitement or to indicate a pause in reading. Ask volunteers to come up and add each ellipsis as you write.

▶ Ask the class to read the sentences aloud with you.

Summarize and Apply

Summarize the learning. Have children try using an ellipsis to build suspense or to indicate a pause.

> When do you use an ellipsis?

▶ Write the principle at the top of the chart.

> Today, look in your writing for a place you want to build suspense or show a pause. If you find one, use an ellipsis in the sentence. Bring your writing to share when we meet later.

> **Use an ellipsis to show a pause or to build excitement.**
>
> I usually feel unlucky . . . but not today.
>
> I heard a mysterious sound . . . woof!
>
> I opened my eyes, and . . . I saw an adorable puppy looking at me!
>
> This was the best day . . . ever!

Confer

▶ During independent writing, move around the room to confer briefly with as many individual children as time allows. Sit side by side with them and invite them to talk about ellipses. Use the following prompts as needed.

- *Show me a place in your writing where something exciting is about to happen.*
- *How will an ellipsis help the reader?*
- *Where will you put an ellipsis?*
- *If you want to try using an ellipsis in this sentence, where might it be placed?*

Share

Following independent writing, gather children in the meeting area. Ask a few volunteers to share their writing.

> Who used an ellipsis in your writing today? Read the part of your writing with the ellipsis and show how you want the reader to pause.

Assessment

After you have taught the minilessons in this umbrella, observe children in a variety of classroom activities. Use *The Fountas & Pinnell Literacy Continuum* to notice, teach for, and support children's learning as you observe their attempts at using punctuation in their writing.

▶ What evidence do you have of children's new understandings related to using punctuation?

- Does children's writing reflect an understanding of how to use periods, question marks, and exclamation points?
- Do children use quotation marks to show dialogue?
- Are they using commas to separate words in a list?
- Are they using apostrophes to show possession?
- Are they able to use an ellipsis to show a pause or to build suspense?
- Are they using vocabulary such as *punctuation*, *sentence*, *end mark*, *period*, *question mark*, *exclamation point*, *quotation marks*, *opening*, *closing*, *talking*, *comma*, *list*, *apostrophe*, *belongs*, *ellipsis*, *pause*, *build suspense*, and *excitement*?

▶ In what ways, beyond the scope of this umbrella, are children's reading and writing behaviors showing an understanding of conventions?

- Do children use punctuation to show voice in their writing?
- Do they use capital letters correctly in their writing?

Use your observations to determine the next umbrella you will teach. You may also consult Suggested Sequence of Lessons (pp. 575–589) for guidance.

EXTENSIONS FOR LEARNING ABOUT PUNCTUATION

▶ Teach minilessons that help children use their voices to reflect punctuation when they read. If you use *The Reading Minilessons Book, Grade 2* (Fountas and Pinnell 2019), see SAS.U3: Maintaining Fluency.

▶ Use mentor texts for examples of different ways that dialogue is shown (e.g., speaker tag at the beginning or ending, no speaker tag when the speaker is known, different words for *said*).

▶ Write the same sentence three times, each with a different punctuation mark. Read the sentences. Then have children talk in small groups about how the sentence changes meaning depending on which punctuation mark is used.

Minilessons in This Umbrella

WML1 Capitalize the first letter of a name.

WML2 Capitalize the word *I*.

WML3 Capitalize the first letter of the first word in a sentence.

WML4 Capitalize the first word and the important words in a title.

Before Teaching Umbrella 4 Minilessons

Before teaching this umbrella, make sure the children have a good understanding of the difference between letters, words, and sentences and of the difference between uppercase (capital) and lowercase (small) letters.

Read and discuss books that the children will enjoy. Use the following texts from *Fountas & Pinnell Classroom™ Shared Reading Collection*. You can also choose books from your classroom library. As much as possible, use enlarged texts, such as published big books or class-made big books, or project the text so that children can see the print.

Shared Reading Collection

Animals with Jobs by Charlotte Rose

The Boy Who Cried Wolf: An Aesop Fable retold by David Edwin

Fur, Feathers, and More by Stephanie Petron Cahill

Night of the Ghost Crabs by Reese Brooks

Rain Forest Surprises by Kelly Martinson

Weather Watch: Rita's Journal by June Schwartz

As you read and enjoy these and other texts together, help children notice which words are capitalized.

WML1

CNV.U4.WML1

Writing Minilesson Principle
Capitalize the first letter of a name.

Using Capital Letters

You Will Need

- a couple of books with examples of proper nouns (people's names, place names, etc.), such as the following from *Shared Reading Collection*:
  - *Animals with Jobs* by Charlotte Rose
  - *Rain Forest Surprises* by Kelly Martinson
- sticky notes (see chart)
- highlighter
- chart paper and markers

Academic Language / Important Vocabulary

- capitalize
- uppercase (capital)
- lowercase (small)
- letter
- name

Continuum Connection

- Use capital letters for the names of people, places, days, months, cities, states

GOAL

Understand that names begin with capital letters.

RATIONALE

When you help children notice that proper nouns are always capitalized, they learn to capitalize proper nouns in their own writing.

ASSESS LEARNING

- Observe whether children capitalize the first letter of each proper noun.
- Look for evidence that children can use vocabulary such as *capitalize, uppercase (capital), lowercase (small), letter,* and *name.*

MINILESSON

Use mentor texts to help children notice that names are capitalized. Use the term (*uppercase* or *capital*) that you prefer. Here is an example.

▶ Show page 13 of *Animals with Jobs*. Read aloud the page.

> What do you notice about the *A* and the *P* in the name *Alison Payne*? Are they uppercase or lowercase?

> Why did the writer use uppercase letters there?

> They are uppercase because they are the first letters in the person's name. The first letters in a person's first name and last name are always capitalized.

▶ Place or have a child place the sticky note labeled *Person's Name* on the chart. Highlight the uppercase letters.

▶ Repeat with the name of the nonprofit organization Helping Hands Monkey Helpers and the sticky note labeled *Company Name*. Guide children to notice that the names of companies, businesses, and organizations are capitalized.

▶ Show the inside back cover of *Rain Forest Surprises*. Read the More About the Rain Forest note.

> Which words in this note start with uppercase letters?

> *Amazon, South America, Kuelap,* and *Peru* are all capitalized. Why do you think the author capitalized these words?

> These words are the names of particular places. Notice that the author did not capitalize *rain forest* because there are many rain forests in the world.

▶ Add the sticky note with the label *Place Name*. Highlight the capital letters.

Have a Try

Invite children to talk to a partner about capitalizing names.

▶ Write a sentence including today's date, such as "Today is Friday, April 9."

> Which words are capitalized in this sentence? Why do you think they're capitalized? Turn and talk to your partner about this.

▶ After time for discussion, invite a few children to share their thinking. Explain that the names of days and months are always capitalized.

Summarize and Apply

Help children summarize the learning. Remind them to capitalize the first letter of a name.

> What did you learn today about writing names?

> A name always begins with an uppercase letter—whether it's the name of a person, a company, a place, a day, or a month.

▶ Write the principle on the chart.

> During writing time today, remember to capitalize the first letter of any names you write. Bring your writing to share when we come back together.

Capitalize the first letter of a name.	
Person's Name	Alison Payne
Company Name	Helping Hands Monkey Helpers
Place Name	Amazon rain forest South America Kuelap, Peru
Days, Months	Friday, April 9

Confer

▶ During independent writing, move around the room to confer briefly with as many individual children as time allows. Sit side by side with them and invite them to talk about capitalizing the first letter of a name. Use prompts such as the following as needed.

- *What is the name of the main character (place) in your story? How should you write the character's name?*

- *Remember that names always start with an uppercase letter, no matter where they are in the sentence.*

Share

Following independent writing, gather children in the meeting area to share their writing.

> Raise your hand if you wrote any names in your book today.

> What names did you write? What did you remember to do when you wrote them?

Using Capital Letters

You Will Need

- two or more books containing the pronoun *I*, such as the following from *Shared Reading Collection*:
  - *Weather Watch: Rita's Journal* by June Schwartz
  - *The Boy Who Cried Wolf* retold by David Edwin
- chart paper and markers
- To download the following online resource for this lesson, visit **fp.pub/resources**:
  - chart art (optional)

Academic Language / Important Vocabulary

- capitalize
- uppercase (capital)

Continuum Connection

- Use capital letters for the names of people, places, days, months, cities, states

---

GOAL

Understand that the pronoun *I* is always capitalized.

RATIONALE

When you help children notice that the pronoun *I* is always capitalized, no matter where it is in a sentence, they learn to capitalize *I* in their own writing.

ASSESS LEARNING

- Observe whether children capitalize the pronoun *I*.
- Look for evidence that children can use vocabulary such as *capitalize* and *uppercase (capital)*.

MINILESSON

To help children think about the minilesson principle, use mentor texts to help them notice that the pronoun *I* is always capitalized. Use the term (*uppercase* or *capital*) that you prefer. Here is an example.

- Show the cover of *Weather Watch* and read the title and subtitle. Display page 2.

  What do you notice about the letter *I* on this page?

  Sometimes the letter is in a word, and it is lowercase. This one (*I can't wait*) and this one (*Dad and I*) are different. What do you notice about them?

  Why do you think the letter *I* is capitalized in these two places?

- Write one of the sentences on chart paper.

  The letter *I* is not just a letter—it is also a word. In this book, the word *I* refers to Rita, who is telling this story. The word *I* is always capitalized when it refers to a person, no matter where it is in a sentence.

- Show the cover of *The Boy Who Cried Wolf* and read the title. Display page 8.

  What do you notice about the *I* in the last sentence?

- Add another example to the chart.

Have a Try

Invite children to talk to a partner about the pronoun *I*.

> What did you learn today about writing the word *I*? What will you remember to do when you write it? Turn and talk to your partner.

▶ After time for discussion, invite one or two volunteers to share their responses. You might have children suggest a couple of sentences to add to the chart to show the capitalization of the word *I*.

Summarize and Apply

Write the principle at the top of the chart. Read it to children, and remind them to always capitalize the pronoun *I*.

> The word *I* should always be capitalized, no matter where it is in a sentence. During writing time today and every day, remember to capitalize the word *I* if you use it in your writing.

Capitalize the word I.

- Dad and I are going on a weather watch every morning this week.

- And I want to have some fun.

Roberto and I are twins!

Elvio and I are twins!

Confer

▶ During independent writing, move around the room to confer briefly with as many individual children as time allows. Sit side by side with them and invite them to talk about capitalizing words. Use prompts such as the following as needed.

- *What are you going to write on this page?*
- *You are writing a memory story, so you will use the word* I.
- *How should you write the word* I?
- *You remembered to capitalize the word* I.

Share

Following independent writing, gather children in the meeting area to share their writing.

> Who would like to read aloud your writing?

> Did you write the word *I* today? How did you write it?

WML3
CNV.U4.WML3

Writing Minilesson Principle
Capitalize the first letter of the first word in a sentence.

Using Capital Letters

You Will Need

- a familiar book with full paragraphs of text, such as *Fur, Feathers, and More* by Stephanie Petron Cahill, from *Shared Reading Collection*
- chart paper prepared with the sentences from page 12 of *Fur, Feathers, and More* (optional)
- marker
- highlighter or highlighter tape
- To download the following online resource for this lesson, visit **fp.pub/resources**:
  - chart art (optional)

Academic Language / Important Vocabulary

- capitalize
- uppercase (capital)
- lowercase (small)
- letter
- word
- sentence

Continuum Connection

- Use a capital letter for the first word of a sentence

GOAL

Understand that a sentence begins with a capital letter.

RATIONALE

When children notice that sentences in books begin with uppercase letters, they understand that they, too, should capitalize the first word in each sentence. They also begin to learn to separate their ideas into multiple sentences, avoiding run-on sentences and making their writing clearer to their readers.

ASSESS LEARNING

- Look at children's writing. Do they begin each sentence with a capital letter?
- Look for evidence that children can use vocabulary such as *capitalize, uppercase (capital), lowercase (small), letter, word,* and *sentence.*

MINILESSON

To help children think about the minilesson principle, use a mentor text to help them notice that a sentence begins with a capital letter. Use the terms (*uppercase* or *capital, lowercase* or *small*) that you prefer. Here is an example.

- Show the cover of *Fur, Feathers, and More* and read the title. Read aloud page 12. Then show the page and point out the letters at the beginning of each line.

  What do you notice about these letters?

  Why are some of the letters uppercase and some lowercase?

  Each sentence begins with a capital letter.

- Invite volunteers to highlight the capital letters. If you are using the Shared Reading book, have children use highlighter tape. If you wrote the sentences on chart paper, have them use either highlighter tape or a highlighter.

  Why do you think it's important to put punctuation at the end of each sentence and start the next sentence with a capital letter?

  This helps the reader read your writing and understand your ideas. If there were no periods or capital letters, readers would not know where one idea ends and the next one begins. The writing would be very confusing to read!

WML3

CNV.U4.WML3

Have a Try

Invite children to talk to a partner about capital letters.

> Which words should you capitalize when you write sentences? Turn and talk to your partner about this.

▶ After children turn and talk, invite a few children to share their thinking. Clear up any misunderstandings as needed.

Summarize and Apply

Write the principle at the top of the chart. Read it to children. Summarize the learning and remind children to capitalize the first letter of the first word in every sentence.

> During writing time today and every day, remember to capitalize the first letter of every sentence you write. If you are working on a book now, check the pages you have written to make sure you capitalized the first letter in each sentence. Bring your writing to share when we meet later.

> Capitalize the first letter of the first word in a sentence.
>
> A frog has wet, slimy skin.
> Slimy skin is smooth
> and stretchy.
> It stretches to help
> a frog croak.

Confer

▶ During independent writing, move around the room to confer briefly with as many individual children as time allows. Sit side by side with them and invite them to talk about capitalizing words. Use prompts such as the following as needed.

- *What is the next sentence you're going to write?*
- *Which letters should be capitalized in that sentence? Why?*
- *Are there any other words in your book that should begin with a capital letter?*
- *You capitalized the first word of every sentence on this page.*

Share

Following independent writing, gather children in triads in the meeting area to share their writing.

> Turn and talk about three words that you capitalized and why.

Writing Minilesson Principle
Capitalize the first word and the important words in a title.

Using Capital Letters

You Will Need

- several familiar books with titles of varying lengths, such as the following from *Shared Reading Collection*:
  - *Animals with Jobs* by Charlotte Rose
  - *Fur, Feathers, and More* by Stephanie Petron Cahill
  - *Night of the Ghost Crabs* by Reese Brooks
  - *The Boy Who Cried Wolf* retold by David Edwin
- chart paper and markers
- highlighter or highlighter tape

Academic Language / Important Vocabulary

- capitalize
- uppercase (capital)
- lowercase (small)
- title

Continuum Connection

- Use a capital letter for the first word, the last word, and most other words in a title

GOAL

Understand that writers capitalize the first word and the important words in a title.

RATIONALE

When children notice that the first word and the important words in published book titles are capitalized, they will learn to properly use capital letters in their own book titles. Note, however, that there are different styles of capitalization for titles, so children might see a word capitalized in one place but not in another place.

ASSESS LEARNING

- Observe whether children capitalize the first and the important words in book titles.
- Look for evidence that children can use vocabulary such as *capitalize, uppercase (capital), lowercase (small),* and *title*.

MINILESSON

To help children think about the minilesson principle, use mentor texts to prompt a discussion about capitalization in titles. Some style guides offer more specifics about which words to capitalize in a title, but this lesson introduces the basic idea that the first word and the important words are capitalized. Use the term (*uppercase* or *capital*) that you prefer.

- Show the cover of *Animals with Jobs* and read the title.

    What do you notice about the letters in this book title?

    Most of the letters are lowercase, but some are uppercase.

- Write the title on chart paper, highlighting (or inviting a child to highlight) the uppercase letters.

- Repeat with *Fur, Feathers, and More* and *Night of the Ghost Crabs*.

    What do you notice about how book titles are written?

    The important words in a title are capitalized. Most little words like *and, of,* and *the* are not capitalized.

- Show the cover of *The Boy Who Cried Wolf* and read the title.

    What do you notice about this title? Which words are capitalized?

- Add the title to the chart. Point out that the word *The* is capitalized in this case because it is the first word in the title.

    The first word in a title is always capitalized, no matter what it is!

Have a Try

Invite children to talk to a partner about which words to capitalize in a title.

> I'm working on a book called *My Favorite Place in the World.* Which words should I capitalize in the title *My Favorite Place in the World?* Turn and talk to your partner about this.

▶ After time for discussion, invite a few children to share their thinking. Ensure that children understand which words need to be capitalized, and add the title to the chart.

Summarize and Apply

Help children summarize the learning and remind them to capitalize the important words in a title.

> What did you learn today about how to write titles?

▶ Write the principle at the top of the chart. Read it aloud.

> When you write the title of your book, remember to capitalize the first word and the important words. Bring your writing to share when we come back together.

Confer

▶ During independent writing, move around the room to confer briefly with as many individual children as time allows. Sit side by side with them and invite them to talk about capitalizing words. Use prompts such as the following as needed.

- *What is the title of your book?*
- *Where will you write the title? How will you write it?*
- *Which words should be capitalized in the title?*
- *Remember to always capitalize the first word in the title, no matter what it is.*

Share

Following independent writing, gather children in the meeting area to share their books. Give everyone a chance to share their titles before asking several children about capitalization.

> Let's go around the circle so that you can each read your title.

> Which words did you capitalize? Why?

Capitalize the first word and the important words in a title.

Animals with Jobs

Fur, Feathers, and More

Night of the Ghost Crabs

The Boy Who Cried Wolf

My Favorite Place in the World

Assessment

After you have taught the minilessons in this umbrella, observe children as they write and talk about their writing. Use *The Fountas & Pinnell Literacy Continuum* to notice, teach for, and support children's learning as you observe their writing skills.

▶ What evidence do you have of new understandings children have developed related to using capital letters?

- Do children capitalize the first letter of proper nouns, the pronoun *I*, and the important words (including the first word) in titles?

- Is there evidence children can use vocabulary such as *uppercase*, *lowercase*, and *capitalize*?

▶ In what other ways, beyond the scope of this umbrella, are children ready to expand their writing skills?

- Are they noticing and using different types of punctuation?

- Do they write a title on their books before publishing them?

Use your observations to determine the next umbrella you will teach. You may also consult Suggested Sequence of Lessons (pp. 575–589) for guidance.

EXTENSIONS FOR USING CAPITAL LETTERS

▶ Encourage children to reread their writing to make sure they have used capital letters correctly. [See WPS.U10: Editing and Proofreading Writing.]

▶ Help children notice that sometimes authors use all caps to indicate yelling or for emphasis.

▶ If children type their writing on a computer, teach them how to use the Shift and Caps Lock keys to make capital letters.

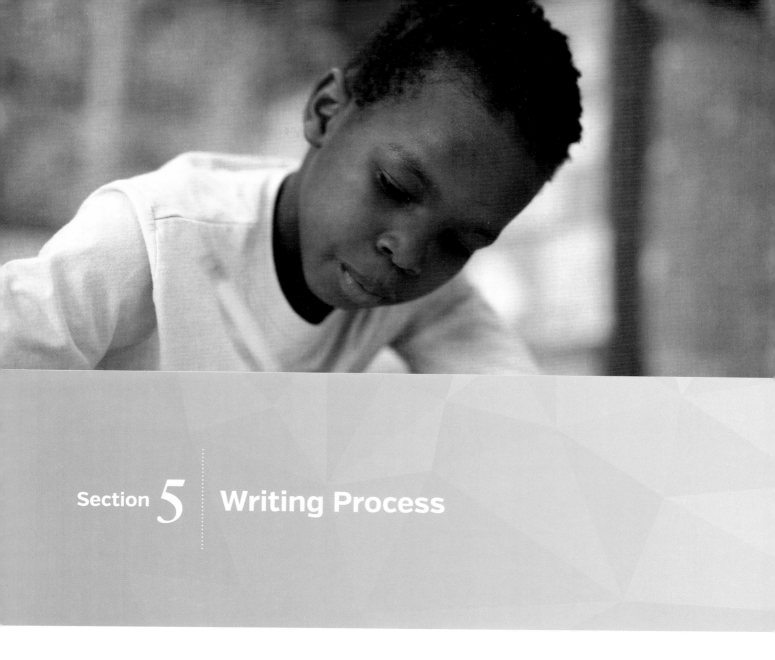

Section 5 | Writing Process

CHILDREN LEARN TO write by writing. As they write, they engage in some aspect of the writing process. They plan what to write, write a first draft and make changes to improve it, check their work to be sure others can read it, and publish it by sharing it with an audience. Not all aspects of the writing process will happen at one time, and they won't always happen in the same order. Writers tend to move back and forth. But over time, each will experience the full writing process. The lessons in this section will help you guide the children in your class through the writing process.

5 Writing Process

Planning and Rehearsing

Drafting and Revising

Editing and Proofreading

Publishing

The Writing Minilessons Book, Grade 2

Minilessons in This Umbrella

WML1 Tell stories about yourself.

WML2 Tell stories about things from your Me Box.

WML3 Tell stories about things you did.

WML4 Tell stories about people and places you don't want to forget.

Before Teaching Umbrella 1 Minilessons

Before children can write, they need to know what to write about. The minilessons in this umbrella use storytelling as inspiration for generating ideas for writing. Oral storytelling shows children that people share what they are thinking through language. By sharing mentor texts and telling your own stories, you plant seeds for children's own storytelling. Oral storytelling yields multiple benefits:

- One person's stories can inspire ideas for more stories.

- Children can rehearse what they want to say and how to say it before writing.

- Children get to know one another through their stories about experiences and interests.

The online resource My Ideas for Writing is used throughout the lessons to capture ideas. Children can keep the resource in a writing folder (see MGT.U4: Introducing Writing Folder Resources) or in a writer's notebook (see WPS.U2: Learning About My First Writer's Notebook).

It is recommended that you do not teach these lessons consecutively so that you can provide opportunities for children to build their repertoire of stories between each of the lessons. Post the chart you will build across the minilessons and refer to it often as a reminder of where children can look for story ideas. For mentor texts, use the books listed below from *Fountas & Pinnell Classroom™ Interactive Read-Aloud Collection*, or choose books from the classroom library that tell stories that are personal to the writers.

Interactive Read-Aloud Collection

Caring for Each Other: Family

Pecan Pie Baby by Jacqueline Woodson

Two Mrs. Gibsons by Toyomi Igus

Finding Your Way in a New Place

Roses for Gita by Rachna Gilmore

The Have a Good Day Cafe by Frances Park and Ginger Park

As you read and enjoy these or other texts together, help children

- discuss how the stories make them think about events in their own lives, and

- talk about what events from an author's own life may have been used as a basis for the stories.

Finding Your Way

Section 5: Writing Process

Writing Minilesson Principle
Tell stories about yourself.

Getting Ideas for Writing Through Storytelling

You Will Need

- a familiar book about something from an author's life, such as *Pecan Pie Baby* by Jacqueline Woodson, from Text Set: Caring for Each Other: Family

- chart paper prepared with My Ideas for Writing (either drawn on or printed out and fastened to the chart paper), with one idea filled in

- markers

- a copy of My Ideas for Writing for each child

- To download the following online resource for this lesson, visit **fp.pub/resources**:
  - My Ideas for Writing

Academic Language / Important Vocabulary

- stories
- remind
- special

Continuum Connection

- Understand that writers may tell stories from their own lives

- Generate and expand ideas through talk with peers and teacher

- Look for ideas and topics in personal experiences, shared through talk

- Tell stories from personal experiences

GOAL

Understand that writers get ideas for stories from their own lives.

RATIONALE

Hearing stories read aloud and listening to others' stories can prompt children to think of their own stories. When children tell stories about themselves, they share something about who they are and how they are similar to or different from each other. From their stories, they learn what makes each one of them a special human being. Getting to know one another through oral storytelling enables children to establish a safe and respectful classroom community.

ASSESS LEARNING

- Observe for evidence that children understand that writers get ideas for stories from their own lives, and they can, too.
- Notice whether children keep a list of writing ideas.
- Look for evidence that children can use vocabulary such as *stories*, *remind*, and *special*.

MINILESSON

Before the lesson, make at least one copy of My Ideas for Writing for each child. Children can either keep the list fastened inside a writing folder or glued in a writer's notebook. Demonstrate thinking about story ideas from books, other people's stories, or children's own stories about their own lives. Here is an example, but talk about your own ideas for writing.

▶ Display a familiar book, such as *Pecan Pie Baby*.

> Jacqueline Woodson wrote *Pecan Pie Baby* based on her own life with her children. She told a story about herself. That makes me think that I could tell a story about myself. Someday, I would like to write a story about when my little brother was born. I was not happy! I'm going to write down my idea so I don't forget about it.

▶ Display the prepared chart paper and add the idea.

> Writers are always looking for ideas to write about. One way to get ideas is to read stories by other people. Another way is to listen to the stories people tell about themselves. Those stories might remind you of a story from your life. _____ told us a story about when she fell and broke her leg. _____'s story made me think of when I fell and hurt myself. I'd like to write about that someday, too.

▶ Add the second idea to the list.

> Notice that first I wrote a number and then I wrote my idea.

▶ Save the chart for the next lesson.

Have a Try

Invite children to talk to a partner about ideas for stories about themselves.

> Turn and talk to your partner about an idea for a story about yourself. Maybe your partner's idea will make you think of another story idea.

▶ After time for discussion, ask several volunteers to share their story ideas.

> If someone has a story idea similar to yours, you two will have something to talk about together!

Summarize and Apply

Summarize the lesson. Prepare children to list ideas on My Ideas for Writing. Eventually, children may need more than one copy.

> Writers are always thinking about what to write about next. With My Ideas for Writing, you'll always have a place to look when you wonder what to write about.

> Today during writing time, write on your list two or three ideas for stories from your life. Bring your list to share later.

My Ideas for Writing

1. My little brother
2. When I fell down and hurt myself

Confer

▶ During independent writing, move around the room to confer briefly with as many individual children as time allows. Sit side by side with them and invite them to talk about their lists of writing ideas. Use the following prompts as needed.

- *What made you think of this idea?*
- *Think about your family. Does that make you think of any story ideas?*
- *What is something that makes you special? You could write that on your list.*
- *What do you like to do when you're not at school?*

Share

Following independent writing, gather children in the meeting area to share their ideas for stories about themselves.

> Who would like to share the ideas you put on your list?

> Do _____'s ideas make you think of any ideas for your own stories?

Writing Minilesson Principle
Tell stories about things from your Me Box.

Getting Ideas for Writing Through Storytelling

You Will Need

- Me Boxes for you and for each child or objects for generating story ideas
- chart paper and markers
- To download the following online resource for this lesson, visit **fp.pub/resources**:
  - My Ideas for Writing

Academic Language / Important Vocabulary

- stories
- Me Box

Continuum Connection

- Understand that writers may tell stories from their own lives
- Generate and expand ideas through talk with peers and teacher
- Look for ideas and topics in personal experiences, shared through talk
- Use talk and storytelling to generate and rehearse language that may be written later

GOAL

Understand that objects can be the inspiration for story ideas.

RATIONALE

Using objects as inspiration for stories is another way for children to generate story ideas. When one person tells a story, other people get ideas for their own stories. Sharing stories not only prompts new story ideas but also helps children get to know one another and build a strong writing community.

ASSESS LEARNING

- Observe whether children get ideas for writing from their own stories and stories that other people tell.
- Notice whether children keep a list of writing ideas.
- Look for evidence that children can use vocabulary such as *stories* and *Me Box*.

MINILESSON

Before the lesson, make at least one copy of My Ideas for Writing for each child. Children can either keep the list fastened inside a writing folder or glued in a writer's notebook. Demonstrate thinking of story ideas from an object and then recording them. Here is an example, but talk about your own ideas for writing.

- Before teaching, have each child prepare a Me Box filled with meaningful objects. Make a Me Box for yourself as well. Alternatively, make sure each child has an object that can be the inspiration for a story.

- Choose an item from your Me Box. Tell a personal story about the object you have chosen. Here is an example of the type of story you might tell.

  > In my Me Box there is a copy of a page from my first piano book. When I was in second grade, I really wanted to play the piano. Finally, I convinced my parents to get a piano. I could write a story about when we got our piano.

- Write your idea on the chart. Then engage children in a discussion about the story you told.

  > Does my story make you think about any ideas for your own stories?

  > Is there something you always wanted to do, and you finally got to do it? Or, do you have a story about when you learned to do something?

  > Hearing someone's story can give you some ideas for your own stories.

- Save the chart for the next lesson.

Have a Try

Invite children to turn and talk about story ideas inspired by objects from their Me Boxes.

> Choose something from your Me Box. Tell your partner about an idea for a story you could tell about it.

▶ After time for discussion, invite a few children to share ideas for their stories.

Summarize and Apply

Summarize the lesson. Have children add ideas for stories inspired by objects in their Me Boxes to My Ideas for Writing.

> If something in your Me Box makes you think of an idea for writing, put it on your list.

> Today during writing time, write on your list two or three ideas for stories about objects from your Me Box. Bring your list to share later.

My Ideas for Writing
1. My little brother
2. When I fell down and hurt myself
3. Getting a piano

Confer

▶ During independent writing, move around the room to confer briefly with as many individual children as time allows. Sit side by side with them and invite them to talk about their lists of writing ideas. Use the following prompts as needed.

- *This looks like something that is special to you. What is a story you could tell about it?*
- *Why did you include this item in your Me Box? That can be an idea for a story.*

Share

Following independent writing, gather children in the meeting area to share their story ideas.

> Who would like to share a story idea you wrote down?

> Does _____'s idea make you think of an idea for a story of your own?

Writing Minilesson Principle
Tell stories about things you did.

Getting Ideas for Writing Through Storytelling

You Will Need

- a book you have read recently that includes familiar experiences, such as *Two Mrs. Gibsons* by Toyomi Igus from Text Set: Caring for Each Other: Family
- chart paper and markers
- To download the following online resource for this lesson, visit **fp.pub/resources**:
  - My Ideas for Writing

Academic Language / Important Vocabulary

- stories
- ideas

Continuum Connection

- Understand that writers may tell stories from their own lives
- Use talk and storytelling to generate and rehearse language that may be written later
- Generate and expand ideas through talk with peers and teacher
- Look for ideas and topics in personal experiences, shared through talk
- Tell stories from personal experience

GOAL

Understand that writers tell stories about things they have done.

RATIONALE

Telling stories about things they have done is another way for children to generate story ideas. When one person tells a story, other people get ideas for their own stories. Sharing stories not only prompts new story ideas but also helps children get to know one another, thereby building a strong writing community.

ASSESS LEARNING

- Observe whether children get ideas for writing from their own stories and stories that other people tell.
- Notice whether children keep and use a list of writing ideas.
- Look for evidence that children can use vocabulary such as *stories* and *ideas*.

MINILESSON

Before the lesson, make at least one copy of My Ideas for Writing for each child. Children can either keep the list fastened inside a writing folder or glued in a writer's notebook. Demonstrate thinking of story ideas from books, other people's stories, or children's own stories about things they have done. Here is an example, but talk about your own ideas for writing.

- Revisit pages 17–20 from *Two Mrs. Gibsons*.

  What does the author, Toyomi Igus, tell about on these pages of *Two Mrs. Gibsons*?

- Read the author's note at the end of the book. Help children understand that the author used ideas from her own life when writing this book.

  This story makes me think about things in my life that I could tell about in a story. My grandmother and I did a lot of things together. She took me on the subway for the first time, she taught me to knit, and we searched for four-leaf clovers together. Those are all things I could write a story about.

- Write your idea on the chart. Then engage children in a discussion about the story you told.

  You don't have to tell a story about a grandmother. You could think of things you have done. For example, I could also tell a story about helping people. I went on a trip to rebuild houses that were destroyed by a hurricane.

- List the second idea on the chart.

Have a Try

Invite children to turn and talk about story ideas about something they did in their lives.

> Think of something you have done in your life. Tell your partner about an idea for a story you could tell about it.

▶ After time for discussion, invite a few children to share ideas for their stories.

Summarize and Apply

Summarize the lesson. Have children add ideas for stories about something they have done to My Ideas for Writing.

> If something you do makes you think of an idea for writing, put it on your list.

> Today during writing time, write on your list two or three ideas for stories about something you have done in your life. Bring your list to share later.

My Ideas for Writing

1. My little brother
2. When I fell down and hurt myself
3. Getting a piano
4. Things I did with Grammy
5. Rebuilding houses

Confer

▶ During independent writing, move around the room to confer briefly with as many individual children as time allows. Sit side by side with them and invite them to talk about the ideas on their lists. Use the following prompts as needed.

• *What story will you tell about this idea?*

• *What made you think of this idea?*

• *Let's look at your list. What idea would you like to write about?*

• *You can think about things you have done a long time ago or just a few days ago.*

Share

Following independent writing, gather children in the meeting area to share their ideas for writing.

> Who would like to share a story idea you listed?

> Does _____'s idea make you think of an idea for a story of your own?

Section 5: Writing Process

WML4
WPS.U1.WML4

Writing Minilesson Principle
Tell stories about people and places you don't want to forget.

Getting Ideas for Writing Through Storytelling

You Will Need

- several familiar books that include people in a setting, such as the following from Text Set: Finding Your Way in a New Place:
  - *Roses for Gita* by Rachna Gilmore
  - *The Have a Good Day Cafe* by Frances Park and Ginger Park
- chart paper and markers
- To download the following online resource for this lesson, visit **fp.pub/resources**:
  - My Ideas for Writing

Academic Language / Important Vocabulary

- stories
- people
- places

Continuum Connection

- Understand that writers may tell stories from their own lives
- Generate and expand ideas through talk with peers and teacher
- Look for ideas and topics in personal experiences, shared through talk
- Use talk and storytelling to generate and rehearse language that may be written later
- Tell stories from personal experience

GOAL

Understand that stories about people and places generate additional ideas for stories.

RATIONALE

Telling stories about familiar people and places is another way for children to generate story ideas. When one person tells a story, other people get ideas for their own stories. Reminding children that ideas for their writing can come from memorable people and places helps them understand that the things they know have value.

ASSESS LEARNING

- Observe whether children get ideas for writing from their own stories and stories that other people tell.
- Notice whether children keep a list of writing ideas.
- Look for evidence that children can use vocabulary such as *stories*, *people*, and *places*.

MINILESSON

Before the lesson, make at least one copy of My Ideas for Writing for each child. Children can either keep the list fastened inside a writing folder or glued in a writer's notebook. Demonstrate thinking of story ideas from books, other people's stories, or children's own stories about people and places. Here is an example, but talk about your own ideas for writing.

- Revisit page 22 of *Roses for Gita*. Read the author's biography on the back cover.

  This story is about a girl who moves to a new country. The neighbor's yard is a special place for her because it reminds her of her grandmother's yard back in India. The author also lived in India and moved to different countries.

- Revisit pages 25–26 of *The Have a Good Day Cafe*. Read the note about the authors on the inside front cover.

  The authors tell a story about a family who set up a cart in the park to sell Korean food that is special to the family. They got the idea from seeing a food cart in a park near their homes.

  What do you notice about where these authors got their ideas for writing?

- Guide children to notice that the authors got their ideas for writing from people and places in their lives that they wanted to remember.

  I could tell a story about a favorite place and person from my childhood. After school, I would walk over to the library. Mrs. Connolly, the librarian, would let me help her. One time, she found a book in which the two main characters had the same names as my brother and I!

- Write your idea on the chart.

Have a Try

Invite children to turn and talk about story ideas about people and places they know.

> Think of someone you know or a place you have been. Tell your partner about an idea for a story you could tell about the person or the place. Your story might be about both.

> ▶ After time for discussion, invite a few children to share ideas for their stories.

Summarize and Apply

Summarize the lesson. Have children add ideas for stories about people and places to My Ideas for Writing.

> You can get ideas for writing from the stories you tell and the stories other people tell.

> Today during writing time, write on your list two or three ideas for stories about people you know or places you have been. Bring your list to share later.

My Ideas for Writing

1. My little brother
2. When I fell down and hurt myself
3. Getting a piano
4. Things I did with Grammy
5. Rebuilding houses
6. Mrs. Connolly the librarian
___ _____
___ _____

Confer

> ▶ During independent writing, move around the room to confer briefly with as many individual children as time allows. Sit side by side with them and invite them to talk about their ideas for writing. Use the following prompts as needed.
>
> * *What story will you tell about this idea?*
> * *What made you think of this idea?*
> * *Let's look at your list. What idea would you like to write about?*
> * *What person (place) do you not want to forget? You could write that on your list.*

Share

Following independent writing, gather children in the meeting area to share their story ideas.

> Share your list of ideas with a partner. Do any ideas on your partner's list inspire you to think of more ideas? If so, add them to your list.

Assessment

After you have taught the minilessons in this umbrella, observe children in a variety of classroom activities. Use *The Fountas & Pinnell Literacy Continuum* to notice, teach for, and support children's learning as you observe their attempts at generating story ideas.

▶ What evidence do you have of new understandings children have developed about getting ideas for writing?

- Can children generate ideas of their own for stories by listening to other people's stories or from hearing stories read aloud?

- Do children list their ideas for stories on My Ideas for Writing?

- Are they using vocabulary such as *stories*, *special*, *Me Box*, *ideas*, *people*, and *places*?

▶ In what ways, beyond the scope of this umbrella, are children writing?

- Are children ready to write memory books?

- Are they trying craft techniques they have noticed authors and illustrators using?

Use your observations to determine the next umbrella you will teach. You may also consult Suggested Sequence of Lessons (pp. 575–589) for guidance.

EXTENSIONS FOR GETTING IDEAS FOR WRITING THROUGH STORYTELLING

▶ Have children bring in photographs from home or provide photos from experiences children have had at school to use for generating story ideas.

▶ Encourage children to rotate partners so they have opportunities to hear different story ideas and get to know different classmates.

▶ Invite a professional storyteller to class to tell stories and talk about ideas for stories.

Minilessons in This Umbrella

Shared Reading

WML1 Collect ideas and writing in your writer's notebook.

WML2 Make a heart map for ideas.

WML3 Try out new ideas in your writer's notebook.

WML4 Collect and write about important things in your writer's notebook.

WML5 Reread your writer's notebook to get ideas.

Before Teaching Umbrella 2 Minilessons

Many writers keep a writer's notebook as a place to collect lists, information about interesting topics, poems, and ideas to inspire their writing. Well-known author Nicola Davies remarked that writers use and organize their writer's notebooks in ways that make them their own (www.authortoauthor.org/author-videos-2). The purpose of this umbrella is to provide children with their first writer's notebook and to begin exploring ways to use it.

Introduce the writer's notebook when children are writing more fluently and beginning to produce multiple writing projects relatively quickly. The writer's notebook is a place to record seeds of ideas for expanded writing and to experiment with quick writes. Expanded writing projects will be done on separate paper, usually kept in a writing folder.

Any notebook can be used—a composition book, for example. Help children develop a sense of pride in and ownership of the writer's notebook by delivering it to them in a momentous way and encouraging them to decorate the cover (see WML1). You may want to add tabs to the writer's notebooks to make sections, such as Getting Ideas, More Writing and Sketching, or the sections that you would like children to have in their notebooks. See pages 79–84 for more information on writer's notebooks.

After WML1, the other lessons may be taught in any order. Each may be reintroduced multiple times across the year in the context of the genre the class is working on. For WML4, use the book listed below from *Fountas & Pinnell Classroom™ Shared Reading Collection*, or choose a book from the classroom library that exemplifies a collection of artifacts or memorabilia as a way to build memories.

Shared Reading Collection
Weather Watch: Rita's Journal by June Schwartz

As you read and enjoy this text together, help children notice the artifacts that appear taped into the book, which catalog and help Rita remember her noticings about weather.

Section 5: Writing Process

WML1
WPS.U2.WML1

Writing Minilesson Principle
Collect ideas and writing in your writer's notebook.

Learning About My First Writer's Notebook

You Will Need

- your own, completed writer's notebook and/or examples from former students or published writers
- a new writer's notebook for you and each child
- white paper and glue sticks or large white stickers for children to label and decorate their notebook covers
- chart paper and markers
- document camera (optional)

Academic Language / Important Vocabulary

- writer's notebook

Continuum Connection

- Use a writer's notebook or booklet as a tool for collecting ideas, experimenting, planning, sketching, or drafting
- Use sketching to support memory and help in planning
- Have a list or notebook with topics and ideas for writing

GOAL

Understand that writers use a notebook to collect ideas and writing.

RATIONALE

When children learn that a writer's notebook is a place to collect and save ideas for writing, they begin to understand that writers are always thinking about topics for their writing. This builds a foundation for children as writers themselves.

ASSESS LEARNING

- Notice evidence that children understand that writers use a notebook to collect ideas and writing.
- Observe for evidence that children are talking about ideas to capture in a writer's notebook.
- Look for evidence that children use vocabulary such as *writer's notebook*.

MINILESSON

Receiving one's first writer's notebook can feel like a rite of passage for young writers. Share your own writer's notebook or examples from former students. Demonstrate the excitement and possibility of a new writer's notebook as you share a new notebook with each child. Here is an example.

- Show the cover of your own writer's notebook. Briefly show the pages, sharing the ideas and the writing you collected.

  I want to show you something important to me as a writer: my writer's notebook. Let's look at a few pages together. What kinds of things do you notice in my writer's notebook?

- Engage children in a conversation about the purpose of a writer's notebook, recording ideas on chart paper.

  Many pages have ideas I could turn into longer pieces of writing, things I tried out as a writer, or some writing about a time I want to remember.

- Display a new writer's notebook. Model the excitement of opening it—the crackling sound of a new composition book or a gently turned first page in a spiral notebook.

  Today is a special day in your writing life—each of you is getting your first writer's notebook! Listen carefully as I open this brand-new notebook.

  Now I am going to give each of you a writer's notebook. Don't open it yet—we all want to open them at the same time.

- Distribute the notebooks in a fun/ceremonial way. When each child has a notebook, indicate they can quietly open them together.

Have a Try

Invite children to turn and talk about making their writer's notebook their own.

> Think about something you might write today. It might be about how you're feeling, what makes you happy, something that you did recently, or anything else. Turn and talk to a partner.

▶ After discussion, ask several volunteers to share. Add ideas to the chart.

Summarize and Apply

Summarize the lesson and write the principle at the top of the chart. Remind children to decorate the cover and write on the first page.

> You learned that writers use a notebook to collect ideas and writing. Today you have two jobs. Write your name on the cover and plan how to or begin to decorate your cover. You don't need to finish today. Then go to the first page in your notebook and write today's date. Begin writing your first entry. Be prepared to share your notebook when we come back together.

> **Collect ideas and writing in your writer's notebook.**
>
> • Notes about days you want to remember
>
> • Memories of trips taken with family
>
> • Papers, stickers, maps, photographs
>
> • Ideas for books you might write
>
> • Poems
>
> • Interesting words
>
> • Things that make you happy

Confer

▶ During independent writing, move around the room to confer briefly with as many individual children as time allows. Sit side by side with them and invite them to talk about their writer's notebooks. Use the following prompts as needed.

- *How are you going to decorate the cover of your notebook?*
- *What are you thinking about writing as your first entry?*
- *Who (what) are the important people (places) in your life? Make a list in your notebook.*
- *What is a time in your life you never want to forget? Write about that in your notebook.*
- *What is something you know a lot about? Write what you know about that.*

Share

Following independent writing, gather children in the meeting area to share their notebooks. Have children hold up their covers for all to see. Then choose several children to talk about their notebooks.

> Tell about what you put on your cover and wrote inside.

Learning About My First Writer's Notebook

You Will Need

- chart paper prepared with the outline of a large heart on it
- markers
- To download the following online resource for this lesson, visit **fp.pub/resources**:
  - Heart Map (optional)

Academic Language / Important Vocabulary

- identity
- heart map

Continuum Connection

- Use a writer's notebook or booklet as a tool for collecting ideas, experimenting, planning, sketching, or drafting
- Use sketching, webs, lists, and freewriting to think about, plan for, and try out writing

GOAL

Create a heart map filled with important pieces of one's identity for the purpose of inspiring writing ideas.

RATIONALE

When children think about who they are and the important pieces of their identity, this information can inspire writing ideas. Adding these ideas to a heart map is a strategy children can use to organize their ideas in a writer's notebook.

ASSESS LEARNING

- Notice evidence that children can create a heart map filled with important pieces of their identity.
- Look for evidence that children are thinking about what aspects of their identity will lend themselves to future writing.
- Look for evidence that children use vocabulary such as *identity* and *heart map*.

MINILESSON

To help children understand that writers get inspiration for their writing by thinking about who they are, demonstrate making a heart map about yourself. Here is an example.

- Display a large heart drawn on chart paper.

  Writers have different ways of collecting ideas for their writing in a writer's notebook. One of these ways is making a heart map. I am going to make a heart map about me. My heart map will show who I am and what I'm like. What are some things about me I can write in my heart map?

- Think aloud as you add authentic elements about yourself to the heart map. Talk about how the words inspire you to think about writing more. Section off the words as you go.

  In this section of the heart I am going to write the words *mother to Andrew and Matthew*. A big part of who I am is being a mother. I'll draw a line to separate off those words. In this next spot on my heart map I am going to write *South Korea*. My husband was born there, and we enjoy many Korean traditions as a family. Another important part of who I am is being a teacher, so I will add that here. I am also going to add *Spanish* to my map because I speak Spanish.

  Notice how I drew lines to separate bits of information. These are the important pieces of myself. I can refer back to the heart map anytime I am looking for ideas for writing.

Have a Try

Invite children to turn and talk to a partner about more elements they could add to a heart map.

> What are some parts of who you are—of your identity—that you could put on your heart map?

▶ After time for discussion, ask a few volunteers to share. Write the ideas outside the heart map for children to consider for their own heart maps.

Summarize and Apply

Summarize the lesson. Remind children to add authentic ideas about themselves to a heart map to inspire ideas for writing. Have children write in their writer's notebooks, using the heart map from online resources or drawing a heart on paper that they can glue into their writer's notebooks.

▶ Write the principle at the top of the chart.

> One of the ways writers collect ideas for their writing is in a heart map. When you write today,
>
> begin to create your heart map. You don't need to finish it today. You will add to your heart map throughout the year. Bring your heart map to share when we meet later.

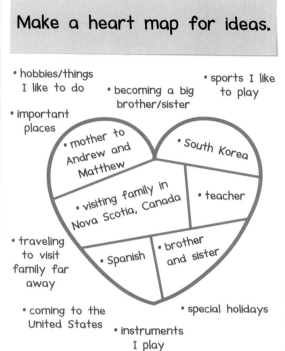

Make a heart map for ideas.

- hobbies/things I like to do
- becoming a big brother/sister
- sports I like to play
- important places
  - mother to Andrew and Matthew
  - South Korea
  - visiting family in Nova Scotia, Canada
  - teacher
- traveling to visit family far away
  - Spanish
  - brother and sister
- coming to the United States
- instruments I play
- special holidays

Confer

▶ During independent writing, move around the room to confer briefly with as many individual children as time allows. Sit side by side with them and invite them to talk about their heart maps. Use the following prompts as needed.

- *What is important about you?*
- *Who is an important person to you?*
- *What is an important place for you?*
- *What has been an important moment for you?*
- *What are experiences you will never forget?*

Share

Following independent writing, gather children in the meeting area to share their heart maps with a partner. Then ask a few to share with the whole class.

> What are some ideas you added to your heart map?
>
> What ideas did you hear from your classmates that you might add to your heart map?

WML3
WPS.U2.WML3

Writing Minilesson Principle
Try out new ideas in your writer's notebook.

Learning About My First Writer's Notebook

You Will Need

- chart paper and markers
- your writer's notebook, with writing prepared in advance linked to one of the topic areas you will add to the chart
- a writer's notebook for each child

Academic Language / Important Vocabulary

- writer's notebook
- experiment

Continuum Connection

- Use a writer's notebook or booklet as a tool for collecting ideas, experimenting, planning, sketching, or drafting
- Use sketching, webs, lists, and freewriting to think about, plan for, and try out writing

GOAL

Use a writer's notebook to experiment with an idea for writing.

RATIONALE

When you teach children that a writer's notebook is a tool used for collecting ideas for writing and experimenting with writing, it helps them to build a lifelong habit as writers. They learn that many writers (including published writers) use this tool.

ASSESS LEARNING

- Observe for evidence that children feel free to experiment with ideas for writing.
- Look for evidence that children use vocabulary such as *writer's notebook* and *experiment*.

MINILESSON

To help children think about using a writer's notebook to try out new ideas, model creating entries. Below is an example. Reintroduce this minilesson throughout the year in relation to a genre or aspect of writing children are learning (e.g., trying interesting leads/endings, gathering ideas for informational writing, describing the setting).

▶ Display blank chart paper and have your prepared writer's notebook nearby.

> Today we are going to think about how you can use your writer's notebook to help you try out ideas for writing. Thinking about important people in your life can help you think about ideas for your writing.

▶ Write *People* on the chart. As you think aloud about important people in your own life, add their names to the chart. When you finish the list, go back and circle the name of the person who will be the subject of your story.

> There are many important people in my life: my sons, Andrew and Matthew; my mom; my nieces and nephew; my friend Molly; my sister; Mrs. Flahive, my teacher-friend. I'd like to write a memory story about Molly, so I will circle her name. I wrote a bit in my writer's notebook about a fun time when she stopped by on a Friday evening.

▶ Display your writer's notebook. Turn to and read from the story you began writing about the referenced person.

> This is not a complete story, but my notebook gives me a place to jot down ideas so I can write more later.

▶ Repeat this process with another category or two, such as birthdays and celebrations.

Have a Try

Invite children to turn and talk about ideas to try out in a writer's notebook.

> What ideas do you want to write about in your writer's notebook? People, celebrations, something I didn't list yet? Turn and talk to your partner about that.

▶ After time for discussion, ask a few volunteers to share. Add new ideas to the chart.

Summarize and Apply

Summarize the lesson. Remind children to try out new ideas in a writer's notebook.

> How can you use your writer's notebook?

▶ Rephrase their comments to be more generative. Write the principle at the top of the chart.

> Today, begin a list of people that are important to you, celebrations, sports memories, or other ideas. Choose an idea, circle it, and begin writing a memory story just like I did. If you write as much as you can about that person, circle another idea and begin writing that memory story. Bring your writing to share when we meet later.

<table>
<tr><td colspan="4">Try out new ideas in your writer's notebook.</td></tr>
<tr><th>People</th><th>Birthdays</th><th>Celebrations</th><th>Sports fun</th></tr>
<tr>
<td>• Andrew
• Matthew
• Mom
• Kiera and Emma
• Josh
• (Molly)
• Peggy
• Mrs. Flahive</td>
<td>• My 6th birthday

• Andrew's first birthday

• Matthew's first birthday</td>
<td>• Peggy's graduation

• Mom and Dad's anniversary</td>
<td>• Scoring my first goal in soccer

• Doing the obstacle course in gym</td>
</tr>
</table>

Confer

▶ During independent writing, move around the room to confer briefly with as many individual children as time allows. Sit side by side with them and invite them to talk about trying out new ideas in a writer's notebook. Use the following prompts as needed.

- *Which one of those ideas do you think you will begin a story about? Tell that story with your voice before you begin writing. Now, write that story.*
- *Who are some important people in your life? Make a list of them.*
- *What are some important places you have visited? Make a list of them.*
- *What do you like to do for fun? Create a list of those things.*

Share

Following independent writing, gather children in the meeting area to share their writing ideas. Have a few children share with the whole class. Add new ideas to the chart.

> What ideas for writing did you hear about from your classmates that you might try?

Writing Minilesson Principle

Collect and write about important things in your writer's notebook.

You Will Need

▶ a book that incorporates creative use of artifacts, such as *Weather Watch* by June Schwartz, from *Shared Reading Collection*

▶ chart paper and markers

▶ your writer's notebook, with examples of artifacts

▶ artifacts children have collected from home or class activities to add to their own notebooks

▶ a writer's notebook for each child

Academic Language / Important Vocabulary

▶ writer's notebook

▶ items

Continuum Connection

▶ Use a writer's notebook or booklet as a tool for collecting ideas, experimenting, planning, sketching, or drafting

▶ Take notes or make sketches to help in remembering and generating information

▶ Participate actively in experiences and recall information that contributes to writing and drawing (using notebooks and artifacts)

GOAL

Understand that a writer's notebook is used to collect artifacts to inspire writing ideas.

RATIONALE

When you teach children that a writer's notebook can be used to collect artifacts from their experiences, it teaches them another way to look for ideas for writing.

ASSESS LEARNING

▶ Observe for evidence that children are using a writer's notebook to collect artifacts to inspire writing.

▶ Look for evidence that children use vocabulary such as *writer's notebook* and *items*.

MINILESSON

To help children think about using a writer's notebook to collect and write about important moments from their lives, encourage them to bring items from home (e.g., photos, stickers, maps, certificates, magazine clippings) that can be placed in their notebooks, or encourage them to make quick sketches to remind them of experiences. Demonstrate using items using your own writer's notebook. Here is an example.

▶ Show *Weather Watch* and read the title.

> This is Rita's journal, or notebook. She uses it to collect information about the weather. What sorts of things do you notice she collects?

▶ Share pages of collected items in your own writer's notebook.

> You can collect items from important moments in your life in your writer's notebook. Each of the items can give you an idea for your writing. Here is my writer's notebook. I have collected stickers from each time I voted. I could write a story about that. This map reminds me of a mountain bike ride with my boys. I definitely could write about that adventure! These photos remind me of my sister. I have so many stories I could write about her. I don't have a picture of her graduation, but I can draw a quick sketch of that to remind me I want to write more about that.

▶ On chart paper, record ideas for writing inspired by items in your notebook.

Have a Try

Invite children to turn and talk about items they might collect in a writer's notebook.

> What items might you collect in a writer's notebook? How will they help you as a writer? Turn and talk to your partner about that.

▶ After time for discussion, ask a few volunteers to share. Add new ideas to the chart.

Summarize and Apply

Summarize the lesson. Remind children to think about collecting and writing about important things in a writer's notebook.

> What have you learned about how you can use your writer's notebook?

▶ Write the principle at the top of the chart.

> Today during writing time, add items you wish to save to your notebook or sketch what you want to remember. Ask yourself what those items help you think about and how you can use them in your writing. Next to the item or sketch, you might want to quickly write down some ideas that you could write about.

Collect and write about important things in your writer's notebook.

- Photos
- Stickers
- Quick sketches
- Magazine or newspaper clippings
- Map from a bike trail
- Pamphlet from a place I visited
- Certificate of swimming lessons
- Ribbon from a race

I Voted !

BIKE TRAIL

Confer

▶ During independent writing, move around the room to confer briefly with as many individual children as time allows. Sit side by side with them and invite them to talk about collecting and writing about important things in a writer's notebook. Use the following prompts as needed.

- *Talk about this item. What does it make you think about?*
- *What idea for writing does this item give you? Talk about that idea before you begin writing. Now begin writing that idea down.*
- *Where are some memories of places you have been? If you don't have an item from that place, what could you sketch quickly to help you remember that place?*

Share

Following independent writing, gather children in the meeting area to share their items and/or quick sketches with a partner and then the class. If children bring items in from home on a later date, provide time for them to quickly share with classmates then.

> What ideas for items did you hear about from your classmates?

Section 5: Writing Process

Learning About My First Writer's Notebook

You Will Need

- your writer's notebook
- small sticky notes
- chart paper and markers
- draft paper and a pencil
- a writer's notebook for each child

Academic Language / Important Vocabulary

- writer's notebook
- reread

Continuum Connection

- Use a writer's notebook or booklet as a tool for collecting ideas, experimenting, planning, sketching, or drafting
- Reread a writer's notebook to select and develop a topic

GOAL

Understand that writers reread their writer's notebook as a way to find ideas for writing.

RATIONALE

When they understand that writers reread their writer's notebooks to help them choose ideas for writing, children learn the importance of continuously collecting ideas for writing in a writer's notebook.

ASSESS LEARNING

- Observe for evidence that children are rereading their writer's notebook to find ideas for writing.
- Look for evidence that children use vocabulary such as *writer's notebook* and *reread*.

MINILESSON

Introduce rereading the writer's notebook when children have several entries they can choose from. Model how you might reread your writer's notebook to pull out an idea for a memory story writing project.

- Show your writer's notebook.

  What should I write about today? When I am not sure, here is something I can do to think of an idea.

- Think aloud as you reread entries in your notebook.

  Here's an idea, but I can't think of enough to write about it. Maybe I'll use that idea later. Here's another idea, but I don't love it. Here's a good one! I love the idea, and I have plenty to write about. I'll put a sticky note on this page.

- Continue in this manner, thinking aloud about two or three more entries.

  What do you notice I just did to find an idea to write about?

- Record their responses on a chart.

  Now I have these sticky notes popping out of my notebook. I will reread each idea and choose one to write about.

- Explain why you chose that entry to write about. Demonstrate getting a piece of draft paper, writing today's date, and beginning a new project.

  What do you notice that I did to start writing?

- Record children's responses on the chart.

Have a Try

Invite children to reread their writer's notebooks and follow the process to find ideas for writing. Give them each three sticky notes and their writer's notebooks.

> Take a few moments to reread some entries in your writer's notebook. Follow the directions on the chart. Can you find two or three entries that might help you to begin writing?

▶ After time for rereading, ask children to share their ideas with a partner.

Summarize and Apply

Summarize the lesson. Remind children to reread their notebooks for ideas.

> What did you explore today about using a writer's notebook?

▶ Write the principle at the top of the chart.

> Today during writing time, continue rereading entries in your writer's notebook. Ask yourself the questions on the chart. Choose one entry, get a piece of draft paper, and begin writing.

Reread your writer's notebook to get ideas.

1. Reread an entry in your notebook.

2. Ask yourself: Do I love this idea? Do I know enough to write about it?

3. If you don't like the idea, keep rereading. If you like the idea, mark it with a sticky note.

4. Choose one entry. Get draft paper. Begin writing.

Confer

▶ During independent writing, move around the room to confer briefly with as many individual children as time allows. Sit side by side with them and invite them to reread and share entries from their notebooks. Use the following prompts as needed.

- *Share some of the entries in your notebook. Which entry might you write about?*
- *On which entries did you place a sticky note? What made you mark those?*
- *Which entry did you decide to use to get started on a new writing project? Why?*

Share

Following independent writing, gather children in the meeting area to share how rereading their notebook helped them think about what to work on today.

> Who would like to talk about how rereading your notebook helped you think about what to work on?

Assessment

After you have taught the minilessons in this umbrella, observe children as they write. Use *The Fountas & Pinnell Literacy Continuum* to notice, teach for, and support children's learning as you observe their attempts at reading and writing.

▶ What evidence do you have of children's new understandings related to using a writer's notebook?

- Do children talk about how writers use a notebook to collect ideas and writing?

- Can they create heart maps for the purpose of inspiring writing ideas?

- How comfortable are children with experimenting with ideas for writing?

- Are they using a writer's notebook as a place to collect memorabilia to inspire writing ideas?

- Do you observe them rereading their ideas to find one to write about?

- Do they understand and use the term *writer's notebook* and related vocabulary such as *heart map*, *identity*, *experiment*, and *reread*?

▶ In what ways, beyond the scope of this umbrella, are children using a writer's notebook?

- Are they expanding the way they collect ideas in their notebook to include webs and lists?

- Do they use their writer's notebooks to collect ideas for narrative writing (e.g., fiction, memory stories) and informational writing?

Use your observations to determine the next umbrella you will teach. You may also consult Suggested Sequence of Lessons (pp. 575–589) for guidance.

EXTENSIONS FOR LEARNING ABOUT MY FIRST WRITER'S NOTEBOK

▶ Provide a quick-write experience for children to try out in their writer's notebooks. For example, they could write a list of facts they know about a certain topic, draw and label a sketch of their bedroom, or make a list of favorite foods and write a quick entry.

▶ Support children in using sketches within a writer's notebook to help them generate ideas for writing or as a strategy to revise their writing. For example, they can sketch the setting of a memory as a way to think about what words to use to describe it.

▶ When you learn something new about a child, suggest that it be added to the heart map [WML2].

Minilessons in This Umbrella

WML1 Make a list of wonderings.

WML2 Make a list of topics you know about.

WML3 Explore a topic to find out if you want to write about it.

WML4 Sketch an object from nature.

Before Teaching Umbrella 3 Minilessons

The purpose of the minilessons in this umbrella is to show children ways of gathering ideas for informational writing. We recommend having children complete the exercises in these minilessons in a writer's notebook, so it will be helpful to have taught WPS.U2: Learning About My First Writer's Notebook before this umbrella. Otherwise, children can use paper and store it in their writing folders. You can invite children to make the lists, webs, and sketches suggested in this umbrella and then extend with quick writes about the same topics. Eventually, children can reread their writer's notebooks and grow an idea into a longer writing project (e.g., an all-about book).

Before teaching this umbrella, read and discuss engaging informational books about a variety of topics that will interest your class. You may also want to set up areas in the classroom for discovery and wondering (e.g., a science corner with various objects from nature) to provide children with ideas for their informational writing.

As you read and enjoy informational texts together, help children

- talk about what they learned from each book,

- share what they wonder about the topic, and

- discuss what they noticed about the illustrations.

Writing Minilesson Principle
Make a list of wonderings.

Gathering Ideas for Informational Writing

You Will Need

- chart paper and markers
- a writer's notebook for each child

Academic Language / Important Vocabulary

- wonder
- list

Continuum Connection

- Use a writer's notebook or booklet as a tool for collecting ideas, experimenting, planning, sketching, or drafting
- Use sketching, webs, lists, and freewriting to think about, plan for, and try out writing

GOAL

Make a list of wonderings to gather ideas for writing.

RATIONALE

Making a list of things they wonder about helps children engage their natural curiosity to come up with ideas for topics for informational writing. If children make lists in their writer's notebooks (or store the lists in their writing folders), they will always know where to find ideas for their writing.

ASSESS LEARNING

- Observe whether children keep a list of wonderings to gather ideas for writing.
- Notice whether they refer to their list of wonderings when choosing a topic for writing.
- Look for evidence that children can use vocabulary such as *wonder* and *list*.

MINILESSON

To help children think about the minilesson principle, engage them in a discussion about things they wonder, and use shared writing to make a list of class wonderings. Here is an example.

- Tell children about something you wonder about similar to the following.

    Yesterday morning I sat in my backyard and looked up at the sky. It was a beautiful day, and there was not a cloud in the sky. I started to wonder, why is the sky blue? That gave me the idea that I could someday write a book about why the sky is blue! I made a note of this wondering in my writer's notebook so I wouldn't forget it.

- Record the wondering on chart paper.

    Do you ever wonder why things are the way they are, or how things work? What are some things you wonder about?

- Record children's responses on chart paper.

Have a Try

Invite children to talk to a partner about things they wonder about a specific topic.

> We made a list of lots of different wonderings. You can also make a list of things you wonder about a specific topic. For example, we've been learning a lot about birds lately. What are some things you wonder about birds? Turn and talk to your partner about this.

▶ After time for discussion, invite children to share their wonderings. Record them on chart paper.

Summarize and Apply

Write the principle at the top of the chart. Summarize the learning. Remind children to make a list of things they wonder in their writer's notebooks or on a sheet of paper to be kept in their writing folders.

> Why is it a good idea to make a list of wonderings?

> Making a list of wonderings will help you remember them, so you can later find the answers to your questions and maybe even write a book about the topic! Today during writing time, make a list of things you wonder in your writer's notebook. Whenever you wonder about something new, add it to your list. Bring your list to share when we come back together.

Make a list of wonderings.

Things I Wonder
- Why is the sky blue?
- Why do giraffes have long necks?
- How many stars are there in the sky?
- Is there life on other planets?
- How deep is the deepest ocean?
- What is the most poisonous animal?

Things I Wonder About Birds
- How many different types of birds are there?
- What is the smallest bird?
- What is the largest bird?
- Why do birds have feathers?
- Where do birds sleep?
- How far can birds fly?

Confer

▶ During independent writing, move around the room to confer briefly with as many individual children as time allows. Sit side by side with them and invite them to talk about things they wonder. Use prompts such as the following as needed.

- *What are some things you wonder about?*

- *What questions do you have about the world?*

- *What do you wonder about _____?*

- *Is there anything on your list that you might like to write a book about?*

Share

Following independent writing, gather children in the meeting area to share their lists.

> Who would like to share something you wrote on your list of things you wonder?

WML2
WPS.U3.WML2

Writing Minilesson Principle
Make a list of topics you know about.

Gathering Ideas for Informational Writing

You Will Need

- a sample list of topics you know about
- chart paper and markers
- a writer's notebook for each child

Academic Language / Important Vocabulary

- topic
- list

Continuum Connection

- Use a writer's notebook or booklet as a tool for collecting ideas, experimenting, planning, sketching, or drafting
- Use sketching, webs, lists, and freewriting to think about, plan for, and try out writing

---

GOAL

Make a list of topics to inspire writing ideas.

RATIONALE

Making a list of topics they know about helps children be aware of what they know and could write about. They will be more likely to write about topics they are interested in and more engaged in the writing process.

ASSESS LEARNING

- ▶ Observe whether children keep a list of topics they know about to gather ideas for writing.
- ▶ Notice whether they refer to their list when choosing a topic for writing.
- ▶ Look for evidence that children can use vocabulary such as *topic* and *list*.

MINILESSON

To help children think about the minilesson principle, share a list of topics you know about and then use shared writing to make a list of topics the class knows about. Here is an example.

> You learned that one way to get ideas for writing is to make a list of things you wonder. You can also get ideas by making a list of topics you know about.

▶ Display the prepared list of topics you know about. Tell children about the topics on your list.

> I made a list of topics I know about. I know about teaching because I am a teacher. I also know a lot about dogs because I have three dogs. I know about science because I studied science in college. And I know about gardening because I spend a lot of time gardening on the weekends.

> Let's make a list of topics that we know about, as a class. What are some topics we've learned about together this year?

▶ Record children's responses on chart paper. Save the chart for WML3.

Have a Try

Invite children to talk to a partner about topics they know about.

> What are some other topics you know about? Turn and talk to your partner about topics you know about.

▶ After children turn and talk, invite several children to share.

Summarize and Apply

Write the principle at the top of the chart. Summarize the learning. Remind children to make a list of topics they know about in their writer's notebooks or on a sheet of paper to be kept in their writing folders.

> During writing time today, make a list in your writer's notebook of topics you know about. Whenever you learn about a new topic, add it to your list. When you are choosing a topic to write about, look at your list to get ideas. Bring your list to share when we come back together after writing time.

Make a list of topics you know about.

Topics We Know About:

- Birds

- Volcanoes

- Penguins

- The moon

- Dinosaurs

- Insects

Confer

▶ During independent writing, move around the room to confer briefly with as many individual children as time allows. Sit side by side with them and invite them to talk about topics they know about. Use prompts such as the following as needed.

- *What are some topics you know about?*
- *What are your hobbies?*
- *What are some things you know how to make or do?*
- *What interesting topics have you learned about this year?*
- *Would you like to write a book about any of the topics on your list?*

Share

Following independent writing, gather children in the meeting area to share their lists.

▶ Ask each child to share one idea.

> Now that you've heard your classmates ideas, is there an idea you would like to add to your list?

Writing Minilesson Principle
Explore a topic to find out if you want to write about it.

Gathering Ideas for Informational Writing

You Will Need

- the chart from WML2
- chart paper and markers
- a writer's notebook for each child

Academic Language / Important Vocabulary

- topic
- explore

Continuum Connection

- Use a writer's notebook or booklet as a tool for collecting ideas, experimenting, planning, sketching, or drafting
- Use sketching, webs, lists, and freewriting to think about, plan for, and try out writing

GOAL

Explore a topic to decide whether to write about it.

RATIONALE

Choosing a topic to write about can be challenging for children. By guiding them to think through a topic before writing about it, you show them how to select an appropriate topic for their writing.

ASSESS LEARNING

- Observe for evidence that children can think through a topic before they write about it.
- Look for evidence that children can use vocabulary such as *topic* and *explore*.

MINILESSON

To help children think about the minilesson principle, talk about about how to explore a topic to decide what to write about. Here is an example.

- Show the chart from WML2.

    When you're thinking about a topic to write about, think about what you might know already. Then think about what you want to know about the topic. Use that information to decide if you want to write about that topic.

    For example, let's think about what we know about penguins. What do you know about penguins?

- Write children's responses in the left-hand column of a two-column chart. Label the column *What You Think You Know*.

    Sometimes what you think you know turns out to be incorrect. You might find that out when you learn more about your topic.

    What would you like to find out about penguins that you don't already know or you're not sure about?

- Write children's responses in the right-hand column. Label the column *What You Want to Find Out*.

    It looks like we think we know a little bit about penguins, and we have some questions about penguins. Penguins might be a topic to write about.

    If you find that you don't have much information or there is nothing you want to find out about a topic, then that topic would not be a good one to write about.

Have a Try

Invite children to talk to a partner about exploring another topic.

> What is another topic you could explore? What do you think you know about it, and what would you want to find out? Talk about that with your partner.

▶ After time for discussion, invite a few pairs to share their ideas. Record ideas on the chart.

Summarize and Apply

Summarize the learning. Remind children to explore a topic to find out if they want to write about it. Children can do their writing in a writer's notebook or on a sheet of paper to be kept in their writing folders.

> What did you learn about choosing a topic to write about?

▶ Write the principle at the top of the chart.

> During writing time today, reread your list of topics. Write down what you think you know and what you would like to find out about your topic. Use that information to decide if you would like to write about that topic. If not, try a different topic. Bring your lists to share when we come back together.

Explore a topic to find out if you want to write about it.	
What You Think You Know	**What You Want to Find Out**
There are different kinds of penguins.	What is the biggest penguin? What is the smallest penguin?
Penguins live in Antarctica.	Do penguins live anywhere else? If so, where?
Volcanoes have lava.	Where is the nearest volcano?

Confer

▶ During independent writing, move around the room to confer briefly with as many individual children as time allows. Sit side by side with them and invite them to talk about the topic they would like to write about. Use prompts such as the following as needed.

- *Let's look at your list of topics you know about. What topic would you like to explore today?*
- *What do you think you know about your topic?*
- *What would you like to find out about _____?*

Share

Following independent writing, gather children in the meeting area to share their lists.

> Who has decided on a topic to write about?

> How did you choose that topic?

Gathering Ideas for Informational Writing

You Will Need

- chart paper prepared with a sketch of an object from nature (e.g., a feather) with labels and notes
- markers
- a large collection of objects from nature (feathers, rocks, leaves, acorns, etc.)
- a writer's notebook for each child
- To download the following online resource for this lesson, visit **fp.pub/resources**:
  - chart art (optional)

Academic Language / Important Vocabulary

- sketch
- nature
- idea

Continuum Connection

- Observe in the environment to notice details or changes
- Use drawings with labels to show how something looks, how something works, or the process or change
- Take notes or make sketches to help in remembering or generating information

GOAL

Use sketching to generate ideas for informational writing.

RATIONALE

When children sketch an object from nature, they take the time to look carefully at the object and ponder it. This can help them generate ideas for informational writing. Making a note of their thoughts and ideas will help children remember them.

ASSESS LEARNING

- Observe whether children sketch objects from nature to generate ideas for informational writing.
- Notice whether they make a note of their thoughts, ideas, and wonderings.
- Look for evidence that children can use vocabulary such as *sketch*, *nature*, and *idea*.

MINILESSON

To help children think about the minilesson principle, use a prepared sketch to engage them in learning how to sketch objects from nature as a way of generating writing ideas. Here is an example.

- Show the sketch you prepared of an object from nature.

  When I was walking through a little park downtown the other day, I found a feather. I thought it looked really interesting, so I decided to sketch it. As I was sketching it, I wondered about what kind of bird it came from and what kind of feather it was. This gave me ideas for my writing. I would like to learn more about feathers and maybe write a book about feathers or about the bird my feather came from. I took some notes so I would remember my thoughts about this feather. What do you notice about what I wrote?

  I wrote where I found the feather, what I noticed about it, and what it made me wonder.

Have a Try

Invite children to talk to a partner about the object from nature.

> What does this feather make you think about or wonder? Does it give you any ideas for writing? Turn and talk to your partner about this.

▶ After time for discussion, invite several pairs to share their thinking. Add any new wonderings to the chart.

Summarize and Apply

Write the principle at the top of the chart. Summarize the learning. Remind children to use sketching to generate ideas for informational writing. Children can do their writing in a writer's notebook or on a sheet of paper to be kept in their writing folders.

> How can sketching an object from nature give you ideas for writing?

> Here are some objects from nature. During writing time today, choose one of these objects and sketch it in your writer's notebook. Make notes about what the object makes you think about or wonder. Bring your notes to share when we meet later.

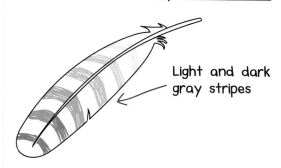

Sketch an object from nature.

Feather I found in a park downtown

Light and dark gray stripes

I wonder . . .
- What kind of feather is this?
- What kind of bird did it come from?
- What are feathers made of?

Confer

▶ During independent writing, move around the room to confer briefly with as many individual children as time allows. Sit side by side with them and invite them to talk about getting ideas for writing from a sketch. Use prompts such as the following as needed.

- *What are you sketching today? Why did you choose that object?*
- *What do you notice about the object?*
- *What does the object make you think about?*
- *What ideas does this object give you for your writing?*

Share

Following independent writing, gather children in the meeting area to share their sketches and ideas.

> Hold up the sketch you made today so everyone can see. What ideas does your object give you for your writing?

Section 5: Writing Process

Assessment

After you have taught the minilessons in this umbrella, observe children as they draw, write, and talk about their writing. Use *The Fountas & Pinnell Literacy Continuum* to notice, teach for, and support children's learning as you observe their writing skills.

▶ What evidence do you have of children's new understandings related to gathering ideas for informational writing?

- Do children refer to lists of wonderings and topics they know about?
- Can they make good decisions about which topics to choose?
- Do they sketch objects from nature to generate ideas for informational writing?
- Do they understand and use vocabulary such as *list, wonder, topic,* and *explore*?

▶ In what other ways, beyond the scope of this umbrella, are children exploring the writing process?

- Are they planning their informational writing?
- Are they interested in adding book and print features to their writing?
- Are they editing and proofreading their writing?

Use your observations to determine the next umbrella you will teach. You may also consult Suggested Sequence of Lessons (pp. 575–589) for guidance.

EXTENSIONS FOR GATHERING IDEAS FOR INFORMATIONAL WRITING

▶ Take the children on a field trip (e.g., to a local business, a park, or a museum). Afterward, invite children to discuss what ideas the experience gave them for informational writing. Encourage children to note their ideas in their writer's notebooks.

▶ Invite a local expert (e.g., firefighter, scientist, business owner, veterinarian) to speak to the class. With children, explore a topic or topics from the presentation as a way to generate ideas for informational writing.

▶ Have children reread their ideas in their writer's notebooks when choosing a topic for a longer writing piece.

Minilessons in This Umbrella

WML1 Make a web of favorite memories.

WML2 Make a map of an important place and think about the stories that took place there.

WML3 Sketch a favorite memory.

Interactive Read-Aloud
Tomie dePaola

Before Teaching Umbrella 4 Minilessons

The purpose of the minilessons in this umbrella is to show children ways of gathering ideas for memory writing that children can grow into a memory book. You do not need to teach the minilessons in this umbrella consecutively. Rather, they can be used whenever you feel your children need some inspiration for their writing. They can also be repeated as needed because they are intended to be generative—for example, when you teach children to make a web of favorite memories, they are also learning that webs can be used to brainstorm other ideas. We recommend having children apply their new thinking in a writer's notebook, so it would be helpful to have taught WPS.U2: Learning About My First Writer's Notebook before this umbrella.

Before teaching this umbrella, read and discuss engaging books in which authors reflect on memories and experiences that are important to them, such as the following books from *Fountas & Pinnell Classroom™ Interactive Read-Aloud Collection*, or choose similar books from the classroom library.

Interactive Read-Aloud Collection

Tomie dePaola: Writing from Life

The Art Lesson

Nana Upstairs & Nana Downstairs

As you read and enjoy these and other books together, help children

- notice that authors write about different types of memories (e.g., scary, sad, exciting, happy), and

- talk about their own ideas for writing about a similar topic or theme.

Writing Minilesson Principle
Make a web of favorite memories.

Gathering Ideas for Memory Writing

You Will Need

- books in which authors reflect on memories and experiences, such as the following by Tomie dePaola from Text Set: Tomie dePaola: Writing from Life:
  - *Nana Upstairs & Nana Downstairs*
  - *The Art Lesson*
- chart paper and markers
- a writer's notebook for each child
- To download the following online resource for this lesson, visit **fp.pub/resources**:
  - Web

Academic Language/ Important Vocabulary

- memory
- story
- web
- ideas

Continuum Connection

- Understand that writers may tell stories from their own lives
- Select a meaningful topic
- Use a writer's notebook or booklet as a tool for collecting ideas, experimenting, planning, sketching, or drafting
- Use sketching, webs, lists, and freewriting to think about, plan for, and try out writing

GOAL

Understand that a web can help generate ideas for a story.

RATIONALE

Teaching children to use a web to collect ideas gives them a tool for getting started on their writing. The hardest part of writing is facing a blank page. Offering a way to fill that page will give children confidence in generating ideas for stories.

ASSESS LEARNING

- Observe whether children use a web to generate ideas for stories.
- Look for evidence that children can use vocabulary such as *memory*, *story*, *web*, and *ideas*.

MINILESSON

To help children think about the minilesson principle, demonstrate organizing ideas in a web to generate story ideas. Below is an example. Have children bring their writer's notebooks or a copy of the web from the online resources to the circle to use in Have a Try.

- Show *Nana Upstairs & Nana Downstairs* and *The Art Lesson*.

    Writers sometimes tell about their own lives in their writing, like in these two books Tomie dePaola wrote about his childhood. What did he share about his childhood in each?

    As a writer, you can get ideas for a memory story from your life, too. You can create webs in your writer's notebook to collect ideas for writing. Let me show you how. Notice the steps I follow to make the web.

- Model building a web, adding to it as you think aloud.

    First, I draw a circle in the middle of the page. I want to write about my memories with my family, so I am going to write *Family Stories* in that circle. Next, I jot notes about my family memories all around that, each in its own circle. When I add a circle, I connect it to the center with a line.

- Write brief descriptions of several memories around the center circle.

    See how it starts to look like a web? These are memories from my family that I can write books about.

- As time allows, and on following days, continue to build webs together, such as for holiday celebrations, pets, friends, or school.

Have a Try

Invite children to talk to a partner about how they can make a web of favorite memories in a writer's notebook.

> Think of some memories that you would like to write about. Make a circle in the middle of a page that says *Memories*. Write your ideas for memories in circles around the center, like I did. Then share your ideas with your partner.

▶ After children turn and talk, invite several children to share the memories they would like to write about to inspire other children.

Summarize and Apply

Summarize the learning. Remind children to think about making memory webs as a way to collect ideas for writing.

> What is one way you can get ideas for writing a memory story?

▶ Write the principle at the top of the chart.

> During writing time today, choose one of the memories you wrote in your web. Make a new web about that memory. Write details in the circles around the center circle. If I wanted to write about finding a baby bird, I might make circles for the people I was with, how I felt, what the bird looked like, and what we did to help the baby bird. Bring your writer's notebook to share when we meet later.

Confer

▶ During independent writing, move around the room to confer briefly with as many individual children as time allows. Sit side by side with them and invite them to talk about their ideas for a memory web. Use prompts such as the following if needed.

- *Talk about your ideas for your memory web.*
- *What will you write in the center circle? What will you write around that?*
- *Do you have any special memories of _____ that you would like to write about?*

Share

Following independent writing, gather children in the meeting area to talk about their writing.

> Share your web with your partner. Talk about what makes that memory special.

Writing Minilesson Principle
Make a map of an important place and think about the stories that took place there.

Gathering Ideas for Memory Writing

You Will Need

- simple map of a place special to you, sketched in advance on 8½ x 11 paper
- chart paper and markers
- tape
- a writer's notebook for each child

Academic Language/ Important Vocabulary

- memory
- story
- map
- ideas

Continuum Connection

- Understand that writers may tell stories from their own lives
- Use a writer's notebook or booklet as a tool for collecting ideas, experimenting, planning, sketching, or drafting
- Use sketching, webs, lists, and freewriting to think about, plan for, and try out writing

GOAL

Create a map of a special place to generate ideas for writing.

RATIONALE

When children learn to create a map of a meaningful place, it allows them to reflect on special moments experienced there. As they develop these memories into books, they gain confidence in generating ideas for stories.

ASSESS LEARNING

- Observe whether children choose to create memory maps to generate writing ideas.
- Look for evidence that children can use vocabulary such as *memory*, *story*, *map*, and *ideas*.

MINILESSON

To help children think about the minilesson principle, demonstrate creating a map of a special place to generate story ideas. Here is an example.

- Hold up your writer's notebook.

  Places can have special memories. Authors sometimes write books about memories that are connected to a meaningful place. As a writer, you can draw a map of a place that is special to you to help you think about your memories from that place. You can write a story about each of your memories. Let me show you a map of a place that is special to me.

- Affix your hand-drawn map to chart paper. Point to specific places on the map as you think aloud about the fond memories they help you recall. Jot a few notes below the map to capture the memories.

  This is the neighborhood where I grew up. Here is the house where I lived. Behind my house were trails that we would sled on every winter. One day we were sledding so fast that we went right into the woods! I'll write *Sledding down the hill and into the woods* here so I can write a story about that later. In the woods there was a huge fir tree whose branches spread out like a tent. We would sit under it and pretend it was our fort. Coral Avenue was hilly. My friends and I would coast down the hill on our bikes and then pedal like crazy to get up the next hill.

  Notice how this map helps me to think of these memories. Each one is something that I can write more about. I will add to this list as I look at the map and think of more memories from my childhood.

Have a Try

Invite children to discuss ideas for a map with a partner, mentioning the experiences they had in that place.

> Turn and talk to your partner about a place that is important to you.

▸ After children turn and talk, invite a few children to share their ideas.

Summarize and Apply

Summarize the learning. Remind children to think about making maps as a way to collect ideas for writing.

> What is one way you can get ideas for writing a memory story?

▸ Write the principle at the top of the chart.

> Today you talked about making a map to help you think of memories. During writing time today, draw a map in your writer's notebook. You might draw the school, your grandparents' house, home, someplace else you have lived, the park, or something else. Underneath the map, write some ideas for stories you could write. Bring your writer's notebook to share when we meet later.

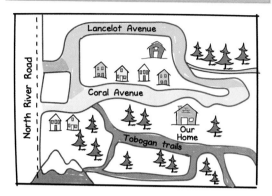

Make a map of an important place and think about the stories that took place there.

- Sledding down the hill and into the woods
- Using a huge tree as a fort
- Coasting down Coral Avenue on our bikes

Confer

▸ During independent writing, move around the room to confer briefly with as many individual children as time allows. Sit side by side with them and invite them to talk about their ideas for a memory map. Use prompts such as the following if needed.

- *Talk about the map that you drew. Why is this a special place for you?*
- *Can you think of some special memories that happened there?*
- *Think of another place that is important to you. Can you draw a map of it?*

Share

Following independent writing, gather children in the meeting area to talk about their writing.

> Who would like to share your map? What did you include on your map? How did your map help you to think about a story?

WML3
WPS.U4.WML3

Writing Minilesson Principle
Sketch a favorite memory.

Gathering Ideas for Memory Writing

You Will Need

- your writer's notebook
- chart paper, pencil, and markers
- a writer's notebook for each child

Academic Language / Important Vocabulary

- memory
- story
- ideas
- sketch
- details
- plan

Continuum Connection

- Use sketching, webs, lists, and freewriting to think about, plan for, and try out writing
- Use a writer's notebook or booklet as a tool for collecting ideas, experimenting, planning, sketching, or drafting

GOAL

Use sketching to generate ideas about a memorable experience.

RATIONALE

When children sketch pieces of a memory, they take the time to visualize the experience and consider various aspects of it. This can help them generate ideas for memory writing and can serve as a talking point to support the development of a piece of writing.

ASSESS LEARNING

- Observe whether children use sketching to generate ideas about a memorable experience.
- Notice whether they are able to add more to a story by talking about a sketch.
- Look for evidence that children can use vocabulary such as *memory*, *story*, *ideas*, *sketch*, *details*, and *plan*.

MINILESSON

To help children think about the minilesson principle, demonstrate making a sketch of a memorable experience to generate story ideas. Below is an example. Have children bring their writer's notebooks to the circle to use in Have a Try.

Before you begin writing a memory story, it helps to make a plan. One way writers do this is by making a sketch of the memory they want to share. You can make a sketch of a memory in your writer's notebook.

- Show an ideas page from your writer's notebook.

Here are some ideas that I've written in my writer's notebook.

- Begin sketching as you think aloud about a memory.

Watch as I sketch my memory about going to the county fair.

I always loved going to the fair with my family. We would see the animals—cows, pigs, chickens, and horses. My favorite thing was to ride on the Ferris wheel. It was scary at the top, but fun!

What do you notice about how I talked about my memory and what I sketched?

Have a Try

Invite children to look at the ideas they have listed in their writer's notebooks, choose a memory, and sketch what happened.

> Which memory will you choose to sketch? Open to a new page and begin to sketch what you remember about what happened.

▶ After a short time for sketching, invite children to share the sketch they are working on with a partner and describe it.

Summarize and Apply

Write the principle at the top of the chart. Summarize the learning. Remind children to use sketching to generate ideas for memory writing.

> How can sketching a memory give you ideas for writing?

> During writing time today, continue to add to the sketch that you started. If you have time you may want to sketch another memory, too. Bring your writer's notebook to share when we meet later.

Sketch a favorite memory.

Confer

▶ During independent writing, move around the room to confer briefly with as many individual children as time allows. Sit side by side with them and invite them to talk about their sketches. Use prompts such as the following as needed.

• *What are you sketching today? Why did you choose to sketch it that way?*

• *Talk about what is happening in your sketch.*

• *Why did you include this detail (item)?*

• *Is there anything else that you would like to add to your sketch?*

Share

Following independent writing, gather children in the meeting area to share their sketches.

> Who would like to share the sketch you made?

> Tell about your memory and the details you included in your sketch.

Assessment

After you have taught the minilessons in this umbrella, observe children as they draw and write. Use the behaviors and understandings in *The Fountas & Pinnell Literacy Continuum* to notice, teach for, and support children's learning as you observe their attempts at reading and writing.

▶ What evidence do you have of children's new understandings related to gathering ideas for memory writing?

- Can children make webs to generate ideas for stories?
- Do they make maps of important places and think about the stories that took place there?
- Do they include details in their sketches that they can write about?
- Do children understand and use vocabulary such as *memory*, *story*, *web*, *ideas*, *map*, *list*, *sketch*, *details*, and *plan*?

▶ In what other ways, beyond the scope of this umbrella, are children ready to expand their writing skills?

- Are they using the techniques in this umbrella to write different kinds of stories?
- Do they need to work on adding details to their sketches to provide information for writing?

Use your observations to determine the next umbrella you will teach. You may also consult Suggested Sequence of Lessons (pp. 575–589) for guidance.

EXTENSIONS FOR GATHERING IDEAS FOR MEMORY WRITING

▶ Invite children to create webs for different areas of the curriculum. For example, they could create a web for something that they are studying in science or social studies. Show them how to use webs to consolidate their thinking and show what they understand.

▶ Encourage children to use sketching in their writer's notebook to generate additional ideas of what to write and also to plan and revise what they will write.

▶ Use published memory stories to model craft decisions that the authors made. For example, Cynthia Rylant repeated the phrase "When I was young in the mountains," which is the title of her book. Elizabeth Fitzgerald Howard used dialogue in her memory story *Aunt Flossie's Hats (and Crab Cakes Later)*. Both books are in the Memory Stories text set in *Fountas & Pinnell Classroom™ Interactive Read-Aloud Collection*.

Minilessons in This Umbrella

WML1 Think about your purpose.

WML2 Think about your audience.

WML3 Think about the kind of writing you want to do.

Before Teaching Umbrella 5 Minilessons

The goal of this umbrella is to make children aware of the relationship between purpose, audience, and genre. Purpose and audience are separate ideas, yet they are intertwined because they both influence the type of writing (genre or form) an author chooses to use. Prior to beginning this umbrella, children should have an idea of the topic they want to write about so they can think about and make connections between their purpose, audience, and genre. Before teaching, it is recommended that you teach or revisit WPS.U2.WML5: Reread your writer's notebook for ideas. As well, it is suggested that you will have formally taught several genres. When addressing audience, encourage children to think beyond the school community (see WML2). These minilessons build on each other, so it is recommended that you teach them in order.

   Children should have read a variety of genres and talked about the choices that the writers made. For mentor texts, use the books listed below from *Fountas & Pinnell Classroom™ Interactive Read-Aloud Collection* and *Shared Reading Collection* or books from the classroom library.

Interactive Read-Aloud Collection

Facing Challenges

Roller Coaster by Marla Frazee

Suki's Kimono by Chieri Uegaki

Seymour Simon: A Scientific Eye

Dogs

Shared Reading Collection

A Piñata Fiesta by Adrián Garcia Montoya

As you read and enjoy these texts together, help children

- talk about what purpose the author may have had for writing, and
- talk about who the writer's intended audience might be.

Interactive Read-Aloud
Facing Challenges

Seymour Simon

Shared Reading

Section 5: Writing Process

Writing Minilesson Principle
Think about your purpose.

Thinking About Purpose and Audience

You Will Need

- a mentor text that tells a story and a mentor text that gives information, such as the following:
  - *Roller Coaster* by Marla Frazee, from Text Set: Facing Challenges
  - *A Piñata Fiesta* by Adrián Garcia Montoya, from *Shared Reading Collection*
- chart paper and markers

Academic Language / Important Vocabulary

- writing
- reason
- topic
- purpose
- tell a story
- give information

Continuum Connection

- Write for a specific purpose: e.g., to inform, entertain, persuade, reflect, instruct, retell, maintain relationships, plan

GOAL

Understand that writers think about why they are writing and how they want their writing to affect their audience.

RATIONALE

When children understand that writers have a purpose for writing, they begin to think about why and what they want to write. They also learn that they have choices in their own writing. Giving children a choice in the topics to write about leads to increased motivation for writing and more authentic writing.

ASSESS LEARNING

- Look for evidence that children understand that writers have a purpose for writing.
- Observe whether children are talking about different purposes for writing.
- Look for evidence that children can use vocabulary such as *writing*, *reason*, *topic*, *purpose*, *tell a story*, and *give information*.

MINILESSON

To help children think about the minilesson principle, talk about why they think the authors chose to write familiar texts. Link that discussion to having children think about their own purposes for writing. Here is an example.

- Prior to this lesson, children should have chosen a topic they want to write about.
- Show the cover and revisit a few pages of *Roller Coaster*.

  Why do you suppose Marla Frazee chose to write *Roller Coaster*?

  A purpose is the reason for doing something. Before you write something, think about your purpose for writing.

- Engage children in a conversation about the author's purpose, guiding them to recognize that the writer's purpose was to tell an entertaining story.
- Begin a list of purposes for writing. Start the list with *Tell a story* and *Entertain*.
- Show the cover and revisit a few pages of an informational book, such as *A Piñata Fiesta*.

  Adrián Garcia Montoya is the writer. What do you think was his purpose for writing?

- Guide the conversation to help children recognize that the purpose was to teach how to make a piñata. Add *Teach* and *Give information* to the chart list.

  Think about some other purposes for writing. Turn and talk about some ideas.

- After time for discussion, ask volunteers for ideas. Add to the chart list.

Have a Try

Invite children to turn and talk about their purposes for writing. Model talking about the way a writer might choose a purpose using the topics chosen by several children. This is just an example.

> Think about the different purposes, or reasons, you might write something about your topic. Cole, you want to write about your favorite pair of shoes. Maybe you want to describe them or tell a story about them. Maybe you want to give information about where you can buy them or share how you feel when you wear them.
>
> Share your topic with your partner and talk about your purpose, or reason, for writing.

▶ After time for discussion, ask children to share their ideas. If they mention any new purposes, add to the chart. Save the chart for WML3.

Summarize and Apply

Summarize the lesson. Encourage children to think about their purposes for writing. Add the principle to the top of the chart.

> Today you talked about some different purposes for writing. During writing time, write down some ideas you have about your purpose for writing. Look at the chart to help you choose a purpose. Plan to share your ideas when we meet later.

Confer

▶ During independent writing, move around the room to confer briefly with as many individual children as time allows. Sit side by side with them and invite them to talk about purpose. Use the following prompts as needed.

- *What ideas do you have for writing about this topic?*
- *What is your purpose for writing?*
- *Let's look at the chart and think about some different purposes.*

Share

Following independent writing, gather children in the meeting area.

▶ Ask children to each share a purpose they wrote down.

> What did you hear from your classmates that you might use when you write?

Think about your purpose.

Purposes for Writing

- Tell a story
- Entertain
- Teach
- Give information
- Plan something (shopping list, to-do list)
- Invite someone to do something
- Explain something
- Change something
- Have someone feel something
- Share feelings
- Describe something using the senses
- Share ideas

Thinking About Purpose and Audience

You Will Need

- a mentor text, such as *Suki's Kimono* by Chieri Uegaki, from Text Set: Facing Challenges
- chart paper prepared with audience groups: *Larger Community, Family, Classmates and Friends*
- sticky notes
- chart paper and markers

Academic Language / Important Vocabulary

- writing
- reader
- audience

Continuum Connection

- Write with specific readers or audience in mind
- Understand that writing is shaped by the writer's purpose and understanding of the audience
- Plan and organize information for the intended readers
- Understand audience as all readers rather than just the teacher

GOAL

Understand that writers think about their intended audience to further define their purpose.

RATIONALE

When children think about their intended audience, they can stay better focused on their purpose for writing and they learn that their words matter. By considering a wider and more genuine audience than just classmates, teacher, or family, children realize that their words can have an impact and be powerful and meaningful.

ASSESS LEARNING

- Look for evidence that children can identify who their audience is.
- Notice whether children can answer some questions about their audience, such as what their audience might want to know about.
- Look for evidence that children understand and use vocabulary such as *writing*, *reader*, and *audience*.

MINILESSON

To help children think about the minilesson principle, use a mentor text to engage them in an interactive conversation about audience. Here is an example.

- Ahead of time, prepare a chart with the names of several audiences that children might be interested in writing for (e.g., friends, classmates, family, larger community).

    Listen as I read through a few pages of *Suki's Kimono*.

- Revisit a few pages of *Suki's Kimono*.

    Who do you think would like this book, adults or children? Why?

    You can tell that she wrote it for children because she uses interesting pictures and chooses words that children might like to read. Children are her audience.

    An audience is the person or group of people you think would like to read something that you write.

- Show and read the prepared audience chart.

    The writer probably wrote this for children your age. An audience can be small, like maybe one friend or grandparent. An audience can also be big.

    Turn and talk about some people you would like to read your writing.

- After time for discussion, ask a few volunteers to share. Place a few examples on sticky notes and add them to the chart.

Have a Try

Invite children to turn and talk about an intended audience for their writing.

> Think about the different audiences that you could write for. Yaa, you could write a book about pizza for the class. Zach, you could write about dolphins for an adult expert.

> Turn and talk about who your audience might be and what they might want to know.

▶ After time for discussion, ask children to share their ideas.

Summarize and Apply

Summarize the lesson. Encourage children to think about the audience they want to write for.

> Today you talked about *who* your audience is and *what* they might want to know.

▶ Write the principle at the top of the chart. Add the two questions (shown on the chart).

> You have chosen your topic and you know your purpose. During writing time, write down the audience you might like to write for. Also write some things your audience might want to know and what you want to share. Bring the ideas you have when we meet later.

▶ Save the chart for WML3.

> ### Think about your audience.
>
> **Larger Community**
>
> nature center, coaches, college teacher, mayor, adult expert
>
> **Who** is the audience?
>
> **Family**
>
> aunt, grandfather
>
> **What** would the audience want to know?
>
> **Classmates and Friends**

Confer

▶ During independent writing, move around the room to confer briefly with as many individual children as time allows. Sit side by side with them and invite them to talk about audience. Use the following prompts as needed.

- *Who will be reading this?*
- *What does your audience know already and what would they like to know more about?*

Share

Following independent writing, gather children in the meeting area to share their writing.

> What ideas do you have about your audience and what they might want to know about? Tell about that.

Section 5: Writing Process

WML3
WPS.U5.WML3

Writing Minilesson Principle
Think about the kind of writing you want to do.

Thinking About Purpose and Audience

You Will Need

- a mentor text on a topic that could be used for a variety of purposes and audiences, such as *Dogs* by Seymour Simon, from Text Set: Seymour Simon: A Scientific Eye
- purpose and audience charts from WML1 and WML2
- chart paper prepared with headings: *Topic, Purpose, Audience, Type of Writing*
- chart paper and markers
- To download the following online resource for this lesson, visit **fp.pub/resources**:
  - Topic, Purpose, Audience, Type of Writing Chart

Academic Language / Important Vocabulary

- writing
- topic
- choice
- purpose
- audience

Continuum Connection

- Tell whether a piece of writing is functional, narrative, informational, or poetic
- Understand how the purpose of the writing influences the selection of genre
- Select the genre for the writing based on the purpose

GOAL

Choose the genre or form of writing based on purpose and audience.

RATIONALE

When children choose the type of writing they want to do by thinking about how it best suits their purpose and audience, they write effectively and with authenticity.

ASSESS LEARNING

- Observe whether children recognize that thinking about purpose and audience can help them decide what type of writing they want to do.
- Look for evidence that children can use vocabulary such as *writing, topic, choice, purpose,* and *audience*.

MINILESSON

To help children think about the type of writing they want to do, engage them in a discussion about how authors think about the purpose and audience for their writing. Here is an example.

- Display the purpose and audience charts from WML1 and WML2.
- Show the cover of *Dogs*.

  Seymour Simon's books are about science and nature. I think he is interested in those topics and wants to share what he knows with other people, especially children. If you wanted to share what you know about something, what type of writing would you choose?

  An all-about book tells information, so that would be a good choice. Seymour Simon's book *Dogs* and many of his other books are all-about books. They are written in a way that children can understand, learn from, and enjoy.

- Show the prepared chart. Add *Seymour Simon: Dogs* in the topic column. Guide the conversation and then, using children's ideas, write Seymour Simon's purpose, audience, and type of writing.

  If, instead, you wanted to write something entertaining about dogs, what type of writing would you choose?

- Talk about how a story or a poem or a cartoon might be choices they could make.

  There are different ways that you can write about the same topic. Choose the way that makes sense for your purpose and audience.

Have a Try

Invite children to turn and talk about purpose, audience, and type of writing.

> Cole wants to write about a pair of shoes. Once he decides his purpose and audience, then he can think about the type of writing he might like to do. For example, if he thinks you should buy shoes just like his, he could make an ad.

> Turn and talk about your topic, your purpose and audience, and what type of writing you are thinking of doing.

▶ After time for discussion, ask volunteers to share their ideas. Add to the chart.

▶ You may want to keep the chart posted and have other children fill it in with their ideas.

Think about the kind of writing you want to do.			
Topic	Purpose	Audience	Type of Writing
Seymour Simon: Dogs	Inform	Children	All-about book
Yaa: Pizza	Teach	Children	How-to book
Cole: Favorite pair of shoes	Share feelings	Class	Poetry
Shoshana: Birthday	Invite	Grandparents	Invitation
Zach: Dolphins	Change something	Adult expert	Letter

Summarize and Apply

Summarize the lesson. Remind children to think about what type of writing best fits their purpose and audience. Write the principle at the top of the chart.

> You have been talking about the type of writing you want to do by thinking about topic, purpose, and audience. During writing time, choose the type of writing you want to do and begin writing. Bring your writing to share when we meet later.

Confer

▶ During independent writing, move around the room to confer briefly with as many individual children as time allows. Sit side by side with them and invite them to talk about their writing. Use the following prompts as needed.

- *What is your purpose for writing? Who will be your audience?*
- *What type of writing is best for your purpose and audience?*
- *You have chosen a topic. Let's look at the charts and choose the type of writing.*

Share

Following independent writing, gather children in the meeting area to share their writing.

> What type of writing did you decide to do today? Talk about how you made your decision.

> What (Who) is the purpose of (audience for) _____'s writing? How do you know?

Assessment

After you have taught the minilessons in this umbrella, observe children as they write and talk about writing. Use *The Fountas & Pinnell Literacy Continuum* to notice, teach for, and support children's learning as you observe their attempts at writing.

▸ What evidence do you have of children's new understandings related to purpose and audience?

- Do children's writing behaviors show that they are thinking about purpose and audience?

- Are children thinking and talking about the kind of writing they want to do?

- Are they using vocabulary such as *writing, reason, purpose, tell a story, give information, reader, audience,* and *choice*?

▸ In what ways, beyond the scope of this umbrella, are children showing an interest in making independent writing choices?

- Do children show an interest in choosing their own topics?

- Are children showing an interest in writing in a variety of genres?

Use your observations to determine the next umbrella you will teach. You may also consult Suggested Sequence of Lessons (pp. 575–589) for guidance.

EXTENSIONS FOR THINKING ABOUT PURPOSE AND AUDIENCE

▸ Share other types of writing (e.g., travel brochure, recipe) with children that have different purposes and intended audiences and have them talk about the purpose and audience.

▸ Have children add sticky notes to the audience chart as they think of new examples of each audience.

▸ If you are using *The Reading Minilessons Book, Grade 2* (Fountas and Pinnell 2019), the related umbrella is LA.U8: Thinking About the Author's Purpose.

Minilessons in This Umbrella

WML1   Write what you think is going to happen.

WML2   Sketch what you observe.

WML3   Write down your observations.

Before Teaching Umbrella 6 Minilessons

Before teaching the minilessons in this umbrella, you will need to choose, plan, and gather materials for a science experiment or activity that you will do with the children over the course of these lessons. These minilessons are based on an activity in which children observe the clouds and use their observations to predict the day's weather. However, you can use any multiday activity or experiment that is relevant to your class's science curriculum.

You might also want to read and discuss nonfiction books related to the science topic you have chosen. If you choose an experiment related to weather, you might use the following text from *Fountas & Pinnell Classroom™ Shared Reading Collection* or books about weather from the classroom library.

Shared Reading Collection

Weather Watch: Rita's Journal by June Schwartz

As you read and enjoy these texts together, help children

- make predictions and inferences,
- notice and discuss details in the illustrations, and
- pose questions and wonderings about the topic.

Section 5: Writing Process

Writing Minilesson Principle
Write what you think is going to happen.

Observing and Writing Like a Scientist

You Will Need

- a plan and materials for a science activity/experiment (e.g., observing the weather)
- a book related to the science experiment, such as *Weather Watch: Rita's Journal* by June Schwartz, from *Shared Reading Collection* (optional)
- chart paper and markers

Academic Language / Important Vocabulary

- science
- experiment
- predict
- prediction

Continuum Connection

- Use vocabulary appropriate for the topic
- Generate and expand ideas through talk with peers and teacher
- Take notes or make sketches to help in remembering or generating information

GOAL

Write a prediction related to a science project.

RATIONALE

When you help children write a prediction for a science experiment, they learn that scientists use what they already know about a topic to make an educated guess about what will happen. They also learn that scientists use writing for a purpose–to record their predictions in order to have a permanent, written record of their scientific process.

ASSESS LEARNING

- Observe children as they talk about science experiments. Do they draw on their existing knowledge to make an educated guess about what will happen?
- Notice whether children can write a prediction for a science experiment.
- Look for evidence that children can use vocabulary such as *science, experiment, predict,* and *prediction*.

MINILESSON

Introduce the science activity that the children are going to conduct (see Before Teaching for more information) and help them make predictions. Here is an example.

- Show the cover of *Weather Watch* and read the title.

    In this book, what do Rita and her dad do every morning?

    Why do they look at the clouds?

    They look at the clouds to predict what the weather will be like each day. They make predictions and then check to see if their predictions are correct. What kinds of clouds did you learn about in this book?

- Revisit the pages about cumulus, cirrus, and stratus clouds.
- Take the children outside, or gather them around a large window.

    We can go on a weather watch just like Rita did. Look at the clouds. What do you think the weather will be like today?

    Why do you think that?

- Record on chart paper the language children use to state their predictions (e.g., *I think . . . because . . .*). Point out that the word *because* introduces the reason for the prediction.

Have a Try

Invite children to talk to a partner about making predictions.

> What did you learn today about making predictions for a science experiment? Turn and talk to your partner about this.

▸ After children turn and talk, invite a few children to share.

Summarize and Apply

Write the principle at the top of the chart. Read it to children. Summarize the learning and remind children to record their predictions.

> It's important to write your prediction down so that you will remember it. At the end of the day, you can read your prediction to see if you were right about today's weather!

> Today during writing time, write your prediction about today's weather. When you finish writing your prediction, continue working on a book you've already started or start a new one.

Write what you think is going to happen.

- I think . . . because . . .

- I predict that . . . because . . .

- My prediction is that . . . because . . .

- I see . . . , which makes me think that . . .

Confer

▸ During independent writing, move around the room to confer briefly with as many individual children as time allows. Sit side by side with them and invite them to talk about their predictions. Use prompts such as the following if needed.

- *What do you think the weather will be like today?*
- *What did you notice that makes you think that?*
- *What words will you use to start your prediction?*
- *Make sure you include a reason for your prediction.*

Share

Following independent writing, gather children in triads in the meeting area to share their predictions.

> Turn and talk to your partners about your prediction and how you made it.

Observing and Writing Like a Scientist

You Will Need

▸ a book related to the chosen science experiment, such as *Weather Watch: Rita's Journal* by June Schwartz, from *Shared Reading Collection* (optional)

▸ materials for the chosen science experiment/activity if needed

▸ chart paper and markers

Academic Language / Important Vocabulary

▸ sketch

▸ observe

▸ label

Continuum Connection

▸ Observe carefully to detect and describe change (growth, change over time in plants or animals, chemical change in food), and talk about observations

▸ Observe in the environment to notice details or changes

▸ Use drawings with labels to show how something looks, how something works, or the process or change

▸ Remember important labels for drawings

▸ Take notes or make sketches to help in remembering or generating information

GOAL

Use drawings with labels to show what has been observed.

RATIONALE

When you help children sketch their scientific observations, they learn to look closely at a subject to observe its many different aspects. They begin to understand that drawings can convey important information, so the drawings must be clear and accurate.

ASSESS LEARNING

▸ Notice the details children include in their sketches of scientific observations.

▸ Look for evidence that children can use vocabulary such as *sketch*, *observe*, and *label*.

MINILESSON

To help children think about the minilesson principle, model sketching scientific observations and engage children in telling what they notice. Here is an example.

▸ Show the cover of *Weather Watch* and read aloud page 4. Point to the illustration.

> What does Rita draw on this page of her weather journal?
>
> She draws fluffy, puffy clouds that are called cumulus clouds. What does she do so she'll remember what they're called?
>
> She labels her drawing with the words *cumulus clouds*.
>
> We can sketch what we observe, just like Rita does.

▸ Take the children outside, or gather them around a large window.

> What do you notice about the clouds today?

▸ Using children's observations, sketch the clouds on chart paper. Think aloud as you add details and label your drawing.

> To help remember what we observed, I must draw the clouds carefully.
>
> I remember that clouds like these are called cirrus clouds, so I will write the label *cirrus clouds*. I will also write today's date so I will remember when we observed these clouds.

Have a Try

Invite children to talk to a partner about sketching scientific observations.

> What do you notice about what I did? What did I draw and write? What kinds of things did I think about? Turn and talk to your partner about what I drew and wrote.

▶ After time for discussion, invite several children to share their thinking. Record responses on chart paper.

Summarize and Apply

Summarize the learning and remind children to sketch their scientific observations.

> What can you do to help remember your observations?

▶ Write the principle at the top of the chart.

> Today during writing time, look closely at the clouds and sketch what you observe. Remember to add labels and today's date. You can also write another prediction about today's weather. Bring your drawing to share when we come back together.

Sketch what you observe.

- Look closely.
- Think about size, color, shape, and texture.
- Carefully draw what you notice.
- Label your sketch.
- Write the date.

Tuesday, October 12

cirrus clouds ↗

Confer

▶ During independent writing, move around the room to confer briefly with as many individual children as time allows. Sit side by side with them and invite them to talk about their observations. Use prompts such as the following if needed.

- *What do you notice about the clouds today?*
- *What shape are they? What color are they? How big are they? What color is the sky?*
- *Does your drawing look like what you saw?*
- *What label could you add to your sketch?*

Share

Following independent writing, gather children in the meeting area to share their sketches.

> Who would like to share your sketch? Tell about what you drew.

> What do you think today's weather will be like?

Writing Minilesson Principle
Write down your observations.

Observing and Writing Like a Scientist

You Will Need

- a book related to the chosen science experiment, such as *Weather Watch: Rita's Journal* by June Schwartz, from *Shared Reading Collection* (optional)
- materials for the chosen science experiment/activity, if needed
- chart paper and markers

Academic Language / Important Vocabulary

- observation
- description
- scientist

Continuum Connection

- Observe carefully to detect and describe change (growth, change over time in plants or animals, chemical change in food), and talk about observations
- Observe in the environment to notice details or changes

GOAL

Observe carefully and record important information about the observations.

RATIONALE

When you help children record their scientific observations, they learn to look closely at a subject and observe its many different aspects. They understand the importance of keeping an ongoing record of scientific observations to capture changes over time.

ASSESS LEARNING

- Notice whether children record their scientific observations in writing.
- Observe for evidence that children can use vocabulary such as *observation*, *description*, and *scientist*.

MINILESSON

To help children think about the minilesson principle, model recording scientific observations. Here is an example.

- Show and read the title of *Weather Watch: Rita's Journal*.

  How does Rita remember what she observes each day?

  She writes down what she sees. What are her descriptions like?

- Read aloud the first sentence on page 4 ("We saw fluffy, puffy clouds that looked like giant pillows") if children need reminding. Point out that Rita chose words carefully to provide an accurate description.

- Take the children outside, or gather them around a large window.

- Model observing the clouds and writing your observations on chart paper. Read aloud your writing as you write it.

  What should you do as a scientist to record your observations?

- Record children's responses on chart paper.

  What did I write at the top of the chart?

  Why is it important to write the date when you write scientific observations?

  Scientists have to be very careful in their work. When they write their observations, they write exactly what they saw and when they saw it.

Have a Try

Invite children to talk to a partner about their observations.

> Did you notice anything else about the sky today? Is there anything else you think I should add to my writing? Turn and talk to your partner about that.

▶ After time for discussion, invite a few children to share their ideas. Add to the chart as appropriate.

Summarize and Apply

Summarize the learning and remind children to write down their scientific observations.

> What do scientists do to remember their observations?

▶ Write the principle at the top of the chart.

> During writing time today, look closely at the sky and write down your observations. You may also add a sketch, if you like. Then write your prediction about today's weather. Bring your writing to share when we come back together.

Confer

▶ During independent writing, move around the room to confer briefly with as many individual children as time allows. Sit side by side with them and invite them to talk about their observations. Use prompts such as the following if needed.

- *What words will help you remember your observations?*
- *What are the clouds shaped like today?*
- *What color is the sky?*
- *Remember to write today's date.*

Share

Following independent writing, gather children in the meeting area to share their observations.

> Who would like to read aloud your observations?

> What do you predict today's weather will be like?

Write down your observations.

Wednesday, October 13

This morning, the clouds are flat and gray. They cover the whole sky like a blanket. They are stratus clouds. The sky looks dark and gloomy.

- Look closely.
- Think about size, color, shape, and texture.
- Write what you notice.
- Include as many details as you can.
- Use describing words.
- Write the date.

Assessment

After you have taught the minilessons in this umbrella, observe children as they write and talk about their writing. Use *The Fountas & Pinnell Literacy Continuum* to notice, teach for, and support children's learning as you observe their attempts at writing.

▶ What evidence do you have of children's new understandings related to observing and writing like a scientist?

- Can children write a prediction for a science experiment?
- Do they sketch and/or record their scientific observations?
- Do children understand and use vocabulary such as *scientist*, *observe*, and *observation*?

▶ In what other ways, beyond the scope of this umbrella, are children ready to write like scientists?

- Are they ready to write different kinds of books about scientific topics (e.g., all-about books, question-and-answer books)?

Use your observations to determine the next umbrella you will teach. You may also consult Suggested Sequence of Lessons (pp. 575–589) for guidance.

EXTENSIONS FOR OBSERVING AND WRITING LIKE A SCIENTIST

▶ Instead of having them sketch their observations, have children take photographs.

▶ Collect children's questions and wonderings that come from their scientific observations. Then help children conduct research or do additional experiments to answer some of the questions and wonderings.

▶ Teach children how to record and present scientific data and observations in tables, charts, and/or graphs.

▶ Help children write conclusions about a science experiment.

▶ Encourage children to write how-to books about how to do a science experiment or all-about books about a science topic.

Minilessons in This Umbrella

WML1   Say your story before you write it.

WML2   Say what you learned in your own words.

WML3   Say the directions before you write them.

Before Teaching Umbrella 7 Minilessons

The purpose of the lessons in this umbrella is to help children rehearse language for stories and topics that they intend to write about. This will help them develop their language and ideas before they put their ideas into writing. It is important to give children the opportunity to rehearse their writing before they start writing as well as throughout the drafting process.

These lessons do not need to be taught consecutively. For example, you may choose to teach WML1 when most of the children are writing narrative texts (e.g., fiction or memory stories) and WML2 when they have chosen a topic and are getting ready to write informational pieces (e.g., all-about books). WML3 should be taught when the children are working on procedural texts (e.g., directions, how-to books, recipes). All the lessons are intended to be generative and may be revisited whenever the children need them.

Before teaching the minilessons in this umbrella, give children plenty of opportunities to listen to stories read aloud and told by you and to share stories of their own. Tell various kinds of stories (e.g., about your own experiences, shared class experiences, retellings of familiar stories) and model effective presentation techniques. It is important for children to have some ideas in mind for what they might write about before these lessons, so you might first want to teach one of the umbrellas on getting ideas for writing in the Writing Process section.

WML1
WPS.U7.WML1

Writing Minilesson Principle
Say your story before you write it.

Rehearsing Your Writing

You Will Need

- an idea for a story based on a personal experience
- chart paper and markers
- To download the following online resource for this lesson, visit **fp.pub/resources**:
  - chart art (optional)

Academic Language / Important Vocabulary

- story

Continuum Connection

- Use talk and storytelling to generate and rehearse language that may be written later
- When rehearsing language for narrative writing, use action and content words appropriate for the story

GOAL

Learn a process for rehearsing language before writing.

RATIONALE

When children rehearse their stories by telling them orally (perhaps across their fingers), they are able to think about what they want to say—even changing how they say it—before writing. This process is particularly supportive for English learners. Children can tell their stories to themselves, to you, or to a partner. Another possibility is to have children record themselves telling the story and then listen to the recording before they write.

ASSESS LEARNING

- ▶ Observe whether children rehearse what they want to say before writing.
- ▶ Notice evidence that children can use vocabulary such as *story*.

MINILESSON

To help children think about the minilesson principle, model telling a story to hear how it sounds before you write it down. Engage children in a discussion about what they notice. Here is an example.

> I want to write a story about what I did last weekend. First, I will tell my story out loud.

▶ Tell a brief story about a personal experience. Think aloud about how you are going to adjust the story when you write it.

> I like how I told all the important things that happened. However, there are a few places where I think I could make my story better. For example, I said that Max knocked over the paint, but I should say that it happened right after I opened the can of paint.

▶ Write the story on chart paper, revising the story as necessary. Read the story aloud when you finish writing.

Have a Try

Invite children to talk to a partner about the process for rehearsing language.

> What did you notice about how I got ready to write my story? What did I do? Turn and talk to your partner about this.

▶ After children turn and talk, invite several children to share their responses. Use their responses to summarize the process on chart paper. Write the principle at the top.

Summarize and Apply

Summarize the learning. Remind children to say their stories before they write them.

> Today during writing time, think of a story you would like to write. First, tell the story to yourself in a whisper voice, to a partner, or to me. After you tell your story, think about whether you would like to change anything. Then write your story. Bring your writing to share when we come back together.

Confer

▶ During independent writing, move around the room to confer briefly with as many individual children as time allows. Sit side by side with them and invite them to tell stories orally. Use prompts such as the following if needed.

- *What do you think about how your story sounded when you said it out loud?*

- *Would you like to record yourself telling a story?*

- *Is there anything you would like to change when you write your story?*

Share

Following independent writing, gather children in the meeting area. Invite a few children to share their writing.

> Who would like to read aloud the story you wrote?

> Was it helpful to say your story before you wrote it? Why or why not?

Painting the Kitchen

Last weekend, I painted my kitchen. I chose a cheery yellow paint. Right after I opened the can of paint, my dog Max ran through the kitchen and knocked over the paint! Quickly, I picked up the can. Luckily, not too much paint spilled. But, Max left a trail of yellow footprints!

Say your story before you write it.

1. Say your story to yourself, a partner, or the teacher.

2. Think about what you said.

3. Think about how you could make your story even better.

4. Write your story.

Writing Minilesson Principle
Say what you learned in your own words.

Rehearsing Your Writing

You Will Need

- an idea for a nonfiction book about a specific topic
- a book or article about the topic
- chart paper and markers
- To download the following online resource for this lesson, visit **fp.pub/resources**:
  - chart art (optional)

Academic Language / Important Vocabulary

- topic
- information
- nonfiction

Continuum Connection

- Use talk and storytelling to generate and rehearse language that may be written later
- When rehearsing language for an informational piece, use vocabulary specific to the topic

GOAL

Learn a process for putting new information in one's own words before writing it down.

RATIONALE

When children say aloud what they have learned in their own words, they are able to communicate their ideas in writing more effectively and naturally. This process helps children synthesize what they learned from research, revise how they want to say something, and use their own words rather than the author's words. Children can tell what they have learned to themselves, a partner, or you. Another possibility is to have children record themselves and then listen to the recording before they write.

ASSESS LEARNING

- Observe whether children can say what they learned about a topic in their own words.
- Notice whether they use their oral rehearsal to help them decide how to write informational texts.
- Notice evidence that children can use vocabulary such as *topic*, *information*, and *nonfiction*.

MINILESSON

To help children think about the minilesson principle, model saying in your own words what you learned about a topic. Engage children in a discussion about what they notice. Here is an example.

> I want to write a nonfiction book about giant pandas. Before I write, I'm going to look in this book for information that I can use in my own book.

- Read aloud a page or two from the book you chose.

> This is very interesting! I'd like to write a page in my book about this. First, I'm going to say what I learned from the book I read.

- Say what you learned in your own words. Think aloud about how you are going to write about the topic.

> I notice that I said that giant pandas tend to stay by themselves. This is exactly the same thing that it says in the book. I need to change that. I don't want to copy what the author wrote because that's not fair to the author. Instead, I will tell the information in my own words. I could write that pandas like to spend a lot of time alone. I also could tell about how pandas communicate with one another by making different kinds of sounds.

- Write the informational piece in your own words on chart paper. Read it aloud.

Have a Try

Invite children to talk to a partner about saying information in their own words before they write.

> What did you notice about how I got ready to write about giant pandas? What did I do? Turn and talk to your partner about this.

▸ After time for discussion, invite several children to share their thinking. Summarize the process on chart paper.

Summarize and Apply

Summarize the learning and remind children to put information in their own words before writing it down.

> What is important to do when you learn information that you want to write in a nonfiction book?

▸ Write the principle at the top of the second chart.

> During writing time today, do some research on the topic for your nonfiction book. Say what you learned about the topic in your own words to yourself in a whisper voice, to a partner, or to me. Then start to write your nonfiction book.

Confer

▸ During independent writing, move around the room to confer briefly with as many individual children as time allows. Sit side by side with them and invite them to talk about their chosen topics. Use prompts such as the following if needed.

- *What topic did you choose?*
- *Say what you learned about the topic in your own words.*
- *Is there anything you would like to change when you write your book?*

Share

Following independent writing, gather children in the meeting area. Invite a few children to share their writing.

> Who would like to read aloud your nonfiction book?

> What did you learn from _____'s book? Say it in your own words.

Giant Pandas

Giant pandas are very shy and like to spend a lot of time alone. When they hear people coming, they usually hide. However, they sometimes talk to other pandas. They can make about eleven different sounds. They can bark, growl, squeal, and make other sounds. Each sound means something different.

Say what you learned in your own words.

1. Read about the topic.
2. Say what you learned in your own words.
3. Think about what you said.
4. Write about the topic.

Section 5: Writing Process

WML3

WPS.U7.WML3

Writing Minilesson Principle
Say the directions before you write them.

Rehearsing Your Writing

You Will Need

- an idea for directions for a simple activity
- a child prepared to act out your directions
- chart paper and markers
- To download the following online resource for this lesson, visit **fp.pub/resources**:
  - chart art (optional)

Academic Language / Important Vocabulary

- how-to book
- directions

Continuum Connection

- Use talk and storytelling to generate and rehearse language that may be written later
- When rehearsing language for an informational piece, use vocabulary specific to the topic

GOAL

Rehearse directions for procedural texts before writing.

RATIONALE

When children rehearse the directions for a procedural text (e.g., a how-to book, a recipe) with a partner, they have the opportunity to get immediate feedback, and they may realize that their directions are unclear or incomplete. This will prepare them to write their directions in a more clear and effective manner later on.

ASSESS LEARNING

- Observe whether children orally rehearse directions for procedural texts before writing.
- Notice whether they use this process and their partner's feedback to revise their directions.
- Notice evidence that children understand and use vocabulary such as *how-to book* and *directions.*

MINILESSON

To help children think about the minilesson principle, model telling directions for a procedural text to a child who is prepared to act out following the directions. Here is an example.

> I want to write directions for how to fold a tortilla into a wrap. Before I write the directions, I'm going to tell them to _____. _____ will pretend to follow my directions. Watch what we do.

- If you use the example in this lesson, you can simulate the directions by using a piece of paper cut into a circle and a few small objects as the filling (e.g., scraps of paper, paper clips).

- Tell the directions to the prepared child. Invite the child to pretend to follow the directions.

> _____, was it easy to follow my directions? Were any of my directions confusing?

> Saying the directions out loud helped me realize that I forgot to say to press down. I will add that when I write the directions.

- Write the directions on chart paper and read them aloud.

Have a Try

Invite children to talk to a partner about the process for rehearsing directions.

> What did you notice about how I got ready to write my directions? What did I do? Turn and talk to your partner about this.

▶ After time for discussion, invite several children to share their thinking. Summarize the process on a second chart.

Summarize and Apply

Summarize the learning. Remind children to rehearse directions for procedural texts before they write them.

> What can you do to help yourself write good directions?

▶ Write the principle at the top of the second chart.

> Today during writing time, think of something that you know how to do and say the directions. Say the steps to me or to a partner, and have your partner act out the directions. Then think about what you might change in your directions to make them better. When you are ready, start to write your how-to book.

Confer

▶ During independent writing, move around the room to confer briefly with as many individual children as time allows. Sit side by side with them and invite them to rehearse directions for procedural texts. Use prompts such as the following if needed.

- *What would you like to teach other people how to do?*
- *Tell me how to do it, and I will pretend to follow your directions.*
- *This part is a little confusing. Should I do _____ before or after _____ ? How do I do _____ ?*
- *Is there anything you would like to change when you write your directions?*

Share

Following independent writing, gather children in the meeting area to share their writing.

> Who would like to read aloud your how-to book?

> Was it helpful to say your directions before you wrote them down? Why or why not?

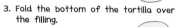

How to Fold a Tortilla

1. Warm the tortilla.

2. Add the filling just below the center. Not too much!

3. Fold the bottom of the tortilla over the filling.

4. Fold in the sides. Press down.

5. Roll up from bottom to top. Press down.

Say the directions before you write them.

1. Say the directions to a partner.

2. Ask your partner to pretend to follow the directions.

3. Think about how you could make the directions better. Ask your partner for help.

4. Write the directions.

Section 5: Writing Process

Assessment

After you have taught the minilessons in this umbrella, observe children as they rehearse language for writing. Use *The Fountas & Pinnell Literacy Continuum* to notice, teach for, and support children's learning as you observe their oral communication and writing.

▶ What evidence do you have of children's new understandings related to rehearsing language for writing?

- Do children rehearse their writing for narrative, informational, and procedural texts?

- Do they evaluate their own oral language and use it to adjust their writing?

- Do they understand and use vocabulary such as *story*, *how-to book*, *information*, and *directions*?

▶ In what other ways, beyond the scope of this umbrella, are children exploring writing?

- Are they ready to think about ways to start or end their books?

- Are they sharing their writing with others?

Use your observations to determine the next umbrella you will teach. You may also consult Suggested Sequence of Lessons (pp. 575–589) for guidance.

EXTENSIONS FOR REHEARSING YOUR WRITING

▶ Oral language can also be useful after children have written their books. Suggest that they read their writing to themselves in a whisper voice so they can hear how it sounds and make changes accordingly.

▶ When children orally tell stories or share ideas, prompt them to give more details with questions such as *What did you do after that? How did you feel when that happened? What did it smell/taste/look/sound like? What did you like about that?*

▶ Encourage children to write and draw about stories or topics that they have shared orally.

Minilessons in This Umbrella

WML1 Use different tools to add to your writing.

WML2 Add details to your drawings.

WML3 Add describing words or phrases to help the reader picture the idea.

WML4 Use connecting words to add more information to your writing.

WML5 Add details to slow down an exciting or important part of the story.

WML6 Add information to help the reader understand your topic.

Before Teaching Umbrella 8 Minilessons

These minilessons help children expand their thinking about ways to revise their writing. It is not necessary to teach the lessons consecutively. Instead, teach them throughout the year whenever children work on revising their writing. Revision is a high-level concept and children will need multiple exposures to these lessons. Continue to have children tell stories orally because they often include details that they may first omit from their writing. These details can be added during the revision process.

These lessons suggest using mentor texts, previously written class writing (i.e., shared writing), and samples of your own writing to model how to look back at writing to find areas for improvement. Use the following texts from *Fountas & Pinnell Classroom™ Interactive Read-Aloud Collection*, or choose books from the classroom library that the children will enjoy.

Interactive Read-Aloud Collection

Caring for Each Other: Family

Two Mrs. Gibsons by Toyomi Igus

Tomie dePaola: Writing from Life

The Art Lesson

Bill and Pete

Exploring Narrative Nonfiction Texts

Salmon Stream by Carol Reed-Jones

Cactus Hotel by Brenda Z. Guiberson

As you read and enjoy these texts together, help children

- think about the author's process to write and revise the book,

- notice interesting details and word choices, and

- discuss what makes the book interesting or exciting.

Interactive Read-Aloud
Family

Tomie dePaola

Narrative Nonfiction

Section 5: Writing Process

WML1

WPS.U8.WML1

Writing Minilesson Principle
Use different tools to add to your writing.

Adding Information to Your Writing

You Will Need

- a book you have prepared that demonstrates a variety of tools for adding to writing (e.g., caret marks, sticky notes, strips of paper, numbered items or asterisks on separate pages)
- chart paper and markers
- strips of paper
- sticky notes

Academic Language / Important Vocabulary

- revise
- add
- tool
- caret
- sticky note
- asterisk

Continuum Connection

- Add words, letters, phrases, or sentences using a variety of techniques: e.g., caret, sticky notes, spider's legs, numbered items on a separate page

GOAL

Learn a variety of tools, including caret marks, sticky notes, spider legs, numbered items, and asterisks, for revising writing by adding information.

RATIONALE

By teaching children a variety of ways to make adding to their writing easier, you make the idea of revision more accessible. When children are armed with the knowledge they need to revise their writing, they will be able to communicate their ideas more effectively.

ASSESS LEARNING

- Observe whether children show a willingness to add to their writing.
- Notice whether they effectively use a variety of tools to add to their writing.
- Look for evidence that children can use vocabulary such as *revise*, *add*, *tool*, *caret*, *sticky note*, and *asterisk*.

MINILESSON

To help children think about the minilesson principle, use a book that you have prepared before class or a piece of shared writing to engage children in an inquiry-based lesson around tools for adding to writing. Here is an example.

- Show the cover of the sample book you prepared (or the class wrote).

  I wrote this book. After I wrote it, I reread my writing and thought about how I could make it even better. When you reread your writing and make changes to it, you are revising it. I'm going to show you how I revised my writing.

- Show a page from your book that shows one tool for adding to writing (e.g., a caret).

  On this page, I added a descriptive word to make my writing more interesting. What do you notice about how I added it?

  I used a caret. A caret looks like an upside-down *V*. You place it right where you want a word to go. Then you write the word right above the caret.

- Record a description and example of the tool on chart paper.
- Show a page that demonstrates another tool (e.g., a strip of paper, or "spider leg").

  What do you notice about how I added to my writing on this page?

  I added a sentence on a strip of paper. This is also called a spider leg! Why do you think I used a spider leg instead of a caret to add to my writing?

- Add the spider leg. Continue in a similar manner to teach other ways to make revising easier (e.g., sticky notes, numbered items or asterisks, added pages).

Have a Try

Invite children to talk to a partner about how to add information to a page.

▶ Tell children about a place in your book where you would like to add more information.

> I would like to add a few more sentences on this page about _____. What tool do you think I should use to add to my writing? Turn and talk to your partner about this.

▶ After time for discussion, invite several pairs to share their thinking. Discuss which tool is most appropriate in this case and why. Demonstrate adding to your writing using the chosen tool.

Summarize and Apply

Write the principle at the top of the chart. Read it to children. Summarize the learning and remind children to use different tools to add to their writing.

> What are some ways you can add to your writing?

> Today during writing time, reread your writing in the book you're working on or the last book you wrote. Think about whether there's anything you'd like to add to your writing to make it even better. If so, decide the best way to add that information. Bring your writing to share when we come back together.

Use different tools to add to your writing.

Tool	What You Can Add	What It Looks Like
Caret	A word	We ate a ^delicious chocolate cake.
Spider leg	A sentence	My dog's name is Rover.
Sticky note	A few sentences	
Numbers or asterisks	More information when there's not much space on the page	My family is from Uganda.[1] [1] Uganda is a country in Africa.
New page	A lot more information	

Confer

▶ During independent writing, move around the room to confer briefly with as many individual children as time allows. Sit side by side with them and invite them to talk about adding to their writing. Use prompts such as the following as needed.

- *Would you like to write more about _____? How could you add that to your writing?*
- *You could add a new page to write more about _____.*
- *I noticed that you used a caret on this page. Why did you choose that tool?*

Share

Following independent writing, gather children in the meeting area to share their writing.

> Raise your hand if you added to your writing today.

> What did you add? How did you add it?

Adding Information to Your Writing

You Will Need

- a familiar book with detailed illustrations, such as *The Art Lesson* from Text Set: Tomie dePaola: Writing from Life
- chart paper and markers
- a sample book you have made
- books the children have made

Academic Language / Important Vocabulary

- detail
- add
- illustration
- reread

Continuum Connection

- Add details to drawings to add information or increase interest
- Create drawings that employ careful attention to detail or color

GOAL

Learn to revise drawings by adding details.

RATIONALE

By observing and discussing details in illustrations, children learn that the details make a difference in what the reader understands about a story or topic. Children learn that the details in their own drawings matter and that it is a good idea to look closely at them to decide if more details are needed.

ASSESS LEARNING

- ▶ Notice whether children are willing and able to add details to their drawings.
- ▶ Look for evidence that children can use vocabulary such as *detail*, *add*, *illustration*, and *reread*.

MINILESSON

To help children think about the minilesson principle, use a familiar book to engage them in a discussion about details in illustrations. Here is an example.

- ▶ Show the cover of *The Art Lesson* and read the title. Show the illustration on page 15.

  Let's look carefully at this illustration. Where is Tommy?

  What time of year is it?

  What is the weather like?

  How do you know about the time of year and the weather?

  Tomie dePaola showed Tommy on a sidewalk, so we know he is outside. The leaves are orange and yellow and are falling, and Tommy is wearing warm clothes, so we know it is fall. We know it is windy because we can see the leaves, Tommy's hair, and the paint being blown around! Tomie dePaola included details about who is in the story, where this part of the story takes place, the time of year, and the weather.

- ▶ Record these types of details on chart paper.
- ▶ Demonstrate thinking aloud about how to add details to a book you wrote.

  I am going to look carefully at each illustration to make sure it has all the details the reader needs to understand that part of the story.

- ▶ Model quickly adding a detail to an illustration.

Have a Try

Invite children to talk to a partner about adding details to illustrations.

▸ Ask children to look at a piece of shared writing or books that they have already written or are currently working on.

> Look carefully at the illustrations. What details could you add to help people understand more about the story or topic? Turn and talk to your partner about your ideas.

Summarize and Apply

Summarize the learning and remind children to add details to their drawings.

> Readers get a lot of information from the illustrations. Check your illustrations to decide whether more details are needed.

▸ Write the principle at the top of the chart.

> Today during writing time, spend some time rereading your writing. Think about if there are any more details you could add to your illustrations to help readers understand your story or topic. Add the details. Bring your writing to share when we come back together.

Add details to your drawings.

- Characters — clothing, hair, face
- Setting — sidewalk, colored leaves, grass
- Weather — cool—jacket, warm clothes
- Season — leaves blowing

Confer

▸ During independent writing, move around the room to confer briefly with as many individual children as time allows. Sit side by side with them and invite them to talk about adding details to their drawings. Use prompts such as the following as needed.

- *What is this page about? What details could you add to your illustration to help the reader understand more about that?*

- *What is the main character of your story like? What details could you add to your drawing to show that?*

- *Where does this part of your story take place? What does that place look like? What is the weather like? Can you add details showing that?*

Share

Following independent writing, gather children in the meeting area to share their writing.

> Share your illustration with a partner. Point out details you added.

Writing Minilesson Principle
Add describing words or phrases to help the reader picture the idea.

Adding Information to Your Writing

You Will Need

- two familiar fiction or nonfiction books with examples of descriptive language, such as the following:
  - *Two Mrs. Gibsons* by Toyomi Igus, from Text Set: Caring for Each Other: Family
  - *Salmon Stream* by Carol Reed-Jones, from Text Set: Exploring Narrative Nonfiction Texts

- markers
- an object or photo and chart paper prepared with a sentence inspired by it (with no descriptive language)
- To download the following online resource for this lesson, visit **fp.pub/resources**:
  - chart art (optional)

Academic Language / Important Vocabulary

- describing
- word
- phrase
- picture

Continuum Connection

- Add descriptive words (adjectives, adverbs) and phrases to help readers visualize and understand events, actions, processes, or topics
- Add words, phrases, or sentences to provide more information to readers

GOAL

Learn to revise writing by adding adjectives and adverbs or descriptive phrases.

RATIONALE

When children notice the information they gain from the descriptive language that authors use in their writing, they begin to understand the importance of it in their own writing. By teaching children about adding adjectives, adverbs, and descriptive phrases, you give them a specific way to think about revising their writing.

ASSESS LEARNING

- Observe whether children can identify descriptive language in other authors' writing.
- Notice whether they add descriptive language to their own writing.
- Look for evidence that children can use vocabulary such as *describing*, *word*, *phrase*, and *picture*.

MINILESSON

To help children think about the minilesson principle, use familiar books to engage them in an inquiry-based lesson around descriptive language. Here is an example.

- Show the cover of *Two Mrs. Gibsons* and read the title. Read pages 5–6.

  What words did the author use to describe the first Mrs. Gibson's hugs?

  What words did she use to describe the second Mrs. Gibson's hugs?

  How do phrases like "great big fat bearskin rug" and "light, down-filled comforter" help you understand what their hugs are like?

  The author used describing words to help you make a picture in your mind of what it is like to be hugged by each Mrs. Gibson.

- Show the cover of *Salmon Stream* and read the title. Read pages 11–12.

  What interesting words and phrases did the author use to help you make a picture in your mind of the salmon stream?

  "Rocky gravel" and "shady pool" are some of the words that help you picture what the salmon stream is like.

- Show a photo or object and the sentence you prepared before class. Read the sentence aloud.

  I wrote this sentence about this picture. What words or phrases could I add to my sentence to help readers make a picture in their minds of this scene? Turn and talk to your partner about your ideas.

- After children turn and talk, invite several children to share their ideas. Add their suggestions about descriptive language to the sentence.

Have a Try

Invite children to talk to a partner about adding descriptive language.

▸ Add several basic sentences to the chart.

   Think about words you could add to these sentences to make them more descriptive. Use your imagination! Turn and talk to your partner about your ideas.

▸ After children turn and talk, invite several children to share their ideas. Add descriptive language to the sentences.

Summarize and Apply

Summarize the learning and remind children to add descriptive language to their writing.

   How do describing words and phrases help readers?

▸ Write the principle at the top of the chart.

   Today during writing time, reread your writing in the book you're working on or the last book you wrote. Try adding some describing words or phrases to help readers make pictures in their minds. Bring your writing to share when we meet later.

Confer

▸ During independent writing, move around the room to confer briefly with as many individual children as time allows. Sit side by side with them and invite them to talk about adding information to their writing. Use prompts such as the following as needed.

   • *What was _____ like?*

   • *What words or phrases could you add to your writing to help readers picture it?*

   • *What tools could you use to add those words to your writing? Would a spider leg work?*

   • *The way you described the _____ as _____ really helps me picture it in my mind.*

Share

Following independent writing, gather children in the meeting area to share their writing.

   Raise your hand if you added describing words or phrases to your writing today.

   Would you like to read aloud your writing, _____?

Writing Minilesson Principle

Use connecting words to add more information to your writing.

Adding Information to Your Writing

You Will Need

- a familiar book with numerous examples of connecting words, such as *Cactus Hotel* by Brenda Z. Guiberson from Text Set: Exploring Narrative Nonfiction Texts
- document camera (optional)
- chart paper and markers
- highlighter
- a brief sample piece of writing that contains examples of connecting words
- To download the following online resource for this lesson, visit **fp.pub/resources**:
  - chart art (optional)

Academic Language / Important Vocabulary

- connecting words
- revise

Continuum Connection

- Use common (simple) connectives (transitional words) for relating ideas and showing meaning through nonfiction texts (*and, but, so, because, before, after*)

GOAL

Understand that writers use connecting words (e.g., *and, but, so, because, before, after*) to add information to improve their writing.

RATIONALE

When you help children notice how authors use connecting words to connect ideas, they learn to use connecting words in their own writing. Connecting words make writing clearer by linking ideas, and they add variety in sentence structures.

ASSESS LEARNING

- Notice whether children can identify connecting words in mentor texts.
- Examine children's writing to see whether they use a variety of connecting words and use them correctly.
- Look for evidence that children can use vocabulary such as *connecting words* and *revise*.

MINILESSON

To help children think about the minilesson principle, use mentor texts to engage them in an inquiry-based lesson around connecting words. Project the text if possible. Here is an example.

- Show the cover of *Cactus Hotel* and read the title. Display page 13 and read the third sentence aloud. Point to the word *and*.

  Why do you think the author used the word *and* here?

  The word *and* is a connecting word. It connects two things that are happening. The woodpecker looks around, *and* he decides to stay.

- Display page 9 and read sentences 2 and 3 aloud.

  The word *but* is also a connecting word. Why do you think the author used the word *but* here?

  The word *but* is used to connect two ideas when there is something surprising, unexpected, or different about the second idea. Can you find the word *but* anywhere else on this page?

  Why do you think the author used the word *but* in this sentence?

- Continue in a similar manner with a couple of other examples of connecting words in the book (e.g., *after, when*). Record each connecting word on chart paper. Discuss its function in the sentence (e.g., *because* signals a reason, *after* and *when* show how two things are related in time).

Have a Try

Ask children to help you add information to a piece of writing using a connecting word. Here is an example.

> Look at this writing I did about our science experiment. Work with your partner to find some connecting words.

▸ After time for discussion, invite several children to highlight the connecting words. Talk about how they work in the sentences.

Summarize and Apply

Summarize the learning and remind children to use connecting words when they add information to their writing.

> What did you learn today about how you can add information to your writing?

▸ Write the principle at the top of the chart and read it aloud.

> During writing time today, reread your writing and think about any information you would like to add. If you add any information to your writing, remember to use connecting words like *and*, *but*, *after*, and *because*. Bring your writing to share when we come back together.

Use connecting words to add more information to your writing.

- and
- but
- after
- when
- then
- because

Water Cycle in a Bag

We wanted to see what the water cycle looks like, so we filled a bag with water and sealed it.

The water evaporated because the sun heated it.

After the water evaporated, it "rained" down in the bag.

Confer

▸ During independent writing, move around the room to confer briefly with as many individual children as time allows. Sit side by side with them and invite them to talk about adding connecting words to their writing. Use prompts such as the following as needed.

- *What word could you use to connect those two ideas?*
- *What did you do after that? What connecting word could you use to show that you did _____ after _____?*
- *Why did _____ happen? What connecting word could you use to connect what happened with the reason it happened?*
- *Do you think you might use a caret or a spider leg to add information?*

Share

Following independent writing, gather children in the meeting area to share their writing.

> Who used a connecting word to add information? Tell about the word you used.

WML5
WPS.U8.WML5

Writing Minilesson Principle
Add details to slow down an exciting or important part of the story.

Adding Information to Your Writing

You Will Need

- two familiar fiction books, such as the following from Text Set: Tomie dePaola: Writing from Life:
  - *Bill and Pete*
  - *The Art Lesson*
- chart paper and markers
- children's own writing
- To download the following online resource for this lesson, visit **fp.pub/resources**:
  - chart art (optional)

Academic Language / Important Vocabulary

- detail
- exciting
- important
- story
- character
- setting

Continuum Connection

- Tell details about the most important moments in a story or experience while eliminating unimportant details
- Identify the most exciting part of a story
- Add words, phrases, or sentences to make the writing more interesting or exciting for readers

GOAL

Understand that authors slow down the action in their stories by adding details.

RATIONALE

When you help children notice how authors slow down the most exciting or important part of a story, they understand that they too can add extra details to their own stories to slow down and emphasize an important part of the story. Slowing down the most exciting part of the story engages the reader by creating interest and suspense.

ASSESS LEARNING

- Observe whether children add details to slow down the most exciting or important part of a story.
- Look for evidence that children can use vocabulary such as *detail*, *exciting*, *important*, *story*, *character*, and *setting*.

MINILESSON

To help children think about the minilesson principle, use mentor texts to engage them in an inquiry-based lesson around how authors slow down the most exciting or important part of a story. Here is an example.

- Show the cover of *Bill and Pete* and read the title.

    What do you think is the most exciting or important part of this story?

    Listen as I read the part of this story when Bill is captured by the Bad Guy.

- Read pages 17–19.

    After Bill is captured by the Bad Guy, do you find out right away what happens to him?

    The author made you wait to find out. Why would an author make you wait to find out what happens in a story?

    How did he make you wait?

- Help children understand that the conversation between the Bad Guy and the butler slows down and stretches out the most exciting part, making the reader eager to continue reading to find out what happens to Bill and Pete.

- Show the cover of *The Art Lesson* and read the title. Read pages 22–27.

    What kinds of details did the author use to slow down the art lesson?

- Help children notice that the author slowed down the action by including dialogue and details about how the characters are thinking and feeling.

- With children's input, make a list on chart paper of the types of details authors might include to slow down an exciting or important part of a story.

Have a Try

Have children talk to a partner about how to slow down the most exciting or important part of their own story.

▶ Make sure each child or pair of children has a story to look at.

> Think about details you could add to slow down an exciting or important part of your story so that your readers want to keep reading to find out what happens. What details might you add? Turn and talk to your partner about your ideas.

▶ After children turn and talk, invite several children to share their ideas. Add any new ideas to the chart.

Summarize and Apply

Summarize the learning and invite children to add more details to slow down the most exciting or important part of their story.

> How can you make your readers want to keep reading your story?

▶ Write the principle at the top of the chart and read it aloud.

> Today during writing time, try adding some details to slow down the most exciting or important part of your story. Bring your writing to share when we come back together.

Add details to slow down an exciting or important part of the story.

Add details about . . .

- What the characters are thinking or feeling
- What the characters are doing
- What the characters are saying
- What the setting is like
- What is going on around the main action

Confer

▶ During independent writing, move around the room to confer briefly with as many individual children as time allows. Sit side by side with them and invite them to talk about adding information. Use prompts such as the following as needed.

- *What is the most exciting or important part of your story?*
- *What details could you add about _____ (e.g., the setting, character's thoughts or feelings)?*
- *What might the characters say to each other during this part of the story? How could you add that to your story?*

Share

Following independent writing, gather children in the meeting area to share their writing.

> Who would like to share how you slowed down the most exciting or important part of your story?

WML 6

WPS.U8.WML6

Writing Minilesson Principle
Add information to help the reader understand your topic.

Adding Information to Your Writing

You Will Need

- a short, simple piece of informational writing that is intentionally vague
- chart paper and markers

Academic Language / Important Vocabulary

- information
- reread
- topic

Continuum Connection

- Reread and revise the draft or rewrite a section to clarify meaning
- Add words, phrases, or sentences to provide more information to readers
- Add words, phrases, or sentences to clarify meaning for readers

GOAL

Add words, phrases, or sentences to help the reader understand the topic.

RATIONALE

When you model how to reread informational writing and add details to make it more clear or informative, children learn how to revise their own informational writing and communicate their ideas more effectively.

ASSESS LEARNING

- Observe whether children reread their informational writing to identify parts that are unclear or missing information.
- Notice whether children show a willingness to add information to their writing.
- Look for evidence that children can use vocabulary such as *information*, *reread*, and *topic*.

MINILESSON

To think about the minilesson principle, use a short, simple, prepared informational text to model adding information to help the reader understand the topic. Here is an example.

- Display the prepared text.

  I am working on a nonfiction book about a topic that I know a lot about: me! I am going to reread what I've written so far and think about what information I could add. Watch what I do.

- Read the text aloud and think aloud about information you could add to help the reader understand the topic.

  I wrote "I am a teacher." This is true, but it doesn't give a lot of information. Is there some information I could add to help my readers know more about my teaching?

  I could add information about what grade I teach and where I teach.

  I wrote "I live in a house." I wonder what else I could say. As a reader, is there anything else you would like to know about this?

  I could add something about the people I live with. I'll add that I live with my husband and our two daughters. I think readers would want to know that.

- Demonstrate adding information to the text.

Have a Try

Invite children to talk to a partner about adding information.

> Is there anything else you think I should add to my writing to help readers understand my topic? Is anything unclear, or is there anything you would like to know more about? Turn and talk to your partner about this.

▶ After time for discussion, invite several pairs to share their thinking. Using their feedback, demonstrate adding additional information.

Summarize and Apply

Help children summarize the learning and remind them to think about what information they could add to their own writing to help readers understand the topic.

> What did you learn today about how you can help readers understand your topic?

▶ Write the principle at the top of the chart.

> Today during writing time, reread a nonfiction book that you are working on or that you've already written. Look to see if you should add some information to help the reader understand your topic. You can ask me or a partner for help. Bring your writing to share when we come back together.

> Add information to help the reader understand your topic.

> My name is Ms. Wallace.

> 2nd grade   at Southwood
> Elementary
> I am a teacher.

> with my husband and
> our two daughters
> I live in a house.

> named Fluff   named Spot
> I have a cat and a dog.

Confer

▶ During independent writing, move around the room to confer briefly with as many individual children as time allows. Sit side by side with them and invite them to talk about adding information. Use prompts such as the following as needed.

- *I am curious about _____. Would you like to add something about that?*
- *Why is _____? How could you add something about that to your book?*
- *This part is a little unclear to me. Let's think about how you could make it more clear to readers.*

Share

Following independent writing, gather children in the meeting area to share their writing.

> Raise your hand if you added information to your book to help the reader understand your topic. What did you add?

Assessment

After you have taught the minilessons in this umbrella, observe children as they draw, write, and talk about their writing. Use *The Fountas & Pinnell Literacy Continuum* to notice, teach for, and support children's learning as you observe their writing skills.

▶ What evidence do you have of new understandings children have developed related to adding to writing?

- Do children understand that they can (and show a willingness to) revise their books to make them better?
- What kinds of details do they add to their drawings to give more information?
- Are they using tools (e.g., caret, strip of paper, number or asterisk on a separate page) to add to their writing?
- Do they use describing and connecting words to add more detail or information to their writing?
- Do they understand what it means to slow down the most exciting or important part of a story?
- Are they using vocabulary such as *detail*, *page*, *book*, *connecting*, and *information*?

▶ In what other ways, beyond the scope of this umbrella, are children exploring the writing process?

- Are they ready to revise their writing in other ways?
- Is there interest in informational writing?

Use your observations to determine the next umbrella you will teach. You may also consult Suggested Sequence of Lessons (pp. 575–589) for guidance.

EXTENSIONS FOR ADDING INFORMATION TO YOUR WRITING

▶ Revise a piece of shared writing that you and the children have written by adding information.

▶ Pull together a small group of children who would benefit from guided instruction on adding to their writing.

▶ Revisit WML4 to teach additional connecting words (e.g., *although, unless, as soon as*). The online resource Planning a Writing Minilesson provides a structure for planning a new lesson.

▶ Teach children how to add to their writing when typing it on a computer.

Minilessons in This Umbrella

WML1   Take out information that does not tell about the important ideas.

WML2   Change or add words to give more information or to make your writing more interesting.

WML3   Skip time to tell only the important things that happened.

WML4   Organize your writing to make sure the order makes sense.

WML5   Group similar ideas together.

Before Teaching Umbrella 9 Minilessons

Help children build the habit of rereading their writing aloud (in a whisper voice) each day before they begin writing more. This will help them hear how their writing sounds and consider what to revise. It is not necessary to teach these minilessons consecutively. Instead, you might choose to teach them throughout the year to support children when they revise their writing. Revision is a high-level concept, and children will need multiple exposures to these lessons.

Children should know how to use headings and write more complex nonfiction texts before you teach WML5. Also give them plenty of opportunities to read texts that are organized with similar ideas grouped together and that may also use headings. To model the principles taught in these minilessons, read aloud the following texts from *Fountas & Pinnell Classroom™ Interactive Read-Aloud Collection*, or choose suitable books from your classroom library.

Interactive Read-Aloud Collection

Seymour Simon: A Scientific Eye

  Cats

  Dogs

The Pleasure of Giving

  Sam and the Lucky Money by Karen Chinn

  The Birthday Swap by Loretta Lopez

Exploring the Natural World: Birds

  Feathers: Not Just for Flying by Melissa Stewart

As you read and enjoy these and other texts together, help children notice that

- all the words and sentences on a page are relevant and connected to the same idea,

- authors often use specific and interesting word choices, and

- the writing is organized in an order that makes sense.

Interactive Read-Aloud
Seymour Simon

Pleasure of Giving

Birds

Section 5: Writing Process

Writing Minilesson Principle
Take out information that does not tell about the important ideas.

You Will Need

▸ a familiar book, such as *Cats* by Seymour Simon, from Text Set: Seymour Simon: A Scientific Eye

▸ chart paper prepared with a sample piece of nonfiction writing that contains a few irrelevant and/or repetitive sentences

▸ markers

▸ To download the following online resource for this lesson, visit **fp.pub/resources**:

  ▪ chart art (optional)

Academic Language / Important Vocabulary

▸ information

▸ idea

Continuum Connection

▸ Change words to make the writing more interesting

▸ Identify vague parts or confusing ideas and provide specificity

---

GOAL

Identify the important ideas and take out information that does not tell about them.

RATIONALE

Some children think that the more they write the better their writing will be. However, including information that is not relevant weakens the writing. When you help children notice that all the information in a nonfiction book is relevant and relates to the main idea of the page or paragraph, they will begin to reread their own writing and remove extraneous information and details.

ASSESS LEARNING

▸ Observe for evidence that children can reread their own writing, identify the most important ideas, and take out information that does not tell about the important ideas.

▸ Look for evidence that children can use vocabulary such as *information* and *idea*.

MINILESSON

To help children think about the minilesson principle, use a familiar nonfiction book to help them notice that all the information on a page tells about the important ideas. Then model revising a brief nonfiction text to take out unimportant information. Here is an example.

▸ Show the cover of *Cats* and read the title. Read aloud page 16.

  What information is on this page?

  This page is about the sounds that cats make. Does the author write about anything else on this page, such as the food that cats eat? Why not?

  All the information on this page tells about the idea that "cats make sounds that tell you or other cats how they're feeling or what they want." This is the most important idea on the page. All the information on the page tells about this idea.

▸ Show the sample nonfiction text that you prepared.

  I am going to reread my writing to see how I can make it better. Let's read the first part together.

  What is the most important idea?

▸ Using children's input, circle the main idea of the paragraph.

  The most important idea in this paragraph is "Cats make wonderful pets." All the other information in this paragraph should tell more about this idea. Does the sentence "My cat is named Fluffy" tell about why cats make wonderful pets?

  The sentence does not tell about the important idea, so I will cross it out.

Have a Try

Invite children to talk to a partner about taking out information.

> Turn and talk to your partner about anything I should take out of the second part.

▶ After children turn and talk, invite several pairs to share their thinking. Discuss whether each piece of information tells about the important ideas. Cross it out if it doesn't.

Summarize and Apply

Summarize the learning. Remind children to reread their writing and take out information that does not tell about the important ideas.

> What should you do when you find information in your writing that does not tell about the important ideas?

▶ Write the principle at the top of the chart.

> During writing time today, work on a book that you already started or a book that you recently finished. Reread your writing, and take out any information that does not tell about the important ideas. Bring your writing when we meet later.

Confer

▶ During independent writing, move around the room to confer briefly with as many individual children as time allows. Sit side by side with them and invite them to talk about revising their writing. Use the following prompts as needed.

* *What is this page of your book about? What are the most important ideas on this page?*
* *Does _____ tell about the important ideas? How?*
* *Remember that all the information on the page should tell about the important ideas.*
* *How can you take out information that doesn't tell about the important ideas?*

Share

Following independent writing, gather children in the meeting area to share their writing.

> Did anyone take out information from your book?

> How did you decide what to take out?

> Take out information that does not tell about the important ideas.

Having a Pet Cat

(Cats make wonderful pets.) It is always fun to watch them play and explore. Many cats are friendly and like to be petted. ~~My cat is named Fluffy.~~

(Having a pet cat is also a big responsibility.) If you get a pet cat, you will have to give it food and water every day. ~~Cats started to be used as pets thousands of years ago.~~ You will also need to clean the litter box every day. ~~Cats purr when they are relaxed.~~

Writing Minilesson Principle

Change or add words to give more information or to make your writing more interesting.

Revising to Focus and Organize Writing

You Will Need

- a familiar book with interesting and specific word choices, such as *Sam and the Lucky Money* by Karen Chinn, from Text Set: The Pleasure of Giving
- chart paper prepared with a shared writing piece written by your class that contains examples of generic language
- markers

Academic Language / Important Vocabulary

- information
- clear
- interesting

Continuum Connection

- Change words to make the writing more interesting
- Identify vague parts or confusing ideas and provide specificity

GOAL

Replace vague words to make writing clear and interesting.

RATIONALE

When you help children notice the interesting and specific words chosen by published authors, they will be more likely to think carefully about the words they choose for their own writing. They will begin to reread their writing and identify and replace generic language.

ASSESS LEARNING

- ▶ Look for evidence that children reread their writing, evaluate their word choices, and change words to make their writing more specific and interesting.
- ▶ Observe for evidence that children can use vocabulary such as *information*, *clear*, and *interesting*.

MINILESSON

To help children think about the minilesson principle, use a familiar book to engage children in an inquiry-based lesson around purposeful and thoughtful word choice. Then revise a piece of shared writing together. Here is an example.

▶ Read the first three paragraphs of *Sam and the Lucky Money*.

How does the author help you make a picture in your mind of the small red envelopes called *leisees*? What do you notice about the words she uses?

She uses interesting words such as "crisp dollar bills," "two golden mandarins," "a slithering dragon," "a giant peach," and "embossed in gold." If the author had just written about envelopes filled with money, you probably wouldn't have as clear a picture in your mind.

▶ Read the piece of shared writing that you selected aloud.

You can reread your own writing and change some of the words. You can use interesting words to give more information. For example, instead of saying "I like fruit," you can give more information about fruits that you like: "I like apples, blueberries, and mangoes." What words could you change to make your writing more interesting and give more information?

▶ Guide children's thinking, as needed, with questions such as the following:

- *What is the name of the park we went to?*
- *What is a more interesting word that means "very big"?*
- *What kinds of birds did we see?*

▶ Using children's responses, demonstrate changing some words.

Have a Try

Invite children to talk to a partner about how to further revise the shared writing piece.

> Is there anything else that you think we should change to give more information or to make our writing more interesting? Turn and talk to your partner about this.

▶ After children turn and talk, invite several pairs to share their ideas. Discuss the suggestions and make the changes if appropriate.

Summarize and Apply

Summarize the learning. Remind children to reread their writing and think about their word choices.

> When you reread your writing and think about how to make it better, you are revising it. What did you learn today about revising your writing?

▶ Write the principle at the top of the chart. Read it to children.

> During writing time, work on a book that you already started or a book that you recently finished. Reread your writing, and think about if there are any words you could change to give more information or to make your writing more interesting.

Change or add words to give more information or to make your writing more interesting.

A Day at the Park

Fairmount Park
Our class went to ~~the park~~ today.

enormous
The park was ~~very big~~.

blue jays and sparrows   caterpillars
We saw lots of ~~birds~~. We also saw ~~bugs~~.

an exciting
It was ~~a good~~ day.

Confer

▶ During independent writing, move around the room to confer briefly with as many individual children as time allows. Sit side by side with them and invite them to talk about revising their writing. Use prompts such as the following as needed.

- *Can you think of a word that is more interesting than* nice? *What else could you say about _____ ?*

- *What is another way to say _____ ?*

- *What word could you use to better describe _____ ?*

Share

Following independent writing, gather children in the meeting area to share their writing.

> Turn to your partner and share how you made. your writing more interesting.

Writing Minilesson Principle
Skip time to tell only the important things that happened.

Revising to Focus and Organize Writing

You Will Need

- a familiar narrative book with clear examples of skipping time, such as *The Birthday Swap* by Loretta Lopez, from Text Set: The Pleasure of Giving
- chart paper prepared with a piece of narrative writing that contains extraneous detail and does not skip time
- markers

Academic Language / Important Vocabulary

- story
- skip

Continuum Connection

- Use time appropriately as an organizing tool
- Take out unnecessary words, phrases, or sentences that are repetitive or do not add to the meaning

---

GOAL

Focus writing by using transitional words to skip time and remove unimportant details.

RATIONALE

When they first try narrative writing, children may write about everything that happens, including many unimportant details. Help them notice that authors often "skip time" and include only important details to keep their readers interested in reading their stories.

ASSESS LEARNING

- Observe whether children focus their stories by using transitional words to skip time and removing unimportant details.
- Look for evidence that children can use vocabulary such as *story* and *skip*.

MINILESSON

To help children think about the minilesson principle, use a familiar narrative book to discuss how the author skips time to focus the story. Then revise a teacher-written piece of writing together. Here is an example.

▷ Read page 13 and the first paragraph of page 14 of *The Birthday Swap*.

> Does the party happen on the same day that Lori sees the piñatas at the market?
>
> How do you know that it happens on a different day?
>
> One page ends with Lori and her mom walking back to the car, and the next page begins with "The next morning."
>
> Why do you think the author didn't tell everything that happened from one day to the next?
>
> The author skipped several hours and gave only details that are important for you to know. When you write your own stories, you don't have to tell everything that happens in a day. You can skip hours, days, weeks, months, or even years so you can tell just the important things that happened.

▷ Show the piece of writing that you prepared. Read it aloud.

> I wrote this piece of writing about a trip to Chicago. I want to make sure that I only tell about the important things that happened. What could I take out to tell just the important things that happened?

▷ Cross out the extraneous details. If needed, ask questions such as the following:

- *Is it important to say that we walked back to our hotel?*
- *Will readers be interested in knowing that we woke up at 9:30?*
- *Is it interesting to include that we got dressed and had breakfast?*

The Writing Minilessons Book, Grade 2

Have a Try

Invite children to talk to a partner about how to add transitional words.

> We took out a lot of unimportant details, but now it's not clear when we went to the museum. What words could I add to make it clear when we went to the museum? Turn and talk to your partner about this.

▶ After time for discussion, invite a few children to share their suggestions. Demonstrate adding a transitional word or phrase.

> You can show that you are skipping time by using words like "The next day," "later that day," or "one week later."

Summarize and Apply

Summarize the learning and remind children that they can skip time to focus their stories.

> Why do authors sometimes skip time in their stories?

▶ Write the principle at the top of the chart. Read it to children.

> Today during writing time, reread a story that you've already written. Look for places to skip time so you can tell only the most important things that happened.

Confer

▶ During independent writing, move around the room to confer briefly with as many individual children as time allows. Sit side by side with them and invite them to talk about how to revise their stories. Use prompts such as the following as needed.

- *Let's reread your story to see if there are any places where you could skip time.*
- *Does the reader need to know about this?*
- *What words could you add to show how much time you are skipping?*

Share

Following independent writing, gather children in the meeting area to share their writing.

> Would anyone like to read aloud a place in your story where you skip time?

> Why did you decide to skip time there?

Skip time to tell only the important things that happened.

My Trip to Chicago

Last summer, I went to Chicago with my family. We spent the whole first day walking around. We saw tall buildings and Lake Michigan. Then we had dinner at an Italian restaurant. ~~After that, we walked back to our hotel. Then we took showers and went to bed.~~

The next day, we
∧~~We woke up at 9:30 the next morning. We got dressed and had breakfast. Then we walked some more. We~~ went to a natural history museum! Then we went to the aquarium. It was an amazing day!

Writing Minilesson Principle
Organize your writing to make sure the order makes sense.

You Will Need

▶ a familiar narrative book with a clear chronological sequence, such as *The Birthday Swap* by Loretta Lopez, from Text Set: The Pleasure of Giving

▶ chart paper prepared with a simple text you wrote that is out of order

▶ markers

▶ To download the following online resource for this lesson, visit **fp.pub/resources**:
  ▪ chart art (optional)

Academic Language / Important Vocabulary

▶ organize

▶ order

Continuum Connection

▶ Rearrange and revise writing to better express meaning or make the text more logical: e.g., reorder drawings, reorder pages, cut and paste

▶ Reorder pages by laying them out and reassembling them

▶ Reorder the information in a text to make the meaning clearer by cutting apart, cutting and pasting, laying out pages, using word-processing

GOAL

Understand that writers reread their writing to be sure the order makes sense, and they reorganize it to make the text more logical.

RATIONALE

When you teach children to reread their writing to make sure the order makes sense, they begin to think about the structure of their writing and they learn to communicate their ideas more effectively.

ASSESS LEARNING

▶ Look for evidence that children reread their own writing to determine if the order makes sense.

▶ Observe whether children are willing to reorganize their writing.

▶ Look for evidence that children can use vocabulary such as *organize* and *order*.

MINILESSON

To help children think about the minilesson principle, revisit a familiar text and discuss how the order of events makes sense. Then discuss the order of events in a simple text you prepared. Here is an example.

▶ Show the cover of *The Birthday Swap* and read the title. Show several pages of the book and help children summarize the major events in the story in order.

> What happens first in this story?

> What happens next?

> What happens at the end?

> What do you notice about the order of the things that happen in the story? How do you think the author decided what order to tell her story in?

> The author, Loretta Lopez, thought carefully about what happens in the story and made sure to organize her writing so the story would make sense.

▶ Show the simple text you prepared. Read it aloud.

> What do you notice about the order of my writing? Does the order make sense? Why or why not?

> What should I change?

Have a Try

Invite children to talk to a partner about how to change the order of writing.

> I need to move "Put the seed in the hole" before "Cover the seed with soil." How can I change the order of my writing? What do you think I should do? Turn and talk to your partner about this.

▶ After children turn and talk, invite several pairs to share their ideas.

▶ Discuss different ways of reorganizing writing (cutting and pasting, circling and drawing an arrow, changing the order of the pages, etc.). Demonstrate reorganizing your writing in a way that makes sense.

Summarize and Apply

Summarize the learning and remind children to reread their writing to make sure the order makes sense.

▶ Write the principle at the top of the chart. Read it to children.

> During writing time today, reread the book you're writing or a book you've already written. Make sure the order makes sense. If it doesn't, put your writing in the right order using one of the ways we talked about.

Confer

▶ During independent writing, move around the room to confer briefly with as many individual children as time allows. Sit side by side with them and invite them to talk about reorganizing their writing. Use prompts such as the following as needed.

- *Let's reread your book together. Does the order make sense? Why or why not?*
- *Does _____ happen before or after _____ ?*
- *Where do you want to move that part of your story?*
- *How can you move it?*

Share

Following independent writing, gather children in the meeting area to share their writing.

> Did anyone change the order of your writing today? Share how you changed it.

Organize your writing to make sure the order makes sense.

How to Plant a Seed

First, fill a pot with soil.
Dig a small hole in the soil.
Cover the seed with soil.
Put the seed in the hole.
Water the seed. Put the pot in a sunny place.
Finally, wait patiently for the seed to grow. Be sure to water it often.

Section 5: Writing Process

Revising to Focus and Organize Writing

You Will Need

- familiar nonfiction texts, with and without headings, such as the following:
  - *Feathers: Not Just for Flying* by Melissa Stewart, from Text Set: Exploring the Natural World: Birds
  - *Dogs* by Seymour Simon, from Text Set: Seymour Simon: A Scientific Eye
- chart paper prepared with a short nonfiction text, organized by category, with one fact out of order
- markers
- document camera (optional)
- To download the following online resource for this lesson, visit **fp.pub/resources**:
  - chart art (optional)

Academic Language / Important Vocabulary

- heading
- group
- author
- similar

Continuum Connection

- Understand that an informational text is ordered by logic (sequence, ideas related to each other)
- Reorder the information in a text to make the meaning clearer by cutting apart, cutting and pasting, laying out pages, using word-processing

---

GOAL

Organize writing so that similar ideas are grouped together.

RATIONALE

When you teach children to reread their writing to make sure similar ideas are grouped together, they begin to think about the structure of their writing. They learn to communicate their ideas more effectively.

ASSESS LEARNING

- Look for evidence that children reread their own writing to make sure similar ideas are grouped together.
- Observe whether children are willing to reorganize their writing.
- Look for evidence that children can use vocabulary such as *heading*, *group*, *author*, and *similar*.

MINILESSON

To help children think about the minilesson principle, use familiar nonfiction texts, with and without headings, to discuss how the authors grouped similar ideas together. If possible, use a document camera so everyone can see the pages. Here is an example.

- Show a book that uses headings to group ideas, such as *Feathers: Not Just for Flying*. Display and read pages 13–14, including the heading.

  What is the book about?

  What are these pages about?

  All the facts on these pages are about how feathers can protect birds from attackers. The author grouped all these facts together in the same place. She wrote the heading "Feathers can distract attackers like a bullfighter's cape . . . or hide a bird from predators like camouflage clothing" to tell what the pages are about.

- Read page 15.

  What is this page about?

  This whole book is about feathers, but each part is about a different job that feathers do.

- Repeat this process with a book that does not use headings, such as *Dogs*. Read pages 11 and 15, and ask children what they are about.

  On page 11, the author grouped together facts about how mother dogs take care of their puppies. On page 15, he grouped together facts about hounds. There are no headings in this book, but the author still grouped similar ideas together.

Have a Try

Invite children to talk to a partner about whether similar ideas are grouped together in your writing.

▶ Display the nonfiction text you prepared. Read it aloud.

> What do you notice about how I organized my ideas in my writing? Is there anything I should fix? Turn and talk to your partner about that.

▶ After children turn and talk, invite several children to share their thinking. If necessary, help children identify the idea that is out of place.

▶ Demonstrate moving the out-of-place idea in whatever way makes the most sense (e.g., cutting and pasting or circling and drawing an arrow).

Summarize and Apply

Summarize the learning and remind children to reread their writing to make sure similar ideas are grouped together.

▶ Write the principle at the top of the chart. Read it to children.

> During writing time today, reread the book you're working on or a book you've already written. Make sure that similar ideas are grouped together. If you find any idea you want to move, move it using one of the ways we talked about.

Group similar ideas together.

Dogs

Dogs are known as best friends to all. They are the most popular pet in the world. Humans and dogs have lived together for thousands of years.

There are more than four hundred breeds of dogs. Some, like the Great Dane, are very big. Others, like the Chihuahua, are tiny. Some can run very fast—much faster than people.

Many dogs have strong, powerful bodies. Some dogs can jump very high. Dogs also have strong teeth and jaws.

Confer

▶ During independent writing, move around the room to confer briefly with as many individual children as time allows. Sit side by side with them and invite them to talk about organizing their writing. Use prompts such as the following as needed.

• *What is this page about? Does _____ have to do with _____ ?*

• *Where should the fact about _____ go?*

• *How can you move that fact?*

Share

Following independent writing, gather children in the meeting area to share their writing.

> Did anyone move any of the ideas in your book? Share how and why you moved them.

Assessment

After you have taught the minilessons in this umbrella, observe children as they draw, write, and talk about their writing. Use *The Fountas & Pinnell Literacy Continuum* to notice, teach for, and support children's learning as you observe their attempts at writing.

▶ What evidence do you have of children's new understandings related to revising writing?

- Do children show a willingness to revise their writing?
- Are they able to evaluate information that does not tell about the important ideas and remove it?
- Do they change or add words to give more information or make their writing more interesting?
- How successful are children at skipping time in their fiction writing?
- Do they understand how to reorder their writing?
- Do they group similar ideas together, with or without headings?
- Do children understand and use vocabulary such as *information*, *idea*, and *organize*?

▶ In what other ways, beyond the scope of this umbrella, are children exploring the writing process?

- Are they writing different kinds of books?
- Are they including different kinds of illustrations and graphics in their nonfiction writing?

Use your observations to determine the next umbrella you will teach. You may also consult Suggested Sequence of Lessons (pp. 575–589) for guidance.

EXTENSIONS FOR REVISING TO FOCUS AND ORGANIZE WRITING

▶ Gather together a guided writing group of several children who need support in a specific aspect of writing, such as reorganizing parts that are out of order.

▶ Teach children how to add information to their writing (see WPS.U8: Adding Information to Your Writing).

▶ Show children how to revise their writing on a computer, using tools such as Cut and Paste.

Minilessons in This Umbrella

WML1 Make sure your writing makes sense.

WML2 Make sure you made your letters easy to read.

WML3 Make sure you wrote the words you know correctly.

WML4 Check your punctuation and capitalization.

WML5 Use a proofreading checklist.

Shared Reading

Before Teaching Umbrella 10 Minilessons

The goal of this umbrella is to help children understand how to proofread and edit their own writing. A basic checklist for proofreading will be built as a chart across the minilessons. Decide whether you will have the children use the online resource Proofreading Checklist during the first four minilessons or wait until WML5. Fasten the checklist inside children's writing folders. Before teaching these lessons, make sure children have had many experiences writing and reading their work. It will also be helpful to have taught CNV.U1–CNV.U4.

Throughout the umbrella, use a writing sample from a child, a piece of shared writing, or the sample provided. Make sure the sample is large enough for everyone to see—either project it or rewrite it on chart paper. In these lessons, the same child's writing sample is used in order to model the entire process a child will use for each piece of writing; however, you could also use a different sample for each lesson if you prefer. Use the book listed below from *Fountas & Pinnell Classroom™ Shared Reading Collection*, or choose books from the classroom library to serve as models.

Shared Reading Collection

Stone Soup: An Old Tale retold by Helen Lorraine

As you read and enjoy this text together, help children notice

- that letters are easy to read,
- spaces between words,
- punctuation and capitalization, and
- print that makes sense.

Editing and Proofreading Writing

You Will Need

- a big book that has clear and simple writing, such as *Stone Soup: An Old Tale* retold by Helen Lorraine, from *Shared Reading Collection*
- a prepared short piece of writing to edit, projected or written on chart paper
- children's writings (one per child or pair of children)
- chart paper and markers
- document camera (optional)
- To download the following online resources for this lesson, visit **fp.pub/resources**:
  - Proofreading Checklist (optional)
  - Sample Text: "Anna's Broken Leg"

Academic Language / Important Vocabulary

- draft
- words
- makes sense
- edit
- proofread

Continuum Connection

- Edit for sentence sense
- Delete text to better express meaning and make the text more logical

GOAL

Proofread and edit writing to make sure sentences make sense.

RATIONALE

Writing is a form of communication from writers to their audience. When the writing does not make sense and cannot be understood by the audience, then it is not effective.

ASSESS LEARNING

- Look for evidence that children understand that readers need to be able to understand what they are reading.
- Observe whether children proofread and edit their writing to make sure it makes sense.
- Look for evidence that children can use vocabulary such as *draft*, *words*, *makes sense*, *edit*, and *proofread*.

MINILESSON

To help children proofread and edit their work, first provide an example of a mentor text with clear writing. Then model how writing can be corrected when it does not make sense. Below is an example. Before teaching, decide whether children will use the Proofreading Checklist now or wait until WML5.

- Show the cover of *Stone Soup* and then read page 2.

  Think about what the writer wrote here. Does it make sense? Do you understand what the writer was trying to say?

- Guide the conversation so children notice that it is clear and easy to understand.

  The writer, Helen Lorraine, proofread, or reread her writing to make sure that her writing made sense. If something did not make sense, she edited, or made changes to, her work.

- Show the prepared writing sample.

  When you do your own writing, check to make sure a reader will understand it. One thing that you check for is whether your writing makes sense. Let's proofread and edit this piece of writing to check if it makes sense.

- Read the excerpt from "Anna's Broken Leg" or other writing, stopping to ask children if what you read makes sense. Show them how to use one line to cross out (not erase) any extra or wrong words and add in missing words using a caret. Reread the writing and ask children to talk about whether it makes sense now.

- Continue with the process for this writing sample until you feel the children understand what to look for and how to fix any errors.

Have a Try

Invite children to turn and talk about checking if their writing makes sense.

▶ Give children a sample of their own writing (or one sample per pair).

> Read your draft to your partner. Together, talk about whether it makes sense.

▶ After time for discussion, ask a few volunteers to share whether they noticed any parts that did not make sense and what ideas they have to correct them.

Summarize and Apply

Summarize the lesson. Encourage children to proofread their writing to check if it makes sense and make edits if needed.

> Today you learned that you can proofread your work to check if it makes sense and edit the parts that don't make sense.

▶ On chart paper, begin a proofreading checklist. On the left, write the principle. On the right, add several examples that children noticed in the sample piece. Keep the checklist posted and continue adding to it throughout this umbrella.

> During writing time today, share your draft with a different partner. If you talk about any parts that do not make sense, cross out any extra or wrong words and add in words so that they do make sense. Bring your writing when we meet later.

Confer

▶ During independent writing, move around the room to confer briefly with as many individual children as time allows. Sit side by side with them and invite them to talk about editing and proofreading. Use the following prompts as needed.

- *Reread this part. Does that make sense?*
- *Let's talk about words that could be added so that this makes sense.*
- *Show me an extra word that could be crossed out.*

Share

Following independent writing, gather children in the meeting area. Ask a few volunteers to share parts of their writing that they have edited.

> Who would like to share your writing? Tell about what you edited.

Writing Minilesson Principle
Make sure you made your letters easy to read.

Editing and Proofreading Writing

You Will Need

- a big book that has clear letters that are written properly, such as *Stone Soup: An Old Tale* retold by Helen Lorraine, from *Shared Reading Collection*

- a prepared short piece of writing that could be edited (the sample from WML1 or a different one) projected or written on chart paper

- chart paper and markers

- chart (proofreading checklist) from WML1

- document camera (optional)

- children's writings (one per child or pair of children)

- To download the following online resources for this lesson, visit **fp.pub/resources**:

  - Proofreading Checklist (optional)

  - Sample Text: "Anna's Broken Leg"

  - Verbal Path for Letter Formation

Academic Language / Important Vocabulary

- letters
- size
- handwriting
- height
- spaces
- sink

Continuum Connection

- Check and correct letter formation

GOAL

Reread writing to check for correct letter formation, proportion, and orientation so the reader can understand the message.

RATIONALE

When children check their writing to be sure their letters are easy to read, paying attention to letter size and orientation, they are better able to get their message across to a reader, and they learn to write in an efficient and proportional manner. They also gain independence and confidence over their own writing.

ASSESS LEARNING

- Look for evidence that children understand the importance of proper letter formation.

- Observe whether children proofread and edit their work to check for letter formation, proportion, and orientation.

- Look for evidence that children can use vocabulary such as *letters*, *handwriting*, *spaces*, *size*, *height*, and *sink*.

MINILESSON

To help children learn to proofread and edit their work, provide samples of mentor texts with proper letter formation, proportionality, and orientation. Model how writing can be corrected when letters are not formed properly. Below is an example. Before teaching, decide whether children will use the Proofreading Checklist now or wait until WML5.

- Show and read page 3 in *Stone Soup*.

  What do you notice about how the letters are written?

- Guide the conversation to help children notice that the letters are written so they are easy to read and go from left to right. Have a conversation about whether letters are tall, small, or sink below the line.

- Show the writing sample.

  Take a look at the letters. What do you notice?

- Engage children in conversation, having them notice any letters that need correction for formation, proportionality, or orientation. As they do, rewrite the pertinent letters and words on chart paper with handwriting lines. Have children guide you through the formation using the verbal path or ask volunteers to come up and write the letters.

  When you do your own writing, make your letters the best that you can so that your reader will understand what you wrote. If you notice a letter that you can write better, cross out the whole word instead of erasing and rewrite it above.

Have a Try

Invite children to turn and talk about proofreading and editing their writing.

▶ Give children a sample of their own writing (or one sample per pair).

Look at the writing. Turn and tell your partner about any letters that should be fixed and how you can fix them.

▶ Remind them that they should cross out the word that has a letter that could be made better and write it clearly above.

Summarize and Apply

Summarize the lesson. Encourage children to proofread their writing and make edits as needed.

▶ Add the principle to the proofreading checklist you began in WML1, along with an example. Read the checklist.

During writing time, read your writing to make sure that you have written each letter the best that you can. If you find a letter that you need to fix, cross the word out neatly and write it correctly above. Bring your writing to share when we meet later.

▶ Save the checklist for WML3.

Confer

▶ During independent writing, move around the room to confer briefly with as many individual children as time allows. Sit side by side with them and invite them to talk about proofreading and editing their writing. Use the following prompts as needed.

• *Are there any letters that you could write differently so a reader can read them better?*

• *Where can you look to know how to make a letter?*

• *Show how you can fix this letter.*

Share

Following independent writing, gather children in the meeting area. Ask a few volunteers to share their writing from today.

Who would like to share your writing?

Did you fix any letters after you proofread your writing? Show what you did.

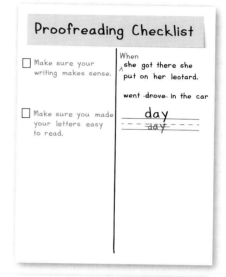

Section 5: Writing Process

Writing Minilesson Principle
Make sure you wrote the words you know correctly.

Editing and Proofreading Writing

You Will Need

- a big book with familiar high-frequency words, such as *Stone Soup: An Old Tale* retold by Helen Lorraine, from *Shared Reading Collection*

- a prepared short piece of writing with spelling errors (the sample from WML2 or a different one)

- document camera (optional)

- chart (proofreading checklist) from WML2

- children's writings (one per child or pair of children)

- To download the following online resources for this lesson, visit **fp.pub/resources**:
  - Proofreading Checklist (optional)
  - Sample Text: "Anna's Broken Leg"

Academic Language / Important Vocabulary

- edit
- proofread
- words
- spelling

Continuum Connection

- Edit for spelling errors by circling words that do not look right and spelling them another way

- Edit for the conventional spelling of known words

- Understand that the more accurate the spelling and the clearer the space between words, the easier it is for the reader to read it

---

GOAL

Reread writing to check or correct spelling so the reader can understand the message.

RATIONALE

When children learn to proofread and then edit by checking for misspelled words, they understand that it is the writer's responsibility to spell the words they know correctly. It is important to encourage children to use temporary, approximated spelling when they don't know conventional spelling in order to expand vocabulary, so help them focus on checking only words they feel confident about and the most important words in the story.

ASSESS LEARNING

- Look for evidence that children understand the importance of correct spelling.
- Observe whether children proofread and edit their work for correct spelling.
- Look for evidence that children can use vocabulary such as *edit*, *proofread*, *words*, and *spelling*.

MINILESSON

To help children learn how to proofread and edit their work, display mentor texts with proper spellings of words children know. Model how writing can be corrected when words they know are spelled incorrectly. Below is an example. Before teaching, decide whether children will use the Proofreading Checklist now or wait until WML5.

- Show and read page 4 in *Stone Soup*.

  What is a word you know on this page?

- Guide the conversation to help children notice familiar words that are spelled correctly.

  You know the words *one* and *day*. Notice that they are spelled here the same way you would spell them. That's how you know what those words are. You also know the words *the* and *pot*. They are spelled the same way each time they are written on this page, which helps the reader know what the words are.

- Show the writing sample.

  Are there any words you know that might not be spelled correctly?

- Guide the conversation to help children notice misspelled familiar words or words that are important to the story (e.g., *want* instead of *went*). Model how to circle the words that don't look right and encourage them to try writing them correctly. Have them check spellings in places they know (e.g., personal word list, word wall).

Have a Try

Invite children to turn and talk about how to correct their spelling.

▶ Give children a sample of their own writing (or one sample per pair).

Look at the writing. Turn and tell your partner about a word you know that should be fixed. How can you fix it?

▶ After time for a brief discussion, ask a few volunteers to share how they can fix any words that are misspelled.

Summarize and Apply

Summarize the lesson. Remind children to proofread their writing and make edits if needed.

▶ Add the principle to the proofreading checklist you began in WML1, along with an example.

Today you learned to proofread by checking to make sure the words you know are spelled correctly. When you do your own writing, it's important to write the words you know correctly so that your reader will understand what you wrote. During writing time, check for spelling by proofreading your writing. Bring your writing to share when we meet later.

▶ Save the checklist for WML4.

Confer

▶ During independent writing, move around the room to confer briefly with as many individual children as time allows. Sit side by side with them and invite them to talk about proofreading and editing their writing. You might wish to have them use the Proofreading Checklist. Use the following prompts as needed.

- *Read this sentence to make sure the words you know are spelled correctly.*

- *What do you notice about this sentence?*

- *How can you fix the spelling of this word?*

- *Show how you used the Proofreading Checklist.*

Share

Following independent writing, gather children in the meeting area to share their writing.

When you proofread, did you find any words that were not spelled correctly? Show what you did to edit them.

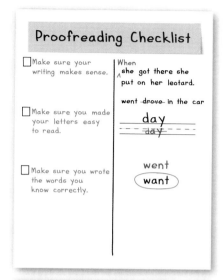

Section 5: Writing Process

Editing and Proofreading Writing

You Will Need

- a big book that shows clear punctuation and capitalization, such as *Stone Soup: An Old Tale* retold by Helen Lorraine, from *Shared Reading Collection*

- a prepared short piece of writing with clear errors (the sample from WML3 or a different one)

- chart (proofreading checklist) from WML3

- document camera (optional)

- children's writings (one per child or pair of children)

- To download the following online resources for this lesson, visit **fp.pub/resources**:
  - Proofreading Checklist (optional)
  - Sample Text: "Anna's Broken Leg"

Academic Language / Important Vocabulary

- writing
- edit
- proofread
- punctuation
- capitalization

Continuum Connection

- Edit for capitalization
- Edit for end punctuation

GOAL

Edit for capitalization and punctuation.

RATIONALE

When children understand that it is a writer's job to proofread and edit for correct capitalization and punctuation, they recognize that they are responsible for making their writing easy for a reader to understand. They learn to take ownership over their own work.

ASSESS LEARNING

- Look for evidence that children understand the importance of capitalization and punctuation.
- Observe whether children proofread and edit their work for proper capitalization and punctuation.
- Look for evidence that children can use vocabulary such as *writing*, *edit*, *proofread*, *punctuation*, and *capitalization*.

MINILESSON

To help children learn how to proofread and edit their work, display a mentor text with proper capitalization and punctuation. Model how writing can be corrected when they notice incorrect punctuation or capitalization. Below is an example. Before teaching, decide whether children will use the Proofreading Checklist now or wait until WML5.

- Show and read page 11 in *Stone Soup*.

  What do you notice about the punctuation and capitalization on this page?

  When does the writer capitalize letters?

  Why has she chosen to use apostrophes in *doesn't* and *I'll*?

  What punctuation do you see at the end of the sentences?

- Show the writing sample.

  Are there any words you know that might not have correct punctuation or capitalization?

- Guide the conversation to help children notice errors. Show them how to add in or cross out punctuation marks and how to cross out letters with incorrect capitalization and rewrite them above.

- Continue with the process for this writing sample until you feel the children understand what to look for and how to fix any errors.

Have a Try

Invite children to turn and talk about how to correct punctuation and capitalization.

▶ Give children a sample of their own writing (or one sample per pair).

Look at the writing. Turn and tell your partner about something you notice that should be fixed. How can you fix it?

▶ After time for a brief discussion, ask a few volunteers to share how they can edit any errors.

Summarize and Apply

Summarize the lesson. Remind children to proofread their writing and make edits if needed.

▶ Add the principle to the proofreading checklist you began in WML1 along with an example.

Today you learned to proofread to make sure that punctuation and capitalization are correct. During writing time, check for correct punctuation and capitalization by rereading what you have written. Bring your writing to share when we meet later.

▶ Save the checklist for WML5.

Confer

▶ During independent writing, move around the room to confer briefly with as many individual children as time allows. Sit side by side with them and invite them to talk about proofreading and editing their writing. You might wish to have them use the Proofreading Checklist. Use the following prompts as needed.

- *Read this sentence to make sure the punctuation and capitalization are correct.*
- *What do you notice about this sentence?*
- *How can you fix that?*
- *Show how you used the Proofreading Checklist.*

Share

Following independent writing, gather children in the meeting area to share their writing.

When you proofread, did you find any punctuation or capitalization that was not correct? Show what you did to fix it.

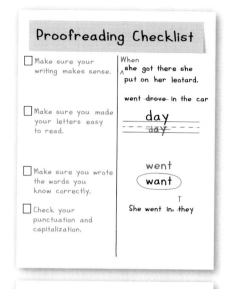

Section 5: Writing Process

Writing Minilesson Principle
Use a proofreading checklist.

Editing and Proofreading Writing

You Will Need

- a prepared short piece of writing with clear errors (the sample from WML4 or a different one)
- chart (proofreading checklist) from WML4
- document camera (optional)
- children's writings (one per child or pair of children)
- a copy of the Proofreading Checklist or a checklist of your own fastened inside each child's writing folder
- To download the following online resources for this lesson, visit **fp.pub/resources**:
  - Proofreading Checklist (optional)
  - Sample Text: "Anna's Broken Leg"

Academic Language / Important Vocabulary

- writing
- edit
- proofreading checklist

Continuum Connection

- Know how to use an editing and proofreading checklist

GOAL

Use a proofreading checklist to make writing clear and easy for the reader to understand.

RATIONALE

A proofreading checklist will remind children that they need to make their writing clear and easy for a reader to understand and show them what to check for and edit in their writing.

ASSESS LEARNING

- Look for evidence that children understand the importance of proofreading and editing their work.
- Observe whether children are using a proofreading checklist.
- Look for evidence that children can use vocabulary such as *writing*, *edit*, and *proofreading checklist*.

MINILESSON

To help children learn how to proofread their work, model how a piece of writing can be corrected by using a proofreading checklist. Below is an example. If the children have been using a proofreading checklist already, you may not need to teach this minilesson.

- Show the writing sample and the checklist from WML4.

   You have been thinking and talking about proofreading and editing your work, and we have created a proofreading checklist. Let's use the checklist to look through the entire piece of writing and see if there is anything to fix.

- Model how to proofread the entire paper using the Proofreading Checklist, including placing a check mark in each box as the step is completed.

- Show a paper copy of the Proofreading Checklist from the online resources. Talk about where children will keep the checklist (in their writing folders).

   After you finish a piece of writing, use the Proofreading Checklist to help you fix any errors.

Have a Try

Invite children to turn and talk about how to use a proofreading checklist.

▶ Give children a sample of their own writing (or one sample per pair) and a copy of the Proofreading Checklist.

> Look at the writing. Use the Proofreading Checklist to read through the writing with a partner. Talk about things you notice that need to be fixed. How can you fix them?

▶ After time for a brief discussion, ask a few volunteers to share their experience using the Proofreading Checklist.

Summarize and Apply

Summarize the lesson. Remind children to proofread their writing and edit if needed.

> Today you learned to use the Proofreading Checklist to look through an entire piece of writing and check for errors. During writing time, use the Proofreading Checklist to check your writing. Bring your writing to share when we meet later.

▶ Remind children where to keep their checklists.

Confer

▶ During independent writing, move around the room to confer briefly with as many individual children as time allows. Sit side by side with them and invite them to talk about using the Proofreading Checklist. Use the following prompts as needed.

- *Which step on the Proofreading Checklist are you working on?*
- *Where will you place the check mark after you complete this step?*
- *Let's look through your writing together using the Proofreading Checklist.*

Share

Following independent writing, gather children in the meeting area. Have them bring their writing from today.

> Turn and talk to your partner about how you used the Proofreading Checklist today.

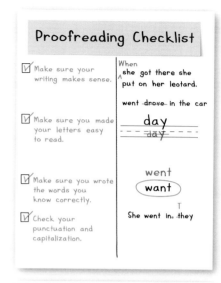

Assessment

After you have taught the minilessons in this umbrella, observe children in a variety of classroom activities. Use *The Fountas & Pinnell Literacy Continuum* to notice, teach for, and support children's learning as you observe their attempts at writing.

▶ What evidence do you have of children's new understandings related to proofreading and editing?

- Do children understand that they should go back and check that their writing makes sense?
- Are children checking to see if they made their letters easy to read?
- Are they writing the words they know correctly?
- Do they check for correct punctuation and capitalization?
- Are you noticing evidence that they are using a proofreading checklist?
- Are they using vocabulary such as *writing, words, makes sense, letters, handwriting, edit, proofread, spaces, between, spelling, punctuation, capitalization,* and *proofreading checklist?*

▶ In what ways, beyond the scope of this umbrella, are children showing an interest in the writing process?

- Are they revising and organizing writing?
- Are they adding information to their writing?

▶ Use your observations to determine the next umbrella you will teach. You may also consult Suggested Sequence of Lessons (pp. 575–589) for guidance.

EXTENSIONS FOR EDITING AND PROOFREADING WRITING

▶ Gather together a guided writing group of several children who need support for a similar aspect of proofreading and editing their writing.

▶ From time to time when you are using big books, ask children to point out the clear writing and correct spelling, punctuation, and capitalization. Talk about how the writer needed to proofread and edit before publishing the book.

Minilessons in This Umbrella

WML1 Write a title and illustrate your cover.

WML2 Write an author page.

WML3 Dedicate your book to someone.

WML4 Make endpapers for your book.

Before Teaching Umbrella 11 Minilessons

The minilessons in this umbrella introduce children to the idea of getting writing ready to share with an audience by adding book and print features. You do not need to teach the minilessons one right after another. Teach them when you observe that the children are ready.

Before teaching these minilessons, give children plenty of opportunities to write and draw freely and without constraints. Read and discuss engaging books from a variety of genres. For these minilessons, use the following books from *Fountas & Pinnell Classroom™ Interactive Read-Aloud Collection*, or choose books with a variety of book and print features from the classroom library.

Interactive Read-Aloud Collection

Caring for Each Other: Family

Pecan Pie Baby by Jacqueline Woodson

Big Red Lollipop by Rukhsana Khan

The Wednesday Surprise by Eve Bunting

Exploring the Natural World: Insects

The Bugliest Bug by Carol Diggory Shields

Bugs for Lunch by Margery Facklam

Exploring Narrative Nonfiction Texts

A Log's Life by Wendy Pfeffer

Salmon Stream by Carol Reed-Jones

Think of an Eel by Karen Wallace

As you read and enjoy these texts together, help children

- use the title to predict what the book will be about,

- notice and talk about author pages, dedications, and acknowledgments, and

- share what they notice about cover illustrations and endpapers.

Interactive Read-Aloud
Family

Insects

Narrative Nonfiction

Section 5: Writing Process

Writing Minilesson Principle
Write a title and illustrate your cover.

You Will Need

- a few familiar books, such as the following from Text Set: Caring for Each Other: Family:
  - *The Wednesday Surprise* by Eve Bunting
  - *Pecan Pie Baby* by Jacqueline Woodson
  - *Big Red Lollipop* by Rukhsana Khan
- chart paper prepared with a book cover (no title)
- marker
- To download the following online resource for this lesson, visit **fp.pub/resources**:
  - chart art (optional)

Academic Language / Important Vocabulary

- cover
- illustrate
- title

Continuum Connection

- Generate multiple titles for the piece and select the one that best fits the content of an informational piece or the plot or characterization in a narrative
- In anticipation of an audience, add book and print features to the text during the publishing process: e.g., illustrations and other graphics, cover spread, title, dedication, table of contents, about the author piece
- Attend to layout of text in final publication

GOAL

Write a title and illustrate the cover of books.

RATIONALE

When children notice that books have a title and a complementary illustration on the front cover, they will learn to add fitting titles and illustrations to their own book covers.

ASSESS LEARNING

- Look for evidence that children understand the purpose of book titles and cover illustrations.
- Notice if children add fitting titles and illustrations to their own book covers.
- Observe for evidence that children can use vocabulary such as *cover*, *title*, and *illustrate*.

MINILESSON

To help children think about the minilesson principle, use several familiar books to start a discussion about book titles and cover illustrations. Below is an example.

- Display the covers of several familiar books.

  The front of a book is called the front cover. What is written on the front cover of each book?

  What do you notice about where the title is written on the cover?

  The title is usually written near the top of the cover, but sometimes it's at the bottom or in the middle. When you're the author, you decide where to put it.

- Display the cover of *The Wednesday Surprise*.

  Why is this book called *The Wednesday Surprise*? What is the Wednesday surprise?

  Look at the illustration on the cover. What makes this a good illustration for the cover of this book?

- Show the cover of *Pecan Pie Baby*.

  Why do you think the author chose the title *Pecan Pie Baby* for this book?

  What do you notice about the illustration?

  How does the illustration help you understand what the book is about?

- Continue in a similar manner with *Big Red Lollipop*.

  The title and the illustration on the cover help you understand what the book is about.

Have a Try

Have children help you write a title for the cover on the prepared chart.

> Here's a book cover that needs a title. The book is about a boy who goes for a walk in the park with Grandpa Joe every Sunday morning. What might be a good title for this book? Turn and talk to your partner about this.

▶ After time for discussion, invite several children to share their ideas. Record all reasonable suggestions on chart paper. Then discuss which title would be the most fitting and why, and discuss where on the cover to put the title. Write the title.

Summarize and Apply

Summarize the learning. Remind children to write a title and draw an illustration on the front cover of their books. Write the principle at the top of the chart.

> During writing time today, write a title and draw an illustration on the front cover of your book.
>
> Make sure to add a title and an illustration that help your readers know what the book is about. Bring your book to share when we meet later.

Write a title and illustrate your cover.

- A Walk in the Park

- My Grandpa and Me

- My Grandpa Joe

- Sunday Morning with Grandpa

- Walking with Grandpa

Confer

▶ During independent writing, move around the room to confer briefly with as many individual children as time allows. Sit side by side with them and invite them to talk about adding a title and cover illustration. Use the following prompts as needed.

- *What is your book about?*

- *What are your ideas for a title? Which title do you think is the best? Why?*

- *What illustration could you put on the cover that would match the title?*

- *Where on the cover will you write the title?*

Share

Following independent writing, gather children in the meeting area. Have everyone hold up their book covers. Then choose several children to talk about them.

> Hold up your book cover so everyone can see.

> Talk about how you decided on the title and cover illustration.

Adding Book and Print Features

You Will Need

- a few familiar books with an author page, such as the following:
  - *Big Red Lollipop* by Rukhsana Khan and *Pecan Pie Baby* by Jacqueline Woodson, from Text Set: Caring for Each Other: Family
  - *A Log's Life* by Wendy Pfeffer, from Text Set: Exploring Narrative Nonfiction Texts
- chart paper and markers
- To download the following online resources for this lesson, visit **fp.pub/resources**:
  - chart art (optional)
  - paper templates (optional)

Academic Language / Important Vocabulary

- author
- author page

Continuum Connection

- Write an author page at the beginning or end of a book to give information about the author
- In anticipation of an audience, add book and print features to the text during the publishing process: e.g., illustrations and other graphics, cover spread, title, dedication, table of contents, about the author piece

GOAL

Write an author page to share information about yourself.

RATIONALE

Helping children study author pages and supporting them in writing their own author pages helps them view themselves as writers. It encourages children to take pride in and celebrate their writing.

ASSESS LEARNING

- ▶ Look for evidence that children understand the purpose of an author page.
- ▶ Notice if children write author pages in their own books.
- ▶ Look for evidence that children can use vocabulary such as *author* and *author page*.

MINILESSON

To help children think about the minilesson principle, study author pages in several familiar texts. Engage children in a discussion about the information that authors share about themselves on an author page. Below is an example.

- ▶ Read aloud the author information on the back flap of *Big Red Lollipop*.

  What is the purpose of this part of the book?

  Talk about the kind of information you find in the author's page.

  What did you learn about the author, Rukhsana Khan, from this part of the book?

  What did you learn about why she wrote this book?

- ▶ Record children's responses in general terms on chart paper.
- ▶ Continue in a similar manner with *Pecan Pie Baby* and *A Log's Life*.

  The page that has information about the author is called the author page. Where in a book might you find the author page?

  The author page may be in the front or back of the book, or on the back cover or back flap. When you write your own books, you can decide where to put the author page.

  Why might an author decide to write an author page?

  Knowing a bit about an author and the reasons the author wrote a book can help you enjoy a book more.

Have a Try

Invite children to talk to a partner about what they would write on their own author page.

> Turn and talk to your partner about what you might write about yourself on the author page in a book you've written.

▶ After time for discussion, invite several children to share their thinking.

Summarize and Apply

Summarize the learning. Remind children that they can write an author page in their own books. When children make their author pages, they can use plain paper or the author page from the paper templates in the online resources.

> What did you learn today about author pages?

▶ Write the principle at the top of the chart.

> During writing time today, think about what you would like your readers to know about you. Write an author page about yourself. Bring your book to share when we come back together.

Write an author page.

- Where the author lives and with whom
- Why the author wrote the book
- Other books the author has written
- The author's website
- Awards the author has won
- The author's other jobs

About the Author

Confer

▶ During independent writing, move around the room to confer briefly with as many individual children as time allows. Sit side by side with them and invite them to talk about their author pages. Use prompts such as the following as needed.

- *What would you like your readers to know about you?*
- *What could you write to share why you wrote the book?*
- *What other books have you written?*
- *Where would you like to put the author page?*

Share

Following independent writing, gather children in the meeting area to share their author pages.

> Who would like to read aloud your author page?

> What did you learn about _____ from the author page?

Adding Book and Print Features

You Will Need

▸ a few familiar books with a dedication, such as the following:

- *Bugs for Lunch* by Margery Facklam, from Text Set: Exploring the Natural World: Insects

- *A Log's Life* by Wendy Pfeffer, from Text Set: Exploring Narrative Nonfiction Texts

- *The Wednesday Surprise* by Eve Bunting, from Text Set: Caring for Each Other: Family

▸ chart paper and markers

▸ To download the following online resource for this lesson, visit **fp.pub/resources**:

- paper templates (optional)

Academic Language / Important Vocabulary

▸ author

▸ dedicate

▸ dedication

Continuum Connection

▸ Dedicate a story to someone and write the dedication inside the cover, on the title page or copyright page, or on a page of its own

▸ In anticipation of an audience, add book and print features to the text during the publishing process: e.g., illustrations and other graphics, cover spread, title, dedication, table of contents, about the author piece

GOAL

Write a dedication to someone or something that is important to you.

RATIONALE

When children study dedications and think about the reasons authors choose to dedicate a book to someone, they understand that authors are real people who care about and are influenced by others. They also begin to think of themselves as authors.

ASSESS LEARNING

▸ Look for evidence that children understand the purpose of a dedication.

▸ Notice if children write dedications in their own books.

▸ Look for evidence that children can use vocabulary such as *author*, *dedicate*, and *dedication*.

MINILESSON

To help children think about the minilesson principle, study dedications in several familiar texts. Engage children in a discussion about dedications. Here is an example.

▸ Read aloud the author's dedication in *Bugs for Lunch*.

> Does anyone know what this part of the book is called?

> This is the dedication. Talk to a partner about what a dedication is.

> Dedicating a book to someone is a way of honoring that person and showing appreciation.

▸ Reread the dedication.

> Why did the author, Margery Facklam, dedicate the book *Bugs for Lunch* to her friend Barbara Lucas?

▸ Generalize children's responses and record them on chart paper.

> She says that Barbara Lucas "would not hesitate to eat a well-cooked bug." Maybe Barbara gave her the idea for the book, or she wants to honor people who would eat bugs for lunch!

▸ Read the dedication in *A Log's Life*.

> Whom did the author, Wendy Pfeffer, dedicate this book to and why?

▸ Record responses on the chart.

▸ Continue in a similar manner with *The Wednesday Surprise*.

> What do you notice about where authors put dedications?

Have a Try

Invite children to talk to a partner about their own dedications.

> Think about the book you're working on or the last book you wrote. Is there someone you would like to dedicate your book to? Why? Turn and talk to your partner about your dedication.

▶ After children turn and talk, invite several children to share their thinking. Add new ideas to the chart.

Summarize and Apply

Summarize the learning. Remind children that they can dedicate their books to someone. When children make their dedication pages, they can use plain paper or the dedication page from the paper templates in the online resources.

▶ Write the principle at the top of the chart.

> Why do authors write dedications?

> During writing time today, think about whether you would like to write a dedication. If you would, write it and decide where you would like to place it in your book. Bring your book to share when we come back together.

Dedicate your book to someone.

- Someone who gave you the idea for the book

- Someone who is interested in the book's topic

> Dedication
> This book is dedicated to all children who have moved a long way from home.

- The person the book is about

- Someone you respect, love, or care about

Confer

▶ During independent writing, move around the room to confer briefly with as many individual children as time allows. Sit side by side with them and invite them to talk about writing a dedication. Use prompts such as the following as needed.

- *Did someone give you the idea to write this book?*
- *Would you like to dedicate it to someone special in your family?*
- *What could you write about why you are dedicating your book to that person?*
- *Where in your book would you like to put the dedication?*

Share

Following independent writing, gather children in the meeting area to share their dedications.

> Who would like to read aloud your dedication? Share why you decided to dedicate your book to _____.

Writing Minilesson Principle
Make endpapers for your book.

You Will Need

- a few familiar books with interesting endpapers, such as the following:

  - *Think of an Eel* by Karen Wallace, from Text Set: Exploring Narrative Nonfiction Texts

  - *The Bugliest Bug* by Carol Diggory Shields, from Text Set: Exploring the Natural World: Insects

- chart paper and markers

- To download the following online resource for this lesson, visit **fp.pub/resources**:

  - chart art (optional)

Academic Language / Important Vocabulary

- endpapers
- illustrator
- author

Continuum Connection

- Provide important information in illustrations

- Create drawings that are related to the written text and increase readers' understanding and enjoyment

- Attend to the language and craft of other writers (mentor texts) in order to learn more as a writer

GOAL

Make endpapers that are related to the meaning of the text and increase readers' understanding and enjoyment.

RATIONALE

When children study endpapers and think about how they relate to the book's meaning, they gain an appreciation for the thought and care that went into creating every aspect of the book. They understand that they, too, can put the same thought and care into creating their own books by adding endpapers.

ASSESS LEARNING

- Look for evidence that children understand that endpapers can add to the meaning of a text and increase the reader's enjoyment.

- Notice if children add endpapers to their own books.

- Observe for evidence that children can use vocabulary such as *endpapers*, *illustrator*, and *author*.

MINILESSON

To help children think about the minilesson principle, study the endpapers in familiar texts. Engage children in a discussion about endpapers. Here is an example.

- Show the cover of *Think of an Eel* and open to the final spread of the book, the endpapers.

  What do you notice about the final pages in this book?

  There are no words on these pages, but there is an illustration. What does this illustration show? Why is it important?

  The illustration shows an eel at different times in its life. These pages remind you of what you learned about an eel's life in this book. The final pages in a book, after the main part of the book ends, are called the endpapers.

- Show the endpapers in *The Bugliest Bug*.

  What do you notice about these endpapers?

  These endpapers give extra facts about different bugs. Why do you think authors and illustrators sometimes add endpapers to their books?

- Record responses on chart paper.

  Some authors and illustrators decide to create endpapers to give you more information or to make the book more fun to read.

Have a Try

Invite children to talk to a partner about their own books.

> Think about the book you're working on or another book you've written recently. What might you put on the endpapers of your book? Turn and talk to your partner about your ideas.

▶ After children turn and talk, invite several children to share their ideas.

Summarize and Apply

Summarize the learning. Remind children that they can make endpapers for their books.

▶ Write the principle at the top of the chart.

> What did you learn today about endpapers?

> During writing time today, make endpapers for your book that will help readers understand the topic or make your book more fun to read. You can make the endpapers on paper and then glue them into your book, or you can make them right in your book. One side of the endpapers is the back of your last page. The other side is the inside of your back cover. Bring your book to share when we come back together.

Make endpapers for your book.

- Remind readers of what they learned

- Give more information

- Make the book more fun to read

Confer

▶ During independent writing, move around the room to confer briefly with as many individual children as time allows. Sit side by side with them and invite them to talk about making endpapers. Use prompts such as the following as needed.

- *Could you draw something that would help readers understand more about the topic?*

- *What could you draw that would make your book even more fun to read?*

- *Why did you decide to put _____ on your book's endpapers?*

Share

Following independent writing, gather children in the meeting area to share their endpapers.

> Turn and talk to your partner about the endpapers you made. How did you decide what to draw?

Assessment

After you have taught the minilessons in this umbrella, observe children as they draw, write, and talk about their writing. Use *The Fountas & Pinnell Literacy Continuum* to notice, teach for, and support children's learning as you observe their bookmaking skills.

▶ What evidence do you have of children's new understandings related to adding book and print features for an audience?

- Do children add a title and an illustration to the front cover of their books?
- Can they write an author page about themselves?
- Have they tried writing a dedication?
- Have they experimented with making endpapers for a book?
- Do they understand and use vocabulary such as *author*, *title*, *illustrate*, *dedicate*, and *endpapers*?

▶ In what other ways, beyond the scope of this umbrella, are children exploring the writing process?

- Are they sharing their writing with others?
- Are they publishing their writing in different ways?

Use your observations to determine the next umbrella you will teach. You may also consult Suggested Sequence of Lessons (pp. 575–589) for guidance.

EXTENSIONS FOR ADDING BOOK AND PRINT FEATURES

▶ To help children know which words to capitalize in their titles, consider teaching CNV.U4.WML4.

▶ Help children make back covers that provide information about what their books are about.

▶ Teach children how to make copyright pages and acknowledgments pages. A copyright page shows when the book was written. An acknowledgments page thanks people who encouraged the author in life or helped the author with the book, perhaps by inspiring the idea or assisting with the writing.

▶ During interactive read-aloud, read aloud author pages, dedications, and acknowledgments. Discuss with children how these features add interest or enjoyment when reading a book.

Minilessons in This Umbrella

WML1 Get ready to share the writing you want to celebrate.

WML2 Celebrate something new you tried.

WML3 Publish your writing in different ways.

Before Teaching Umbrella 12 Minilessons

The purpose of the minilessons in this umbrella is to prepare children to choose pieces they are proud of to publish and share. Teach these lessons when children are ready to publish their writing. Some ways that children can share their books include reading them aloud to the whole class or a small group, inviting the children's parents or caregivers to a class celebration in which children share their books, or sharing with another classroom or grade level. Some children might enjoy "publishing" their work by typing and printing it. However, we recommend that this process be reserved for special occasions, as children's work should generally speak for itself. We want children's writing to look like children's writing!

The minilessons in WPS.U11: Adding Book and Print Features enhance the minilessons in this umbrella. Consider teaching some of the lessons alongside this umbrella or as an extension. It would also be helpful for you to make some sample books to use for demonstrating this umbrella's principles.

As you read aloud and enjoy books together, help children

- be aware of how you read aloud to them (read with expression, speak so they can understand, show the illustrations), and

- talk about how authors make their books ready for others to read.

Section 5: Writing Process

Writing Minilesson Principle

Get ready to share the writing you want to celebrate.

Celebrating Writing

You Will Need

- a book that you have made as an example
- chart paper and markers
- To download the following online resource for this lesson, visit **fp.pub/resources**:
  - chart art (optional)

Academic Language / Important Vocabulary

- celebrate
- proofread
- author's page
- dedication
- practice

Continuum Connection

- Share a text with peers by reading it aloud to the class
- Select best pieces of writing from one's own collection and give reasons for the selections

GOAL

Choose a book to celebrate and prepare to share it with an audience.

RATIONALE

Before children can share their work with an audience, they must first choose which piece to share and get it ready to share. This lesson helps them think about the criteria they can use to evaluate their work. When children think carefully about choosing pieces, they are more likely to select work that they are truly proud of and confident about sharing.

ASSESS LEARNING

- ▶ Listen to children's reasons for choosing pieces to celebrate.
- ▶ Notice how they get ready to share their writing.
- ▶ Look for evidence that children can use vocabulary such as *celebrate*, *proofread*, *author's page*, *dedication*, and *practice*.

MINILESSON

To help children think about the minilesson principle, share why you have chosen to celebrate a particular book and help them generate a list of guidelines for getting ready to share their own writing. Here is an example.

> Sometimes you might want to celebrate a special piece of writing by sharing it with others.

▶ Display the example book that you prepared.

> This is a book that I wrote and illustrated and that I'd love to celebrate by sharing with you. I'm very proud of it! It's about a topic that I care a lot about, and I think you will be interested in it, too. I worked very hard on my book. I got ready to share my book by rereading my writing carefully to make sure that it shows my best work. I also made an author's page and wrote a dedication. Then I practiced reading the words aloud. What do you notice about why I chose this book to celebrate?
>
> How did I get ready to share my book?

▶ Record children's responses on chart paper.

Have a Try

Invite children to talk to a partner about a piece of writing they would like to celebrate.

> Think about the pieces of writing you have worked on lately. Which one would you like to celebrate by sharing with other people? Why? Turn and talk to your partner about this.
>
> Now talk about how you will get ready to share it. What will you do?

Summarize and Apply

Write the principle at the top of the chart. Summarize the learning and invite children to get ready to share a piece of writing they want to celebrate.

> Today you learned about choosing a piece of writing to celebrate. You also learned how to get ready to share it. During writing time today, choose a piece of writing to share with your classmates and get ready to share it. Bring your writing to share when we meet later.

Get ready to share the writing you want to celebrate.

- Choose a piece of writing that makes you proud.

- Reread your writing.

- Add an author's page and a dedication.

- Practice reading the words aloud.

My story is about . . .

Confer

▶ During independent writing, move around the room to confer briefly with as many individual children as time allows. Sit side by side with them and invite them to talk about the writing they will celebrate and how they will share it. Use prompts such as the following as needed.

- *Which piece of writing would you like to share?*
- *What have you written that you are proud of?*
- *Why do you want to celebrate this book?*
- *How are you going to get ready to share it?*

Share

Following independent writing, gather children in the meeting area to share their writing.

> Who would like to share a special piece of writing?
>
> Why did you decide to celebrate that piece?

Writing Minilesson Principle
Celebrate something new you tried.

Celebrating Writing

You Will Need

- several examples of children's work that show something new the writers tried (e.g., speech bubbles, borders, sidebars, collage)
- chart paper and markers

Academic Language / Important Vocabulary

- celebrate
- writing
- illustration

Continuum Connection

- Self-evaluate writing and talk about what is good about it and what techniques were used

GOAL

Identify and celebrate trying new writing techniques.

RATIONALE

Encouraging children to share the new things they have tried in their writing makes it more likely that other children will try similar things. Identifying the risks children have taken in their writing makes that writing worth celebrating.

ASSESS LEARNING

- Observe children's attempts at trying something new in their writing and illustrating.
- Notice whether children identify and celebrate new writing or illustrating techniques they have tried.
- Look for evidence that children can use vocabulary such as *celebrate*, *writing*, and *illustration*.

MINILESSON

To help children think about the minilesson principle, engage them in talking about new techniques they have tried in their writing and illustrating. Here is an example.

- Display one of the examples of children's work that you selected before class.

  _____ worked hard on this book and is very proud of it. He tried something new in this book. What did you try, _____?

- Record the example on chart paper.

- Continue sharing examples of new techniques the children have tried in their writing and illustrating. Add them to the chart.

Have a Try

Invite children to talk to a partner about something new they have tried in their writing or illustrating.

> Turn and talk to your partner about something new you have tried recently in your writing or illustrations.

▶ After time for discussion, ask several volunteers to share their responses. Add any new ideas to the chart.

Summarize and Apply

Write the principle at the top of the chart to summarize the learning. Remind children to celebrate new techniques they have tried.

> During writing time today, spend some more time thinking about new things you have tried in your writing or illustrations. If you are proud of something new you tried, you might want to celebrate that piece by sharing it with other people. Bring your writing to share when we meet later.

Celebrate something new you tried.

- Speech bubbles
- Thought bubbles
- Captions
- Borders
- Sidebars
- Characters talking

Confer

▶ During independent writing, move around the room to confer briefly with as many individual children as time allows. Sit side by side with them and invite them to talk about something new they would like to celebrate. Use prompts such as the following if needed.

- *Did you try anything new in this piece of writing? What did you try?*
- *You made a sidebar for the first time in this book. What do you like about it?*
- *What have you tried in your writing or illustrations that you want to share?*
- *What piece of writing would you like to celebrate? Why?*

Share

Following independent writing, gather children in the meeting area to share the new techniques they have tried in their writing.

> Who would like to share something new you tried in your writing or illustrations?

Section 5: Writing Process

Writing Minilesson Principle
Publish your writing in different ways.

You Will Need

- a book that has been typed and printed and has a cardboard cover that you have prepared
- an informational book shaped like the topic it is about (e.g., a circle-shaped book about the solar system) that you have prepared
- a typed poem of yours that has been framed or mounted
- chart paper and markers

Academic Language / Important Vocabulary

- publish
- type
- cover
- title
- author

Continuum Connection

- Select a poem, story, or informational book to publish in a variety of appropriate ways: e.g., typed/printed, framed and mounted or otherwise displayed

GOAL

Learn a variety of ways to publish writing.

RATIONALE

When you teach children different ways to make their writing accessible to others, they begin to understand that bookmaking is a process that involves several steps beyond writing the words and drawing the pictures. They also begin to conceptualize the idea of writing not just for themselves but also for an audience.

ASSESS LEARNING

- Observe whether children experiment with different ways of publishing their writing (e.g., adding a cover, framing or mounting a poem, making a shape book).
- Look for evidence that children can use vocabulary such as *publish*, *type*, *cover*, *title*, and *author*.

MINILESSON

To help children think about the minilesson principle, engage them in a discussion about different ways to publish their writing. Here is an example.

- Display the typed and printed book that you prepared. Draw attention to the cover.

    I published my writing to get it ready for others to read. What do you notice about how I did it?

    I put a cardboard cover on my book so it won't tear easily. What did I write on the cover?

- Add to the chart as you discuss each way of getting writing ready to share.
- Display the book you prepared that is shaped like the topic it is about.

    This is another book that I published so I can share it with others. What do you notice about it?

    This book is about the solar system, so I made each page a circle shape, just like the planets in the solar system! This is called a shape book because it is shaped like the topic.

- Display the framed or mounted poem.

    How did I publish my poem?

    I typed my poem and put it on a piece of construction paper to make it look nice.

Have a Try

Invite children to talk to a partner about how they would like to publish their writing.

> Think about a special piece of writing that you would like to celebrate. How would you like to publish it so others can read it? Turn and talk to your partner about this.

Summarize and Apply

Write the principle at the top of the chart to summarize the learning. Remind children to think about different ways of publishing their writing.

> Today we talked about different ways you can publish your writing so other people can read it. During writing time today, think of how you want to publish one of your books or poems. I can help you.

Confer

▷ During independent writing, move around the room to confer briefly with as many individual children as time allows. Sit side by side with them and invite them to talk about publishing their writing. Use prompts such as the following as needed.

- *How would you like to publish your writing?*
- *Would you like to type it?*
- *Would you like to frame your poem? How can you frame it?*
- *What is your book about? Could you make a shape book?*

Share

Following independent writing, gather children in the meeting area to talk about publishing their writing.

> Who would like to share the writing you worked on today?
>
> How will you publish it?

Publish your writing in different ways.

- Add a cardboard cover.
- Make a shape book.
- Type it.
- Frame it.

Mars

Assessment

After you have taught the minilessons in this umbrella, observe children as they draw, write, and talk about their writing. Use *The Fountas & Pinnell Literacy Continuum* to notice, teach for, and support children's writing development.

▶ What evidence do you have of children's new understandings related to celebrating writing?

- Are children able to choose a piece of writing to share with an audience?
- How do they prepare to share their writing?
- What new writing and illustrating techniques have they tried?
- How do they publish their writing?
- Do they understand and use vocabulary such as *book, poem, share, publish,* and *celebrate*?

▶ In what other ways, beyond the scope of this umbrella, are children exploring the writing process?

- Are they revising, editing, and proofreading their writing?
- Are they adding book and print features to their books?

Use your observations to determine the next umbrella you will teach. You may also consult Suggested Sequence of Lessons (pp. 575–589) for guidance.

EXTENSIONS FOR CELEBRATING WRITING

▶ Help children identify and talk about different text features in published books (e.g., title page, table of contents, glossary). Invite them to add the same features to their own books (see CFT.U9: Using Text Features in Nonfiction Writing and WPS.U11: Adding Book and Print Features).

▶ Dedicate a section of the classroom library or area of the school (e.g., hallway or lobby) to displaying and celebrating children's own books.

▶ Teach children how to put books or stories together into an anthology or collection.

Appendix:

Suggested Sequence of Lessons

The Suggested Sequence of Lessons is also available on the Fountas & Pinnell Online Resources site (**fp.pub/resources**).

Suggested Sequence of Lessons

This sequence shows when you might teach the writing minilessons across the year. It also aligns these lessons with the texts from *Fountas & Pinnell Classroom™ Shared Reading Collection* and *Interactive Read-Aloud Collection*, as well as the reading minilesson umbrellas from *The Reading Minilessons Book, Grade 2.* You do not need these other resources to teach the lessons in this book, but this comprehensive sequence helps you see how all these pieces can fit together and think about how you might organize reading and writing across the year. Note that the number of days refers to approximately how long it will take to teach the lessons. It does not indicate how long your students might spend applying new ideas or experimenting with new kinds of writing.

Suggested Sequence of Lessons

Months	Texts from *Fountas & Pinnell Classroom™ Shared Reading Collection*	Text Sets from *Fountas & Pinnell Classroom™ Interactive Read-Aloud Collection*	Reading Minilessons (RML) Umbrellas	Writing Minilessons (WML) Umbrellas	Teaching Suggestions for Extending Learning
Months 1 & 2	Animals with Jobs	The Importance of Friendship	MGT.U1: Working Together in the Classroom	**MGT.U1: Working Together in the Classroom (9 days)**	If you are using *The Reading Minilessons Book, Grade 2*, you do not need to teach the lessons that repeat in MGT.U1. Both RML and WML establish basically the same routines. However, be sure to take time to build community in your classroom. The opening page of the writing minilessons umbrella MGT.U1 offers a suggestion for a writing project students might work on throughout the umbrella to get to know each other while practicing these important routines.
		Caring for Each Other: Family	MGT.U2: Using the Classroom Library for Independent Reading		

Key

MGT: Management   GEN: Genres and Forms   CFT: Craft   CNV: Conventions
WPS: Writing Process

Months	Texts from *Fountas & Pinnell Classroom™ Shared Reading Collection*	Text Sets from *Fountas & Pinnell Classroom™ Interactive Read-Aloud Collection*	Reading Minilessons (RML) Umbrellas	Writing Minilessons (WML) Umbrellas	Teaching Suggestions for Extending Learning
Months 1 & 2 (cont.)	Smokey Bear: A True Story		MGT.U3: Engaging in Classroom Literacy Work	WPS.U1: Getting Ideas for Writing Through Storytelling, WML1–WML2 (2 days)	WPS.U1 helps children get to know one another and continue to build community while generating ideas for writing through oral storytelling. Teach the minilessons in WPS.U1 over several days so that children have time to tell stories in between the lessons. Use the time you usually take to teach a minilesson to give children the opportunity to tell their stories. You can also invite them to tell their stories in partnerships and small groups.
				MGT.U2: Using Drawing and Writing Tools (3 days)	MGT.U2 can be taught in conjunction with GEN.U1. You may choose to teach it before or integrate it with the lessons in GEN.U1. Children can apply what they learn about using drawing and writing tools to the picture books they are making.
	Side by Side: A True Story			GEN.U1: Getting Started with Making Books (4 days)	Invite and encourage children to make books about anything they want. Suggest that they draw and write the stories they have been sharing orally and collecting on their ideas lists.
		Finding Your Way in a New Place		CFT.U11: Learning to Draw (5 days)	The lessons in CFT.U11 support children in making representational drawings as well as in learning new drawing techniques. The lessons can be applied as children continue to make books.
			LA.U1: Thinking and Talking About Books	WPS.U11: Adding Book and Print Features, WML1 (1 day)	The first minilesson in WPS.U11 helps children think about how to choose titles and make covers for their picture books. Teach the remaining minilessons throughout the rest of the year.
				MGT.U3: Establishing Independent Writing (6 days)	We suggest introducing MGT.U3 after children have had time to experiment with bookmaking so they understand one way to use their time during independent writing. Once children are comfortable with the routine of making books at an established time of day, it will be easy to establish the routines for independent writing.

Months	Texts from *Fountas & Pinnell Classroom™ Shared Reading Collection*	Text Sets from *Fountas & Pinnell Classroom™ Interactive Read-Aloud Collection*	Reading Minilessons (RML) Umbrellas	Writing Minilessons (WML) Umbrellas	Teaching Suggestions for Extending Learning
Months 1 & 2 (cont.)			LA.U22: Understanding Plot	**MGT.U4: Introducing Writing Folder Resources (3 days)**	Introduce writing folder resources whenever you think children will find them helpful. Children are more likely to use the resources once they are comfortable with the routines of independent writing and bookmaking. They can keep the books they are making in their writing folders.
		Memory Stories		**GEN.U8: Writing Poetry, WML1 (1 day)**	Teach the lessons in GEN.U8 over time so you are teaching about poetry throughout the year. You may want to establish a time weekly to explore poetry during writers' workshop. The first lesson in GEN.U8 introduces children to their own poetry books—a place to collect, illustrate, write, and respond to poetry.
				CNV.U1: Using Good Handwriting (3 days)	Repeat the lessons in this umbrella as needed across the year.
				WPS.U1: Getting Ideas for Writing Through Storytelling, WML3–WML4 (2 days)	Teach the rest of WPS.U1 to infuse more storytelling into the classroom in preparation for writing memory books. Help children see that the stories they tell about their memories can be made into books. Provide time in between these lessons for children to tell their stories. For example, for a few days, start writing time with storytelling instead of teaching a minilesson.
		Tomie dePaola: Writing from Life	LA.U3: Studying Authors and Illustrators, RML1	**GEN.U2: Making Memory Books (5 days)**	Encourage children to revisit stories they have told (WPS.U1) to get ideas for their memory books. Invite children to write several memory books over a couple of weeks. Revisit this umbrella throughout the year as you build more complex understandings of reading and writing. Later in the year, children will use a writer's notebook to help generate ideas for more memory books.
			SAS.U1: Monitoring, Searching, and Self-Correcting	**CFT.U4: Adding Dialogue to Writing (3 days)**	Invite children to add dialogue to the memory books they are making. You may also want to teach CNV.U3.WML2, which addresses how to punctuate dialogue. Alternatively, you can revisit the use of quotation marks when you teach the entire CNV.U3 umbrella a little later in the year.

Months	Texts from *Fountas & Pinnell Classroom™ Shared Reading Collection*	Text Sets from *Fountas & Pinnell Classroom™ Interactive Read-Aloud Collection*	Reading Minilessons (RML) Umbrellas	Writing Minilessons (WML) Umbrellas	Teaching Suggestions for Extending Learning
Months 1 & 2 (cont.)			LA.U23: Understanding Characters' Feelings, Motivations, and Intentions	**CNV.U2: Learning How to Write Words (5 days)**	Teach this umbrella all at once or teach each lesson based on need. Revisit the minilessons later in the year as needed. Encourage children to apply what they learn about writing words directly to the pieces they are writing.
				WPS.U12: Celebrating Writing (3 days)	Through this umbrella, children learn that they can celebrate their writing in several ways: share a piece with an audience, celebrate a risk they have taken in their writing, or publish their writing more formally. They can apply these lessons to any type of writing they have completed, or you might want to use this umbrella as an opportunity for children to specifically celebrate their memory books.
Months 3 & 4	Weather Watch: Rita's Journal	Exploring the Natural World: Insects		**CFT.U1: Reading Like a Writer and Illustrator (3 days)**	This umbrella helps children look at the decisions writers and illustrators make. They can apply these lessons to whatever writing they are currently working on, including memory books. This umbrella builds on the author studies they may have experienced if you are using *The Reading Minilessons Book, Grade 2*.
	A Raindrop's Journey	Exploring Narrative Nonfiction Texts	LA.U12: Studying Narrative Nonfiction	**GEN.U8: Writing Poetry, WML2 (1 day)**	The second lesson in GEN.U8 recommends using texts that are introduced later in the year based on the sequence for the *Interactive Read-Aloud Collection*. Read the recommended books ahead of this umbrella and then repeat them as part of the text set later in the year. They offer strong examples of poetry that students will benefit from hearing more than once across the year.
				WPS.U2: Learning About My First Writer's Notebook (5 days)	Once children have had several experiences making books, you might choose to introduce the writer's notebook as a tool for generating and trying out new ideas for writing.

Suggested Sequence of Lessons (cont.)

Months	Texts from *Fountas & Pinnell Classroom™ Shared Reading Collection*	Text Sets from *Fountas & Pinnell Classroom™ Interactive Read-Aloud Collection*	Reading Minilessons (RML) Umbrellas	Writing Minilessons (WML) Umbrellas	Teaching Suggestions for Extending Learning
Months 3 & 4 (cont.)	Paws and Claws		LA.U6: Understanding Fiction and Nonfiction Genres	**WPS.U7: Rehearsing Your Writing, WML1 (1 day)**	After children have begun collecting ideas in their writer's notebooks and have reread their writer's notebooks for ideas (WPS.U2), invite them to orally rehearse the story they plan to write before they write it down. This lesson builds on the oral storytelling they have done through WPS.U1. In this lesson, they learn that it is helpful to say your story before you write it. We recommend teaching the other lessons in this umbrella when you introduce informational (all-about books) and procedural (how-to books) writing, respectively.
	Inside a Cow				
	Night of the Ghost Crabs		WAR.U1: Introducing a Reader's Notebook	**CFT.U5: Exploring Different Ways Authors Start Books (6 days)**	Children can apply these lessons to any type of writing they are drafting or revising, or they can revisit old pieces of writing to try out new ideas. Invite children to use their writer's notebooks to try different beginnings before adding them to their books.
	The Amazing Seahorse	Seymour Simon: A Scientific Eye		**WPS.U8: Adding Information to Your Writing (6 days)**	Use WPS.U8 to teach practical ways to add details (e.g., use a caret mark, attach a strip of paper). Teach this umbrella to help students learn how to revise their writing by adding details to the important parts of their writing. Children can apply these lessons to the stories they are writing. Teach and revisit lessons on revision whenever students need them.
			LA.U3: Studying Authors and Illustrators, RML1	**CNV.U3: Learning About Punctuation (5 days)**	This umbrella supports children in editing their work for punctuation. These lessons can be revisited throughout the year. You may also choose to teach the lesson on using quotation marks earlier, when you introduce dialogue. Children can apply these lessons to anything they are currently writing or revisit books they have written to apply the minilessons.
	Big Bites			Revisit **WPS.U12: Celebrating Writing (1 day)**	Revisit any of the lessons in WPS.U12 to give children the choice to publish any of the books they have been making or to celebrate new things they are trying in their writing.

Months	Texts from *Fountas & Pinnell Classroom™ Shared Reading Collection*	Text Sets from *Fountas & Pinnell Classroom™ Interactive Read-Aloud Collection*	Reading Minilessons (RML) Umbrellas	Writing Minilessons (WML) Umbrellas	Teaching Suggestions for Extending Learning
Months 3 & 4 (cont.)		Finding Beauty in the World Around You	LA.U2: Expressing Opinions About Books, RML1–RML3	**GEN.U8: Writing Poetry, WML3 (1 day)**	GEN.U8.WML3 helps students broaden their definition and understanding of poetry. Invite them to continue to build their poetry books by collecting and responding to poems and writing their own poems.
	Busy Beavers			**WPS.U3: Gathering Ideas for Informational Writing (4 days)**	Invite children to gather ideas in their writer's notebooks in preparation for making all-about books. It is important to note that children will not necessarily write about all the ideas gathered through this umbrella; rather, the minilessons encourage them to explore various topics of interest.
		The Pleasure of Giving		**WPS.U7: Rehearsing Your Writing, WML2 (1 day)**	Teach this minilesson either before or alongside GEN.U3 when you teach children how to take notes in their own words.
				GEN.U3: Making All-About Books (5 days)	The first lesson in this umbrella invites children to read through their writer's notebooks to find a topic for an all-about book. Encourage children to make several all-about books over the next several days.
	Bigger or Smaller?		LA.U4: Giving a Book Talk	**CFT.U9: Using Text Features in Nonfiction Writing, WML1–WML2 (2 days)**	Choose whether to introduce how to make headings and a table of contents as children are making all-about books. Some children find that writing headings helps them organize their information into categories. Alternatively, wait to teach the entire umbrella later in the year after you teach reading minilessons about text features. If you choose to introduce these concepts now, introduce a few of the texts that would come later in the year according to the sequence. We recommend reading them both now and as part of their text set later.
				CFT.U10: Expanding Nonfiction Writing (4 days)	Encourage children to apply the minilessons from this umbrella to the all-about books they are making. If you have the *Shared Reading Collection*, read *The Perfect Beak* before this lesson and again later in the year.

Months	Texts from *Fountas & Pinnell Classroom™ Shared Reading Collection*	Text Sets from *Fountas & Pinnell Classroom™ Interactive Read-Aloud Collection*	Reading Minilessons (RML) Umbrellas	Writing Minilessons (WML) Umbrellas	Teaching Suggestions for Extending Learning
Months 3 & 4 (cont.)			WAR.U2: Using a Reader's Notebook	**CFT.U13: Using Illustrations and Graphics in Nonfiction Writing (2–5 days)**	The lessons in this umbrella can be applied to the all-about books students are making. If you are using *The Reading Minilessons Book, Grade 2*, consider waiting to teach WML3–WML5 until later in the year when you teach reading minilessons about illustrations and graphics. If your students are ready, teach the entire umbrella now and use reading minilessons to revisit these ideas later in the year. You will also want to read *Eaglets in the Nest* (if you have the *Shared Reading Collection*) before this umbrella and again at the end of the year.
				CFT.U6: Exploring Different Ways Authors End Books (4 days)	Children can apply the minilessons in CFT.U6 to both fiction and nonfiction writing. You may want them to try different endings for their all-about books in their writer's notebooks. Alternatively, they can revisit other pieces of writing to try new endings. Revisit this umbrella throughout the year to give children the opportunity to try a variety of endings for different types of writing.
			LA.U5: Getting Started with Book Clubs	**WPS.U9: Revising to Focus and Organize Writing, WML1 (1 day)**	This umbrella can be taught over the course of the year based on the needs of your students. The lessons in this umbrella support children in learning different reasons to revise their work. Invite children to apply this lesson to writing they have already drafted, helping them learn that writers revise their writing.
				CNV.U4: Using Capital Letters (4 days)	This umbrella can be taught at any time of the year based on students' needs. Notice that this umbrella uses books from the *Shared Reading Collection* introduced later in the sequence. It is not necessary to read these books ahead of this umbrella because the lessons are not tied to the content of the books. Children can apply these lessons to the books they are making or to writing in their writer's notebooks.

Months	Texts from *Fountas & Pinnell Classroom*™ *Shared Reading Collection*	Text Sets from *Fountas & Pinnell Classroom*™ *Interactive Read-Aloud Collection*	Reading Minilessons (RML) Umbrellas	Writing Minilessons (WML) Umbrellas	Teaching Suggestions for Extending Learning
Months 3 & 4 (cont.)				Revisit **WPS.U12: Celebrating Writing (1 day)**	Choose any one of the minilessons in WPS.U12 to help children celebrate their writing. Invite them to celebrate one of the all-about books they have written.
Months 5 & 6	Stone Soup: An Old Tale	Jan Brett: Creating Imaginary Worlds	WAR.U3: Writing Letters About Reading	**GEN.U7: Writing Friendly Letters (3 days)**	If you are using *The Reading Minilessons Book, Grade 2*, this umbrella will support and build on understandings developed in WAR.U3. Children can apply the lessons they learn in GEN.U7 to writing any type of friendly letter. If you choose, invite them to write letters about their reading in a reader's notebook. Respond with letters of your own that stretch children's thinking.
	The Boy Who Cried Wolf: An Aesop Fable		LA.U3: Studying Authors and Illustrators, RML1	**WPS.U4: Gathering Ideas for Memory Writing (3 days)**	Use WPS.U4 with writer's notebooks to help children generate and record more ideas for memory books or small-moment writing.
	The Blind Men and the Elephant: A Tale from India	Exploring Different Cultures: Folktales		Revisit **GEN.U2: Making Memory Books (1–5 days)**	Select lessons from GEN.U2 that would be beneficial to review with your students as they revisit memory writing. Encourage children to write several memory books over several days.
	Watch Out, Rabbit! An Indonesian Tale		LA.U26: Studying Illustrations in Fiction Books	**CFT.U12: Adding Information to Illustrations (5 days)**	Encourage children to apply these lessons to their memory books.
	Jackal and Lion: An African Folktale	Exploring Trickster Tales	SAS.U2: Solving Words	**CFT.U7: Making Powerful Word Choices (5 days)**	Children can apply these lessons to their memory books or to any type of writing. Word choice is particularly important in poetry. Encourage children to apply the minilessons to poems they write in their poetry books as well. If you are using *The Reading Minilessons Book, Grade 2*, LA.U9: Analyzing the Writer's Craft also addresses aspects of word choice. You might choose to teach some of these lessons now or teach them later in the sequence to reinforce and revisit these concepts.
			LA.U19: Studying Trickster Tales		

Months	Texts from *Fountas & Pinnell Classroom™ Shared Reading Collection*	Text Sets from *Fountas & Pinnell Classroom™ Interactive Read-Aloud Collection*	Reading Minilessons (RML) Umbrellas	Writing Minilessons (WML) Umbrellas	Teaching Suggestions for Extending Learning
Months 5 & 6 (cont.)	Monkey and Rabbit: A Tale from Brazil		LA.U21: Thinking About Where Stories Take Place	**CFT.U3: Crafting a Setting (3 days)**	If you are using *The Reading Minilessons Book, Grade 2*, CFT.U3 will complement LA.U21. Invite children to think about setting in the memory books they are writing.
	Bananas, Bananas: Based on a Philippine Folktale			**WPS.U9: Revising to Focus and Organize Writing, WML2–WML3 (2 days)**	WPS.U9.WML2 will help children apply what they have learned in CFT.U7 to revising their writing. WML3 offers a suggestion for revising on a bigger scale. Invite children to choose one of their memory stories to apply this revision technique. Revisit these lessons whenever students need them.
				Revisit **CNV.U2: Learning How to Write Words (1–5 days)**	Revisit one or more minilessons in CNV.U2 as needed.
	Sun, Wind, and Moon: A Tale From India		WAR.U4: Writing About Fiction Books in a Reader's Notebook (RML1–RML4)	**WPS.U10: Editing and Proofreading Writing (5 days)**	Teach the lessons in WPS.U10 whenever they would be most helpful for your students. We recommend this umbrella at this point in the sequence because children can use what they have learned from minilessons about conventions. Invite them to apply the minilessons in WPS.U10 when they prepare to publish a book.
	The Tricky Turtle: A Hopi Tale	Humorous Characters		Revisit **WPS.U12: Celebrating Writing (1 day)**	Revisit any of the lessons in WPS.U12 as needed or simply provide a time to celebrate student writing. Consider inviting another class, sharing with administrators, or hosting a writing celebration with families.
				Revisit **WPS.U3: Gathering Ideas for Informational Writing, WML2 (1 day)**	In preparation for procedural writing (e.g., writing how-to books), revisit WPS.U3.WML2 to help students brainstorm topics that are familiar and interesting.
	A Piñata Fiesta			**WPS.U7: Rehearsing Your Writing, WML3 (1 day)**	Teach this minilesson either before or alongside GEN.U4 to help children orally rehearse steps in a sequence before writing them.
				GEN.U4: Making How-to Books (3 days)	Encourage children to make several how-to books on a variety of topics.

Months	Texts from *Fountas & Pinnell Classroom™ Shared Reading Collection*	Text Sets from *Fountas & Pinnell Classroom™ Interactive Read-Aloud Collection*	Reading Minilessons (RML) Umbrellas	Writing Minilessons (WML) Umbrellas	Teaching Suggestions for Extending Learning
Months 5 & 6 [cont.]		Helen Lester: Learning a Lesson	LA.U11: Noticing Text Resources	Revisit **CFT.U5: Exploring Different Ways Authors Start Books (1–6 days)**	Revisit any of the lessons in CFT.U5 to help students learn to make their writing more interesting.
				WPS.U9: Revising to Focus and Organize Writing, WML4 (1 day)	Invite children to apply this lesson to one of their how-to books. Sequence and order is particularly important in procedural writing. Revisit this lesson to help children see how it also applies to other genres and forms. Review any other lessons in WPS.U9 that you think would help your students revise their writing.
				Revisit any **Conventions** lessons that apply or **WPS.U10: Editing and Proofreading Writing (1–3 days)**	After children have had the opportunity to revise their writing, encourage them to proofread and edit one of their how-to books. Revisit any of the Conventions lessons or WPS.U10 to support them in the editing and proofreading process.
				WPS.U11: Adding Book and Print Features, WML2– WML3 (2 days)	If you are using *The Reading Minilessons Book, Grade 2*, LA.U11 works well with WPS.U11 to provide children with a strong understanding of text resources and how to use them in their own writing.
			LA.U3: Studying Authors and Illustrators (RML1– RML2)	Revisit **WPS.U12: Celebrating Writing (1 day)**	Revisit any of the lessons in WPS.U12 as needed. Provide a time to celebrate student writing. For example, you might invite students to use their how-to books to teach an audience how to do something.
Months 7 & 8		Facing Challenges	SAS.U3: Maintaining Fluency	**GEN.U10: Experimenting with Writing in New Ways, WML1 (1 day)**	This minilesson helps children see that they can use the same topic for different types of writing. The next umbrella helps them think about their purpose and audience to determine the type of writing they want to do.
		The Importance of Determination	LA.U24: Understanding Character Traits	**WPS.U5: Thinking About Purpose and Audience (3 days)**	It is important to give students plenty of opportunities to select their own genres for writing based on their purpose and audience. Children will revisit the idea of purpose and audience in reading minilessons LA.U7 and LA.U8 toward the end of the year. Over the next couple of weeks, encourage children to write several different pieces, possibly based on ideas in their writer's notebooks.

Months	Texts from *Fountas & Pinnell Classroom™ Shared Reading Collection*	Text Sets from *Fountas & Pinnell Classroom™ Interactive Read-Aloud Collection*	Reading Minilessons (RML) Umbrellas	Writing Minilessons (WML) Umbrellas	Teaching Suggestions for Extending Learning
Months 7 & 8 (cont.)	Rain Forest Surprises Surprises on a Coral Reef Surprises on the Savanna	Simple Biography	WAR.U4: Writing About Fiction Books in a Reader's Notebook, RML5–RML6	**CFT.U8: Writing with Voice in Fiction and Nonfiction (3 days)**	Invite children to apply the lessons in CFT.U8 to the writing they are doing. Alternatively, you may choose to introduce this later in the year along with reading minilesson umbrella LA.U10: Looking Closely at Print. It will be important to revisit this aspect of writing more than once from the perspective of both reading and writing.
			LA.U25: Thinking About Character Change	**CFT.U14: Making Illustrations Interesting, WML1–WML2 (2 days)**	CFT.U14 offers students different ways to craft their illustrations and books. Introduce these lessons over time so students have time to experiment with the ideas and you can provide them with the materials they need.
			WAR.U4: Writing About Fiction Books in a Reader's Notebook, RML7	**WPS.U11: Adding Book and Print Features, WML4 (1 day)**	Children can use some of the techniques they have learned in CFT.U14 to make endpapers for their books. Invite them to make endpapers for a book they are currently working on or to add them to a book they have finished.
				Revisit **WPS.U12: Celebrating Writing (1 day)**	Revisit any of the lessons from WPS.U12 as needed. Provide an opportunity to celebrate writing within your classroom or with an external audience (e.g., parents, administrators, another class)
		Gail Gibbons: Exploring the World Through Nonfiction	LA.U13: Understanding Simple Biography	**GEN.U10: Experimenting with Writing in New Ways, WML2–WML3 (2 days)**	Continue to teach GEN.U10 over time to inspire new writing in the classroom. Children will have fun playing with some of these new ideas.
			LA.U3: Studying Authors and Illustrators, RML1	**WPS.U6: Observing and Writing Like a Scientist (3 days)**	Besides helping children write about scientific experiments, WPS.U6 can also inspire ideas for future nonfiction writing. You may also introduce this type of writing earlier in the year if it supports science activities in your classroom.
		Exploring the Natural World: The Earth		**GEN.U8: Writing Poetry, WML4 (1 day)**	After children have had the opportunity to observe and write like scientists, help them to see that close observation can also give them ideas for poetry (WML4). You may need to pull from texts that are listed a little later in the *Interactive Read-Aloud Collection*, but children will benefit from hearing these texts multiple times across the year.

Months	Texts from *Fountas & Pinnell Classroom™ Shared Reading Collection*	Text Sets from *Fountas & Pinnell Classroom™ Interactive Read-Aloud Collection*	Reading Minilessons (RML) Umbrellas	Writing Minilessons (WML) Umbrellas	Teaching Suggestions for Extending Learning
Months 7 & 8 (cont.)			LA.U15: Thinking About the Topic in Nonfiction Books	Revisit **WPS.U3: Gathering Ideas for Informational Writing, WML1–WML3** (1–3 days)	Revisit any or all of the first three minilessons in WPS.U3 to inspire more writing ideas for informational writing. Invite children to use their writer's notebooks to collect ideas.
				GEN.U6: Making Slide Presentations (5 days)	Ask children to reread their writer's notebooks for ideas for a slide presentation. You can also ask them to revisit their writing about scientific experiments (WPS.U6) to put into presentation form. Encourage children to make a few slide presentations about a variety of topics.
				GEN.U5: Making Question-and-Answer Books (5 days)	GEN.U5 offers children the opportunity to explore another text structure for organizing and telling information in nonfiction writing.
				CFT.U9: Using Text Features in Nonfiction Writing, WML3–WML4 (2 days)	If your children are ready, teach them how to use sidebars and captions to provide more information in their question-and-answer books. Alternatively, you can wait until later in the year when you teach about text features in reading minilessons (LA.U17).
				Revisit **WPS.U8: Adding Information to Your Writing** (1–3 days)	Revisit any of the lessons in WPS.U8 to help children revise their writing. They can apply these lessons to the question-and-answer books they are writing.
			WAR.U5: Writing About Nonfiction Books in a Reader's Notebook, RML1–RML3	Revisit **WPS.U10: Editing and Proofreading Writing** (1–5 days)	Revisit any of the lessons in WPS.U10 to help children edit their writing. Invite them to apply these lessons to one of the question-and-answer books they are writing.
				Revisit **WPS.U12: Celebrating Writing** (1 day)	Revisit one of the lessons in WPS.U12 as needed or simply provide a time for children to celebrate their writing with an audience. Encourage them to celebrate one of their question-and-answer books.
				GEN.U8: Writing Poetry, WML5 (1 day)	Invite children to apply WML5 to writing poems in their poetry books. Help children understand that some of what they learn about poetry can also be applied to other forms of writing.

Months	Texts from *Fountas & Pinnell Classroom™ Shared Reading Collection*	Text Sets from *Fountas & Pinnell Classroom™ Interactive Read-Aloud Collection*	Reading Minilessons (RML) Umbrellas	Writing Minilessons (WML) Umbrellas	Teaching Suggestions for Extending Learning
Months 9 & 10	Fur, Feathers, and More The Perfect Beak Eaglets in the Nest Amazing Nests	Living and Working Together: Community Exploring the Natural World: Birds	LA.U7: Thinking About the Author's Message SAS.U4: Summarizing LA.U8: Thinking About the Author's Purpose LA.U9: Analyzing the Writer's Craft LA.U14: Noticing How Authors Organize Nonfiction WAR.U5: Writing About Nonfiction Books in a Reader's Notebook (RML4–RML6)	**GEN.U10: Experimenting with Writing in New Ways, WML4 (1 day)**	This last minilesson in GEN.10 offers a new way for children to think about writing. WML4 invites them to think about different ways to communicate a message. If you are using *The Reading Minilessons Book, Grade 2*, this lesson will be a nice complement to learning about author's message in LA.U7.
				Revisit **WPS.U5: Thinking About Purpose and Audience (3 days)**	By this point in the year, children have a large repertoire of familiar genres and forms. Encourage them to choose the genre and form that fit their purpose and audience. Revisiting these lessons will also complement LA.U8 if you are using *The Reading Minilessons Book, Grade 2*.
				Revisit any **Craft** umbrellas **(1–3 days)**	Support children as they experiment with various genres and forms. Revisit craft lessons that support children in their writing work.
				Revisit any lessons in the **Conventions** umbrellas **(1–3 days)**	Support children as they experiment with various genres and forms by revisiting Conventions lessons.
				Revisit **WPS.U12: Celebrating Writing (1 day)**	Revisit WPS.U12 or simply provide an opportunity for students to share one of the pieces they have written.
				GEN.U8: Writing Poetry, WML6 (1 day)	WML6 offers new ways to inspire poetry writing. When you infuse your classroom with poetry throughout the year, you see it permeate all genres and forms of writing.
				Revisit **WPS.U3: Gathering Ideas for Informational Writing (1–3 days)**	Revisit WPS.U3 to gather more ideas for informational writing.
				Revisit **GEN.U3: Making All-About Books (1–5 days)**	Invite children to revisit Making All-About Books now that they have had exposure over the course of the year to different nonfiction text features and graphics.

Months	Texts from *Fountas & Pinnell Classroom™ Shared Reading Collection*	Text Sets from *Fountas & Pinnell Classroom™ Interactive Read-Aloud Collection*	Reading Minilessons (RML) Umbrellas	Writing Minilessons (WML) Umbrellas	Teaching Suggestions for Extending Learning
Months 9 & 10 (cont.)			LA.U17: Using Text Features to Gain Information	Revisit **CFT.U9: Using Text Features in Nonfiction Writing (1–4 days)**	If you are using *The Reading Minilessons Book, Grade 2*, LA.U16 and LA.U17 provide children with opportunities to look at nonfiction text features and graphics as readers. Revisiting CFT.U9 and CFT.U13 will reinforce children's ability to use graphics and text features as writers.
			LA.U16: Learning Information from Illustrations and Graphics	Revisit **CFT.U13: Using Illustrations and Graphics in Nonfiction Writing (1–5 days)**	Revisit CFT.U13 as needed to help students integrate graphics, such as maps, close-ups, and diagrams, into their all-about books.
				WPS.U9: Revising to Focus and Organize Writing, WML5 (1 day)	Teach children how to revise their writing to group similar ideas. Invite children to apply this lesson to their all-about books.
	Scout, the Chicken Guard	Amazing Places: The World of Fantasy	WAR.U5: Writing About Nonfiction Books in a Reader's Notebook (RML7, RML8)	Revisit **WPS.U11: Adding Book and Print Features (1–4 days)**	In preparation for publishing a piece of writing, perhaps an all-about book, children might choose to add a book or print feature. Revisit any lesson from WPS.U11 to support them in doing so.
				Revisit **WPS.U12: Celebrating Writing (1 day)**	Invite children to celebrate one of their all-about books. Revisit any lessons from WPS.U12 as needed.
			LA.U20: Understanding Fantasy	Revisit **WPS.U4: Gathering Ideas for Memory Writing (1–3 days)**	Teach WPS.U4 to inspire new ideas for narrative writing. The minilessons in this umbrella will help children think about real-life events that they may be able to turn into realistic fiction stories (see GEN.U9).
		Exploring Realistic Fiction	LA.U18: Studying Realistic Fiction	**GEN.U9: Writing Fiction (5 days)**	Children will love having the opportunity to write short fiction. Building on what they know about narrative writing from their memory stories, GEN.U9 helps them understand some of the important elements of fiction. After children have had the opportunity to write realistic fiction, you might invite them to try writing fantasy.
			LA.U2: Expressing Opinions About Books (RML4, RML5)	**CFT.U2: Describing Characters (4 days)**	Encourage children to apply the lessons in CFT.U2 to their realistic fiction stories.

Months	Texts from *Fountas & Pinnell Classroom™ Shared Reading Collection*	Text Sets from *Fountas & Pinnell Classroom™ Interactive Read-Aloud Collection*	Reading Minilessons (RML) Umbrellas	Writing Minilessons (WML) Umbrellas	Teaching Suggestions for Extending Learning
Months 9 & 10 (cont.)		Steve Jenkins: Exploring the Animal World	LA.U3: Studying Authors and Illustrators, RML1, RML3	Revisit **CFT.U3: Crafting a Setting** if needed **(1–3 days)**	Revisit CFT.U3 as needed to help children develop the setting of their fiction texts.
			LA.U10: Looking Closely at Print	Revisit **CFT.U8: Writing with Voice in Fiction and Nonfiction (3 days)**	Use the lessons in CFT.U8 to emphasize the importance of voice in writing. These lessons work together with LA.U10 from *The Reading Minilessons Book, Grade 2,* to reinforce how authors use punctuation and print to create voice.
				Revisit **WPS.U8: Adding Information to Your Writing** and/or **WPS.U9: Revising to Focus and Organize Writing (1–4 days)**	Choose any of the revision lessons from WPS.U8 and WPS.U9 that will benefit your students.
				CFT.U14: Making Illustrations Interesting, WML3– WML5 (3 days)	Use the last three minilessons in CFT.U14 to give children options for making their illustrations more appealing to their readers. Invite children to apply what they learn to realistic fiction books or any other genre they are writing.
				Revisit **WPS.U10: Editing and Proofreading Writing (1–3 days)**	Choose any lessons from WPS.U10 that would benefit children. Invite them to apply the lessons to a realistic fiction book they want to publish for the classroom library.
				GEN.U8: Writing Poetry, WML7 (1 day)	Teach children another way to get ideas for writing poetry through the last minilesson in GEN.U8.
				Revisit **WPS.U12: Celebrating Writing (1 day)**	Revisit WPS.U12 as needed. Provide a time for children to celebrate what they have learned as writers across the year.

Glossary

all-about book A nonfiction book that tells about only one subject or topic.

alphabet book/ABC book A book that helps children develop the concept and sequence of the alphabet by pairing alphabet letters with pictures of people, animals, or objects with labels related to the letters.

alphabet linking chart A chart containing upper- and lowercase letters of the alphabet paired with pictures representing words beginning with each letter (*a*, *apple*, for example).

assessment A means for gathering information or data that reveals what learners control, partially control, or do not yet control consistently.

audience The readers of a text. Often a writer crafts a text with a particular audience in mind.

behaviors Actions that are observable as children read or write.

bold / boldface Type that is heavier and darker than usual, often used for emphasis.

book and print features The physical attributes of a text (for example, font, layout, and length). Also, elements of a book (for example, acknowledgments, author page, dedication, and endpapers).

character An individual, usually a person or animal, in a text.

chronological sequence An underlying structural pattern used especially in nonfiction texts to describe a series of events in the order they happened in time.

compose Think about the message and how to say it.

concepts of print Basic understandings related to how written language or print is organized and used—how it works.

construct Write the message that has been composed together; includes sharing the pen.

conventions In writing, formal usage that has become customary in written language. Grammar, usage, capitalization, punctuation, spelling, handwriting, and text layout are categories of writing conventions.

craft In writing, how an individual piece of writing is shaped. Elements of craft are organization, idea development, language use, word choice, and voice. See also *voice*.

dialogue Spoken words, usually set off with quotation marks in text.

directionality The orientation of print (in the English language, from left to right).

directions (how-to) Part of a procedural nonfiction text that shows the steps involved in performing a task. A set of directions may include diagrams or drawings with labels. See also *how-to book*.

drafting and revising The process of getting ideas down on paper and shaping them to convey the writer's message.

drawing In writing, creating a rough image (i.e, a drawing) of a person, place, thing, or idea to capture, work with, and render the writer's ideas.

editing and proofreading The process of polishing the final draft of a written composition to prepare it for publication.

elements of fiction Important elements of fiction include narrator, characters, plot, setting, theme, and style.

elements of poetry Important elements of poetry include figurative language, imagery, personification, rhythm, rhyme, repetition, alliteration, assonance, consonance, onomatopoeia, and aspects of layout.

English learners People whose native language is not English and who are acquiring English as an additional language.

family, friends, and school story A contemporary realistic text focused on the everyday experiences of children of a variety of ages, including relationships with family and friends and experiences at school.

fiction Invented, imaginative prose or poetry that tells a story. Fiction texts can be organized into the categories realism and fantasy. Along with nonfiction, fiction is one of two basic genres of literature.

figurative language An element of a writer's style, figurative language changes or goes beyond literal meaning. Two common types of figurative language are metaphor (a direct comparison) and simile (a comparison that uses *like* or *as*).

font In printed text, the collection of type (letters) in a particular style.

form A kind of text that is characterized by particular elements. Mystery, for example, is a form of writing within the realistic fiction genre. Another term for form is *subgenre*.

friendly letter In writing, a functional nonfiction text usually addressed to friends or family that may take the form of notes, letters, invitations, or email.

functional text A nonfiction text intended to accomplish a practical task, for example, labels, lists, letters, and directions with steps (how-to).

genre A category of written text that is characterized by a particular style, form, or content.

graphic feature In fiction texts, graphic features are usually illustrations. In nonfiction texts, graphic features include photographs, paintings and drawings, charts, diagrams, tables and graphs, maps, and timelines.

guided writing Instructional support for a small, temporary group of writers who have similar needs.

high-frequency words Words that occur often in spoken and written language (for example, *the*).

how-to book A procedural nonfiction text that describes the procedure for making or doing something. It often includes a list of materials, ordered steps, and illustrations.

illustration Graphic representation of important content (for example, art, photos, maps, graphs, charts) in a fiction or nonfiction text.

independent writing A text written by children independently with teacher support as needed. Also, a time during writers' workshop for children to write on their own.

informational text A nonfiction text in which a purpose is to inform or give facts about a topic. Informational texts include the following genres: biography, autobiography, memoir, and narrative nonfiction, as well as expository texts, procedural texts, and persuasive texts.

innovate on a text Change the ending, the series of events, the characters, or the setting of a familiar text.

interactive read-aloud An instructional context in which students are actively listening and responding to an oral reading of a text.

interactive writing A teaching context in which the teacher and students cooperatively plan, compose, and write a group text; both teacher and students act as scribes (in turn).

italic (italics) A styling of type that is characterized by slanted letters.

label A written word or phrase that names the content of an illustration.

layout The way the print and illustrations are arranged on a page.

learning zone The level at which it is most productive to aim one's teaching for each student (the zone of proximal development).

lowercase letter A small letterform that is usually different from its corresponding capital or uppercase form.

main idea The central underlying idea, concept, or message that the author conveys in a nonfiction text. See also *message*.

memory story A story about something experienced personally.

mentor texts Books or other texts that serve as examples of excellent writing. Mentor texts are read and reread to provide models for literature discussion and student writing.

message An important idea that an author conveys in a fiction or nonfiction text. See also *main idea*.

modeled writing An instructional technique in which a teacher demonstrates the process of composing a particular genre, making the process explicit for students.

nonfiction Prose or poetry that provides factual information. According to their structures, nonfiction texts can be organized into the categories of narrative and nonnarrative. Along with fiction, nonfiction is one of the two basic genres of literature.

organization The arrangement of ideas in a text according to a logical structure, either narrative or nonnarrative. Another term for organization is *text structure*.

organizational tools and sources of information A design feature of nonfiction texts. Organizational tools and sources of information help a reader process and understand nonfiction texts. Examples include tables of contents, headings, indexes, glossaries, appendices, author bios, and references.

picture book An illustrated fiction or nonfiction text in which pictures work with the text to tell a story or provide information.

planning and rehearsing The process of collecting, working with, and selecting ideas for a written composition.

plot The events, action, conflict, and resolution of a story presented in a certain order in a fiction text. A simple plot progresses chronologically from start to end, whereas more complex plots may shift back and forth in time.

poetry Compact, metrical writing characterized by imagination and artistry and imbued with intense meaning. Along with prose, poetry is one of the two broad categories into which all literature can be divided.

principle A generalization that is predictable. It is the key idea that children will learn and be invited to apply.

print feature In nonfiction texts, features that include the color, size, style, and font of type, as well as various aspects of layout.

procedural text A nonfiction text that explains how to do something. Procedural texts are almost always organized in temporal sequence and take the form of directions (or how-to texts) or descriptions of a process.

prompt A question, direction, or statement designed to encourage the child to say more about a topic.

publishing The process of making the final draft of a written composition public.

punctuation Marks used in written text to clarify meaning and separate structural units. The comma and the period are common punctuation marks.

purpose A writer's overall intention in creating a text, or a reader's overall intention in reading a text. To tell a story is one example of a writer's purpose, and to be entertained is one example of a reader's purpose.

question and answer A structural pattern used especially in nonfiction texts to organize information in a series of questions with responses. Question-and-answer texts may be based on a verbal or written interview or on frequently arising or logical questions about a topic.

repetition Repeated words or phrases that help create rhythm and emphasis in poetry or prose.

rhyme The repetition of vowel and consonant sounds in the stressed and unstressed syllables of words in verse, especially at the ends of lines.

rhythm The regular or ordered repetition of stressed and unstressed syllables in poetry, other writing, or speech.

sequence See *chronological sequence* and *temporal sequence*.

setting The place and time in which a fiction text or biographical text takes place.

share the pen At points selected by the teacher for instructional value, individual children take over or "share the pen" with the teacher.

shared reading An instructional context in which the teacher involves a group of students in the reading of a particular big book to introduce aspects of literacy (such as print conventions), develop reading strategies (such as decoding or predicting), and teach vocabulary.

shared writing An instructional context in which the teacher involves a group of students in the composing of a coherent text together. The teacher writes while scaffolding children's language and ideas.

sidebar Information that is additional to the main text, placed alongside the text and sometimes set off from the main text in a box.

slide presentation A series of slides or pages often prepared on a computer and presented on a screen. Slides contain minimal print and (if on a computer) possible audio or video that can be played to enhance the presentation.

small moment Part of a memory that a writer focuses on. For example, rather than writing about a whole event, the writer writes in detail about one thing that happened during the event.

speech bubble A shape, often rounded, containing the words a character says in a cartoon or other text. Another term for *speech bubble* is *speech balloon*.

story A series of events in narrative form, either fiction or nonfiction.

story map A representation of the sequence of events from a text using drawings or writing.

style The way a writer chooses and arranges words to create a meaningful text. Aspects of style include sentence length, word choice, and the use of figurative language and symbolism.

survey Asking a question and recording the responses.

syllable A minimal unit of sequential speech sounds composed of a vowel sound or a consonant-vowel combination. A syllable always contains a vowel or vowel-like speech sound (e.g., *pen/ny*).

temporal sequence An underlying structural pattern used especially in nonfiction texts to describe the sequence in which something always or usually occurs, such as the steps in a process or a life cycle. See also *procedural text.*

text features Parts of a text designed to help the reader access or better understand it (for example, tables of contents, headings, sidebars, captions).

text structure The overall architecture or organization of a piece of writing. Another term for text structure is *organization.*

thought bubble A shape, often rounded, containing the words (or sometimes an image that suggests one or more words) a character thinks in a cartoon or other text. Another term for *thought bubble* is *thought balloon.*

tools In writing, references that support the writing process (dictionary, thesaurus). Also, a physical means of revising or editing a piece of writing, such as a caret, a spider leg, or a numbered list.

topic The subject of a piece of writing.

uppercase letter A large letterform that is usually different from its corresponding lowercase form. Another term for *uppercase letter* is *capital letter.*

verbal path Language prompts paired with motor movements to help children learn to form letters correctly.

viewing self as writer Having attitudes and using practices that support a student in becoming a lifelong writer.

voice In writing, the unique way a writer "sounds" as a result of word choice, point of view, and arrangement of words and sentences.

word boundaries The space that appears before the first letter and after the last letter of a word and that defines the letter or letters as a word. It is important for young readers to learn to recognize word boundaries.

wordless picture book A form in which a story is told exclusively with pictures.

writer's notebook A notebook of bound pages in which students gather ideas for writing and experiment with writing. A writer's notebook is a record of children's writing across the year. It may have several different sections to serve a variety of purposes.

writers' workshop A classroom structure that begins with a whole-group minilesson; continues with independent writing, individual conferences, and small-group instruction; and ends with a whole-group share.

writing Children engaging in the writing process and producing pieces of their own writing in many genres.

writing about reading Children responding to reading a text by writing and sometimes drawing.

writing folder A two-pocket folder with brads in the middle. Writing that is in progress is stored in the pockets. Resources, such as checklists and spelling lists, are fastened in the middle. When a piece of writing is finished, it is removed from the folder and placed in a hanging file.

writing process Key phases of creating a piece of writing: planning and rehearsing, drafting and revising, editing and proofreading, and publishing.

Credits

Cover image from *A Log's Life* by Wendy Pfeffer with illustrations by Robin Brickman. Text copyright © 1997 by Wendy Pfeffer. Illustrations copyright © 1997 by Robin Brickman. Reprinted with the permission of Simon & Schuster Books for Young Readers, an imprint of Simon & Schuster Children's Publishing Division. All rights reserved.

Cover image from *A Weekend with Wendell* by Kevin Henkes. Copyright © 1986 by Kevin Henkes. Used by permission of HarperCollins Publishers.

Cover image from *Abuela's Weave* by Omar S. Castenada, illustrated by Enrique O. Sanchez. Copyright © 1993 Omar S. Castenada and Enrique O. Sanchez. Permission arranged with Lee & Low Books, Inc., New York, NY 10016.

Cover image from *All for Me and None for All* by Helen Lester. Text copyright © 2012 by Helen Lester. Illustrations copyright © 2012 by Lynn Munsinger. Reprinted by permission of Houghton Mifflin Harcourt Trade Publishing.

Cover image from *Amelia's Road* by Linda Jacobs Altman, illustrated by Enrique O. Sanchez. Copyright © 1993 Linda Jacobs Altman and Enrique O. Sanchez. Permission arranged with Lee & Low Books, Inc., New York, NY 10016.

Cover image from *Armando and the Blue Tarp School* by Edith Hope Fine, illustrated by Herman Sosa. Copyright © 2007 Edith Hope Fine and Herman Sosa. Permission arranged with Lee & Low Books, Inc., New York, NY 10016.

Cover image from Author: *A True Story* by Helen Lester. Copyright © 1997 by Helen Lester. Reprinted by permission of Houghton Mifflin Harcourt Trade Publishing.

Cover image from *Bigmama's* by Donald Crews. Copyright © 1991 by Donald Crews. Used by permission of HarperCollins Publishers.

Cover image from *Bugs for Lunch* by Margery Facklam, illustrated by Sylvia Long. Copyright © Charlesbridge Publishing, Inc. All rights reserved. Used with permission of Charlesbridge Publishing, Inc. www.charlesbridge.com.

Cover image from *Cactus Hotel* by Brenda Guiberson. Illustration © 1991 by Megan Lloyd. Reprinted by permission of Henry Holt Books for Young Readers. All rights reserved.

Cover image from *Cats* by Seymour Simon. Copyright © 2004 by Seymour Simon. Used by permission of HarperCollins Publishers.

Cover image from *Dogs* by Seymour Simon. Copyright © 2004 by Seymour Simon. Used by permission of HarperCollins Publishers.

Cover image from *Dolphins* by Seymour Simon. Copyright © 2009 by Seymour Simon. Used by permission of HarperCollins Publishers.

Cover image from *Earrings!* by Judith Viorst with illustrations by Nola Langner Malone. Text copyright © 1990 by Judith Viorst. Illustrations copyright © 1990 by Nola Langner Malone. Reprinted with the permission of Atheneum Books for Young Readers, an imprint of Simon & Schuster Children's Publishing Division. All rights reserved.

Works Cited

Fletcher, Ralph. 2017. *Joy Write: Cultivating High-Impact, Low-Stakes Writing*. Portsmouth, NH: Heinemann.

Fountas, Irene C., and Gay Su Pinnell. 2001. *Guiding Readers and Writers: Teaching Comprehension, Genre, and Content Literacy*. Portsmouth, NH: Heinemann.

————. 2012. *Genre Study: Teaching with Fiction and Nonfiction Books*. Portsmouth, NH: Heinemann.

————. 2017. *Guided Reading: Responsive Teaching Across the Grades*, 2nd ed. Portsmouth, NH: Heinemann.

————. 2017. *Phonics, Spelling, and Word Study System, for Grade 2*. Portsmouth, NH: Heinemann.

————. 2017, 2022. *The Fountas & Pinnell Literacy Continuum: A Tool for Assessment, Planning, and Teaching*. Portsmouth, NH: Heinemann.

————. 2018. *Fountas & Pinnell Classroom™ Interactive Read-Aloud Collection*. Portsmouth, NH: Heinemann.

————. 2018. *Fountas & Pinnell Classroom™ Shared Reading Collection*. Portsmouth, NH: Heinemann.

————. 2018. *Fountas & Pinnell Classroom™ System Guide, Grade 2*. Portsmouth, NH: Heinemann.

————. 2018. *The Literacy Quick Guide: A Reference Tool for Responsive Literacy Teaching*. Portsmouth, NH: Heinemann.

————. 2019. *The Reading Minilessons Book, Grade 2*. Portsmouth, NH: Heinemann.

Glover, Matt. 2009. *Engaging Young Writers, Preschool–Grade 1*. Portsmouth, NH: Heinemann.

Heard, Georgia. 1999. *Awakening the Heart: Exploring Poetry in Elementary and Middle School*. Portsmouth, NH: Heinemann.

————. 2016. *Heart Maps: Helping Students Create and Craft Authentic Writing*. Portsmouth, NH: Heinemann.

Heard, Georgia, and Jennifer McDonough. 2009. *A Place for Wonder: Reading and Writing Nonfiction in the Primary Grades*. Portsmouth, NH: Stenhouse.

Johnston, Peter, Kathy Champeau, Andrea Hartwig, Sarah Helmer, Merry Komar, Tara Krueger, and Laurie McCarthy. 2020. *Engaging Literate Minds: Developing Children's Social, Emotional, and Intellectual Lives, K–3*. Portsmouth, NH: Stenhouse.

Stilton. Geronimo. 2021. *Mysterious Eye of the Dragon*. NY: Scholastic.

VanDerwater, Amy. 2018. *Poems Are Teachers: How Studying Poetry Stengthens Writing in All Genres*. Portsmouth, NH: Heinemann.

Vygotsky, Lev. 1979. *Mind in Society: The Development of Higher Psychological Processes*. Cambridge, MA: Harvard University Press.